SO-DRF-035

The papers published in this book are
printed from camera-ready copy supplied
by the contributing authors who are
solely responsible for the contents of
their individual paper.

B
15
33
987

# FRONTIERS
# OF
# ENTREPRENEURSHIP
# RESEARCH
## 1987

Proceedings of the Seventh Annual Babson College
Entrepreneurship Research Conference

Sponsored by
Center for Entrepreneurial Studies
Babson College
Wellesley, Massachusetts 02157
and
Co-sponsored by
School of Business Management
Pepperdine University
Malibu, CA 90265

Edited by
**NEIL C. CHURCHILL**
Babson College
**JOHN A. HORNADAY**
Babson College
**BRUCE A. KIRCHHOFF**
Babson College
**O. J. KRASNER**
Pepperdine University
**KARL H. VESPER**
University of Washington

bson College 1987

# PUBLICATIONS

The following books are published by the Center for Entrepreneurial Studies, Babson College, Wellesley, Massachusetts 02157:

| Title | ISBN No. |
| --- | --- |
| Frontiers of Entrepreneurship Research 1981 | 0-910897-01-8 |
| Frontiers of Entrepreneurship Research 1982 | 0-910897-02-6 |
| Frontiers of Entrepreneurship Research 1983 | 0-910897-03-4 |
| Frontiers of Entrepreneurship Research 1984 | 0-910897-04-2 |
| Frontiers of Entrepreneurship Research 1985 | 0-910897-05-0 |
| Frontiers of Entrepreneurship Research 1986 | 0-910897-07-7 |
| Frontiers of Entrepreneurship Research 1987 | 0-910897-08-5 |
| Entrepreneurship Education 1985, Karl H. Vesper | 0-910897-06-9 |

# TABLE OF CONTENTS

COMPARATIVE STUDIES OF ENTREPRENEURSHIP

SUCCESS PROFILES

NEW VENTURES

COMPUTER INDUSTRY VENTURES

CORPORATE VENTURING

INTERNATIONAL COMPARATIVE

EDUCATION AND ENTREPRENEURSHIP

UNIVERSITY BASED VENTURES

# ACKNOWLEDGEMENTS

The editors of this volume wish to express thanks to the 1987 Conference participants for their work which makes this book possible. Seventy-one papers were presented this year, the greatest number in the seven years of the conference. The contributions of the participants continue to show growing concern for quality of content and breadth of topic, thereby assuring that this volume contains the leading edge of research in the field of entrepreneurship.

The Conference this year was jointly sponsored with and held at Pepperdine University in California, where a large number of people contributed to the organization and presentation of a successful conference. Most significant among these was Jean Sandlin who was responsible for the local arrangements with the assistance of many co-workers, faculty members, and students.

The great geographical distance between the Pepperdine and Babson campuses created more than the usual problems with coordination but Irene McCarthy managed the overall arrangements especially well. We are particularly indebted to Irene this year for her excellent contribution. She was assisted at Babson by Connie Stumpf and the Word Processing Department, Debbie Curran, Barbara Ward, and Mary O'Donnell.

A special thanks goes this year to Neil Churchill and Jack Hornaday for their contribution of the index to all seven volumes of Frontiers of Entrepreneurship Research. This index required considerable time and patience since it not only lists each paper but also categorizes all by topic. The index appears at the end of this seventh volume.

At Pepperdine, the Conference received enthusiastic support from President David Davenport and Dean of the School of Business and Management, James Wilburn. And, at Babson, Academic Vice President Mel Copen and President William Dill continued their essential roles as supporters of the Conference. We thank them all.

Neil C. Churchill
John A. Hornaday
Bruce A. Kirchhoff
O. J. Krasner
Karl H. Vesper

# INTRODUCTION

The Seventh Annual Babson College Entrepreneurship Research Conference was held at Pepperdine University in April, 1987. This volume is a compilation of full papers and summaries of the papers presented at that Conference. The purpose of the Annual Conferences is to stimulate and report research in entrepreneurship. The stimulating process has proven quite successful as the number of paper proposals submitted, papers accepted and participants increased again this year. In 1987, 138 proposals were received, 71 papers were presented with 146 authors and coauthors contributing, and 128 participants attended the Conference. Of the authors and coauthors, 65 percent were contributing to the Conference for the first time. Thirty-eight of the 71 papers were judged of superior quality and are presented in their entirety within this volume. Thirty-two papers appear in summary form since resources limit the number of papers which can be published in their entirety.

This introduction provides descriptions of two features which are new to the Conference and proceedings. First, we present a description of the paper reviewing process which has evolved over the years into a more formal, academically rigorous process. Second, we describe the "Topic Index" which has been included in this seventh volume.

## PAPER REVIEW PROCESS

As the number of research papers has increased over the years, the Conference Directors have increasingly focused attention on quality. This year, 138 research paper proposals were received. Given the limit of 71 for presentation at the Conference, we decided to use a traditional academic review process to assure that the best quality papers would be selected.

Each research paper proposal was read and evaluated by two independent reviewers; when the two reviewers agreed, their decision was considered final. When the two disagreed, a third reviewer read the proposal and made the final decision. In this way, 71 papers were selected for presentation at the Conference.

When the final drafts of the 71 papers were received, each was again sent to two independent reviewers. If both agreed, their decision was final. When the two reviewers disagreed, the paper was read

by a third reviewer who made the final decision. This independent
review process resulted in the selection of the 38 papers whose full
text is presented in this volume of Frontiers of Entrepreneurship
Research.

Although somewhat inflexible, this type of review process suc-
ceeds in assuring every author an equal chance at being selected.
Furthermore, it allows the Conference Directors to spread the work of
paper reviewing among a large number of colleagues; the work load has
become too much to be handled by a few of us gathered around a table
with our morning coffee.

The review process has the further benefit of establishing academic merit for the papers which appear here. The summaries published
herein have been academically reviewed and accepted on the basis of
their merit. The full papers published herein have been academically
reviewed twice and accepted twice on the basis of their merit.
Authors of summaries and full papers can be proud of the positive
peer review they have received.

## TOPIC INDEX TO SEVEN VOLUMES OF FRONTIERS

As a special feature of this seventh volume, we are including a
categorized index of all the papers published in volumes one through
seven of Frontiers of Entrepreneurship Research. This index was prepared by Neil Churchill and Jack Hornaday. They prepared this index
as part of their paper entitled "Current Trends in Entrepreneurial
Research" which appears as the first paper in this volume. Their analysis of all papers published in previous volumes required considerable work; yet, they were willing to contribute further work by
extending their analysis to include the papers in this seventh volume.
Their categorized index appears at the end of this volume. We are
especially indebted to Neil and Jack for this significant contribution.

The reader will find the topical index, organized by twenty
topic categories, useful in determining the author, title, volume and
page of every paper published in the seven volumes of Frontiers of
Entrepreneurship Research. Within each topic category, papers are
listed in the order of year of publication and then alphabetically by
first author's last name.

It is our hope that this index will be used by future
researchers to better understand the variety of topics within
entrepreneurship research and, once understood, stimulate even more
research on a broader range of topics.

We want participation in the Babson Entrepreneurship Research Conference to grow over the years to come. The field is still new and new participants are encouraged to join us. We will continue the research proposal and paper review process as described above for at least one more year. Unless we find that the process is stifling research creativity, we will likely continue it indefinitely.

At the same time, it seems undesirable to either lengthen the Conference or shorten the time available for each paper's presentation. Thus, if participation continues to grow and new people join us, we need to find a format for expanding the opportunities for participation. We are opening up the invitation process for the 1988 Conference to include past participants who either chose not to offer a paper, or whose paper does not pass the review process. In this way, we can be assured that paper acceptance will be dependent on quality of research, yet those who have established a track record of research will not be excluded from attending. This assures a good mix of old and new participants which should provide a creative environment.

Given resource limitations, it is likely that the number of full text papers published in Frontiers will continue to range between 35 and 40. However, as the number of submissions increases, the quality of published papers should also increase. Furthermore, we hope to prepare and publish a topic index, such as the one in this volume, every four or five years.

The future of entrepreneurship research looks ever brighter; we hope that Frontiers of Entrepreneurship Research can continue to make a useful contribution to this growing field.

# CURRENT TRENDS IN ENTREPRENEURIAL RESEARCH

John A. Hornaday, Babson College**
Neil C. Churchill, Babson College*

## ABSTRACT

This paper examines the 227 studies published in the 1981 through 1986 volumes of Frontiers of Entrepreneurship Research and classifies each by year published, topic addressed, methodology used, and objective attempted (contribute to theory, practice, or methodology) and degree of centrality of the research to our understanding the nature of entrepreneurship in theory or in practice. Among the findings were:

o   The most studied topic was the Personal Characteristics of Entrepreneurs

o   Surveys were by far the most common research methodology used and the methodologies chosen changed over time

o   Some two-thirds of the studies were, not suprisingly, intended to be contributions to theory

o   Surprisingly, only 14% of the studies (17% of those aimed at theory) were deemed to be converging on the central problems of entrepreneurship.

## INTRODUCTION

This work is an extension of three papers (Ronstadt,[1] Hornaday,[2] and Churchill & Lewis.[3]) published within recent years analyzing the

---

*   On leave from Southern Methodist University
** As of September 1987, with Daniel Webster College

[1]Robert Ronstadt, "Introduction," Frontiers of Entrepreneurship Research, 1986, Babson College, Wellesley, MA, pp. xii-xviii.

[2]John A. Hornaday, "The Corporate Entrepreneur Revisited," in Donald L. Sexton and Raymond W. Smilor, eds., The Art and Science of Entrepreneurship, Ballinger Press, Cambridge, MA, 1986, pp. 265-269.

[3]Neil C. Churchill and Virginia L. Lewis, "Entrepreneurship Research: Directions and Methods," in Donald L. Sexton and Raymond W. Smilor, eds., The Art and Science of Entrepreneurship, Ballinger Press, Cambridge, MA, 1986, pp. 333-366.

nature of entrepreneurial research as it appears in publications in the field. Ronstadt analyzed the Babson Research Conference proceedings by number, number of authors, number of new authors, percent of papers published, and size of data bases used. Hornaday urged an increased systematic attention to the development of theory in entrepreneurial studies and cited the need for more hypothetico-deductive reasoning in developing research designs and in selecting problems to be attacked. Churchill & Lewis surveyed the entrepreneurship/small business litera-ture from 1980 through 1984 including the first _four_ volumes of the Babson Research Conference proceedings. The objective of this paper is to extend the Churchill & Lewis analysis so that it includes all six years of the Babson Research Conference in order to see from this six year data base if there are signs that we are (a) moving toward more theoretical reports or (b) beginning to develop a comprehensive theory of entrepreneurship.

THE DATA

The 227 articles published in _Frontiers of Entrepreneurship Research_ from 1981 - 1986 were evaluated on four characteristics and "year of publication." The result was a categorization by the following five characteristics:

1. Year of publication (1981 - 1986)

2. Topic (20 topics categories were used - see Table 1)

3. Methodology used (9 research methods - see Table 2)

4. Objective of the research (3 objectives - see Table 3)

5. Centrality, the extent to which the studies contributed to our ability to understand the central, core issues in entrepre-neurship (3 measures of convergence toward the core of the field - see Table 4)

Other than the year of publication, there is, obviously and unavoidably, considerable subjectivity in the judgments used to place a paper in any, and particularly the last, of these categories. In the Churchill & Lewis study, Lewis made the basic judgments using guidelines developed by both authors. In the present study Churchill made the basic judgments with back-up from Hornaday. The degree of consistency in these judgments is demonstrated, positively, by the similarity between the two studies of centrality (the most subjective of the five categories) - see Table 4A. The percentages of "Not Convergent" versus the sum of "Convergent" and "Marginally Convergent" were essentially identical. On the other hand, the frequency of assignment to the category "Convergent" differed considerably. The five classifications of each paper permit ten paired comparisons. The implications of the data through these ten comparisons make up the body of this paper.

## Topics

The topics published in the six years of the Research Conference are shown in Table 1. The percentages of papers devoted to a topic in each year's <u>Frontiers</u> are shown in separate columns. For any one year, the number of papers on each topic as a percent of all papers on that particular topic in the six year period, is shown under the number of papers on that topic for that year. For example, of the 39 papers in the 1981 volume, four or 10% dealt primarily with Topic 1, (T-1) Personal Characteristics of Entrepreneurs, and this was 12% of the 33 papers which dealt with this topic over the six years. The column on the far right shows that this was the most popular topic studied; 15% of the total papers (33 out of 227) in the six volumes dealt with this topic.

Most of the topics occur relatively infrequently in the six volumes so that no significant trend for them is discernible. Four topics accounted for 44% of the papers - Personal Characteristics of Entrepreneurs (T-1), Characteristics of Start-ups (T-4), Venture Capital Firms (T-5), and Incubators and Other University Support to Entrepreneurs (T-11). The related topics, Factors Supporting Entrepreneurship - Government (T-13) and Non-Government (T-12), if combined, account for 24 or 11% of the total. Thus these six topics account for over half (55%) of all papers. Finally, if the two topics on start-ups (Topics 3 and 4) are combined, they involve another 13% of the papers. Thus eight of the twenty "topics" account for two-thirds of publications instead of the "expected" 40%.

Over the six-year period there has been some change in the topics published. Topic 1, Personal Characteristics of Entrepreneurs, the single most popular topic (15% of all papers) varied between 3% (1985) and 30% (1986) of the topics chosen in any one year but with no discernible trend. The two second-most popular topics, Venture Capital (T-5) and Incubators/University Support to Entrepreneurship (T-11), differed a bit. Venture Capital (T-5) was reasonably consistent over the six years while Incubators (T-11) showed some decline - as did Managing the Business (T-7). Topic 10, Corporate Venturing (Intrapreneurship) on the other hand had a "bell-shaped" pattern over the six years.

Some diversity could be expected since the individuals responsible for selecting the papers to be published changed during the period - Karl Vesper was primarily responsible in 1981 & 1982; Jeff Timmons in 1983, 1984, & 1985; and Bob Ronstadt in 1986. This variability was mitigated, however, by the diversity and relative stability of the committee of referees, which numbered from four to six and included Vesper for the whole six-year period and Hornaday for the last five years.

3

## Methodologies

As with topics, a few methodologies dominated the research efforts. Examination of Table 2 shows that Questionnaire or Telephone Surveys (M-1) and In-Depth Surveys/Interviews (M-2) were used in 60% of the papers while two methodologies, (M-5) and (M-9), were used only 2% of the time. In contrast with topics, the methodologies used showed significant trends over the six year period.

Mail and Telephone Questionnaires (M-1) were used in only 23% of the articles in the 1981 <u>Frontiers</u> but this percentage increased yearly - 26%, 39.39%, 39.47%, 55%, to 68% in 1986. In-depth Surveys/ Interviews (M-2) also have increased. The first three years account for only 40% of the total studies using this methodology.

One reason for the increase in questionnaires and telephone interviews may stem from the fact that it is relatively easy to conduct surveys of students, practitioners, participants at conferences, or alumni. A second reason might be that the first research of someone new to the field is often a survey of questions of particular interest to them (this was true of both authors by the way) and that an increasing number of people are becoming interested in entrepreneurship and hence are new to the field. A third reason may be the requirement for attendance at the Babson Entrepreneurial Research Conference - a data-based paper. Field research or longitudinal studies take considerably more time than questionnaires but the conference is a good place to network and to keep up on the field.

In contrast to surveys and interviews, three methodologies showed a considerable decline from the early to the later years. If the first three years are contrasted with the last three, Field Studies (M-3), Personal Observation/Contemplative Theory (M-6), Literature Surveys (M-7), and Vignettes or Reportage (M-8) show substantial decreases in usage. Indeed the first three years account for 62%, 75%, 77%, and 62% respectively of the total use of each methodology.

The lack of field research is, in the authors' view, unfortunate given the paucity of data in entrepreneurship. This is most likely attributable to the high cost in time, effort, and money needed to do research in the field. It seems to the authors that more emphasis on field studies and in-depth interviews is preferable to "another survey on an available population" which addresses a small part of a specific problem.

The decreases in literature surveys is more understandable. In the year or two following the decade of the 1970's, researchers were again turning their attention to the study of entrepreneurship and a number of studies were conducted on the extant literature. Once the literature is evaluated, it can be expected that energies are turned somewhere else. The decrease in "theory contemplation and synthesis and hypotheses formulation from personal observation" may be due in part to the same phenomena and in part to the Conference's focus on data-based papers. One of the messages of this paper, which we will focus on later, is the need for more attention to the core issues of entrepreneurship. It is the opinion of the authors[4] that the accumulation of the past few years' research has produced sufficient empirical data to allow some development of theoretical constructs.

## Objectives

The desirability of studies directed toward developing theoretical constructs is recognized by others dealing with entrepreneurial research. This is indicated by Table 3 which shows that the objective of the majority of papers each year was to develop the theory of entrepreneurship. Indeed, starting with 1983, the percentage of theory-directed papers rose from 50 plus percent to two-thirds or more of those included in Frontiers. While this can be expected in the proceedings of a research conference, what struck the authors as unusual in such a new field is that only four papers attempted to extend research methodology.

## Centrality

Although two-thirds of the authors focused on theory, not all of these papers moved our understanding of entrepreneurship forward to any considerable extent. Table 4 reveals a relatively low percentage, albeit with a generally rising trend, of papers that were central to the development of a theory of entrepreneurship - those that advanced to some modest degree our understanding of the basic nature of entrepreneurs and entrepreneurship.[5] This is, unfortunately, a rather subjective judgment of (a) the degree to which the paper addressed a problem central to this understanding and (b) whether or not the paper accomplished this to some extent. A number of the papers were well done on criteria (b) and even dealt with well specified problems that would be of interest to some audiences, but they were tangential to understanding the nature of small business start-ups; the process of entrepreneurship and commercial innovation; the forces that nurture or retard entrepreneurship; or what factors lead to successful versus unsuccessful enterprises.

If the categories of "Convergent" and "Marginally Convergent" are combined, which is probably more relevant given the subjectivity of the judgements, Table 4 shows that a relatively constant sixty-plus percent of the papers fall into this category over the years with 1983 and 1984 having the highest convergent percentages. While these ratings are quite subjective, Churchill and Lewis found the same combined percentage in their 1980-81 study[6] although there were considerable differences between the "Convergent" and "Marginally

---

[4]Hornaday, op. cit.

[5]For a more complete description of "centrality" and "convergence toward the core" see Churchill and Lewis, op. cit.

[6]Churchill & Lewis, op. cit., Table 11-6, p. 351.

Convergent" categories. For this reason, and because of other differences already cited, the present study cannot be considered a
direct replication of the earlier work.

RESULTS - INTERACTIONS

## Topics and Methodologies

The most striking relationship between topics studied and
methodologies used to research them is the concentration of methodology by topic (see Table 5). This is exemplified by the heavy use of
questionnaires (M-1) in exploring the personal characteristics of
entrepreneurs (T-1). 76% of all the research papers on this topic
were based on questionnaires. Similarly, Vignettes/Reportage (M-8)
accounted for 40% of the studies of Incubators/University Support to
Entrepreneurship (T-11), and this topic accounted for 48% of the use
of that methodology.

The pattern in Table 5 is that most topics are studied using,
primarily, one to three methods. For topics studied nine times or
more (the number of methods available), all of them had at least 50%
of the studies done by no more than two methodologies and in all but
two of these topics three methodologies accounted for over 70% of the
papers in that topic - 100% for two of them. The only two exceptions
to this concentration of methodology seems to be Surveys (T-1) and
In-Depth Surveys (M-2). Surveys (43% of all studies) accounted for
50% more of the papers in eight topics and In-Depth Surveys (17%)
accounted for 33% or more of the papers in 5 topics.

## Topics and Objectives

As would be expected in a unversity-based research conference,
contributing to the theory of entrepreneurship would be the principal
objective and, as discussed above, 67% of the papers published had
this objective. Looking at objective by topic, Table 6 shows that
over half of the papers in 16 of the 20 topics had theory as their
objective - and 14 of the 20 topics had better than two-thirds of
their papers oriented toward theory. In three of the other four
topics, 100% of the papers dealt with practice - and for the fourth,
practice was 80% of the papers. The practice-oriented topics were
High Tech Ventures (T-8), Incubators/University Support for
Entrepreneurship (T-11), Governmental Factors Influencing
Entrepreneurship (T-13), and Entrepreneurship Education (T-16).
Improving methodology was the subject of only four papers, of which
half dealt with Entrepreneurial Research (T-17). It is interesting to
note that almost all of the studies in Personal Characteristics of
Entrepreneurs (T-1) had Contribution to Theory as their objective.
Unfortunately, the extent to which the objective was fully realized
was limited as the next section demonstrates.

## Topics and Centrality

Centrality is a judgement of the degree to which a research study moves us toward understanding the theory, or the practice, of entrepreneurship - convergence to the core of our area of interest. Centrality is neither the measure of quality in an abstract sense nor a judgement of the importance of a research study to any particular group of people. The authors believe that research on the central issues of entrepreneurship should be encouraged and the following analysis may serve, in part, as a guide to such issues.

Table 7 shows a wide divergence in centrality in the studies of different topics. Of the 11 topics which were addressed by 10 or more papers, three had none that were convergent - Personal Characteristics (T-1), Women and Minority Entrepreneurs (T-14), and Entrepreneurial Education (T-16). They were also the only topics of all 20 with a "Some Convergence" score (the sum of Convergent and Marginally Convergent) below 40%. It is of value to compare these three low-scoring topics with those judged least interesting in the study by Ronstadt.[7] The topic, Women and Minority Entrepreneurs, was selected by Ronstadt's participants as the least interesting and Personal Characteristics of Entrepreneurs as third least interesting. Entrepreneurial Education, which the current study deemed 19th out of 20 in centrality, scored slightly above the median in interest with Ronstadt's particpants. It should be re-emphasized that lack of Convergence to the Core does not imply a lack of interest in the topic, only that it does not further our understanding of the entrepeneurial phenomena to any great degree. The topics that scored high on the "Some Convergence" score were, for the 11 heavily studied topics:

| | | |
|---|---|---|
| T-10 | Corporate Venturing | 86% |
| T- 6 | Financing Startups | 85% |
| T- 5 | Venture Capital | 84% |
| T-12 | Factors Influencing Startups (Non-Governmental) | 82% |
| T- 4 | Startups - Data, Rates, etc. | 76% |
| T- 3 | Managerial Characteristics of Entrep./Startup Mgrs. | 75% |

Three other Topics earned a 100% "Some Convergence" score but they were studied by only 6, 3, and 2 papers respectively.

To the extent the above, admittedly subjective, judgements are valid, this paper suggest some topics that should be considered in launching the reader's next research project.

## Methodologies and Objectives

As there seemed to be a relationship between Methodology and Topic, so it appears that there is a relationship between Methodology and Objective although Table 8 shows Surveys (M-1) to be ubiquitous across all Objectives. One methodology, In-depth Surveys (M-2), was

---

[7] Ronstadt, op. cit., p. xiv.

used 82% of the time in Theoretically-oriented studies while another, Vignette/Reportage (M-8), was employed in 95% of the studies directed toward Practice; which was 28% of all Practice-oriented papers. In addition, the third most utilized methodology in Practice-directed papers was Observation/Contemplative Theory (M-6) - 13% and this accounted for 45% of all uses of this research approach. While little can be said about the four studies aimed at improving methodology, Table 8 does indicate a relationship between methodology and purpose. The authors believe that the choice of objective generally dictates the methodology selected.

## Methodology and Centrality

All of the methodologies except two were used in studies deemed to be near or above the average (65%) of the "Some Convergence" measure - see Table 9. These two were Vignettes/Reportage (M-8) at 57% and Observation/Contemplative Theory (M-6) at 50%. Both of these were heavily used in Practice-oriented studies and, as we shall see in the next section, these Practice-oriented studies fare slightly less well than Theory-oriented studies in achieving centrality. On the other hand two methodologies achieved over 30% on Convergence - against an average of 14% in that category. They were both field-directed methodologies - In-depth Surveys (M-2) and Analysis of Data Bases (M-4). A third methodology, Field Study (M-3), was the only other methodology to rank above the mean of the nine methodologies. The data in Table 9 suggest, first, that an author who wishes to contribute to the advancement of entrepreneurship should do in-depth surveys, field projects or case studies, or analyze rather extensive data bases. This, in turn, implies that a high priority be given to data collection or ferreting out extant but obscure data bases since there is a paucity of data available for systematic research at the present date. A second conclusion from the data is that research relying on Vignettes or Contemplative Theory has to be well done if it is to contribute very much to entrepreneurship.

Finally, a comment is warranted on Surveys (M-1). Surveys are by far the most widely used methodology yet Surveys have one of the lowest Convergence ratings. One reason may be the use of surveys on the nearest available population (undergraduates) rather than on a population that is more representative of entrepreneurs and entrepreneurship. A second reason may be the inability to build upon such surveys since the population is unspecified along a number of dimensions that may be of interest to other researchers. While the problem of nonspecification is not limited to surveys alone, it certainly is applicable to this methodology. Fortunately it is being addressed in a project initiated by Robert Brockhaus which is reported upon at this conference.

## Objective and Centrality

The data in Table 10 show essentially the same degree of "Some Convergence" in the studies directed at Theory and those directed at Practice. There is considerable variation, however, in the categories of convergence. Studies whose objective was Practice had a far smaller percentage classified as "Convergent," This was due, in part, to the difficulty the authors had in categorizing a study directed at Practice as "Convergent." In addition, it was a little harder to score a Practice-oriented study as "Non-Convergent." Thus the middle classification was more frequently applied to Practice-oriented studies. What is disappointing is the low number (17%) of theoretical studes that were contributing substantially to the advancement of the theory of entrepreneurship.

## CONCLUSION

Analyses of the six volumes of studies selected from the Babson Conference on Entrepreneurship Research have shown that substantial progress is being made toward understanding entrepreneurs and entrepreneurship. There seems to be considerable diversion of research from the central problems of the field. This seems to stem from a focus on one or two methodologies and an unwillingness to venture out into the field where entrepreneurs do their work. There are a number of hypotheses as to why progress in understanding the field moves so slowly. Some of these are:

o   Lack of good data
o   Pressure by universities to publish or perish and thus the
     motivation to do research in a way which eliminates the long
     period usually needed to gather meaningful data
o   The complexity and unstructured nature of the field and the
     need to be integrative in researching it rather than deeply
     skilled in a discipline
o   Inexperience of many individuals now entering the field
o   Desire to attend the Babson Conference and hence the need to
     present a paper each year

The authors believe that the results of this study suggest that attention to the following recommendations in future research studies would increase our understanding the field of entrepreneurship:

o   A thorough study of the literature relative to a particular
     area of research will avoid duplication and will make
     possible a more systematic building upon the foundation that
     has now become fairly extensive in the entrepreneurial field.
o   One should think in terms not only of the unit of research to
     be done but also its contribution to the development of a
     theoretical structure and, ideally, its possibility of lead-
     ing to the core of entrepreneurship.
o   The data for studies are more promising for contributing
     information to the core problems if they are obtained from,
     or designed to be, extensive data banks developed, where
     possible, from the field.
o   As a method of research, one should avoid the use of a survey
     unless it is in enough depth to shed light on basic issues
     and deals with a population relevant to the subject under
     examination.

9

## TABLE 1
### ANALYSIS OF TOPICS BY YEAR PUBLISHED

| | TOPIC | 1981 | 1982 | 1983 | 1984 | 1985 | 1986 | TOTAL |
|---|---|---|---|---|---|---|---|---|
| 1 | Personal Characteristics of Entrepreneurs--Psychological & Environmental | 4 / 12% | 3 / 9% | 8 / 24% | 4 / 12% | 1 / 3% | 13 / 39% | 33 / 100% / 15% |
| 2 | Economic & Demographic Characteristics of Small or Entrepreneurial Firms | 0 / 0% | 1 / 33% | 0 / 0% | 0 / 0% | 2 / 67% | 0 / 0% | 3 / 100% / 1% |
| 3 | Managerial Characteristics of Entrepreneurs & Managers of Start-ups | 3 / 25% | 1 / 8% | 1 / 8% | 3 / 25% | 2 / 17% | 2 / 17% | 12 / 100% / 5% |
| 4 | Start-ups--Data on Characteristics, Rate of Formation, etc. | 3 / 18% | 3 / 18% | 4 / 24% | 3 / 18% | 3 / 18% | 1 / 6% | 17 / 100% / 7% |
| 5 | Venture Capital--Characteristics of V.C. Industry, Role in Bus. Formation, etc. | 3 / 12% | 4 / 16% | 2 / 8% | 4 / 16% | 7 / 28% | 5 / 20% | 25 / 100% / 11% |
| 6 | Financing Start-ups Other Than Through Venture Capitalists | 1 / 8% | 2 / 15% | 4 / 31% | 3 / 23% | 3 / 23% | 0 / 0% | 13 / 100% / 6% |
| 7 | Managing the Business--Turnaround, Harvest, Contractions, Acquisition, etc. | 3 / 33% | 2 / 22% | 0 / 0% | 3 / 33% | 1 / 11% | 0 / 0% | 9 / 100% / 4% |
| 8 | High Technology Ventures (per se) | 0 / 0% | 0 / 0% | 0 / 0% | 0 / 0% | 1 / 50% | 1 / 50% | 2 / 100% / 1% |
| 9 | Strategy & Growth in Entrepreneurial Businesses | 0 / 0% | 3 / 50% | 0 / 0% | 0 / 0% | 1 / 17% | 2 / 33% | 6 / 100% / 3% |
| 10 | Corporate Venturing | 2 / 14% | 0 / 0% | 3 / 21% | 5 / 36% | 2 / 14% | 2 / 14% | 14 / 100% / 6% |
| 11 | Incubators & Other University Support to Entrepreneurship | 5 / 20% | 6 / 24% | 1 / 4% | 5 / 20% | 5 / 20% | 3 / 12% | 25 / 100% / 11% |
| 12 | Factors Influencing Entrepreneurship & Start-ups (Non-Government) | 1 / 9% | 2 / 18% | 2 / 18% | 0 / 0% | 0 / 0% | 6 / 55% | 11 / 100% / 5% |
| 13 | Factors Influencing Entrepreneurship & Start-ups (Government) | 6 / 46% | 1 / 8% | 2 / 15% | 3 / 23% | 0 / 0% | 1 / 8% | 13 / 100% / 6% |
| 14 | Women & Minorities in Entrepreneurship | 2 / 17% | 3 / 25% | 2 / 17% | 2 / 17% | 1 / 8% | 2 / 17% | 12 / 100% / 5% |
| 15 | Failures & Ex-Entrepreneurs | 0 / 0% | 0 / 0% | 0 / 0% | 1 / 50% | 0 / 0% | 1 / 50% | 2 / 100% / 1% |
| 16 | Entrepreneurial Education | 3 / 27% | 2 / 18% | 1 / 9% | 1 / 9% | 4 / 36% | 0 / 0% | 11 / 100% / 5% |
| 17 | Entrepreneurial Research | 2 / 22% | 2 / 22% | 0 / 0% | 1 / 11% | 2 / 22% | 2 / 22% | 9 / 100% / 4% |
| 18 | Crosscultural Studies | 0 / 0% | 0 / 0% | 1 / 33% | 0 / 0% | 0 / 0% | 2 / 67% | 3 / 100% / 1% |
| 19 | Networks | 0 / 0% | 0 / 0% | 1 / 33% | 0 / 0% | 1 / 33% | 1 / 33% | 3 / 100% / 1% |
| 20 | Entrepreneurship & the Social Good | 1 / 25% | 0 / 0% | 1 / 25% | 0 / 0% | 2 / 50% | 0 / 0% | 4 / 100% / 2% |
| | TOTALS AND PERCENTAGE BY YEAR | 39 / 100% | 35 / 100% | 33 / 100% | 38 / 100% | 38 / 100% | 44 / 100% | 227 / 100% |

TABLE 2

ANALYSIS OF METHODOLOGY BY YEAR

| METHODOLOGY | 1981 | 1982 | 1983 | 1984 | 1985 | 1986 | TOTAL |
|---|---|---|---|---|---|---|---|
| 1 Survey--Questionnaires by Mail or Telephone | 9<br>9%<br>23% | 9<br>9%<br>26% | 13<br>13%<br>39% | 15<br>15%<br>39% | 21<br>22%<br>55% | 30<br>31%<br>68% | 97<br>100%<br>43% |
| 2 In-depth Survey or Interview | 8<br>21%<br>21% | 3<br>8%<br>9% | 4<br>11%<br>12% | 9<br>24%<br>24% | 6<br>16%<br>16% | 8<br>21%<br>18% | 38<br>100%<br>17% |
| 3 Field Study or Field Case | 5<br>24%<br>13% | 4<br>19%<br>11% | 4<br>19%<br>12% | 1<br>5%<br>3% | 4<br>19%<br>11% | 3<br>14%<br>7% | 21<br>100%<br>9% |
| 4 Analysis of Data Base(s) | 1<br>6%<br>3% | 6<br>38%<br>17% | 3<br>19%<br>9% | 3<br>19%<br>8% | 2<br>13%<br>5% | 1<br>6%<br>2% | 16<br>100%<br>7% |
| 5 Computer Simulation or Modeling | 0<br>0%<br>0% | 1<br>33%<br>3% | 1<br>33%<br>3% | 0<br>0%<br>0% | 0<br>0%<br>0% | 1<br>33%<br>2% | 3<br>100%<br>1% |
| 6 Personal Observation or Contemplative Theory | 8<br>40%<br>21% | 4<br>20%<br>11% | 3<br>15%<br>9% | 2<br>10%<br>5% | 3<br>15%<br>8% | 0<br>0%<br>0% | 20<br>100%<br>9% |
| 7 Literature Survey or Research | 3<br>33%<br>8% | 1<br>11%<br>3% | 3<br>33%<br>9% | 2<br>22%<br>5% | 0<br>0%<br>0% | 0<br>0%<br>0% | 9<br>100%<br>4% |
| 8 Vignette or "Reportage" of a Particular Situation | 5<br>24%<br>13% | 7<br>33%<br>20% | 1<br>5%<br>3% | 6<br>29%<br>16% | 2<br>10%<br>5% | 0<br>0%<br>0% | 21<br>100%<br>9% |
| 9 Analysis of Company Financial Data or Business Plans | 0<br>0%<br>0% | 0<br>0%<br>0% | 1<br>50%<br>3% | 0<br>0%<br>0% | 0<br>0%<br>0% | 1<br>50%<br>2% | 2<br>100%<br>1% |
| TOTAL AND PERCENT BY YEAR | 39<br>100% | 35<br>100% | 33<br>100% | 38<br>100% | 38<br>100% | 44<br>100% | 227<br>100%<br>100% |

11

TABLE 3

ANALYSIS OF OBJECTIVE BY YEAR

| OBJECTIVE | 1981 | | 1982 | | 1983 | | 1984 | | 1985 | | 1986 | | TOTAL | |
|---|---|---|---|---|---|---|---|---|---|---|---|---|---|---|
| 1 Contribution to Theory | 23 | 59% | 19 | 54% | 24 | 73% | 25 | 66% | 25 | 66% | 35 | 80% | 151 | 67% |
| | 15% | | 13% | | 16% | | 17% | | 17% | | 23% | | 100% | |
| 2 Contribution to Practice | 16 | 41% | 15 | 43% | 9 | 27% | 12 | 32% | 12 | 32% | 8 | 18% | 72 | 32% |
| | 22% | | 21% | | 13% | | 17% | | 17% | | 11% | | 100% | |
| 3 Contribution to Methodology | 0 | 0% | 1 | 3% | 0 | 0% | 1 | 3% | 1 | 3% | 1 | 2% | 4 | 2% |
| | 0% | | 25% | | 0% | | 25% | | 25% | | 25% | | 100% | |
| TOTALS & % BY YEAR | 39 | 100% | 35 | 100% | 33 | 100% | 38 | 100% | 38 | 100% | 44 | 100% | 227 | 100% |

## TABLE 4

### ANALYSIS OF CENTRALITY BY YEAR

| CENTRALITY | 1981 | 1982 | 1983 | 1984 | 1985 | 1986 | TOTAL |
|---|---|---|---|---|---|---|---|
| 1 Convergent Toward the Core | 5<br>16%  13% | 5<br>16%  14% | 6<br>19%  18% | 8<br>25%  21% | 4<br>13%  11% | 4<br>13%  9% | 32<br>100%  14% |
| 2 Marginally Convergent Toward the Core | 19<br>16%  49% | 17<br>15%  49% | 18<br>16%  55% | 19<br>16%  50% | 18<br>16%  47% | 25<br>22%  57% | 116<br>100%  51% |
| Some Convergence Toward the Core ( 1 + 2 ) | 24<br>16%  62% | 22<br>15%  63% | 24<br>16%  73% | 27<br>18%  71% | 22<br>15%  58% | 29<br>20%  66% | 148<br>100%  65% |
| 3 Not Convergent Toward the Core | 15<br>19%  38% | 13<br>16%  37% | 9<br>11%  27% | 11<br>14%  29% | 16<br>20%  42% | 15<br>19%  34% | 79<br>100%  35% |
| TOTALS & % BY YEAR | 39<br>100%  100% | 35<br>100%  100% | 33<br>100%  100% | 38<br>100%  100% | 38<br>100%  100% | 44<br>100%  100% | 227<br>100%  100% |

13

## TABLE 4A

### ANALYSIS OF CENTRALITY BY REVIEWER

| CENTRALITY | CHURCHILL & LEWIS | PRESENT AUTHORS |
|---|---|---|
| 1 Convergent Toward the Core | 56.7% | 14.1% |
| 2 Almost Convergent Toward the Core | 8.7% | 51.1% |
| Sum of 1 and 2 | 65.3% | 65.2% |
| 3 Not Convergent Toward the Core | 34.7% | 34.8% |
| TOTAL PERCENTAGES | 100.0% | 100.0% |

TABLE 5
ANALYSIS OF TOPIC BY METHODOLOGY

METHODOLOGY

| TOPIC | 1 | 2 | 3 | 4 | 5 | 6 | 7 | 8 | 9 | TOTAL |
|---|---|---|---|---|---|---|---|---|---|---|
| 1 | 25 26% / 76% | 4 11% / 12% | 0 0% / 0% | 2 13% / 6% | 0 0% / 0% | 2 10% / 6% | 0 0% / 0% | 0 0% / 0% | 0 0% / 0% | 33 15% / 100% |
| 2 | 1 1% / 33% | 0 0% / 0% | 0 0% / 0% | 1 6% / 33% | 0 0% / 0% | 1 5% / 33% | 0 0% / 0% | 0 0% / 0% | 0 0% / 0% | 3 1% / 100% |
| 3 | 4 4% / 33% | 4 11% / 33% | 3 14% / 25% | 0 ·0% / 0% | 0 0% / 0% | 1 5% / 8% | 0 0% / 0% | 0 0% / 0% | 0 0% / 0% | 12 5% / 100% |
| 4 | 3 3% / 18% | 5 13% / 29% | 2 10% / 12% | 3 19% / 18% | 1 33% / 6% | 0 0% / 0% | 2 22% / 12% | 0 0% / 0% | 1 50% / 6% | 17 7% / 100% |
| 5 | 9 9% / 36% | 5 13% / 20% | 1 5% / 4% | 4 25% / 16% | 2 67% / 8% | 1 5% / 4% | 0 0% / 0% | 2 10% / 8% | 1 50% / 4% | 25 11% / 100% |
| 6 | 9 9% / 69% | 0 0% / 0% | 2 10% / 15% | 0 0% / 0% | 0 0% / 0% | 0 0% / 0% | 0 0% / 0% | 2 10% / 15% | 0 0% / 0% | 13 6% / 100% |
| 7 | 1 1% / 11% | 4 11% / 44% | 1 5% / 11% | 0 0% / 0% | 0 0% / 0% | 1 5% / 11% | 1 11% / 11% | 1 5% / 11% | 0 0% / 0% | 9 4% / 100% |
| 8 | 2 2% / 100% | 0 0% / 0% | 0 0% / 0% | 0 0% / 0% | 0 0% / 0% | 0 0% / 0% | 0 0% / 0% | 0 0% / 0% | 0 0% / 0% | 2 1% / 100% |
| 9 | 1 1% / 17% | 3 8% / 50% | 2 10% / 33% | 0 0% / 0% | 0 0% / 0% | 0 0% / 0% | 0 0% / 0% | 0 0% / 0% | 0 0% / 0% | 6 3% / 100% |
| 10 | 5 5% / 36% | 2 5% / 14% | 2 10% / 14% | 1 6% / 7% | 0 0% / 0% | 3 15% / 21% | 1 11% / 7% | 0 0% / 0% | 0 0% / 0% | 14 6% / 100% |
| 11 | 8 8% / 32% | 2 5% / 8% | 3 14% / 12% | 0 0% / 0% | 0 0% / 0% | 1 5% / 4% | 1 11% / 4% | 10 48% / 40% | 0 0% / 0% | 25 11% / 100% |
| 12 | 4 4% / 36% | 2 5% / 18% | 1 5% / 9% | 2 13% / 18% | 0 0% / 0% | 2 10% / 18% | 0 0% / 0% | 0 0% / 0% | 0 0% / 0% | 11 5% / 100% |
| 13 | 5 5% / 38% | 1 3% / 8% | 0 0% / 0% | 0 0% / 0% | 0 0% / 0% | 4 20% / 31% | 1 11% / 8% | 2 10% / 15% | 0 0% / 0% | 13 6% / 100% |
| 14 | 7 7% / 58% | 2 5% / 17% | 0 0% / 0% | 3 19% / 25% | 0 0% / 0% | 0 0% / 0% | 0 0% / 0% | 0 0% / 0% | 0 0% / 0% | 12 5% / 100% |
| 15 | 1 1% / 50% | 1 3% / 50% | 0 0% / 0% | 0 0% / 0% | 0 0% / 0% | 0 0% / 0% | 0 0% / 0% | 0 0% / 0% | 0 0% / 0% | 2 1% / 100% |
| 16 | 3 3% / 27% | 1 3% / 9% | 1 5% / 9% | 0 0% / 0% | 0 0% / 0% | 1 5% / 9% | 1 11% / 9% | 4 19% / 36% | 0 0% / 0% | 11 5% / 100% |
| 17 | 3 3% / 33% | 1 3% / 11% | 1 5% / 11% | 0 0% / 0% | 0 0% / 0% | 3 15% / 33% | 1 11% / 11% | 0 0% / 0% | 0 0% / 0% | 9 4% / 100% |
| 18 | 2 2% / 67% | 0 0% / 0% | 1 5% / 33% | 0 0% / 0% | 0 0% / 0% | 0 0% / 0% | 0 0% / 0% | 0 0% / 0% | 0 0% / 0% | 3 1% / 100% |
| 19 | 2 2% / 67% | 1 3% / 33% | 0 0% / 0% | 0 0% / 0% | 0 0% / 0% | 0 0% / 0% | 0 0% / 0% | 0 0% / 0% | 0 0% / 0% | 3 1% / 100% |
| 20 | 2 2% / 50% | 0 0% / 0% | 1 5% / 25% | 0 0% / 0% | 0 0% / 0% | 0 0% / 0% | 1 11% / 25% | 0 0% / 0% | 0 0% / 0% | 4 2% / 100% |
| TOTALS | 97 100% | 38 100% | 21 100% | 16 100% | 3 100% | 20 100% | 9 100% | 21 100% | 2 100% | 227 100% |

## TABLE 6
### ANALYSIS OF TOPIC BY OBJECTIVE

| TOPIC | THEORY | | PRACTICE | | METHODOLOGY | | TOTAL | |
|---|---|---|---|---|---|---|---|---|
| | OBJECTIVE | | | | | | | |
| 1 | 31 94% | 21% | 1 3% | 1% | 1 3% | 25% | 33 100% | 15% |
| 2 | 3 100% | 2% | 0 0% | 0% | 0 0% | 0% | 3 100% | 1% |
| 3 | 12 100% | 8% | 0 0% | 0% | 0 0% | 0% | 12 100% | 5% |
| 4 | 14 82% | 9% | 2 12% | 3% | 1 6% | 25% | 17 100% | 7% |
| 5 | 19 76% | 13% | 6 24% | 8% | 0 0% | 0% | 25 100% | 11% |
| 6 | 9 69% | 6% | 4 31% | 6% | 0 0% | 0% | 13 100% | 6% |
| 7 | 7 78% | 5% | 2 22% | 3% | 0 0% | 0% | 9 100% | 4% |
| 8 | 0 0% | 0% | 2 100% | 3% | 0 0% | 0% | 2 100% | 1% |
| 9 | 6 100% | 4% | 0 0% | 0% | 0 0% | 0% | 6 100% | 3% |
| 10 | 13 93% | 9% | 1 7% | 1% | 0 0% | 0% | 14 100% | 6% |
| 11 | 5 20% | 3% | 20 80% | 28% | 0 0% | 0% | 25 100% | 11% |
| 12 | 6 55% | 4% | 5 45% | 7% | 0 0% | 0% | 11 100% | 5% |
| 13 | 0 0% | 0% | 13 100% | 18% | 0 0% | 0% | 13 100% | 6% |
| 14 | 10 83% | 7% | 2 17% | 3% | 0 0% | 0% | 12 100% | 5% |
| 15 | 2 100% | 1% | 0 0% | 0% | 0 0% | 0% | 2 100% | 1% |
| 16 | 0 0% | 0% | 11 100% | 15% | 0 0% | 0% | 11 100% | 5% |
| 17 | 6 67% | 4% | 1 11% | 1% | 2 22% | 50% | 9 100% | 4% |
| 18 | 3 100% | 2% | 0 0% | 0% | 0 0% | 0% | 3 100% | 1% |
| 19 | 3 100% | 2% | 0 0% | 0% | 0 0% | 0% | 3 100% | 1% |
| 20 | 2 50% | 1% | 2 50% | 3% | 0 0% | 0% | 4 100% | 2% |
| TOTAL | 151 | 100% | 72 | 100% | 4 | 100% | 227 | 100% |

## TABLE 7
## ANALYSIS OF TOPIC BY CENTRALITY

CENTRALITY

| TOPIC | CONVERGENT | | MARGINALLY CONVERGENT | | : | SOME CONVERGENCE | | NOT CONVERGENT | | TOTAL | |
|---|---|---|---|---|---|---|---|---|---|---|---|
| 1 | 0<br>0% | 0% | 13<br>39% | 11% | : | 13<br>39% | 9% | 20<br>61% | 25% | 33<br>100% | 15% |
| 2 | 0<br>0% | 0% | 2<br>67% | 2% | : | 2<br>67% | 1% | 1<br>33% | 1% | 3<br>100% | 1% |
| 3 | 3<br>25% | 9% | 6<br>50% | 5% | : | 9<br>75% | 6% | 3<br>25% | 4% | 12<br>100% | 5% |
| 4 | 4<br>24% | 13% | 9<br>53% | 8% | : | 13<br>76% | 9% | 4<br>24% | 5% | 17<br>100% | 7% |
| 5 | 5<br>20% | 16% | 16<br>64% | 14% | : | 21<br>84% | 14% | 4<br>16% | 5% | 25<br>100% | 11% |
| 6 | 4<br>31% | 13% | 7<br>54% | 6% | : | 11<br>85% | 7% | 2<br>15% | 3% | 13<br>100% | 6% |
| 7 | 2<br>22% | 6% | 3<br>33% | 3% | : | 5<br>56% | 3% | 4<br>44% | 5% | 9<br>100% | 4% |
| 8 | 0<br>0% | 0% | 2<br>100% | 2% | : | 2<br>100% | 1% | 0<br>0% | 0% | 2<br>100% | 1% |
| 9 | 1<br>17% | 3% | 5<br>83% | 4% | : | 6<br>100% | 4% | 0<br>0% | 0% | 6<br>100% | 3% |
| 10 | 5<br>36% | 16% | 7<br>50% | 6% | : | 12<br>86% | 8% | 2<br>14% | 3% | 14<br>100% | 6% |
| 11 | 2<br>8% | 6% | 15<br>60% | 13% | : | 17<br>68% | 11% | 8<br>32% | 10% | 25<br>100% | 11% |
| 12 | 2<br>18% | 6% | 7<br>64% | 6% | : | 9<br>82% | 6% | 2<br>18% | 3% | 11<br>100% | 5% |
| 13 | 1<br>8% | 3% | 6<br>46% | 5% | : | 7<br>54% | 5% | 6<br>46% | 8% | 13<br>100% | 6% |
| 14 | 0<br>0% | 0% | 3<br>25% | 3% | : | 3<br>25% | 2% | 9<br>75% | 11% | 12<br>100% | 5% |
| 15 | 1<br>50% | 3% | 1<br>50% | 1% | : | 2<br>100% | 1% | 0<br>0% | 0% | 2<br>100% | 1% |
| 16 | 0<br>0% | 0% | 3<br>27% | 3% | : | 3<br>27% | 2% | 8<br>73% | 10% | 11<br>100% | 5% |
| 17 | 1<br>11% | 3% | 4<br>44% | 3% | : | 5<br>56% | 3% | 4<br>44% | 5% | 9<br>100% | 4% |
| 18 | 0<br>0% | 0% | 2<br>67% | 2% | : | 2<br>67% | 1% | 1<br>33% | 1% | 3<br>100% | 1% |
| 19 | 1<br>33% | 3% | 2<br>67% | 2% | : | 3<br>100% | 2% | 0<br>0% | 0% | 3<br>100% | 1% |
| 20 | 0<br>0% | 0% | 3<br>75% | 3% | : | 3<br>75% | 2% | 1<br>25% | 1% | 4<br>100% | 2% |
| TOTAL | 32 | 100% | 116 | 100% | : | 148 | 100% | 79 | 100% | 227 | 100% |

TABLE 8
ANALYSIS OF METHODOLOGY BY OBJECTIVE

| METHOD-OLOGY | OBJECTIVE | | | | | | | |
|---|---|---|---|---|---|---|---|---|
| | THEORY | | PRACTICE | | METHODOLOGY | | TOTAL | |
| 1 | 71 73% | 47% | 23 24% | 32% | 3 3% | 75% | 97 100% | 43% |
| 2 | 31 82% | 21% | 7 18% | 10% | 0 0% | 0% | 38 100% | 17% |
| 3 | 16 76% | 11% | 5 24% | 7% | 0 0% | 0% | 21 100% | 9% |
| 4 | 12 75% | 8% | 3 19% | 4% | 1 6% | 25% | 16 100% | 7% |
| 5 | 1 33% | 1% | 2 67% | 3% | 0 0% | 0% | 3 100% | 1% |
| 6 | 11 55% | 7% | 9 45% | 13% | 0 0% | 0% | 20 100% | 9% |
| 7 | 6 67% | 4% | 3 33% | 4% | 0 0% | 0% | 9 100% | 4% |
| 8 | 1 5% | 1% | 20 95% | 28% | 0 0% | 0% | 21 100% | 9% |
| 9 | 2 100% | 1% | 0 0% | 0% | 0 0% | 0% | 2 100% | 1% |
| TOTALS | 151 | 100% | 72 | 100% | 4 | 100% | 227 | 100% |

18

TABLE 9
ANALYSIS OF METHODOLOGY BY CENTRALITY

| METHOD-OLOGY | CONVERGENT | | MARGINALLY CONVERGENT | | : | SOME CONVERGENCE | | NOT CONVERGENT | | TOTAL | |
|---|---|---|---|---|---|---|---|---|---|---|---|
| 1 | 7 | 22% | 55 | 47% | : | 62 | 42% | 35 | 44% | 97 | 43% |
| | 7% | | 57% | | : | 64% | | 36% | | 100% | |
| 2 | 12 | 38% | 14 | 12% | : | 26 | 18% | 12 | 15% | 38 | 17% |
| | 32% | | 37% | | : | 68% | | 32% | | 100% | |
| 3 | 4 | 13% | 12 | 10% | : | 16 | 11% | 5 | 6% | 21 | 9% |
| | 19% | | 57% | | : | 76% | | 24% | | 100% | |
| 4 | 5 | 16% | 7 | 6% | : | 12 | 8% | 4 | 5% | 16 | 7% |
| | 31% | | 44% | | : | 75% | | 25% | | 100% | |
| 5 | 0 | 0% | 2 | 2% | : | 2 | 1% | 1 | 1% | 3 | 1% |
| | 0% | | 67% | | : | 67% | | 33% | | 100% | |
| 6 | 2 | 6% | 8 | 7% | : | 10 | 7% | 10 | 13% | 20 | 9% |
| | 10% | | 40% | | : | 50% | | 50% | | 100% | |
| 7 | 0 | 0% | 6 | 5% | : | 6 | 4% | 3 | 4% | 9 | 4% |
| | 0% | | 67% | | : | 67% | | 33% | | 100% | |
| 8 | 2 | 6% | 10 | 9% | : | 12 | 8% | 9 | 11% | 21 | 9% |
| | 10% | | 48% | | : | 57% | | 43% | | 100% | |
| 9 | 0 | 0% | 2 | 2% | : | 2 | 1% | 0 | 0% | 2 | 1% |
| | 0% | | 100% | | : | 100% | | 0% | | 100% | |
| TOTALS | 32 | 100% | 116 | 100% | : | 148 | 100% | 79 | 100% | 227 | 100% |

CENTRALITY

19

TABLE 10
ANALYSIS OF OBJECTIVE BY CENTRALITY

CENTRALITY

| OBJECTIVE | CONVERGENT | MARGINALLY CONVERGENT | SOME CONVERGENCE | NOT CONVERGENT | TOTAL |
|---|---|---|---|---|---|
| THEORY | 25 74% 17% | 75 66% 50% | 100 68% 66% | 51 65% 34% | 151 67% 100% |
| PRACTICE | 5 15% 7% | 39 34% 54% | 44 30% 61% | 28 35% 39% | 72 32% 100% |
| METHODOLOGY | 4 12% 100% | 0 0% 0% | 4 3% 100% | 0 0% 0% | 4 2% 100% |
| | 34 100% | 114 100% | 148 100% | 79 100% | 227 100% |

20

TABLE 11

ANALYSIS OF "SOME CONVERGENCE" BY OBJECTIVE AND BY REVEIEWER

| CENTRALITY | CHURCHILL & LEWIS | PRESENT AUTHORS |
|---|---|---|
| 1 Contribution to Theory | 67% | 76% |
| 2 Contribution To Practice | 61% | 46% |
| 3 Contribution to Methodology | 100% | 100% |

SUMMARY

ENTREPRENEURSHIP RESEARCH POPULATIONS - WHO ARE THEY?

Authors

    Robert H. Brockhaus
    Randolph A. Pohlman

Addresses

    School of Business
    St. Louis University
    3674 Lindell Boulevard
    St. Louis, MO 63108
    (314) 658-3826

    College of Business Administration
    Kansas State University
    Manhattan, Kansas 66506
    (913) 532-7190

Principal Topics

The results of a summary research workshop will be presented and discussed with the objective to be a further distillation and increased awareness of the need to fully describe research populations. A more complete description will allow for a better understanding of the significance of research on entrepreneurs. With this better understanding, future research efforts can more effectively examine the voids in our knowledge.

One of the frequent complaints about current research on "small business owners" and "entrepreneurs" is the lack of a widely accepted definition of these terms. The lack of clarity of these terms is a problem which will probably continue to haunt us - just as the definition of when human life begins or ends haunts medical, religious, and legal experts. Thus, it was not the focus of this workshop to attempt to define these terms.

However, a major improvement in research methodology would occur if all empirical research included a complete description of the population being studied. The purpose of this workshop was to fully examine various factors which could be used to describe the subjects being studied and to ascertain the level of description about each factor.

For example, is ownership of a business an important factor in the description of the population? If so, is a simple "yes" or "no" an adequate level of description about ownership. Or, should the percent of ownership be presented? If yes, to what degree of precision? Are categories of 0%, 1-25%, 26-50%, 76-99% or 100% adequate or should it be in increments of 10% or 1% or 50%?

## Major Findings and Implications

The workshop participants suggested a list of 40 factors and levels of description which will enable future research to be more useful to subsequent researchers. Indeed, it may move us one small step closer to generally agreed definitions of entrepreneurs and small business owners.

SUMMARY

GREEK - AMERICAN ENTREPRENEURSHIP:
TRAITS, MOTIVES, BEHAVIOR AND VALUES

Author

   Charal. C. Kanellopoulos

Addresses

   24 Kleomenous Street
   10676 Athens, Greece
   Tel. 7236584
   or
   Management Dept.
   Hofstra University
   Hempstead, N.Y. 11550

Principal Topics

   Entrepreneur: Age, Education, "Origin", Cultural Perception.
   Enterprise: "Age" of Firm, Employees, Sales, Industry.
   Entrepreneurial Past: Start Motives, Starting Age, Parents
   Attitude, Start Strengths, Start Weaknesses and Way of Overcoming,
   Numbers of Starts.
   Entrepreneurial Present-Work and Leisure Habits: Day Start Time, A
   Working Day's First Task, Evening and Weekend Occupations, Vacation
   per Year, Work Hours per Week, Managerial Functions, Business
   Functions/Activities.
   Entrepreneurial Present - Preferences and Perceptions: Appealing
   Entrepreneurial Aspects, Frustrating Entrepreneurial Aspects,
   "Important Lessons" learned, Innovativeness and Entrepreneurship,
   Environmental Factors of Influence, Fatal Entreprepneurial Mistakes
   and Traits, Terminal and Instrumental Values.

Major Findings

   Under the condition of representativeness of the data collected
   through this survey, American-Greek entrepreneurs are mainly (70.5%)
   between 46 and 65 years of age and hold at least a College degree
   (76.3%). In their majority (58.8% - 65.6%) they are second generation and regard themselves rather as Americans (76.65%).

   American-Greek firms in their majority (52.1%) had in 1986 a life of
   11-30 years and employed less than 20 employees (53%) and less than
   75 (80%). They made in 1985 between $60,000 and $2 million 52%
   less than $6 million 71%.

Self-actualization needs (Ambition, Creativity, Independence)
account for 65.6% of the motives for starting their own business,
while money only for 9.5%. At that time most of these new entrepreneurs (51.5%) were between 21 and 30 years old and faced a positive
attitude from their parents (80.3%). They regard as their main
starting strengths Energy/hard work and Desire to succeed.

The sample entrepreneurs start their work day either at 8:00 - 8:30
(29.6%) or at 9:00 - 9:30 (23.4%) with planning their day activities
(23.8%) or with their daily mail (19.0%). They spend their "free"
time in the evenings reading/studying (18%) or continuing their work
(15%) and socializing (13%), while on weekends they take care of
their family (14%), relax (14%) socialize (10%) and read/study (9%).

Their vacation is usually between 1-3 weeks (41.2%) and they prefer
to spend quite a long time at work (more than 50 hours/week) 64.4%
or over 60 hours/week (23%).

Their Terminal Values are:  1) Health, 2) Family Security, 3)
Comfortable Life and 4) A Sense of Accomplishment.  Their
Instrumental Values are:  1) Responsible, 2) Honest, 3) Capable and
4) Ambitious.

# A TALE OF TWO PARKS
## KEY FACTORS INFLUENCING THE LOCATION DECISION PROCESS OF NEW ENTREPRENEURIAL COMPANIES AT RENSSELAER (NEW YORK STATE) AND PLASSEY (IRELAND) TECHNOLOGY PARKS

Pier A. Abetti, Rensselaer Polytechnic Institute
Joyce O'Connor, National Institute for Higher Education
Lisa M. Ehid, Rensselaer Technology Park
Joseph L. Rocco, General Electric Company
Barry J. Sanders, New York State Energy R&D Authority

## ABSTRACT

Most new entrepreneurial companies get started in temporary quarters, which range from the proverbial garage to more sophisticated Incubator facilities. As soon as they achieve initial success, these companies outgrow (physically and psychologically) their original home and seek more permanent locations. Since these new ventures are major contributors to local economic growth, employment and area renewal, they are eagerly sought as desirable tenants by a variety of private and public real estate organizations and economic/industrial development authorities. Technology Parks, which specialize in attracting high-tech new ventures or new intrapreneurial branches of established companies, are now a world-wide phenomenon.

This paper investigates the key factors which have influenced new entrepreneurial (or intrapreneurial) companies to locate at two recently formed and highly successful parks: Rensselaer Technology Park in North Greenbush, New York and Plassey Technological Park in Limerick, Ireland. An 50-question survey was developed at Rensselaer Polytechnic Institute in order to determine the key factors which influenced the decision of a company to locate at the Rensselaer Technology Park. This questionnaire was administered during personal interviews with the principal decision makers of 23 tenants (out of 28 total) during the Summer of 1986. The same questionnaire was administered to 22 tenants (out of 31 total) of Plassey Technological Park in the Fall of 1986. The results of the two surveys were analyzed separately using frequency tables to summarize the data and highlight trends in factor importance. Chi-square analysis was used to determine significant correlations between survey parameters, and between company demographics and factor importance levels. Additional analyses were performed to determine significant similarities and differences between the two Technology Parks. Conclusions are drawn which should be useful to:

(1)    technical entrepreneurs seeking a more permanent
location, who are bewildered by the variety of possible
choices and the competition between sundry real estate,
economic and industrial development organizations

(2)    managers of Technology (and similar) Parks who are
striving to attract these entrepreneurs to their
location.

INITIAL TEMPORARY LOCATIONS:  GARAGES, INCUBATORS AND SKUNK WORKS

Most new entrepreneurial companies get started in temporary
quarters with a minimum of technical and business equipment,
facilities, comforts and amenities.  American and European folklore
is replete with stories of founders who got started in the proverbial
garages, lofts, cellars or abandoned mills and then moved to plush
offices and superbly equipped laboratories among landscaped grounds
provided with all modern amenities for sport and recreation.  The
histories of Apple, EDS, ROLM are modern versions of the tale of
Cinderella who, however, has now become a princess through her own
efforts, rather than through the magic intervention of a Prince
Charming.

High-tech entrepreneurship is a relatively new phenomenon,
which appeared in the USA and in the United Kingdom around 1950.  It
then spread to Canada, Sweden, France, Japan, the Republic of Ireland
and subsequently to many other countries all over the world.  New
entrepreneurial ventures have made major contributions to the
national economies, through the creation of new markets, new
industries, new jobs and new export opportunities.  Because of the
pervasive impact of technology in the modern world and its
contribution to international competitiveness, major emphasis is now
being given in many countries to the creation of new high-tech
ventures through private and public initiatives.  In parallel, these
initiatives have tried to recreate, with greater or lesser degree of
success, the environmental conditions where successful new ventures
originated by chance rather than by design.  This is the primary
objective of an Incubator facility, or Innovation Center.[1]

In order to nurture the entrepreneurial spirit, many
Incubators strive to duplicate the environment and physical
facilities of the initial "heroic era" of entrepreneurship.  Thus, by
design or convenience, many incubators are located in old mills (for
instance, the Kodak Incubator in Rochester, New York), in abandoned
industrial facilities, often in decaying neighborhoods (for instance,
several Control Data Incubators) or in unused offices and schools

---

[1]R.W. Smilor and M.D. Gill, Jr., <u>The New Business
Incubator</u>, Lexington Books, Lexington, MA, 1986.

owned by local governments (for instance in Calgary, Alberta). The more successful Incubators try to combine the spartan facilities of the proverbial garage with sophisticated technical and business tools, such as computers, word processors, model shops, data bases, technical and management consulting, which are made available to all Incubator tenants. It is believed that this marriage of simple physical facilities with up-to-date technical business assistance will improve the probability of success of the Incubator companies. Obviously, as implied by its name, an Incubator is strictly a temporary facility for its tenants. In fact, the goal of the "incubating" entrepreneurs should be to grow the company rapidly and successfully and thus outgrow their initial facilities, moving to larger quarters. The goal of the Incubator management is to "graduate" rapidly and successfully the Incubator tenants, in order to have them move away and leave room for the next generation of start-ups, and to repeat this process many times.

It is well-known that most high-tech (and some not so high-tech) ventures have originated as spinoffs from universities or established companies.[2] In many cases, the sales and profits of the spinoffs have greatly exceeded those of the parent organization. This constant stream of spinoffs has created two technopoleis: Route 128 around Boston, Massachusetts and Silicon Valley in the San Francisco area.[3] This spinoff phenomenon is naturally a major concern to the parent companies. In fact, the parent suffers a triple loss: 1) the loss of creative and entrepreneurial people, 2) the opportunity loss of new products which could have been developed by the parent itself, and 3) the rise of entrepreneurial and aggressive competitors, usually serving the same markets with innovative products. Thus, large mature companies have tried a variety of approaches in order to stop or at least staunch this bleeding off of some of their best people, and at the same time to encourage potential entrepreneurs to remain within the company and develop new products, processes, services and new businesses under the company's sponsorship, as "intrapreneurs."[4]

Most approaches to intrapreneurship strive to combine the organic, even chaotic environment of independent new venture creation with organized and disciplined availability of ample resources from the company, in terms of skilled manpower, sophisticated equipment,

---

[2]E.M. Roberts, "Influences Upon the Performance of New Technical Enterprises" in A. Cooper and J. Komives (editors), Technical Entrepreneurship: A Symposium. Center for Venture Management, Milwaukee, WI, 1972.

[3]Rogers, E.M. and J.K. Larsen, Silicon Valley Fever, Basic Books, Inc., New York, NY, 1984.

[4]Pinchot, G. III, Intrapreneuring, Harper & Row, New York, NY, 1985.

sources of capital, technical, marketing and management consulting, etc. One approach is to separate, physically and psychologically, the "organic" intrapreneurial team from the "segmented" mechanistic organization with its inherent bureaucratic inertia, resistance to change, and fear of innovation. This can be achieved by setting up "Skunk Works" (for instance, Data General), Independent Business Units remote from the parent (for instance, the IBM Personal Computer unit) or by detaching a small group on the campus of a leading research university. In summary, it appears that the nature, structure and location of the initial facility is a major consideration in setting up new entrepreneurial (or intrapreneurial) ventures, and that this decision affects their chances of initial success. The case history of the Incubator Program of Rensselaer Polytechnic Institute (RPI) in Troy, New York clearly illustrates this point.[5]

## TRAINING INTERVENTIONS IN ENTREPRENEURSHIP : THE EXAMPLE OF IRELAND

Ireland is one of the lesser developed regions of the European Community and, in contrast to the United States, lacks culture, traditions and role models which favor the development of entrepreneurship. Therefore, a conscious effort is being made at Plassey Technological Park to train potential entrepreneurs who would start their own companies and locate in the Park.[6]

The training course in question was launched in January 1983. Shannon Development Company (SFADCo) and National Institute for Higher Education (NIHE), Limerick, jointly sponsored this course, both agencies having education and training responsibilities. The course is unique both at regional and national level in Ireland as it highlights the role of training intervention as a key component in the industrial strategy for indigenous company formation.[7]

---

[5]Abetti, P.A., C.W. LeMaistre and W.A. Wallace, "The Role of Technological Universities in Nurturing Innovation: the RPI 'Model'" in D.O. Gray, T. Solomon, W. Hetzner (editors), Technological Innovation-Strategies for a New Partnership, Elsevier Science Publishers (North-Holland), Amsterdam, 1986, pp. 251-260.

[6]J. O'Connor, "Can Entrepreneurs Be Found, Trained and Fostered in Peripheral Regions of the (European) Community?" in J.M. Gibb (Editor), Science Parks and Innovation Centres: Their Economic and Social Impact, Elsevier, Amsterdam, The Netherlands, 1985.

[7]O'Connor, J. High Technology Entrepreneurship: A Case Study of Training Intervention, Social Research Centre, N.I.H.E., Limerick, 1984.

The main elements are the interactions between (1) training intervention, (2) potential entrepreneurs and (3) mediating factors. The course ran for twenty-two weeks. Two sessions were held each week. The sessions typically were of 3 hours duration and it was expected that each participant would spend an additional 15 hours per week on work related to the course, e.g., meeting with fellow team members, developing a business plan. The focus of the course related to:

o Orientation to market needs
o Team formation
o Preparation of a business plan

In all 30 people, all males, joined the course initially, and 22 people completed it. What was the outcome? By January 1986 the short-term evaluation showed that the training course facilitated the creation of three entrepreneurial teams and enterprises. A further venture has been formed by a participant who remained on his own during the course but subsequently formed a team with someone outside the course.

A similar project funded under the European Social Fund Pilot Scheme has been launched to train 9 young graduates, in methods and techniques for innovation and entrepreneurship. These graduates are engineers, 4 are from Queen's University, Belfast, Northern Ireland and 5 from Irish third level institutions. The aim of the project is to develop export-oriented small industries in the North and South of Ireland. It is a joint programme between NIHE (Limerick) and Queen's University, Belfast, and the development agencies Shannon Development Company and LEDU, the Small Business Agency for Northern Ireland. The focus of the course is on:

o product development
o preparation of a business plan.

This project is in its early stages of development and, if successful, could lead to further projects in different industrial sectors and between different technical and third level (university) institutions. As an example of technology transfer this is a new initiative that will be evaluated and assessed for its effectiveness and reproductibility in other regions of the European Community.

THE MOVE TO MORE PERMANENT LOCATIONS; INDUSTRIAL, SCIENCE AND TECHNOLOGY PARKS

Ambitious and farsighted entrepreneurs strive for a fast growth rate, in order to pass the critical threshhold represented by sales above $1 million/year.[8] Thus, as soon as they achieve some

---

[8] J.A. Timmons, New Venture Creation, 2nd edition, Irwin, Homewood, IL, 1985.

initial success, new high-tech ventures, outgrow (physically and psychologically) their original homes and are faced with the decision of finding a more suitable, hopefully permanent location.

Moving to a new place, whether a new home or a new business location, is generally a trying experience. For entrepreneurs, who work long hours and are often fighting for survival, the extra effort of relocating their business and possibly their family, may be a traumatic experience. Thus, to minimize the negative effects of such a move, entrepreneurs prefer to relocate within the area, that is, within commuting distance of their initial location. Thus they are able to maintain the extensive network of contacts which they have already developed and their ongoing relationships with local universities, banks, legal, financial, business and technical advisors, customers and suppliers, government offices, chambers of commerce, service clubs, relatives, friends and acquaintances.

On the other hand, certain geographical areas may lack the infrastructure needed for the creation and development of successful high-tech ventures, such as the presence of a major technological university, the availability of venture capital, government incentives, and pools of skilled labor. In such cases, the entrepreneur may be forced to relocate to a distant area, such as the technopoleis of Route 128 near Boston, Silicon Valley in California, the North Carolina Research Triangle, the San Antonio-Austin, Texas area or the surroundings of Cambridge, England. These technopoleis have created major sources of wealth for the region and for the nation, and major efforts are being made by national, state and local governments to create the conditions for the rise and growth of Industrial, Science and Technology Parks which could develop into new technopoleis.[9] In many cases the initial effort consisted in making available land and sometimes physical facilities near universities and offering various financial and non-financial incentives to attract established companies from other locations, usually from other states or even countries. As the number of such local initiatives increased, it became clear that this was a zero-sum game. Therefore, the effort has now shifted towards attracting innovative entrepreneurs, or newly formed high-tech entrepreneurial companies, which create jobs directly and also through the growth of suppliers and support services. It has been estimated that one new high-tech job "pulls through" five to ten support jobs.

Not all of these Science and Technology Parks have been successful. Some have failed to develop despite substantial investments, others have grown very slowly. Even the now highly successful Research Triangle Park of North Carolina did not really

---

[9]Gibb, J.M. (editor), Science Parks and Innovation Centres: Their Economic and Social Impact, Elsevier, Amsterdam, The Netherlands, 1985.

"take off" until fifteen years after it was launched.  Cox states[10]
that the essential ingredients for success of Science and Technology
Parks are:
      1) a desirable living environment
      2) a major technological university
      3) major institutional research facilities
      4) a skilled labor force.
To these four factors we would add:
      5) community support
      6) an executive champion.

We will now discuss two recently formed Technology Parks
which have grown very successfully since their inception, in spite of
the lack of some of the ingredients listed by Cox.  These parks are:
      1)    Rensselaer Technology Park in North Greenbush, New York
           (USA) and
      2)    Plassey Technological Park in Limerick, Republic of
           Ireland.
Both these projects have concentrated their efforts on attracting
innovative entrepreneurs, newly formed high-tech ventures and support
companies, and entrepreneurial (or intrapreneurial) branches of
technologically-intensive established companies.

<u>Rensselaer Technology Park</u>

The Capital District of New York State has suffered a drastic
loss of employment since 1970.  All the textile factories in Cohoes
and Troy have closed down and castle-like empty mills remain as
symbols of a bygone era.  The employment level of the General
Electric Company (USA) in Schenectady has decreased from 29,000 in
1974 to 14,000 in 1986, and still continues to decline.  Local
mechanical, pharmaceutical and automotive industries are also
shrinking.  George Low, former President of Rensselaer Polytechnic
Institute (RPI), a private university founded in 1824, realized that
there was no hope to reverse this precipitous decline of industrial
employment in the New York Capital District by appealing to the large
mature firms to remain in the area and expand their facilities.
Rather, new jobs could only be created by entrepreneurial, innovative
high-tech ventures.  Thus arose the RPI Incubator and the Rensselaer
Technology Park (RTP).  Studies were initiated in 1979 by Michael
Wacholder (now Director of RTP) to convert several hundred acres of
pasture and woodland owned by RPI, about 5 miles south of the campus,
and only 15 minutes drive from Troy, Albany and Albany Airport.
While these studies were in progress, the Incubator Program
experienced significant success and it became apparent that the
development of the Technology Park should proceed.  RPI decided to

------------------------------

[10]Cox, R.N., "Lessons from 30 Years of Science Parks in the
USA" in reference 9 above, pp. 17-24.

invest several million dollars of its endowment funds to develop the first 100 acres of the Park, and work was started in 1982.

To maintain strict control of the environment, Rensselaer Technology Park does not sell land, but leases it on a long-term basis (49-99 years). All buildings must conform to rigid specifications and only R&D, service, and light manufacturing activities are allowed. The first tenant for the park was National Semiconductor's Optoelectronics Division in 1983. It had acquired a local company specializing in epitaxial GaAs light sources. National Semiconductor had to decide whether to move this company from Latham, NY to California or whether to move its own plant from Silicon Valley to the Rensselaer Technology Park. When it found that housing and related costs in the Capital District were one-third of those in Silicon Valley, the answer was clear. For the graduating incubator companies and other small or medium companies, who did not require an entire building, RPI has built five multi-tenant buildings that offer short-term lease space. An additional incentive was developed, a creative funding program instituted by the Town of North Greenbush, where HUD Small Cities Block Grant funds are utilized for seed capital investments (up to $100,000) in young companies which plan to increase employment.

The results of the first four years (1983-86) of the Rensselaer Technology Park have been very rewarding. Thirty-four companies are located in the Park, including six graduates from the Incubator Program, and together they employ about 350 people. Employment will increase to 700 in the Spring of 1987, when NYNEX (New York and New England Telephone Company) will occupy its new data center in a new building in the Park. As with the Incubator Program, there is close interaction between most companies and RPI faculty and students.

## Plassey Technological Park

Plassey Technological Park consists of some 500 acres of parkland, 311.3 of which are developed to date. The aim of the Park is to create a network of technological, manufacturing, research and development and educational support services in a single location. The objective of the Park is to foster close links between education and industry with a view to establishing and promoting steady growth of commercially viable, science-based industries. Located within the Park are two third-level educational institutions, a number of research and development organizations, a range of industrial support services, a variety of high technology manufacturing companies and the regional offices of the national development agencies. At present there are 31 organizations on the Park.

The National Institute for Higher Education (NIHE) is, in the technological sphere, the academic heart of Plassey Technological Park. Modelled after leading technological universities in North America and Europe, the NIHE was established in 1972 to help meet Ireland's growing need for special expertise and leadership in areas

arising from the new technologies.  Its three constitutent colleges:
Engineering and Science, Business, and Humanities provide programmes
of teaching and research to Batchelors, Masters and Doctorate level.
The 40,000 m$^2$ (450,000 square feet) complex, financed by the World
Bank and the European Investment Bank, houses Ireland's largest
complex of high technology education and research facilities in some
80 different laboratories.  The following are special target areas
for teaching and research:  microelectronics, information technology,
materials, manufacturing productivity and international trade.

In essence, Plassey Technological Park arose out of the perceived
need for a close working link between industry and the educational
sector in an effort to create a supportive environment for
entrepreneurship.  It is now a distinct part of Irish industrial
strategy.  It facilitates the industrial exploitation of research
and, at the same time, presents new, applied focii to research.  As
it operates, the Park aims to improve the level and usage of
technology in existing Irish industry and commerce and to create
around it the kind of work and living environment where future
leaders of Irish business, industry and the professions are being
educated.

Table I compares the most significant characteristics of the
two Parks.

TABLE I
COMPARISON OF RENSSELAER AND PLASSEY TECHNOLOGY PARKS

|  | Rensselaer | Plassey |
|---|---|---|
| Date Founded | 1982 | 1981 |
| Size |  |  |
| - total | 1200 acres | 500 acres |
| - developed to date | 150 acres | 311 acres |
| Number of Companies |  |  |
| (as of July 1986) | 28 | 31 |
| R&D and Manufacturing | 12 | 21 |
| Services | 16 | 10 |
| Total employment - July 1986 | 350 | 900* |
| Estimated employment - July 1987 | 700 | N/A** |
| Population of area | 500,000 | 250,000 |
| Technological University | Yes | Yes |
| Major R&D facilities | Yes | No |
| Other universities | Yes | Yes |
| Skilled labor force | Yes | Yes |
| Community support | Yes | Yes |
| Executive Champion | Yes | Yes |

*Excluding NIHE   **N/A = Not Available

## ANALYSIS OF THE LOCATION DECISION PROCESS OF
## NEW ENTREPRENEURIAL COMPANIES

As we have seen, new entrepreneurial companies, particularly if considered high-tech, are eagerly sought after as desirable tenants by a variety of private and public real estate organizations and economic or industrial development authorities. Therefore, the principals of such companies face a bewildering spectrum of choices in selecting prospective permanent locations. From discussions with entrepreneurs or intrapreneurial managers of newly created branches of established companies, the RPI authors developed a 50 item questionnaire to determine the key factors which influence the location decision process of US entrepreneurs.

Subsequent discussions with entrepreneurs at Plassey Technological Park indicated that the same factors were also considered valid by Irish entrepreneurs. The 50 questions are grouped into 6 categories:
1) -Company Demographics (employees, revenues, space, years in operation, type of company)
2) -Financial Considerations (lease rates and terms, space availability, cost of employees, etc.)
3) -Location (geographic location; buildings and grounds; area image, transportation; employee skills; interaction with customers, suppliers, services, government; recreational and cultural activities, etc.)
4) -Funding (local, state, federal government funding; tax incentives; private sources, banks and venture capital)
5) -University Connections (technical and management support, personal ties, students as employees, faculty consultants, image)
6) -Miscellaneous (alternate facilities, publicity, etc.)

The questionnaire was administered by RPI MBA students during personal interviews with the Chief Executives or key decision makers of each tenant company. The interviews ranged in duration between 30 minutes and one hour. Additional questions were raised to solicit more information from the respondents and key response items were recorded by the interviewers. The data was collected in July 1986 from 23 tenants of Rensselaer Technology Park, out of 28 total. The same questionnaire was administered by interviewers of the Social Research Centre of the National Institute of Higher Education to the principals or key decision makers of 22 tenants, out of 31 total, at Plassey Technological Park.

The results of the survey were accumulated separately for the two Parks, and used as inputs for analysis with a mainframe computer. The data were analyzed according to various statistical techniques, including chi-square and frequency testings. From the statistical analysis and the impressions gained during the interviews, conclusions were drawn separately for the two Parks. Finally, a comparison was made, using the statistical t-test, of corresponding variables of the two Parks, in order to highlight significant differences and similarities.

RESULTS: RENSSELAER TECHNOLOGY PARK

As stated above, 23 out of 28 companies were interviewed, or 82% of the total population. This percentage is sufficiently large to state that the sample selected is representative of the entire Park. However, a sample size of 23 is quite small for a reliable statistical analysis. To compensate for potential errors due to this cause, the confidence level was increased from 95% to 98%. To increase the response frequency, the data was rescaled into two levels: the first level grouping the "very important" and "important" responses, the second level maintaining the "unimportant" response. The results of the RTP survey are shown in the Appendix and are summarized below.

(1) Company Demographics
Of the 23 companies interviewed 35% are engaged in R&D and manufacturing, 65% in services. Sixty-five percent of the companies are less than 2 years old, 87% have less than 15 employees, 83% have annualized revenues less than $2 million, and 57% occupy less than 3000 square feet (270 m$^2$). These demographic data show that young, new entrepreneurial ventures comprise the majority of the Park tenants.

(2) Financial Considerations
Among the seven items included as financial considerations, four were considered significantly important, with response rates above 75%. These are (in parentheses is the percentage of respondents rating the item "very important" or "important"):
2.1 space availability for quick occupancy (87%)
2.2 landlord flexibility and approachability (83%)
2.3 length of lease term (78%)
2.4 lease rates (78%)
    Two items showed response rates between 50 and 75%:
2.5 ability to accommodate space growth (74%)
2.6 space flexibility (70%).

(3) Location
Among the 22 items included as location considerations, only two showed response rates above 75%:
3.1 building quality (83%)
3.2 appearance of grounds (83%)
    Ten items showed response rates between 50 and 75%:
3.3 geographic location (70%)
3.4 location to knowledge base, such as universities (70%)
3.5 quality of long-distance transportation (61%)
3.6 interaction with other tenants in the Park (61%)
3.7 employee commuting factors, such as traffic and roadways (57%)

3.8  education level of local employee base (57%)
3.9  location to suppliers and services (57%)
3.10 location near employee base (52%)
3.11 experience level of local employees (52%)
3.12 location to customer base (52%).
     Surprisingly, location to recreational and cultural
facilities showed low response rates (26% and 39%,
respectively).

(4) Funding
None of the six items comprising the importance of locating near
funding sources received a response rate higher than 50%:
Location to state and local government funding were rated 48% and
43% respectively, to venture capital and federal funding both at
35%, to local lending institutions at 30%, and to private capital
at 17%.

(5) RPI Connection
Of the 6 items measuring the importance of the Park being
associated with RPI, one was considered significantly important,
with response rate higher than 75%:
-connection with RPI image (78%)
and four showed responses higher than 50%:
-availability of technical support from RPI (57%)
-availability of RPI amenities, such as athletic facilities,
 tickets to hockey games, seminars, entertainment, etc. (57%)
-availability of RPI students as part-time or full-time
 employees (57%)
-availability of RPI faculty consultants (52%).

(6) General Summary
Table II summarizes all the RTP & PTP responses by the four main
categories, and shows the means and standard deviations.

TABLE II
SUMMARY OF RESPONSES BY FACTOR CLASSIFICATION

| Factor Classification | Number of Factors | Rensselaer Mean | S.D.* | Plassey Mean | S.D.* | S.S.D** |
|---|---|---|---|---|---|---|
| Financial | 7 | 72% | 17% | 68% | 12% | No |
| Location | 22 | 48% | 17% | 64% | 20% | Yes |
| Local Funding | 6 | 35% | 9% | 39% | 20% | No |
| Univ. Connection | 6 | 57% | 13% | 74% | 10% | No |

 * S.D. = Standard Deviation
** S.S.D. = Statistically Significantly Difference to the 98%
   confidence level

The summary data presented in Table II lead to some significant conclusions:

1. Even though the purpose of the Rensselaer Technology Park is different from that of a conventional real estate project, the success of the Park is based upon the recognition that the "real estate" considerations must be competitive. Therefore financial factors have the greatest influence in the entrepreneurs' location decision process.

2. The RPI Connection is next in importance. This category differentiates RTP from all other developments in the area.

3. Location is considered less important, despite the fact that this factor is rated as key by commercial real estate developers.

4. Location to local funding sources is the least important. This apparently surprising result may be explained by the fact that there are limited funding sources for new ventures in the New York Capital District, while venture capital is available from major nearby financial centers, specifically New York City and Boston.

(7)     Chi-Square Analysis of Correlation

The chi-square method of statistical analysis was utilized to determine significant correlations among demographics and factor importance. Due to the limited sample population, a minimum confidence level of 98% (rather than 95%) was chosen to filter the chi-square results and further enhance the reliability of the analysis. The following relationships were determined to be both significant and to have business implications:

1. Companies with less than 15 employees and those with revenues less or equal to $2 million annualized considered the connection with the RPI image to be important in their decision to locate at the Park.

2. Companies with less than 15 employees considered the availability of RPI technical support to be important. Technical support is defined to include the use of the library, computer center and of the RPI staff and students for applied research work and consulting.

3. Companies with annualized revenues less than or equal to $2 million thought that the availability of RPI consultants was important.

4. Service companies considered interaction with the fellow tenants important.

5. Companies with more than 15 employees considered the location to product transportation resources to be important.

In summary, the first 3 items above show that the RPI connection is most important for new ventures in their early stage of growth, which are a primary marketing target as desirable Park tenants.

The results of the Plassey Technological Park (PTP) survey are shown in the Appendix. Rather than summarize the entire survey, we will highlight only those data and factors where the two Parks appear to be different.

At PTP, 22 out of 31 companies were interviewed, or 71% of the total population. Here again, the percentage is sufficiently large to state that the sample size is representative. In addition, since the sample sizes of the two Parks are almost equal, the results are directly comparable.

(1) <u>Comparison of Company Demographics</u>
Of the 22 PTP companies interviewed, 64% are engaged in R&D and manufacturing, 36% in services. This is just about the opposite of the distribution at Rensselaer Technology Park (RTP) where service companies represent 65% of the total, perhaps reflecting the fact that Ireland is still in the stage of industrial development, while the US is already a service-oriented economy. Sixty-five percent of the PTP companies are less than 4 years old (compared to 64% at RTP less than 2 years old). Sixty-four percent of the PTP companies have less than 15 employees (compared to 87% at RTP). Sixty-two percent of the PTP companies occupy less than 3000 square feet (compared to 57% at RTP). Thus, PTP companies are somewhat older and larger than RTP companies, but small entrepreneurial firms comprise the majority of tenants at both Parks.

(2) <u>Comparison of Location Factors</u>
Table II above summarizes all the responses of the PTP survey, and shows the means and standard deviations. The t-test was utilized to evaluate the mean responses from each park and determine if each pair was statistically different. Comparison of each pair of means to a standard t distribution, and use of a 98% confidence level, identified only the Location Factors as statistically different. The Financial, Local Funding, and University Connection factors were not statistically significantly different between the parks.

We will now discuss those individual location factors which show major differences among the two Parks.

(3) <u>Financial Considerations</u>
Six of seven factors were rated as "important" or "very important" by tenants of both parks. However, cost of employees was important for PTP and not important for RTP.

(4) <u>Location</u>
As we have seen, the statistically significant differences between the two Parks are only in this category. Plassey tenants rated the importance of location factors higher than the tenants

at Rensselaer (means of 64% and 48% respectively).  In
particular, the neighborhood and location to metropolitan areas
factors were considered very important by PTP tenants, and not
important by RTP tenants.

(5) <u>University Connection</u>
Tenants of both parks considered the University connection to be
important, perhaps more so at Plassey than at Rensselaer.


## GENERAL CONCLUSIONS


We believe that this comparative study of two recently formed
highly successful technology parks has uncovered some significant
factors which affect the decision location process of new
entrepreneurial ventures.  It is well known that new high-tech
entrepreneurial companies tend to flock together in desirable
locations in order to enhance their networking opportunities, their
ability to attract venture capital, skilled employees, advisors,
etc.  For instance, there are now 700 computer related companies in
the Boston-Route 128 area.  Thus entrepreneurs may decide to locate
in an existing technopoleis for the above reasons and also because of
the "herd instinct" and "follow the leader" syndrome.  Since both
Rensselaer Technology Park and Plassey Technology Park are quite new
compared to Route 128, Silicon Valley and North Carolina Research
Triangle, the decision location process of the entrepreneurs located
at Rensselaer and Plassey was not affected by this syndrome and,
therefore, should have been more objective.  Hence, the importance of
the results of this preliminary study, in spite of the limited sample
sizes.
Our conclusions are:
  (1) The Rensselaer and Plassey Technology Parks are located
      on opposite sides of the Atlantic Ocean, in countries
      with a common language, but with different cultural,
      social, political and economic characteristics.
      Nonetheless, the responses of the tenants of both Parks
      were surprisingly the same, with a statistically
      significant difference only in the location category.
      This may be due to the fact that young entrepreneurial
      companies are a strong majority in both parks, and
      entrepreneurs are essentially the same kind of people,
      driven by the same forces, in USA and Ireland.
  (2) Managers of Technology Parks should realize that they
      operate in the industrial real estate business.
      Therefore, the necessary but not sufficient condition for
      success of their Park is to be competitive in terms of
      lease rates and terms, space availability and
      flexibility, building quality, ground appearances and
      geographic location.
  (3) Connection with a nearby technological educational
      institution is very important as an "extra incentive" to
      attract desirable park tenants.  This connection is

particularly important for small newly created ventures.It includes image, availability of faculty, staff and students for technical work and consulting, use of the library, computer center, etc. and of the university recreational facilities.

(4) Location is important in Ireland, but less so in the USA. The most important factors are geography, neighborhood, availability of long-distance transportation, employee commuting factors, availability of educated and skilled employees and proximity to knowledge base. Less important are recreational and cultural activities, probably because entrepreneurs have little time available for such amenities.

(5) Surprisingly, location near funding sources, whether government agencies, banks, private or venture capital does not appear to be important. This may be due to the fact that entrepreneurs are apt to start with their own savings and funds from friends and relatives. As soon as they have achieved initial success, they may obtain venture capital from major financial centers regardless of location.

(6) Service companies tend to locate in Technology Parks in order to be close to their high-tech customers.

(7) High-tech entrepreneurs faced with the decision of finding a more permanent home after achieving initial success, should shop around for the best real estate deal they can get, provided there is a solid ongoing connection with a major technological educational institution.

ACKNOWLEDGEMENT


The authors gratefully acknowledge the cooperation and assistance of Michael H. Wacholder, Director of Rensselaer Technology Park and his staff.

41

APPENDIX

LOCATION FACTORS

PERCENTAGE OF SURVEY POPULATION RESPONDING
"VERY IMPORTANT" OR "IMPORTANT"

| Factor Description | Rensselaer (n=23) | Plassey (n=22) |
|---|---|---|
| FINANCIAL: | | |
| Lease Rates | 78% | 57% |
| Lease Terms | 78 | 55 |
| Landlord Flexibility | 83 | 75 |
| Space Availability | 87 | 86 |
| Space Flexibility | 70 | 58 |
| Accommodate Space Growth | 74 | 76 |
| Cost of Employees | 35 | 58 |
| LOCATION: | | |
| Geographic Location | 70% | 86% |
| Building Quality | 83 | 86 |
| Grounds | 83 | 82 |
| Employee Base | 52 | 77 |
| Neighborhood | 48 | 82 |
| Commuting Factor | 57 | 68 |
| Local Employees: | | |
| Education Level | 57% | 91% |
| Experience Level | 52 | 77 |
| Regional Cost of Living | 43 | 50 |
| Quality of Local Public Transp. | 22 | 41 |
| Quality of Long-Distance Transp. | 61 | 59 |
| Location to Knowledge Base | 70 | 91 |
| Interaction with Tenants | 61 | 77 |
| Location to Metropolitan | 43 | 82 |
| Customer Base | 52 | 41 |
| Customers - Park | 26 | 36 |
| Supplier/Services - Area | 57 | 62 |
| Supplier/Services - Park | 22 | 47 |
| Product Transportation | 30 | 52 |
| Government | 30 | 30 |
| Recreational Facilities | 26 | 52 |
| Cultural Activities | 39 | 43 |

-continued-

## LOCATION FACTORS

### PERCENTAGE OF SURVEY POPULATION RESPONDING
### "VERY IMPORTANT" OR "IMPORTANT"

| Factor Description* | Rensselaer (n=23) | Plassey (n=22) |
|---|---|---|
| FUNDING: | | |
| *North Greenbush/Shannon Free Area Development Company | 43% | 55% |
| *NYS Government/Industrial Development Authority | 48 | 44 |
| *Federal Government/Tax Incentives | 35 | 53 |
| Local Lending Institutions | 30 | 55 |
| Private Sources | 17 | 0 |
| Venture Capital | 35 | 18 |
| | | |
| *RPI/NIHE CONNECTION | | |
| Technical Support | 57% | 71% |
| Amenities | 57 | 76 |
| Previous Ties | 39 | 62 |
| Students as Employees | 57 | 52 |
| Faculty Consulting | 52 | 85 |
| Image Connection | 78 | 85 |

* First item pertains to Rensselaer, second item to Plassey.

NETWORK SUPPORT SYSTEMS: HOW COMMUNITIES
CAN ENCOURAGE ENTREPRENEURSHIP

David H. Holt, James Madison University

## ABSTRACT

Networking is important for new venture creation, and while there
has been much written about networks, few implications have been drawn to
suggest ways in which community leaders can actively encourage entrepreneurship. This study focuses networking and how community support systems
can benefit entrepreneurs when making location and start-up decisions. By
asking questions of a sizeable sample of business owners and new venture
managers, more than a hundred suggestions evolved for community programs.
These response formed the core of a three-phase Delphi study with convergence of opinions on ten rank-ordered community support activities. Panel
participants also rank-ordered the most important considerations related
to business location decisions.

## PERSPECTIVE OF NETWORKS

Networks are associations of individuals or groups that facilitate
access to information or resources.  These associations range from family
ties to innovative computer-linked telecommunications, but most networks
are social or cultural in nature. Historically, immigrants have relied on
ethnic bonds to find jobs or start new businesses; the cultural ties that
exist among ethnic groups suggest a vibrant networking process.  There is
substantial evidence that many minority enterprises and ethnic-based ventures rely on strong coalitions.[1]  In a social sense, a growing number
of focal groups, such as those aimed at helping women, have been formed
in recent years.[2]  Examples of these are the American Women's Economic

---

[1]Ivan Light, Ethnic Enterprise in America: Business and Welfare
among Chinese, Japanese, and Blacks, University of California Press,
Berkeley, CA, 1972; Albert Shapero and Lisa Sokol, "The Social Dimensions
of Entrepreneurship," in Calvin A. Kent, Donald L. Sexton, and Karl H.
Vesper (eds) Encyclopedia of Entrepreneurship, Prentice-Hall, Inc.,
Englewood Cliffs, NJ, 1982, pp. 72-90.

[2]Jeffry A. Timmons, Leonard E. Smollen, and Alexander L. M.
Dingee, Jr. New Venture Creation: A Guide to Entrepreneurship, 2nd ed.,
Richard D. Irwin, Inc., Homewood, IL, 1985, pp. 46-47.

Development Corporation, the Association of Women Entrepreneurs, and the National Association of Women Business Owners.

Social networks include regional associations, such as the Smaller Business Association of New England, and, of course, there are many local clubs and chapters of national organizations that provide many opportunities for business affiliations. Educational programs have gained wider acceptance and have brought together business persons, entrepreneurs, and educators; the MIT Enterprise Forum is perhaps the most notable alliance. Student networks provide yet another dimension, evidenced by the national Association of Collegiate Entrepreneurs (ACE).

Conceptually entrepreneurs are individualistic, and while they are stereotyped as independent risk takers who avoid group enterprise, recent studies have refuted this. The evidence suggests that entrepreneurs rely heavily on business and social contacts to gain access to important material resources, information, customers, and capital.[3]

If we accept entrepreneurship, in part, as an opportunity seeking activity, then it follows that more opportunities emerge through greater social interaction. This viewpoint is not speculative but is supported by careful sociological research.[4] This may be more accute for minority and women entrepreneurs who generally have less business experience and fewer professional contacts than non-minority men in similar circumstances.[5] However, recognizing opportunities is important only to the extent that resources can gathered to transform opportunities into plausible commercial ventures.

The transformation process often focuses on start-up money, and in this sense, professional associations coupled with strong networking can be crucial.[6] A more pervasive list of resource gathering efforts would include accessing information, attracting equity investors, securing debt

----

[3]Howard Aldrich and Catherine Zimmer, "Entrepreneurship Through Social Networks," in Donald L. Sexton and Raymond W. Smilor (eds) The Art and Science of Entrepreneurship, Ballinger Publishing Company, Cambridge, MA, 1986, pp.3-23; Mark Granovetter,"The Strength of Weak Ties: A Network Theory Revisited," in Peter V. Marsden and Nan Lin (eds) Social Structure and Network Analysis Sage Publishing, Beverly Hills, CA 1982, pp.105-113.

[4]Donald M. Dible, Up Your Own Organization! Reston Publishing Company, Reston, VA, 1986, pp. 59-62, 70-71; Linton C. Freeman, "Centrality in Social Networks: Conceptual Clarification," Social Networks, Vol. 1, 1979, pp.215-239.

[5]Robert D. Hisrich and Candida Brush, "The Woman Entrepreneur," Journal of Small Business Management, (January, 1984), pp. 30-37.

[6]Albert V. Bruno, Tysoon T. Tyebjee, and James C. Anderson, "Finding a Way Through the Venture Capital Maze," Business Horizons, (January-February, 1985), pp.12-19.

underwriting, contacting vendors and key suppliers, and obtaining legal, professional, and technical support. In most instances, networking in and through informal associations is antecedent to, and essential to, entrepreneurial success.[7] Many initial contacts become middlemen who introduce aspiring entrepreneurs to third parties.[8]

Research has also shown that individuals who leave corporate life to new start businesses have elaborate networks comprised of colleagues, business persons, and technical specialists.[9] Professionals, such as bankers, attorneys, and accountants, are prominent in business networks, but social contacts may be equally important and include family members, friends, work associates, and perhaps competitors.[10] It is not surprising to find that "weak ties" are crucial for venture success. Weak ties are third-party "friends of friends" who are accessible through mutual affiliations.[11] There are also strong alliances among technical occupation groups with congruent role sets.

## FRAMEWORK OF STUDY

Recognizing the importance of networks, this study was implemented in 1986 to investigate two specific questions using a Delphi framework to encourage selected participants to provide indepth responses. The first question was concerned with factors most important to new venture managers for making location decisions. The second question encouraged ideas for community leaders and how they might help enterprises start up or to locate in their areas. The format of the study and summary of recommendations are provided in the appendix without elaboration on methodology or results.

---

[7]Karl H. Vesper, New Venture Strategies, Prentice-Hall, Inc., Englewood Cliffs, NJ, 1980, pp.27-55; William E. Wetzel, Jr., "Informal Risk Capital in New England," Frontiers of Entrepreneurship Research, 1981, pp. 217-245.

[8]Bill Sloan, "How Middlemen Help Raise Money," Venture (February 1981), pp. 50-51.

[9]David A. Garvin,"Spin-offs and the New Firm Formation Process," California Management Review, Vol.25, No.2, 1983, pp. 3-20; also, Bengt Johanaisson, "New Venture Creation -- A Network Approach," Frontiers of Entrepreneurship Research, 1986, pp. 236-238.

[10]Howard Aldrich, Ben Rosen, and William Woodward, "Social Behavior and Entrepreneurial Networks," Frontiers of Entrepreneurship Research, 1986, pp. 239-240.

[11]Mark Granovetter, "The Strength of Weak Ties," The American Journal of Sociology, Vol.78, No.6 (May, 1973), pp. 1360-1380.

## The Study

Two open-ended questions, asked in the first round, provided lists of responses that were combined into short statements. Initially, there was a great deal of duplication with more than a hundred answers for each question. After combination, question #1 reflected 38 items; question #2 reflected 25 items. The results were sent to respondents for round two in which they were asked to rank-order survey responses by assigning numbers from one to ten (1 = highest, 10 = lowest). Participants were encouraged to rank all items for each question, but nearly all assigned rankings for only their first ten choices. Each person could also add to the list by expressing new ideas for further consideration.

The third and final round instrument summarized rankings from the second round, and participants were asked to reconcile their rank-orders with one-to-ten scoring. In each instance, participants were encouraged to clarify their statements which was valuable for interpretation.

## The Participants

The initial survey was sent to 973 individuals from 22 chapters of the International Management Council. The chapters from IMC Divisions II, III, and V represented firms in Maryland, New Jersey, New York, Virginia, and Pennsylvania. Of those surveyed, 278 responded (28.6%). There were

TABLE I

| Summary of Participants in Study[*] (1st round n = 278; 3rd round n = 93) | | | | |
|---|---|---|---|---|
| Category of Enterprise | Number in Study | Mean Years in Firm | Legal Form | Gross Sales (x 1000) |
| Manufacturing | 86 (27) | 18.7 ( 7.8) | S-2,P-3,C-81 (S-0,P-1,C-26) | $14,260 (11,020) |
| Retail Merchandising | 71 (19) | 13.4 ( 4.4) | S-7,P-6,C-58 (S-7,P-0,C-11) | 1,050 (1,011) |
| Personal Services | 69 (24) | 14.1 ( 6.9) | S-36,P-15,C-18 (S-12,P-1,C-11) | 191 (157) |
| Computer Sales and Services | 21 (8) | 3.4 (3.8) | S-1,P-12,C-8 (S-0,P-1,C-7) | 367 (412) |
| Professional Services | 18 (9) | 9.8 (4.7) | S-2,P-11,C-5 (S-1,P-7,C-1) | 370 (441) |
| Construction | 13 (6) | 8.2 (5.3) | S-3,P-1,C-9 (S-0,P-0,C-6) | 426 (419) |

[*] Third-round data in ( ); S-Proprietor, P-Partner, C-Corporation.

59 surveys returned undelivered (6.1%) due to address changes or lack of mailing information. By coincidence, not design, all 278 respondents were men. A profile of the respondents was determined by asking the legal form of enterprise, type of product or service, estimated gross sales for the previous year, and length of time each individual had been with the firm. Table I summarizes this information and also indicates the attrition from 278 to 93 participants between the first and final round of inquiry. This may seem like a large drop in numbers, but for a study requiring written responses, the initial 28.6% response was much better than expected, and the retention of 93 in a "panel" format was almost too large.

## RESULTS

Ranking ordering was accomplished for both questions based on the number of respondents assigning the highest priorities to items. Where a score was the same for two or more items, the second highest priority was taken into account. A pattern emerged consistent with this approach that supporting rankings for all ten items in each question. As shown in the tables that follow, the total number of top ten ratings in each item also supported the results.

### Location Decisions

Table II replicates Question #1 and the ten most important factors for making location decisions. Actual scoring from third-round results is shown to illustrate the relative emphasis placed on each item. Using the highest rank-order, several interesting results emerged.

The single most important factor concerned local wage and salary data reflecting, in part, a concern for attracting employees at reasonable costs. Commentary by respondents also indicated that the "structure" of wages and salaries was important in terms of union activity and potential human resource problems. There was also an indication that wage and salary data were vital from a marketing standpoint reflecting, in part, a concern for a healthy economic environment with effective demand.

The second ranked response indicated a concern with local networks of business organizations and professionals. Actual difference between this and the wage and salary item was slight. While commentary was brief on this point, participants emphasized the need for collegial groups such as the IMC; manufacturers' associations were singled out together with a number of social groups (Rotary and chapters of the National Association of Accountants).

The third-ranked area encompassed logistics and transportation. It was not unusual to note a concern with access to logistics and transportation facilities, but it is important to note that this item was not concerned with "travel;" it was focused on freight and shipping issues.

The fourth ranked item was not expected. The participants placed great weight on knowing something about patterns of business success and past failures. There were few insights how this data could be generated,

TABLE II

| Question #1: Locating a business enterprise involves many important questions. Please list at least three factors that you feel new business venture managers must consider when making a location decision. |
| --- |

| Response Category in Summary Form: | Summary of Rank Order | | | | | | | | | | All (n) |
| --- | --- | --- | --- | --- | --- | --- | --- | --- | --- | --- | --- |
| | 1 | 2 | 3 | 4 | 5 | 6 | 7 | 8 | 9 | 10 | |
| 1. Advantages of local wage and salary structures. | 15 | 13 | 7 | 9 | 9 | 9 | 3 | 5 | 5 | 6 | (80) |
| 2. Business organizations, networked professionals. | 14 | 13 | 7 | 7 | 7 | 8 | 6 | 5 | 7 | 4 | (78) |
| 3. Logistics: roads, rail, trucking, freight, air. | 13 | 12 | 7 | 9 | 8 | 6 | 2 | 9 | 10 | 3 | (78) |
| 4. Patterns success/failure for area businesses. | 13 | 11 | 8 | 7 | 8 | 5 | 2 | 8 | 6 | 2 | (70) |
| 5. Subcontractor services, fabrication, supplies. | 11 | 11 | 9 | 7 | 7 | 4 | 1 | 7 | 7 | 6 | (70) |
| 6. Predisposition of banks, financial institutions. | 8 | 7 | 12 | 8 | 6 | 4 | 0 | 1 | 10 | 9 | (65) |
| 7. Proximity to airline & public transportation. | 7 | 7 | 9 | 11 | 6 | 4 | 2 | 2 | 9 | 11 | (68) |
| 8. Available technical and professional services. | 7 | 5 | 12 | 8 | 7 | 5 | 1 | 1 | 8 | 12 | (66) |
| 9. Tax advantages compared with other areas. | 3 | 6 | 8 | 10 | 9 | 10 | 7 | 3 | 5 | 13 | (74) |
| 10. Water supply, sewage, & commercial disposal. | 2 | 6 | 6 | 10 | 10 | 3 | 2 | 2 | 11 | 1 | (65) |
| Totals: | 93 | 91 | 85 | 85 | 76 | 58 | 26 | 43 | 78 | 79 | (714) |

but the issue created interest during the survey so that nearly a third of all respondents placed it in the top five categories.

Subcontracting networks, including those for services, fabricated materials, and supplies, was ranked fifth. There was strong support for this factor category with nearly half of the participants rating it among the five most important issues. Commentary that accompanied the response indicated that firms would not have located in their communities without substantial support from subcontractors and vendors.

Those factors ranked sixth, seventh, and eighth were perceptional in nature with ambiguous definitions: "Predisposition" of bankers to help new businesses, "proximity" of public transportation, and "availability" of support technical and professional services. There was no indication how to evaluate the predisposition of bankers to help new businesses, but clearly the respondents formed opinions about financial services in their areas. Proximity of public transportation and airline facilities was just as vague, yet perceived as important. Those who pressed for technical and professional services commented on engineering services, computer systems support, and consulting.

Tax considerations as a category was ranked ninth, and while state and local taxes can be easily determined, the participants indicated an interest in "comparative" data that suggested a more refined information base. The final item in the top ten concerned water, sewage, and disposal services. (Other utilities, gas and electric, formed a separate item but were not among the top ten rankings.)

## Community Support

Table III replicates Question #2 and summarizes suggestions by the participants for improved community support services. The suggestion with the highest rating was for a convenient data base that would include tax trends, labor rates, wages, assessments and licenses. These are economic in nature but also reflect concerns for social and political issues. The second highest rated suggestion for an entrepreneurial network to provide access to capital and professional support was rated lower than the data base by only the narrowest of margins.

The third most important was surprising and opened a new area for consideration. The participants were strongly in favor of a "facilities locator" -- a data base with search characteristics that would locate and profile available physical facilities. Commentary reflected some concern that entrepreneurs had little clear information about reasonable location opportunities, leases, rent, plant sites, and the infrastructure of real property. This would include legal use restrictions, covenants, zoning, and technical considerations such as water tables, potentially hazardous conditions, EPA compliance, and community expansion plans that influence location decisions.

The fourth highest ranked suggestion focused on analyses of trans-portation and logistics. This was consistent with question #1 responses where participants noted significant concern for similar issues and would include access to freight outlets, highways, trucking, rail services, and air services.

The fifth suggestion was entirely consistent with their perceived need for a network of subcontractors and vendors. This was not surprising given the crucial aspect of securing material resources, inventory, and supplies. However, the sixth ranked suggestion encompassed economic data that, for the most part, are available from many public or private publi-cations. Economic data is clearly of value, perhaps more important than indicated, but respondents felt it was available, hence less vital.

TABLE III

Question #2: Many communities are interested in helping new ventures get started and located in their areas. List at least three ways in which communities can help new firms start up or locate in their areas.

| Suggestions by Participants: | Summary of Rank Order | | | | | | | | | | All n= |
|---|---|---|---|---|---|---|---|---|---|---|---|
| | 1 | 2 | 3 | 4 | 5 | 6 | 7 | 8 | 9 | 10 | |
| 1. Data base on taxes, labor, wages, other. | 16 | 15 | 12 | 10 | 10 | 9 | 6 | 2 | 1 | 1 | (82) |
| 2. Network to capital & professional support. | 16 | 14 | 11 | 11 | 8 | 8 | 6 | 2 | 0 | 1 | (77) |
| 3. Facilities "locator" for new ventures. | 15 | 14 | 12 | 11 | 7 | 8 | 4 | 1 | 1 | 7 | (80) |
| 4. Transport & logistics analyses. | 11 | 13 | 12 | 9 | 10 | 11 | 2 | 5 | 5 | 1 | (79) |
| 5. Subcontractor list & relevant capabilities. | 11 | 11 | 9 | 10 | 9 | 12 | 5 | 6 | 0 | 4 | (77) |
| 6. Economic analyses for broad-based issues. | 7 | 9 | 9 | 8 | 12 | 15 | 10 | 7 | 3 | 0 | (80) |
| 7. Commercial and private travel, commuters. | 6 | 7 | 10 | 7 | 12 | 9 | 8 | 4 | 9 | 9 | (81) |
| 8. Historic development, expansion & change. | 5 | 4 | 6 | 7 | 6 | 7 | 10 | 11 | 7 | 13 | (76) |
| 9. Manufacturers' Assn. with specific help. | 4 | 4 | 5 | 8 | 9 | 5 | 3 | 3 | 4 | 11 | (56) |
| 10. Professional service listings. | 2 | 2 | 5 | 7 | 7 | 5 | 5 | 7 | 10 | 4 | (54) |
| Totals: | 93 | 93 | 91 | 88 | 90 | 89 | 59 | 48 | 40 | 51 | (742) |

Air transportation became a prominent consideration and reflected travel requirements. It was ranked seventh with specifications for data on commercial as well as private accommodations. Several comments focused on hub routes and ease of access to commuter airlines.

The eighth suggestion was unusual. It emphasized historic development coupled with information about patterns of change and plans for future community expansion. A lengthy comment that accompanied the initial suggestion implied that few entrepreneurs think deeply enough about those social and political forces that can often drastically change the course of business. Entrepreneurs, according to the respondent, often wear "cost blinders" when looking for a location and seldom consider vital community characteristics.

Ninth was the suggestion for a manufacturers' association network with a specific string attached that the MA should be able to assist with analyses related to business decisions. It was surprising to find this in the top ten suggestions since most communities represented in the survey had active manufacturing associations, or their equivalent. However, by hand matching responses on the issue, it became apparent that respondents from the manufacturing sector did not rate this suggestion high; the top 30 responses (values between one and five) were entirely in the service sectors (professional services, computer sales and service, or personal services). This prompts an unresolved question whether existing manufacturing associations network effectively with their service counterparts.

The final category suggested a network list of professional services coupled with a narrative of specific skills. Some concern was voiced by a respondent in the final round that such a listing would be difficult to create and to maintain unless all community services were included; to do otherwise would create undue advantage to only those listed. Several participants suggested it would be a form of advertising unless equitably administered by a responsible public agency.

## DISCUSSION

The lists of considerations that emerged from the study indicate a need for rather extensive information services, and these are focused on noneconomic issues. Aside from wage data and tax comparisons, the central interests from question #1 reflected operational requirements that would influence location decisions. Suggestions derived from question #2 indicated a pattern of community services that, in most instances, focused on noneconomic issues. These issues reflected a community's infrastructure, notably its social, legal, political, and demographic characteristics.

Participants clearly favored social and business networks, but not necessarily networks in which membership is required to access essential information. For example, a "facilities locator" implies access but not membership -- perhaps a data based system with for-fee services. The same applies to manufacturers' listings, subcontractor and vendor references, transportation and logistics data, and historic or planning scenarios.

Reliance on social and business networks is consistent with empirical studies, and in those instances when participants emphasized professional associations, the results are plausible. Just as intriguing is the number of factors and suggestions, initially listed and taken into round two, that were systematically ignored in the final analysis. The appendix notes the final rank order for each item in each question. Many of these are intuitively important considerations, however, they were set aside by participants as either relatively less critical to entrepreneurs or of a nature to be easily accessed through existing channels.

The listings also include a number of cultural considerations, and while these issues did not rank among the top, they attracted interest by a number of respondents. The "image" of a town, for example, was found to be of great importance to several participants. Several others suggested that quality schools, recreation, lower crime rates, and drug enforcement were critical. Compliance regulations, particularly those concerned with hazardous material disposition and employment were among the higher-rated considerations even though not among the top ten categories.

Economic theory suggests that businesses locate near their markets or primary resources. The results of this study do not strictly support this except through a general interpretation of response that emphasized transportation and logistics. The response pattern more readily supports an interest in sociocultural factors that were seen to influence start-up and location decisions.

## CONCLUSIONS

The study accomplished its intended purpose to investigate factors that are important to new venture managers when considering location, and further, to generate suggestions for community activities that encourage new ventures. Several of the ten most important factors in each instance are refreshing and may enrich community development efforts. For example, a "facilities locator" could be sponsored, perhaps through a university or government agency, to maintain a search-based index of property, plant locations, and location-specific information vital to entrepreneurs when making location decisions.

A network for subcontractors and vendor services may be a valuable addition in any community, and the relative importance of these services noted by participants indicates a perceived gap in existing sources. The same can be said of a professional services association, although such an association may be sensitive to create and maintain.

The Delphi responses suggest ample opportunities for new research by those interested in public policy and economic development, and there is much more work to be accomplished in network evaluation. As a summary statement, it should be recognized that while there was a convergence of opinions by participants, there was not complete agreement. Convergence is not the same as consensus, but there was a strong pattern of ratings for both location issues and suggestions for community support.

## Question 1: Location Issues (25 rank-ordered)

20 Local government attitude to welcome new ventures and businesses.
25 Availability of business incubator facilities.
 9 Tax advantages and comparisons with other areas.
24 Business taxes and license requirements compared to other areas.
19 Costs associated with insurance for property, fire, and liability.
12 Quality of local schools and reputation for children's education.
23 Recreation facilities and proximity to entertainment & shopping.
 6 Predisposition of bankers and financial mgrs. to help new businesses.
21 Labor supply related to skills and availability of competent workers.
13 Ability to attract and retain technical and managerial personnel.
 1 Advantages of local wage and salary structures.
22 Union profile and "right to work" legislation.
10 Water supply, sewage configuration, and commercial disposal service.
18 Utility rates and supplies (gas & electric) with forecasted growth.
14 Regulations governing hazardous waste, disposal, and compliance.
 3 Logistics: highways, rail, trucking, freight, and air transport.
 5 Advantages of local subcontracting, fabrication, and vendor supplies.
 7 Proximity to public and private air, air hubs, and commuter services.
16 Image of town, name recognition, address and proximity to major city.
 2 Business organizations with network linkage for professionals.
 4 Patterns of success and failure for similar businesses in area.
 8 Availability of technical and professional support services.
15 Trends for crime and crime rates, trends toward drug enforcement.
17 Market proximity and economic activity related to domestic sales.
11 Employment, compliance, local regulations, state compensation.

## Question 2: Suggestions for Communities (17 rank-ordered)

17 Inducements to lower start-up costs for rezoning or tax relief.
 9 Manufacturers' associations formal programs to help new ventures.
15 Demographic data for state and local population trends.
10 Professional service listings with narrative of skills/services.
 1 Data base on tax trends, labor rates, wages, assessments, licenses.
 5 Mfg list and search base for subcontractors, vendors, suppliers.
13 Profile of schools, education, and elementary/high school facilities.
 4 Analysis for transportation and logistics, routes to cities and hubs.
 7 Data access for commercial air travel and private air transport.
 2 Network for entrepreneurs to access capital and professional support.
 3 Facilities locator data base with infrastructure of location options.
11 Accessible data base on state and local laws and regulations on
   hazardous waste, filing, compliance, licensing, etc.
16 Procurement index to raw materials, supplies, contracted services.
12 Family life-style information on schools, recreation, wellness, etc.
14 Comparative data on crime, violence, drug abuse, and civil disorders.
 8 Historic profile on change, development, plans, boundary changes, new
   patterns of social activity.
 6 Economic data analyses: prices, housing, interest rates, producer
   prices, disposable income, unemployment, construction, etc.

# REFERENCES

Aldrich, Howard and Zimmer, Catherine, "Entrepreneurship Through Social Networks," in Sexton, Donald L. and Smilor, Raymond W. (eds) The Art and Science of Entrepreneurship, Ballinger Publishing Company, Cambridge, MA, 1986, pp. 3-23.

Aldrich, Howard, Rosen, Ben, and Woodward, William, "Social Behavior and Entrepreneurial Networks," Frontiers of Entrepreneurship Research 1986, pp. 239-240.

Bruno, Albert V., Tyebjee, Tysoon T., and Anderson, James C., "Finding a Way Through the Venture Capital Maze," Business Horizons (January-February, 1985), pp. 12-19.

Dible, Donald M. Up Your Own Organization! Reston Publishing Company, Reston, VA, 1986, pp. 59-62, 70-71.

Garvin, David A., "Spin-offs and the New Firm Formation Process," California Management Review, Vol. 25, No. 2, 1983, pp. 3-20.

Granovetter, Mark, "The Strength of Weak Ties," The American Journal of Sociology, Vol. 78, No. 6 (May 1973), pp. 1360-1380.

Granovetter, Mark, "The Strength of Weak Ties: A Network Theory Revisited," in Marsden, Peter V. and Lin, Nan (eds) Social Structure and Network Analysis, Sage Publishing, Beverly Hills, CA, 1982, pp. 105-113.

Freeman, Linton C., "Centrality in Social Networks: Conceptual Clarification," Social Networks, Vol. 1, 1979, pp. 215-239.

Hisrich, Robert D. and Brush, Candida, "The Woman Entrepreneur," Journal of Small Business Management, (January, 1984), pp. 30-37.

Light, Ivan, Ethnic Enterprise in America: Business and Welfare among Chinese, Japanese, and Blacks, University of California Press, Berkeley, CA, 1972.

Johannisson, Bengt, "New Venture Creation -- A Network Approach," Frontiers of Entrepreneurship Research 1986, pp. 236-238.

Shapero, Albert and Sokol, Lisa, "The Social Dimensions of Entrepreneurship," in Kent, Calvin A., Sexton, Donald L., and Vesper, Karl H. (eds) Encyclopedia of Entrepreneurship, Prentice-Hall, Inc., Englewood Cliffs, NJ, 1982, pp. 72-90.

Timmons, Jeffry A., with Smollen, Leonard E. and Dingee, Alexander L. M., Jr. New Venture Creation: A Guide to Entrepreneurship, 2nd ed., Richard D. Irwin, Inc., Homewood, IL, 1985, pp. 46-47.

Sloan, Bill, "How Middlemen Help Raise Money," Venture (February, 1981) pp. 50-51.

Vesper, Karl H., "New Venture Ideas: Do Not Overlook the Experience Factor," Harvard Business Review, Vol. 79, No. 4 (July-August, 1979), pp. 164-167.

Vesper, Karl H., New Venture Strategies, Prentice-Hall Inc., Englewood Cliffs, NJ, 1980, pp. 27-55.

Wetzel, William E. Jr., "Informal Risk Capital in New England," Frontiers of Entrepreneurship Research 1981, pp. 217-245.

# EXAMINING ENTREPRENEURSHIP'S ROLE IN ECONOMIC GROWTH

Bruce A. Kirchhoff, Babson College
Bruce D. Phillips, U. S. Small Business Administration

## ABSTRACT

The U. S. has created new jobs at a rate greater than other western nations during the last 25 years. The reasons for this have been previously unclear. This paper provides some recent data and analysis that shows that small firms have created most of the new jobs and that new firm entry is a major component of job creation. Firm exits are relatively stable over time; thus, variations in new entries account for the differences between economic expansions and contractions. Furthermore, firm dynamics of entry, exit, expansion and contraction cause three job additions and two losses for each net new job created. These dynamics fit Schumpeter's model of capitalism well. Barriers to new entries may be caused by government policies such as regulation. Conversely, deregulation may explain the rapid rise in firm entry rates and the attendant increase in small business' share of total net new jobs since 1980.

## INTRODUCTION

The United States displayed an outstanding ability to create new jobs during the past 15 years, especially when compared to Western Europe. Civilian employment increased 33.5 percent in the United States from 1970 to 1984 while it increased only 2.4 percent in France, 6.9 percent in Italy, and declined 8.2 percent in Great Britain and 5.8 percent in West Germany.[1]

Entrepreneurship has been given a leading role among the many explanations cited for the United States' outstanding job creation performance. The popular media has drawn considerable attention to entrepreneurship; best selling books have been published on entrepreneurship; magazines and journals have been formed solely to focus upon entrepreneurship; and newspapers have added sections or columns to focus on entrepreneurship. However, most of the evidence

---

1. Denis P. Doyle and Terry W. Hartle, "Job Creation in the United States: An overview." Prepared for Public Policy Week - 1985. American Enterprise Institute for Public Policy Research, Washington, D.C., October, 1985.

offered in these sources to support the "entrepreneurship belief" is anecdotal, not rigorously empirical. In fact, in 1985, after reviewing the existing empirical research, the Organization for Economic Co-operation and Development concluded: "The job-creation potential of small firms is an issue that has received considerable attention in recent years. Unfortunately, the evidence on this topic . . . is somewhat contradictory and difficult to interpret."[2]

This paper bridges some of the theoretical and empirical gaps in the analysis of entrepreneurships' contribution to job growth. First, the paper compares employment growth in the U. S. and other western nations so as to demonstrate that job growth in the U. S. is an economy-wide phenomena, not merely a phenomena of a particular sector or industry. Second, the paper reviews the job generation research in the U. S. so as to confirm that small businesses have been the source of most job generation. Third, the paper combines the concept of job generation with firm entry and exit so as to show that the dynamics of the U. S. economy comply with Schumpeter's descriptive theory of capitalism. Finally, the role of government policy in affecting flexibility is explored.

## U. S. EMPLOYMENT GROWTH

Table 1 shows employment changes in eight major western nations for 1960 through 1980, 1970 through 1980 and 1980 through 1982. First, note that from 1960 through 1980, the U. S. had the highest growth in total civilian employment, even exceeding Japan's growth. In fact, of the eight nations, only three, the U. S., Japan, and the Netherlands had employment growth in excess of ten percent.

Given the unprecedented scale of the 1960's economic expansion in the U. S. and the equally renowned lackluster "stagflation" of the 1970's, one might assume that most of the U. S. employment growth occurred in the 1960's. However, the 1970 through 1980 changes shown in column two of Table 1 reveal that the U. S. had the highest percent change in employment during the decade of the 1970's. Even Japan lags far behind the U. S. in employment changes. Only the U. S. exceeds ten percent growth.

The recession of the early 1980's substantially dampened the U. S. employment growth rate as noted in the third column of Table 1. However, the world wide recession also dampened the growth of the other seven nations. In fact, the U. S. had the second highest percent growth among the eight nations. Only the U. S. and Japan show positive change. All others show zero or negative changes in civilian employment.

---

2. Organization for Economic Cooperation and Development, OECD Employment Outlook (Paris, October, 1985), pp. 64.

TABLE 1

PERCENT TOTAL AND MANUFACTURING JOB GROWTH:
UNITED STATES AND SELECTED OTHER
INDUSTRIALIZED NATIONS, 1960-1982

=================================================================

|  | Change in Number of Jobs | | |
|---|---|---|---|
| Nation | 1960-1980 | 1970-1980 | 1980-1982 |
|---|---|---|---|
| (Total Employment) | | | |
| United States | 19.5% | 24.9% | 0.3% |
| Japan | 14.8% | 8.7% | 1.8% |
| France | 9.4% | 3.9% | -0.9% |
| Germany | 1.6% | -1.4% | -2.4% |
| Great Britain | 2.7% | 1.3% | -6.3% |
| Italy | -4.9% | 7.0% | 0.0% |
| Netherlands | 12.4% | 1.9% | -3.1% |
| Sweden | 7.1% | 9.8% | -0.3% |
| (Manufg. Employment) | | | |
| United States | 20.1% | 5.8% | -7.5% |
| Japan | 45.8% | -0.9% | 0.8% |
| France | 7.8% | -3.8% | NA |
| Germany | 9.8% | -9.5% | NA |
| Great Britain | -4.6% | -18.1% | -16.0% |
| Italy | 10.0% | 3.6% | -3.8% |
| Netherlands | 4.0% | -19.7% | NA |
| Sweden | -5.0% | -37.0% | -7.7% |

=================================================================

Note:  NA means not available.

Source:  Bureau of Labor Statistics, Statistical Supplement
to International Comparison of unemployment bulletin,
September, 1983.  As cited in U. S. Congress, Joint Economic
Committee, "Industrial Policy Movement in the United States:
Is It the Answer?", 98th Congress, 2nd Session, 1984, S. Prt.
98-196, p. 31.

The U. S. has obviously fared quite well in employment growth compared to these seven nations. And, this growth, especially in the 1970's, occurred in the face of significant increases in the U. S. trade deficit. Thus, even though the U. S. was buying more goods and services from these seven nations, the net effect of such trade is not evident in its relative increases in employment growth within its domestic economy.

## Services or Manufacturing

The popular view is that most, perhaps all, new jobs in the U. S. have been created in services rather than in manufacturing. According to analysis of the U. S. Small Business Administration's (SBA) data base, 48.3 percent of the 17 million new jobs created between 1976 and 1984 were in services. However, contrary to popular belief, the U. S.'s manufacturing employment has also increased, far more than most realize. Again using SBA's data base, 6.4 percent of the new jobs from 1976 through 1984 were created in manufacturing.

The lower half of Table 1 shows these changes in manufacturing employment in the U. S. compared to other nations from 1960 to 1982. Note that during 1960 to 1980, the U. S. showed the second greatest increase in manufacturing jobs among the eight nations, exceeded only by Japan. Japan is the clear leader in manufacturing employment growth during these 20 years but no country is even close to the U. S.'s second position.

Furthermore, all of Japan's growth in manufacturing employment is attributable to the decade of the 1960's. From 1970 to 1980 (column two in Table 1) Japan experienced a decline in manufacturing employment. Only the U. S. and Italy experienced growth in manufacturing employment during the decade of the 1970's. The other six nations experienced declines.

All of the 1970's gain in U. S. manufacturing employment was lost in the recession of 1980 to 1982 despite some offsetting growth among small firms. But similar, or even more severe losses are experienced by three of the four other nations reporting. Only Japan weathered the recession with a slight growth in manufacturing employment. Thus, although much of the U. S.'s employment growth has been in services, especially during the 1980 to 1982 recession, compared to the other economically developed nations, the U. S. has had exceptional growth in manufacturing employment during the 1970's.

Outstanding growth in overall employment bolstered by exceptional growth in manufacturing employment demonstrated by these data suggests that the U. S. economy has characteristics that other nations would like to define and emulate. The characteristic suggested by recent research reported in the popular media is that the U. S. has an "entrepreneurial" economy. However, the popular media tends to rely upon anecdotal information and when the OECD reviewed the more rigorous research, it remained skeptical of entrepreneurship's role.[3]

## FIRM SIZE AND EMPLOYMENT GROWTH

Employment growth in any economy can occur in two ways: first, existing firms can grow and add employees; second, new firms can form and grow thereby initially acquiring and then adding employees. Let us first examine the growth of overall employment as a net indicator of these two phenomena and then isolate the formation and growth phenomena for separate analysis.

### Growth in Employment by Firm Size

Since Birch[4] first published his innovative micro analysis of job growth, a flurry of other studies replicating his methodology have appeared. Those available to the OECD in 1985 are neatly summarized in OECD Employment Outlook.[5] It is this summary that led to OECD's confusion and doubt about the meaning of these studies, confusion resulting from the lack of uniformity in definitions of size, base year and length of time period analyzed. In the U. S., OECD notes four studies which show that firms with less than 100 employees accounted for between 269 percent and 39 percent of jobs created. Birch's original study reports 82 percent of new jobs were created by firms with less than 100 employees.

However, recent work by the SBA expands upon Birch's findings to create a uniform set of definitions of firm size, base year and time period. First, all firms are defined by size of enterprise. An enterprise contains all establishments (individual places of work) under the same ownership or control such as separate factories, subsidiaries, or multiple offices. This is an important distinction since many large firms (enterprises) own, operate and control many places of work; the employment growth of a small manufacturing plant owned by a large firm would not be considered small firm growth within the enterprise definition.

Second, the base year is uniformly taken every two years and the time period is two years corresponding to the updating cycle of firms by Dun and Bradstreet. Thus, there is comparability between time periods. This is important since firms move into larger size classes as they grow and the longer the time period, the greater the percentage of job growth which may be attributed to smaller firms.

---

3. op. cit., OECD.

4. David L. Birch, "The Job Generation Process," a report prepared by the Massachusetts Institute of Technology Program on Neighborhood and Regional Change (Cambridge, Mass., 1979).

5. op. cit., pp. 72-78.

For example, if one defined all firms as small or large on a base year of 1950 and analyzed their job growth until 1980, the growth of many of our giant corporations would be included in the small firm category. Xerox, Polaroid, Control Data, Digital Equipment and many others were "small" or started small after 1950. Such a base year and time period would create unrealistic distortion of the intent of the analysis of the small category.

A summary of the job generation research is shown in Table 2. Note that the first base year (1969) and time period (3 years) are not uniform. This is because Birch's data file begins with 1969, not 1970 as would be desirable. However, in spite of this minor distortion, the table clearly shows that small enterprises contribute a major share of total net new jobs in the U. S. economy.

The results in Table 2 show that small firms make their greatest percentage contribution during recessionary periods. Note that economic recessions occurred in 1969-70, 1973-75 and 1980-82. The percentage of jobs created in 1969-72, 1974-76, and 1980-82 are among the highest in the table, 82, 66 and 100 percent respectively. Apparently, small firms experience disproportionately larger employment increases during recessions than large firms. Thus, although fewer net new jobs are created during a recession, a larger percentage of these are created by small firms. In 1980-82, all of the net new jobs were created by small firms.

Small firms' contribution to employment varies by stage of the business cycle. Immediately after recessions, 1976-78 and 1982-84, small firms still contributed a major share of net new jobs. However, late in an expansionary period, 1978-80, small firms contributed a much smaller percent of new jobs. Apparently, the high growth of small firms stimulated during a recession carries into the early stages of recovery while large firms do not experience significant growth until later in an expansion period. This evidence derives from only two recession-expansion cycles so these conclusions remain tentative.

Thus, not only has the U. S. experienced an outstanding growth in employment compared to other developed nations, but most of this growth has occurred through the activities of small firms. This evidence of small firms at the core of economic growth is clearly conclusive for the U. S.

Firm Formation and Growth

As noted earlier, employment growth can occur because of growth in existing firms or because of new firm formation. Although the difference in these two may seem unimportant to many who are concerned solely with overall growth, investigation into the formation phenomena has revealed that it is a significant component of and determinant of economic growth rates.

TABLE 2

JOB GENERATION IN THE U. S. BY FIRMS
WITH FEWER THAN 100 EMPLOYEES

==================================================================

| Period of Observation | Percent of Jobs Generated by Firms with Fewer than 100 Employees |
|---|---|
| 1969-1972a/ | 82% |
| 1972-1974a/ | 53% |
| 1974-1976a/ | 65% |
| 1976-1978b/ | 56% |
| 1978-1980b/ | 38% |
| 1980-1982b/ | 100% |
| 1982-1984b/ | 66% |

==================================================================

a/ Data from:  David L. Birch and Susan MacCracken, " Corporate
Evolution:  A Micro-based Analysis."  A report prepared for the
U. S. Small Business Administration by the MIT Program on
Neighborhood and Regional Change under SBA award no. 1451,
January 1981.  Some of the establishments added to the files
from 1969 to 1976 represent new listings rather than the
creation of new jobs.

b/ U. S. Small Business Administration, Office of Advocacy, Small
Business Data Base.  The Small Business Data Base meassures
changes from the first quarter of one period to the first
quarter of the next period of observation.

Let us begin by examining the components of "net" new firm formation, i. e. the growth in total number of firms. The process of net new firm formation consists of new firm formation minus firm discontinuances; discontinuances can be firm terminations for a variety of reasons with bankruptcy being only one of these. Firms also voluntarily terminate. But, to sterilize the terminology so as to avoid debates on why or how firms discontinue, we chose the terms "entry" and "exit."

The data source for the following U. S. statistics is the Small Business Data Base of the Office of Advocacy within the Small Business Administration. This data base provides longitudinal data on individual firms. This allows us to trace each firm from entry through expansion and possible exit. And, since the raw data for this data base comes from Dun and Bradstreet Inc., the firms in the data base are real operating businesses, not tax shelters.[6]

The results of analysis shown in Table 3 are taken from Katherine Armington's innovative work with SBA's data base on firm entry and exit. The Table compares rates in the United States with the United Kingdom. The table shows that overall, the U. S. has shown entry rates higher than exit rates in three of the four time periods studied. Only 1978-80 shows a zero net change. The fourth column in Table 3 shows the growth in gross national product (GNP) in each of these time periods. Note the striking relationship between GNP growth and net change in firm formations. In years of greatest GNP growth, the net new formations are also greatest. Apparently, net new firm formation is a significant contributor to GNP growth.[7]

Armington notes that entry rates range from low period to high period by 1.3 to 2.1 percent. Exit rates, however, vary less than one percent from period to period. Exit rates are more stable from period to period than entry rates. Changes in "net change" percentages are largely due to variations in formation rates rather than exit rates.[8] Thus, entrepreneurial activity, i. e. new firm formation, is an important contributor to GNP growth.

Table 3 also shows entry/exit rates and economic growth for the United Kingdom (UK). Here again, net change in entry/exits is

---

6. For a detailed description of the U. S. Small Business Administration's Data Base, see: The State of Small Business: A Report of the President, (U. S. Government Printing Office; Washington, D.C.), 1984, pp. 405-22.

7. Catherine Armington, "Entry and Exit of Firms: An International Comparison," Unpublished paper prepared for the U. K. Conference on Job Formation and Economic Growth, London, England, March, 1986, pp. 11-17.

8. ibid., pp. 12-13.

TABLE 3

UNITED STATES AND UNITED KINGDOM -- FIRM ENTRY
AND EXIT RATES, ANNUAL PERCENT CHANGE FROM
FIRM POPULATION AT START OF YEAR

| | Entry | Exit | Net Change | GNP or GDP Growth |
|---|---|---|---|---|
| United States: | | | | |
| 1976-78 | 11.7% | -9.6% | 2.1% | 5.2% |
| 1978-80 | 10.4% | -10.4% | 0.0% | 1.2% |
| 1980-82 | 10.4% | -10.2% | 0.2% | 0.2% |
| 1982-84 | 12.5% | -9.7% | 2.8% | 5.2% |
| Average | 11.3% | -10.0% | 1.3% | 2.9% |
| United Kingdom: | | | | |
| 1979-80 | 12.1% | -10.9% | 1.2% | -2.2% |
| 1980-81 * | 11.3% | -9.4% | 1.9% | -1.1% |
| 1981-82 * | 12.0% | -9.8% | 2.2% | 1.9% |
| 1982-83 | 12.0% | -8.6% | 3.4% | 3.4% |
| Average | 11.9% | -9.7% | 2.2% | 0.5% |

* Exits in these years were adjusted by shifting 0.5 percentage
  points, or 7000 closures, from 1982 to 1981 to correct for the
  estimated effect on deregistration counts of a 1981 civil
  service strike.

Source: Catherine Armington, "Entry and Exit of Firms:  An
International Comparison." An unpublished paper prepared for the
U. K. conference on Job Formation and Economic Growth, London,
England, March, 1986, p. 16.

related positively to Gross Domestic Product (GDP), where GDP is GNP less imports and exports. Armington notes that in those years where net changes are greatest, GDP is also greatest.[9] Notice that the magnitude of the exit rates are about the same for both nations but in the U. K., the entry rates in 1979-80 and 1981-82 are greater and therefore the net changes are also greater. Nevertheless, the overall net changes in GDP are lower than those for U. S. GNP suggesting that the entry/exit phenomena of the two countries differs in its contribution to overall economic activity. Perhaps the U. K. has not yet built as large a base of entrepreneurial activity or as efficient a mechanism to channel resources into newer entrepreneurial opportunities. It is also possible that the large firm employment base is deteriorating more rapidly in the U. K. than in the U. S.

These results suggest that the lower rates of growth in manufacturing employment may be related to the differences in entry/exit rates. However, the data are inadequate to test this hypothesis. Armington concludes that micro data should be developed in more nations so that the role of entry and exit in determining economic growth can be determined.[10]

Firm Dynamics and Job Changes

The affect of entry and exit upon the creation of jobs can be extracted from SBA's data by examining the number of job changes due to the dynamics of entries, exits, contractions and expansions. The information for 1976 through 1984 is shown in Table 4.

Confirmation of Armington's findings is shown by noting that 37,578,000 new jobs were created by new establishment formations (entries column total) and of these, 54.6 percent (20,504,000) were entries by firms with less than 500 employees. During this same time period, expansions of existing establishments created 13,190,000 jobs and of these 56.8 percent (7,490,000) were created by firms with less than 500 employees. In terms of the net jobs created, small firms contributed 61.5 percent.

At first glance, the last row of Table 4 seems to misrepresent the data since the percentages exceed 100. But, what Table 4 reveals is the extent to which the dynamics of entry, exit, expansion and contraction contribute to the overall "flow" of jobs. The "flow" is the total number of job changes, the sum of the gains and the losses. Table 4 shows that there were 33,759,000 jobs lost by the combination of exits and contractions, and 50,768,000 jobs created by entries and expansions for the net increase of 17,009,000. Thus, in total, 84,527,000 job changes were necessary to create a net gain of 17,009,000. In other words, for every net job gained, three

---

9. ibid., p. 19.

10. ibid., p. 37.

new jobs were created and two were lost.

Overall, entries created 74.0 percent of all new jobs while expansions created 26.0 percent. The greater role of entries in job creation fits well with Armington's finding that firm entry rates decline at the same time that economic growth declines. Armington also noted that exit rates remain stable from period to period. This suggests that job loss rates may also remain stable from period to period. Thus, a decline in economic activity may merely reflect a decline in entry rates rather than a rise in exits or contractions. In other words, during recessions new jobs are not created fast enough to absorb the relatively constant rate at which jobs are lost from exits and contractions.

The total flows are much larger than expected and they show just how important dynamics of our economy are to creating net increases in employment. Furthermore, Table 4 does not detail interindustry changes, that is the movement of jobs from one industry to another. Lustgarten and Thomadakis examined the flows among industries and found that flows across industry boundaries are even greater than the net flows represented in Table 4.[11] Apparently, a very large amount of change is necessary for a modest amount of real growth to occur.

## SCHUMPETER'S MODEL OF GROWTH THROUGH ENTRY

The above observations fit well with Schumpeter's model of capitalistic economies. He proposed that competition in capitalistic economies was not characterized by market place give and take as described by classical economics, but instead consisted of entrepreneurs using innovations to enter established markets. Such entry entails risk of failure. However, when entrepreneurs succeed, the existing market structures/relationships among established firms in the industry are destroyed. This he called "creative destruction." The net result of such entry and expansion dynamics would be the contraction and failure of some of the new and old firms. But, overall, economic growth would emerge as demand and supply are increased. He hypothesized that when entrepreneurial entry declined, so would growth.[12] The flows of job changes among entries, exits, expansions and contractions shown in Table 4 would not surprise Schumpeter.

---

11. Steven Lustgarten and Stavros Thomadakis, "Firm Size and Resource Mobility." An unpublished paper prepared for the U. S. Small Business Administration under contract number SBA-7153-0A-83, 1985.

12. Joseph A. Schumpeter, Capitalism, Socialism and Democracy (New York: Harper and Row), 1942.

TABLE 4

COMPONENTS OF NET CHANGES IN NUMBER OF JOBS FROM 1976 THROUGH 1984
CLASSIFIED BY FIRM SIZE AND ESTABLISHMENT DYNAMICS

(Data in Thousands)

Changes in Establishment Employment

| Firm Size Number of Employees | Entries | | Exits | | Expansions | | Contractions | | Total Changes | |
|---|---|---|---|---|---|---|---|---|---|---|
| | Number | % | Number | % | Number | % | Number | % | Number | % |
| < 20 | 9285 | 24.7% | -6741 | 25.3% | 3339 | 25.3% | -930 | 13.1% | 4953 | 29.1% |
| 20-99 | 6163 | 16.4% | -4116 | 15.4% | 2384 | 18.1% | -1340 | 18.9% | 3091 | 18.2% |
| 100-499 | 5056 | 13.5% | -3455 | 13.0% | 1767 | 13.4% | -1120 | 15.8% | 2248 | 13.2% |
| > 500 | 17074 | 45.4% | -12366 | 46.4% | 5700 | 43.2% | -3692 | 52.1% | 6716 | 39.5% |
| Total | 37578 | 100.0% | -26678 | 100.0% | 13190 | 100.0% | -7082 | 100.0% | 17008 | 100.0% |
| Row % | 220.9% | | -156.9% | | 77.6% | | -41.6% | | 100.0% | |

Note: Detail may not add to totals due to rounding.

Source: U. S. Small business Administration, Office of Advocacy, Small Business Data Base,
USEEM file, unpublished data, 1987.

## Contemporary Innovation

Schumpeter perceived technological innovation as the principle mechanism of entrepreneurial entry. Most anecdotal evidence in the popular press also stresses technological innovation as the primary mechanism. Yet, some have cast doubt on the entire entrepreneurial thesis because the rates of technological change, though high, cannot explain the phenomenal growth in number of new firms arising in the last 15 years.

Bishop's analaysis provides a partial answer to this question. Bishop analyzed the differences in U. S. and European job growth for the last 25 years and in so doing developed a model of entrepreneurial innovation that is market, not technology, based. He examines the supply side and the demand side of the labor markets. He concludes that the relatively free U. S. labor markets responded to high unemployment with a reduction in the real wages paid to workers. Because government pursued an expansionary course, the excess supply in the markets was absorbed by small firms that had the flexibility to take advantage of the decline in real wages. Meanwhile, large firms were often inflexible in setting wages due to established policies or union influences. He attributes the substantial growth in small firm employment (as we reported in Table 2) to small firm entry and growth based upon their ability to use the reduction in real wages and the abundance of skilled labor available as large firms laid off more employees when faced with declining demand.[13] Bishops analysis, however, fails to adjust for the large increases in voluntary part time employment during the 1970's which contributed to the lowering of real wages.

In Europe, he notes, governments intervened in the labor markets to prevent high unemployment and thwarted the decline in real wages. This government intervention was reinforced by the increasing strength and militancy of European labor unions. The net result is a much lower growth in employment among European nations.[14] Also, as Armington's preliminary data for four European nations suggest, it may have resulted in much lower rates of firm entry and exit.

Bishop's model fits well with Schumpeter's description of innovative entrepreneurial entry. In the U. S., many entrepreneurs found entry innovations in simply supplying similar products/services as large firms but with a labor force hired at substantially lower wages. The entrepreneurial entry of new, low fare airlines shortly after airline deregulation is an obvious example of new firm

---

13. John Bishop, "American Job Growth: What Explains It?" as published in, Portfolio: International Economic Perspectives (Washington, D.C.: U. S. Information Agency, in press, June, 1987.)

14. ibid., pp.36-47

formation using this entry innovation. Viewed as a Schumpeteran creative destruction process, these new low cost airlines entered an established industry and created new competition that drove down prices, expanded services, and eventually destroyed several established firms while greatly expanding the demand for and supply of airline travel.

Yet, capitalistic economic phenomena as theorized by Schumpeter may not be the only mechanism operating here. It may be that deregulation activities during the Carter and Reagan administrations created the entry opportunities. No amount of cheap labor would allow entry of a new trucking firm or new airline while regulatory agencies maintained a barrier of laws, regulations and codes. Government policy can and does make a difference, not only labor policy as described by Bishop but also regulatory policies.

## SUMMARY AND CONCLUSIONS

We began by describing how the U. S. has had greater employment growth than most developed nations of the world and how this growth has been broadly based including manufacturing. Next, we examined the data on the relative contribution of small and large firms to the U. S. job growth. Here we find conclusive evidence that small firms are the major source of net new job creation with strongest performance in periods of economic recession.

Further understanding of small firm job creation is obtained when we examine firm entry and exit data. Here we find that variations in firm entry rates are the major determinant of net new firm formations since the exit rates are relatively stable from period to period. Entrepreneurial activity, the formation of new firms, is the major cause of net increases in the number of firms. Furthermore, evidence from the U. S. and U. K. suggests that net firm formation activity is positively related to overall economic activity.

Next we examine the role of entry, expansion, exit and contraction upon job creation. Here we find that entry is the major source of new job creation. The positive correlation of firm entry rates and economic growth shows that new business formation is the major determinant of economic growth as hypothesized by Schumpeter. As further evidence of a Schumpeter like economy, we find that the magnitude of entry, exit, expansion and contraction are far greater than the net changes in jobs imply. Three jobs are created and two lost for each net new job formed. Creation of new jobs along side the destruction of existing jobs fits Schumpeter's model well.

Government policies can and have affected this creative destruction process. Bishop's research concludes that government policies of controlling labor markets decreased economic flexibility in Europe. This prevented small firms from taking advantage of the decline in real wages. In the U. S. open labor markets led to more

jobs and far greater economic growth than that experienced in
Europe.

Since entries create over half of new jobs and economic
growth is related to the rise and fall of entry rates, we conclude
that entrepreneurial entry is a necessary requirement for economic
growth. And, entrepreneurial entry is affected by government
policies, for example by industry regualtion or labor policies. But,
historically, government policy has not considered small firm entry
as a central issue. Regulatory policy, for example, typically
addresses consumer interests without recognizing that regualtions
create a barrier to entry of new firms. Deregulation has the
opposite effect as experienced in the trucking and airline industries
since deregualtion.

Furthermore, the entrepreneurial economy incorporates a
Schumpeter like creative destruction dynamic characterized by a great
deal of turbulence in labor markets with three jobs created and two
lost for every one net new job. Since this entails considerable
worker movement from job to job, such labor turbulence may be seen by
policy makers as undesirable. For example, policy makers have
recently proposed policies to protect workers from job loss due to
contractions and exits. But, such policies, as demonstrated in
recent European experience, will also construct barriers to
entrepreneurial entry. The result may be a decline in small firm
entry and a decline in economic growth.

Instead of protecting specific jobs, appropriate policies are
those that facilitate movement and reduce the suffering of workers
when they involuntarily move from job to job. Adequate unemployment
compensation for short term unemployed, fully vested and portable
pension plans, and retraining programs are examples of policies that
allow the labor market to remain flexible while reducing the negative
affect on those who involuntarily lose jobs.

SUMMARY

THE SYNERGISM OF INDEPENDENT HIGH-TECHNOLOGY BUSINESS STARTS

Authors

    William J. Dennis, Jr.
    Bruce D. Phillips

Addresses

    The NFIB Foundation
    600 Maryland Ave., SW, Ste. 700
    Washington, D.C. 20024
    (202) 554-9000

    Director of Data Development
    Office of Advocacy
    Small Business Administration
    1441 L St., NW
    Washington, D.C. 20416
    (202) 654-7550

Principal Topics

The principal issue addressed in the paper is whether high tech
birth rates are greater in economic environments in which the birth
rates of other type businesses are comparatively large as well, or
do high high-technology birth rates tend to occur in an economic
vacuum unrelated to other business start activity. Thus, the paper
examines the relationship between birth rates of high-technology
businesses and 1. birth rates of non-high technology businesses and
2. factors frequently associated with high-technology births.
Supplementing a static analysis is an exploration of lead-lag relationships to ascertain the sequence of high-technology birth rates
and selected variables.

Data and Methodology

Data on business starts, available in even-numbered years from 1976
- 1984, are drawn from the Small Business Administration's Small
Business Data Base. Other variables used in the analysis, e.g.
scientific Ph.D.'s per capita, existence of a small business/high-
tech financing program, percent of the population urbanized, migra-
tion per capita, personal income per capita, Defense Department
procurement per capita, are generally gathered from common data
sources such as the Statistical Abstract of the United States.
Using state-by-state high-technology starts as the dependent

variables (one equation for the 1976 - 1980 period and one for the 1980 - 1984 period), a series of multiple regressions are constructed to test the hypothesized relationships.

## Major Findings

High technology births are not a leader on average in creating economic growth. Quite the opposite. High technology births seemed to lag general economic growth during 1980 - 1984 at least as measured by employment gains. However, the only industry start rate related to technology starts was manufacturing and manufacturing birth rates appeared to lead. Curiously, the service birth rate was inversely related to high-technology birth rates. But results of the regressions are as surprising for what they do not show as for what they do. For example, no relationship exists between the high-technology birth rate and the various measures of education; nor is any found with wealth or DOD procurement. None was found with the existence of special government programs nor legal geographic restrictions on the banking system. In fact, no factor other than employment growth and manufacturing birth rates were related in any manner to the high-technology birth rate.

## Implications

High high-technology birth rates do not occur in an economic vacuum. Start rates appear highest where economic activity is already robust. Yet, what stimulates economic activity in the first place? Thus, we may be asking the wrong question. The major implication of this study at least for public policy is that it would be a major error to place one's primary economic development effort on advancing high-technology births at least until the entire economic development process is well under way.

# MAKING THE TRANSITION FROM ENTREPRENEURIAL
## TO PROFESSIONAL MANAGEMENT

Michael J. Roberts, Harvard University

## ABSTRACT

This paper examines the phenomenon of "the transition from entrepreneurial to professional management." It develops a conceptual framework that defines this phenomenon as a change in the firm's--and the entrepreneur's--strategy of coordination. Based on this concept, the transition is examined through the lens of an information processing model, wherein the change in coordination strategy is viewed as a response to an excess of information processing requirements relative to capacity. This paper discusses the factors that determine capacity and requirements, and how information processing capacity can be increased-- via the transition--to yield more effective performance.

## INTRODUCTION

The phrase "the transition from entrepreneurial to professional management" is widely used to describe the set of changes that organizations experience as they grow and mature.[1] Yet, this transition remains poorly understood. At the heart of the problem lies a basic uncertainty about what the terms _really_ mean, and whether this transition is good or bad.

This dilemma is highlighted by the recent succession at Apple Computer. Some complained that Sculley's ascendancy "...cut the heart

---

[1] Hofer, Charles W., and Charan, Ram, "The Transition to Professional Management: Mission Impossible?" _American Journal of Small Business_ (IX), Summer 1983, pp. 1-11. Flamholtz, Eric G., and Duncan, Clay, "Making the Transition from an Entrepreneurship to a Professionally Managed Firm, _American Management Association Management Review_, January, 1982, pp. 57-62. Sexton, Donald L. and Bowman, Nancy, _From Entrepreneurial to Professional Management: Key Factors in the Transition Process_, Presentation at the International Colloquium on Entrepreneurship, Ecole Des Hautes Etudes Commerciales, University of Montreal, Montreal, Canada, April 1-4, 1963.

out of Apple and substituted an artificial one. We'll just have to see how long it pumps".[2] Others maintained that, under Jobs, Apple was out of control: "The process at the top of Apple Computer was a joke."[3]

This confusion is compounded by our intuitive sense that somehow, "professional management" must be better than the alternatives. Yet, if this is so, why is it that so many large, professionally-managed firms yearn to return to their entrepreneurial routes via approaches such as "intrapreneurship"?[4]

If we look to the literature to resolve these issues, our uncertainty only increases. Some scholars argue that entrepreneurial management is defined by the individual's psychological characteristics;[5] the firm's function;[6] or, the firm's performance.[7] Others attempt to define professional management according to the firm's structural characteristics;[8] the manager's behavior;[9] or, the manager's background and training[10]. Such definitions make it difficult to define a transition; surely firms can be undergoing a transition even while the manager's personality, background and training remain constant. And, a transition should not necessarily imply a diminution in firm

[2]Uttal, Bro., "Behind the Fall of Steve Jobs," Fortune, August 5, 1985, pp. 20-24.

[3]Pava, Calvin and Mayer, James, John Sculley at Apple Computer A&B, Harvard Business School Cases #9-486-001 and 002, Boston, MA.

[4]Pinchot, Gifford III, Intrapreneuring, Harper & Row, New York, 1985.

[5]McClelland, David C., The Achieving Society, C. Van Nostrand, Princeton, 1961. Collins, Orvis F., and Moore, David, The Enterprising Man, Bureau of Business and Economic Research, Graduate School of Business Administration, Michigan State University, East Lansing, MI, 1964.

[6]Schumpeter, J.A., The Theory of Economic Development, Oxford Press, New York, 1961. Cole, A.H., Business in Its Social Setting, Harvard University Press, Cambridge, MA, 1959.

[7]Drucker, Peter, F., Innovation and Entrepreneurship, Harper & Row, New York, 1985.

[8]Chandler, Alfred D., The Visible Hand, The Belknap Press, Cambridge, MA, 1977.

[9]Gulick, Luther, "Notes on the Theory of Organization," in Gulick, Luther H. and Urwick, L. (eds.) Papers on the Science of Administration, Institute of Public Administration, Columbia University, New York, 1937. Mintzberg, Henry, The Nature of Managerial Work, Harper & Row, New York, 1973.

[10]Schon, Donald A., The Reflective Practitioner, Basic Books, NY: 1983.

performance.

Clearly, what is needed is a definitional scheme that permits the researcher to:

- focus on the transition <u>process</u> by examining key dimensions of the organization and its management that may change during growth;

- examine both the firm and the entrepreneur, as well as the relationship between these two critical aspects of the process; and

- investigate the phenomenon in a non-judgmental fashion, without a definition that assumes the superiority of one management form over the other.

In order to develop such a scheme, and a model of the transition process itself, exploratory research was undertaken. This work examined several firms that had grown rapidly, and which had attempted a change in management approach. The primary research questions were:

1. What pressures force a change in the firm's coordination strategy?; and

2. How can firms and entrepreneurs deal with these pressures and successfully make the transition?

It is important to note that a successful transition is defined in terms of both the individual entrepreneur and the firm. That is, if a succession takes place, and the firm makes a transition under new leadership, that transition is <u>not</u> defined as successful, even though the firm itself may be successful.

This research resulted in the findings presented below, which should be viewed as hypotheses.

The remainder of this paper will:

- present a conceptual scheme that allows us to define entrepreneurial and professional management; and
- describe a model of the transition based upon information processing as the driving process underlying the transition.

DEFINING ENTREPRENEURIAL AND PROFESSIONAL MANAGEMENT

By examining the purpose of the firm, we can develop a definitional scheme that is more descriptive of the phenomenon in question, and more amenable to research. This definitional scheme is based on the notion of the <u>firm as a coordinating mechanism</u>.[11]  The characteristics that much of the literature uses to define entrepreneurial and professional management all represent <u>features of the manner in which the firm chooses to coordinate its efforts</u>.  This suggests that the transition from entrepreneurial to professional management is a fundamental shift in the approach to coordination in terms of both managerial behavior and organization structure and process.

The fundamental notion of the firm as a coordinating mechanism is well established in the literature.  Indeed, many management theorists suggest that coordination is <u>the</u> key management task.  Gulick (1937:1), for instance, maintains that

> The theory of organization, therefore, has to do with the structure of organization imposed upon the work division units of the enterprise.

## The Strategy of Coordination

We can build on this rich tradition that views the firm as a coordinating mechanism and define entrepreneurial and professional management as different "strategies of coordination."  The literature highlights two dimensions of this strategy of coordination.  Mintzberg (1979:2) makes the point most clearly:

> Every organized human activity--from the making of pots to the placing of a man on the moon--gives rise to two fundamental and opposing requirements: the <u>division of labor</u> into various tasks to be performed and the <u>coordination</u> of these tasks to accomplish this activity.  <u>The structure of an organization can be defined simply as the sum total of the ways in which it divides its labor up into distinct tasks and then achieves coordination among them</u>.

This idea is obviously behind many of the important concepts in organization theory, from Sloan's "decentralization with coordinated control"[12] to Lawrence and Lorsch's "differentiation and integration".[13]

Thus, we can define two dimensions of the firm's strategy of coordination as shown in FIGURE 1: 1) the manner in which responsibilities are delegated; and 2) the degree of formality with which those divided tasks are controlled.  These two dimensions define

---

[11]Williamson, Oliver, E., <u>Markets and Hierarchies</u>, The Free Press, New York, 1975.  Also, see note 8.

[12]Sloan, Alfred P. Jr., <u>My Years With General Motors</u>, McFadden Books, New York, 1963.

[13]Lawrence, Paul and Lorsch, Jay, <u>Organization and Environment</u>, Richard D. Irwin, Homewood, IL, 1969.

the strategy of coordination:

FIGURE 1

The Strategy of Coordination

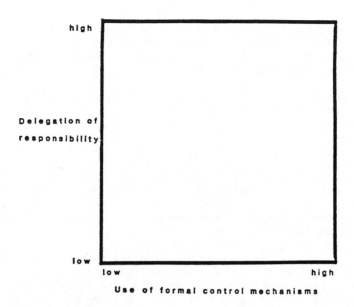

high

Delegation of
responsibility

low

low                                    high

Use of formal control mechanisms

The axes are defined broadly to encompass the full range of decisions that constitute the firm's choice about how to coordinate its efforts.

The term "delegation of responsibility" is used rather than the more traditional centralization/decentralization because it conveys an important sense of the impact of the individual manager's own behavior on the division of responsibilities within the firm. This term is used to describe:

-    The structural elements of the organization: the way in which responsibilities are divided and distributed to subunits;

-    Subunit roles and strategies; what the roles and objectives are for each of those organizational subunits;

-    The degree of latitude that each subunit has in influencing its own objectives;

-    The degree of authority that each subunit has to pursue its agreed upon objectives; and

-   The manager's own behavior in the day-to-day decision-making process.

The term "use of formal control mechanisms" is used to describe:

-   The nature of the objectives set for managerial performance;

-   The type of information that is collected to insure performance against those objectives;

-   The level of detail at which data is collected;

-   The nature and timing of feedback that individuals receive regarding their performance;

-   The reward and incentives that are used to motivate behavior, and the extent to which those rewards are tied to objectives and tangible measures;

-   The nature and extent of policies and procedures; and,

-   The entrepreneur's own behavior in the control process.

## Defining Entrepreneurial and Professional Management

Having defined the dimensions of the strategy of coordination, we can see that there are four primary archetypical strategies, as shown in FIGURE 2: 1) the direct strategy of coordination, that uses neither delegation of responsibility nor formal control mechanisms; 2) the laissez-faire strategy of coordination, that uses delegation but not formal control mechanisms; 3) the bureaucratic coordination strategy, that uses form control mechanisms but not delegation; and, 4) the indirect coordination strategy, that relies on both delegation and formal control.

# FIGURE 2

## Different Strategies of Coordination

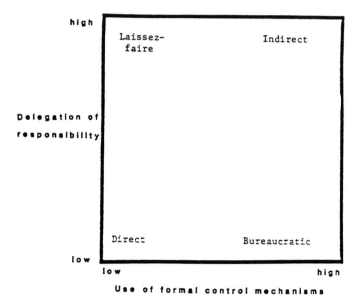

Based on this conceptual framework, entrepreneurial and professional management can be defined as two different strategies of coordination:

- Entrepreneurial management is the direct strategy of coordination;

- Professional management is the indirect strategy of coordination.

With this definition of entrepreneurial and professional management, we can begin to explore the process that underlies this phenomenon.

## UNDERSTANDING THE TRANSITION PROCESS

In order to build a process model, we need to identify the underlying variables that influence change, as well as the process through which change occurs. Given the conceptual framework presented in the last chapter, it makes sense to think of the shift in the coordination strategy as a response to the demand for increased coordination capacity. The question then becomes: what variables determine the firm's ability to coordinate its efforts? A stream of literature has identified information processing as the key process underlying coordination because:

- Coordination requires decision-making:  The coordination of the organization's activities clearly requires decision-making on the part of management;[14]

- The firm faces uncertainty:  As open system theorists[15] have long argued, organizations face uncertainty:

    Uncertainty appears as the fundamental problem for complex organizations, and coping with uncertainty, the essence of the administrative process.[16]

- Decision-making in the face of uncertainty requires information processing:  As Galbraith (1973:4) has argued most convincingly, uncertainty begets the need for information processing:

    ...the greater the task uncertainty, the greater the amount of information that must be processed among decision-makers...

In order to understand how the concept of information processing helps us explain the transition process, we can develop a supply and demand model that revolves around the concepts of information processing capacity and information processing requirements.

The model, described in more detail on the following pages, assumes that:

- information processing requirements are primarily a function of uncertainty;

- information processing capacity is primarily determined by the choice of a coordination strategy;

- if information processing requirements exceed information procession capacity, certain dysfunctional symptoms result;

- the response to these symptoms to correct the imbalance by either increasing capacity or decreasing requirements.

This model is shown graphically in Figure 3.

---

[14]Simon, Herbert A., _Administrative Behavior_, The Free Press, New York, 1976.

[15]Weick, Karl, _The Social Psychology of Organizing_, Addison-Wesley, Reading, MA, 1980.  Katz, Daniel, and Kahn, R.L., _The Social Psychology of Organizations_, Wiley & Sons, New York, 1966.  Thompson, James D., _Organizations in Action_, McGraw-Hill, New York, 1967.

[16]See note 15, 159.

FIGURE 3

AN INFORMATION PROCESSING MODEL OF THE TRANSITION PROCESS

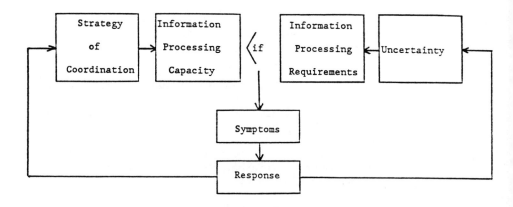

## Information Processing Requirements

First, if we accept the notion that information processing underlies coordination, it follows that the firm's information processing capacity must be sufficient to meet the requirements of that coordination task. As Tushman and Nadler (1978:622) have argued,

> ...subunits must choose from a feasible set of
> structural alternatives, a particular set of
> organizational arrangements to most effectively deal
> with their information processing requirements.

These requirements for information processing are largely determined by the degree of uncertainty the firm faces. Organizational theorists[17] have identified three primary sources of uncertainty:

- Subunit task characteristics: The complexity, predictability and intra-unit interdependence of tasks;

- Subunit task environment: The complexity and dynamism of task environments;

- Inter-unit task interdependence: The degree to which a

---

[17]Tushman, Michael L., and Nadler, David, "Information Processing as an Integrating Concept in Organizational Design," _Academy of Management Review_, July 1978, pp. 613-624.

subunit is dependent upon other subunits in order to perform its task effectively.

Firms typically grow by selling new products to new customers in new markets, and by adding new organizational units to accomplish these tasks. These steps increase uncertainty by:

- making the task environment more diverse and complex;

- increasing the interdependence of tasks _within_ subunits as work becomes more and more specialized; and

- increasing interdependence _between_ subunits as these units become more and more responsible for their own decision-making.

Thus, growth increases the requirements for information processing by increasing uncertainty.

## Information Processing Capacity

Information processing capacity is largely determined by the choice of coordination strategy. With the direct strategy information processing capacity is limited by the entrepreneur's own mind. Without formal policies and procedures to eliminate the need for making certain decisions, and with the necessity for all decisions to percolate to the top, the individual entrepreneur becomes the limiting constraint on the firm's ability to process information.

It is worth noting that this capacity--limited though it may be--is often sufficient during the firm's early stages. Indeed, it is probably the best and only possible approach; the firm lacks the resources to hire middle management to whom responsibility could be delegated and has not yet learned enough about its operations to implement formal policies and procedures. As information processing requirements expand due to growth, however, they may soon exceed the individual entrepreneur's capacity.

## Symptoms of Imbalance

In response to an increase in information processing requirements, the firm and its management will experience certain symptoms. These range from excess demands on the individual entrepreneur, and a consequent overload and dissatisfaction, to organizational disarray and a lack of responsiveness. Details seem to fall through the cracks; efforts are duplicated, while some important tasks remain undone; and, the organization seems unresponsive, missing opportunities and discovering problems when it is too late to do anything about them.

## A Range of Responses

In response to this excess of information processing requirements over capacity, the entrepreneur can take several steps, including:

- opting out of the problem by initiating a succession or selling the company;

- managing the demand side of the imbalance by slowing or reversing the growth of the business; or, by simplifying the business by paring back marginal product lines, customers and regions; or,

- managing the supply side of the imbalance by increasing the firm's information processing capacity.

It is this last approach that is commonly referred to as the transition from entrepreneurial to professional management.

## Increasing Information Processing Capacity

Movement along each of the dimensions that defines the coordination strategy can increase the firm's capacity to process information. Increased delegation of responsibility can expand capacity in a number of ways:

- The delegation of responsibility to middle managers: The delegation of responsibility and authority to subordinates removes the necessity for transferring information up the hierarchy and back down. As more individuals are vested with decision-making responsibility, communication channels are shortened. Information processing capacity is increased most significantly when decision-making authority is vested at the first locus of the information required for sound decisions.

- The delegation of authority and resources: In order for delegation to achieve its intended effect on information processing capacity, the subordinate must be sufficiently empowered with both authority and resources to make and implement decisions, rather than merely allowed to submit recommendations for suggested action.

- The delegation of responsibility to deal with relevant contingencies: The firm's ability to process information will be enhanced when jobs are defined to include the responsibility for dealing with relevant contingencies. When individuals are forced to deal with these sources of uncertainty, they are required to think about and adapt to these contingencies. The more individuals in the organization charged with doing this, the more information processing capacity the firm will have.

- The creation of lateral integrating mechanisms: The delegation of specific responsibilities to subunits that serve as lateral integrating mechanisms will allow communication to be truncated and information processed at a lower level.

- The creation of self-contained tasks: The creation of self-contained tasks reduces interdependencies between subunits, and thus decreases uncertainty. Communication channels are shortened, and managers have responsibility for a more focused task.

The use of formal control mechanisms also increases the firm's ability to process information:

- The use of information systems: Rules and systems for collecting and transferring information speed communication through organizational channels, improving the capacity of the firm to process information. These systems typically specify exactly what information is to be collected, array it in standardized form, communicate it to points in the organization where it is required, and assure the use of information in situations where it should be considered.

- Standardization: The standardization of jobs, products and processes in the firm eliminates the need for decision-making and thus information processing. Individual employees do not have to think and decide--or consult with superiors about--what to do. They merely act in a predetermined fashion in response to certain stimuli. By standardizing work, the firm eliminates the need for communication and decision-making in many areas.

- The use of performance objectives, measures, and incentives: The use of performance objectives and incentives increases the organization's ability to process information because it gives subordinates an incentive to act in the best interests of the firm, reducing the need for monitoring their behavior. Moreover, employees' performance can be monitored merely by comparing results with objectives, rather than assuring that specific individual actions are correct.

- The use of policies: Policies that specify how certain decisions are to be made eliminate uncertainty and even the need to make certain classes of decisions. Other classes of policies can ease the decision-making task by specifying factors that are to be considered or objectives that are to be met.

The delegation of responsibility and the use of formal control mechanisms increases the firm's information processing capacity. This change in coordination strategy is a necessary component of successful growth; the transition is required in order to meet the increased information processing requirements wrought by growth.

85

The phrase, "the transition from entrepreneurial to professional management," describes a very real phenomenon. Unfortunately, the use of these terms does little to facilitate understanding. The phenomenon itself is fundamentally a change in approach to coordinating the activities of the firm: from a direct to an indirect approach.

This change requires very basic--and very difficult--changes on the part of both the entrepreneur and the organization. Although we often think of the transition as involving changes in the firm's structure and systems, it requires far more. These artifacts of the organization arise chiefly out of the entrepreneur's behavior; if s/he wants to use a certain system, or vests an individual with authority and responsibility, these organizational characteristics come into being. Without a change in the individual entrepreneur's behavior, any such changes are ineffectual.

A successful transition requires both the delegation of responsibility to a layer of middle managers, and the introduction of formal control mechanisms. Together, these tools permit the coordination of the firm's activities and efforts as they become increasingly complex.

# THE COMPETITIVE TACTICS OF ENTREPRENEURIAL FIRMS IN HIGH- AND LOW-TECHNOLOGY INDUSTRIES

Dennis P. Slevin, University of Pittsburgh
Jeffrey G. Covin, Georgia Institute of Technology

## ABSTRACT

This study examined the competitive tactics employed by 79 recently-created entrepreneurial firms. The purposes of this study were to identify (1) differences in the competitive tactics used by entrepreneurial firms in high- and low-technology industries, and (2) performance differences associated with the use of individual competitive tactics among entrepreneurial firms in high- and low-technology industries. Results indicate that while some competitive tactics are equally common (or uncommon) among entrepreneurial firms in high- and low-technology industries, other tactics are much more common in one industry type or the other. Furthermore, the relationship between certain competitive tactics and firm performance can differ significantly between entrepreneurial firms in high- and low-technology industries. However, relatively few competitive tactics are significantly different for high- and low-performing firms in the two types of industries.

## INTRODUCTION

An increasing amount of research in recent years has focused on strategy content issues.[1] Several attempts have been made to empirically define the content or components of business-unit and corporate strategy.[2,3,4,5] Most of this research has been based on samples of

---

[1] J. Fahey and H. K. Christensen, "Evaluating the Research on Strategy Content," Journal of Management, 12 (2), (1986), pp. 167-183.

[2] C. R. Anderson and C. P. Zeithaml, "Stage of Product Life Cycle, Business Strategy, and Business Performance," Academy of Management Journal, 27, (1984), pp. 5-24.

[3] C. S. Galbraith and D. Schendel, "An Empirical Analysis of Strategy Types," Strategic Management Journal, 4, (1983), pp. 153-173.

[4,5] See next page

large, established firms. Relatively less is known about the content of strategies pursued by new ventures or entrepreneurial firms.[6]

This paper reports the results of a study in which the competitive tactics (which define the content of strategies) of entrepreneurial firms in high- and low-technology industries were examined. The study was designed to answer two questions. First, are there significant differences between the competitive tactics used by entrepreneurial firms in high- and low-tech industries? Second, do high-performing entrepreneurial firms in high-tech industries rely on specific competitive tactics to a different extent than do low-performing entrepreneurial firms? Likewise, do high-performing entrepreneurial firms in low-tech industries rely on specific competitive tactics to a different extent than do low-performing entrepreneurial firms?

THEORETICAL BACKGROUND

A basic premise of strategic management is that the content of strategies must be determined in light of current and predicted environmental conditions. As such, different strategies and competitive tactics may be appropriate for firms operating in different industry settings. The strategies of firms competing in industries which are dynamic, concentrated, competitive, and hostile may be quite different from the strategies of firms in stable, diffuse, noncompetitive, and benevolent industries.

A key dimension on which industries differ is technological sophistication. Certain industries are commonly regarded as "high-tech" industries (e.g., advanced electronics industries) while others are typically considered to be "low-tech" industries (e.g., construction, agriculture). Given the aforementioned argument that competitive tactics should be chosen in light of industry conditions, it seems reasonable to expect that many of the competitive tactics used by entrepreneurial firms in high-tech industries will differ from those used by entrepreneurial firms in low-tech industries. Accordingly, the following null hypothesis can be stated:

H1: There are no differences in the competitive tactics of entrepreneurial firms in high- and low-technology industries.

---

[4]R. A. Bettis,"Performance Differences in Related and Unrelated Diversified Firms," Strategic Management Journal, 2, (1981), pp. 379-394.

[5]D. Miller and P. H. Friesen, "Organizations: A Quantum View," Englewood Cliffs, NJ: Prentice-Hall, (1984).

[6]A. C. Cooper, "Strategic Management: New Ventures and Small Business," in Strategic Management: A New View of Business Policy and Planning, D. E. Schendel and C. W. Hofer (eds.), Boston: Little, Brown and Company, (1979), pp. 316-327.

The issue of effectiveness should also be considered when examining differences in the competitive tactics used by entrepreneurial firms in high- and low-tech industries. One would expect that regardless of any differences in the technological sophistication of industries, high-performing firms will rely on certain competitive tactics to a greater or lesser extent than low-performing firms. Furthermore, it is conceivable that specific competitive tactics may be associated with high performance for firms in both high- and low-tech industries, or only for firms in high-tech industries, or only for firms in low-tech industries. The possibility that performance differences within different types of industries (i.e., either high-tech or low-tech) may be associated with the use of specific competitive tactics is incorporated in the following null hypothesis:

H2: There are no differences in competitive tactics of high- and low-performing entrepreneurial firms in high-technology industries, nor are there any differences in the competitive tactics of high- and low-performing entrepreneurial firms in low-technology industries.


METHODS


## The Sample

Data were collected from 79 recently-created entrepreneurial firms. All the firms have been in business for five years or less and are either members, clients, or affiliates of three independent Pittsburgh-based organizations which share the purpose of promoting business activity and economic development in the western Pennsylvania area. Thirty-eight of the firms are primarily manufacturing-oriented. Forty-one of the firms are primarily service-oriented. The average annual sales revenue for these firms is approximately $4 million. The average number of employees is 32.

A questionnaire was mailed to the senior-most executive within each firm (typically the firm's president and/or CEO). Included with each questionnaire were a cover letter which explained the research and a self-addressed return envelope. One follow-up letter was sent to all non-responding firms. The final response rate was 28.1%.

## The Measures

Competitive Tactics. A 50-item instrument was used to measure the firms' competitive tactics. This instrument is included in the Appendix. The items of this instrument were generated following a review of relevant strategic management literature. This instrument is similar to the strategy measures developed by Bourgeois[7], Robinson and

---

[7]L. J. Bourgeois, "Performance and Concensus," Strategic Manage-Journal, 1, (1980), pp. 227-248.

Pearce[8], and Dess and Davis[9], but is intended to be more comprehensive in terms of the number and types of competitive tactics examined. The tactics included in this instrument fall into seven categories: financial tactics (items 1 - 9), marketing tactics (items 10 - 21), operations tactics (items 22 - 25), product/service tactics (items 26 - 31), external control tactics (items 32 - 42), planning and decision making tactics (items 43 - 45), and personnel tactics (items 46 - 50).

Technological Sophistication. A 2-item scale, developed by Khandwalla[10], was used to measure the technological sophistication of the firms' industries. This scale is included in the Appendix. The respondents' ratings on these two items were averaged to arrive at a single technological sophistication index for each firm's industry. The higher the index, the more sophisticated the firm's industry. The inter-item reliability coefficient of this scale is .81. This scale has a mean value of 4.96, a standard deviation of 1.71, and a range of 1.0 to 7.0.

Firm Performance. Performance was measured with a modified version of an instrument developed by Gupta and Govindarajan[11]. The respondents were first asked to indicate on a 5-point Likert-type scale, ranging from "of little importance" to "extremely important", the degree of importance their firm attaches to each of the following financial performance criteria: sales level, sales growth rate, cash flow, return on shareholder equity, gross profit margin, net profit from operations, profit to sales ratio, return on investment, and ability to fund business growth from profits. The respondents were then asked to indicate on another 5-point Likert-type scale, ranging from "highly dissatisfied" to "highly satisfied", the extent to which their firm's top managers are currently satisfied with their firm's performance on each of these same financial performance criteria. The "importance" scores were used to weight the "satisfaction" scores in the calculation of a weighted average performance index for each firm. The inter-item reliability coefficient of this scale is .89. This scale has a mean value of 10.82, a standard deviation of 4.00, and a range of 3.78 to 21.67.

---

[8]R. B. Robinson and J. A. Pearce, "The Structure of Generic Strategies and Their Impact on Business-unit Performance," Academy of Management Proceedings, (1985), pp. 35-39.

[9]G. G. Dess and P. S. Davis, "Generic Strategies as Determinants of Strategic Group Membership and Organizational Performance," Academy of Management Journal, 27, (1984), pp. 367-388. Porter's (1980).

[10]P. N. Khandwalla,"The Design of Organizations", New York: Harcourt Brace Jovanovich.

[11]A. K. Gupta and V. Govindarajan, "Business Unit Strategy, Managerial Characteristics, and Business Unit Effectiveness at Strategy Implementation," Academy of Management Journal, 27, (1984), pp. 25-41.

The Analytical Techniques

Hypothesis 1 was tested by splitting the sample into firms in high-tech industries and firms in low-tech industries according to whether each firm's technological sophistication index was above or below the mean value of this index. T-tests were then used to compare the two subgroups in terms of their mean scores on each competitive tactic.

Hypothesis 2 was tested by splitting the sample into firms in high- and low-tech industries, then splitting these subgroups into high-performing and low-performing firms. The mean values on the technological sophistication and firm performance indices were used for the first and second splits, respectively. T-tests were then used to compare the high- and low-performing firms in both high- and low-tech industries in terms of their mean scores on each competitive tactic.

## RESULTS AND DISCUSSION

Tables 1 and 2 present the results of the tests conducted for hypotheses 1 and 2, respectively. Clearly, null hypothesis 1 must be rejected. There are significant differences between many of the competitive tactics of entrepreneurial firms in high- and low-technology industries (see Table 1). On the other hand, the data do not clearly indicate that null hypothesis 2 should be rejected. While there are significant differences between several of the competitive tactics of high- and low-performing entrepreneurial firms in both high- and low-tech industries, the overall proportion of tactics that differs for high- and low-performing firms is relatively small (see Table 2).

As can be determined from Table 1, 15 of the 50 competitive tactics were significantly different ($p < .05$ or better) for entrepreneurial firms in high- and low-tech industries. Specifically, entrepreneurial firms in high-tech industries agree more strongly with these items than do their counterparts in low-tech industries.

2.  We maximize use of outside financing.

4.  We frequently explore for new sources of funds.

9.  We emphasize long-term profitability.

10. We engage in heavy promotional activities.

13. We use advertising which differentiates our products/ services from those of competitors.

16. We emphasize the building of brand image/identification.

21. We actively attempt to predict customer requirements/ tastes.

27. We use product or process patents and/or copyrights to provide a competitive advantage.

28.  We offer superior product/service warranties.

30.  We emphasize new product/service development.

47.  We attract and retain highly skilled technical personnel.

In contrast, entrepreneurial firms in high-tech industries more strongly disagree with the following items than do their lower-tech counterparts:

23.  We emphasize the improvement of employee productivity and operations efficiency.

40.  We actively attempt to create stable, nonfluctuating levels of demand for our products/services.

41.  We actively attempt to minimize our dependence on any supplier.

48.  We use personnel training and development programs.

It might be argued from the above list that the high-tech firms "do a lot more" in terms of the different types of proactive competitive tactics that are used. It is interesting to note that the items where low-tech firms score higher imply a more mechanistic, efficiency, stability of demand, stability of supply sort of world. Indeed, the only item in which they scored higher that one might argue is not strongly mechanistic concerns their higher use of personnel training and development programs. However, even this item might reflect the more mechanistic approach if this training focused on lower level repetitive tasks. In general, it appears as though the dynamic environment does encourage "organic" competitive tactics. It is clear that the high-tech firms are more financially aggressive, more focused in their marketing efforts, more on the offensive in their product/service tactics and more oriented toward staffing with highly skilled personnel. In summary, they seem to "attack" their industries rather than assume a more dormant competitive posture.

As can be determined from Table 2, 6 competitive tactics differed significantly for high- and low-performing firms in high-tech industries, while 4 competitive tactics differed for high- and low-performing firms in low-tech industries. It should be noted that by splitting the sample into four subgroups (as was done to test hypothesis 2) rather than two subgroups (as was done to test hypothesis 1), the statistical significance of differences in the mean scores of individual competitive tactics was probably reduced due to the reduction in the relevant sample sizes. This fact notwithstanding, the single most remarkable result of the analysis conducted to test hypothesis 2 is the general lack of significant differences among the tactics used by high- and low-performing firms in high- and low-tech industries. While there are highly significant differences between a few of the tactics employed by these firms, the number of tactics in which these differences occur is not that much greater than the number one would expect by chance. Even for those tactics in which there are statistically significant differences between the high- and low-performing firms, the general pattern of the findings is not necessarily clear nor theoretically meaningful as was the case for the findings discussed above. As such, a post hoc rationalization of the meaning of the specific results presented in Table 2 is probably not warranted.

The general lack of significant findings when the relationship between individual competitive tactics and firm performance is the focus of the analysis has a number of potential explanations. First, those competitive tactics which differentiate between high- and low-performing firms in high- and low-tech industries may not have been well-represented in the competitive tactics instrument. This explanation, while possible, is not highly plausible given the number and diversity of competitive tactics included in the instrument. Second, the measures used to assess firms' competitive tactics and performance may not be valid. While this explanation must be considered, there is no clear evidence which suggests that this is the case. Third, while high- and low-performing firms may, in general, engage in roughly the same competitive tactics, perhaps high-performing firms are better than low-performing firms at <u>executing</u> those tactics. The extent to which particular tactics are well-implemented may be a better predictor of firm performance than the mere presence or absence of those tactics, per se. As such, many more significant differences between the competitive tactics of high- and low-performing firms in high- and low-tech industries may have been found if data could have been collected on the firms' efficacy in implementing competitive tactics rather than just the existence or non-existence of particular tactics. This explanation of the results is intuitively appealing and certainly warrants additional research.

A final explanation of the general lack of significant "performance" findings could be that the overall profile of competitive tactics is a much better predictor of firm performance than any single tactic or small set of tactics. In order to test this possibility a discriminant analysis of the data was conducted. While a presentation of the results of this analysis is beyond the scope of this paper, preliminary findings support the potential conclusion that firm performance differences are better revealed through an examination of overall competitive profiles than through a "disaggregated" examination of individual tactics.

CONCLUSIONS

In conclusion, the findings of this study highlight the fact that industry context will influence the choice of competitive tactics used by entrepreneurial firms. Specifically, entrepreneurial firms in high-tech industries tend to attack their environments, adopting a proactive, aggressive, innovative, focused and future-oriented strategic posture. On the other hand, entrepreneurial firms in low-tech industries adopt a more mechanistic, structured, and standardized approach to their environments, apparently preferring the certainty and predictability of such a strategic posture. Concerning the performance issue, most of the competitive tactics of high-performing firms were not significantly different from those of low-performing firms. This was true for firms in both high- and low-tech industries. While it would be unwarranted to conclude from this finding alone that firm performance is not significantly affected by the specific competitive tactics used by a firm, this finding raises interesting issues concerning the importance of effectively implementing business strategies. Indeed, the results of the analysis can be interpreted as suggesting that "doing things right" is as important as "doing the right things."

Table 1

T-TESTS FOR HYPOTHESIS 1

| COMPETITIVE TACTIC | MEAN SCORE OF FIRMS IN: | | SIGNIFICANCE LEVEL |
| | HI-TECH INDUSTRIES | LO-TECH INDUSTRIES | |
| --- | --- | --- | --- |
| 1 | 2.81 | 2.56 | |
| 2 | 3.51 | 2.55 | .0005 |
| 3 | 2.91 | 2.93 | |
| 4 | 3.38 | 2.75 | .01 |
| 5 | 2.64 | 2.78 | |
| 6 | 4.30 | 4.38 | |
| 7 | 3.13 | 2.94 | |
| 8 | 3.33 | 3.39 | |
| 9 | 4.15 | 3.78 | .05 |
| 10 | 3.00 | 2.47 | .05 |
| 11 | 2.47 | 2.31 | |
| 12 | 3.64 | 3.25 | |
| 13 | 3.72 | 3.19 | .05 |
| 14 | 1.83 | 2.03 | |
| 15 | 2.61 | 2.25 | (.1) |
| 16 | 3.96 | 3.38 | .05 |
| 17 | 4.45 | 4.25 | |
| 18 | 3.57 | 3.28 | |
| 19 | 3.77 | 3.91 | |
| 20 | 3.84 | 3.78 | |
| 21 | 4.23 | 3.88 | .05 |
| 22 | 3.87 | 4.06 | |
| 23 | 3.96 | 4.41 | .01 |

| | | | |
|---|---|---|---|
| 24 | 4.30 | 4.34 | |
| 25 | 4.09 | 3.75 | (.1) |
| 26 | 4.51 | 4.50 | |
| 27 | 3.27 | 2.25 | .0005 |
| 28 | 3.62 | 2.81 | .005 |
| 29 | 3.17 | 3.03 | |
| 30 | 4.00 | 3.19 | .0005 |
| 31 | 3.79 | 3.94 | |
| 32 | 4.55 | 4.47 | |
| 33 | 2.87 | 2.78 | |
| 34 | 2.78 | 2.63 | |
| 35 | 3.13 | 3.10 | |
| 36 | 3.37 | 3.09 | |
| 37 | 3.98 | 3.69 | (.1) |
| 38 | 2.50 | 2.25 | |
| 39 | 2.04 | 1.72 | (.1) |
| 40 | 3.21 | 3.68 | .05 |
| 41 | 3.62 | 3.84 | |
| 42 | 4.13 | 4.47 | .05 |
| 43 | 2.96 | 3.03 | |
| 44 | 3.34 | 3.06 | |
| 45 | 3.79 | 3.72 | |
| 46 | 3.94 | 3.63 | (.1) |
| 47 | 4.13 | 3.53 | .005 |
| 48 | 2.98 | 3.44 | .05 |
| 49 | 4.04 | 3.94 | |
| 50 | 3.60 | 3.95 | (.1) |

Table 2

T-TESTS FOR HYPOTHESIS 2

| COMP. TACTIC | HI-TECH IND. HI-PERF | HI-TECH IND. LO-PERF | LO-TECH IND. HI-PERF | LO-TECH IND. LO-PERF | SIGNIFICANCE LEVEL HI-TECH | SIGNIFICANCE LEVEL LO-TECH |
|---|---|---|---|---|---|---|
| 1 | 2.77 | 2.84 | 2.87 | 2.47 | | |
| 2 | 3.27 | 3.72 | 2.57 | 2.60 | | |
| 3 | 2.82 | 3.00 | 2.75 | 3.14 | | |
| 4 | 3.32 | 3.44 | 2.73 | 2.67 | | |
| 5 | 2.86 | 2.44 | 2.80 | 2.80 | (.1) | |
| 6 | 4.05 | 4.54 | 4.47 | 4.27 | .05 | |
| 7 | 3.32 | 2.96 | 2.93 | 2.87 | | |
| 8 | 3.36 | 3.29 | 3.64 | 3.20 | | |
| 9 | 4.14 | 4.17 | 3.73 | 3.87 | | |
| 10 | 3.09 | 2.92 | 2.47 | 2.33 | | |
| 11 | 2.77 | 2.20 | 2.20 | 2.27 | .05 | |
| 12 | 3.50 | 3.76 | 2.93 | 3.47 | | |
| 13 | 3.77 | 3.68 | 3.00 | 3.27 | | |
| 14 | 2.23 | 1.48 | 1.80 | 2.27 | .005 | |
| 15 | 2.55 | 2.67 | 2.20 | 2.07 | | |
| 16 | 3.82 | 4.08 | 3.40 | 3.13 | | |
| 17 | 4.18 | 4.68 | 4.33 | 4.07 | .01 | |
| 18 | 3.59 | 3.56 | 3.47 | 3.00 | | |
| 19 | 3.68 | 3.84 | 3.93 | 3.93 | | |
| 20 | 3.64 | 4.04 | 3.47 | 4.00 | (.1) | (.1) |
| 21 | 4.18 | 4.28 | 3.87 | 3.80 | | |
| 22 | 3.59 | 4.12 | 4.00 | 4.07 | .05 | |
| 23 | 3.73 | 4.16 | 4.47 | 4.33 | (.1) | |

| | | | | | | |
|---|---|---|---|---|---|---|
| 24 | 4.28 | 4.36 | 4.27 | 4.33 | | |
| 25 | 4.00 | 4.16 | 3.60 | 3.73 | | |
| 26 | 4.45 | 4.56 | 4.53 | 4.40 | | |
| 27 | 3.14 | 3.40 | 2.07 | 2.47 | | |
| 28 | 3.86 | 3.39 | 2.80 | 2.87 | (.1) | |
| 29 | 3.73 | 2.68 | 3.20 | 2.60 | .005 | (.1) |
| 30 | 3.91 | 4.08 | 3.40 | 2.73 | | .05 |
| 31 | 4.00 | 3.60 | 4.07 | 3.80 | (.1) | |
| 32 | 4.45 | 4.64 | 4.53 | 4.40 | | |
| 33 | 2.86 | 2.88 | 3.13 | 2.33 | | (.1) |
| 34 | 2.91 | 2.67 | 2.73 | 2.40 | | |
| 35 | 3.18 | 3.09 | 3.21 | 3.00 | | |
| 36 | 3.55 | 3.21 | 3.13 | 2.93 | | |
| 37 | 4.09 | 3.88 | 3.47 | 3.80 | | |
| 38 | 2.64 | 2.38 | 2.40 | 2.13 | | |
| 39 | 2.09 | 2.00 | 2.13 | 1.40 | | .05 |
| 40 | 3.23 | 3.20 | 3.80 | 3.53 | | |
| 41 | 3.64 | 3.60 | 4.00 | 3.73 | | |
| 42 | 4.18 | 4.08 | 4.60 | 4.27 | | (.1) |
| 43 | 3.09 | 2.84 | 3.07 | 3.13 | | |
| 44 | 3.55 | 3.16 | 3.13 | 3.00 | | |
| 45 | 3.77 | 3.80 | 3.73 | 3.60 | | |
| 46 | 4.14 | 3.76 | 3.87 | 3.40 | (.1) | .05 |
| 47 | 4.18 | 4.08 | 3.47 | 3.67 | | |
| 48 | 2.86 | 3.08 | 3.40 | 3.53 | | |
| 49 | 3.82 | 4.24 | 4.20 | 3.60 | (.1) | .05 |
| 50 | 3.82 | 3.40 | 4.00 | 3.87 | | |

## THE COMPETITIVE TACTICS INSTRUMENT

Below are listed several statements which describe methods for conduting business operations or competing in an industry. Please indicate by circling the appropriate number the degree to which you agree or disagree with each statement as it pertains to your firm's current overall business strategy.

The following scale applied to all statements:

| STRONGLY DISAGREE | DISAGREE | NEUTRAL | AGREE | STRONGLY AGREE |
|---|---|---|---|---|
| 1 | 2 | 3 | 4 | 5 |

1.  We have a highly liquid financial position.
2.  We maximize use of outside financing.
3.  We have a highly leveraged financial position.
4.  We frequently explore for new sources of funds.
5.  We extend generous customer credit.
6.  We constantly try to increase cash flow.
7.  We emphasize long-term capital investments.
8.  We emphasize immediate profitability.
9.  We emphasize long-term profitability.
10. We engage in heavy promotional activities.
11. We use frequent advertising.
12. We use sharply-focused advertising.
13. We use advertising which differentiates our products/services from those of competitors.
14. We use widespread, broad-based advertising.
15. We offer our products/services at a high price relative to our competitors.
16. We emphasize the building of brand image/identification.
17. We provide extensive customer service/support.
18. We engage in novel, innovative marketing techniques.
19. We attract customers away from competitors.
20. We encourage new customers to enter the market.
21. We actively attempt to predict customer requirements/tastes.
22. We emphasize cost reduction in all facets of business operations.
23. We emphasize the improvement of employee productivity and operations efficiency.
24. We emphasize strict quality control.
25. We use innovative operating techniques or technologies.
26. We offer products/services of superior quality.
27. We use product or process patents and/or copyrights to provide a competitive advantage.
28. We offer superior product/service warranties.
29. We offer a wide range of products/services.
30. We emphasize new product/service development.
31. We emphasize the development and refinement of existing products/ services.

32. We emphasize the building of company image and reputation within our industry.
33. We influence or control sources of supplies/raw materials.
34. We influence or control distribution channels.
35. We engage in "networking" activities to reduce environmental uncertainty.
36. We actively attempt to predict competitors' moves.
37. We actively attempt to predict industry trends.
38. We stockpile materials and/or supplies in order to meet fluctuating demand.
39. We maintain large inventories of finished goods.
40. We actively attempt to create stable, nonfluctuating levels of demand for our products/services.
41. We actively attempt to minimize our dependence on any supplier.
42. We actively attempt to minimize our dependence on any single customer.
43. We use formalized management information systems to support decision making.
44. We use long-term forecasting and planning techniques.
45. We set explicit performance goals for our business.
46. We attract and retain highly competent top managers.
47. We attract and retain highly skilled technical personnel.
48. We use personnel training and development programs.
49. We reward employees based upon the attainment of performance goals.
50. We use a participative, group, or democratic approach to business decision making.


## THE TECHNOLOGICAL SOPHISTICATION SCALE

How would you characterize the external environment within which your firm functions?

| An environment demanding little in the way of technological sophistication | 1 to 7 | Technologically, a very sophisticated and complex environment |
|---|---|---|

How much research and development activity takes place within your firm's principal industry?

| Virtually no R & D in industry (e.g., bakery, publishing, real estate) | 1 to 7 | Extremely R & D oriented industry (e.g., telecommunications, space. drugs) |
|---|---|---|

# REFERENCES

Anderson, C. R. and Zeithaml, C. P. (1984) Stage of product life cycle, business strategy, and business performance. Academy of Management Journal, 27, 5-24.

Bettis, R. A. (1981) Performance differences in related and unrelated diversified firms. Strategic Management Journal, 2, 379-394.

Bourgeois, L. J. (1980) Performance and concensus. Strategic Management Journal, 1, 227-248.

Cooper, A. C. (1979) Strategic management: New ventures and small business, in Strategic management: A new view of business policy and planning, Schendel, D. E. and Hofer, C. W. (eds.), Boston: Little, Brown and Company, 316-327.

Dess, G. G. and Davis, P. S. (1984) Porter's (1980) generic strategies as determinants of strategic group membership and organizational performance. Academy of Management Journal, 27, 367-388.

Fahey, L. and Christensen, H. K. (1986) Evaluating the research on strategy content. Journal of Management, 12 (2), 167-183.

Galbraith, C. S. and Schendel, D. (1983) An empirical analysis of strategy types. Strategic Management Journal, 4, 153-173.

Gupta, A. K. and Govindarajan, V. (1984) Business unit strategy, managerial characteristics, and business unit effectiveness at strategy implementation. Academy of Management Journal, 27, 25-41.

Khandwalla, P. N. (1977) The design of organizations, New York: Harcourt Brace Jovanovich.

Miller, D. and Friesen, P. H. (1984) Organizations: A quantum view, Englewood Cliffs, NJ: Prentics-Hall.

Robinson, R. B. and Pearce, J. A. (1985) The structure of generic strategies and their impact on business-unit performance. Academy of Management Proceedings, 35-39.

SUMMARY

EVOLVING MARKETS AND ENTREPRENEURIAL SUCCESS -
IS TIMING OF THE ESSENCE?

Author

   Mahesh Bhave

Address

   Maxwell School, Technology and Information Policy Program
   Syracuse University
   Syracuse, NY 13244
   (315) 471-7893/ (315) 423-1890

Method and Principal Topics

   This paper is based on empirical case data obtained through open-
   ended interviews of 27 entrepreneurs in Upstate New York.   In
   starting a business venture, I propose that "correct" timing in an
   entrepreneur's personal life must be congruent with correct timing
   with respect to the technology.  Under certain circumstances, which
   are considered in this paper, a new business lags or leads the
   market.  The project is either a shade too early or a shade too
   late with respect to the needs of the market.  In either case, a new
   firm faces challenges that may jeopardize its very existence.  While
   an entrepreneur may have control over some factors in his personal
   environment, the technology at any given point is a given, and
   beyond the powers of most entrepreneurs to control.

Major Findings and Conclusion

   In conclusion, we note that the nature and magnitude of entrepreneurial success may not wholly depend on initiative, energy, managerial skills or available resources.  Success may depend on
   environmental conditions.  When a product is new and unfamiliar to
   users, an entrepreneur has to create a market for it.  The rate at
   which the users will accept a new product will determine an
   entrepreneur's success.   In general, it is difficult to predict how
   users will respond to the introduction of a new product.  Creating
   markets involves educating customers, and requires enormous resources.  When a product is technology-based, however, an entrepreneur
   can make judgments about the likely rate of acceptance of his/her
   product, if he/she can "locate" the product on the trajectory of the
   technology system.

Technologies evolve at different rates, and the trajectory of a technology system can be one indicator of the rate of market acceptance of a product. Timing the introduction of a product is crucial to success, especially when the "market learning curve" is evolving rapidly, driven by underlying technological forces. Technological forces, however, are but one element in market evolution and change.

# A CONTINGENCY THEORY OF PRODUCT LIFE CYCLE, RELATEDNESS AND RESULTING SYNERGIES

## Author

Diana L. Day

## Address

Wharton School
University of Pennsylvania
34th & Spruce Streets
Philadelphia, PA 19104
(215) 898-3022

## Principal Topics

Previous studies of relatedness and synergy typically look at the degree of overall relatedness of a firm and its financial performance to determine if related diversification pays. This paper argues that in all diversification moves based on internal venturing, the unit of focus should be the individual venture and not the total corporation. In addition, this paper argues that it is not simply the overall degree of relatedness between the venture and its parent company but the specific ways in which the venture is related and the nature of the venture's competitive environment which will determine whether the relationship will result in positive or negative synergies. More specifically, the strength and direction (positive or negative) of these synergies from these different types of relatedness are contingent on the stage of the product life cycle. Finally, this paper looks at these synergistic effects in the form of market and financial performance from both start-up and long-term synergies.

## Method and Data Base

The specific hypothesis tested in this study are based on an underlying theoretical assumption: relatedness results in synergies which affect venture performance. Sub-group analysis with Fisher's Z-test were used to test individual hypotheses about benefits from specific types of relatedness and Chow tests were used to test for overall effects.

## Major Findings

The study concludes that the value of different types of relatedness is contingent upon the stage of the product life cycle especially for synergistic benefits in terms of market benefits.  These
findings indicate strong support for Hofer's argument that life
cycle stage may be one of the single most important variables to
consider strategy research.

SUMMARY

ENTREPRENEURIAL SUCCESSION:
AN EMPIRICAL STUDY REVIEW

Author

Eugene G. Gomolka

Address

University of Dayton
Department of Management
300 College Park
Dayton, Ohio 45469
(513) 229-2021

Principal Topics

Succession in entrepreneurial firms, literature review of research findings on succession, and a summary of survey results on succession planning.

Major Findings

The results presented indicate some agreement with, and some extension of the previous results surveyed. Factors important in the succession planning process are identified and relatively ordered.

The composite firm in the surveys reported is a small company, founded by a person or persons, with unquoted stock or shares, and only one location. The individual owner-manager in the sample is pictured as a male, 35 to 44 years old, born in the United States with a U.S. born father, a college graduate, a tenure of 8 years as the head of his company, and the founder of his firm.

Only 34.4% to 39% of the firms surveyed have a formal succession plan. The smallest size firms have the greatest likelihood of not having a succession plan, and those firms which tended to designate a successor are likely to be principal units, have unquoted stock, and choose a member of the present management team or a son or daughter.

Major Implications

The data reported reveal some interesting validations and extensions of the classic description of succession in the literature. Future studies of succession need to build upon and extend the type of analyses reported in the paper.

SUMMARY

ETHICAL ENTREPRENEURSHIP

Author

Wayne Smeltz

Address

Rider College
School of Business Administration
2083 Lawrenceville Road
Lawrenceville, NJ 08648
(609) 895-5548

## Principal Topics

This paper develops a model that examines the role of ethical motivation in the entrepreneurial process.  The argument for developing
such a model is that ethical motivation is seen as a potentially
significant competitive advantage when identifying market niches.
It is hypothesized that ethical individuals are often driven to
entrepreneurship because of their lack of satisfaction of important
personal needs.  If it is found that like-minded networks who these
individuals interact with are also experiencing this persistent need
deprivation then a market niche has been identified.  This process
is then contrasted with a typical entrepreneurial model to determine similarities and differences.  Differences would be expected to
be found in determining the firms' mission and subsequent strategies.

## Major Findings

The sample chosen for initial examination are entrepreneurs from the
natural food industry.  This sample was chosen because the food
industry has had a long history of entrepreneurship and the natural
food segment has experienced significant growth.  In addition,
dietetic laws based on ethnic and religious differences are seen to
be significantly linked to ethical beliefs.

Preliminary findings lend support to the ethical model.  Respondents
have indicated that their primary reason for starting a business was
their individual dissatisfaction with a particular product or service.  Findings also indicate disagreement among entrepreneurs over
the ethical value of other's undertakings.

## Major Implications

Preliminary results indicate the need for further research to better understand the make-up of ethical entrepreneurs. Through interviews the following issues will be addressed. (1) The motivations and doubts of ethical individuals as they consider an entrepreneurial undertaking. It must be remembered that many of these individuals tend to be reluctant entrepreneurs. (2) The compromises that ethical entrepreneurs face when trying to run a successful organization. (3) Whether ethical enterprises begin to approximate typical firms over time and is the ethical foundation a help or hindrance.

As many large corporations grapple with their values and culture, a firm begun from ethical principles may provide a large contribution to society. This contribution is not only in product and service but also in its adherence to a set of principles and values. This research seeks to further examine this possibility.

OPPORTUNITY RECOGNITION:
THE CORE OF ENTREPRENEURSHIP

Jeffry A. Timmons, Babson College
Daniel F. Muzyka, Harvard University
Howard H. Stevenson, Harvard University
William D. Bygrave, Babson College

## ABSTRACT

Little has been said concerning opportunity screening and evaluation, and, any common characteristics of <u>successful</u> (as opposed to selected) entrepreneurial ventures. This paper documents empirical research bearing on this question. Specifically, the paper develops a series of formal propositions concerning the criteria and parameters appropriate to the evaluation and selection of investment opportunities.

## INTRODUCTION

The venture capitalist's success in searching for potentially successful ventures is a key determinant of performance of the fund he controls. Venture capitalists have been largely unwilling or unable to articulate the detailed characteristics they associate with successful ventures, the specifics of any formal models or frameworks they utilize and the very mechanisms behind the successful performance of venture funds (see Stevenson et al., 1986).

Why are the characteristics associated with successful ventures so difficult to uncover? Why can't we rely on formal models such as the competitive strategy models (Porter, 1980; Hofer and Schendel, 1978) to evaluate potential entrepreneurial ventures? Based on our research, a number of answers appear to be appropriate to these questions. First, systematic research into the characteristics of successful ventures has only begun, partly as a result of the unwillingness of venture capitalists to discuss them and partly as a result of the small database from which to generalize. Second, venture capitalists noted that they did not find the competitive strategy frameworks and other policy models to be directly and easily transferable to their environment.

Some of the difficulty experienced by venture capitalists might be associated with the underlying databases used by researchers. Research in industrial organization economics and strategic management has not focused on new venture development and performance. Most of the industrial organization studies have been based on firm and industry data related to large enterprises (Fortune 500 sized). Strategic management research, consulting and practice have similarly provided few concrete guidelines for the use of venture capitalists in identifying potentially profitable ventures and have left underdeveloped the notions regarding new business creation and venturing.

Previous research in entrepreneurship has provided venture capitalists with some insights but is generally exploratory in nature and presents somewhat contradictory results. There have been several studies directed at determining what factors are used by venture capitalists to evaluate venture proposals and how venture characteristics relate to venture success. These studies (e.g., Wells, 1974; Poindexter, 1976; Tyebjee and Bruno, 1981; MacMillan et al., 1985) are directed at determining what factors are used by venture capitalists in selecting ventures from the population of proposals they receive. They tend to support the traditional wisdom that the key evaluation criteria, and presumably the key success factor, were primarily related to the characteristics of the entrepreneur. Another stream of studies have attempted to link venture characteristics with venture performance (e.g., Hoban, 1976; Sandberg and Hofer, 1986). The research in this stream tends to support the notion that product-market characteristics were more directly related to venture success than the characteristics of the entrepreneur.[1]

The new venture capital climate in the 1980's has been accompanied by both innovative investing practices and approaches, particularly in start up and early stage investments (Timmons and Gumpert, 1982). Building on his earlier research and cumulative practical experience, Timmons (1985, Chapter 3) introduced specific criteria and a framework for venture selection and evaluation. This framework provides a basis for the propositions developed here.

RESEARCH DESIGN

The purpose of our research was to try to develop a more complete understanding, from the perspective of the venture capitalists, of the characteristics of "successful" ventures. It was our hope that we could (1) extend and link the work done by those reviewing deal selection criteria and the structure-strategy-performance link; (2) develop a practitioner originated list of the common characteristics of high performing ventures; (3) provide researchers with as complete as possible a list of the possible factors leading to higher performance in entrepreneurial ventures; and (4) develop an initial list of

---

[1]A more expansive version of this paper may be obtained from the second author by asking for Harvard Business School Working Paper #87-045.

characteristics for venture capitalists to use in their screening and selection of investment opportunities. We wished to seek an operational definition of the factors affecting venture success and, therefore, adopted relatively unstructured research methods.

We selected a sample of 47 sites for interview purposes. Included in the total sample of 47 firms and investors were 18 private investors, four international venture capital firms, and 21 venture capitalists recognized as having highly innovative and diverse portfolios (see Timmons, Fast and Bygrave (1984)). The investors included in the sample represent a broad range of investment interests, orientations, industry participation, and performance.

The research process was exploratory in nature. Unstructured interviews were conducted with principals of the venture capital firms. The characteristics for discussion and the definition of a "successful venture" were supplied by the venture capitalists being interviewed, since any pre-defined and exact performance standard might have introduced unwanted bias. A series of general and "fatal flaws" propositions were developed based on the information from the field interviews. The propositions discussed in the following section were developed with a minimum of reliance on formal paradigms (e.g., Porter's (1980) competitive strategy paradigm). The propositions were, however, grouped by the authors into logical categories. No attempt was made to rank the characteristics or propositions since a major objective of the study was to outline a complete set of characteristics common to successful ventures across markets and industries. (As a general point, the term industry is used as in Porter (1980) to describe the group of firms producing products that are substitutes for each other (e.g., computer industry) and includes many markets (e.g., word processing work stations)). Finally, as part of our research effort we attempted to compile a list of "fatal flaws" or characteristics venture capitalists associated with ventures which had a high likelihood of failure.

## RESEARCH FINDINGS

Five groups of characteristics were identified as a result of the interviews: product-market characteristics, competitive dynamics, business economics, business performance and management. The propositions that follow were found to apply across venture industries.

### Product-Market Structure

Venture capitalists note that a thorough and complete understanding of the product-market characteristics is an essential element of a proper evaluation of a venture opportunity. The first proposition is fundamental to the success of any venture -- the <u>identification of the true market</u> for the venture's product. What venture capitalists have noted as more important than a "market" for the venture product is a well defined notion of the actual customers, the customers' rationale for purchasing the new product or service, and benefits and economic payback realized by the customer (see Muzyka et al., 1986; Lilien and Kotler, 1983). Many individuals discussing the problems of applying the concepts organized under the title of competitive strategy (Porter, 1980; Bogue and Buffa, 1985; Hofer and Schendel, 1978) have noted the problem of market definition.

> **Proposition 1:** Ventures which will have a product/service with a clearly identified and enthusiastic customer population are more likely to succeed than ventures which have a vague or poorly defined customer population.
>
> **Proposition 2:** Ventures which will provide a product with a clear payback to the customer in less than 18 months is more likely to succeed than a venture with a product having ill-defined economic returns to the customer.

Another major product-market factor is simply the size of the market to be served by the venture. Markets that are too small appear to give little room for growth and competition. In many cases, venture capitalists note, venture plans which describe businesses which will address relatively small markets contain unrealistically high expectations for long-run market share. Markets for proposed ventures

> **Proposition 3:** Ventures which are likely to serve a clearly defined market with an annual size between $10MM and $100MM are more likely to succeed than a venture serving a very small or very large market.

that are too large appear to be an undesirable characteristic of a new venture for several reasons: (1) that large market expectations are the result of inadequate research or unbridled enthusiasm, and (2) that ventures which appear to have a potentially large market for their product tend to attract and end up competing with large corporations in their market. Major corporations, armed with the necessary market, financial and technical information, can often rapidly transfer learning or experience from related businesses (Spence, 1981) in order to be low cost producer in a new market.

Another product-market characteristic that is of importance to the financial success of a venture is the market growth rate. As with

> **Proposition 4:** Ventures which will serve a market with a potential growth rate of 30% to 60% are more likely to succeed than ventures serving markets with very slow or high growth rates.

market size, market growth rates that are too low do not provide enough opportunity for venture growth (and, therefore, return) while markets with excessive growth rates tend to attract many (sometimes too many as Sahlman and Stevenson (1985) noted) new entrants. Furthermore, markets with excessively high growth rates require that venture management not only manage the creation of a business but potentially madcap growth. Also, expected profits in potentially large, fast growing markets may be sufficient for established industry competitors to overcome the risks of entry (Stonebraker, 1976). The notion that fast growth is associated with the markets served by successful or selected ventures can be found in both Sandberg and Hofer (1986) and MacMillan et al., (1986).

The final point addressed by venture capitalists regarding product-market structure is the differentiation of the product vis-a-vis the competition. Legal restrictions or key protected (either

> Proposition 5: Ventures which are based on a product which incorporates or is manufactured by a process that incorporates legally protected or highly unique technologies or features are likely to be more successful than ventures which rely on more generic product features or technologies.

through patents or trade secrets) technologies can represent a formidable barrier to market entry (see Waterson, 1984). MacMillan et al., (1986) identified this as a major consideration in the selection of new ventures.

A related issue is the distinctiveness of the features of the proposed product or service as compared to similar ones (close substitutes) that may exist in the marketplace. It has been shown (Brander and Eaton, 1984; Schmalensee, 1978) that existing competitors in a

> Proposition 5.1: Ventures whose product or service features can be served by similar products or services or the easy combination of similar products or services are less likely to be successful than ventures with a product or service with new features.
>
> Proposition 5.2: Ventures whose product or service can be duplicated by the relatively immediate extension of the product line of an existing competitor are less likely to be successful than ventures with a product or service with unique features.

market can and will compete on the basis of an interlocking series of differentiated products. If existing competitors have a product line in place with products that have different groupings of features, existing customers may be well served by purchasing products with a bundle of features near those of the product proposed as part of the new venture. Also, the existing competitor may have a shared cost advantage from producing other similar products (Porter, 1985; Bogue and Buffa, 1986).

One of the most discussed dimensions along which a company can differentiate its product is quality (Waterson, 1984). As the literature (Garvin, 1983; Buzzell et al., 1981; Crosby, 1979) would suggest, high product quality has a double benefit. Superior quality not only

> Proposition 5.3: Ventures which produce products or services of higher quality than substitute or competitive products have a higher likelihood of success than ventures with ventures that produce products of moderate or low quality.

113

permits the business to differentiate its product but it also permits the total cost (direct production, service and warranty cost) of products to be lower in the long run.

Competitive Dynamics

Venture capitalists made a number of common points concerning the history and state of competition in the industry. The first major point made by the venture capitalists that we interviewed was that an assessment must be made of the <u>reaction to new competitors</u> in the marketplace. Research has shown that predatory behavior is a common

Proposition 6: Ventures that would face strong and vindictive competitors in their served market segment or adjacent market segments are less likely to succeed than potential ventures with limited or passive competition.

and effective, albeit economically irrational at times, barrier to entry as noted by some researchers (Milgrom and Roberts, 1982).

Another proposition developed from our interviews involved the <u>basis of competition</u> in the market for a proposed venture. Venture capitalists consistently made it clear that ventures that initially

Proposition 7: Ventures which compete in the marketplace on the basis of product differentiation and technological innovation are more likely to be successful than ventures which compete on price.
Proposition 7.1: Ventures which compete on the basis of technological innovation or a differentiated product are more successful if the technologies or products are not perceived to be as threatening to the competitors or have an inherently long lead time for competitive response.

planned to compete strictly on the basis of price were less likely to succeed than those which relied on product differentiation and research and development. Venture capitalists also claimed that ventures which proposed to offer an existing product or service in a geographic area where it is currently not offered (focus strategy as defined by Porter (1980)), were less likely to succeed than those who adopted a "differentiation" strategy. This is consistent with Sandberg's and Hofer's (1986) findings regarding venture strategy.

In addition to the product-market characteristics noted in the previous section, venture capitalists we interviewed indicated that ventures which had a strong likelihood of achieving and maintaining a <u>dominant position in the marketplace</u> were more likely to succeed.

Proposition 8: Ventures which have a potential to attain and maintain a dominant position (high relative market share) in the market are more likely to succeed.
Proposition 8.1: Ventures which have the potential to acquire and sustain a market share (in a clearly defined market) in excess of 20% are more likely to be successful.

Proposition 8.2: Ventures which are likely to exercise price leadership based on share position are likely to be more successful.

Proposition 8.3: Ventures which can attain and maintain a low or the lowest cost position are more likely to be successful.

The wisdom from industrial organization economics (Waterson, 1984), strategic management research (Buzzell et al., 1975) and practice (Henderson, 1979) which relates market share, concentration and profitability seems to hold true as related to entrepreneurial ventures.

Another major concern of venture capitalists assessing competitive dynamics is the nature of the barriers to entry in the marketplace. As previous research would indicate, high barriers to entry permit competitors to realize higher profits (Bain, 1972).

Proposition 9: Ventures which can grow in a market niche protected by extensive entry barriers are more likely to succeed than those competing in a market without protective barriers.

Proposition 9.1: Ventures with low barriers to initial entry and, therefore, lower cost are more successful.

Higher profit potential leads to the potential for more successful ventures. As noted by venture capitalists, these same barriers to entry take on another role when considering the initiation of a new venture in an existing market. It takes time, money and energy, or a novel idea or concept, to surmount high barriers without a large expenditure of funds.

The discussion with venture capitalists regarding the strategic options faced by ventures contains many of the same elements as the literature on low market share companies following a "niche" strategy (Hamermesh et al., 1978; Woo and Cooper, 1981). The suggestion has been made in our discussions and the literature on low share firms that they should establish themselves within the confines of a protected market within an industry. In effect, there must be mobility barriers (Waterson, 1984) that prevent existing industry competitors from competing in the specific market served by the venture. The industry "U" (Porter, 1980; Muzyka and Crittenden, 1985) or "V" (Bogue and Buffa, 1986) curve is consistent with this notion. What our research indicates is that successful ventures appear to have identified lucrative markets within an industry, found gateways to entry (Yip, 1982) through the barriers protecting the markets, taken dominant share positions in the specific market while ensuring that their costs are the lowest of any competitor serving the specific market, and have attempted to grow and maintain barriers to protect the chosen markets.

A final consideration under the category of competitive dynamics is the product line growth path for the venture. The data from investors with regard to successful ventures was that from the outset,

Proposition 10: Ventures which rely on one innovative product with little or no possibility for expansion or extension are less likely to succeed than ventures which rely on a product concept which can lead to a product line.

they had a clear product line growth path. An alternative issue with respect to growth is that the market opportunity the entrepreneur sees may not have been previously addressed for good economic reasons: growth beyond the single product may not have been possible without resorting to another, completely new technology.

## Business Economics

Venture capitalists identified a major set of comments we have categorized under the title "business economics." The major groups of propositions included in this section are associated with the economic value created by the business. The first set of propositions are related to the <u>determination of the "value added" stream</u> the venture will be part of. Venture capitalists confirm that it is important,

> Proposition 11: Ventures with a clearly defined position in a value added stream and a durable and high value added have a better chance of success than those with low value added.
> Proposition 11.1: Ventures which expect stable gross margins of between 20-50+% have a greater chance for success than ventures with gross margins less than 20% or with volatile gross margins.

particularly with regard to proposed ventures in industrial markets to understand the nature, size and durability of the value added position of the venture (see Porter (1985) or Bogue and Buffa (1986)). Venture capitalists went on to note that ventures with low or volatile value added and, therefore, low margins were unlikely to be successful. Low margin ventures required efficiency as well as effectiveness on the part of the management team initiating the venture, providing little slack for management to work with.

Related propositions deal with the relationship and nature of the elements of the value added stream adjacent to those addressed by the venture. Venture capitalists noted the real need to understand the value added of the proposed business vis-a-vis suppliers and buyers. Entrepreneurial ventures which were critically dependent upon

> Proposition 11.2: Ventures having clearly defined inputs and multiple factor inputs and sources of supply for these inputs have a greater chance for success than those which must develop sources of supply or that must determine how to best manufacture or provide the product/service.
> Proposition 11.3: Ventures that have clearly defined, accessible, and established product distribution channels are more likely to be successful than ventures with poorly defined or non-existent product distribution channels.
> Proposition 11.4: Ventures which have an exclusive or unique relationship with suppliers and/or distribution channels are more likely to be successful.

developing sources of supply or were dependent upon developing channels of distribution and/or special relationship with suppliers and/or
distributors. The issue that seems somewhat at variance with the
literature is the wisdom that both supplier and buyer power should be
weak (Porter, 1976; Lustgarten, 1975; Waterson, 1984). With regard to
ventures there would appear to be some intermediate, optimal level of
supplier and buyer power.

The second set of propositions under the category of business
economics are those related to the nature of the investment stream
required to create the business. Ventures which required planned
major, "lumpy" investments up-front were not usually successful.

> Proposition 12: Ventures which require multiple rounds of funding
> and have capital requirements between $300,000 and $1,000,000 per
> round, tend to be more successful than ventures requiring only
> small or very large investments, or those with very irregular
> capital requirements (e.g., large funding up-front with little
> required in additional rounds).
> Proposition 12.1: Ventures which are planned, proposed and
> funded largely in a single investment stage are typically less
> successful than those segmented for both planning and funding
> purposes into smaller logical segments with discrete and measur-
> able performance criteria.

Venture capitalists cited many problems with such ventures, including
the fact that real monitoring of performance was difficult in ventures
where there was major up-front investment.

In addition, venture capitalists related that highly asset
intensive ventures did not perform well. Venture capitalists noted

> Proposition 12.2: Ventures which are asset intensive are typi-
> cally less successful than ventures with moderate or low asset
> intensity.

that this seemed too true for several reasons: (1) ventures requiring
major asset development put a major strain on potentially untried
management, and (2) venture capitalists noted that the acquisition and
development of assets such as plant and equipment provided little competitive advantage for new ventures.

The final value-related issue is the requirement that the venture capitalist have mechanisms to capture the value created by the
business. The main issue for venture capitalists was that ventures

> Proposition 13: Ventures with no clear exit path, be it an IPO or
> sale to another firm, are typically less successful than ventures
> which have a clear economic value to another firm or which can be
> configured in such a fashion that they will have a clear and
> reasonable chance of operating as a separate entity.
> Proposition 13.1: Ventures which are funded with the expecta-
> tion that the best exit option for the venture capitalist is a

buyback by the management are less likely to succeed than ventures with an externally and independently apparent value.

could not, by definition, be successful if the economic value that was thought to be created in the business was not recognized by others. In essence, the value did not exist and the venture could not be successful if a market did not exist for the venture itself. These propositions are consistent with Tyebjee's and Bruno's (1981) and MacMillan's et al. (1986) findings.

## Business Performance

In addition to the propositions already noted, venture capitalists outlined performance standards associated with successful ventures. The performance characteristics of a proposed venture are obviously related to the structure and conduct characteristics outlined previously. However, venture capitalists noted that they also contain certain additional information concerning management behavior and expectations and resource management.

The first set of performance standards identified as part of the research were time related standards. Ventures with very short

> Proposition 14: Ventures planned for final disposition (IPO or sale to another company) within four to seven years are likely to be more successful than ventures with unusual life cycles involving early sale or longer term disposition.
> Proposition 15: Ventures with a reasonably planned time to breakeven of between 18 months (or less) to 36 months are more likely to succeed than ventures with long or very short breakeven periods.
> Proposition 15.1: Ventures with exceedingly short breakeven periods are likely to serve product-market segments with few barriers to entry and are likely to be less successful.
> Proposition 15.2: Ventures with exceedingly long breakeven periods are likely to have intrinsically risky and possibly unrealistic assumptions concerning long-term payouts making them generally less successful.

expected periods to IPO sometimes contained unrealistic assumptions concerning the difficulty of initiating the venture or overcoming industry entry barriers. Also, venture capitalists noted that some ventures with short periods to IPO are typically entering industries with few barriers to entry. These ventures have a low value at offering time since they can be easily replicated. Ventures with exceedingly long expected periods to IPO were generally identified as being very risky for a variety of reasons, including the threat of obsolescence of the underlying technology.

Venture capitalists interviewed indicated certain cash flow and profit plan standards which successful ventures generally met.

> Proposition 16: Ventures which have a reasonable chance of attaining durable after tax profits in the 10-15+% range are more

likely to be successful than ventures with exceedingly low or
exceedingly high expectations.

Proposition 16.1: Ventures with long-term profit expectations
less than 5% are less likely to be successful than ventures with
higher profit expectations.

Proposition 16.2: Ventures with excessively high profit expectations are unlikely to be successful in the long-run due to
heightened competitive interest in the product-market or unrealistic long-run expectations concerning the cost structure.

Venture capitalists noted that extraordinary profit expectations did
not indicate a sound plan. Excessively high returns would attract
competition to the industry, lowering the eventual returns for all
competitors (Stonebraker, 1976; Masson and Shaanan, 1982; Caves,
Fortunato and Ghemawat, 1984). On the other hand, low profit expectations left little "slack" in the financial statements to meet negative operating contingencies or variances from plan, making the
management task more difficult.

The other clear cash flow and profit plan measure generally
associated with successful ventures was the time until positive cash

Proposition 17: Ventures with planned positive cash flows
beginning between 18 and 36 months after investment are more
likely to succeed than ventures exhibiting longer periods until
positive cash flow.

flow. Ventures with long planned periods until positive cash flow
were found to be very risky investments to be made with a new management team.

The final category of performance measures indicated by venture
capitalists were the "return" measures. Venture capitalists noted

Proposition 18: Venture plans which exhibit a return in the range
of 10x initial investment in five years are associated with more
successful ventures.

Proposition 19: All factors considered, ventures with an initial
ROI expectation of 25-30% generally have the greatest chance of
success. Ventures with ROI's less than 10% or excessively high
proposed returns are less successful than ventures with more moderate returns.

that ventures with higher planned returns were either the creation of
an overly optimistic planning process or were likely to attract a
great deal of competition (assuming low barriers to entry).

Management

Venture capitalists interviewed as part of this research uniformly noted that the most important factor which is a potential prior
determinant of venture success is the management team. Just as many
researchers in strategic management emphasize that the formulation of

an effective corporate strategy can only lead to the realization of a successful corporate strategy if the implementation is successful (Hamermesh, 1986), venture capitalists uniformly agree that venture success is critically dependent upon implementation: a poor venture concept can sometimes be rescued by good management but a good venture concept will not rescue poor management.

The first proposition we state is one which was reiterated in each of our interviews: venture success is more likely if the management team is more likely to work together and has a proven track record in the proposed business area.

> Proposition 20: Ventures with a proven, integrated management team with high integrity are more likely to succeed than those with a totally inexperienced management team with no proven track record.
> Proposition 20.1: Ventures with key management team members having extensive experience with the venture technologies, market and/or products are more likely to succeed than ventures with management teams with limited or no experience in the key venture technologies or products.
> Proposition 20.2: Ventures which include one or more "industry superstars" (with prior profit and loss, marketing and/or technological experience in the industry) in their top management teams are more likely to succeed.

The types of prior experience that venture capitalists noted as most important were (1) experience with general management in a start-up environment, and (2) industry experience. In addition, the presence on the proposed management team of an industry "superstar" with extensive technical and/or operating experience appears to be a major contributor to venture success.

A second major and associated point is the integration and orientation of the management team.

> Proposition 21: Management teams which can work in a complementary fashion toward achieving the overall objective are more likely to succeed than ones composed of individuals with different objectives and/or only a limited ability to work together.
> Proposition 21.1: Management teams with a uniform orientation toward opportunity rather than resource control are more likely to be successful than management teams oriented toward control and/or management of acquired resources.

Venture capitalists associate a prior degree of understanding and a common set of objectives with regard to the business as the most important prior predictors of whether a management team will cooperate. Finally, venture capitalists indicated that managers who exhibit "trustee" behavior (see Stevenson, et al., 1985) or an orientation toward acquiring and protecting assets are unlikely to foster the environment necessary to achieve success.

Certain general management skills appear to be most critical to venture success including the ability to focus the venture organization's efforts to provide the organization strong leadership (Zaleznick, 1977), to dynamically manipulate incentives for employees and fellow managers, and to provide the minimal, essential administrative systems (Hamermesh, 1984). Those venture capitalists we spoke to stated that they were able to evaluate managers on their abilities in these areas by careful review of the venture objectives and plan, review of the prior performance and career paths and discussions with the proposed management team.

Proposition 22: Ventures with strong general management and appropriate general management incentives are more likely to succeed than ventures with "unfair" or poor incentives and mediocre general management.
Proposition 22.1: Ventures with a general manager who is able to identify and maintain organizational and management focus on the factors key to the success of the venture are more likely to be successful.
Proposition 22.2: Ventures with a general manager who exhibits strong leadership skills and projects a strong vision of the overall venture objectives are more likely to be successful.
Proposition 22.3: Ventures with a general manager who understands how to manipulate incentives for fellow employees are more likely to be successful.
Proposition 22.4: Ventures with general manager skilled at configuring, implementing, and operating appropriate (and minimal) organizational systems for monitoring and resource allocation are more likely to be successful.

Of particular interest in our discussion with venture capitalists was the role of proper incentives. Consistent with the literature on agency theory, our data suggests that the proper alignment of personal and venture goals and expectations through realistic and reasonable incentives is a critical determinant of venture success (Pratt and Zeckhauser, 1985; Jensen and Meckling, 1976).

The conventional wisdom of the venture capital market is echoed in these comments regarding management: management and implementation are issues with a pervasive influence on venture success. In particular, our research would suggest that it is experience and the proven ability to apply it that are two of the most important characteristics of the lead entrepreneur and the management team in general. Some studies (e.g., Sandberg and Hofer, 1986) find little or no relationship between venture performance and entrepreneur or management characteristics. Our research would suggest that the definitions used in some studies to operationalize the entrepreneur's characteristics do not capture all of the dimensions associated with what venture capitalists perceive as "experience" and "ability" or the role of the management team as a group.

## Fatally Flawed Ventures

As indicated earlier, in the course of our research we also attempted to compile a list of "fatal flaws" -- individual character-istics often associated with ventures that fail.  These fatal flaws

TABLE 1

Fatal Flaws

Product-Market Structure:
° Very small or very large market for the product or service.

Competitive Dynamics:
° Overpowering competition and high cost of entry.
° Inability to expand beyond a one-product company.

Business Economics:
° Overwhelming financial requirements.
° Inability to produce a product at a cost that will make it competitive.
° Lack of influence and control over product development and component prices.
° Inability to harvest the opportunity profitably.

were identified by asking what factors usually led to the ultimate failure of the venture (see Table 1) and should be considered in con-junction with the proposition outlined above.  These "fatal flaws" are somewhat different than those presented by MacMillan et al., (1985) whose orientation was directed more toward what apparent factors would lead to rejection of a venture proposal.

## IMPLICATIONS FOR PRACTITIONERS

There are a number of preliminary implications for practition-ers from this research.  The most important implication is that the identification of potentially successful ventures requires the careful consideration of a constellation of factors.  It is clear from our interviews that venture capitalists felt that each of the elements discussed previously (i.e., product-market strategy, business econom-ics, competitive dynamics, business performance and management) con-stitute a multi-dimensional "venture screen."  The notion that venture success is tied to the interaction of many economic and organizational factors is parallel to the notions found in the business policy literature regarding successful business performance (e.g., Andrews (1980)).  The competitive strategy literature notes that the creation of sustainable competitive advantage (Porter, 1985; Bogue and Buffa, 1986) is also the result of the alignment of a number of different factors.  Our exploratory research findings are consistent with those of research into the factors leading to higher levels of performance in larger, established enterprises:  successful performance is the result of the interaction of many factors but most particularly the quality and actions of management (Chandler, 1977).

There are three additional findings. The second major implication for entrepreneurs and venture capitalists is a restatement of an
oft forgotten idea: good venture ideas (many venture plans are simply
statements of ideas) do not equate to good venture opportunities. A
sound product or idea is a necessary but not sufficient condition for
launching, building and eventually harvesting an economically successful venture. The third implication of our research for fund managers
and investors is that a basic understanding of the target market for a
potential venture's products and the value added to the customer of the
products are essential. Venture capitalists should strive to understand the basic economics of the product and the business before
investment. Our final key finding for practitioners is that the
existence of a good concept and product-market strategy does not
guarantee the existence of a good venture opportunity. The entrepreneur and management team were the most critical elements for venture
success cited in our research. The top management of the proposed
venture must demonstrate basic general management skills and the
ability to manage under uncertainty.

## IMPLICATIONS FOR RESEARCHERS

The challenge for us as researchers is to integrate these propositions, with our understanding of competitive strategy and to
further our understanding of competitive strategy as it applies to
emerging businesses. Our objective should be to create a complete
"structure-conduct-performance" framework for entrepreneurial ventures. We have attempted to begin the process here by providing
researchers with propositions which can be useful in guiding future
research efforts.

Our research would appear to have implications for the nature
and type of research to follow. First, we would suggest that further
work must be done to understand the linkage between the structural
characteristics of funded ventures and their eventual performance.
Extensive field research will be required to accomplish this since we
cannot rely on the observations made by those who have done past work
in linking structure, conduct and performance -- they have, for the
most part, relied on aggregate computerized data from large established concerns (e.g., COMPUSTAT data). Second, the challenge for
researchers in exploring the link between venture characteristics and
venture success would appear to be avoiding the temptation to be
"reductionist" in the search for the factors having the greatest
influence on venture performance. Venture success appears to be
related to and interrelated multi-disciplinary set of dynamic factors,
not a single static relationship.

## REFERENCES

Given the long list of references and the constraints on paper
length, references may be obtained by writing to the second author.

YOUNG AND NUMEROUS:   RETAIL/SERVICE ESTABLISHMENTS
IN THE GREATER LOS ANGELES AREA[1]

Allan W. Wicker, The Claremont Graduate School
Jeanne C. King, The Claremont Graduate School

## ABSTRACT

Five counties in the greater Los Angeles area -- Los Angeles, Orange, Riverside, San Bernardino, Ventura -- encompass the leading retail/service sector in the state.  New data from the registration records of the California State Board of Equalization on over 150,000 area retail/service establishments provide initial insights into the dynamics of new venture creation and business failure in this population of predominantly small businesses.  A central finding is that the population is characterized by relatively many young establishments but relatively few old ones, across counties, business types, and ownership forms.  Establishments in Los Angeles County and establishments owned by corporations are relatively old, whereas establishments in Riverside and San Bernardino counties and those owned by partners are relatively young.  The most common establishments share an emphasis on service rather than on essential commodities, and the most precarious futures are faced by various specialty shops.  Additional investigations to be based on these findings are described.

## INTRODUCTION

The State of California and the greater Los Angeles area are dominant forces in the retail and service economy of the United States. According to data compiled by the Los Angeles Area Chamber of Commerce,[2] California leads the nation in retail sales and selected service industry receipts -- the combined output of over 400,000 establishments. Almost half of the state's retail sales are contributed by businesses in the greater Los Angeles area.

------

[1]This research was supported by a grant from the John Randolph Haynes and Dora Haynes Foundation, Los Angeles.  Order of authorship is arbitrary; both authors made equal contributions to this work.

[2]Los Angeles Area Chamber of Commerce, The Los Angeles Area: Dimensions of a World-Class Market, Los Angeles Area Chamber of Commerce, Los Angeles, Ca., 1984.

The vital role played by the retail/service sector in the robust California economy has often been overlooked, possibly because most retail and service businesses are small operations that individually command little economic power. Eighty percent of the retail and service establishments in the United States have fewer than five employees, and most of the new businesses started each year are small.[3]

Although neglected, small businesses make substantial economic contributions, particularly as a venue for new job generation and for minority employment and training. In recent years, small businesses have generated most of the new private sector jobs in the United States; California retailers (operating mostly small establishments) continue to create jobs at a rate that exceeds the average for all industries.[4] These new positions are often filled by members of certain groups (youth, older citizens, women, the less well-educated, the previously unemployed) who lack attributes and skills desired by large corporations. Small businesses also have important social impacts: They provide job and entrepreneurial training to first-time workers and opportunities for owners to further their managerial abilities and needs for self-expression and independence.[5]

This paper is the first from a research program on the dynamics of business creation and failure among the mostly small retail and service establishments in the greater Los Angeles area. The data presented are drawn from the January 1, 1985, master file of business registration records maintained by the California State Board of Equalization (SBE), the agency that collects and redistributes state sales and excise taxes.[6] A variety of nonfinancial information on each establishment can be derived from these records, including location, type of business, form of ownership, and age (calculated from the sales tax account start date).

Here we provide background data on the entire population of Los Angeles area retail and service establishments with emphasis on the numbers and ages of establishments by county, by type of establishment (e.g., clothing stores, car dealerships, repair shops), and by ownership form (single proprietorships, partnerships, corporations). More detailed analyses of age and type patterns by locality (counties,

---

[3]U. S. Small Business Administration, Annual Report on Small Business and Competition, U. S. Government Printing Office, Washington, D. C., 1984.
[4]Security Pacific Bank, "A Look at California's Retail Trade," Southern California, Vol. 62, No. 11 (November, 1983).
[5]U. S. Small Business Administration, Annual Report on Small Business and Competition, U. S. Government Printing Office, Washington, D.C., 1984.
[6]The SBE master registration file provides the most complete, accurate, and timely information on the California retail/service population. The file is updated daily, only about 5% of businesses are estimated to operate without tax licenses, and the overwhelming majority of owners register within a month of opening for business.

selected cities) are provided elsewhere.[7]

## OVERVIEW OF THE POPULATION OF RETAIL/SERVICE ESTABLISHMENTS

Over 150,000 retail and service establishments[8] are located in the five-county Los Angeles area alone, according to our data from the State Board of Equalization (Table 1). In raw numbers, Los Angeles County clearly dominates the area, with approximately eight million residents and 100,000 retail/service outlets. Sixty-four percent of the establishments in the five-county area are located in Los Angeles County. Only 17 percent are located in Orange County; Riverside, San Bernardino, and Ventura counties together account for the remaining 19 percent.

When the number of establishments is adjusted for the size of the population in each county, however, a different pattern emerges. Orange and Riverside counties have the most retail/service outlets (130 and 129 per 10,000 residents), Los Angeles County is third (126), followed by San Bernardino and Riverside counties (118 and 112, respectively).

TABLE 1

RETAIL/SERVICE ESTABLISHMENTS IN THE GREATER LOS ANGELES AREA

| County | No. Estab. | Percent of Five- County Total | No. Residents[a] | No. Estab. per 10,000 Residents | Estab. in Years Mean | Median |
|--------|-----------|-------------------------------|------------------|--------------------------------|-----------|--------|
| Los Angeles | 100,117 | 63.9% | 7,952,700 | 126 | 7.2 | 4.6 |
| Orange | 27,119 | 17.3 | 2,088,400 | 130 | 6.1 | 4.2 |
| Riverside | 10,290 | 6.6 | 794,800 | 129 | 6.0 | 3.7 |
| San Bernardino | 12,467 | 8.0 | 1,053,800 | 118 | 6.3 | 3.7 |
| Ventura | 6,613 | 4.2 | 589,500 | 112 | 6.2 | 4.2 |
| All Counties | 156,606 | 100.0% | 12,479,200 | 125 | 6.8 | 4.3 |

[a]Data from California Department of Finance. January 1, 1985, estimates.

----

[7]Allan W. Wicker and Jeanne C. King, "A Profile of the Retail and Service Establishments in Five Southern California Counties" (Report No. 2755), Social and Behavioral Sciences Documents, Vol. 16, No. 1 (1986), p. 18.

[8]The unit of analysis is the establishment, an individual business location or outlet, rather than the firm, which may have more than one establishment.

# AVERAGE AGES OF RETAIL/SERVICE ESTABLISHMENTS

Although retail and service establishments are numerous in the greater Los Angeles area, their existences are often precarious and their life spans are typically short. Our research program explores the life cycles of these organizations in some detail.[9] Here we present data on the ages of firms that existed at a fixed time -- January 1, 1985.

In the population of retail/service establishments, there are relatively many young businesses and relatively few old ones. This kind of distribution -- called "positively skewed" by statisticians -- characterizes virtually all lines of business, all ownership types, and all localities in our population. In such a distribution, the arithmetic mean is greater than the median. (The median is the number that splits a distribution into halves; half of the values in the distribution are smaller and half are larger than the median.) To illustrate, the mean age of establishments in the five-county area is 6.8 years; the median age is 4.3 years (Table 1). In this paper, analyses are based on median age.

The characteristic age distribution is depicted by Figure 1, which presents combined data for the five counties. The percentage of establishments in each age category is indicated by the vertical line opposite its location on the vertical scale. Thus, for example, on January 1, 1985, 17.5 percent of establishments in the five-county area were less than one year old (i.e., they started in 1984), 12.9 percent were between one and two years old (started in 1983), and so on. The shape of the figure indicates that the the the number of establishments drops with each successive age category. Only a very few establishments (3.4%) had survived 25 or more years.

Despite the overall similarity of the distributions for each of the five counties, some interesting age differences exist. Retail/ service establishments in Los Angeles County are generally older than establishments in the other four counties. Establishments in Riverside County are youngest, followed closely by those in San Bernardino County (Tables 1 and 2). Twenty-five percent of the establishments in Los Angeles county are 10 years old or older, compared to 19 to 21 percent for the other counties. In all counties, a majority of businesses is less than five years old; the range is from 60 percent in Riverside County to 53 percent in Los Angeles County.

---

[9]Allan W. Wicker and Jeanne C. King, "Life Cycles of Behavior Settings," Research in the Social Psychology of Time (J. E. McGrath, Ed.), Sage Publications, Newbury Park, Ca., in press.

FIGURE 1

## AGE DISTRIBUTION OF RETAIL/SERVICE ESTABLISHMENTS
## IN THE FIVE-COUNTY SOUTHERN CALIFORNIA AREA

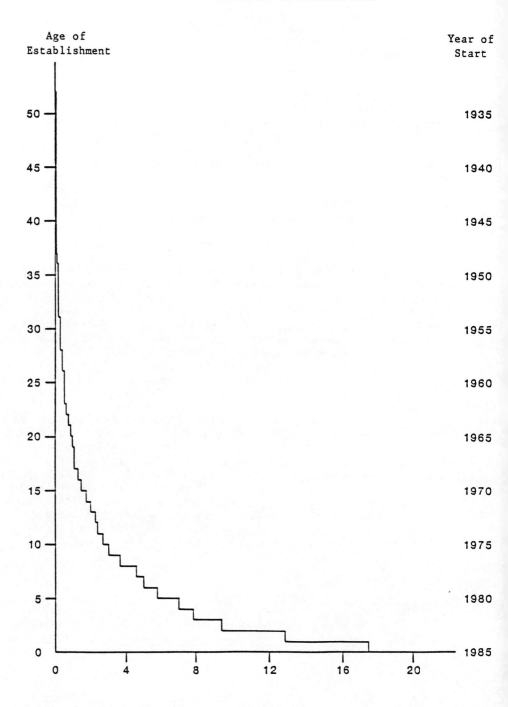

TABLE 2

PERCENT OF RETAIL/SERVICE ESTABLISHMENTS IN VARIOUS AGE CATEGORIES:
DATA FOR FIVE LOS ANGELES AREA COUNTIES

| Age Category | Los Angeles | Orange | Riverside | San Bernardino | Ventura | All Counties |
|---|---|---|---|---|---|---|
| 10 years or older | 25.0 | 20.3 | 19.3 | 21.0 | 19.6 | 23.3 |
| Less than 10 years | 75.0 | 79.7 | 80.7 | 79.0 | 80.4 | 76.7 |
| Less than 5 years | 53.1 | 55.9 | 59.6 | 59.5 | 56.0 | 54.6 |
| Less than 4 years | 46.3 | 48.8 | 52.6 | 52.3 | 48.3 | 47.0 |
| Less than 3 years | 38.5 | 40.9 | 44.8 | 43.3 | 40.6 | 39.9 |
| Less than 2 years | 29.3 | 31.2 | 35.1 | 33.3 | 30.4 | 30.4 |
| Less than 1 year | 16.8 | 18.0 | 20.3 | 19.2 | 18.0 | 17.5 |

The average age of retail/service establishments in an area may be due in part to recent demographic trends such as growth in population and residential units. Los Angeles County, for example, has experienced a slower population growth rate than the other four counties, and as noted above, its retail/service establishments tend to be older. More generally, we might expect rapidly developing areas to have newer establishments and more stable areas to have older establishments. To examine this idea, we calculated the relationship between median age of establishment and the percentage of dwelling units built between 1970 and 1979 for each city in the five-county area.[10]

As expected, cities whose housing stock has recently increased also tend to have younger retail and service establishments. The computed statistical relationship was strongest for San Bernardino County and Ventura County, and for the entire five-county area. In more technical terms, the variance in median establishment age accounted for by the proportion of dwelling units built in each city during the 1970's was as follows: San Bernardino County, 43% ($n$ = 23); Ventura County, 39% ($n$ = 10); all counties combined, 23% ($N$ = 168); Orange County, 15% ($n$ = 30); Riverside County, 14% ($n$ = 20); Los Angeles County, 9% ($n$ = 85).[11]

---

[10]Median age was used because it is less sensitive to the positive skew in the age distribution. The dwelling unit completion rates are from the 1980 U.S. Census of Population and Housing Information, which are the most recent available figures. Four cities with missing data or outlying values were excluded.

[11]Of course, these relationships are based on data from different sources and from different time periods. The magnitude of the reported relationships is therefore likely to be affected by these factors.

The numbers and ages of various types of establishments provide a more differentiated view of the Los Angeles area retail/service sector. Twenty-seven research categories were derived by refining the classification scheme used by the SBE.[12] Most of the category names that we will present below are self-explanatory; examples of business types in categories with broad or ambiguous labels are given in Table 3.

TABLE 3

TYPES AND EXAMPLES OF RETAIL/SERVICE ESTABLISHMENTS
IN SELECTED RESEARCH CATEGORIES

Fulltime specialty
    Art supplies and original art; Pet stores; Toy stores; Tombstone retailers;
    Hearing aids; Cosmetic stores; Coin dealers; Ship chandlers;
    All specialty retail stores not elsewhere classified

Specialty foods
    Bakeries; Fresh produce stands; Health foods; Candy and nut stores;
    Delicatessens; Bottled water dealers

Repair shops
    Recreational vehicle repair; Refrigerator repair shops;
    Picture framing shops; Radio and appliance repair

Personal services
    Portrait studios; Barber and beauty shops; Dress making and alterations;
    Laundries and cleaners; Massage and reducing salons; Golf courses;
    Card rooms; Skating rinks, swimming pools; Theatres, bowling alleys;
    Marinas; Health clubs

Miscellaneous
    Low-price sundries; Country general stores; Newspaper and magazine stands;
    Farm equipment stores; Garden supply and equipment; Nurseries;
    Fuel and ice dealers

---

[12]The research categories were based on the 57 categories in the SBE Sales Tax Business Classification Code used to classify retail and service establishments. The point of the reduction was to generate generally distinct business types, although this was not completely successful for some categories (as illustrated in Table 3). The reduction procedure is described at length elsewhere [Allan W. Wicker and Jeanne C. King, "A Profile of the Retail and Service Establishments in Five Southern California Counties" (Report No. 2755), Social and Behavioral Sciences Documents, Vol. 16, No. 1 (1986), p. 18].

The most common types of business in the five-county area share an emphasis on service (Table 4). For every 10,000 residents in the five counties, there are 22 eating and drinking places (17.6% of all establishments), 11 repair shops (9.0%), between 10 and 11 personal service establishments (8.4%), and 10 automotive repair shops (8.1%). Businesses that specialize in providing essential commodities are less numerous. For example, for each 10,000 residents there are nine clothing stores (7.4% of all establishments), about six home furnishing stores (4.6%), between five and six grocery stores and service stations (each 4.4%), three building and decorating businesses (2.4%), and two drug stores (1.8%). Also relatively few in number are department stores and car or recreational vehicle dealers, which typically are larger in size, serve wider areas, and require more substantial capital investments than other types of retail/service businesses.

Although not as numerous as most other types of establishments, department stores and drug stores are generally the oldest in the five-county population. Their median ages are 8.2 and 7.8 years, respectively, compared with 4.3 years for establishments of all types. The youngest business types are specialty foods (3.2 years), fulltime specialty stores such as pet shops and art supply stores (3.3. years), and eating and drinking places (3.5 years). The ages of other types are between these extremes (last column of Table 4). Some speculations about the causes of these age differences are presented in the concluding section of this paper.

## FORMS OF OWNERSHIP OF RETAIL/SERVICE ESTABLISHMENTS

Virtually all retail/service establishments are organized under one of three types of ownership: single proprietorship, partnership, or corporation. In the greater Los Angeles area, 44 percent of establishments are single proprietorships, 33 percent are corporations, and 23 percent are partnerships (Table 5). In median age, corporations are the oldest (5.5 years for all counties), partnerships are the youngest (3.2 years), and single proprietorships are in between (4.2 years).

An examination of ownership patterns for various types of establishments produces a more refined view that for some types contradicts the general findings (Table 5). For example, partnerships account for only 23 percent of all establishments, but are the predominant form of ownership in one type of business -- package liquor stores. And, although 33 percent of all establishments are owned by corporations, this form of ownership predominates among 12 types of business, typically ones that require higher investments of capital to open and operate (e.g., department stores, car dealers, grocery stores). Smaller operations such as gift and specialty stores and repair shops are predominantly owned by single proprietors.

131

## TABLE 4

## TYPES OF RETAIL/SERVICE ESTABLISHMENTS IN THE GREATER LOS ANGELES AREA

| Establishment Type | No. Estab. | Percent of Five-County Total | No. Estab. per 10,000 Residents | Median Age of Estab. in Years |
|---|---|---|---|---|
| Clothing stores | 11,560 | 7.4% | 9.3 | 3.9 |
| Department stores | 1,632 | 1.0 | 1.3 | 8.2 |
| Gift stores | 3,492 | 2.2 | 2.8 | 3.8 |
| Sporting goods | 1,857 | 1.2 | 1.5 | 4.8 |
| Florist shops | 1,785 | 1.1 | 1.4 | 4.1 |
| Music stores | 1,365 | 0.9 | 1.1 | 5.2 |
| Stationery, book stores | 2,645 | 1.7 | 2.1 | 5.2 |
| Jewelry stores | 2,356 | 1.5 | 1.9 | 5.1 |
| Office equipment | 2,215 | 1.4 | 1.8 | 3.8 |
| Fulltime specialty | 11,817 | 7.5 | 9.5 | 3.3 |
| Grocery stores | 6,838 | 4.4 | 5.5 | 4.3 |
| Specialty foods | 3,204 | 2.0 | 2.6 | 3.2 |
| Package liquor | 3,144 | 2.0 | 2.5 | 3.8 |
| Eating and drink- ing places | 27,552 | 17.6 | 22.1 | 3.5 |
| Drug stores | 2,223 | 1.4 | 1.8 | 7.8 |
| Home furnishings | 7,261 | 4.6 | 5.8 | 5.2 |
| Appliance stores | 1,991 | 1.3 | 1.6 | 5.7 |
| Secondhand stores | 1,744 | 1.1 | 1.4 | 6.0 |
| Building, decorating | 3,833 | 2.4 | 3.1 | 6.2 |
| Car dealers | 3,026 | 1.9 | 2.4 | 5.9 |
| Automotive supply | 3,881 | 2.5 | 3.1 | 5.0 |
| Service stations | 6,889 | 4.4 | 5.5 | 5.2 |
| Recreational vehicles | 1,640 | 1.0 | 1.3 | 5.2 |
| Automotive repair | 12,690 | 8.1 | 10.2 | 4.2 |
| Repair shops | 14,035 | 9.0 | 11.2 | 5.2 |
| Personal services | 13,190 | 8.4 | 10.6 | 4.2 |
| Miscellaneous | 2,741 | 1.8 | 2.2 | 6.2 |
| All types | 156,606 | 100.0 | 125.5 | 4.3 |

TABLE 5

PREDOMINANT OWNERSHIP FORMS FOR ESTABLISHMENTS OF VARIOUS TYPES
IN THE GREATER LOS ANGELES AREA

| | Single Proprietorship | Corporation | Partnership |
|---|---|---|---|
| Number | 68,414 | 51,243 | 36,169 |
| Percent of All Estab. | 43.7% | 32.7% | 23.1% |
| Median Age | 4.2 | 5.5 | 3.2 |

| | | |
|---|---|---|
| Gift stores (5) | Clothing stores(5) | Package |
| Sporting goods (4) | Department stores (5) | liquor (4) |
| Florist shops (2) | Music stores (2) | |
| Jewelry stores (3) | Stationery, book | |
| Fulltime specialty (5) | stores (5) | |
| Specialty foods (2) | Office equipment (5) | |
| Eating and drinking | Grocery stores (4) | |
| places (2) | Drug stores (5) | |
| Home furnishings (5) | Appliance stores (4) | |
| Secondhand stores (5) | Building, decorating (5) | |
| Service stations (2) | Car dealers (3) | |
| Automotive repair (5) | Automotive supplies (5) | |
| Repair shops (5) | Recreational vehicles (5) | |
| Personal services (5) | | |

Note.—Given in parentheses is the number of counties for which the stated
ownership type was predominant.


Median ages for the various business types under each form of
ownership are presented in Table 6. The typical age pattern associated
with ownership form described above tends to be replicated for each
business type, with a few exceptions worth noting. Businesses operated
by corporations are usually oldest, but in four cases (gift stores,
florist shops, service stations, repair shops) the oldest establishments
are run by single proprietors. More dramatically, across business lines
the youngest establishments are owned by partners, although in two
categories (department stores, grocery stores) partnerships fall between
corporations and single proprietorships in age.

Some other interesting patterns can be discerned in Table 6.
For example, certain businesses operated by single proprietors
(appliance stores, service stations, repair shops) are much older than
expected by the median age for single proprietorships as a whole.
Similarly, gift stores, florist shops, and office equipment stores run
by corporations are much younger than would be predicted from the
overall age for this ownership form.

TABLE 6

MEDIAN AGES OF ESTABLISHMENTS OF VARIOUS TYPES HAVING DIFFERENT
FORMS OF OWNERSHIP IN THE GREATER LOS ANGELES AREA

| Establishment Type | Single Proprietorship | Corporation | Partnership |
|---|---|---|---|
| Clothing stores | 3.2 | 4.8 | 3.2 |
| Department stores | 4.7 | 10.5 | 5.4 |
| Gift stores | 4.0 | 3.7 | 3.6 |
| Sporting goods | 4.8 | 5.7 | 3.7 |
| Florist shops | 4.5 | 3.8 | 3.8 |
| Music stores | 5.0 | 5.8 | 4.3 |
| Stationery, book stores | 4.7 | 5.5 | 3.9 |
| Jewelry stores | 4.3 | 6.2 | 3.7 |
| Office equipment | 3.7 | 4.2 | 2.2 |
| Fulltime specialty | 3.5 | 3.8 | 2.5 |
| Grocery stores | 2.7 | 8.7 | 3.2 |
| Specialty foods | 2.9 | 4.2 | 2.8 |
| Package liquor | 3.4 | 6.5 | 3.2 |
| Eating and drinking places | 2.9 | 5.3 | 2.7 |
| Drug stores | 6.9 | 8.6 | 6.7 |
| Home furnishings | 5.0 | 5.7 | 4.6 |
| Appliance stores | 5.7 | 6.9 | 3.0 |
| Secondhand stores | 5.5 | 8.5 | 4.2 |
| Building, decorating | 5.2 | 7.5 | 4.6 |
| Car dealers | 4.0 | 10.0 | 2.0 |
| Automotive supply | 5.0 | 5.2 | 3.5 |
| Service stations | 6.3 | 5.2 | 3.3 |
| Recreational vehicles | 5.3 | 5.5 | 4.0 |
| Automotive repair | 4.4 | 4.9 | 3.0 |
| Repair shops | 5.8 | 5.5 | 3.5 |
| Personal services | 4.3 | 4.9 | 3.3 |
| Miscellaneous | 5.0 | 9.2 | 4.3 |
| All Forms | 4.2 | 5.5 | 3.2 |

## DISCUSSION OF SELECTED FINDINGS

Our study of retail/service establishments constitutes a more
detailed examination of this population than has previously been
available.  We conclude the paper by highlighting certain findings and
by indicating the place of this study in our larger program of research.

Over half of all retail/service establishments in the five-
county Los Angeles area are five or fewer years old, and approximately
77 percent are 10 or fewer years old.  This age pattern is compatible
with estimates from other sources of the mortality rates of small

businesses[13] and with the common belief that it is difficult for a business to survive the first critical years. Two dynamics are likely to account for the generally young ages of these establishments: the continuing growth of counties and cities in the area and/or a high rate of business turnover. Our subsequent work will attempt to clarify the relative contributions of these dynamics.

The data presented also indicate considerable variation in the numbers and ages of establishments of different types and ownership forms. With respect to business type, we noted that establishments providing services are relatively more numerous than establishments selling merchandise. It may be that, compared to retail sales operations, service businesses (such as eating and drinking places, repair shops, personal services) can survive with less capital and more personal efforts -- time, energy, and talents -- of the owner and employees. Moreover, the finding that certain businesses (appliance stores, service stations, repair shops) owned as single proprietorships are unusually old may reflect the wisdom of the local merchant's philosophy to emphasize service over sales in attracting and retaining a clientele.

For ownership form, we found that single proprietorships generally are more numerous than other types of ownership. Single proprietorships also are most numerous among service businesses and among retail shops dealing in specialized lines of merchandise. These data further suggest the importance of a business founder's motivation and expertise. It may be no coincidence, for example, that eating and drinking places which are most frequently run as single proprietorships, are among the youngest type of business. The apparent simplicity of running a small restaurant may seduce a novice entrepreneur into a business failure.

Certain establishments are able to survive longer than others, probably because these types are associated with more managerial experience and larger amounts of start-up capital and profit reinvestments. Thus, business types that require considerable managerial oversight and investments of capital for operating space, equipment, and merchandise (such as department stores, appliance stores, car dealerships in our population) are more likely to reach advanced ages. The fact that most businesses owned by corporations are generally older than those run as single proprietorships or partnerships is likely to reflect such differences in capitalization. Interestingly, a few business types (gift and florist shops, office equipment stores) owned by corporations are unusually young, perhaps indicating the emergence of franchise operations in business lines formerly dominated by independent neighborhood proprietors.

---

[13]A. B. Cochran, "Small Business Mortality Rates: A Review of the Literature," Journal of Small Business Management, Vol. 19, No. 4 (1981), pp. 50-59.

In addition to having been founded on a more stable economic base, corporations may last longer because there is a formal structure for negotiating differences among the owners. Partnerships, on the other hand, are generally youngest among all business types. The relative youth of these establishments may reflect high rates of dissolution due to conflicts among partners on how the business is to be organized and on how decisions are to be made.[14] Partners also may disagree on whether business income is to be reinvested or used as a means of livelihood. Some partnerships may be terminated because they cannot provide a livelihood for more than one owner. Partnerships involving spouses may be particularly vulnerable because marital strain, often exacerbated by the pressures of working together, can lead to dissolution of the marriage and of the business.[15]

## MORE DYNAMIC AND DETAILED STUDIES OF CHANGE
## IN RETAIL AND SERVICE ESTABLISHMENTS

Our age data from one time period (January 1, 1985) are the result of as yet unknown dynamic patterns of change over time in the population of retail/service establishments. In subsequent research we will analyze such population changes to uncover the nature of these dynamics. By tracking the movement of particular establishments in and out of the population, we expect to be able to estimate more precisely the life expectancies of businesses according to locality, business type, and ownership type.

The differences in life expectancies of various types of establishments that we expect to uncover in our longitudinal analyses will be explored further in studies of businesses and of owners. In one investigation using telephone interviews, we ask owners and managers from a random sample of new establishments to provide information on characteristics of their employees and on their own previous entrepreneurial activities. In addition to identifying the employment patterns of these new businesses, we will relate the survey information, including information on business type and ownership type, to their two-year survival. In later intensive interviews, we will explore in more detail the plans and actions taken by founders as they organize their new businesses. We also plan to examine business terminations through interviews with owners who are closing their shops.

Thus, the "static" picture presented here serves as a base from which to explore other more dynamic and more detailed aspects of this population, of the individual establishments that make up the population, and of the entrepreneurs and employees who create and staff the establishments.

---

[14]R. Buck, "Business Divorces," The Seattle Times (August 11, 1985), pp. C1, C8.
[15]Ellen Wojahn, "Divorce Entrepreneurial Style," Inc. (March, 1986), pp. 55-64.

REFERENCES

Buck, R., "Business Divorces," The Seattle Times (August 11, 1985), pp. Cl, C8.

Cochran, A. B., "Small Business Mortality Rates: A Review of the Literature." Journal of Small Business Management, Vol. 19, No. 4 (1981), pp. 50-59.

Los Angeles Area Chamber of Commerce, The Los Angeles Area: Dimensions of a World-Class Market, Los Angeles Area Chamber of Commerce, Los Angeles, Ca., 1984.

Security Pacific Bank, "A Look at California's Retail Trade," Southern California, Vol. 62, No. 11 (November, 1983).

U. S. Small Business Administration, Annual Report on Small Business and Competition, U.S. Government Printing Office, Washington, D.C., 1984.

Wicker, Allan W., and King, Jeanne C., "Life Cycles of Behavior Settings," Research in the Social Psychology of Time (J. E. McGrath, Ed.), Sage Publications, Newbury Park, Ca., in press.

Wicker, Allan W., and King, Jeanne C., "A Profile of the Retail and Service Establishments in Five Southern California Counties" (Report No. 2755), Social and Behavioral Sciences Documents, Vol. 16, No. 1 (1986), p. 18.

Wojahn, Ellen, "Divorce Entrepreneurial Style", Inc. (March, 1986), pp. 55-64.

VENTURE SURVIVABILITY:   AN ANALYSIS OF
THE AUTOMOBILE, SEMICONDUCTOR, VACUUM TUBE
AND AIRLINE INDUSTRIES

Kenneth E. Knight, University of Texas
Michael J. Dowling, University of Texas
James B. Brown, University of Texas

## ABSTRACT

In this paper, we argue that the pattern of new venture creation is neither a new nor uncommon phenomenon, but is fairly regular and predictable.  To illustrate this pattern we discuss some of the forces that stimulate the growth of firms in a new industry.  Then we examine firm growth patterns in the automobile, semiconductor, vacuum tube and airline industries.  Finally, we relate these patterns to the literature on product and corporate life cycles, and product/process innovation.

## INTRODUCTION

Entrepreneurship is one of the most popular topics in business, academia, and government today.  Suddenly the new American heroes are the entrepreneurs--Steven Jobs of Apple Computer, Donald Burr of People Express, and many more.  This new fascination with entrepreneurship is reflected in the dozens of books, articles and how-to guides that promise "Entrepreneurial Megabucks" or "How to Succeed as an Entrepreneur" (1).  This interest is also reflected in new programs designed to teach entrepreneurship.  According to a 1984 survey, over 250 universities offer courses in entrepreneurship, up from 160 in 1980 (2).  But, in fact, entrepreneurship is not a new phenomenon at all, rather what is happening is a popularization of a phenomenon that has always been a part of American culture.  Today's entrepreneurial heroes are not much different than the Ben Franklins, Eli Whitneys and Henry Fords of yesterday.

Unfortunately most of the popular literature on entrepreneurship has focused on the "how to," success stories, or on the personality characteristics of entrepreneurs.  For example, the following description appeared in a recent book on entrepreneur success stories (3).

> Entrepreneurs drive quickly, take early flights, avoid maintenance breakdowns or other time eaters, speak rapidly, and walk at a quick pace.  Entrepreneurs are rarely significantly overweight, because they do not overeat.

Such a description paints entrepreneurs not only as heroes, but as supermen, which although interesting, does not tell us much about the process of entrepreneurship.

Even the academic literature on the subject has tended to focus on the individual characteristics of entrepreneurs (4). Psychological characteristics that have been studied include the need for achievement, locus of control, and risk taking propensity. In addition, some researchers have looked at the backgrounds of entrepreneurs examining such factors as job satisfaction, previous work experience, entrepreneurial parents, education and age (5).

This research, which attempts to show how things entrepreneurial differ from all things non-entrepreneurial, is useful, but gives an incomplete picture of the nature of entrepreneurship. Although it might be true, that overall entrepreneurial activity is increasing, especially as private sources of venture capital grow, it is still neither a new nor uncommon phenomenon. Rather, the entry and exit of firms, a central concept in economic theory, follows regular patterns that have been ignored in studies of entrepreneurship. However, an area of research that has explicitly examined the creation of new organizations is population ecology (6). Population ecologists have focused on the formation of new firms in relation to their environments, rather than on the individual characteristics of entrepreneurs. This research implies that variations in entrepreneurial activity can be explained by socio-economic factors. For example, a recent study of birth frequencies in three industries in 70 urban area in the United States showed that occupational and industrial differentiation, percentage of immigrants, size of the industry, and size of the urban area were critical for predicting the creation of new organizations (7). Another study of nineteenth century creation of newspapers in Argentina and Ireland suggested that environmental conditions, such as political turbulence, accounted for new firm creations (8).

In this paper, we will argue that the pattern of new venture creation is fairly regular and predictable, and due not only to environmental conditions, but also to market forces. In particular, we contend that in any new industry, the number of entrants will grow rapidly at first, and then peak as firms fail, leave the industry, or are consolidated. To illustrate this pattern we will first discuss some of the forces that stimulate the growth of firms in a new industry. Then we will examine in more detail the pattern of firm growth in the automobile, semiconductor, vacuum tube and airline industries. Finally, we will discuss the implications of this data for the study of entrepreneurship.

FORCES THAT STIMULATE NEW VENTURE GROWTH

There are a variety of forces that potentially stimulate the growth of new firms in an industry. For example, three forces are as follows:

## New Technology

Of course, one of the most powerful forces that often leads to the creation of new firms is innovation, or the introduction of a new technology. Economists have shown in a number of studies that technological change can lead to changes in productivity (9). This in turn stimulates the growth of new firms or hasten the decline of existing ones, a force that Schumpeter aptly called "creative destruction" (10). More recently, Porter has observed:

> Technological change is one of the principle drivers of competition. It plays a major role in industry structural change as well as in creating new industries. It is also a great equalizer, eroding the competitive advantage of even well entrenched firms and propelling others to the forefront (11).

Foster has shown in his studies of technological transition that existing firms usually discount the importance of new technologies and often fail to survive in the industries that develop around new technologies (12).

## New Markets

Another powerful source of new ventures is the application of an existing technology or product to a new area or market. For example, the personal computer industry was completely based on existing technology but applied in a new way to open up new markets (homes, schools, small businesses, etc.) that had been ignored by the large computer manufacturers.

## Deregulation or Shifts in Government Regulation

Another less obvious force behind venture creation that has become increasingly prevalent in recent years is the deregulation or changes in the regulation of tightly controlled industries. Examples include the growth of new airlines since the removal of entry barriers in the air line industry during the late 1970s and the recently deregulated long distance telephone service industry.

## INDUSTRY TRENDS

To examine the impact of these forces in more detail it is useful to look at the growth of new firms in several industries. To do this we have collected data on four industries: automobiles, semiconductors, vacuum tube and airlines, and constructed four kinds of graphs:

1. the number of new start-up firms per year over time.
2. the number of firms still in business over time.
3. the total number of firms created over time.
4. the percent of firms still in business over time.

Automobiles

Data on the birth and death of firms in the entrepreneurial stage of the automobile industry were taken from a study conducted in the 1920s by Epstein and extended with other historical accounts (13). Figure 1 shows the number of new automobile companies per year from 1903 to 1940. This figure shows that there was a lot of entrepreneurial activity between 1903 and 1920 which reflected both the introduction of new technologies, namely the internal combustion engine and mass production, and the application of those technologies to new markets, i.e., mass marketing of automobiles. This entrepreneurial activity led to a steady growth in the number of firms producing automobiles which peaked in 1921. After that point, economic pressures, environmental conditions, etc. led to a consolidation of the industry through mergers and exit of firms. Steep decreases in the number of firms are observed following the panic of 1920-21 and again during the Great Depression of the 1930s. By 1940 there were only 10 manufacturers of automobiles left in the U.S. industry which has declined even further to four companies today.

Figure 3 shows the cumulative number of firms created by year over the same period which again shows a very regular pattern of growth and eventual leveling off. This curve has the familiar S-shape of the life cycle curves that have been shown to exist for products, firms, and industries (14). Finally, the consolidation in the industry is reflected in Figure 4 showing the percentage of firms surviving by year which fits very well to a straight line (R2 = .96).

FIGURE 1

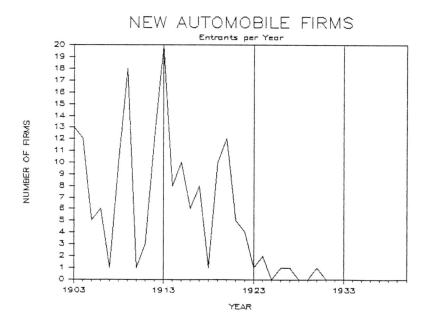

FIGURE 2

NUMBER OF AUTOMOBILE FIRMS IN BUS.
90
80
70
60
50
40
30
20
10
NUMBER OF FIRMS
1903
1913
1923
1933
YEAR

FIGURE 3

TOTAL AUTOMOBILE FIRMS CREATED
190
180
170
160
150
140
130
120
110
100
90
80
70
60
50
40
30
20
NUMBER OF FIRMS
1903
1913
1923
1933
YEAR

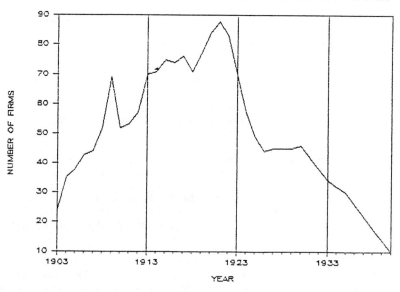

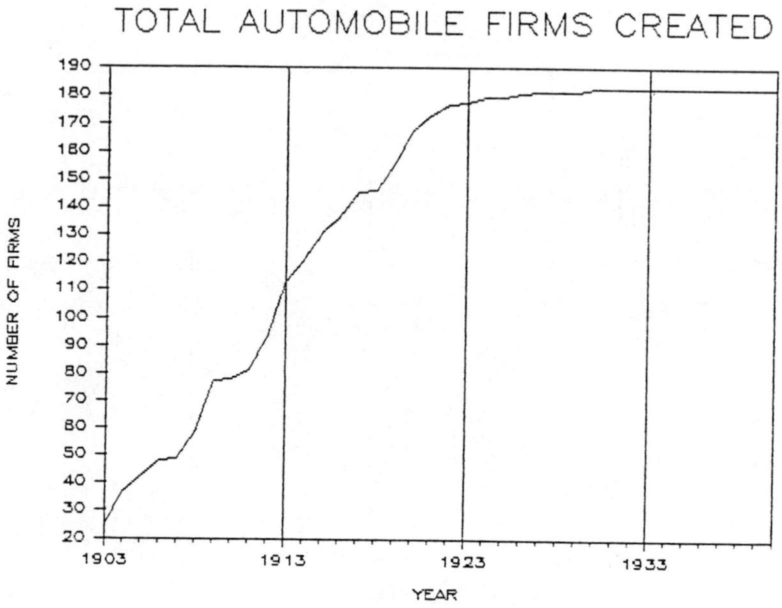

FIGURE 4

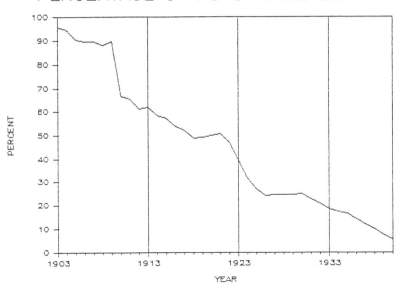

# PERCENTAGE OF AUTO FIRMS SURVIVING

## Semiconductors

Data on the semiconductor industry was collected as part of a study by Brittain (15). Figure 5 shows the number of new semiconductor firms created from 1945 to 1981. There is a slow build up in entrepreneurial activity in the 1940s and 1950s, followed by large numbers of new firms entering the industry in the 1960s. This growth reflects both the introduction of new product and process technologies in semiconductors and the expanding application of semiconductors to new markets. This activity then began to drop off in the 1970s. This pattern is very similar to the one shown for the automobile industry in Figure 1.

In Figure 6, the growth in the number of firms in business is given. This graph is similar to the 1903-1920 period of the automobile industry as shown in Figure 2, but it does not show a decline in firms simply because the industry was still growing up until 1981. In the last few years, the industry has begun to consolidate and we would expect a continued decline of the number of firms in business. Figure 7 again shows the S-shape curve of total firms created. The top of the curve has not yet flattened out as was shown in the more mature automobile industry curve in Figure 3. Finally, Figure 8 shows the percentage of firms surviving, again closely fitting a straight line (R2 = .82).

FIGURE 5

# NEW SEMICONDUCTOR FIRMS

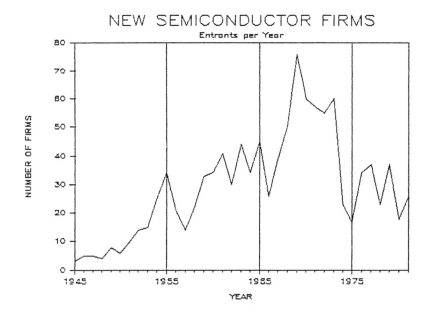

FIGURE 6

# SEMICONDUCTOR FIRMS IN BUSINESS

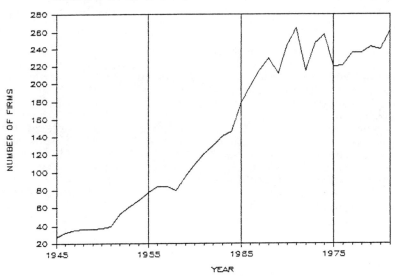

FIGURE 7

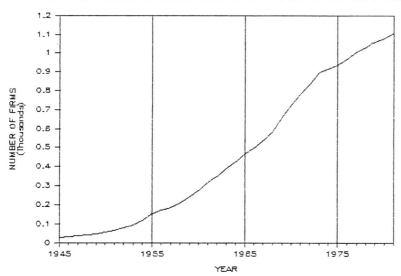

## TOTAL SEMICONDUCTOR FIRMS CREATED

FIGURE 8

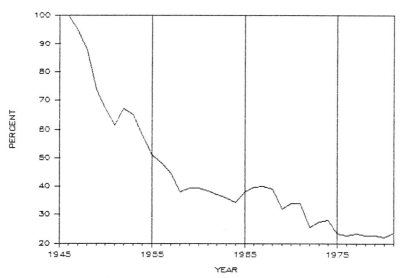

## PERCENTAGE SEMICOND. FIRMS SURVIVING

145

## Vacuum Tubes

Data on the vacuum tube industry were also collected as part of Brittain's study.  Figures 9, 10, 11, and 12 show the complete life cycle of the industry from its birth in the 1920s, through a highpoint in the late 1950s, and its steep decline in the 1960s and 1970s as semiconductors replaced vacuum tubes in most applications.  These curves are the best examples of how a technological discontinuity can lead to the death of an existing industry.

FIGURE 9

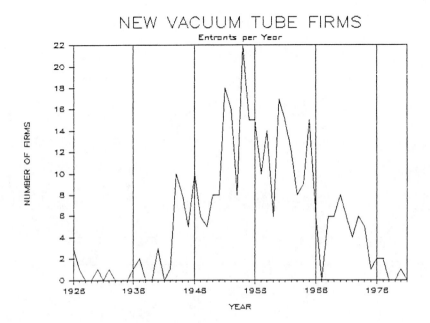

NEW VACUUM TUBE FIRMS

FIGURE 10

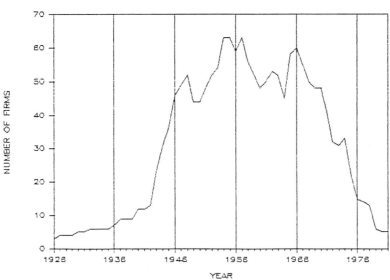

VACUUM TUBE FIRMS IN BUSINESS

FIGURE 11

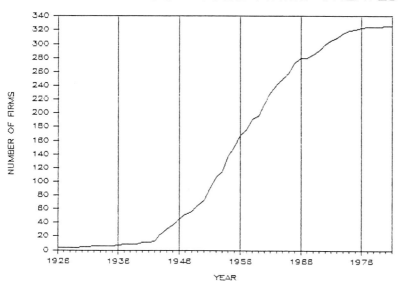

TOTAL VACUUM TUBE FIRMS CREATED

FIGURE 12

## PERCENTAGE OF TUBE FIRMS SURVIVING

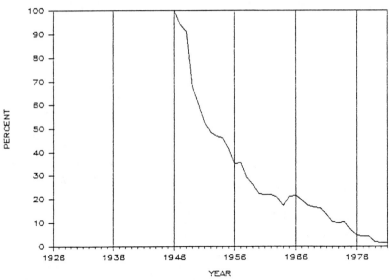

### Airlines

The last set of curves constructed for the airline industry were based on data collected by the Civil Aeronautics Board (CAB) (16). Figure 13 shows the number of new airlines created by year between 1937 and 1984. The two obvious peaks after 1945 and 1977 reflect the growth in new airlines due to returning pilots after World War II who started new airlines, and the explosive growth after deregulation of the airlines in 1978. Figure 14, which shows the gradual decline in the number of airline firms in business from 1938 until 1977 reflects the fact that the CAB restricted the entry of new firms preferring to give new routes to established companies. Normal consolidation of the industry led to this gradual decline until deregulation again allowed new entrants. The effect of deregulation is also clearly seen in Figures 15 and 16 which show the total number of airlines created and percentage surviving over the same period. These data illustrate the powerful effect government policy can have on new venture creation in an industry.

FIGURE 13

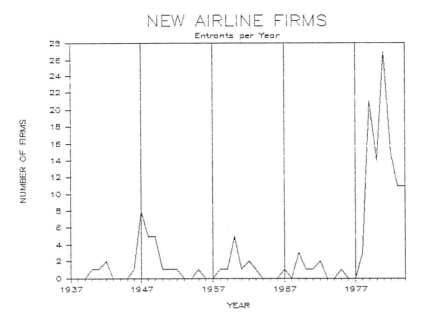

# NEW AIRLINE FIRMS
Entrants per Year

FIGURE 14

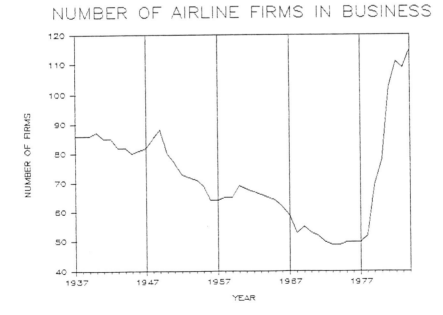

# NUMBER OF AIRLINE FIRMS IN BUSINESS

FIGURE 15

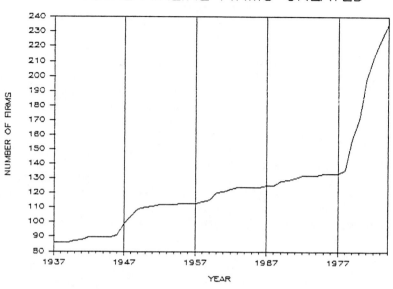

TOTAL AIRLINE FIRMS CREATED

FIGURE 16

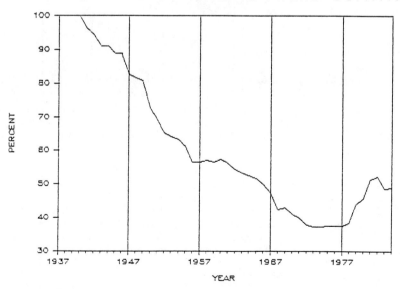

PERCENTAGE OF AIRLINE FIRMS SURVIVING

# DISCUSSION AND CONCLUSIONS

The data presented here on the automobile, semiconductor, vacuum tube, and airline industries illustrate the regular patterns of new firm creation in the early stages of an industry's development, and then the eventual exit of firms as an industry matures and consolidates. These patterns can be explained in terms of a variety of market forces including technological change, development of new markets, and changes in government policy, etc.

In addition we believe that these industry life cycles of the birth and death of new firms can be related to earlier theoretical and empirical research on product and organizational life cycles. For example in a recent study, Thietart and Vivas used data from the PIMS data base to study the affects of different strategies for consumer and industrial product firms at various stages on the product life cycle including: growth, maturity and decline (17). They found that for a set of strategic actions, firm success depended on the stage of the product life cycle.

Miller and Friesen reviewed the current theoretical literature on corporate or organizational life cycles and identified five life stages: (18)

1.  the birth phase
2.  The growth phase
3.  The maturity phase
4.  The revival phase
5.  The decline phase

They then conducted an empirical study of 36 firms classified into different life cycle stages. They found that there were differences in strategy and firm characteristics over different stages of the life cycle. For example, firms in the birth phase usually placed a high emphasis on product innovation, and had fluid, organic structures. Firms in the maturity phase had much less emphasis on innovation and tended to adopt bureaucratic structures. However, innovation often became more important as firms attempted to revive themselves in the revival phase.

This pattern relating stage of development to innovation fits very well the dynamic model of innovation presented by Utterback and Abernathy (19). They argue that in a new industry, the rate of major product innovation wil be high at first and gradually decrease as major process innovation increases.

Such changes in product and process innovation, strategy and structure along the product and corporate life cycles, and the market forces discussed earlier, may all be contributing factors to the regular growth and decline patterns illustrated in the four industries presented here. In other words, the inability of some firms to manage the necessary changes in innovation and strategic orientation across life cycle stages may lead to their failure and exit from an industry. For as Michael Porter has observed:

Industry evolution takes on critical importance for formulation
of strategy.  It can increase or decrease the basic
attractiveness of an industry as an investment opportunity,
and it often requires the firm to make strategic adjustments
(20).

In conclusion, in this paper we have shown that the phenomenon
of new venture creation or entrepreneurship is neither new nor
uncommon, but rather, environmental conditions, market forces,
government policy, life cycles, and innovation can all play important
roles in encouraging or discouraging the growth of new firms.  We
believe that further research is needed concerning these factors that
affect new venture creation and survivability.  Such research will, we
expect, expand and enrich the study of entrepreneurship.

## REFERENCES

(1) David Gumpert, "Probing the Venture Creation Process,"
_Harvard Business Review_, (March-April, 1984), pp. 22-30 and "Stalking
the Entrepreneur," _Harvard Business Review_, (May-June, 1986), pp. 32-
36.

(2) "B-Schools Try to Churn Out Entrepreneurs," _Business Week_
(March 5, 1984), p. 102.

(3) Gumpert, 1986, p. 33.

(4) Arnold Cooper and William Dunkelberg, "Entrepreneurship
and Paths to Business Ownership," _Strategic Management Journal_, Vol.
7, (1986), pp. 53-68.

(5) William Gartner, "A Conceptual Framework for Describing
the Phenomenon of New Venture Creation," _Academy of Management Review_,
Vol. 10, No. 4, (1985), pp. 696-706.

(6) M. T. Hannan and J. H. Freeman, "The Population Ecology of
Organizations," _American Journal of Sociology_, Vol. 82, (1977), pp.
929-964.

(7) Johannes Pennings, "Organizational Birth Frequencies:  An
Empirical Investigation," _Administrative Science Quarterly_, 27 (1982),
pp. 120-144.

(8) Jacques Delacroix and Glenn R. Carroll, "Organizational
Foundings:  An Ecological Study of the Newspaper Industries of
Argentina and Ireland," _Administrative Science Quarterly_, Vol. 28
(1983), pp. 274-291.

(9) Edwin Mansfield, _The Economics of Technological Change_,
Norton, New York, 1968.

(10) Joseph Schumpeter, _The Theory of Economic Development_, Harvard University Press, Cambridge, MA, 1934.

(11) Michael Porter, _Competitive Advantage_, The Free Press, New York, 1985, p. 164.

(12) Richard Foster, _Innovation:  The Attacker's Advantage_, Summit Books, New York, 1986.

(13) R. C. Epstein, _The Automobile Industry:  Its Economic and Commercial Development_, A. W. Shaw Chicago, 1928, and J. B. Rae, _The American Automobile Industry_, G. K. Hall, Boston, 1984.

(14) A. C. Hax and N. S. Majluf, _Strategic Management:  An Integrative Perspective_, Prentice Hall, Englewood Cliffs, N.J., 1984.

(15) Jack Brittain, _High Tech Stakes in Silicon Chips:  Winning and Losing in the Semiconductor Industry_, manuscript, University of Texas at Austin, 1986.

(16) Civil Aeronautics Board, _Handbook of Airline Statistics_, Washington, D.C. 1967 and 1973 editions.

(17) R. A. Thietart and R. Vivas, "An Empirical Investigation of Success Strategies for Businesses Along the Product Life Cycle," _Management Science_, Vol. 30, No. 12 (December 1984), pp. 1405-1423.

(18) Danny Miller and Peter H. Friesen, "A Longitudinal Study of the Corporate Life Cycle," _Management Science_, Vol. 30, No. 10, (October, 1984), pp. 1161-1183.

(19) James M. Utterback and William J. Abernathy, "A Dynamic Model of Process and Product Innovation," _Omega_, Vol. 3, No. 6, (1975), pp. 639-656.

(20) Michael Porter, _Competitive Strategy_, The Free Press, New York, 1980, p. 156.

# THE IMPACT OF SOCIAL NETWORKS ON BUSINESS FOUNDINGS AND PROFIT: A LONGITUDINAL STUDY[1]

Howard Aldrich, University of North Carolina at Chapel Hill
Ben Rosen, University of North Carolina at Chapel Hill
William Woodward, University of North Carolina at Chapel Hill

## ABSTRACT

This paper describes a longitudinal study conducted with one hundred and sixty-five active and prospective entrepreneurs over a nine-month period. The study's purpose was to examine and explore the importance of social network characteristics, such as size, accessibility, and diversity to business founding and business profitability. Results show that network accessibility is a significant variable in predicting business foundings. Different variables were found to predict profitability in old and newly founded businesses.

## INTRODUCTION

Networks and networking have become fashionable topics among entrepreneurs. Defined as the process of sharing contacts and obtaining resources, networking is touted as an essential building block of entrepreneurial success. Until recently , however, the role of networks in entrepreneurship has not received much scholarly attention. Traditional approaches to explaining entrepreneurial activity relied on personality approaches[2] and socio-cultural explanations[3]. The first looks at entrepreneurial activity as a function of psychological processes; the second finds entrepreneurial stimulus in ethnic group or in child rearing practices. Neither of these approaches have validly predicted who starts businesses or who is successful[4]. The problem with these approaches is that they ignore the essential dependence that entrepreneurs have on their social networks for resources.

---

[1] We wish to thank Rollie Tillman, Director of the Institute of Private Enterprise, for his support of this and earlier research.

[2] McClelland, David C. "Need for Achievement and Entrepreneurship: A Longitudinal Study," Journal of Personality and Social Psychology 1(1965): pp. 389-92.

[3] Fleming, W.J. "The Cultural Determinants of Entrepreneurship and Economic Development," Journal of Economic History, XXXIX, No.1 (March, 1979).

During the past five years, researchers have begun exploring the role of social networks in entrepreneurship. Aldrich and Zimmer (1986) and Johannisson (1986)[5] have provided some initial theoretical perspectives, and Birley (1985)[6], Aldrich, Rosen, and Woodward (1986)[7], and Johannisson (1986) have conducted some initial statistical studies. The results of these efforts provide beginning steps for developing a social network perspective on entrepreneurship.

The social network perspective rests on two fundamental premises. First, entrepreneurs succeed because they are able to identify opportunities and obtain scarce resources from their environments. These resources include everything entrepreneurs require to start and build businesses, including money, social support, product ideas, markets, and information. Second, resources are obtained through exchange relationships between entrepreneurs and their social networks. Relatives loan money, husbands or wives grant permission to use family resources, colleagues or business contacts become partners or customers, and acquaintances give advice about lawyers, accountants, and bankers. Accordingly, prospective entrepreneurs who have social networks rich in resources should succeed more often than those who do not.

Empirical research into the social network perspective has only begun, but initial results support social network importance. Birley (1985) showed that business owners rely on informal contacts rather than formal sources to start their businesses. Johannisson's (1986) case study of Swedish businesses showed how prospective entrepreneurs use business colleagues as customers for new businesses. Aldrich, Rosen, and Woodward (1986) documented the importance of family and non-business connections in entrepreneurs' networks. The strength of these studies comes from the maps they provide of entrepreneurs' social networks. Their weakness lies in their retrospective and cross-sectional nature. They support the value of a social network perspective, but cannot give causal evidence for the significance of social networks in starting and building businesses. Concrete support for the social network perspective must come from longitudinal research which examines the role of social networks in business formation over time.

---

[4] Aldrich, Howard and Zimmer, Catherine, "Entrepreneurship through Social Networks." In Entrepreneurship  Edited by Raymond Smilor and Donald Sexton. New York: Ballinger, 1985.

[5] Johannisson, Bengt, "New Venture Creation - A Network Approach," Frontiers of Entrepreneurial Research. Wellesley, MA: Babson College, 1986.

[6] Birley, Sue "The Role of Networks in the Entrepreneurial Process," Frontiers of Entrepreneurial Research (1985). Wellesley, MA: Babson College.

[7] Aldrich, Howard; Rosen, Ben; and Woodward, William. "Social Behavior and Entrepreneurial Networks," Frontiers of Entrepreneurial Research (1986). Wellesley, MA: Babson College.

This paper takes an important step in providing longitudinal support for the importance of social networks in entrepreneurship. It reports initial findings from a nine-month study of entrepreneurs and prospective entrepreneurs. The study focuses on two major questions:

(1) Do social network variables effect business foundings?

(2) To what degree do social network variables predict profit-making in newly founded businesses?

## Network Characteristics

Current theory suggests social networks vary in their ability to provide resources to prospective entrepreneurs (Aldrich, Rosen, and Woodward, 1986). Research in social network analysis identifies three important dimensions of social networks that have relevance for entrepreneurial performance. First, the amount of resources in a network determines limits the ability of entrepreneurs to obtain enough resources to found businesses. Networks with more resources should be more helpful than those with less. Second, networks with diverse resources helps entrepreneurs because the business formation process requires a wide variety of resources. To simply get started, entrepreneurs must identify opportunities, find markets, establish legal and governmental identity, and obtain financial support. Accordingly, prospective entrepreneurs with diverse social networks should have more success than those with homogeneous resources. Finally, entrepreneurs need access to resources. Having large amounts of diverse resources does no good unless the resources are accessible. Consequently, entrepreneurs who have easily accessible resources should be more successful than those who do not.

Entrepreneurial success occurs in several ways. First, we can define success as founding a new business. Although starting operations is no guarantee of later success, beginning operations means that essential resources have been obtained. Accordingly, we expect networks of entrepreneurs who actually begin operations to have differ significantly from those who do not. Specifically, we predict:

H1: Prospective entrepreneurs who start businesses will have networks with more members, with higher levels of activity, with higher diversity than those who do not start businesses.

A second approach is to define success as establishing a profitable business. Current statistics suggest that a high proportion of businesses fail in the first years[8]. Simply beginning operations, therefore, may not be a sufficiently rigorous measure of eventual success. Based on our earlier arguments, we believe that social networks should have a significant effect on a business's success, particularly in the early years of operation. Consequently, we predict:

H2: Profitability in newly founded businesses will be positively associated with network size, diversity, and accessibility, but weakly, if at all, in older businesses.

## Introduction

The results reported in this paper come from a nine-month study of prospective and active entrepreneurs in the Research Triangle area of North Carolina. The initial study, conducted in February, 1986, provided base-line data on the social networks and the business status of two hundred and eighty-five respondents[9]. The follow-up study, conducted in December, 1986, surveyed two hundred and twelve participants from the first survey who agreed to further contact. Using a short post-card format, we gathered information on business status, entrepreneurial intentions, past business history, and financial performance during the study period.

## Subjects

Respondents are members or have attended meetings of the Research Triangle Council for Entrepreneurial Development (CED). The CED is an association dedicated to encouraging entrepreneurship in the Research Triangle area of North Carolina. The first survey was sent to over seven hundred names taken from the CED mailing list in February, 1986. The second survey was sent to two hundred and twelve respondents of the first survey who agreed to be contacted again.

Information was obtained about one hundred and eighty-five participants (87.3%). One hundred and eleven (60.0%) returned the post cards, fifty-five (29.7%) were contacted by telephone, fifteen (8.1%) have moved from the area without forwarding addresses, and two (1.0%) had died. In all, we obtained usable information from one hundred and sixty-five (77.8%) participants.

Of the one hundred and sixty-five first-wave respondents who also responded to the second survey, one hundred and twenty-one (72.5%) own businesses, forty-one (24.6%) are employed by someone else, and five (3.0%) are unemployed. Sixty-six respondents expressed intentions about starting a new or another business: thirty (47.6%) had no interest, sixteen (25.4%) were thinking about starting a business, and seventeen (27.0%) were in the process of starting a business. Seventy (56.5%) of the business owners were managing their first business; eighty (64.5%) said they had made a profit during the past nine months.

## Design

Answers were obtained through a mailed questionnaire sent to respondents of the first survey who agreed to further contact.  A

---

[8] U. S. Small Business Administration. The State of Small Business. Washington, D.C.: U.S. Government Printing Office, 1985.

9.  Aldrich, Rosen, and Woodward, Frontiers, 1986.

summary of the findings of the first survey accompanied the
questionnaire. Subjects who had not returned the questionnaire were
contacted by telephone.

The questionnaire asked four questions. Two questions, business
intentions and employment status, were the same as in the first survey.
"Business intentions" were obtained by asking respondents to choose all
appropriate answers from a list of five statements (see Appendix A).
Answers included having no plans to start a business, thinking about
starting a business, and being in the process of starting a business.
In addition, respondents could say that they were already operating a
business they had started or had bought from someone else. "Employment
status" asked whether the respondent was unemployed, self-employed,
owner/manager of a business, or an employee of someone else. Multiple
answers were allowed. Two other questions were not asked before: one
asked for the number of businesses started before and one asked whether
respondents made a profit.


VARIABLES


Independent Variables

The study had three independent variables: (1) amount of
resources in the network, (2) diversity of resources in the network, and
(3) accessibility of resources in the network.

Amount of resources describes the quantity of resources available
to and was measured by the size of the entrepreneur's network. Subjects
were asked how many people they talked to about starting or running
their businesses in the six months prior to the survey.

Diversity of resources refers to the variety of resources
available to the entrepreneur. Research in social network analysis has
shown that networks in which members are not well acquainted tend to
have more varied resources[10]. This approach at measuring diversity,
known as the theory of weak ties, argues that network members who are
friends of each other are more likely to have similar ideas, points-of-
view, and information. People generally make friends with people who
are similar to them. Conversely, network members who are not friends are
more likely to be different from each other and have different ideas,
points-of-view, and information. Thus networks made up of people who do
not know each other should contain more diverse information than those
networks that are made up of close friends.

Resource diversity was measured by asking subjects to identify
the five people with whom they felt most comfortable in discussing ideas
for business formation and operation. Subjects were then asked to

_____

[10] Granovetter, Mark. "The Strength of Weak Ties." In Social
Structure and Network Analysis, pp. 105-130. Edited by Peter V. Marsden
and Nan Lin. Beverly Hills, CA: Sage, 1982.

describe the relationship between each of the ten pairs of network members. Choices included friends, acquaintances, strangers, and unknowns. The measure, average strength of ties, was constructed by taking a weighted average of the three types of possible relationships (unknowns were ignored). The measurement varied from 1, which meant that all the members of the network were good friends, to 3, which meant that all the members of the network were strangers. Higher numbers show more potential diversity in available resources.

Resource accessibility is the degree to which entrepreneurs can obtain resources. Resource accessibility was measured by looking at the amount of time entrepreneurs spent in developing and maintaining business contacts, and by the number of interrelationships among the five identified network members.

Using amount of time and frequency of contacts as a measurement of accessibility is based on the argument that the more time and energy entrepreneurs spend on trying to obtain resources, the more likely they are to be successful. Accordingly we asked subject to tell us how many hours each week do they spend developing and maintaining contacts with people with whom they can discuss business matters. In addition, we asked subjects to report the number of times each week they discussed business matters with their five closest network members. We constructed a measure by taking a simple average of contacts per week.

The number of linkages among the five closest network members is known as the 'density' of the network. As connections increase between network members, communication should increase, and information sharing should increase. Highly dense networks have more easily accessible information (resources) than networks with low density. Accordingly, we measured density by constructing a 1,0 variable that took the average of the number of connections. Scores of '1' meant that all network members were connected by either friendship or acquaintance; scores of '0' meant that there were no contacts between network members.

## Dependent Variables

The study includes two dependent variables: business foundings and profitability.

Business Founding is defined as the starting a business. In the second survey, respondents were asked to give the date of of their latest business founding, if any. Business founding represents businesses founded during the nine months of the study as well as those businesses being started at the time of the second survey.

Profit is defined as making money after taxes and expenses. Subjects were asked in the second survey to choose one of three answers: (1) made a profit, (2) did not make a profit, and (3) unsure.

## Network Characteristics and Changes in Entrepreneurial Intentions

The study is a preliminary look at the longitudinal effects of social network characteristics on entrepreneurship. In a nine-month period we expected only small changes in the population, and we were mainly interested in general trends. Consequently we used simple dichotomous variables and $X^2$ statistics[11]. Continuous variables were divided into two categories based on sample medians to control for outliers. (We plan more sophisticated analyses later.)

The study population experienced considerable change between the time of the first study (March, 1986) and the follow-up (January, 1987). Sixteen new businesses were started and four businesses failed. Significant change occurred in respondents' business intentions as well as their employment status (see Tables 1A and 1B). For example, only one-half of the seventeen respondents who said they were starting businesses in the first survey report they are still starting a business. The rest are now less active, with forty-one percent identifying no intention at all. Similar change occurred among the

TABLE 1A

## Changes in Respondents' Intentions to Start A Business--
## February, 1986 to January, 1987

### 1987 Intentions

| 1986 Intentions | No Stated Intention | No Plans | Thinking About | Currently Starting | Total % | Total N |
|---|---|---|---|---|---|---|
| No Stated Intention | 87% | - | 4% | 9% | 100 | 102 |
| No Plans | 7% | 63% | 23% | 7% | 100 | 30 |
| Thinking About | 6% | 12% | 63% | 19% | 100 | 16 |
| Currently Starting | 41% | - | 12% | 47% | 100 | 17 |

Note: No stated intention means that respondents did not choose any of the first three choices for Question 1.

---

[11]. SAS Institute Inc. SAS User's Guide: Statistics, Version 5 Edition. Cary, NC: SAS Institute Inc., 1985, pp. 403-432.

sixteen respondents who were "Thinking About" starting a business in the first survey. Ten still report they have the same intention; two now have "No plans," and one expressed no intention whatever.

Two categories, "No Stated Intention" and "No Plans," show relatively little change. Examination of the two groups' characteristics offers some possible reasons. All but one of the respondents who chose "no plans" in both surveys were business owners who checked one of the other two choices in Question 1: "currently running a business that I started" or "I have taken over an ongoing business." We suspect that this group includes business owners who were mainly engaged in operating their businesses and were not concerned one way or the other about starting another business when they answered the questions. The other group that had little change were those respondents who said they had no plans to start a business in the first survey. Of the nineteen people who said they had no plans in both surveys, seventeen (90%) are full-time executives in firms. These managers are in the sample because they were sent by their firms to the CED to discover potential entrepreneurial ideas and to look for business opportunities.

TABLE 1B

Changes in Respondents' Employment Status -- Feb., 1986 to Jan., 1987

| Employment Status (1986) | Employment Status(1987) | | | | | |
|---|---|---|---|---|---|---|
| | Employee | Bus. Owner | BusOwner/ Employee | Unempl. | Total % | Total N |
| Employee | 84% | 5% | 12% | - | 101 | 43 |
| Business Owner | 3% | 91% | 5% | 2% | 101 | 108 |
| Business Owner and Employee | 14% | 43% | 43% | - | 100 | 7 |
| Unemployed | - | 60% | - | 40% | 100 | 5 |

Note: Business owners and employees are respondents who both have businesses and work for someone else.

Change can also be seen in the respondents' employment status (See Table 1B). Seven (16%) of the forty-three employees in the first survey now report they have begun businesses. Six (5%) of the one hundred and fifteen business owners in February, 1986, now say they are employees or unemployed. Three of the five respondents who were unemployed have since started businesses. Finally, three of the seven people who both worked for someone else and operated businesses have quit their jobs -- presumably to work full-time in their businesses.

These tables show that the change among the research population during the nine month period was generally isolated to two groups. Two populations, business owners and full-time employees, showed the least change in both employment status and business intentions. Most changed were respondents who had jobs and businesses, and those who were unemployed.

As interesting as these tables are, however, they fail to explain the source of the sixteen business foundings. First, only nine of those subject who said they were starting a business in the first survey failed to give any intentions in the second. It is unlikely that all of them actually succeeded in starting operations. A check of these nine people show that only five of them succeeded during the nine months; four had given up. Second, the change in employment status only can account for five of the sixteen starts -- two by employees and three by subjects who were unemployed in the first survey. Thus we are left with the question: where did the other six business founding come from?

To find the answer to the question of where the new business starts came from, we identified those respondents who had started businesses during the research period and traced their answers to the intentions and employment status questions. The findings have implications for the reliability of "intention" surveys as well as the volatility of entrepreneurial populations (see Table 2).

The first implication is that stated intentions are not a reliable guide to later outcomes, unless respondents say they have no plans to start a business. Only five (23%) of the twenty-two respondents who said they were starting businesses in the first survey had begun operations at the time of the follow-up. Four expressed no intention at all, two now say they had no plans to start a business, three have moved back to only "thinking about" starting a business, and eight report they are still starting. Of the twenty-three people who said they were thinking about starting a business, only three (13%) moved ahead with their plans. Ten (44%) respondents are still thinking, seven (30%) said they had given up ("no plans"), and three (13%) expressed no intention.

Not only do people's stated intentions provide poor guides for later action; the lack of clear intentions is equally poor as a predictor of business behaviors. Of the business formations that occurred among the respondents during the nine months, one-half came from people who expressed no intention whatever about starting a business in the first survey (See Table 2). Clearly, a person's intentions have little to do with eventual business outcomes.

The second implication is that the business formation process can happen quickly. For one-half of the business formations in our sample, entrepreneurs apparently formulated the idea for starting a business and began operations in fewer than nine months. Two respondents started one business and are already in the process of starting another. This volatility suggests that a significant part of the business formation process may have more to do with sudden opportunity than with long-term planning.

TABLE 2

Intentions of Respondents Who Started Businesses
(February, 1986 to January, 1987)

| Intentions | | | Number of |
| February 1986 | January 1987 | N | Business Foundings |
| --- | --- | --- | --- |
| No stated intention | No stated intention | 89 | 7 |
| Starting | No stated intention | 9 | 5 |
| No stated intention | Starting | 7 | 1 |
| Starting | Starting | 8 | 1* |
| Thinking | No stated intention | 4 | 1 |
| Thinking | Thinking | 10 | 1* |

* Respondents started one business and are thinking about or in process of starting another.

## Network Characteristics and Business Foundings

Our first hypothesis predicts that actual business foundings would be associated with large, diverse, and accessible networks. Results are found in Tables 3A and 3B. The first part reports the $X^2$ values for each of the comparisons: the second part shows percentages for the three significant relationships.

Three variables appear to be slightly predictive: people who started businesses reported a significantly (p=.03) higher average number of contacts per week with core network members than did those persons who did not start businesses. Business founders also spent more time developing contacts (p=.07). Finally, business starters had networks that were more closely linked than those who did not start businesses (p=.09). These findings document the relationship of accessibility to business formation, but do not support network size or diversity as important elements in business foundings.

## TABLE 3A

Relationship between Network Variables and Business Foundings

| Network Variable | $\chi^2$ | Probability |
|---|---|---|
| Network Size | .43 | .50 |
| Hours per week developing contacts | 3.24 | .07 |
| Hours per week maintaining contacts | .05 | .82 |
| Average contacts per week with core network members | 4.51 | .03 |
| Density | 2.83 | .09 |
| Average strength of ties | 1.23 | .27 |

## TABLE 3B

Percentage of Subjects Founding Businesses During Nine Months

| Variables | Level[1] | % | N |
|---|---|---|---|
| Hours developing contacts [2] | low | 10 | 83 |
| | high | 20 | 82 |
| Density [3] | low | 10 | 88 |
| | high | 19 | 77 |
| Average Contacts per Week with Core Network [4] | low | 9 | 88 |
| | high | 21 | 77 |

[1] Levels were established by dividing at the median.
[2] p=.07  [3] p=.09  [4] p=.03

## Business Formation and Profitability

Our second hypothesis predicted that networks would be effective in helping newly-founded businesses become profitable. To test this prediction, we compared those entrepreneurs making a profit with those who weren't across the six network variables. Past research has shown, however, that business age is highly associated with profitability. Consequently, we divided the sample along the median -- three years old -- and conducted separate statistical tests for each group.

Results are found in Tables 4A and 4B. For businesses three years old and younger, three variables show significance. Two accessibility measures, hours maintaining contacts (p=.04) and density (p=.004), suggest that entrepreneurs who maintain high levels of contact with networks whose members are interconnected are more likely to make a profit. The third measure, which represents diversity (p=.04), suggests that profit makers have networks whose members are closely associated -- contrary to the prediction.

TABLE 4A

Relationship between Network Variables and Profitability by Business Age

| Network Variable | Business Age | | | |
| --- | --- | --- | --- | --- |
| | <= 3 Years | | > 3 Years | |
| | $x^2$ | P= | $x^2$ | P= |
| Network Size | .00 | .90 | 14.07 | .000 |
| Hours per week developing contacts | .44 | .51 | .05 | .83 |
| Hours per week maintaining contacts | 4.18 | .04 | .02 | .89 |
| Average contacts per week with core network members | .11 | .74 | .33 | .56 |
| Density | 8.36 | .004 | .26 | .61 |
| Average strength of ties | 4.18 | .04 | 1.03 | .31 |

Results are completely different for businesses more than three years in age. No variables show any significance except network size (p=.000), which is highly significant in the direction predicted by the hypothesis. According to this result, entrepreneurs who own businesses older than three years make profits when they maintain large networks of people they can talk to about business progress.

## TABLE 4B
### Percentage of Businesses Making Profits

| Variables | Level[1] | <=3 Years | | >3 Years | |
|---|---|---|---|---|---|
| | | % | N | % | N |
| Network Size | low | 63 | 11 | 51[2] | 37 |
| | high | 62 | 29 | 90 | 40 |
| Density | low | 43[3] | 23 | 69 | 35 |
| | high | 88 | 17 | 74 | 42 |
| Hours Maintain Contacts | low | 48[4] | 21 | 72 | 36 |
| | high | 79 | 19 | 71 | 41 |
| Average strength of ties | low | 48 | 21 | 67 | 42 |
| | high | 79[4] | 19 | 77 | 35 |

[1] Levels were established by dividing at the median.
[2] p=.000   [3] p=.004   [4] p= .04

## Discussion

The results of this study suggest two conclusions, point out a weakness in the theory, and raise a puzzling question. First, the study supports the validity of the social network perspective because it predicts clear relationships between network variables and entrepreneurial outcomes. Network variables had significant relationships with business foundings and profitability. Further, the accessibility and size variables showed consistent variation across the stages of business. For example, "developing contacts" was significant for business foundings, but not for profitability. "Maintaining contacts," however, was a significant predictor for early profit, but not for founding. This relationship makes sense when we realize that founding stages are times of network development while maintaining contacts become more important after the start-up of operations. Further support is found in the differences between important variables for young businesses and older ones. Thus network variables appear to support the notion that entrepreneurship is a process of incremental stages in which requirements change as business progress.

A second conclusion suggested by the study is that the business formation process is volatile and heterogeneous. Based on the changes in the intention data, it appears that a significant portion of business formation happens rapidly and without major planning. Some of these rapid start-ups came from entrepreneurs who were founding their second or third businesses, but five of the sixteen business foundings came from first-time entrepreneurs. This finding raises questions about the value of entrepreneurial education that focuses on careful, long-term planning as a necessity of founding a business. Perhaps we should be teaching people how to recognize opportunities and how to quickly build resource-rich networks.

The theory's major weakness is in the performance of the diversity variable, strength of ties. According to our predictions, successful entrepreneurs should have networks with diverse resources. According to social network analysis, diversity is greater when network members are not tightly linked. The results of this study show, however, exactly the opposite. Only 48% of those entrepreneurs who have networks with higher proportions of weak ties make a profit compared to nearly 80% of those who have strong tie networks.

There are several possibilities for this finding. One problem arises from the measurement we used. Restricting the measurement to a weighted average of the types of linkages between entrepreneurs' five nearest network members may not be a reliable way to determine the proportion of weak ties. About one-third of the network members in the sample are family members who should know each other. Further, the subjects reported an average of 17 contacts with whom they discussed business matters -- taking the closest five may be too restrictive. Perhaps if we were able to map out the relationships of more network members we would find that weak ties are a better predictor. In addition, other measures of diversity, such as age and sex diversity among network members, might show more consistent relationships. A second possibility is we measured diversity correctly but that strength of ties is not a useful characteristic in entrepreneurial networks. Johannisson (1986) emphasizes the importance of close ties in entrepreneurial networks, and our finding supports his contention.

The results showing the differences in the relationship between profitability and network characteristics for different age businesses raise a puzzling question. The results for younger businesses (less or equal to three years old) are as we predicted for "maintaining contacts" and "density," and opposite for "average strength of ties." The striking finding is the high significance for network size in businesses older than three years. Not only does the result show the highest significance for any variable in the entire study, but we cannot find any logical reason for network size to be the only important variable for older business profitability. Before we speculate any further, we need to test for possible confounding variables. Two possible candidates, industry type and business size, have been tested. Industry type does not have a significant relationship with profit in our sample, but business size is significant (p=.08). Whether controlling for size will negate the importance of network size remains to be seen.

# CONCLUSIONS

The purpose of this study was to test support for a social network perspective on entrepreneurship. The initial findings of this longitudinal study suggest that social interaction is an important contributor to both business foundings and profits. These findings contrast strongly with traditional perspectives that focus only on psychological, socio-cultural, or economic variables as contributing to entrepreneurial outcomes. Further research is necessary to confirm and explore these findings, but the social network perspective on entrepreneurship has received important support.

The practical implications of the results suggest that entrepreneurship involves several stages of activity, each with its own requirements and opportunities. In the stages before start-up, entrepreneurs should spend time in developing networks whose members have a high level of interaction. Following start-up, entrepreneurs need to spend time maintaining the networks and encouraging interaction between members.

## APPENDIX A: FOLLOW-UP SURVEY QUESTIONS

1. Current business situation (circle all appropriate answers)

    1  I have no plans to start a business
    2  I am thinking about starting a business in the next year or two
    3  I am currently in the process of starting a business, but have not started operations.
    4  I currently run a business I started    Date started:
    5  I have taken over an ongoing business   Date takeover:

2. Current employment status (circle all appropriate answers)

    1  unemployed                    4  owner manager of business
    2  full time student             5  I work part time for someone else

    3  self-employed                 6  I work full time for someone else
       (no other employees)

BUSINESS OWNERS ONLY:

3. Past business history

    1  This is my first attempt at starting a business
    2  I have started other businesses previously.
              How many? ____

4. Do you think you made a profit during the past nine months?

    1  yes          2  no          3  unsure

# THE USE OF PEER NETWORKS IN THE START-UP PROCESS[1]

Bradley L. Rush, The University of Calgary
James B. Graham, The University of Calgary
Wayne A. Long, The University of Calgary

## ABSTRACT

Fifteen entrepreneurs, who were initially strangers, took part in an entrepreneurial management program called "Action Learning for Owner/Managers". The participants attended a series of seminars and met regularly in three small groups to discuss their own particular business problems. While the end goal of the program was to promote growth in the successful, owner-managed, small firm, three new ventures emerged from one group.

Empirical research conducted with that group of five owner-managers over a period of six months indicated what a cohesive peer network could contribute to new venture development. Five major roles played in the start-up process were identified. Findings are discussed in the context of a non-traditional, university-based, management development program. Ideas for new venture creation using the power of a peer network are suggested.

## INTRODUCTION

In this paper, we report the findings of a longitudinal study on the use of a peer network in the start-up process. Over a period of six months, we closely followed the evolution of a small group of entrepreneurs who were initially strangers and we examined the affect of that group on new venture development. During the course of our research, a number of important issues emerged: Can a group actually facilitate the start-up process? What are the key roles played by a "strong-tie" network of owner-managers over time? How can we use networks for repeated new venture creation? What is the social context necessary for success?

---

[1]We would like to acknowledge the valuable contributions made by Karl Vesper (for the idea which initiated this paper) and Ed McMullan (for editorial comments on an earlier draft).

An entrepreneurial management program called "Action Learning for Owner/Managers" was created as a basis for a Ph.D. dissertation[2]. The empirical research described in this paper formed part of that study, which tracked the process of change in owners of successful small-to-medium-sized enterprises.

Action Learning for Owner/Mangers consisted of eleven half-day seminars and twelve small group meetings spread over a period of six months. This university-based program was aimed at growth-oriented owners of companies which had annual sales or operating revenues ranging from $1 million to $10 million. Seventeen owner-managers enrolled and 15 completed the program. Three small groups formed, two of six owner-managers and one of five. Later one person from each of the larger groups dropped out leaving three groups of five. The small groups met 12, 14 and 17 times respectively.

This paper focuses on one part of that overall study. We report on the use of a peer network in the start-up process. We examine one of the three groups in the program, the "Sanderson Group" named after its unofficial leader (not his real name). We try to explain why that group was able to facilitate the development of three new ventures from within that group.

Data was collected primarily by participant observation over a period of six months. At least one of us attended all 17 small group meetings held by the Sanderson group and often there were two, particularly in the early stages of group development. Meetings were tape-recorded to allow further analysis. In addition, we engaged in one-to-one sessions with most of the group members, attended all the seminars, and met regularly to compare views and interpretations. Essentially, it was a "grounded theory" approach; results emerged from the data[3].

Three pencil and paper instruments were also used to collect data: a rating sheet on group effectiveness was administered at three different times; Kolb's Learning Style Inventory (LSI) was completed by the participants early in the program[4] and the Myers-Briggs Type

---

[2]Rush, Bradley L. (1987) Action Learning for Owner/Managers. Unpublished doctoral dissertation, The University of Calgary, Calgary, CAN

[3]Glaser, Barney G. and Strauss, A. L. (1967) The Discovery of Grounded Theory, Hawthorne, NY: Aldine

[4]Kolb, David A. (1976). Learning Style Inventory Technical Manual. Boston, MA: McBer & Co.

Indicator (MBTI), Form G, was answered in the fifth month[5] Later, we attempted to link our findings with other theoretical foundations. Overall, we sought to achieve a high degree of concurrent validation.

## SOCIAL CONTEXT

Action Learning for Owner/Managers provided, in our opinion, the social context which enabled one group to facilitate the development of three new ventures. A basic understanding of the program is thus helpful. Essentially, its overall goal was to promote growth in the owner-managed firm. We proposed to accomplish this by helping the participants undergo the transition needed to take their companies from an early-to-intermediate stage of development to a later stage. We wanted to help owner-managers develop successful growth businesses. Our underlying premise was that if the firm is to grow, it must change and most of the time the owner-manager must change or be changed. The literature is quite clear on this point: producing a winner usually requires a major change on the part of the firm's founder[6]. We aimed to provide an environment where this could happen.

### Action Learning Model

Action Learning for Owner/Managers was based, in part, on the work of Reg Revans and his action learning programs for middle-to-senior managers in large companies in England and Europe[7]. Typically, each participant would investigate and implement something which his or her superior had indicated was important to the success of the company. The participants would then spend the majority of their time working on their own particular projects, using small group meetings to advance each project. Also, the participants would attend a seminar or a block of seminars at the beginning of the program in order to obtain a common theoretical framework[8].

We adapted that model for owner-managers and added ideas gleaned from theories of experiential learning, adult learning, and humanistic psychology/organization development. These ideas affected

---

[5]Myers, Isabel Briggs (1980). Introduction to Type Palo Alto, CA: Consulting Psychologists Press

[6]Clifford, Donald K. & Cavanagh, R.B. (1985). The Winning Performance New York: Bantam.

[7]Revans, Reginald W. (1980). Action Learning: New techniques for Management. London: Blond and Briggs.

[8]Casey, David & Pearce, D. (Eds) (1977). More Than Management Development. London: Gower Press.

the seminar content and the manner in which we interacted with the groups.

## Experiential Learning

Basically, "action learning" may be conceived as a learning community approach in which a learner works on (and solves) a previously unresolved organizational problem. It is a method of "experiential learning", the process whereby knowledge, skills and attitudes are created or changed through the transformation of experience. The fact that learning is a process whereby concepts are derived from and modified by experience has important educational implications. It implies that all learning is "relearning" and, one's job as an educator is not only to implant new ideas, but also to dispose of or modify old ones[9]. Argyris has argued that in order to achieve company growth and personal growth, entrepreneurs "have to break the frames that they normally would use to understand and act in their world"[10].

Our seminars sought to help the participants engage in a process of framebreaking; they aimed to provide owner-managers with alternative ways of viewing the reality of their situations. Rather than giving a lot of new information, the seminars largely presented the owner-managers with useful conceptual frameworks so that each could "reorganize" his or her knowledge. Additionally, instead of being subject-oriented (i.e. Finance, Marketing, Production, etc.) the seminars were problem-oriented. They examined issues which we had identified as being critical to self-development and company growth. Topics included: finding appropriate markets, formulating and implementing a growth strategy, developing a corporate culture to enhance growth, making a transition from one phase of company growth to another, building a top team, developing alternative frames of reference, and managing change.

## Adult Learning and Humanistic Psychology

Important concepts underlying the program also came from the field of adult learning, which suggest that adults learn by experience and the readiness of an adult to learn is closely related to the developmental tasks of his/her social role, such as building an organization. Adult educators have argued that adults accumulate a growing reservoir of experience which produces a rich resource for learning and that adults are more problem-centered than subject-centered in their

---

[9] Kolb, David A. (1984). Experiential Learning Englewood Cliffs, N.J.: Prentice Hall.

[10] Argyris, Chris (1982). Reasoning, Learning and Action. San Francisco: Jossey Bass, 44

learning[11]. These ideas have clear educational implications for the design of any program aimed at adults.

Related propositions drawn from the principles of humanistic psychology (e.g. Carl Rogers, Abraham Maslow) further influenced our action learning model. For example, these theories suggest that the source of knowledge lies in the experience itself, group interaction is an important vehicle of learning, and attention to process issues produces more longer term benefits than attention to content. Organization development (OD) is an applied field which makes use of these principles and, in a way, our program may be described as an OD effort.

## Learning in Groups

These interrelated concepts strongly indicated that, in practice, managers and other people could learn a great deal from their peers and expecially in the context of active problem-solving and solution implementation. Revans described the process as "learning to learn-by-doing with and from others who are also learning to learn-by-doing"[12]. Our program emphasized this.

The small groups met regularly to examine and discuss a series of organizational issues which each participant brought to the meetings (only two of the 15 restricted themselves to one project). The faculty role in these groups was not to lead but rather to observe and help the group develop. The group advisor focused more on how the group was working than on what it was discussing. He facilitated the social processes by which the owner-managers helped each other to learn. As described by an observer of the process, "his role was to behave as differently from a business school lecturer as humanly possible"[13]

## Top Management Development

Support for an experiential learning/action-based program which integrated principles of adult learning and humanistic psychology/OD, came from a seminal study on the development of chief executive officers[14]. Glickman and his colleagues found that the "top management" development process is separate from and more than an extension of a

---

[11]Knowles, Malcolm S. (1972), The Modern Practice of Adult Eduction, (Revised ed.). New York: Association Press.

[12]Revans (1980) 288, op. cit.

[13]Mant, Alistair (1981). Developing effective managers for the future: Learning through experience. In C.L. Cooper (Ed.), Developing Managers for the 1980's 79-87. London: MacMillan.

[14]Glickman, Albert S., Hahn C.P., Fleishman, E.A and Baxter B. (1968). Top Management Development and Succession. Washington D.C.: American Institutes for Research.

firm's management development process. The two formed entirely different concepts. The conventional wisdom of management development, which has been described by reviewers as being in a "sad state"[15], appeared to be inappropriate as a practical guide for top management. Most executives in the Glickman study accepted the proposition that there is no one right way of managing. Top managers were allowed to develop their own style; they learned in action[16]. Our owner-managers, too, learned in action, except that the process was facilitated by a program designed specifically for them, a program which generally opposed the conventional wisdom of management development (e.g. an emphasis on changing perspectives vs. acquiring new information; the use of actual problems vs. reading case studies).

## THE SANDERSON GROUP

Each of the three groups self-selected during the second seminar. The Sanderson group got together quickly, but later, before their first meeting, asked a member of another group to join them She did, and a group of six was formed. Over a period of six months, this group of owner-managers, who were initially strangers, met 17 times. However, after meeting number eight, one of the group members, Bates, withdrew from the program.

We chose to focus on the Sanderson group for several reasons. First, three new ventures emerged from that group, more than from either of the other two groups. It was considered to be the most productive group. Second, based on self report measures, its members saw their group as the most cohesive of the three groups. Our observations strongly supported this perspective; there seemed to be greater commitment by members to seek solutions to each other's problems. Third, the Sanderson group had at least one of each of the four types of learning styles (i.e. accommodator, assimilator, converger, diverger). This was consistent with the theory which argued that the strengths of all four styles were necessary for effective problem solving[17]. The Royce group had only two and the Lane group three of the four styles. Fourth, the Sanderson group had a comfortable and workable blend of similarity and diversity vis-a-vis its "psychological types". According to Myers, success for any enterprise demanded a variety of types, but , she emphasized, the best teams consisted of

---

[15]Goldstein, Irwin L. (1984). Training in work organizations. Annual Review of Psychology, 35, 519-551.

[16]Glickman et al (1968), op. cit.

[17]Kolb (1984), op. cit.

individuals who shared some preferences[18]. Results from the Myers-Briggs Type Indicator (MBTI) demonstrated that the Sanderson group fortuitously fit the bill. The Royce group had a great many differences among its members while the Lane group had a lot of similarities. The Sanderson group's greater productivity therefore was also consistent with the theory. The chart summarizes some key characteristics of the group's members:

|  | LSI | MBTI | New Venture |
|---|---|---|---|
| Sanderson | Accommodator | ENTP | No |
| Peters | Diverger | ISTJ | Yes |
| Mason | Assimilator | INTJ | Yes |
| Carter | Converger | ESTJ | Yes |
| Mahoney | Assimilator | INTP | No |
| Bates | Diverger | - | Withdrew |

TABLE 1:   Some Characteristics of Group Members

Myers wrote extensive descriptions of all 16 psychological types and Kolb did the same for his four learning styles. They are incorporated into the following description of the Sanderson group's members:

Hal Sanderson, age 47, BSc in Mechanical Engineering. Owned 100% of a contracting company which provided a number of services to commercial builders. Played professional football and worked as an industrial engineer and plant manager. Had own company for 8 years. Current sales $3.0 million, 25 employees. Psychological type, ENTP: an intuitive, innovative organizer; aggressive, analytic, systematic. Learning style, accommodation: good at initiating the problemsolving process and at implementation; opposite strength to the assimlator.

Mary Peters, age 44, BA in Agricultural Economics plus a Diploma of Commercial Design. Had a background in the management of shopping centres. Owned her own businesses for five years. Owned two chocolate, nut and candy shops plus was a regional franchisor for a chain of specialty food shops. Sales revenue $1.0 million, 18 employees. Proposed to start her own unique, franchisable new venture in the fast food arena. Psychological type, ISTJ: an analytical manager of facts and details, dependable, decisive, painstaking and systematic; stable and conservative, makes up her own mind as to what should be accomplished and works toward it steadily. Learning style, divergent: good at collecting information and generating ideas and alternatives; opposite strength to the converger.

---

[18]Myers, Isabel Briggs (1980). Gifts Differing. Palo Alto, CA: Consulting Psychologists Press.

Dan Mason, age 37, BSc in Statistics and Computer Science. Previously a founding partner of a high-tech office equipment company that grew to $10 million in sales with 100 employees in eight years but left him with only a minor equity position. He had been on his own for less than six months before the program began. Was in the process of acquiring and using newly developed text and graphics technology as the basis for a start-up company for producing and selling a family of hardware and software. Forecasted sales, over $100 million in three years. Psychological type, INTJ: a logical, critical, decisive innovator of ideas; serious, intense, highly independent, determined and often stubborn; may not look for the things that conflict with his goal; can easily overlook relevant facts. Learning style, assimilation: excellent at defining the problem and formulating models for solving it; opposite strength to the accommodator.

John Carter, age 29, BA in Economics. Went to work for father's electrical contracting company after university and took over company five years ago. Sales $2.5 million, 25-45 employees. Played an active role in the family's property investment business. Proposed an entirely new venture: a series of gas bar/car wash/food store operations. Psychological type, ESTJ: a fact-minded practical organizer; aggressive, analytic, systematic; likes to achieve immediate, visible and tangible results; more interested in getting the job done than in people's feelings; does not listen to his own intuition very much, so needs an intuitive type around to sell him on the value of new ideas and possibilities. Learning style, convergent: strong at evaluating the consequences of the various solutions offered and then picking the best solutions; opposite strength to the diverger.

Dennis Mahoney, age 38, no formal education. Was self-employed for over 12 years in automotive related industries. Took over a bumper plating company five years ago and has increased sales six-fold through acquisitions. He is the lead entrepreneur and CEO but only owns 30%. Sales $1.1 million, 18 employees. Psychological type, INTP: an inquisitive analyzer, reflective, independent, curious; more interested in organizing ideas than situations or people. Learning style, assimilation: excels at defining the problem and formulating models for solving it; opposite strength to the accommodator.

Chuck Bates, age 37, BSc in Mechanical Engineering. Founded an engineering company with an equal partner eight years ago. Sales $6.0 million, 45 employees. Dropped out of the program in third month. Learning style, divergent: good at generating ideas; opposite strength to the converger.

Generally, our observations coincided with the LSI (administered in the first month) and with MBTI (administered in the fifth month). Consistent with the theory, we too found that individuals with different learning styles and opposing types (E/I, S/N, T/F, J/P) experienced tension and had difficulty communicating with one another. However, our major findings have to do with group affects on new venture development.

The main findings which emerged from the data centered on the distinction between a strong-tie and a loose-tie network, the stages of group development, the value of conflict and, most importantly, group roles in the start-up process.

## Strong-Tie Networks

We distinguish between a strong-tie and a "loose-tie" (i.e. multiple business contacts) network.    A strong-tie network may be described as a cohesive group.  And cohesiveness is simply the attractiveness of a group for its members.  It is probably the single most important factor of a high performing group.  Group cohesiveness results in better group attendance, greater participation of members, greater member satisfaction, a high degree of influence among members, and significantly better productivity[19].

Cohesiveness directly affects productivity (in this case, new venture development)  because the more attracted one is to the group, the more one respects the judgement of the group, and the more one will attend to and take seriously any discrepancy between one's self-esteem and one's public-esteem as provided by a group of peers.  A discrepancy between the two will create a state of dissonance for that individual, and one will initiate activity to remove that dissonance. This activity is usually positive as it is far more common for a group to evaluate one more highly than one evaluates oneself[20].  Thus, the cohesive group often has the effect of increasing one's aspirations in order to mitigate the dissonance between public and personal views of esteem.  A strong-tie network indeed can mobilizes powerful forces which produce effects of utmost importance to individuals[21].  The Sanderson group displayed evidence of this.

## Stages of Group Development

In order to become a cohesive, high performing entity, a group goes through a number of growth stages, rather similar to the life cycle.  There is considerable consistency regarding the basic phases of group development.  Broadly, a group goes through an initial stage of orientation, characterized by a search for structure and goals.  Next,

---

[19] Jewell, Linda N. & Reitz, H.J. (1981) Groups Effectiveness in Organizations. Glenview, Ill:  Scott, Foresmen

[20] Yalom, Irvin D. (1985) The Theory and Practic of Group Psychotherapy (3rd Edition) NY: Basic Books

[21] Cartwright, Dorwin P. & Lippitt, R. (1957).  International Journal of Group Psychotherapy 7, 86-102

a group encounters a stage of conflict when the preliminary, and often false, consensus on purposes, roles, norms and behaviors is challenged and re-established. At this stage a lot of personal agendas are revealed and a certain amount of inter-personal hostility is generated. Thereafter, at a group's third stage, the group becomes increasingly concerned with inter-member harmony, while differences are often submerged in the service of group cohesiveness. At this stage, the group needs to establish norms and practices: when and how it should work; what type of behavior, what degree of openness, trust and confidence is appropriate. Only when the three previous stages have been successfully completed will the group be at full maturity and be able to be fully and sensibly productive. Some kind of performance will be achieved at all stages of development, but it is likely to be impeded by the other developmental tasks. Finally, there is a separation or termination phase. These five stages have been identified as: forming, storming, norming, performing and adjourning[22], and were pertinent to our research.

After following the development of the Sanderson group during its 17 "official" meetings (there were also quite a few "unofficial" sub-group meetings), we found that a life-cycle model provided a useful tool for analysis. In our view, the Sanderson group had worked through the stages of forming, norming and storming and had largely reached the performing stage. Each of these stages of the group's life represented a developmental task confronting the group at that time. However, we found that the issues relating to the group's development were better viewed as a series of spirals, some wide and some narrow. Issues were not settled "once and for all" but rather resurfaced again and again. When a recurring issue, such as conflict (i.e. storming), occupied the group's attention as a major developmental task, that issue tended to have a wide spiral at that time and a smaller spiral at other times.

The Value of Conflict

In contrast to the other two groups, the Sanderson group had moved beyond the storming stage. It had worked through the two major problem areas confronting most groups: the issues of leadership and cohesion. Because we adopted a relatively passive role in the group, actual leadership had to be determined by group members. On the whole, the group shared most of the leadership functions and thereby achieved greater control of its own destiny. However, after two months, Sanderson later emerged as the unofficial and unstated group leader. We found this indicative of the group taking responsibility. This aspect was clearly demonstrated after meeting number ten (a particularly stormy one) had concluded: one group member said to the facilitator "Thank you for attending our meeting."

---

[22]Tuckman, Bruce W. & Jensen, M.A C (1977). Stages of small-group development revisited. Group and Organization Studies, 2(4), 419-427.

The Sanderson group became more cohesive by handling two conflictual situations that appeared early in the group's life. The first open conflict arose when it became apparent that Mason needed immediate short-term bridging finance of some $300,000, otherwise his new venture would be seriously retarded, or worse. Two group members saw this as an opportunity to pick up a substantial ownership in a high potential company very cheaply (e.g. the five year forecast was $300 million in sales). Two other group members thought they might be able to help Mason. The factions were at odds with each other and with Mason for "not getting his act together". Within a couple of weeks, many unofficial sub-group meetings took place and the conflict was openly discussed in the official group meetings. Just as this situation appeared to be resolved, Chuck Bates withdrew from the program. His letter denigrating the value of the program and of the group meetings produced a tension which was only resolved after frequent inter-member phone calls and much group discussion. Working through these conflicts certainly helped the group develop greater cohesion and become a performing, strong-tie network.

Group Roles in the Start-Up Process

Because of its cohesion, the group facilitated the development of three new ventures considerably. The group strongly believed that the probability of success for each was enhanced. We concurred. The members of the Sanderson group offered and received five types of help for their new ventures: 1) the transformation of a dream; 2) increased aspiration level; 3) stimulating ideas; 4) practical help; and 5) a sense of support.

First, we saw the group as playing a valuable yet unexpected role in the envisioning process. The group helped Peters transform what she later described as "just a dream" into a possible reality. It pushed Peters to come up with her own idea for a franchisable fast food concept. Subsequently, in an electrically charged presentation, she described her vision to the group. She then translated that into a business plan outline, an artist's rendition of a store, sample menus and a store design with equipment specifications. She has conducted consumer research on both the protypical facilities design and on the menu offerings. She has put in a lot of time and effort to make her new venture idea a reality. The group has had a powerful and transformational affect.

Increasing aspirations was a second role which emerged. Amazingly, but consistent with the theory, two successful owner-managers actually had their level of aspiration increased by the group. Peters' self-concept moved from that of holding an "area franchise" and obtaining income from a limited number of stores to a position where she now sees herself as being the lead entrepreneur of a her own chain. Carter's initial presentation of a gas bar/car wash/food store development located in a section of a large site was expanded to a redevelopment of the entire site and a plan to use the operation as a prototype for a series of similar businesses. Carter's self-concept has moved from running a business started by his father to creating and managing a new venture of his own which promised to produce greater returns than the electrical business. Clearly the group fostered dissonance between Carter's and Peters' self-esteem and public-esteem. Carter and Peters removed that dissonance by adjusting their aspirations, for their new ventures, and their self-esteem, upward. Personal change in matters of utmost importance to the two individuals has been an impressive outcome.

The group saw itself as playing a third important role in the start-up process by stimulating ideas. The group offered an occasion to change one's perception, be intellectually challenged, gain new insights, and find new opportunities. Whenever this occurred, an aura of excitement permeated the meeting; sometimes there was even a feeling of surprise. Mason's perceptions of the problems likely to be encountered with his proposed new venture in the high-tech graphics field were altered drastically as a result of group input. The sophistication of Carter's gas bar/car wash/food store site redevelopment appreciated greatly over the six month period. Finally, new markets were identified for Peters' venture idea. These new directions have helped advance the new ventures substantially

Another role played by the group in the start-up process was the provision of down-to-earth, practical help. The group offered an opportunity to identify and solve problems, practice skills (e.g. presentations) and receive concrete, practical suggestions. From a relatively ethereal venture plan, Mason's project has been advanced considerably. The group helped him acquire short-term bridging finance to take over a small Arizona plant which had all the equipment necessary for building prototypes and providing limited production. The group helped him prepare a more realistic business plan, in language understood by the group. The group assisted in the hiring of a key technical person. Generally, the group helped Mason overcome many of the limitations in his original proposal. Peters and Carter also received useful advice. Carter accomplished a higher level of market research that likely will help his food store. Peters changed her ideas of location completely, from being located only in shopping centres to being more market driven. In all three cases, the new ventures have benefited.

A fifth role played by a cohesive group of peers in the new venture development process is one of support. The Sanderson group seemed to supply a very strong sense of support. The group meetings provided a place where the members could share discouragements and have success appreciated, where confidence and energy could be renewed, and where they could feel less alone. Although the program formally ended after six months, the Sanderson group still continued to meet regularly every two weeks. Apparently, the group has met a felt need for support which has affected the process of new venture development in a positive manner.

The five roles played by the members of the Sanderson group encapsulate our major findings. Therefore, we found it useful to examine the theoretical foundations of our hypotheses. Also, we plot the relative progress of the three new ventures, comment on the influence of our action learning program and suggest some implications.

## Links with Theory

Having determined the key roles played by a cohesive group in the start-up process, we attempted, albeit very cursorily, to match our findings with other theoretical constructs. Primarily, we were interested in theory backed by empirical research. We found strong links in four of the five roles we had identified.

While there were a number of general statements in the purported value of the group in the envisioning process, we could not find any empirical evidence of this role. On the other hand, the group role of increasing aspiration level is well documented in the psychotherapy literature; the role relating to new ideas and changing perspectives is extensively catalogued in the group dynamics and creativity literature; the role of practical help has been given ample evidence by the self-help groups; and the role of support has been written about in both the group dynamics and entrepreneurship literature[23].

## Progress of the New Ventures

The progress of each of the three new ventures can be plotted schematically over time. Peters mentioned that she would come up with an idea for a new venture early in the second month and then proceeded to describe her new venture to the group later in the month. There seemed to be little progress until she produced an outline of a plan. The next step came when she produced a sample of menus and a protypical design in the fifth month. The last jump occurred when Peters decided that her concept should be market-driven rather than shopping centre-oriented.

Carter's new venture seemed to have three milestones: the first occurred when he was in the process of negotiating with several oil companies and the group was able to offer valuable suggestions; the second took place when he outlined his concept for a chain of gas bar/car wash/food store operations; and the third happened when the original development was transformed into a complete site development.

Mason's new venture did not seem to be progressing at all until the group examined his financial needs more closely and "suggested", to

---

[23]See for example, Aldrich, Howard and Zimmer, C. (1986) Entrepreneurship though social networks. In D. L. Sexton and R. Smilor (Eds.), The Art and Science of Entrepreneurship (pp. 3 - 24). Cambridge, MA. : Ballinger.

put it mildly, that he had "better get his act together".  After some members of the group helped provide short-term bridging finance, Mason's new venture generally proceeded on an upward track, with the next milestone being the production of a business plan.

Although Mason's new venture appeared to be better developed than Carter's at the start of the program,  Carter has made much more progress.  Peters started with a dream and has made a substantial advancement.  However, she will not likely be in a position to earn revenue until well after Carter and Mason do, unless she decides to engage in a test-market.  Carter appears to be on track to produce revenue before Mason (see Figure 1)

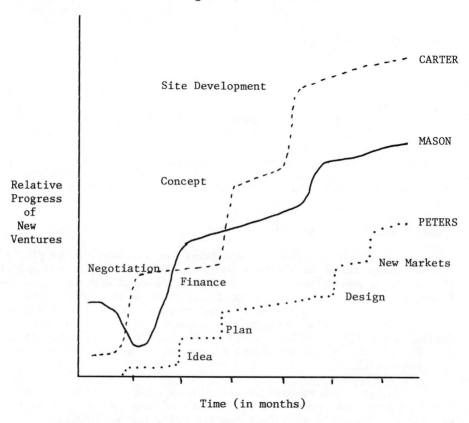

Figure 1:          Progress of New Ventures in Six Months

Influence of Action Learning Program

Although we have largely attributed the progress of three new ventures to the cohesiveness of the Sanderson group, we believe that these findings were very much related to the social context in which the group was formed and by which its members were affected.  There was a definite interaction between the seminars and the small group meetings. For example, frameworks presented in the seminars were examined and discussed in the group. It seemed to us that the program, Action Learning for Owner/Managers, provided the social context in which the Sanderson group could facilitate the development of new ventures.

## Implications of Findings

We believe that the implications for facilitating further new venture developments are clear: combine a number of successful owner-managers with a number of people with new venture ideas (say four or five of each); ensure a blend of learning styles and psychological types; help them become a mature, cohesive group through the use of a skilled facilitator; and have them enter an action learning program similar to the one described above. This will likely result in repeated new venture creation.

## CONCLUSION

We found that a strong-tie, peer network can contribute signficantly to new venture development. The network accomplishes this by playing five key roles in the start-up process:

1.  It can actually help transform a dream into a reality. It can help one envision a new venture.

2.  It can increase one's level of aspiration and therefore substantially advance the scope of a new venture.

3.  It can stimulate ideas, encourage creativity, and give one a different perspective. It can help one find new opportunities. It can enhance a new venture considerably.

4.  It can provide practical, concrete assistance. It can overcome shortcomings and increase a new venture's probability of success.

5.  It can supply a support system which can reduce or remove the sense of loneliness common to many founders. Indirectly, it can help add value to the new venture.

While a peer network can make a positive and powerful contribution to new venture development, the social context for success likely resides in a program similar to Action Learning for Owner/Managers. We propose to do follow-up research with our owner-manager program participants and alumni. This will help validate (or disconfirm) our preliminary findings on the use of peer networks in the start-up process.

SUMMARY

M.D.'S WHO HAVE GIVEN UP CLINICAL PRACTICE TO BECOME ENTREPRENEURS:
CIRCUMSTANCES, EXPERIENCE-TO-DATE, AND RISK PROPENSITY PROFILES

Authors

    O. Jay Krasner
    Michael S. Krasner
    Scott A. Krasner

Address

    School of Business and Management, Pepperdine University
    3415 Sepulveda Blvd.
    Los Angeles, CA 90034
    (213) 425-5551

Principal Topics

This paper examines a sample of M.D.s who, after completion of medical school and residencies, and performing in clinical practice for a number of years, give up a generally lucrative practice to found and manage new business enterprises. What circumstances led to the "launch"? What has been the "track record" to date, and what problems have been perceived to be the most severe so far? What risk-taking propensities do they exhibit, particularly in comparison with non-entrepreneurial MBA candidates?

Method and Data Base

Depth interviews were conducted with each of fifteen M.D. Entrepreneurs. In addition to descriptive responses as to biography, circumstances surrounding the decision to launch, and experiences since, responses were obtained on a risk-propensity instrument ("Dilemmas of Choice") and a "Problem Severity Perception" instrument used in four previous studies of non-M.D. entrepreneurs.

Interviewees were located by: (a) Alumni records at Medical Schools at U.C., San Diego, and University of Arizona, (b) Alumni records of the Presidential and Executive MBA programs at Pepperdine University; (c) Listings of CEO's in various directories; and (d) informal networks. Interviewees' current ages range from mid-thirties to mid-sixties, and their M.D. degrees from 1949 to 1979. Decisions to leave clinical practice date from 1971 to 1986. The individual time-interval between completion of medical school and decision-to-launch ranges from 1 year to 25 years (Median: 9 years; mid-range: 7 to 15 years). Three of the 15 recently completed MBA degrees, all after launching their enterprises.

The enterprises have been operating from 1 to 16 years (Mid-Range: 4 to 9 years). Eight of the fifteen produce tangible products for health care diagnosis/delivery, three more produce non-medical tangible products. The four others deliver health care related services. Information obtained on interview has been analyzed primarily through descriptive statistics; qualitative classification logic has also been used.

Major Findings

1. Circumstances Leading to "Launch": The marketabilty of the product/service was estimated by: (a) being in, or close to, the technological breakthrough (5 enterprises), (b) sensing a need as a clinician (5), (c) government studies/reports (2), (d) favorable responses from friends (2). Only one used a formal, "textbook" opportunity search.

Regarding the technology required: (a) it was founder-developed (8 enterprises), (b) licensed from the developer (4), (c) did not require licensing (3). Regarding the Key People Consulted: (a) Experts in the technology (13 enterprises), (b) Experts in Finance/Accounting (4), (c) Experts in Legal Aspects (2), (d) Experts in General Management (2), and (d) one sought no experts ("M.D. arrogance").

Regarding initial assumptions as to Financial Needs the amounts needed ranged from $25,000 to $2,800,000 (Mid-range: $150,000 to $500,000). Sources sought/provided: Private Placements (5 enterprises), Founder Funding (3), Venture Capitalist Firms (3), Close Friends (2), Vendor and 3rd-party asset funding (1), and Government Grant (1). Annual income from clinical practice the year prior to launching: Nine interviewees provided the information: Median income: $140,000 (Mid-range $100,000 to $200,000).

2. "Track-Record-to Date". Number of persons on the payroll seemed the best indicator of growth, in a few instances, sales revenue was used. Profitability data was largely unavailable. Three of the 15 are in their first year, two others have had essentially no growth over their 3 to 6 years. Of the other ten enterprises, the median annual rate of growth is 33%!. The mid-range is 25% to 47% growth per year!

3. Problem Severity Perceptions. The findings here will be discussed in detail in the full paper, since the date covers each respondent's perceptions of severity in each of 38 problem areas, in each of three phases of the enterprise's history. A few highlights here of the problems perceived to be most severe.

```
     -"At launch":   First, problems in product/service development,
                     reliability, and cost-effectiveness of perfor-
                     mance.
                     Second, financing problems.
     -"Now":         First, financing problems.
                     Second, marketing and sales problems.
```

Differences in problem perception profiles between the fastest and
"slowest" growing enterprises do not appear to be significant.
There are some significant differences from the profiles of non-M.D.
enterprises (previous studies).

4. Risk Propensities. On each of the following scenarios, comparisons between these respondents and non-entrepreneurial M.B.A.'s
are summarized:

-Locating a New Plant: Home country v. foreign country; and
Starting a New Firm. On both of these scenarios, M.D. entrepreneurs
are significantly more risk-aversive than non-entrepreneurial
M.B.A.'s.

-Heart Operation v. Restrictive Life-Style: M.D. entrepreneurs are
extremely risk-aversive here, and significantly above non-
entrepreneurial M.B.A.'s.

-"Cashing-out" Present Position and Re-investing in New Firm: M.D.
entrepreneurs are significantly risk-aversive here; non-
entrepreneurial M.B.A.'s are risk-seeking here.

## Major Implications

These entrepreneurs are different from "traditional". They are not
immigrants, not locked within corporate hierarchies, not frustrated
by little autonomy, and certainly not facing a limited financial
future "working for someone else". Further, many of their enterprises are significant new employers in an increasingly technology-base
new venture dependent economy.

We need to learn more about them and their ventures.

WOMEN ENTREPRENEURS:   A LONGITUDINAL STUDY

Robert D. Hisrich, The University of Tulsa
Candida G. Brush, Brush & Coogan Associates

## ABSTRACT

While the area of women entrepreneurs is receiving increased attention in terms of government concern, research activity and media coverage, there has been little effort to evaluate the entrepreneurial process of either men or women over time.

This paper explores this important topic in the case of women entrepreneurs, the fastest growing group of entrepreneurs, by analyzing the results of a longitudinal study of women entrepreneurs throughout the United States.  Not only are such areas as personal characteristics, family background, management skills, the entrepreneurial venture, and problems investigated, but as well the success rate and growth (or lack thereof).

## INTRODUCTION

Forming, ramping up, and growing a new venture is difficult under any circumstances.  The experience is filled with hard work, loneliness and uncertainty.  For the woman entrepreneur, the process of starting and operating a new enterprise can be even more difficult because they often lack the skills, education and support systems that can facilitate their efforts.  In 1972, Bureau of Census statistics indicated that female-owned businesses accounted for only 4.6 percent of all firms in the United States.  Even though they make up a relatively small proportion of the total number of entrepreneurs, the recent growth of women entrepreneurs has been significant.  The Small Business Administration reports that the number of self-employed women increased by 35 percent between 1977 and 1982.

### Background

Research on women entrepreneurs is limited with most previous studies usually focusing on male entrepreneurs.  However, interest in women business owners is increasing, with areas such as backgrounds, motivations for starting their own companies and business problems having been investigated.

One study of twenty female entrepreneurs identified several major motivations for starting a business: the need to achieve, the desire to be independent, the need for job satisfaction and economic necessity. These female entrepreneurs tended to have an autocratic style of management, with their major problem during start up being credit discrimination. Underestimating operating and/or marketing costs was a subsequent problem.[1]

Another study focusing on demographic characteristics, motivations and business problems of twenty-one women entrepreneurs found that they had particular problems with collateral, obtaining credit, and overcoming society's belief that women are not as serious as men about business.[2]

The characteristic of women entrepreneurs and differences by type of business was explored in another study. The results indicated that women entrepreneurs were older and more educated than either the general populace or the respondents in previous studies. They also had very supportive parents and husbands. Female entrepreneurs in nontraditional business areas (finance, insurance, manufacturing and construction) also differed from their counterparts in more traditionally "female" business areas (retail and wholesale trade), with those in the more traditional areas having particular difficulty in acquiring external financial sources.[3]

A study of 20 female entrepreneurs with one or more years operating a retail or service firm indicated that female entrepreneurs had problems in obtaining funds to start and operate the business as well as operational problems in the areas of record keeping, financial management, and advertising.[4]

A final study of women entrepreneurs indicated that the woman entrepreneur is typically the first born child of middle class parents who starts her first business venture in the service area at the age of

---

[1]Eleanor B. Schwartz, "Entrepreneurship: A New Female Frontier," Journal of Contemporary Business, (Winter, 1979), pp. 47-76.

[2]Robert D. Hisrich and Marie O'Brien, "The Woman Entrepreneur from a Business and Sociological Perspective," Proceedings, 1981 Conference on Entrepreneurship, (June, 1981), pp. 21-39.

[3]Robert D. Hisrich and Marie O'Brien, "The Woman Entrepreneur as a Reflection of the Type of Business," Proceedings, 1982 Conference on Entrepreneurship, (June, 1982), pp. 54-67.

[4]Eric T. Pellegrino and Barry L. Reece, "Perceived Formative and Operational Problems Encountered by Female Entrepreneurs in Retail and Service Firms," Journal of Small Business Management, (April, 1982), pp. 15-24.

35 after obtaining a liberal arts degree and raising children. Typical weaknesses were in finance, marketing, and business operations.[5]

The basic characteristics, problems, and prescriptions for success for women entrepreneurs who start and grow a company as well as the mechanisms needed for so doing are covered in a recent book. In addition to presenting methods for a potential entrepreneur assessing their risk taking ability and feelings on independence and control, aspects of starting a business such as developing a business plan, obtaining a bank loan or venture capital, and establishing a support system and network are discussed.[6]

While all this research has provided valuable insights into the nature and characteristics of the woman entrepreneur and her business, many questions remained unanswered: How successful are the ventures they create? Do women entrepreneurs grow their firms in an aggressive manner? Do the businesses continue to have increasing sales and profits? What is the legal form of the business? Have there been any changes in major business problems since the venture was started? To what extent do women entrepreneurs plan?

RESEARCH DESIGN

In order to provide answers to these questions and in effect to ascertain the nature of successful and unsuccessful businesses of women entrepreneurs, a questionnaire was developed which contained a mixture of scaled, dichotomous, multiple choice, open-ended, and rank-order questions. The questions assessed the characteristics of the business including the age, legal form, financial aspects, sales, number of employees, and income derived. Also aspects of the woman entrepreneur such as management skills, networking, resources used, personal and business problems, and selected demographic characteristics.

This questionnaire was sent to the 344 women entrepreneurs who were identified in the original nationwide sample of 468 women entrepreneurs.

---

[5]Robert D. Hisrich and Candida Brush, "The Woman Entrepreneur: Implications of Family, Educational, and Occupational Experience," Proceedings, 1983 Conference on Entrepreneurship, (April, 1983), pp. 255-270.

[6]Robert D. Hisrich and Candida G. Brush, The Woman Entrepreneur: Starting, Managing, and Financing a Successful New Business, Lexington Books, Lexington Mass, 1986.

The findings from the survey will be discussed in four major areas: the demographic composition and background of the entrepreneurs; the nature of the present venture; the changes that have occurred in the business venture; and the present entrepreneurial situation.

## Demographic Composition and Background

Of the women entrepreneurs sampled, 143 responded. However, this paper is based on the responses of 136 as 7 arrived too late to be included in the analysis. The majority of the respondents were between 38 and 48 years old, with an average age of 46 years. Fifty-six percent indicated they were married (an increase of 3% from the original survey)[7] while the proportions of divorced, engaged, never married, and widowed showed little change. Forty-two percent had children and the majority of their children were over 20 years old. Fifty percent of the respondents were first born and typically came from middle class backgrounds.

Over 62% had attended college; of these, nearly 70% majored in liberal arts in a variety of areas. Engineering and science were infrequent areas of study. Thirty-three percent had graduate degrees with business and law the most commonly specified majors. The parents of the women entrepreneurs also tended to be well educated, particularly their fathers with over half having attended college. Only a small percentage of the parents were blue collar workers; instead one-third of the fathers were self-employed and nearly one-half of the mothers were housewives. Like the parents of the women entrepreneurs, the spouses had attained a high level of education (68% had college or graduate degrees); however, they were most often employed in professional or technical occupations (60%). For 80% of the respondents, the entrepreneurial venture was their first and 64% of the total sample had experience in the field of their present venture. Most recent occupations were service oriented, typically in administration, teaching, retail, or secretarial, reflecting their liberal arts college education.

The majority of the respondents had a current personal income of less than $50,000 (64%) with 10% earning over $100,000 annually. This is a significant increase from the original survey 5 years ago as the original study indicated 83% earned less than $50,000 per year. The income of the spouses increased in nearly the same proportion as that of the women entrepreneur, with the spouses still earning more money.

---

[7] Robert D. Hisrich and Candida G. Brush, "The Woman Entrepreneur: Management Skills and Business Problems," Journal of Small Business Management, Vol. 22, No. 1 (January, 1984), pp. 30-37.

## Nature of Present Venture

The majority of the women entrepreneurs responding operated services businesses (87%) while 9% were engaged in manufacturing and 4% in financial businesses. This breakdown approximates the responses of the original survey where corresponding percentages were: 90%, 7%, and 3% respectively. The average age of the venture was again consistent with the elapsed time in the studies as the majority of the businesses are now over 7 years old versus 27% being in this category in 1982. While the nature of the business venture varied from electrical construction to harp manufacturer, the most popular areas of business were retail sales, consulting, personnel, business services and public relations. The majority of the businesses were not based on revolutionary innovations. Rather, the most frequently stated competitive strengths were quality of service/product, experience and specialization in the market.

The average gross revenues of the businesses of the women entrepreneurs were between $99,000 and $500,000 with average revenues of about $100,000 (see Table 4). Most of the businesses were funded initially by personal sources of financing rather than outside sources. Personal assets (71%) and savings (37%) were most frequently mentioned personal sources while for outside funds, twenty-five percent relied on bank loans at start-up and nine percent received loans from their spouses. Not surprisingly, both venture capital and government funding were employed in less than one percent of the cases at start-up. Similarly in the INC. magazine report of the 500 fastest growing privately held companies, only two percent utilized venture capital and four percent government loans in their start-up phases.

TABLE 1

Personal and Outside Sources of
Financing at Start-up

| Personal Sources* | | Outside Sources | |
|---|---|---|---|
| Personal Assets | 71% | No Outside Financing | 43% |
| Savings | 37% | Bank Loan | 27% |
| Other (family, | | Spouse | 11% |
| clients, insur.) | 11% | Other (credit cards) | 11% |
| None | 7% | Business Associate | 4% |
| Stocks | 7% | Relative | 2% |
| Home Mortgage | 6% | Government | 1% |
| Retirement Funds | 4% | Venture Capital | 1% |
| Average | $17,248 | Average | $33,000 |
| Mode | $ 5,000 | Mode | $ 5,000 |

TOTAL CAPITALIZATION: AVERAGE $23,000
53% INVESTED LESS THAN $5,000

*Total is greater than 100% due to multiple responses.

Although the range of total capitalization for the businesses started by the women entrepreneurs was from 0 to $271,000, the average amount is relatively low as 53% started their businesses with less than $5,000 (see Table 1). Half of the women invested $4,000 or less of their personal resources and, of those who went beyond personal resources, 50% used $10,000 or less from outside sources. Most important, 43% did not seek any outside capital at start-up and 26% have never employed outside financing. These statistics are not surprising given the size and type of most of the businesses. Service businesses such as management consulting, personnel services or interior design do not require large amounts of working capital or need to purchase expensive equipment to open their doors. However, it is apparent that many of the women entrepreneurs needed working capital or start-up funds in the early stages of development as 52% indicated they had applied for outside financing in the first three years of operation (see Table 2). For current financing, 51% of the women entrepreneurs use current profits reinvested and 56% have used bank loans. Government funds and venture capital are still used by less than 1%.

TABLE 2

Age of Business When First Sought Outside Financing

| less than 1 year | 31% |
| 1 to 3 years | 21% |
| 4 to 5 years | 10% |
| 6 to 8 years | 7% |
| 9 to 12 years | 4% |
| Never used outside financing | 26% |

Thirty-four percent of the women entrepreneurs indicated they had difficulty in raising funds for their businesses. They felt their inability to secure funds was due to: lack of a credit line (22%), lack of collateral (18%), and loan bias (18%). While it is difficult to verify specific instances of actual loan discrimination, rejection due to perceived loan bias may in fact be due to the lack of a credit history, inadequate management experience, insufficient collateral or lack of a business track record.[8] Since many more male entrepreneurs have a personal credit rating, own assets, have experience with bank loans and possess management experience, women entrepreneurs may be at a disadvantage (but are not necessarily being discriminated against) in securing outside capital. For example, 55% of the women able to obtain bank loans after building their venture, thereby fulfilling bank loan requirements.

---

[8]Len Furtuck, "Survey of Small Business Lending Practices," Journal of Small Business Management, Vol. 20 (October, 1982), p. 34.

The nature of business problems under present operations are fairly typical of any small business 7-10 years old. Personnel, inadequate time at administrative activities, cash flow, market research, high operating expenses and training employees were frequently a problem (see Table 6). The most pressing problem was time needed to accomplish administrative activities; as one woman entrepreneur stated: "I overestimated my energy level and underestimated the paperwork."

While many respondents noted personnel difficulties as a frequent problem in the scaled questions, nearly 25% indicated difficulties with finding and keeping good employees in response to the open-ended question regarding biggest obstacle encountered. A typical comment: "I thought establishing my business would be the most difficult part - this is not the case; finding loyal employees and managing them well is more difficult." There is a bit of a paradox in this problem in light of the original survey indicating that dealing with people was a business strength for the woman entrepreneur. This may either reflect a lack of experience in managing employees or simply an initial overrating when self-assessing a business strength. Regardless, personnel problems and the other difficulties cited by the respondents are actually not gender based but common to any small 7 to 10 year old business. Areas frequently mentioned as not being a problem included decision making (40%), inadequate facilities (28%), credit lines (34%) and high debt (30%).

While the planning function was most often the sole responsibility of the woman entrepreneur (64%), many respondents indicated that participative planning was practiced with either employees, a management team, board of directors or co-owners. The high proportion of respondents assuming total planning responsibility reflects the small number of employees - 83% indicated they had less than 10 employees. The nature of business planning did vary from annual budgeting (58%), to long range - 2-5 year forecasts (35%), to strategic planning (42%). On the other side of the continuum, 2% indicated no planning, 2% "seat of the pants planning", and 6% had unwritten plans.

Changes that Have Occurred in the Venture

In the 5 years that elapsed between the surveys, several changes occurred in the business ventures of the women entrepreneurs in areas of legal form, size in terms of employees and revenues, scope of markets served, and business problems.

At the time of the first survey, 55% of the businesses were sole proprietorships, 23% were incorporated, and an additional 10% operated as S corporations. This changed significantly as today 51% are now incorporated, 8% are S corporations, and 33% remain as sole proprietorships. The change to a more formal legal structure is fairly typical of growing enterprises. In terms of controlling interest in this business structure, only 14% own less than 50% of their enterprise.

The size of the businesses have increased only slightly in numbers of employees in the past 5 years (see Table 3). The typical business employed less than 10 part- and full-time employees in 1981 and the

same is true for current operations.  There is a decrease in the percentage of responses in the "none" category from 31% to 23% reflecting some
growth.


TABLE 3


Numbers of Employees 1981-1986

| | 1981 | | 1986 | |
|---|---|---|---|---|
| | Full-Time | Part-Time | Full-Time | Part-Time |
| None | 31% | 29% | 23% | 29% |
| 1-10 | 53% | 62% | 60% | 64% |
| 11-20 | 14% | 7% | 11% | 5% |
| 21-30 | 3% | 4% | 4% | 1% |
| 51-100 | 1% | 0 | 1% | 2% |


There has been steady growth in gross revenues for the women
business owners in the past 5 years (see Table 4).  In the original
study, 47% grossed less than $100,000 while only 16% grossed over
$500,000.  In the follow-up study, 29% of the respondents had revenues
of under $100,000, 26% over $500,000.  The mode was in the $100,000-
$499,999 bracket and the average has grown from $65,000 to $100,000,
reflecting an increase of 54% in six years or an average annual growth
rate of about 7% per year.


TABLE 4


Gross Revenues 1981-1986

| | 1980 | 1981 | 1984 | 1985 | 1986 |
|---|---|---|---|---|---|
| <29,999 | 23% | 17% | 17% | 14% | 11% |
| 29,999-99,999 | 25% | 25% | 20% | 14% | 17% |
| 100,000-499,999 | 36% | 40% | 54% | 57% | 46% |
| 500,000-999,999 | 9% | 10% | 6% | 9% | 17% |
| 1,000,000-4,999,999 | 7% | 8% | 3% | 6% | 9% |
| >5,000,000 | 0 | 0 | 0 | 0 | 0 |

1980 average $ 65,000
1981 average $ 72,000
1984 average $ 79,000
1985 average $ 86,000
1986 average $100,000

Compared to the 1982 U.S. Economic Census which found that half of all women-owned businesses earned under $5,000, this is a significant increase. Still, the typical business of the woman entrepreneur is relatively small and growing moderately. When revenues are compared to other groups, for example the delegates to the White House Conference on Small Business in 1986 (35% female, 65% male), 68% of that group earned over $500,000.

Another important measure of growth is changes in the scope of the business and plans for expansion (see Table 5). Seventy-three percent of the businesses served only local markets while only 7% and 3% served national and international markets respectively 5 years ago. Currently, 48% operate on a local scope while 17% and 15% serve national and international markets, a good indication of expansion and growth. In addition, women entrepreneurs also show their interest in moving forward by their willingness to add new products or services and drop older ones. Twenty-five percent indicated they had dropped mature products or services and 72% presently have plans to expand by: adding new services/products, moving to larger facilities, increasing volume, and/or servicing new markets. Nearly 25% planned to sell their venture while 17% intend to acquire another business and 8% hoped to sell a division or product.

TABLE 5

Scope of the Business at Start-up
and Present Operations

|               | Start-up | Present Operations |
|---------------|----------|--------------------|
| Local         | 73%      | 48%                |
| State         | 10%      | 14%                |
| Regional      | 7%       | 14%                |
| National      | 7%       | 17%                |
| International | 3%       | 15%                |

While the growth in sales and employees has been moderate, there is certainly evidence of growth in scope of business as well as the sophistication of management planning. The women entrepreneurs often commented on the importance of planning, moving ahead, not getting lazy and maintaining an external focus. One representative comment was: "Constantly reevaluate your priorities - make decisions in reference to that. Follow your intuition as to what you want to spend your time doing in the future, don't drift too far from your area of competence, and these will influence you to stay the course, sell or expand."

Change in the nature of the business is also indicated in the types of problems encountered at start-up compared to those occurring during current operations (see Table 6). The earlier study identified start-up problems predominately related to management experience and obtaining financing, while current operating difficulties measured in the second survey have shifted towards personnel and marketing as well as finance. It is interesting to note it is not so much the availability of credit that is the financial obstacle, rather difficulties in managing the capital resources of the enterprise. While this is commonly a problem for small businesses, women entrepreneurs may have greater difficulties in sophisticated financing not only because of their lack of experience and background, but also because of perceived risk. At start-up, 65% viewed their greatest risk as financial while psychic risk was second at 23%. The perceived psychic risk decreased to 8% in current operations, but the financial risk is still perceived as very high for 54% of the respondents. Also, 17% felt "Other Risks" (such as personnel, competition and markets) were factors in current operations. One woman entrepreneur offered this explanation for women's difficulties in managing finances and taking financial risks: "Because of our socialization, we are not comfortable being with money. We need to assess our own attitudes about how we feel money, because we sometimes subconsciously plan for whatever we grew up with; feasting and famines, tight budgets, cash abundance, leverage, or whatever."

TABLE 6

Business Problems at Start-up and
Current Operations

Start-up

| Lack of Experience in Financial Planning | 30% |
| Obtaining Credit | 27% |
| Lack of Business Training | 27% |
| Demands on Personal Time | 22% |
| Lack of Guidance and Counsel | 22% |
| Weak Collateral Position | 21% |
| Lack of Management Experience | 21% |

Current Operations

| Inadequate Time for Managerial Functions | 31% |
| Lack of Working Capital | 28% |
| Selection and Supervision of Personnel | 27% |
| Fluctuations in Cash Flow | 26% |
| Training and Developing New Employees | 23% |
| High Operating Expenses | 23% |
| Slow Collections | 22% |
| Market Research | 22% |

## Present Entrepreneurial Situation

For women entrepreneurs, there has been little change in their management skills and support systems over the five year period. The self-assessment of business skills for the respondent group reflected interesting changes particularly in the area of dealing with people. In the original survey, this skill was self-assessed as being very good to excellent for the majority. In the second survey, self-assessed ratings were only average. This reflects the previously stated problems in finding, training and maintaining personnel which may have lessened the confidence of the respondents in this self-assessment. The current assessment of other business skills shows slightly higher ratings in marketing and idea generation, which were rated excellent. Finance and business operations are still rated only average.

Women entrepreneurs do show a continued willingness to seek business guidance and education to compensate for any skill weaknesses. Nearly 80% of the respondents have attended seminars in business to obtain or improve business skills. In addition, 65% have utilized expert advice, 62% used self-help books, and 61% have participated in trade workshops. This willingness is reflected in following comments: "Contact financial people for advice, seek professional marketing expertise and in general hire the best experts for your needs." "Continue to learn techniques and keep up by joining associations, trades, support groups, and attending seminars." The respondents rated their best source of business guidance as other entrepreneurs (58%), while accountants were second (43%), and women in business and other experts were rated nearly equal with 38% and 39% respectively.

The types of support systems and networks remained nearly the same. The results of both surveys showed spouses, business associates, and friends as the biggest moral supporters. Sources of business guidance also remained fairly similar with 55% participating in women groups and a slightly greater number participating in trade associations (an increase from 49% to 57%). Friends and social acquaintances decreased in importance for business guidance as the enterprise became more established.

### SUMMARY AND CONCLUSION

The typical woman entrepreneur operating an established venture is 46 years old, married, has 2 children over 20 years old and has operated her service-oriented business for 8 years. She is college educated, usually in liberal arts, and has had occupational experience in the service area. Her personal income averages $50,000 per year and she maintains a controlling interest in the business which is her first entrepreneurial effort.

Characteristics of an established venture owned by the typical woman business owner are: gross revenues of $100,000, start-up funding mainly through personal assets, and a total investment of $5,000 at start-up. Most ventures rely on profit reinvestment and bank loans for current financing. The biggest business problems are lack of adequate time for administrative activities, cash flow and personnel. Planning is conducted by the entrepreneur alone and is frequently strategic in nature.

The findings of this longitudinal study indicate that the majority of the businesses operated by women entrepreneurs have been moderately successful, providing increases in revenues of about 7% per year. Of the original sample, between 30-40% have failed or are no longer in business for themselves. This is certainly a much lower failure rate than the frequently mentioned national average of 75% of all new businesses failing in the first five years. Nevertheless, the size of the typical woman owned enterprise remains small with 10 or less employees and gross revenues of less than $500,000. On the other hand, the geographic and market scope of the business is expanding rapidly and the woman entrepreneur continues to improve her business skills, and practices strategic planning.

What are the implications of these findings? Although there are some differences in established enterprises of male and female entrepreneurs, these are mainly attributable to the type of venture and its length of time in operation rather than to the gender of the entrepreneur. The problems, support systems, and planning function are essentially the same. However, since the woman entrepreneur more often lacks business experience and a financial track record at start-up, obstacles in the financial area are often more difficult for her to overcome. As the woman entrepreneur gains experience and knowledge, her ability to obtain financing and manage the business improves.

But, why do the businesses of women entrepreneurs remain small in terms of revenues and number of employees, and still experience financial difficulties? There are several possible explanations ranging from lack of market potential, to desire to maintain equity control, to contentedness with present growth patterns. The lack of education and occupational experience typical of most women entrepreneurs as well as a perceived high financial risk probably contributes to a more conservative approach to financial matters. Women entrepreneurs either have not had the opportunity to obtain the resources, have lacked the business skills and track record, or have not had the confidence to create a fast growing multi-million dollar enterprise. There are also many women who consider the importance of quality of their work lives over "bigness" as stated by one woman entrepreneur: "Relax and enjoy it! Structure your business so it makes money, a smaller volume and forget empire building."

This approach has resulted in the women entrepreneurs' businesses experiencing steady growth, solid planning, adaptation to changing markets as well as a lower percentage of business closings. A major obstacle yet to be overcome for most is continued difficulties in cash flow and working capital. One of the keys to continued success is the manager's ability to obtain resources, deploy them creatively and manage them effectively. The best suggestion for overcoming these obstacles is for women entrepreneurs to work on building a personal credit rating and business track record in early operations. Hiring experts, taking courses, and collecting information and opinions from the financial community can help the woman entrepreneur obtain skills and be better informed in her decisions as well. The importance of planning also cannot be stressed - three-fourths of the women mentioned careful planning as their advice to aspiring women entrepreneurs.

Research on women entrepreneurs should continue as more information is needed on: the nature of the businesses that failed, the availability of seed capital, and psychological perceptions of women and their attitudes towards risk and money. Comparisons of male and female entrepreneurial enterprises, their problems and success by industry would also provide valuable information.

None of the women entrepreneurs in either study regretted their efforts. Many admitted to "taking their lumps", hard work, commitment, and frustration, but the majority said they would do it again - start another business if they sold their present one. The following quote reflects the opinions of many of the respondents: "My biggest misconception was that it was a risk. In retrospect, ONLY working for others is risky. It is better to steer the motorcycle than to sit on the back."

## REFERENCES

Furtuck, Len, "Survey of Small Business Lending Practices," Journal of Small Business Management, Vol. 20 (October, 1982), p. 34.

Hisrich, Robert D. and Candida Brush, "The Woman Entrepreneur: Implications of Family, Educational, and Occupational Experience," Proceedings, 1983 Conference on Entrepreneurship, (April, 1983), pp. 255-270.

Hisrich, Robert D. and Candida G. Brush, "The Woman Entrepreneur: Management Skills and Business Problems," Journal of Small Business Management, Vol. 22, No. 1 (January, 1984), pp. 30-37.

Hisrich, Robert D. and Candida G. Brush, The Woman Entrepreneur: Starting, Managing, and Financing a Successful New Business, Lexington Books, Lexington Mass, 1986.

Hisrich, Robert D. and Marie O'Brien, "The Woman Entrepreneur as a Reflection of the Type of Business," Proceedings, 1982 Conference on Entrepreneurship, (June, 1982), pp. 54-67.

Hisrich, Robert D. and Marie O'Brien, "The Woman Entrepreneur from a Business and Sociological Perspective," Proceedings, 1981 Conference on Entrepreneurship, (June, 1981), pp. 21-39.

Pellegrino, Eric T. and Barry L. Reece, "Perceived Formative and Operational Problems Encountered by Female Entrepreneurs in Retail and Service Firms," Journal of Small Business Management, (April, 1982), pp. 15-24.

Schwartz, Eleanor B., "Entrepreneurship: A New Female Frontier," Journal of Contemporary Business, (Winter, 1979), pp. 47-76.

SUMMARY

NEW VENTURE FUNDING FOR THE FEMALE
ENTREPRENEUR:  A PRELIMINARY ANALYSIS

Authors

> Professor Nancy Bowman-Upton
> Alan L. Carsrud, Ph.D.
> Kenneth W. Olm, Ph.D.

Addresses

> Center for Entrepreneurship
> Hankamer School of Business, Suite 307
> Baylor University
> Waco, Texas 76798
> (817) 755-2265
>
> Entrepreneur Program, BRI 6
> Graduate School of Business Administration
> University of Southern California
> Los Angeles, California 90089-1421
> (213) 743-2098
>
> Management Department, CBA 4.202
> Graduate School of Business
> The University of Texas at Austin
> Austin, Texas 78712
> (512) 471-3676

Principal Topics

> Female Entrepreneurs, Financial Institutions, Bank Cooperation, Sex
> Discrimination, Spousal & Family Support

Major Findings and Implications

> Previous research on new venture creation has indicated that female
> entrepreneurs perceive securing capital and obtaining credit as
> significant external barriers to new venture initiation.  The
> current survey-based study explores the nature of start-up funding
> for a sample of female entrepreneurs in the southwestern United
> States.
>
> Variables associated with acquiring funding were identified and ana-
> lyzed.  These variables included the:  (1) organizational form of
> the venture; (2) formal education of the entrepreneur; (3) perceived

cooperation of financial institutions; and (4) percentage of ownership by the male spouse. The specific focus of the research was on the interrelationship of these variables in initial funding decisions by financial institutions. Results indicated that successful female entrepreneurs perceived financial institutions as being cooperative.

SUMMARY

## WHAT MAKES ENTREPRENEURS TICK:  AN INVESTIGATION OF ENTREPRENEURS' VALUES

Authors

>   Ellen A. Fagenson
>   Lyn L. Coleman

Address

>   School of Management
>   State University of New York
>   Binghamton, NY 13901
>   (607) 777-6861

Principal Topics

Very little research has been conducted to determine how male and female entrepreneurs differ from one another.  In an effort to shed some light on this matter, the values of male and female entrepreneurs were examined.  As values have been shown to predict behavior and drive individuals' activities, they were considered appropriate and critical for studying the matter at hand.

Method and Data Base

Rokeach's value survey was used to investigate the entrepreneurs' value systems.  Role theory predicted that no differences would be found in the values of the entrepreneurs.  The sex role socialization perspective, in contrast, predicted that the values of the males and females would diverge.

In order to test these hypotheses, entrepreneurs in urban and rural areas in the Northeast were mailed a survey.  The survey requested respondents to complete a shortened version of the Rokeach (1973) value instrument.  The revised instrument contained 15 terminal and 14 instrumental values.  Respondents were asked to rank order the two sets of values.  In addition to completing the value survey, respondents were also asked to provide information about their companies, their careers, and their personal backgrounds.

One hundred and ten entrepreneurs answered the survey.  Sixty-six of the respondents were female and 44 were male.  The entrepreneurs owned businesses in a variety of industries with the majority being located in the service sector.  All owned a significant percentage

of the businesses they created.  Most of the businesses were profitable, small and had been in existence for at least five years.  The
majority of entrepreneurs were white and college educated.

## Major Findings

The results of the study provided scant support for the sex role
socialization hypothesis and a great deal of support for role
theory.  More specifically, t-tests revealed that the male and
female entrepreneurs ranked only three of the 29 values significantly different.  These values were "family security," "equality"
and "helpful."  These finding contrasted greatly with Rokeach's
(1973) study of the values of males and females in the general population.  In that investigation males and females were found to
differ significantly in their rankings of 20 out of the 29 values
measured.

## Major Implications

The results of the study suggest that male and female entrepreneurs
are more alike than they are different.  While their values differ
to some extent, in general, they concur.

# ENTREPRENEURIAL HIRING AND MANAGEMENT OF EARLY STAGE EMPLOYEES

D. Kirk Neiswander, Case Western Reserve University
Barbara J. Bird, Case Western Reserve University
Peter L. Young, Case Western Reserve University

## ABSTRACT

The early hiring practices of 52 entrepreneurs in different industries and of different ages are examined. With an emphasis on the first five employees and the earliest managers hired, this study finds that earlier employees tend to be given a wider range of responsibilities than later hires. As managers are hired, the focus is on operations, administration and sales, with the manager of personnel and human resources being the least important and last hired. Issues of finding and motivating "entrepreneurial spirit," delegation, and compensation are discussed as are some of the changes in organizational structure that occur with increasing size. Industry, age of firm, and background of the entrepreneur appear to influence early human resource practices.

## INTRODUCTION

What ingredients are needed to start a successful business? Three core elements always seem to be present:

1) A product or service for which people will pay
2) Money, and
3) People (good management) to make the business happen.

There have been numerous studies on the physical, emotional, psychological and biographical make-up of the entrepreneur who founds a business. There are also plenty of studies which look at how new businesses are capitalized and where potential money sources can be found. And yet very little research can be found on how the entrepreneur goes about acquiring one of the most crucial of assets - early stage employees. These employees are the people who will have the greatest impact on whether or not the company goes on to greatness. They will also pose the earliest of management challenges to the entrepreneur. Over the life of the business, employee related matters will create the biggest problems facing the management of a smaller enterprise. [1]

Early hires will have to adapt to and grow with the company, be extremely productive, learn to make decisions, fit in with the character of the company, and implement the dream of the founding entrepreneur all the while using their own creativity in order to fend off the multitude of problems they will face in their own job.

Where does an entrepreneur find employees like this? How important is it to find the right employees early on? (One respondent to this survey who is presently operating a successful company indicated that he started originally with all the wrong people so he fired them all and started over again with the same business concept.)

This research project was undertaken to look more closely at the early stage hiring practices of the entrepreneur and the importance of these new employees to the success of the firm.

In addition to the questions posed above, this research sought answers to the following:

o What were the hiring and recruiting practices used to find new employees?
o What was the role of the first employee and what function did he or she serve?
o What was the sequence of managerial hires by function?
o What employee issues were the most important in the early years of being in business?
o What methods were used to train, motivate, compensate and delegate to employees?
o How did the organizational structure evolve as the company grew?
o Where could assistance be provided to the entrepreneur in the hiring process?

We felt the answers to these questions would provide valuable information to those entrepreneurs about to embark on a new venture and provide an interesting benchmark for those entrepreneurs already in business.

RESEARCH DESIGN

In order to obtain information on the hiring environment at the time of an organization's inception, the founder/owners of independent start-up companies were surveyed.

---

[1] Lewis, J.L., Sewell, C.H. & Dickson, C.L. Identification and Evaluation of Problems and Needs of Small Manufacturing Management. Atlanta, GA: Georgia Institute of Technology, 1961.

The objective of this study was to learn more about the entrepreneur's management role in finding and working with early stage employees.  While there is some information on the importance of internal teams in new ventures,[2] very little is known about the specific relationships or the sequence of team building events. As a result, an open-ended survey was constructed.

## The Survey

A seven-page questionnaire with 15 questions was designed. An additional five page survey with 12 questions was created as an "optional survey."  Each questionnaire was designed to take a respondent 15-20 minutes to complete.  Five pre-tests of the questionnaire were conducted through personal interviews.

## The Sample

The sample for this study consisted of 350 businesses that were founded within the telephone area code 216 (Northeast Ohio). The sample was constructed by merging listings from Harris's Ohio Industrial Directory, Ward's 51,000 Largest U.S. Corporations, Crain's Cleveland Business, "Financial Survey of Middle Market Publicly Held Companies in Northeast Ohio" (Alexander Grant & Co.), Inc. magazine, and Dun & Bradstreet's Million Dollar Directory. Additional firms were added from newspaper articles and from discussions with members of the local business community.

## Methodology

The questionnaires were mailed during the last week of November, 1986, with a one-page cover letter explaining the nature of the survey, who was conducting it, and identifying what employee and type of company should respond.  If a recipient of the survey realized he or she was ineligible to respond (i.e., not an independent start-up company or wasn't around at the founding of the company) then he or she was encouraged to return the survey materials to us with an explanation.  To obtain as high a response rate as possible, two follow-up telephone calls were placed to each person who hadn't returned the questionnaire.

Of the initial mailing to 350 firms, 52 disqualifications were obtained as well as 9 direct refusals.  The data provided in this report is based on 52 completed and usable questionnaires received (18% response rate), and 38 responses (13% return rate) on the optional questionnaire.

In addition to frequencies of response on various items in the questionnaire, some results will be reported by type of industry, entrepreneurial management background, and by age of the company.

---

[2]Martin, M.J.C., Managing Technological Innovation and Entrepreneurship.  Reston, VA: Reston Publishing, 1984.  Vesper, K.H., New Venture Strategies, Englewood Cliffs, NJ: Prentice-Hall, 1980.

Respondents in each industrial category included manufacturing (27), wholesale and retail trade (17), and service (19). (Some of those firms listed in manufacturing also categorized themselves in services or in retail/wholesale trades.) Entrepreneur's work experience was divided into those with management experience only (25 respondents) and those with management and technical/engineering experience (23 respondents). Respondents in each age category included those companies less than 10 years old (19), 10-19 years old (17), and over 20 years old (15). The average age of the companies was 14.3 years. No allowance was made in this research for the time value of money in the older companies. Also, respondents from older firms may have had more difficulty remembering events surrounding the early stage development of their companies.

## SUMMARY OF FINDINGS

### Who were the respondents?

The entrepreneurs studied generally had an undergraduate degree or better, were male, had a company that averaged 14 years of age, did an average of $19.3 million in revenue in 1986, and had about 35 employees. In their first year of operation, the respondents did an average of $465,000 in revenue and had 7 employees. Table 1 below gives a better breakout of where respondents were categorized.

### TABLE 1

### Subcategorization of Respondents

|  | Mfr. | Wholesale/retail Trade | Service Industries | Total |
|---|---|---|---|---|
| Entrepreneurs with mgmt. experience | 12 | 5 | 8 | 25 |
| Entrepreneurs with mgmt. plus tech experience | 15 | 3 | 5 | 23 |
| TOTAL | 27* | 8 | 13 | n=48 |
| Avg. age of company | 17.9 yrs. | 2.1 yrs. | 10.8 yrs. | 14.3 yrs. |

* (Some of these firms did indicate that they operated in multiple categories (i.e., service and manufacturing). In findings reported elsewhere in this research, their input has been represented from both categories.)

## 1) What are the early stage recruiting and hiring practices of entrepreneurs?

In most cases the entrepreneur's means of finding early stage employees is simply hit or miss. Money is not a luxury that entrepreneurs have to spend on "executive search" help. Quite often, early workers tend to be family or friends. Most entrepreneurs find that the best candidate referrals come from business associates, especially those associates operating in a similar industry. Early hires quite often were business associates or came from related industries or competition.[3]

When hiring for an early stage managerial/ administrative position, the entrepreneurs reviewed an average of 12.6 resumes, interviewed 4.5 qualified candidates, and generally asked the eventual hire back to a second and sometimes a third interview.

## Interviews

During the first interview, the most important information to the entrepreneur dealt with the candidate's goals and objectives and where he or she wanted to be in five years. Second in importance and yet still very valuable was the candidate's experience, ability to solve particular problems, initiative, drive, motivation and ability to learn and perform quickly. In the second interview, qualified candidates would be asked "What else can you contribute?" and "Why do you want to work here?" If the candidate responded adequately, the entrepreneur, out of anxiety to get somebody on the job as soon as possible, often gave the position to the candidate on the spot.

One thing that tended to be overlooked and which had long range implications to the company was the "fit" of the candidate into the company culture. Also overlooked and harder to assess was the candidate's ability to grow into new positions and handle new responsibilities. Early hires were usually brought on board to be responsive to a set need at that time.

When asked what the most important characteristics or attributes should be for a prospective early stage manager/ administrator, over 2/3 of the respondent entrepreneurs indicated the following list of traits: entrepreneurial attitude, drive, self-motivation, initiative, and action orientation. A candidate's qualifications and past work experience were the most important information needed by an entrepreneur prior to hiring. One third of the entrepreneurs participating in this study indicated that a reference check was done. Proper candidates were hired and others were eliminated based on intuition and how a candidate handled the interview process.

---

[3]Based on findings from research on "The Origins of Successful Start-up Firms in Northeast Ohio," D. Kirk Neiswander and John M. Drollinger, 1986.

## 2) What was the role of the first employee and what functions did he or she serve?

At the time in which the first employee was hired the capitalization rate in 2/3 of the respondent companies was under $25,000. In 75% of the cases the entrepreneur was dealing with his own money (9 of the respondents had financed their businesses 100%) which should give the reader an idea of how conservative the entrepreneur's approach might be in the spending of money to hire an employee.

In 50% of the cases studied, the first employee was hired in the same month as the first sale, with some interesting differences based on the respondent firm's age. Among firms less than twenty years old, all had hired their first employee prior to or at about the same time as the first sale. In companies 20 years or older the first hire was made within 6 months after the first sale 50% of the time. This indicates an even more conservative attitude about hiring initial help in the 1960's vs. today.

### The First Hire

The first person hired had an average of 2.3 functional job responsibilities (i.e., this might mean an employee would have responsibilities in three functional areas such as marketing, engineering, and accounting). The most important functions which warranted hiring the first employee included operations (production), secretarial/ administrative, and sales. As each additional employee was hired the number of functional responsibilities decreased. By the time the fifth employee was hired, only one functional job responsibility was being assigned. A trend was also evident for firms created in the 70's and 80's which seemed to show more functional duties being assigned to initial hires vs. yesteryear companies when a person was initially hired to handle one specific function.

As might be expected those entrepreneurs with technical backgrounds tended to hire initial employees into engineering and/or technical positions. Those companies created within the last ten years seemed to put a much heavier demand on an initial employee providing a sales function.

### Observations on Employees 1-5

o For employee number one, chances were good that an entrepreneur with a technical background would hire an operations person before hiring a secretary. A non-technical entrepreneur would do the opposite.
o Manufacturing respondents seemed to hire many or all of their first 5 employees to do operation/production related duties.
o Sales responsibilities were expected of many of the early hires.
o The accounting function became an important consideration with the third employee.
o Businesses created within the last 10 years initially hired employees to handle sales related matters whereas those firms started earlier hired operations people early on. The implication is that the entrepreneur/CEO's role has evolved from that of being the direct

salesman to that of in-house chief operating manager and that new businesses have become more marketing oriented.

## Advice on Hiring Employee #1

Based on hindsight the entrepreneurs from this survey suggested the following advice:

1) Hire a person who shares the same values, principles, work ethic, drive, ambition and initiative. Get to know the candidate on a personal basis.
2) Hire a candidate with experience in the function he or she is asked to perform. Hire someone who has worked in a small business environment. Eliminate costly training, put them to work and expect productivity right away (sure, mistakes will be made but an employee will learn faster "on the job").
3) Hire the candidate that brings the most talent to the table in the way of education and intelligence.
4) Hire a candidate who can grow as the company grows. Find someone that plans to stay for at least five years, and likes the challenges, and risk/rewards that come with a young firm.

## 3) What was the sequence of managerial hires by function?

Different kinds of companies have different reasons for hiring employees and at different stages of development. An operations manager, office manager, and sales manager seemed to be listed as one of the top three hires on everyone's list. Whereas the marketing manager would be hired fifth, and the purchasing manager would be hired sixth, the controller who was hired later, had a higher perceived value. (This may be explained by the proportionally higher number of manufacturing firms in the sample.) Graph I gives a visual view of the perceived importance of each position and the time after the initial sale in which that managerial position would be hired.

## Observations

o Growth rates of companies will impact hiring practices and vice versa.
o Those companies started over 20 years ago generally waited over 10 years to hire a controller, while younger companies hired a controller within the first 2-3 years.
o Those entrepreneurs with no technical background hired technical/engineer managers in the first year at about the same rate as those entrepreneurs with technical backgrounds.
o Technical entrepreneurs hired accounting/finance managers sooner than management entrepreneurs.
o Technical entrepreneurs seemed less concerned with hiring office management.
o Younger firms show a need for an office manager within the first year of operations.
o Purchasing managers are being hired much earlier by young firms vs. older firms which hired these people in later years.

GRAPH I

## THE IMPORTANCE AND ORDER OF HIRING A
## MANAGER FOR EACH OF THE FOLLOWING FUNCTIONS

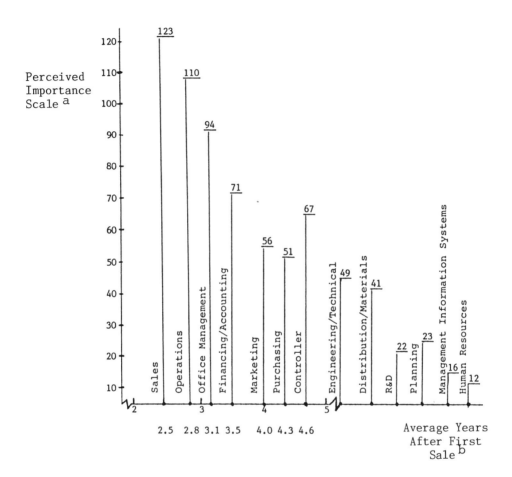

a The perceived importance point total was found in the following manner: Each respondent was to pick the order in which they hired 13 managers for functional positions. Each first hire vote received five points, second hire (4 points) down to fifth hire (1 point) so the perceived importance was a function of two things - 1) Number of respondent votes (per func-tional position) for number 1-5 managerial hires, and 2) The order in which the 1-5 choices were made.

b Since this is an average it shows a proper order and relationship to each other, but not necessarily an accurate figure for years after first sale in which to hire someone for this functional position.

4) **What employee issues were the most important in the early years of being in business?**

The following list ranks employee issues as seen by the entrepreneur, with the most important issues listed first:

1) Hiring an employee
2) Morale
3) Motivation
4) Productivity
5) Turnover
6) Training
7) Compensation.

Hiring was by far and away the most important issue for all respondents. This held true across industry lines, age of the company, and by the entrepreneur's work experience. Training seemed to be more important in the businesses created in the 1980's. Compensation seemed to be the least of the entrepreneur's worries. This is not surprising considering that entrepreneurs themselves tend to work long hours for little take home pay, especially in the early years and expect the same from others.

5) **What methods were used to train, motivate, compensate, and delegate to employees?**

Training

In the early years of the business, training was a luxury that the entrepreneur could not afford. Only 17.6% of the respondents mentioned "enhancing employee skill levels." Those who were hired had already been trained and/or could learn quickly on the job and produce immediate results.

Motivation

Many entrepreneurs perceive a major factor limiting the growth of their company is a lack of an "entrepreneurial spirit" among employees. Furthermore, they feel this is not something that is easily taught; you have it or you don't. If an employee "has it", the founder needs to foster and channel it so that the employee can contribute to growth, both corporate and personal.

Results from the research confirm the notion that employee motivation and productivity were very important issues which challenged respondents during their firms' early years.[4]

How were motivational issues dealt with? Four important tools or methods used to maintain an entrepreneurial spirit for employees were evident from the research:

---

[4]Weighted mean scores of 1.9 on a rating scale from 1 to 5, with 1 being extremely important.

1)  Nearly 77% mentioned providing a "creative atmosphere," coupled with "few rules", "freedom to create a challenging job," and "fostering involvement in your job." Nearly 24% of the respondents mentioned they "treated their employee's fairly" and "like adults." This data may lend support to one conclusion documented in the literature that many entrepreneurs felt frustrated and stifled in former jobs or careers and desired to create a company they would want to work for. [5]

2)  Exactly 50% of the respondents mentioned that the "potential for ownership or incentive compensation" was an important motivational tool. Similarly, nearly 27% of the respondents currently provided "top pay scale programs, benefits, or other financial opportunities." In a few cases the entrepreneur suggested hiring an employee with more talent than what was needed for the job at the time.

3)  Nearly 27% of the respondents suggested that the setting of individual and company goals in a teamwork setting was an important motivational tool. Nearly 21% of the respondents also mentioned "public recognition of excellent work results."

4)  Nearly 18% of the respondents mentioned the fact that their company was a "planned industry leader" and used this as a motivating tool. This seems to suggest that "getting in on the ground floor" is a motivation for employees to get involved with small businesses and become an important player in advancing the firm to preeminence.

## Delegation

The issue of delegating responsibility to subordinates was easy for some of the respondents and quite tough for others, especially in the early years of the business when many entrepreneurs got the feeling that if they wanted it done right they needed to do it themselves.

- 41% indicated that delegation depended on work volume and the amount of trust developed.
- 30% said that delegation was difficult until employees had developed and could produce and yet delegation usually came earlier than anticipated in response to an entrepreneur's overwhelming workload.
- 18% said they could handle everything in those early years.
- 18% said they just let their employees "go for it" and that delegating fit their management style.
- 18% said it was hard to let go!

Entrepreneurs sometimes taught themselves how to delegate by backing away slowly on a step-by-step basis. The process was very systematic and cautious and the "learning to live with other's mistakes" was very frustrating. Entrepreneurs also learned the art of delegation from their past work experiences, from talking to others, and from courses.

---

[5] Collins, O.F. & Moore, D.G., The Enterprising Man. East Lansing, MI: MSU Business Studies, 1964.

## Compensation

The following incentive compensation programs were mentioned as being available to employees most often by survey respondents:

- Profit sharing available to all employees (71.4%)
- Stock awarded to key employees (32.4%)
- Bonuses available to all employees (30%)
- Bonuses available to key employees (26.7%)

## 6) How did the organizational structure evolve as the company grew?

Table 2 offers a good visual look at how the respondent companies have evolved by revenue. Table 3 shows the median number of employees, the median number of employees reporting to the CEO, the average number of reporting levels in the company, and the median number of employees departing the company (for whatever reason).

### TABLE 2

Average Annual Sales*

|  | (000) Year 1 | (000) Year 5 | Yr.1–Yr.5 (times original sales) | (000) Year 10 | Today | Avg. Age |
|---|---|---|---|---|---|---|
| Total respondents (n=44) | $465 | 3,064 | 6x | 7,923 | 19,316 | 14.3 |
| Mfr. Industries (n=25) | $563 | 3,638 | 7x | 5,895 | 12,196 | 12.9 |
| Wholesale/Retail Trade Industries (n=7) | $250 | 1,125 | 5x | 1,929 | 33,300(1) | 22.1 |
| Service Industries (n=12) | $386 | 1,639 | 4x | 7,429 | 12,583 | 10.8 |
| Entrepreneur with mgmt. experience (n=23) | $448 | 3,625 | 7x | 8,536 | 18,677 | 14.4 |
| Entrepreneur with mgmt. & tech experience (n=20) | $486 | 2,390 | 5x | 7,188 | 20,083 | 14.2 |

\*  Figures are based on a mid point from a revenue scale in which the respondent was asked to check.

(1) The reason this figure is so high is because Retail/Wholesale companies have been around for an average of 22 years vs. an average of 14 years for the other enterprises.

TABLE 3

Median From All Respondents*

|  | Year 1 | Year 5 | Today |
|---|---|---|---|
| Employees in the company(1) | 7 | 19 | 34 |
| Employees reporting to CEO(2) | 2 | 8 | 8 |
| Reporting levels in the company(3) | 1.8 | 2.5 | 3.7 |
| Employees departing the company(4) | 3 | 6 | 13 |

\* Based on total database of 51 respondents

(1) Based on 40 responses
(2) Based on 46 responses
(3) Based on 43 responses
(4) Based on 31 responses


Observations

Sales

    Manufacturing firms (SIC's 20-25, 26-29) tended to exhibit a pattern
    of higher annual sales growth than did firms in the trade or service
    sectors.  (Manufacturing firms did 7 times their first year sales in
    year five vs. 4 and 5 times sales for service and retail/wholesale
    respectively.)

Number of Employees

    Firms in the manufacturing industries tended to exhibit a pattern of
    higher employment and growth from year one to the present.

    Firms headed up by respondents with managerial and engineering/
    technical experience tended to exhibit a pattern of higher employ-
    ment and growth from year one to the present.

    Firms that have been in commercial operation only since 1976 tended
    to exhibit a pattern of higher employment and growth in their first
    5 years of operation than did those firms begun over 10 years ago.

Employees Reporting Directly to CEO

    Generally, 3-4 employees on average reported to the CEO of newly
    formed independent start-ups during their first year of commercial
    operation.  In service industries (SIC's 46-49, 60-67, 70-89), more
    often only 2-3 employees reported directly to the CEO.

By year 5 of commercial operation, 6-8 employees on average reported
to the CEO of independent start-ups. In service industries or companies founded since 1976, more often only 4-5 employees reported
directly to the CEO.

For many companies in 1986, the growth curve for the number of
employees on average reporting directly to the CEO had either
leveled off or decline slightly.

Turnover

Generally, 3 employees out of 10 (on <u>average</u>) either voluntarily or
involuntarily left the newly formed independent start-up during the
firm's first year of commercial operation. There seems to be some
tendency shown for higher turnover in firms founded since 1976 and
for firms headed by respondents with both engineering/technical and
managerial experience in year one.

By year 5, firms headed by respondents with managerial experience
were losing fewer employees (2 out of 16 employees) than those
firms headed by a respondent with both engineering and management
experience (10 out of 22 employees, almost 50%). There are three
possible explanations. a) The entrepreneur with the technical
background may be harder to get along with. b) The type of
industry in which the technically oriented entrepreneur operates
is more conducive to switching jobs or even allowing employees an
opportunity to leave and create their own new businesses. c) Those
with only managerial experiences make management systems a higher
priority than the technical entrepreneur. These systems, in turn,
provide stability and low turnover.

Manufacturing firms today (those from this survey reporting in 1986)
are experiencing a 20% turnover rate vs. close to 50% for services
and wholesale/retail trade industries. As expected, manufacturing
has more employment stability than that of trades or services, but
the percentage of turnover seems high in all categories.

Organization Complexity

Newly formed independent start-ups tended to have 1-2 reporting
levels in their organization charts during their first year of
operation. By year 5 of operation, the growth in organizational
complexity was mixed:

* Firms in the manufacturing sector experienced a growth to
  approximately 3 reporting levels on average while firms in
  wholesale/retail trades and services continued to report
  1-2 levels on average.
* Firms formed since 1976 experienced a growth to approximately
  3-4 reporting levels on average while firms formed prior to
  1976 reported approximately 2 organizational levels on
  average.

## 7) Where could assistance be provided to the entrepreneur in the hiring process?

Table 4 refers to where entrepreneurs perceive help can be given to them in the hiring process. Looking for candidates and providing prescreened lists of resumes were deemed to be extremely valuable. Also of interest is the relative unimportance in receiving a large number of candidate resumes for perusal! Younger firms were interested in receiving help in testing candidates (1.7 rating) and service firms chose help with interviewing to be their second most important category (2.1 rating).

### TABLE 4

Recruiting and Hiring Functions
(in which the entrepreneur could use help)*

| Function | Entrepreneurial Rating (1) |
|---|---|
| 1) Providing prescreened lists of resumes | 1.7 |
| 2) Looking for candidates | 1.8 |
| 3) Reference checking | 2.2 |
| 4) Testing candidates | 2.2 |
| 5) Interviewing candidates | 2.6 |
| 6) Reviewing resumes | 3.3 |
| 7) Evaluating requirements of a new position | 3.0 |
| 8) Writing job descriptions | 3.2 |
| 9) Providing large quantities of resumes for review | 3.5 |

* 1-5 scale with 1 being extremely high time or money savings to the entrepreneur and 5 meaning no time or money savings at all

(1) Respondent base of 42

This research indicates that the processes involved in early stage human resource management are complex and varied, and depend on the skills of the entrepreneur, the type of industry, the rate and type of growth of the firm, and the social, cultural and economic conditions into which the new venture is born.

Effective entrepreneurial hiring, like all hiring, involves a three-way matching of (1) organizational culture and resources, (2) jobs, responsibilities, and authority, and (3) people with their skills, experiences, and personalities. Some hiring questions are more complex for the entrepreneurial organization versus the larger more stable firms. In the entrepreneurial setting, the organization is coming into being and very uncertain (i.e., Will it continue? What are its future resources?) and jobs are multidimensional, shifting, and stressful.[6] Finally, during the early stages the personal values, skills, and interpersonal style of the entrepreneur play a central role in both the organizational-level of the firm and the job-level variables affecting all employees.

This research shows that entrepreneurs approach the hiring process with some ambivalence. In the earliest days there are probably two motives for hiring:

1) to have the new hire do what the entrepreneur was doing before and thus relieve the entrepreneur's time to handle more pressing problems
2) to hire a new employee who has skills that the entrepreneur does not have and yet are needed by the company.

In addition, there is often pressure to hire quickly for urgent and current needs. This can result in the entrepreneur failing to consider (or deciding to ignore) the future time horizon (e.g., "Does this employee fit my personal style?" Will this employee be able to grow with the firm?")

Failure to think ahead can result in hiring the wrong people, promoting the wrong people (loyal old-timers who lack management or leadership skills for the now larger organization), and as a result voluntary and involuntary departures take place which are often personally painful. It is interesting to note that turnover does not seem to be much of a concern (and there is a great deal of it) and that hiring a human resource manager was perceived to be last in importance despite other research with suggests that this role along with hiring for the future are critical to growth.[7]

---

[6]Kets de Vries, M.F.R., "Can you survive an entrepreneur?", Cambridge, MA: Harvard Business School Teaching Note 9-484-081, 1984.
[7]Hambrick, D.C. & Crozier, L.M., "Stumblers and stars in the management of rapid growth," Journal of Business Venturing, 1 (1), pp. 31-45.

This study suggests that early employees need to be flexible, jacks-of-all-trades, with experience, preferably in a small business, while later employees tend to be hired for increasingly specialized functions (suggesting a potential "rift" between old-timers and later hires). Despite the generalist expectations of early hires, there is some indication that entrepreneurs, especially technically-based entrepreneurs, might be prone to building a "look alike" team, which while comfortable because of shared backgrounds and values, may have serious limitations if growth is an objective. [8]

This study reports some differences between older and younger firms. These differences might be due to the different social and economic conditions facing new firms in the 1960's compared with the 1980's. Alternatively, entrepreneurs with longer histories might have selective and erroneous remembrances of the early days.

Additional Conclusions

1) The entrepreneur needs to allocate responsibility to employees and let them become entrepreneurs in their own right by letting them be creative, take risks, and take pride and authorship in their own creations.

2) Employees become more productive and responsible when they've got something at stake like ownership or incentive compensation.

3) High turnover is very much in evidence in the companies surveyed and the cause may be traced back to initial hiring mistakes and/or the lack of a Human Resources Manager, for whom the entrepreneur perceives little value.

4) A self-sustaining not-for-profit program can be established to assist entrepreneurs in identifying early stage employees.

---

[8] Bird, B.J., _Entrepreneurial Behavior_. Boston, MA: Little Brown, in press.

# USE OF A SELF-ASSESSMENT PROFILE TO DIFFERENTIATE AMONG PROFESSIONAL GROUPS ON ENTREPRENEURIAL CHARACTERISTICS

Thomas C. Dandridge, SUNY at Albany
Michael A. Ford, University of Auckland

## ABSTRACT

This study combines 50 questions related to characteristics of entrepreneurs into a profile. The composite instrument was then completed by individual respondents in three groups; engineering students, commerce students, and career government officials. Results were analyzed by group, and provided a basis for differentiating among the groups. The profile of the government officials was closest to that which would generally be expected for entrepreneurs. Responses for the group of engineers were analyzed separately to determine underlying factors in the answers, but clear distinctions which might be expected were not found.

## INTRODUCTION

Both researchers and authors of texts on entrepreneurship have tried to identify a profile of the typical entrepreneur.
Often the intention is to provide a "test" which can be administered, or which is self administered, and assesses how well an individual's profile matches that of some group of identified entrepreneurs' results, some theoretical profile, or prior global test results. These instruments try first to determine what the actual relevant features are, and second, how well the person in question matches, that is, qualifies as a potential entrepreneur. The study reported here used questions based on past research and existing profile questions to try to differentiate among three groups of people rather than to specifically profile individuals. All of the people included in the survey had expressed some interest in entrepreneurship but in different contexts and at different career points. In this paper we are trying to relate entrepreneurial potential of a group of people to the group's response on our questionnaire. At present, the inference of a relationship is indirect (See Fig. 1). We recognize that we seek correlates of entrepreneurship which may not extend directly to a causal relationship. Thus potential seen may not be realized in starting a business, or in its ultimate success. However, we may still compile measures of characteristics relevant for

differentiation. We believe from other work that entrepreneurial orientation may be capable of differentiation in a broad sense, and that the population groups chosen should differ.

Groupings of answers into assumed patterns or categories of responses is generally intuitive by the instrument designer. The study reported here also factor analyzes the answers of one set of respondents to see if the groupings on answers which is normally assumed by the profile designers actually are portrayed in the results.

A review of any series of texts on entrepreneurship will show that most try to consider the issue of "What is the typical entrepreneur like?" The opinions and the research which they cite vary as they focus on innate behavioral characteristics, on personal background, or on lifestyle and current environment as the most critical ingredients. As examples of relevant studies, Hornaday and Aboud (1975) looked for objective measures to identify entrepreneurial characteristics, using interviews, self assessment, and accepted objective tests such as the Kuder Occupational Interest Survey. Their sample was of operators of existing businesses. Such a comprehensive approach is more likely to produce meaningful results which provide support for the author's interpretation. In a broader study of occupational choices of college graduates after ten years, McClelland (1965) found support for the idea that entrepreneurship can be assessed by measuring need or achievement.

A survey designed for Venture used 15 questions related to current lifestyle. Such an instrument is brought into question as successful entrepreneurs in a study by Fierro (1982) failed the test. A questionnaire designed by the Center for Entrepreneurial Management and administered to over 2500 members (Mancuso 1983) used 26 questions that centered on work relationships and risk taking behavior. No specific validation of the range of questions or the centrality of these categories was provided. The New York Daily News, typical of many popular media, offered a quiz which focussed on organizational abilities and physical stamina, but with no research base or analysis of any results.

Efforts to identify characteristics of entrepreneurs or to differentiate these individuals from the rest of the population, or from small business owners (eg. Hoy and Carland, 1983) have been the focus of entire sections of the Babson Conference on Entrepreneurship in previous years. Some of these do use individual tests to differentiate between groups. For example, Ronstadt (1983) looked for differences between students that did start businesses versus those that did not. Sexton and Bowman (1983) found differences between students majoring in entrepreneurship and those that had other majors. In the study we report here, we also find that there are differences in questionnaire response between the groups studied. From this we are assuming that our questionnaire is able to detect entrepreneurial orientation or potential. It is accepted that there are also alternative explanations or paradigms which could describe the result, as there are with the use of other instruments mentioned above. A problem with attempting to "dissect" apart components of people's makeup which lead to entrepreneurship, is that the components may well not exist in isolation. Entrepreneurship might be a holistic interaction of many features, in which cause and effect may blur together, leaving just correlations. With this limitation in mind, the study can still claim to use broadly accepted components to create composite profiles of groups, and to see if these groups differ.

Various texts in the field use the authors own experience and the results of questionnaires such as those described above to draw conclusions as to relevant characteristics, or to conclude that characteristics are so variable that we can draw only implications of the broadest composite nature. Schollhammer and Kuriloff (1979) for example conclude that need for achievement "..always seems to emerge as central to the requirements for successful entrepreneurship." (p. 13). Greenfield (1986) concludes "..entrepreneurial characteristics vary widely from person to person and from sample to sample." (p.20). In this study we sought to derive a broader composite test and to see if it could differentiate among groups of individuals. We used elements for this composite which have separately been credited as having some relation to entrepreneurship. This study does not test for the individual's profile match to a "standard", nor do we compare those interested in entrepreneurship with an outside group. We instead look for comparisons of groups interested in entrepreneurship through the combined profile of their members and try to broadly assess which group most closely matched the characteristics we generally associate with entrepreneurs.

FIGURE 1

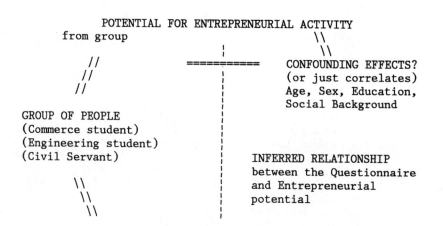

POTENTIAL FOR ENTREPRENEURIAL ACTIVITY
from group

CONFOUNDING EFFECTS?
(or just correlates)
Age, Sex, Education,
Social Background

GROUP OF PEOPLE
(Commerce student)
(Engineering student)
(Civil Servant)

INFERRED RELATIONSHIP
between the Questionnaire
and Entrepreneurial
potential

PROFILE OF GROUP ON QUESTIONNAIRE

## THE SAMPLE

During 1986 the first author conducted the following:

a two semester course in entrepreneurship for 50 undergraduates in the School of Commerce at the University of Auckland, New Zealand. Approximately one third of the students were women, and their average age is estimated to be 20 years.

two seminars each of two days duration for a total of 38 upper and middle level executives in national government in New Zealand. Approximately 10% of the participants were women. The group's average age is estimated to be 40.

a lecture on entrepreneurial behavior to approximately 160 undergraduate engineering students in their last term at the University of Auckland. Approximately 20% of the group were women. The average age of the class is estimated to be 20.

In each case, the instrument that is described below was administered on a voluntary basis early in the first session. The participants were advised that the results were primarily for their own insight and a page showing the answers of "typical" entrepreneurs were subsequently provided. These answers were based on ones that had been provided by the National Center for Research in Vocational Education (1985) with their statement "The answers you see here are what studies show to be the responses commonly given by small business owners." (p.40) This statement of expected results is not relevant to this study, but merely indicates the context and request which the respondents faced.

The following numbers of usable responses were collected. Response sheets were screened by the first author and ones with obviously spurious answers were discarded:

Engineering students  114
Government officials   37
Commerce students      36

The entrepreneurship course was an elective, and one that did not relate specifically to requirements for a degree, hence it is claimed that the participants were essentially there out of interest in the subject. The government seminars required payment of a fee, absence from work by the participants for two full days, and longer than usual work hours. The seminars were offered to teach middle and upper level career managers in government the concept of entrepreneurial behaviour and how to increase such behaviour. While few of them expressed an interest during the seminar in starting their own businesses (a few had part-time businesses at present or had been in business for themselves in the past), they were uniformly interested in such behaviour. The engineering student sample is more suspect. This group was participating in a course on business administration in the engineering school and the lecture was provided as guidance in how an engineer can start his or her own business, given the belief that such students were more likely than others to produce inventions of marketable value. The course administrator claimed that attendance was high, and subsequent informal discussion indicated that participants were interested. Other that a New Zealand cultural tendency to look favorably on the self employed or those who start their own businesses, there is no other basis for concluding this group had a strong interest in entrepreneurship.

While we are interested in justifying the inclusion of these groups based on interest, note that there is no need for interest to exist in order for potential to be determined. In other words, a truly viable instrument should be able to profile groups to assess match to an entrepreneurial group, or to differentiate based on such a composite, regardless of present interest.

## THE INSTRUMENT

A fifty question "Entrepreneurship Self-assessment Profile" was designed by The National Center for Research in Vocational Education (1985) and was used as the basis for the instrument derived for this study. While no justification was provided other that subjective judgement, the authors of the above profile selected questions which they believed fit into three subject areas. These were "personal background", "behavior patterns", and "Life-styles". We made some subjective judgements of our own, based on experience and review of relevant literature, and produced the fifty questions which are described in Table 1. The NCRVE instrument was used as the basis because in the authors' judgement it considered many factors broadly accepted as relevant and was in a simple format to administer. To analyze the results, we changed from their two-point categorical response to a five point scale. The NCRVE instrument was only a basis as the questions were heavily modified for two reasons. First, existing questions were modified to make them more understandable or more specific. For example, the question "Do you take rejection personally?" was modified to read "Do you take rejection of projects or ideas as if they were personal rejections?". In total, 21 questions were used unmodified and 19 questions were used in modified forms. Ten questions were replaced with those of the authors' design in order to broaden the subjects covered. The new questions are indicated by (#) just at the end of the appropriate questions on Table 1. Other students and faculty in the School of Commerce participated informally in the instrument design by taking prior drafts or by interpreting proposed questions to the author, thus confirming intended meaning.

## STATISTICAL METHODS

Statistical Analysis was carried out using the SAS computer package (SAS 1982,1985). The various methods employed are first described, followed by the results of this analysis.

## Methods for Differentiating Groups

Multivariate Analysis Of Variance - MANOVA - (Bartlett 1947, Chatfield and Collins 1980), is an analogue of traditional Analysis of Variance, with the major difference being that in MANOVA the combined effects of many variables are used at once, rather than each variable being used individually. This has the advantage that only a single significance test needs to be used. In MANOVA each group in a sample is represented by its Centroid, a vector of the means for the group of all the variables, and the matrix of variance/covariance from differences between group centroids is compared with variance/covariance within the groups, and a significance test for differences between groups can be performed.

Canonical Variate Analysis - CVA - (Chatfield and Collins 1980) (also known as Canonical Discriminant Analysis (SAS 1982)) involves the generation of a sub-space within the many dimensions of the original variables, which best describes differences between group centroids detected by MANOVA. The dimensions of this sub-space are called Canonical Variates, and can be related to the original variables through coefficients which show the effects that the original variables have on the derivation of the canonical variates, or through the correlations between the variates and the original variables. The groups distinguished along variates may be seen through scatter plots of canonical variate scores by groups, and by group means of the canonical variates. Group separation represented by canonical variates can then be related to the original variables through the Canonical Coefficients, or by correlations - and so the variables strongly involved in difference between particular groups can be seen.
When the original variables have strong intercorrelation, canonical coefficients may only leave one of a family of intercorrelated variables representing the family. Correlations between variables and variates will include all variables in such a group, and potentially show a clearer pattern.

## Methods for Detecting Relationships Between Variables Within a Group

Factor Analysis - FA - is potentially a means of detecting patterns in how variables take on relatable, or unrelatable, values to each other. Groups of variables might be found, representing a few underlying trends in response to a questionnaire. Opinions differ about the utility of FA. It may be that because of contradictory results through small changes in method or data, it should only be used with caution (Chatfield and Collins 1980, Seber 1984). A related, but distinct technique, is Principal Component Analysis, - PCA - which makes far fewer assumptions and gives the same type of result as many users of FA require, and is generally a better alternative. However, a weakness of PCA is that its "Components" can become indistinct and arbitrary in definition if the cloud of data points is circular in a plane where Components could be formed (Pimentel 1979). This can occur in questionnaire data.

The analysis involved two steps, firstly the search for group differences, secondly an examination of patterns within one group. The first step relates to the paper's primary objective of using an instrument to differentiate relevant groups. The second relates primarily to an analysis of the instrument itself to determine patterns and relate these to the patterns assumed in other profiles and in the original design of the instrument. Together the steps give insight into the group differences and some marginal insight into the structure of the profile. Lack of volume of the data limits the application of this technique and the level of real interpretation of the results.

## Group Differences

MANOVA showed significant difference occurring between the three groups ($p < 0.0001$). The differences between groups could be described by two Canonical Variates, CAN1 and CAN2, both of which contained significant Canonical Correlation (for both together, p is < 0.0001; for the smaller CAN2 alone,  p is < 0.01). A plot of the data, by group, in the new space of CAN1 and CAN2, showed the groups to be fairly distinct from each other. Figure 2 provides a general representation of the relationships found in the two Canonical Variates.

CAN1 differentiated between the Government group (mean score on it: 2.4) and the student groups (means: 0.2 (Commerce) and -0.9 (Engineering)). CAN2 showed the smaller difference between the Commerce students (mean score 1.6) and the rest (means: -0.3 (Engineering) and -0.5 (Government)).

The cause, in terms of the original variables, of these low scores can be seen from correlations between variables and the variate (see TABLE 1). The students tend to give low responses, while government employees give higher responses, to (in order of decreasing relationship):

V29 ...Have you deliberately exceeded your authority at work
V37 ...Do you enjoy being able to make your own decisions on the job
V45 ...Do friends or associates come to you for unique ideas on problems
V10 ...Do you often come up with new ideas
V38 ...Do you wake up happy most of the time
V49 ...Have you been divorced or separated
V21 ...Were you expected to do odd jobs at home before 10 years of age
V02 ...Do you watch more than 1/2 hour television on most days
V26 ...Are you an immigrant to this country
V32 ...Do you enjoy tackling a task without knowing all the potential problems

V15 ...Did you participate in competitive school activities or
         sports
V18 ...Will you deliberately seek a direct confrontation to get
         needed results
V09 ...Have you ever been sacked from a job
V33 ...Do you persist when others tell you it cant be done
V30 ...Do you try to find the benefits of a bad situation
V06 ...Do you believe in organizing your tasks before getting
         started

and the students give high responses, while the government group give
low responses, to:

V36 ...Are you likely to work evenings or weekends to complete a
         work project
V46 ...Do you think of your work as if it was a line, between two
         points or stages
V41 ...Do you believe that innovators take a very big risk
V13 ...Were you a very good student at college or university
V39 ...Do you prefer to let a friend decide on a location for
         lunch, or social activities
V31 ...Do you tend to blame others when something goes wrong
V27 ...Do you avoid problems or situations which have no obvious
         solution
V42 ...Do you feel that successful managers must have advanced
         college degrees
V35 ...Do you believe that good luck explains many of your
         successes
V34 ...Do you take rejection of projects or ideas as if they were
         personal rejections
V28 ...Do you enjoy socializing regularly
V12 ...Did you like formal education

Tentatively, it might be proposed that these differences
separate the groups based on some composite entrepreneurial
orientation or potential.  The first group of variables, to which the
government respondents gave higher, or more positive responses, are
ones the literature generally associates with positive responses from
entrepreneurs.  The second group of variables, to which the students
gave high responses (positive) are ones to which we generally assume
entrepreneurs give lower responses.

The contrast between Commerce students compared with
Engineering students and Government workers, as seen in CAN2, seems to
be due to the commerce group giving high ratings (and the other two
groups giving low ratings) to:

V22 ...Do you get bored easily
V07 ...Are you out of work often due to illness
V25 ...Do you, on occasion, need pep talks from others to keep
         you going
V09 ...Have you ever been sacked from a job
V05 ...Has someone in your family shared their experience of
         starting a business with you

V02 ...Do you watch more than 1/2 hour television on most
        days
V29 ...Have you deliberately exceeded you authority at work
V28 ...Do you enjoy socializing regularly
V18 ...Will you deliberately seek a direct confrontation to get
        needed results
V40 ...Have you moved personal funds from one savings account to
        another to gain 2 percentage points of interest
V35 ...Do you believe that good luck explains many of your
        successes
V47 ...Do you prefer to be a loner in your final decision

The explanation of these variables as a group is less obvious
than for CAN1. An impression can be drawn of high scores being
associated with a successful <u>manager</u> more than a profile of an
entrepreneur. CAN2 is also due to commerce students rating low (or
the others rating high):

V24 ...Can you concentrate for extended periods of time on a
        subject
V19 ...Were you the firstborn child
V26 ...Are you an immigrant to this country
V45 ...Do friends or associates come to you for unique ideas on
        problems
V17 ...Is job security an important factor in your selection of a
        position.

Except for the last variable (the least important) this group
includes characteristics which we associate with entrepreneurs.
Overall, this second pattern of differentiation found in CAN2 might be
a dimension in which the type of entrepreneurial activity differs -
between people who have set out to do business, versus those who seek
to do other things, such as perform technical activity - with business
possibly arising as a consequence.

There are also variables which correlate with both variates,
indicating more complex interaction that could be better examined with
larger samples.

Combining the insights of the two canonical variates into
Figure 2, we see the commerce students farther from the profile we
associate with entrepreneurs on each one. We also see that in each
variate the type of answers which we would expect from entrepreneurs
is the same as those received from government officials. Engineering
students are similar to entrepreneurs on one variate but not the
other.

FIGURE 2

CANONICAL VARIATE ONE

```
                                   HIGH                        LOW

                      I              I                        I
                      I              I                        I
   CANONICAL          I              I COMMERCE               I
              HIGH I              I                        I
   VARIATE           I              I                        I
                     ─────────────────────────────────────────
                      I              I                        I
                      I              I                        I
   TWO                I GOVERNMENT,  I  ENGINEERING           I
              LOW I ENTREPRENEURS I                        I
                      I              I                        I
                     ─────────────────────────────────────────
```

Within The Groups

The largest group, the Engineering students, was also examined for internal patterns between variables. This group was chosen solely because it was the only group for which we had sufficient responses. The opportunity to compare internal patterns was statistically not available. A PCA on the group correlation matrix, produced many components with similar variance. Amounts of total variance explained were, PC1 (Principal Component 1) 10%, PC2 7%, PC3 6%, PC4 5%, PC5 5%. From this, there did not appear to be simple patterns in the variables, although the first PC could be interpreted.

As an alternative, the FA approach was then tried. A Principal Factor Analysis was performed on the correlation matrix, using Squared Multiple Correlations between variables and the other variables as prior communality estimates. The factors from this expained: 17% (factor1), 10% (factor2), 9% (factor3), 7% (factor4), 7% (factor5), of variance in the reduced correlation matrix. Again only the first, largest, trend is distinct from the others.

Somewhat arbitrarily, the three largest factors were treated as if they represented the most important trends, and VARIMAX rotated in an attempt to get three new factors, each of which had stronger relationships to unique groups of original variables, and so could be better interpreted. Factor 1 is still made up from similar variables to those in PC1 of the PCA. Probably the two are analagous. From the pattern of Factor loadings (See TABLE 2), this first factor is mainly due to correlation in answer to:

V37 ...Do you enjoy being able to make your own decisions on the job
V30 ...Do you try to find the benefits of a bad situation
V24 ...Can you concentrate for extended periods of time on a subject
V45 ...Do friends or associates come to you for unique ideas on problems

V43 ...Do you try to think of past mistakes as a learning proce.
V36 ...Are you likely to work evenings or weekends to complete ·
     work project

     No clearly understood profile emerges from this group of
variables. They generally describe a hard working, positive sort of
person. It may be worth noting that all are behavioural
characteristics, omitting lifestyle or historical variables. As is
generally true with self-assessment on behavioural variables, there i
a risk the respondent tended to give answers seen as desirable, and
the desirability of positive answers may be the thing these have in
common. The argument against this in general is that many of these
variables were important in differentiating among the three groups on
the canonical correlation. The other two factors might also be
investigated. But it is likely that changes in the amount of the dat.
included in the analysis, or the use of a different method, could
produce different factors, so exploration with the present data set
could be mis-leading.

TABLE 1.

Actual questions, and their correlation with Canonical Variates

| Original Variable | CAN 1 | CAN 2 |
|---|---|---|
| 1. Do you worry about what others think of you? | .10 | .13 |
| 2. Do you watch more than ½ hour television on most days? # | .22** | .21** |
| 3. Do you take the stairs even when an elevator is nearby? # | -.05 | -.13 |
| 4. Do you find it easy to ask others to do something for you who are not employees? | .12 | -.03 |
| 5. Has someone in your family shared their experience of starting a business with you? (Through observation or discussion) | .03 | .23** |
| 6. Do you believe in organizing your tasks before getting started? | .14* | -.11 |
| 7. Are you out of work often due to illness? | -.06 | .26** |
| 8. Do you enjoy doing something just to prove you can? | .01 | -.07 |
| 9. Have you ever been sacked from a job? | .18* | .24** |
| 10. Do you often come up with new ideas? | .31*** | -.02 |
| 11. Would you picture work as a time circle, repeating itself regularly? # | .07 | .06 |
| 12. Did you like formal education? | -.15* | -.12 |
| 13. Were you a very good student at college or university? | -.26** | .01 |
| 14. Were you part of a close group in high school or college? | -.10 | .12 |
| 15. Did you participate in competitive school activities or sports? | .19** | .02 |
| 16. Do you enjoy taking care of details? | -.08 | -.06 |
| 17. Is job security an important factor in your selection of a position? | .05 | -.14* |
| 18. Will you deliberately seek a direct confrontation to get needed results? | .19** | .19** |
| 19. Were you the firstborn child? | -.04 | -.31*** |
| 20. Was your father mostly present during your early life at home? | -.09 | .13 |
| 21. Were you expected to do odd jobs at home before 10 years of age? | .24** | -.03 |
| 22. Do you get bored easily? | -.03 | .29*** |
| 23. Do you forego holidays or earned vacation days? | -.02 | .09 |
| 24. Can you concentrate for extended periods of time on a subject? | -.08 | -.39*** |
| 25. Do you, on occasion, need pep talks from others to keep you going? | -.10 | .25** |
| 26. Are you an immigrant to this country? # | .22** | -.16* |

| Original Variable | CAN 1 | CAN 2 |
|---|---|---|
| 27. Do you avoid problems or situations which have no obvious solutions? | -.19** | .05 |
| 28. Do you enjoy socializing regularly? | -.16* | .20** |
| 29. Have you deliberately exceeded your authority at work? | .58*** | .20** |
| 30. Do you try to find the benefits of a bad situation? | .16* | .11 |
| 31. Do you tend to blame others when something goes wrong? | -.21** | .05 |
| 32. Do you enjoy tackling a task without knowing all the potential problems? | .20** | -.19** |
| 33. Do you persist when others tell you it can't be done? | .17* | -.03 |
| 34. Do you take rejection of projects or ideas as if they were personal rejections? | -.16* | -.01 |
| 35. Do you believe that good luck explains many of your successes? | -.16* | .19** |
| 36. Are you likely to work evenings or weekends to complete a work project? | -.34*** | -.07 |
| 37. Do you enjoy being able to make your own decisions on the job? | .36*** | -.11 |
| 38. Did you wake up happy most of the time? | .31*** | -.03 |
| 39. Do you prefer to let a friend decide on a location for lunch, or social activities?# | -.21** | -.01 |
| 40. Have you moved personal funds from one savings account to another to gain 2 percentage points of interest?# | -.05 | .19** |
| 41. Do you believe that innovators take a very big risk? | -.32*** | -.02 |
| 42. Do you feel that successful managers must have advanced college degrees? | -.18* | .13 |
| 43. Do you try to think of past mistakes as a learning process? | 0 | .01 |
| 44. Are you likely to tell people of your goal prospects or possible successes prior to their coming to pass?# | -.06 | -.06 |
| 45. Do friends or associates come to you for unique ideas on problems?# | .35*** | -.16* |
| 46. Do you think of your work as if it was a line, between two points or stages?# | -.33*** | -.01 |
| 47. Do you prefer to be a loner in your final decision? | -.11 | .15* |
| 48. Do your conversations discuss people more than events or ideas? | .02 | .08 |
| 49. Have you been divorced or separated? | .27** | -.12 |
| 50. Do you sleep as little as possible? | -.03 | .10 |

Variables unique to this study are shown by (#)
Significance of difference from no correlation:  *** = p< 0.0001;
** = p< 0.01; * = p< .05

TABLE 2

Varimax Rotated Factor Pattern for Engineering student group.

| | FACTOR1 | FACTOR2 | FACTOR3 |
|---|---|---|---|
| Variable 37 | 0.62 | -0.00 | -0.05 |
| Variable 30 | 0.53 | -0.40 | -0.00 |
| Variable 24 | 0.49 | -0.31 | 0.07 |
| Variable 45 | 0.47 | -0.24 | 0.33 |
| Variable 43 | 0.46 | 0.07 | 0.09 |
| Variable 36 | 0.45 | 0.10 | 0.01 |
| Variable 10 | 0.41 | -0.25 | -0.07 |
| Variable 4 | 0.38 | -0.13 | 0.27 |
| Variable 18 | 0.38 | -0.00 | -0.03 |
| Variable 50 | 0.38 | -0.07 | -0.34 |
| Variable 5 | 0.38 | 0.03 | 0.09 |
| Variable 23 | 0.38 | 0.10 | -0.28 |
| Variable 40 | 0.37 | 0.02 | -0.12 |
| Variable 33 | 0.36 | -0.24 | -0.20 |
| Variable 29 | 0.35 | -0.18 | -0.32 |
| Variable 6 | 0.34 | 0.20 | 0.25 |
| Variable 16 | 0.32 | 0.14 | 0.26 |
| Variable 8 | 0.27 | -0.21 | 0.09 |
| Variable 15 | 0.24 | -0.07 | 0.18 |
| Variable 46 | 0.24 | 0.02 | -0.18 |
| Variable 21 | 0.21 | -0.14 | -0.12 |
| Variable 44 | 0.17 | -0.15 | 0.03 |
| Variable 20 | -0.35 | -0.21 | 0.14 |
| Variable 27 | -0.19 | 0.50 | -0.09 |
| Variable 11 | 0.09 | 0.48 | -0.00 |
| Variable 25 | -0.07 | 0.47 | -0.12 |
| Variable 17 | -0.04 | 0.45 | 0.38 |
| Variable 1 | -0.09 | 0.41 | 0.17 |
| Variable 41 | 0.07 | 0.40 | -0.10 |
| Variable 2 | -0.22 | 0.29 | 0.14 |
| Variable 35 | -0.14 | 0.26 | -0.16 |
| Variable 34 | 0.12 | 0.25 | -0.23 |
| Variable 48 | -0.01 | 0.19 | 0.16 |
| Variable 42 | 0.07 | 0.15 | 0.03 |
| Variable 3 | -0.10 | -0.12 | -0.06 |
| Variable 19 | 0.04 | -0.28 | 0.13 |
| Variable 32 | 0.11 | -0.61 | -0.09 |
| Variable 14 | 0.10 | 0.08 | 0.59 |
| Variable 13 | -0.08 | -0.07 | 0.44 |
| Variable 12 | 0.13 | 0.08 | 0.41 |
| Variable 38 | 0.08 | -0.27 | 0.40 |
| Variable 28 | 0.19 | -0.03 | 0.40 |
| Variable 39 | -0.17 | 0.15 | 0.28 |
| Variable 26 | 0.04 | 0.09 | 0.25 |
| Variable 49 | -0.08 | -0.10 | 0.15 |
| Variable 7 | 0.01 | 0.06 | -0.10 |
| Variable 22 | 0.02 | 0.10 | -0.29 |
| Variable 31 | -0.22 | 0.17 | -0.29 |
| Variable 47 | 0.30 | -0.12 | -0.34 |
| Variable 9 | 0.14 | -0.08 | -0.41 |

We have produced results that clearly differentiate among three groups of respondents; groups that were initially perceived to differ in their training, aspirations, and career positions. We can also assume the responses which entrepreneurs would give, based on prior studies. Thus we conclude the government group is more similar to the entrepreneur in a composite of behaviour, lifestyle and background than the other two groups. It is possible that other differences in the compositions of the groups could also be causing the differences in response, and hence be confounding our inference. The government employee group would have been different in several ways. It contains older people, somewhat more likely to be male, who might not have been as highly educated as the students, might be from different social backgrounds, had good job security, and some reason for staying in their job despite attractive alternatives in the private sector. Although these factors could be causing the difference in response, they are also heavily entwined with entrepreneurship itself, as authors continually find people with just such characteristics choosing entrepreneurship or staying with their small business. The government group made the most direct investment in participation in the seminar. Thus they can be seen as representing a strong interest in entrepreneurship, even if still within the government. So potential confounding differences in the groups may just be other correlates of entrepreneurial potential. Despite this, there is still work to do with design of such questionnaires and understanding the relation of results to as complex a concept as entrepreneurship.

The individual questions used could be examined again in view of what patterns of response, if any, they fell into, but the questionnaire has not been applied to enough diverse groups or large enough populations within any group for any question to be discarded, yet. The effect of applying questions in differing orders could be examined, although the current order was an attempt to remove patterns.

Relating questionnaire results to other groups or types of activity is desirable. One possibility is to apply the questionnaire to participants in educational seminars on business start-up, along with some more background questions on previous activity. Existing entrepreneurs might also be studied directly, and compared to other groups, perhaps with some case matching on the basis of age, sex, and background, so other features of a person, apart from questionnaire response, which associate with activity, might be isolated.

We believe that instruments such as this are of value in adding insight into differences and similarities among career groups in general, but are of particular value when we have confidence the composite bears some relationship to entrepreneurs. Related work by the authors (in progress) looks for _geographical_ variations in a group's entrepreneurial propensity, and for cultural or sub-cultural variations. Hofstede (1984) provides an excellent example of careful cross cultural analysis of work related values, identifying one dimension which relates to entrepreneurship. The initial study described here could support more focussed comparison of entrepreneurial orientation, based on a broader array of characteristics.

## REFERENCES

Balogh, Judy, M.C. Ashmore, N. Ross, J. Bebris, L.M. Fischer, and P. Baker, Beyond a Dream: an instructor's guide for small business exploration, Columbus, Ohio: The National Center for Research in Vocational Education, 1985

Bartlett, M.S. 1947. "Multivariate Analysis". Journal of the Royal Statistical Society 9(suppl.) p176-197.

Chatfield, C. and A.J. Collins. 1980. Introduction to multivariate analysis.New York: Chapman and Hall, 246pp.

Fierro, Daniel R. , The New American Entrepreneur: How to get off the Fast Track into a Business of Your Own New York: Morrow, 1982

Greenfield, W.M., Calculated Risk, A Guide to Entrepreneurship, Lexington, Mass: D.C. Heath and Co., 1986

Hofstede, G., Culture's Consequences. Beverly Hills, Ca: Sage, 1984

Hornaday, John A. and John Aboud, "Characteristics of Successful Entrepreneurs," in Entrepreneurship and Venture Management, Clifford M. Baumback and Joseph R. Mancuso, eds., Englewood Cliffs, NJ: Prentice Hall, 1975, pp. 11-21.

Hoy, Frank, and James W. Carland, Jr., "Differentiating Between Entrepreneurs and Small Business Owners in New Venture Formation", in Frontiers of Entrepreneurship Research, John A Hornaday, Jeffry A. Timmons, and Karl H. Vesper, eds., Wellesly Mass.: Babson College, p. 157-166.

New York Daily News, August 7, 1983

Mancuso, Joseph, Center for Entrepreneurial Management, 1983, as cited in Greenfield, W.M., Calculated Risk, A Guide to Entrepreneurship, Lexington, Mass: D.C. Heath and Co., 1986

McClelland, D.C., "Achievement and Entrepreneurship", Journal of Personal and Social Psychology, Vol. 1, (1965) pp. 389-392.

Pimentel, R.A. 1979. Morphometrics the multivariate analysis of biological data. Kendall/Hunt Publishing Co. Dubuque, Iowa. 276pp.

Ronstadt, Robert C.,"The Decision Not to Become An Entrepreneur" in Frontiers of Entrepreneurship Research, John A Hornaday, Jeffry A. Timmons, and Karl H. Vesper, eds., Wellesly Mass.: Babson College, p. 192-212.

SAS Institute Inc. 1982. SAS User's Guide: Statistics, 1982 Edition, SAS Institute Inc. Cary N.C. 584pp.

SAS Institute Inc. 1985. SAS/STAT Guide for Personal Computers, Version 6 Edition, SAS Institute Inc. Cary N.C. 378pp.

Schollhammer, Hans, and Arthur H. Kuriloff, Entrepreneurship and Small Business Management, New York: John Wiley & Sons, 1979

Seber, G.A.F. 1984. Multivariate Observations, New York: John Wiley and Sons, 686 pp.

Sexton, Donald L. and Nancy B. Bowman, "Comparative Entrepreneurship Characteristics of Students:  Preliminary Results", in Frontiers of Entrepreneurship Research, John A Hornaday, Jeffry A. Timmons, and Karl H. Vesper, eds., Wellesly Mass.: Babson College, p. 213-232.

SUMMARY

## A MODEL FOR ASSESSING THE RELATIONSHIP BETWEEN
## ENTREPRENEURIAL NEED FOR ACHIEVEMENT AND LOCUS OF CONTROL

Authors

Richard K. Hay
Michelle J. Walker

Address

O. Gene Bicknell Center for Entrepreneurship
Pittsburg State University
Pittsburg, KS 66762
(316) 231-7000, Ext. 4598

Principal Topics

Locus of control
Achievement and goal setting
Entrepreneurial characteristics

Method and Data Base

378 Entrepreneurs were interviewed in depth by students in entrepreneurial courses.

Three instruments: A questionnaire survey selected characteristics of the entrepreneur and the venture; the locus of control instrument developed by Rotter; and a life goals questionnaire were used.

Respondents were classified into two groups based upon locus of control.

Major Findings

Major findings of this study include:

Personal characteristics of the two groups were approximately the same except that the externals tended to be somewhat better educated, relatively younger, and had slightly fewer children.

Business experience and venture characteristics were also similar except that internals were more likely to have been fired, tended toward longer work weeks, and were more likely to be in their first five years with their present venture.

More significantly, externals and internals were equally likely to consider their current venture either successful or very successful.

On an instrument designed to compare the ranking of life goals, significant differences in the composite mean rankings existed for independence and pleasure, which were ranked relatively higher by internals, and for wealth, security, affection, self-realization and expertness, which were ranked relatively higher by externals.

Internals are more likely than externals to pursue an entrepreneurial venture but are not less likely to perceive themselves as successful in that venture.

Externals and internals may well have different measures of success as suggested by the differing rankings of the goals.

## Implications for Practitioners

Major implications for practitioners include:

Locus of control is not necessarily an adequate predictor of entrepreneurial success in that internals who do become entrepreneurs tend to perceive success of their ventures at about the same rate as do externals.

Entrepreneurs, regardless of locus of control, can find the entrepreneurial venture as one means of life goal attainment.

## Implications for Further Research

Suggestions for further research include:

Further conceptualization and modeling of the role of the entrepreneurial venture as a vehicle for goal attainment.

Further investigation of the differing view of success of entrepreneurs when internal versus external locus of control is needed.

# A COMPARATIVE ANALYSIS OF THE EFFECTS OF THE DESIRE FOR PERSONAL CONTROL ON NEW VENTURE INITIATIONS

David B. Greenberger, Ohio State University
Donald L. Sexton, Ohio State University

## ABSTRACT

This paper presents the results of two studies designed to demonstrate the role of personal control as a predisposing variable and a precipitating event in the new venture initiation decision. In the first study of 200 students, it was found that the amount of personal control desired was strongly associated with the anticipation of new venture initiation. In the second study of 56 entrepreneurs and 51 managers, personal control possessed was found to be significantly higher for entrepreneurs than for managers. These results were found despite first the statistical removal of the variance associated with locus of control. Implications for future research on personal control for all stages of the entrepreneurial process are discussed.

## INTRODUCTION

A number of researchers have attempted to answer the question, "Why do some people initiate new ventures while others in similar circumstances do not?" Models for new venture initiation have been developed by Cooper[1] and Martin[2] which indicate that a number of factors affect the venture decision, but researchers have tended to emphasize psychological predisposition and thus often neglect the role of other

---

[1]Arnold C. Cooper, "Strategic Management: New Ventures and Small Business," in Dan E. Schendel and Charles W. Hofer, Strategic Management: A New View of Business Policy and Planning, Little Brown and Co., Boston, MA, 1979, pp. 316-327.

[2]Michael J. C. Martin, Managing Technological Innovation and Entrepreneurship, Reston Publishing Co., Reston, VA, 1984, p. 269.

factors.  Further, as Churchill and Lewis[3] point out, only a small percentage of the articles related to the personal characteristics of entrepreneurs demonstrated the extent to which the research converged on the core issues in the field.

Studies of the psychological characteristics of entrepreneurs have been numerous and varied.  A variety of traits have been evaluated by administering different test instruments to persons included in a number of different definitions of an entrepreneur.  Three trait measurement tests that have been used most frequently have been those related to risk-taking[4], need for achievement[5], and locus of control[6]. Although neither locus of control nor need for achievement were found to be significant in differentiating entrepreneurs from managers, Sexton and Bowman-Upton[7] found in a recent study that when other more carefully validated test instruments were used, that intensity level of some psychological characteristics differentiated entrepreneurs from managers.

The use of instruments with questionable validity, small sample sizes, inconsistent definitions of the entrepreneur, and a paucity of comparable studies have resulted in persons concluding that this particular research stream generally is inadequate.  Van de Ven[8] suggests that these studies are similar to the early leadership research in which taxonomies of personality traits were developed to characterize effective leaders.  The same problems and conflicting results apparent in these

---

[3]Neil C. Churchill and Virginia L. Lewis, "Entrepreneurship Research:  Directions and Methods" in Donald L. Sexton and Raymond W. Smilor, eds., The Art and Science of Entrepreneurship, Ballinger Publishing Co., Cambridge, MA, 1986, pp. 333-365.

[4]N. Kogan and M. A. Wallach, Risk Taking, Holt, Rinehart and Winston, New York, 1964.

[5]D. C. McClelland, "Achievement Motivation Can be Developed," Harvard Business Review, November-December 1965.

[6]Julian B. Rotter, "Generalized Expectancies for Internal Versus External Control of Reinforcement," Psychological Monographs, 80, 1966, (1, Whole No. 609).

[7]Donald L.Sexton and Nancy B. Bowman-Upton, "Validation of a Personality Index:  Comparative Psychological Characteristics Analysis of Female Entrepreneurs, Managers, Entrepreneurship Students and Business Students," in Robert Ronstadt, John A. Hornaday, Rein Peterson, & Karl H. Vesper, eds., Frontiers of Entrepreneurship Research, Babson College, Wellesley, MA, 1986, pp. 40-51.

[8]Andrew H. Van de Ven, "Early Planning, Implementation and Performance of New Organizations," in J. R. Kimberly and R. Miles, eds., The Organization Life Cycle, Jossey Bass, San Francisco, 1980, pp. 83-134.

early studies[9] are also evident in the entrepreneurship literature that has taken this similar approach. Because these leadership studies did not consider the importance of situational factors, the entrepreneurial research, which also concentrates primarily on the description of personality traits and does not consider the moderating effect of situational factors[10], is similarly inadequate.

Sexton and Bowman-Upton[11] also discuss an additional problem: it is common for successful business persons to be internal on the locus of control scale and to have high needs for achievement. That is, whether or not they initiate their own venture, it is likely that most successful business persons exhibit many of the same personality characteristics, on these and other dimensions, as the entrepreneurs. Thus, if the set of personality characteristics is not unique to the entrepreneur, then the value of this line of research is problematic.

Finally, although researchers in this and other management areas have relied on these personality instruments, there exists real concerns about the psychometric properties of these instruments. Mirels[12] and Gurin, Gurin, and Morrison[13], for example, have empirically demonstrated the multidimensional nature of the locus of control scale. Thus, the possibility of spurious results from unreliable instruments can not be overlooked.

In sum, much of the research which has sought to develop psychological profiles of entrepreneur is descriptive, poorly defined, and methodologically imprecise. Researchers may have developed a general composite of the entrepreneur, but this composite is probably quite similar to the composite of many other successful managers. Some recent, comparative research studies have identified a number of psychological characteristics which differentiate entrepreneurs from managers, but psychological characteristics, while necessary, are not sufficient to predict a new venture initiation decision.

---

[9]See Arthur G. Jago, "Leadership: Perspectives in Theory and Research," Management Science, 28, 1982, pp. 315-336.

[10]Van de Ven, op. cit.

[11]Donald L. Sexton and Nancy B. Bowman-Upton, "Validation of a Personality Index: Comparative Psychological Characteristics Analysis of Female Entrepreneurs, Managers, Entrepreneurship Students and Business Students," in Robert Ronstadt, John A. Hornaday, Rein Peterson, & Karl H. Vesper, eds., Frontiers of Entrepreneurship Research, Babson College, Wellesley, MA, 1986, pp. 40-51.

[12]Herbert L. Mirels, "Dimensions of Internal Versus External Control," Journal of Consulting and Clinical Psychology, 36, 1970, pp. 40-44.

[13]Gurin, P., G. Gurin and B. M. Morrison, "Personal and Ideological Aspects of Internal and External Control," Social Psychology, 41, 1978, pp. 275-296.

As indicated, Martin's[14] recent model of new venture initiation includes a number of variables, as well as psychological pre-disposition, which are likely to aid in the understanding of the uniqueness of the new venture initiation process. Research already has examined some of the twelve areas which are hypothesized to interact to influence the new venture initiation decision, but most have not been studied. Two of the most important areas appear to be psychological predispositions and precipitating events.

## PERSONAL CONTROL

Although existing psychological approaches to entrepreneurship have so far met with limited success, this is not to suggest that such an approach is necessarily misdirected. Instead, utilization of psychological theories and their constructs, other than those based upon personality traits, can provide new insights into the prediction of new venture initiation. The relevance of many of these different psychological approaches to the study of new venture initiation rests in the underlying assumption that many of these psychological states change according to the situation. Thus, the individuals perceptions of certain key events in the environment may alter their psychological states and thereby precipitate the initiation of new ventures.

As the relevance of the psychological pre-disposition changes according to situational factors, so do the precipitating events in Martin's model. Precipitating events include factors such as lay-off, dismissal, or job frustration. Lay-off and dismissal are either-or finite situations, while job frustration or job dissatisfaction are relevant, situation factors. A study by Cooper and Dunkelberg[15] of high tech start-ups noted that the engineers who started the new ventures were satisfied with their current salaries and opportunities for future advancements in their existing organizations. This might lead to conclusions that factors other than compensation and future opportunities contribute to the precipitating event of job frustrations. Unfortunately, until recently, attempts to quantify the job frustration factor had met with limited success.

Recent advances in psychological research on personal control, and the application of this research in the study of behavior in organizations has indicated that one of the most important variables affecting an individual's behavior is their perception of personal

---

[14]Martin, op. cit.

[15]Arnold C. Cooper and William C. Dunkelberg, "A New Look at Business Entry: Experience of 1805 Entrepreneurs" in Karl Vesper, ed., Frontiers of Entrepreneurship Research, Babson College, Wellesley, MA, 1981, pp. 1-20.

control[16]. It is hypothesized that perceptions of personal control are critical components of the two areas of the Martin model: the psychological predisposition and the frustrating event which precipitates the new venture initiation decision.

Greenberger and Strasser[17] define personal control as "an individual's beliefs, at a given point in time, in his or her ability to effect a change, in a desired direction, on the environment." In essence, they suggest that persons perceive themselves as possessing control when covariation (a relationship) is perceived by them to exist between their actions and their outcomes. That is, individuals will feel a sense of personal control when they believe that their actions will result in desired outcomes.

Because of its similarity to a number of management constructs, it is important to distinguish personal control from power (and influence) and locus of control. Personal control and the constructs like power or influence[18], while similar conceptually, differ in important ways. For example, power is often defined as an objective commodity possessed by organizational members. The objective nature of power is grounded in organizational hierarchy, formally defined lines of authority, status or role definitions, information possessed, etc. In contrast, personal control is primarily a cognitive construct; its perceived presence may be a function of objective reality, but also the individual's beliefs, personality, vicarious observations, and biases. Thus, unlike power, personal control may or may not be veridical. Second, power involves influence attempts from one person to another person. Personal control, a subjective perception, may or may not involve actual attempts to influence. Third, Langer[19] notes that the need for power often varies greatly across the individual's life. Some persons, for example, have no need for power. In contrast, although situational events influence its magnitude, personal control is something most persons desire on an ongoing basis. Because of these differences,

---

[16]Max H. Bazerman, "Impact of Personal Control on Performance: Is Added Control Always Beneficial?", _Journal of Applied Psychology_, 67, 1982, pp. 472-479. Greenberger, D. B. & S. Strasser, "The Development and Application of a Model of Personal Control in Organizations," _Academy of Management Review_, 11, 1986, pp. 164-177. Jackson, S. C., "Participation in Decision Making as a Strategy for Reducing Job Related Tension," _Journal of Applied Psychology_, 68, 1983, pp. 3-19.

[17]Greenberger and Strasser, _op. cit._

[18]J. R. P. French & B. Raven, "The Bases of Social Power," in D. Cartwright and A. Zander, eds., _Group Dynamics_, Harper and Row, New York, 1968. Mowday, R. T., "The Exercise of Upward Influence in Organizations," _Administrative Science Quarterly_, 23, 1978, pp. 137-156.

[19]Ellen J. Langer, _The Psychology of Control_, Sage, Beverly Hills, CA, 1983.

power and personal control do not have to be highly correlated. Langer[20] provides the example of a CEO's first day in this position. The CEO clearly possesses great power, but he or she may perceive him/herself as possessing little control.

Personal control also differs from the personality variable, locus of control. Locus of control[21] is conceptualized to be a relatively stable propensity to locate causality for outcomes either in the self or in the external world. Rotter suggested that individuals differ in their expectations about the sources of positive and negative reinforcements for their behaviors. Individuals who view themselves as having the ability to affect reinforcing events are labelled "internals," whereas those persons who see reinforcing events as resulting from luck, chance or others are labelled "externals." Personal control, in contrast, reflects the ongoing ebb and flow of one's perceptions about covariation between action and a variety of outcomes. As such, there are four essential differences between these constructs. First, locus of control refers an individual difference in propensity to make attributions about reinforcing outcomes; personal control is concerned with any of a variety of outcomes. Second, locus of control concerns the origin of these outcomes; personal control perceptions are the beliefs about the occurrence of the event. Third, locus of control is hypothesized to be relatively stable, whereas personal control has the potential for changing as the individual is exposed to new environments. Fourth, regardless of the individual's locus of control, virtually all persons are motivated to see themselves as controlling aspects of their environment. Therefore, if two persons are high in personal control, one may believe that only her hard work is the cause of her achieving desired outcomes, whereas the other may believe that luck dictates her achievement of desired outcomes. Nevertheless, Fiske and Taylor[22] suggest that individuals' reactions to control-based interventions (such as therapies to alleviate stress or depression) may differ according to the individual's locus of control. Thus, locus of control may influence the perceptions of the action-outcome relationship.

Greenberger[23] suggested that there are two critical components of control perceptions: the control desired and the control possessed. Greenberger and Strasser[24] maintain that a person's control perceptions and resulting responses can be understood in terms of their overall level of desires and the attainment of personal control. That is, the

---

[20]Langer, op. cit.

[21]Rotter, op. cit.

[22]Susan T. Fiske & Shelley E. Taylor, Social Cognition, Random House, New York, 1984.

[23]David B. Greenberger, Personal Control at Work: Its Conceptualization and Measurement, University of Wisconsin-Madison ONR Tech. Rep. 1-1-4-1982.

[24]Greenberger and Strasser, op. cit.

interaction of how much control a person wants and how much he/she perceives him/herself as possessing may be an important determinant of his/her cognition and behaviors. When control desired exceeds control possessed, "a state of imbalance is created and employees move to the reaction stage of the model." In this reaction stage, the individual attempts (because persons are motivated to seek control) to gain greater control through whatever means are available. Greenberger and Strasser suggest that many organizations provide opportunities for their employees to increase their control productively (i.e., in ways consistent with organizational goals). When the organization does not provide these opportunities, the employees still attempt to increase their control, but this time in unanticipated (and often, undesirable) ways.

## PERSONAL CONTROL AND NEW VENTURE INITIATION

The authors suggest that existing entrepreneurs and potential entrepreneurs (those who anticipate initiating a new venture) have a greater desire for personal control than do most managers. Further, because of this high level of personal control desired, it is unlikely that any single organization, particularly one in which this individual is in a subordinate role, will possess the opportunities necessary for this person to achieve his/her desired level of control. Thus, the only way in which this person can accomplish his/her desired outcomes, is to initiate a new venture. This venture is hypothesized to be initiated when some event makes the levels of control possessed and control desired salient to them. From this salient precipitating event, the individuals come to realize that the amount of control they desire is in a grossly imbalanced state with the amount of control they see themselves as possessing. In turn, the ownership of their own business should result in high levels of control possessed.

The two studies presented in this paper represent a first test of the impact of personal control on the new venture initiation process. In study 1, the impact of personal control desired on the anticipated decision to initiate a new venture is examined. Samples of business students enrolled as entrepreneurial majors (budding entrepreneurs) and as general business majors (budding managers) were asked to indicate the likelihood of their initiating a new venture after graduation. Because entrepreneurs are expected to have much higher levels of control desired than the average manager, it is hypothesized that personal control desired among the student groups would be positively associated with anticipated new venture initiation. Because of the similarity of personal control and locus of control, the individuals' locus of control score is entered first in the regression equation. The removal of variance associated with locus of control therefore allows the reader to be certain that personal control desired has a unique impact on the anticipated decision to initiate a new venture.

In study 2, a sample of existing managers and entrepreneurs are compared to assess the relative importance of personal control desired and personal control possessed for each group. Again, after removing the variance associated with locus of control, the ability to discriminate between these two samples is assessed with the two variables: control desired and control possessed. It is hypothesized that entrepreneurs will exhibit higher levels of personal control possessed than managers who do own their own business. In addition, because of their greater underlying need to control outcomes, it is hypothesized that entrepreneurs will exhibit slightly higher levels of control desired than managers.

## STUDY 1

### Method

Subjects. The subjects were 242 undergraduate and graduate students majoring in entrepreneurship or the more functional business majors at two large universities. Approximately the same number of students participated from the two universities (112 versus 130). Of the total, 117 students were majoring in entrepreneurship. There were 59 undergraduates and 183 graduate students. Finally, there were nearly twice as many males as females in the sample (163 versus 79, respectively).

Procedure. Students were asked to complete a short questionnaire during their regularly scheduled class. Participation was voluntary. Nearly all students who were present completed the questionnaire. The questionnaire asked some basic background information about sex, major and undergraduate/graduate level; students were not asked to place their names on the questionnaire.

Measures. Control desired was assessed by the 11 item (Likert format) control desired scale developed by Greenberger[25]. The questions ask how much control, influence, and freedom of action the individual would like to have in a wide variety of work related areas. These include: the variety of tasks performed, decisions as to when things will be done in the work unit, the quality of the individual's work, performance standards in the unit, and the way equipment is arranged in the work area. The eleven items were unit weighted, summed, and divided by 11 to derive the scale score. This scale has shown excellent psychometric properties in previous research. In the present study, Cronbach's alpha was .87.

Locus of control was measured by 13 items from Rotter's[26] scale. Shortened more valid forms of the locus of control scale were utilized for the present study. The number of items included in the scale was reduced on the basis of the work of Mirels[27] and Gurin, Gurin, and

---

[25]Greenberger, op. cit.

[26]Rotter, op. cit.

[27]Mirels, op. cit.

Morrison[28] who found multiple dimensions in the original 24 item locus of control scale. The items selected were those without high loadings on the political control subscales. These subscales (which ask questions about the individual's beliefs about their ability to influence political decisions) appear to be less relevant to behavior in organizations (and questionable relevance in most situations). The locus of control scale in the present study had a coefficient alpha of .70.

The individual's anticipated entrepreneurial behavior was assessed by a single, Likert format question. If the person did not already own his/her own business they were asked: "How likely are you to start your won business within 5 years after your graduation?" Responses ranged from definitely would not start my own business to definitely would start my own business.

Results

Means, standard deviations, and zero order correlations for the major study variables are presented in Table 1.

TABLE 1

Means, Standard Deviations, and Correlations for Major Study Variables

| Variable | Mean | S.D. | 1 | 2 | 3 |
|---|---|---|---|---|---|
| 1. Anticipated New Venture Initiation | 3.67 | 1.17 | 1.00 | | |
| 2. Control Desired | 4.14 | .50 | .33 | 1.00 | |
| 3. Locus of Control | 21.95 | 2.43 | .30 | .39 | 1.00 |

The principle hypothesis was that the amount of control desired would significantly predict the initiation of new ventures. Recall that the desire to initiate new ventures was assessed by asking individuals to indicate the likelihood that they would start their own business in the next five years. Those persons who already owned their own business, were not included in this analysis. As can be seen in Table 2, control desired significantly predicts anticipated initiation of new ventures. This is a particularly impressive result because the effect of locus of control was held constant. That is, even with the correlation of .39 between personal control desired and locus of control, personal control desired uniquely predicts the anticipated initiation of new ventures. The relationships were in the predicted direction: the greater the amount of control desired, the greater the individual's anticipation that he/she would initiate his/her own venture.

---

[28]Gurin, et al., op. cit.

TABLE 2

Results of Regression Analysis of the Effects of Personal Control Desired
and Locus of Control on Anticipated Initiation of a New Venture

| Independent Variable | B | $R^2$ | $F_R2$ | dR2 | FdR2 |
|---|---|---|---|---|---|
| Locus of Control | .21** | .09 | 18.21*** | .09 | 18.31*** |
| Personal Control Desired | .25*** | .14 | 15.22*** | .05 | 11.27*** |

N = 200
** p<.01
*** p<.001

A second set of analysis was performed on the small sample of
students who already owned businesses. Because these students were only
asked whether or not they "now have your own business," it can not be
ascertained whether the individual him/herself initiated this particular
venture or whether it was initiated by someone else. Since many of these
ventures were initiated by the individual respondent, this measure
provides an additional (and very conservative) measure for this study.
Because of the small sample size (only 42 respondents had their own
business), locus of control was not examined in this analysis. As
expected, control desired was significant associated with business
ownership ($r$ = .14; $p$ < .05). The greater the control desired, the more
likely individuals were to own their business.

STUDY 2

Method

Subjects. The subjects were 107 managers and entrepreneurs in
different businesses in the central Ohio area. The sample was composed
of 56 entrepreneurs and 51 managers. The entrepreneurs were defined as
owners or founders of firms that had five or more employees and annual
revenues in excess of $250,000.00. The managers were defined as either
the top executive in firms with annual revenues of five million dollars
or less, vice-presidents in firms with revenues between five and ten
million dollars, and middle level managers in firms with revenues greater
than ten million dollars.

The sample composition was quite similar. The educational level
of the managers averaged 3.5 years of college verses 3.1 years for the
entrepreneurs. The managers were younger with 35% less than 30 years,
70% less than 40 and 94% less than 50 years of age. The age distribution
for the entrepreneurs was 7% under 30 years. 40% under 40, and 69% less
than 50 years of age.

The type of businesses represented by the entrepreneurs and managers were very closely matched. Differences of two percent or less between the two groups were found in retail operations (30%), services (25%), restaurants and food processing (14%), real estate and construction (14%), manufacturing (12%), and transportation (5%).

Procedure. The entrepreneurs and managers were asked to complete a short questionnaire administered by students as a networking project in an entrepreneurship class. All students were required to interview six individuals: three entrepreneurs and three managers. Participation in the questionnaire was voluntary.

Measures. Control desired was assessed by same 11 item (Likert format) control desired scale developed by Greenberger[29]. The eleven items were unit weighted, summed, and divided by 11 to derive the scale score. In the present study, Cronbach's alpha was .86.

Control possessed was assessed by an 11 item (Likert format) control possessed scale developed by Greenberger[30]. These 11 items were identical to those in the control desired scale, except they asked how much control the individual though he/she possessed (rather than how much he/she would like). The eleven items were unit weighted, summed, and divided by 11 to derive the scale score. In the present study, Cronbach's alpha was .85.

Locus of control was measured by same 13 items from Rotter's (1966) scale as was utilized in the previous study. The locus of control scale in the present study had a coefficient alpha of .65.

Results

A discriminant analysis was performed on the data. In the analysis, the two groups were entrepreneurs and managers; the discriminating variables were locus of control, personal control possessed and personal control desired. The eigenvalue for the one discriminant function was .089; the Wilks lambda was .917 ($X^2$ = 8.18; $p < .05$).

The standardized canonical discriminant function coefficients are presented in Table 3.

---

[29]Greenberger, op. cit.

[30]Ibid.

TABLE 3

Standardized Canonical Discriminant Coefficients for Function

| Variables | Discriminant Coefficients |
|---|---|
| Locus of Control | .090 |
| Control Possessed | 1.368 |
| Control Desired | -0.833 |

As can be seen, the coefficient for locus of control was quite small which indicates a relatively weak influence on the dependent variable. This finding tends to support the research by Brockhaus and Nord[31] while adding to the growing list of studies which indicate that locus of control is a necessary trait but not one which is unique to the entrepreneur[32]. The functions for control possessed and control desired apparently are more meaningful. When these coefficients are examined with respect to the group centroids (for the managers = -.32; for the entrepreneurs = .28), it can be seen that managers and entrepreneurs possess and desire differing levels of control. Managers indicate that they possess less control than do entrepreneurs, but the managers desire more control than do the entrepreneurs. The mean level of control possessed for the managers (Mean =4.22) was found to be significantly different from the mean level of control possessed for the entrepreneurs (Mean = 4.56) ($F$ =6.02; $p$ < .05). The mean level of control desired for the two groups was nearly identical.

## DISCUSSION

The data clearly suggest that the amount of personal control is strongly predictive of past and future initiation of new ventures. Personal control desired was found to be strongly associated with anticipated new venture initiation; personal control possessed enables one to discriminate between those persons who owned and initiated their own business and those persons who were managers in businesses owned and begun by someone else. The one hypothesis which was not supported by the data concerned the failure to find differences between entrepreneurs and

---

[31]Robert H. Brockhaus and W. R. Nord, "An Exploration of the Factors Affecting the Entrepreneurial Decision: Personal Characteristics vs. Environmental Conditions," _Proceedings_, Atlanta: Academy of Management, 1979.

[32]Donald L. Sexton and Nancy B. Bowman, "Comparative Entrepreneurial Characteristics of Students: Preliminary Results" in John Hornaday, Jeffry Timmons, and Karl Vesper, eds., _Frontiers of Entrepreneurship Research_, Babson College, Wellesley, MA, 1983, pp. 213-232.

managers on personal control desired. One possible explanation for the similarity across the two samples is that when persons perceive themselves as possessing large amounts of control, the amount of control they desire is diminished. Thus, successful entrepreneurs believe they possess a large amount of control, and in turn, feel less motivation for control at this time.

The data from the two studies are particularly impressive in view of the fact that locus of control was statistically controlled. The removal of variance associated with this variable, which has been used previously in a number of studies of entrepreneurship, indicates that components of personal control, by themselves, are predictive of entrepreneurial behavior.

Although supportive of the hypotheses, this is nevertheless a limited, first test of the role of personal control in the new venture initiation process. As suggested, the authors believe that the relationship of personal control desired to personal control possessed plays a critical role not only as a predictor of who is likely to initiate a new venture, but also as a factor in the determination of job frustration in the precipitating event suggested by Martin[33]. A salient event which highlights the individual's low level of control possessed may precipitate a review of control feelings and thereby impel the individual to move into a position of greater control. A longitudinal study of potential entrepreneurs, for example, could demonstrate that those who initiate a new venture have greater desires for personal control, find control to be more salient, and have greater anticipation that the initiation of a new venture will result in a desired outcome (i.e., lead to greater control) than those not initiating a new venture.

Finally, a longitudinal study of entrepreneur could also provide data on another important implication of personal control and the entrepreneur. One of the continuing problems in many rapidly growing businesses occurs in later stages of organizational development[34]. As the business grows and the organization evolves into a very different format, the entrepreneur is often forced to confront a problem of delegation. According to Thain, when the organization moves from the small and simple, stage 1 (the "one man show") to the large and complex, stage 3 (the "multi-unit general office and decentralized divisions"), leaders often refuse to delegate power and authority. The psychological construct, personal control, may explain this reluctance to delegate power and authority to subordinates. As indicated, it is likely that entrepreneurs have high needs and desires for control and that they already have learned that they can achieve desired outcomes in their business. Entrepreneurs thus may be afraid that by relinquishing their authority, they will possess less of the control they so strongly need. Ultimately, when they voluntarily or involuntarily delegate control, they my actually find themselves in possession of too little control. The

---

[33]Martin, op. cit.

[34]Donald H. Thain, "Stages of Corporate Development," The Business Quarterly, 1969, pp. 32-45.

salience of this perception, in turn, may precipitate either an attempt to regain control in the previous venture or the initiation of a new venture.

REFERENCES

Bazerman, Max H., "Impact of Personal Control on Performance: Is Added Control Always Beneficial?", Journal of Applied Psychology, 67, 1982, pp. 472-479.

Brockhaus, Robert H. and W. R. Nord, "An Exploration of the Factors Affecting the Entrepreneurial Decision: Personal Characteristics vs. Environmental Conditions," Proceedings, Atlanta: Academy of Management, 1979.

Churchill, Neil C. and Virginia L. Lewis, "Entrepreneurship Research: Directions and Methods" in Donald L. Sexton and Raymond W. Smilor, eds., The Art and Science of Entrepreneurship, Ballinger Publishing Co., Cambridge, MA, 1986, pp. 333-365.

Cooper, Arnold C., "Strategic Management: New Ventures and Small Business," in Dan E. Schendel and Charles W. Hofer, Strategic Management: A New View of Business Policy and Planning, Little Brown and Co., Boston, MA, 1979, pp. 316-327.

Cooper, Arnold C. and William C. Dunkelberg, "A New Look at Business Entry: Experience of 1805 Entrepreneurs" in Karl Vesper, ed., Frontiers of Entrepreneurship Research, Babson College, Wellesley, MA, 1981, pp. 1-20.

Fiske, S. T. & S. E. Taylor, Social Cognition, Random House, NY, 1984.

French, J. R. P. & B. Raven, "The Bases of Social Power," in D. Cartwright and A. Zander, eds., Group Dynamics, Harper and Row, New York, 1968.

Greenberger, David B., Personal Control at Work: Its Conceptualization and Measurement, University of Wisconsin-Madison ONR Rep. 1-1-4-1982.

Greenberger, David B. & Stephen Strasser, "The Development and Application of a Model of Personal Control in Organizations," Academy of Management Review, 11, 1986, pp. 164-177.

Gurin, P., G. Gurin and B. M. Morrison, "Personal and Ideological Aspects of Internal and External Control," Social Psychology, 41, 1978, pp. 275-296.

Jackson, S. C., "Participation in Decision Making as a Strategy for Reducing Job Related Tension," Journal of Applied Psychology, 68, 1983, pp. 3-19.

Jago, Arthur G., "Leadership: Perspectives in Theory and Research," _Management Science_, 28, 1982, pp. 315-336.

Kogan, N. and M. A. Wallach, _Risk Taking_, Holt, Rinehart and Winston, New York, 1964.

Langer, E. J., _The Psychology of Control_, Sage, Beverly Hills, CA, 1983.

McClelland, David C., "Achievement Motivation Can be Developed," _Harvard Business Review_, November-December 1965.

Martin, Michael J. C., _Managing Technological Innovation and Entrepreneurship_, Reston Publishing Co., Reston, VA, 1984, p. 269.

Mirels, Herbert L., "Dimensions of Internal Versus External Control," _Journal of Consulting and Clinical Psychology_, 36, 1970, pp. 40-44.

Mowday, Richard T., "The Exercise of Upward Influence in Organizations," _Administrative Science Quarterly_, 23, 1978, pp. 137-156.

Rotter, J. B., "Generalized Expectancies for Internal Versus External Control of Reinforcement," _Psychological Monographs_, 80, 1966, (1, Whole No. 609).

Sexton, Donald L. and Nancy B. Bowman, "Comparative Entrepreneurial Characteristics of Students: Preliminary Results" in John Hornaday, Jeffry Timmons, and Karl Vesper, eds., _Frontiers of Entrepreneurship Research_, Babson College, Wellesley, MA, 1983, pp. 213-232.

Sexton, Donald L. and Nancy B. Bowman-Upton, "Validation of a Personality Index: Comparative Psychological Characteristics Analysis of Female Entrepreneurs, Managers, Entrepreneurship Students and Business Students," in Robert Ronstadt, John A. Hornaday, Rein Peterson, & Karl H. Vesper, eds., _Frontiers of Entrepreneurship Research_, Babson College, Wellesley, MA, 1986, pp. 40-51.

Thain, Donald H., "Stages of Corporate Development," _The Business Quarterly_, 1969, pp. 32-45.

Van de Ven, Andrew H., "Early Planning, Implementation and Performance of New Organizations," in J. R. Kimberly and R. Miles, eds., _The Organization Life Cycle_, Jossey Bass, San Francisco, pp. 83-134, 1980.

SUMMARY

## BUSINESS INITIATION AND SUCCESS:  A SIMULATION STUDY OF PERSONALITIES AND ORGANIZATIONAL DESIGN

Authors

    Alan L. Carsrud, Ph.D.
    Kenneth W. Olm, Ph.D.
    Barbara G. Dodd, Ph.D.
    Connie Marie Gaglio, M.S.

Addresses

    Entrepreneur Program, BRI 6
    Graduate School of Business Administration
    University of Southern California
    Los Angeles, California 90089-1421
    (213) 743-2098

    Management Department, CBA 4.202
    Graduate School of Business
    The University of Texas at Austin
    Austin, Texas 78712
    (512) 471-3676

    Educational Psychology Department, EDB 540
    College of Education
    The University of Texas at Austin
    Austin, Texas 78712
    (512) 471-4155

    Department of Psychology
    University of Chicago
    contact at:
        Levi Strauss & Company LS/4
        1155 Battery Street
        San Francisco, CA 94120
        (415) 544-3995

Principal Topics

    Business Initiation, Simulation Study, Entrepreneurial Personality,
    Organizational Structure, Research Methodology.

## Major Findings and Implications

The data reported in this paper are based on a laboratory simulation of business initiation and start-up operation. The study attempts to replicate, under controlled conditions, previous research by Carsrud and Olm on the factors affecting success in start-up of entrepreneruial ventures. The study attempts to demonstrate complex interactions between multidimensional achievement motivation, personality traits, and the success of students' "start-up firms".

Success in this study is defined as the net profit and capital stock surplus after eight "quarters" of playing a business start-up simulation game. Regression analyses indicated that multidimensional achievement motivation, need for power and influence, and need for external reinforcement had complex relationships to success at various periods of time. In fact, the greatest effect of personality variables were during the initiation phase of the business.

Findings are compared to data from previous studies of successful entrepreneurs. Results are discussed in terms of the potential limitation of using simulations in studying entrepreneurial development and success. Additional discussion addresses the differences in situational demands between simulations and data from actual entrepreneurs.

SUMMARY

## PROPENSITIES FOR RISK:  A COMPARATIVE STUDY OF RISK ACCEPTANCE LEVELS OF THREE GROUPS:  ENTREPRENEURS, CORPORATE EXECUTIVES AND BUSINESS TEACHERS/CONSULTANTS

Author

   Theodore R. Hartley

Address

   555 Dryad Road
   Santa Monica, CA 90402
   (213) 459-0435

### Principal Topics

What is the risk propensity of entrepreneurs who manage their own
business as compared to that of salaried executives who do not have
an applicable ownership stake in their companies?  How do the risk
profiles of these two groups of executives compare with that of a
group of business teachers who do business consulting and are,
therefore, likely to be influential advisors to business executives
on matters of risk?  Do entrepreneurs have a higher risk tolerance
over all than the other two groups?  If not, is it higher in identifiable situations; if so, is their higher risk propensity apparent
in every case or, for example, in certain business matters only?
What are the principal differences in risk attitudes between these
three groups of business professionals?  Are there subgroupings
within these three classes which have risk characteristics substantially different from each other, for example, older executives versus younger, businessmen of all three groups versus female
executives?

### Method and Data Base

The well documented Kogan and Wallach series of dilemma-of-choice as
modified by O. Jay Krasner was rewritten and restructured for this
study.  Eight dilemmas-of-choice, each with a different level and
kind of risk were presented to individuals in three discrete groups
of business professionals.  The individuals were asked to consider
two response actions in each dilemma situation and to indicate what
level of assurance of success (0% to 100%) he/she would require to
recommend the riskier choice.

As part of the data gathering instrument (a 5 page questionnaire), respondents were asked age, sex, length of service with company, title, how many employees supervised, degree of growth for their company, and their feelings about their contribution to that growth. In succeeding pages the eight dilemmas of choice were presented as mini-case studies and the respondent was asked to circle a % after each dilemma that indicated the level of assurance he/she would need to recommend the more risky choice.

Four tables and one chart present the mean, the arithmetic average and mid-range of the risk assurance responses of the three groups, as well as the make-up by sex and age and experiences of each group. A fifth table reports on a supplemental question regarding risk aversion as it relates to death.

The population studied was made up of 21 successful entrepreneur managers, 18 corporate executives/senior corporate staff and 16 teachers who were also business consultants.

## Major Findings

The entrepreneur group required a lower level of assurance (lower odds) as requisite to recommend the riskier action than either the executive group or the teacher/consultants except in two situations: 1) In a life/death situation relating to surgery, the entrepreneurs required odds of a successful outcome that was as high as the teacher/consultants demanded. 2) In advising a talented music student on a choice between business and music, the entrepreneurs required substantially higher assurance of success as a concert musician than did the executive/employee group.

The teacher/consultants had a risk profile spread across the eight dilemmas that was approximately parallel to that of the entrepreneurs but much more risk avoiding.

There was no discernible overall similarity in risk avoidance patterns between entrepreneurs and executive/employees.

The highest risk avoidance (most favorable odds required to recommend an action) group and situation in the study was the teacher/consultant group advising an experienced executive about his plan to leave a secure job and enter the mail order business. The lowest required odds (perceived as least risk) were 1) by the entrepreneurs in giving up a $125,000 a year job for a much lower paying job and a chance to win the Nobel Prize, and 2) by the non-entrepreneur executives counseling a gifted music student toward a concert career.

## Major Implications

1. Entrepreneurs may be more risk aversive than other groups, including their advisors, in facing serious threats to life and health, and less risk aversive than others in reaching for opportunities for awards and recognition (Nobel Prize).

2. Business teachers as consultants may have attitudes about acceptable risks roughly similar to entrepreneurs except when security
and established position are placed in jeopardy.

3. Entrepreneurs are generally less risk aversive than other corporate executives.

4. Entrepreneurs are willing to accept greater risk if greater gain
is possible. This may not be true for other executives.

5. Women executives are more concerned with security in risk
situations than their male counterparts who are more concerned with
potential gain.

THE CORRIDOR PRINCIPLE: INDEPENDENT ENTREPRENEURS
VERSUS CORPORATE ENTREPRENEURS

David Kopcso, Babson College
Robert Ronstadt, Babson College
William Rybolt, Babson College

ABSTRACT

The Corridor Principle states that many entrepreneurs start new
ventures because they see new opportunities after they've started their
first venture.  This paper extends the original work by examining the
relative propensities of independent entrepreneurs versus corporate
entrepreneurs to pursue the Corridor Principle.  A major hypothesis is
that independent entrepreneurs enjoy longer entrepreneurial careers
compared to corporate entrepreneurs because it is easier for them to
take advantage of the Corridor Principle.  This study is based on
approximately 1100 independent and 150 corporate entrepreneurs.

INTRODUCTION

Background

The Corridor Principle states that many entrepreneurs start new
ventures because they see new opportunities after they've started their
first venture.  Second, third, and subsequent ventures are created when
entrepreneurs move down new venture corridors that are not open to them
until they get into business.

The existence and ubiquitousness of the Corridor Principle was
documented recently by Ronstadt[1].  This paper extends this earlier work
by examining the relative propensities of independent entrepreneurs
versus corporate entrepreneurs to pursue the Corridor Principle.  A
major hypothesis of this paper is that independent entrepreneurs enjoy
longer entrepreneurial careers compared to corporate entrepreneurs
because the later cannot take advantage of the Corridor Principle as
frequently as independent entrepreneurs.  In other words, some corporate
entrepreneurs may have less latitude shifting to a new venture either by

---

[1]Robert Ronstadt, "The Corridor Principle and Entrepreneurial
Time", Journal of Business Venturing, forthcoming 1987.

a massive redirection of an existing business or by creating a new business entity, where such a shift becomes necessary.

## Prior Research

Corporate entrepreneuring bears a striking similarity to independent entrepreneuring along at least one dimension: the more one scrutinizes corporate entrepreneurship, the more one observes a variety of venture types and apparent reasons for success and failure.

In fact, larger corporations have used a variety of organizational approaches to foster entrepreneurship with varying success.[2] [3] [4]   Perhaps the most studied vehicle is the new venture unit.  Testimony coming from various sources indicates that most corporate venture divisions have experienced a poor performance record. [5] [6] [7]   Nevertheless, examples of effective corporate venture groups also exist (3M, Ralston Purina, Exxon).

Although venture units have attracted considerable attention, most large corporations do not possess new venture units . . . about 70% use some other mechanism or nothing according to one survey.[8]  For these companies, "corporate entrepreneuring" may mean several other possibilities.  For example, the mechanism may refer to acquired companies still run by founders without much interference from the parent company.  This approach has been successful according to one report.

---

[2]Roberts, Edward B., "New Ventures for Corporate Growth," Harvard Business Review.  Vol. 58/No. 4, July/August 1980,  pp. 134-142.

[3]Fast, Norman D., and Pratt, Stanley E., "Individual Entrepreneurship and Large Corporations," Frontiers Of  Entrepreneurship Research 1981, (hereafter FOER),  Ed.  Karl H. Vesper, Wellesley, MA: Babson Center for  Entrepreneurial Studies, 1981, pp. 443-451.

[4]MacMillan, Ian C., Block, Zenas, and Narasimha, P.N., "Corporate Venturing: alternatives, Obstacles Encountered, and Experience Effects,  Journal Of Business Venturing, Spring, 1986.

[5]Shapero, Albert, "Corporate Heroes or 'Lousy Managers'?" The Wharton Magazine.  Fall, 1978, pp. 33-37.

[6]Fast, Norman D., "A Visit to the New Venture Graveyard," Research Management.  Vol. XXII/No. 2, March 1979, pp. 18-22.

[7]Brennan, Peter J., "How Entrepreneurs Outdo Corporations," Venture.  June, 1980.

[8]Hisrich, Robert D., and Peters, Michael P., "Establishing A New Venture Unit Within A Firm," Journal Of Business Venturing, Fall,  1986.

"Wholly-owned subsidiaries, headed by founding
intrapreneurs, reportedly become profitable faster and
with less investment than corporate divisions."[9]

Other approaches include new product groups, joint ventures or
"strategic partnerships (minority investment positions in
entrepreneurial enterprises), or venture spin-offs (from technology or
marketing ideas developed by the parent corporation). All have
experienced varying degrees of success, but not to the extent that any
single approach is generally preferred over another.

Just as the approaches to corporate intrapreneuring vary, so do
the apparent reasons for success. An early paper by Kierulff pointed to
the human dimension.[10] The basic message was find and hold good
entrepreneurs. This emphasis was reaffirmed recently in a quantitative
analysis that showed a positive association between a venture's
financial success and the prior experience of its team.[11] Lest we think
the formula for successful "intrapreneuring" is so straightforward, a
much larger set of success factors have been proposed by various
researcher.[12] [13] According to Kanter, one successful stratagem of
corporate venturing is a "dry hole" or portfolio approach... i.e.,
multiple investments in several ventures are better than putting all
one's eggs in a single basket.

## This Research

The Corridor Principle is actually an entrepreneur's imperfect
interpretation of the portfolio approach. For example, we know some
entrepreneurs pursue multiple ventures simultaneously. Others approach
each venture sequentially, often risking less in the earlier ventures.
While these proportions are not clear yet, it does appear that a strong
majority of all seasoned entreprenuers do create multiple ventures,
sometimes finding a "dry hole," sometimes encountering limited success,
and occasionally striking a gusher.[14]

---

[9]Shapero, op. cit.

[10]Kierulff, Herbert E.,"Finding--And Keeping-- Corporate
Entrepreneurs," Business Horizons, February, 1979.

[11]Sykes, Hollister B., "The Anatomy of a Corporate Venturing
Program: Factors Influencing Success." Journal Of Business Venturing,
Fall, 1986.

[12]Hobson, Edwin L., and Morrison, Richard M., "How Do Corporate
Start-Up Ventures Fare?" FOER 1983.

[13]Kanter, Rosabeth, M. "Supporting Innovation And Venture
Development In Established Companies," Journal Of Business Venturing,
Winter, 1985.

[14]Ronstadt, op. cit.

This research builds on perhaps the one point of general agreement about successful corporate (and independent) entrepreneurship. That is, success is usually a longer term process. Successful ventures, particularly high growth ones, usually take many years to ripen and prove their financial contribution. This paper is concerned similarly with a longer term view, but one that goes beyond the life of an individual venture.

Finally, we should note that the study examines only one of many potential factors influencing entrepreneurial success, whether it be corporate or independent. This examination is also a general one insofar as multiple kinds of corporate and independent entrepreneurs are included in the study.

## Database

The data for this study were abstracted from a larger database of 4100 respondents. All the respondents were alumni of four colleges (Babson College, Bentley College, Georgetown University, and Rensselaer Polytechnic Institute) who were participating in Phase I of the National Entrepreneurship Study directed by Robert Ronstadt.

Respondents were included in our sample if:

a) they identified themselves as "independent entrepreneurs" who started their ventures from scratch or "corporate entrepreneurs" who started ventures within a corporation while working for that corporation versus several other possibilities.[15]

b) they identified themselves as practicing entrepreneurs versus several other possibilities.[16]

The set of corporate entrepreneurs in this sample pursued "intrapreneuring" exclusively during their careers. They did not pursue "mixed" careers in the sense that they also had experience as "independent entrepreneurs, acquirers, or anyone of several other possibilities.

---

[15]The other possibilities excluded were acquirers, successors to family businesses, franchiser, franchises, non-profit entrepreneurs, self-employed individuals.

[16]The groups excluded were individual respondents who stated they were never entrepreneurs or serious nonstarters. Also, practicing entrepreneurs were excluded if they identified themselves as partners, members of an entrepreneurial team, a director, or some other designation unless they also identified themselves as founders, cofounders, or lead entrepreneurs.

Another set included individuals who stated they had acted as corporate entrepreneurs as well as some other type of entrepreneur. For example, respondents stated in some instances that they started as corporate entrepreneurs and then became independent entrepreneurs. In other cases, just the reverse was true.

This research attempts to determine if the Corridor Principle is more prevalent among more successful entrepreneurs, whether they be independent or corporate entrepreneurs. One way to measure success, albeit an imperfect one, is to use career length, restrict our analysis to those who were still active (as of 1984), and examine the notion of "seasoned entrepreneurs."

"Seasoned entrepreneurs," whether independent or corporate, are defined as individuals who have at least 6.5 years of experience as entrepreneurs. The particular cutpoint chosen (6.5 years) reflects the amount of time it takes for the majority of ex-entrepreneurs to leave their entrepreneurial careers.

Time is of course only one proxy for success. It is neither a perfect nor an all-encompassing proxy. However, studies show that a tendency exists among independent entrepreneurs to remain entrepreneurs as long as possible rather than shift to another career. "Once an entrepreneur, always an entrepreneur" seems to hold true for the large majority. Even a large share of those who've gone back to work for someone else, look forward to the day when they can be entrepreneurs again. Perhaps more telling, most entrepreneurs who chose not to start another venture but leave their entrepreneurial careers relatively quickly (under 6.5 years) to work for someone else, do so for negative, displacement reasons.[17]

The study's limitations are:

a) the respondents who designated themselves as corporate entrepreneurs cover a variety of types of corporate entrepreneurs. Several types of corporate entrepreneurs are grouped together, yet significant differences may exist between them. The reader should not infer that the study's findings refer solely to independent entrepreneurs pursuing high growth ventures or corporate entrepreneurs who are members of new venture groups.

b) we have no data on the size or type of companies which housed the corporate entrepreneurs, while most prior research has focused on intrapreneuring in larger (Fortune 1000) companies.

c) we have no other data reflecting the relative financial success of the respondents with their various ventures.

---

[17] Ronstadt, Robert, "Exit, Stage Left: Why Entrepreneurs End Their Entrepreneurial Careers Before Retirement," Journal Of Business Venturing, Fall, 1986.

d) although four schools were involved in the study, the number of individuals surveyed by each school differed. In this instance about 40% of the sample are Rensselaer Polytechnic Institute graduates.

## The Hypotheses

A number of hypotheses were developed which, taken as a group, might help reveal the impact of the corridor principle on independent versus corporate entrepreneuring.

Hypothesis #1: The number of ventures started by independent entrepreneurs will be greater than those started by corporate entrepreneurs.

Reason: Independent entrepreneurs have more latitude to shift to new ventures.

Hypothesis #2: The entrepreneurial career lengths of independent entrepreneurs will be longer than those of corporate entrepreneurs.

Reason: Higher numbers of ventures are associated with longer careers.

Hypothesis #3: Independent entrepreneurs start their entrepreneurial careers at an earlier age than corporate entrepreneurs.

Reason: Higher numbers of ventures are associated with earlier startups.

Hypothesis #4: Independent entrepreneurs are more likely to have anticipated their entrepreneurial careers than corporate entrepreneurs.

Reason: Anticipated careers are longer.

Hypothesis #5: Corporate entrepreneurs are more likely to have had technical as opposed to business educational backgrounds than are independent entrepreneurs.

Reason: Technical training and related careers cause later starts and less ventures.

Hypothesis #6: Both independent and corporate entrepreneurs with technical backgrounds are likely to be one-shot entrepreneurs.

Reason: "Nontechnical" individuals will start earlier and thus be able to start more ventures.

## Hypothesis #1

The number of ventures started by independent entrepreneurs will be greater than those started by corporate entrepreneurs.

On face value one would expect the opportunities for new entrepreneurial ventures to be greater for independent entrepreneurs than for corporate entrepreneurs since the latter are encumbered by corporate bureaucracy and shackled by the firms restricted product lines.

The data do not support this hypothesis. There is only a slightly larger average number of ventures started by the independents (2.48 compared to 2.26) (number of independents entrepreneurs = 1115, number of corporate entrepreneurs = 153, $t = 1.35$, $p = 0.179$, D.F. = 220.4)

Examining the histograms in Exhibit 1, one sees the distribution of ventures is relatively the same for both groups. What are the implications for the Corridor Principle? In essence the Corridor Principle seems to apply equally to corporate and to independent entrepreneurs.

However if one examines those entrepreneurs with mixed corporate and independent careers one sees a significantly larger number of ventures, 3.24 on the average. Those with mixed careers have significantly more entrepreneurial opportunities. (See Exhibit 1.) For seasoned entrepreneurs the results remain essentially the same. (See Exhibit 1.)

## Hypothesis #2

The entrepreneurial career lengths of independent entrepreneurs will be longer than those of corporate entrepreneurs.

The data support this hypothesis. The average career length for independent entrepreneurs was 12.3 years as compared to 9.8 years for corporate entrepreneurs. (See Exhibit 2.) This is statistically significant. (number of independents entrepreneurs = 1116, number of corporate entrepreneurs = 177, $t = 3.64$, $p = 0.0003$, D.F. = 237.9)

This difference in conjunction with the results of Hypotheses #1 can be interpreted to mean that independent entrepreneurs spend more time with each venture since they lack the logistic support that corporate entrepreneurs enjoy. It is probable that the independent entrepreneur spends a considerable amount of time handling or establishing structures to handle the operational details of his endeavor.

Mixed entrepreneurs exhibit an even longer career length. (See Exhibit 2.) Further investigation is planned to discover if this extended life is due to having an entrepreneurial startup acquired by a corporation such as McCormick and Dodge by Dun and Bradstreet or due to renegade employees striking out on their own in the manner in which PRIME was formed from Honeywell.

Hypothesis #3

Independent entrepreneurs start their entrepreneurial careers at an earlier age than corporate entrepreneurs.

Again the data support our hypothesis. The independent entrepreneurs start their careers at a statistically significant younger age than their corporate counterparts do. (number of independents entrepreneurs = 1114, number of corporate entrepreneurs = 162, t = -2.66, p = 0.0085, D.F. = 203.3)

However the average ages themselves and the magnitude of the difference between them was surprising. The average age of practicing independent entrepreneurs at the beginning of their first entrepreneurial venture was 31.4 years. The average age of practicing corporate entrepreneurs at the beginning of their first venture was 33.4 years. That's a mere two years difference as an average!

Examination of the distributions in Exhibit 3 shows that the corporate group had a larger variation in start-up age than did the independent group. Additionally the independents cluster closer to the minimum age value. The fact that the mixed career entrepreneurs had a startup age similar to their independent counterparts lends credence to the corporate acquisition theory postulated above.

It should be noted that the restriction of a minimum age of 15 and a maximum age of 63 was imposed on the entire data base to eliminate outliers and to reflect a more mainstream view.

Hypothesis #4

Independent entrepreneurs are more likely to have anticipated their entrepreneurial careers than corporate entrepreneurs.

Although the data indicate that 21.7% of the independent entrepreneurs anticipated their careers while only 19.6% of the corporate entrepreneurs did, this minor difference is not large enough to be due to factors other than chance. (number of independents entrepreneurs = 975, number of corporate entrepreneurs = 168, t = 0.63, p = 0.531, D.F. = 233.1)

Essentially one out of five entrepreneurs anticipates the entrepreneurial aspect of their careers. Some corporations, such as 3M, recognize and promote entrepreneurial desire. Rather than lose a talented employee these companies provide the infra-structure necessary to evaluate and when appropriate, to bring to fruition entrepreneurial vision.

Mixed career entrepreneurs overall exhibited a similar (one out of four chance) of having anticipated their entrepreneurial careers. When seasoned entrepreneurs are considered the difference between the independent and the mixed becomes smaller. However the difference between seasoned corporate entrepreneurs and the seasoned mixed entrepreneurs becomes significant. The proportion of seasoned corporate entrepreneurs who anticipated the entrepreneurial aspects of their careers drops from approximately 20% to approximately 15%.

Hypothesis #5

Corporate entrepreneurs are more likely to have had technical as opposed to business educational backgrounds than are independent entrepreneurs.

The data do not support this hypothesis. Seventy-nine percent of the independent entrepreneurs had technical backgrounds and seventy-eight percent of the corporate entrepreneurs did. (number of independents entrepreneurs = 977, number of corporate entrepreneurs = 191, t = 0.43, p = 0.665, D.F. = 265.2)

This seemingly high percentage of entrepreneurs with technical undergraduate educations is at least in part due to the make up of the database. Of the four colleges who participated in Phase I of the National Entrepreneurship Study, one offers only a technical undergraduate degree. Two of the remaining three are located in the center of most heavily concentrated high tech area in the eastern seaboard. Consequently many of their MBA candidates have technical undergraduate degrees.

Even when the definition of business educational background is extended to include those with MBA's, the high proportion of independent, corporate, and mixed entrepreneurs with technical backgrounds is essentially identical, ranging from 60% to 64%. (See Exhibit 4.)

Hypothesis #6

Both independent and corporate entrepreneurs with technical backgrounds are likely to be one-shot entrepreneurs.

The data do not support this hypothesis. (See Exhibit 5.) Thirty-nine percent of the independent entrepreneurs with a technical background had started only one venture, while forty-six percent of the corporate entrepreneurs had started only one venture. The difference is not large enough to be other than chance. (number of independents entrepreneurs = 1115, number of corporate entrepreneurs = 153, Yates corrected Chisquare = 2.765, d.f.= 1, p = .0964.)

It is surprising that over half of all corporate entrepreneurs with a technical background have started more than one venture! For the independents with a technical background over 60% started more than one venture. However, for the mixed career entrepreneurs with a technical background over 75% started multiple ventures.

## IMPLICATIONS

When a broad definition of corporate entrepreneurship is used, no evidence exists that corporations inhibit entrepreneurial activities by implicit strategies that prevent the selection of employees who anticipate such activities. Among practicing entrepreneurs both corporate and independent, the percent who anticipated their entrepreneurial activities was essentially identical.

Corporate entrepreneurs spend less total time on entrepreneurial activities, but are involved in the same number of ventures. This suggests that within corporate structures individuals spend less time in each venture.

One could argue that according to the Corridor Principle the opportunities are more quickly brought to fruition as one starts down the Corridor. After the same number of ventures as independent entrepreneurs, corporate entrepreneurs seem to leave the corridor.

This may be because the corporate entrepreneurs get a later start. The implications are that both corporate and independent entrepreneurs seem to leave the corridor at about the same time.

If this conclusion is not an artifact of the data sample and corporations want to promote entrepreneurial ventures, then they should encourage employees to get an earlier start into entrepreneurial pursuits.

## REFERENCES

Brennan, Peter J., "How Entrepreneurs Outdo Corporations," Venture. June, 1980.

Fast, Norman D., "A Visit to the New Venture Graveyard," Research Management. Vol. XXII/No. 2, March 1979, pp. 18-22.

Fast, Norman D., and Pratt, Stanley E., "Individual Entrepreneurship and Large Corporations," Frontiers Of Entrepreneurship Research 1981, (hereafter FOER), Ed. Karl H. Vesper, Wellesley, MA: Babson Center for Entrepreneurial Studies, 1981, pp. 443-451.

Hisrich, Robert D., and Peters, Michael P., "Establishing A New Venture Unit Within A Firm," Journal Of Business Venturing, Fall, 1986.

Hobson, Edwin L., and Morrison, Richard M., "How Do Corporate Start-Up Ventures Fare?" FOER 1983.

Kanter, Rosabeth, M. "Supporting Innovation And Venture Development In Established Companies," Journal Of Business Venturing, Winter, 1985.

Kierulff, Herbert E.,"Finding--And Keeping-- Corporate Entrepreneurs," Business Horizons, February, 1979.

MacMillan, Ian C., Block, Zenas, and Narasimha, P.N., "Corporate Venturing: alternatives, Obstacles Encountered, and Experience Effects, Journal Of Business Venturing, Spring, 1986.

Roberts, Edward B., "New Ventures for Corporate Growth," Harvard Business Review. Vol. 58/No. 4, July/August 1980, pp. 134-142.

Ronstadt, Robert, "Exit, Stage Left: Why Entrepreneurs End Their Entrepreneurial Careers Before Retirement," Journal Of Business Venturing, Fall, 1986.

Ronstadt, Robert, "The Corridor Principle And Entrepreneurial Time," Journal Of Business Venturing, forthcoming, 1987.

Shapero, Albert, "Corporate Heroes or 'Lousy Managers'?" The Wharton Magazine. Fall, 1978, pp. 33-37.

Sykes, Hollister B., "The Anatomy of a Corporate Venturing Program: Factors Influencing Success." Journal Of Business Venturing, Fall, 1986.

EXHIBIT 1

Number of Ventures Started

Histograms

```
        Independent (N=1115)      Corporate  (N= 153)
             H                         X
             HH                        X
             HH                        XX
             HHH                       XX
             HHHH                      XXX
             HHHHHHHHHHHH   H     H    XXXXXXX   X
             1------------------20  1------------------10
               H =  73 CASES            X =  12 CASES
```

Analysis of Variance

| Groups | Average Ventures | Size of Group |
|---|---|---|
| Independents | 2.48 | 1115 |
| Corporate | 2.26 | 153 |
| Mixed | 3.24 | 272 |

| F-Value | p-value | DF |
|---|---|---|
| 13.25 | 0.000 | 2,1537 |

p-values for multiple t-tests
| | |
|---|---|
| Independent vs Corporate | .271 |
| Corporate vs Mixed | .000 |
| Mixed vs Independent | .000 |

Analysis of Variance For Seasoned Entrepreneurs

| Groups | Average Ventures | Size of Group |
|---|---|---|
| Independents | 2.85 | 734 |
| Corporate | 2.72 | 72 |
| Mixed | 3.73 | 189 |

| F-Value | p-value | DF |
|---|---|---|
| 8.83 | 0.000 | 2,992 |

p-values for multiple t-tests
| | |
|---|---|
| Independent vs Corporate | .698 |
| Corporate vs Mixed | .006 |
| Mixed vs Independent | .000 |

EXHIBIT 2

## Entreprenurial Career Length

Histograms

```
          Independent (N=1116)        Corporate (N= 177)
               H H                          X
              HH HH                         XX
              HHH HH                        XXX
              HHHHHHHHH H                   XXX X
              HHHHHHHHHHH H                 XXXXXXX X X
              HHHHHHHHHHHHHHHHHH   H        XXXXXXXXXXXXXXX
              0------------------48   1-------------------36
                  H =   27 CASES              X =   7 CASES
```

Analysis of Variance

| Groups | Career Length | Size of Group |
|---|---|---|
| Independents | 12.32 | 1116 |
| Corporate | 9.81 | 177 |
| Mixed | 14.11 | 273 |

| F-Value | p-value | DF |
|---|---|---|
| 12.68 | 0.000 | 2,1163 |

p-values for multiple t-tests

| | |
|---|---|
| Independent vs Corporate | .001 |
| Corporate vs Mixed | .000 |
| Mixed vs Independent | .003 |

Analysis of Variance For Seasoned Entrepreneurs

| Groups | Career Length | Size of Group |
|---|---|---|
| Independents | 16.35 | 764 |
| Corporate | 15.91 | 90 |
| Mixed | 18.11 | 197 |

| F-Value | p-value | DF |
|---|---|---|
| 4.44 | 0.012 | 2,1048 |

p-values for multiple t-tests

| | |
|---|---|
| Independent vs Corporate | .61 |
| Corporate vs Mixed | .027 |
| Mixed vs Independent | .005 |

EXHIBIT 3

Age At First Venture

Histograms

```
        Independent (N=1114)      Corporate  (N= 162)
              HHHH
          H  HHHH                        X
          HHHHHHH                      XX X
          HHHHHHHHHH H                 XXXXX X
          HHHHHHHHHHHHHH             XXXXXXXXXXX X
          HHHHHHHHHHHHHHHHHHHHH    XXXXXXXXXXXXXXXXX X
          15-----------------63   15-----------------63
              H =   23 CASES           X =    5 CASES
```

Analysis of Variance

| Groups | Starting Age | Size of Group |
|---|---|---|
| Independents | 31.37 | 1114 |
| Corporate | 33.44 | 162 |
| Mixed | 30.83 | 274 |

| F-Value | p-value | DF |
|---|---|---|
| 4.85 | 0.008 | 2,1547 |

p-values for multiple t-tests
| | |
|---|---|
| Independent vs Corporate | .005 |
| Corporate vs Mixed | .003 |
| Mixed vs Independent | .368 |

Analysis of Variance For Seasoned Entrepreneurs

| Groups | Starting Age | Size of Group |
|---|---|---|
| Independents | 30.54 | 735 |
| Corporate | 33.10 | 80 |
| Mixed | 29.12 | 188 |

| F-Value | p-value | DF |
|---|---|---|
| 7.12 | 0.001 | 2,1000 |

p-values for multiple t-tests
| | |
|---|---|
| Independent vs Corporate | .006 |
| Corporate vs Mixed | .000 |
| Mixed vs Independent | .029 |

EXHIBIT 4

## Educational Backgrounds

|            | Independent | Corporate | Mixed |
|------------|-------------|-----------|-------|
| Business   | 248         | 47        | 60    |
| Technical  | 210         | 51        | 62    |
| Technical MBA | 156      | 31        | 44    |

Pearson Chisquare = 2.084, d.f. = 4, p = .7203.

## EXHIBIT 5

## Entrepreneurs with Technical Backgrounds

| Ventures      | Independent | Corporate |
|---------------|-------------|-----------|
| One           | 435         | 71        |
| More than one | 680         | 82        |

Yates Corrected Chisquare = 2.765, d.f. = 1, p = .0964.

EXHIBIT 1

## Number of Ventures Started

Histograms

```
            Independent (N=1115)        Corporate  (N= 153)
                    H                           X
                   HH                           X
                   HH                          XX
                  HHH                          XX
                 HHHH                         XXX
             HHHHHHHHHHHH  H      H       XXXXXXX  X
             1------------------20  1-------------------10
                  H =  73 CASES              X =  12 CASES
```

Analysis of Variance

| Groups | Average Ventures | Size of Group |
|--------|-----------------|---------------|
| Independents | 2.48 | 1115 |
| Corporate | 2.26 | 153 |
| Mixed | 3.24 | 272 |

| F-Value | p-value | DF |
|---------|---------|-----|
| 13.25 | 0.000 | 2,1537 |

p-values for multiple t-tests
| | |
|---|---|
| Independent vs Corporate | .271 |
| Corporate vs Mixed | .000 |
| Mixed vs Independent | .000 |

Analysis of Variance For Seasoned Entrepreneurs

| Groups | Average Ventures | Size of Group |
|--------|-----------------|---------------|
| Independents | 2.85 | 734 |
| Corporate | 2.72 | 72 |
| Mixed | 3.73 | 189 |

| F-Value | p-value | DF |
|---------|---------|-----|
| 8.83 | 0.000 | 2,992 |

p-values for multiple t-tests
| | |
|---|---|
| Independent vs Corporate | .698 |
| Corporate vs Mixed | .006 |
| Mixed vs Independent | .000 |

TOWARDS UNDERSTANDING YOUNG FOUNDERS

Lois Stevenson, Acadia University

## ABSTRACT

This paper explores the start up experiences of a group of ten young founders who had started a business between 1980-84, at the time being under 30 years of age. The paper will discuss the process of venture formation for these founders, identifying the variables or influences most critical in the formation decision. It will focus on the major difficulties encountered by these founders, as well as the strategies adopted in coping with obstacles. The difficulties are also discussed in terms of the reaction of the business support system to these young founders and their ideas.

## INTRODUCTION

Timmons, Smollen, and Dingee (1985) point out that people who start businesses, are more likely to be over 30 than under 30 when they are able to attract the caliber of partners and financial backers necessary to launch and grow a significant venture. They are more likely to have 8-10 years of experience than less than five. By this time they have accumulated the general management, marketing, and profit and loss experience to impress professional investors and bankers, and have found and nurtured the relevant business and other contacts and networks that contribute to the ultimate success of the venture. As well they have accumulated enough net worth to fund the start up entirely, or at least to some extent - if not, their track records are impressive enough to give creditors and investors the necessary confidence to provide funding.

However, it is becoming more common for people under 30 to start their own businesses. There is even some evidence to suggest that earlier starts are better, at least in a career continuance sense, than later start ups (Ronstadt, 1984). Although the initiation of a venture at an earlier age often means a smaller start up, younger entrepreneurs are in a better position to start second or third ventures and remain in an entrepreneurial career mode longer than those considering a later career start.

The increase in number of people under 30 who are starting businesses is outstripping the total number of start ups. In Canada, between 1976-1980, the number of people under 30 who were classified as business proprietors[1] increased 26%, at a time when the total number of business proprietors increased by 16.5%[2]. In the U.S., it is also reported that the average age of self employed persons has dropped in recent years, and data for the 70's suggest that younger workers place a higher premium on being self employed earlier than those of prior generations.[3] However, those aged 45 and over continue to account for a large share of all self employed workers (42%).[4] In the U.S. in 1983, 4.5% of total self employed males were 16-24. This percentage was 5.8% for women 16-24.[5] In Canada, in 1984, Statistics Canada reported that 5.0% of the total self employed were males 15-24, and 5.2% of total self employed were females 15-24, a total of 148,000 Canadians.[6] (The percentage of these young people who could actually be considered "founders" is probably quite low since these figures include people self employed as babysitters and paper carriers).

Increasingly, more of our young people are being encouraged to start businesses at a much earlier age, with the perspective of developing entrepreneurial careers. On the one hand the environment, government, educationsl institutions, business leaders, and the media are purporting to be in favour of this, on the other hand there is evidence that not much change has taken place in terms of attitudes towards the risk or potential for success of a venture headed by a lead entrepreneur who is under 30 years of age - that magic number.

Not much research has focused on the young founder and consequently, not much is known about their predispositions to start a business, the nature of the entrepreneurial process for them, their perceptions regarding the experience of starting a venture, and the special problems they face. This paper presents findings from a case study investigation of the start up experiences of 10 young founders - 5 men and 5 women who started businesses before they were 30 years of age. This is exploratory research, in the preliminary stages of analysis, and the findings perhaps raise more questions than answers, which may lead to further investigation of this group of founders.

---

[1]Business proprietors are defined as those people who derive at least 50% of their income from self employment.

[2]Statistical Profile of Small Business in Canada, 1983, Small Business Secretariat, DRIE, Ottawa, 1983, p. 45.

[3]The State of Small Business Report, A Report of the President United States Government Printing Office, Washington, D.C., 1986, p. 114-115.

[4]Ibid, p. 115.

[5]Ibid, Table 4.9, p. 125.

[6]Statistics Canada, Labour Force Survey Division, The Labour Force, Minister of Supply and Services, Ottawa, February 1985.

These young founders were interviewed utilizing a semi-structured interview design. Interviews were taped and later transcribed into manuscripts. These 50-80 page manuscripts were then content analyzed using procedures outlined by Glaser and Strauss (1967) and Turner (1981) as being appropriate for the analysis of qualitative material. Several categories of information were developed for each founder and then individual responses were compared for the set of founders to identify consistent patterns and themes that described the experiences of these young founders. The findings of the analysis provides a greater understanding of the elements critical in their efforts to get a business established. All of these young founders were interviewed within a 60 mile radius of Halifax, Nova Scotia, a city with a metropolitan population of about 250,000. These interviews were conducted as part of a more extensive qualitative study on entrepreneurship, and the businesses were selected on the basis that they had been started in 1980 or after, that the business employed at least one person besides the owner of the business, that the founder was the lead entrepreneur in the formation of the business, and that the owner had not started a previous business prior to 1980. Ten of the owners in the larger study happened to be young founders.

The first section of this paper describes the businesses started by these owners, the second part focuses on the young founders themselves and discusses backgrounds, motivations for starting the business, events leading up to the decision to start a business, and the factors which helped or hindered most in getting the business established. It also looks at the complicating factor associated with being a young "female" founder.

## A DISCUSSION OF THE FINDINGS

### Type of Business

The industries represented are diverse. There were 3 businesses in retail (designer clothing, computer hardware and software, natural body care products), 2 in service businesses (restaurants, insurance services), 2 in aquaculture (domestic raising of salmon, trout, and mussels), 2 in wholesale trade (cosmetics, T-shirts) and 1 in manufacturing (furniture). Six of the founders had experience somehow related to the business they founded and four did not. The businesses were all started between 1980-1984. Five of the founders were involved in more than one business, 1 of the women and 4 of the men.

### Sales Volume

It was difficult to generate an average sales volume for this group of founders because they were all interviewed at different times. The author has generated an average sales volume for these firms by including the sales volume indicated by the owner for the accounting year prior to the interview, in most cases this was 1985 or 1986. The average sales volume per firm was $458,000 with a range from $53,000 to $1,500,000.

## Number of Employees

These businesses employed a total of 64 workers, an average of 6.4 per firm, plus a number of casual, seasonal, and part time employees. This latter category of employees was difficult to deal with because of one firm which employed 400 such people. Small firms in Canada employ an average of 4-5 employees so it is evident that these young founders are significant job creators.

## Years in Business

These founders had had their own full time business for an average of 3 years and 3 months. The average for women was 2.5 years and for the men, almost 4 years. However in five cases, the business owned at the time of the interview was not the owners first venture, or first attempt at self employment.

## Age of Founder at Startup

The average age at startup was 24.7 years and this ranged from 22 to 28. There was no difference between the men and women on this dimension.

## Parental Background

As is the case in other studies of entrepreneurs, many of these young founders came from families where the parents had owned a business or engaged in some type of self employment activity. Four of the founders grew up with family businesses. For two others, while the fathers worked in paid jobs, the founders commented that "he was always involved in some other activity, doing something on his own to earn more money". Another founder's father started a business in 1979 and convinced the young son to join him in a 3 way partnership. The son did, and a year later started his own business supplying that firm with product.

These founders do feel that growing up in an entrepreneurial family was a major influence on what they are doing now but of course it does not explain the event for the other 3 young founders.

Five founders had mothers who did not work outside the home and only one had a mother who was self employed in her own business. This mother later became a partner in another business with her daughter.

The backgrounds of these owners reinforced at least to some extent, the theory outlined by Kets de Vries (1977) on absent fathers and impoverished childhoods. For four of the owners very definite mention is made of the fact that the father was rarely around, mostly because he was always working, and that very little time growing up was spent with the father.

The relationship between "absent" fathers and entrepreneurial behaviour is a tentative but interesting one and is worthy of further investigation.

## Birth Order

Five of these owners are first born and four are youngest children. Much prior research indicates a disproportionate number of founders who are first born. Is this changing?

## Education

In the case of these young founders, there is a high incidence of attendence at university - a total of 8 founders had at least some university. Four had university degrees (B.N., B. Comm., and 2 B.Sc.), another was 1½ credits short of a B. Comm. and 3 others had at least one year of university exposure. Two founders were educated at the community college level and only one young man had the distinction of only completing high school.

There does not seem to be a pattern here which relates educational attainment to entrepreneurial propensity. Three of the male owners had a Commerce background but do not feel that the courses they took were of much help in their businesses.

These young people made career choices based to a certain extent on what their parents wanted them to do or wanted them to go. Many did not want their children to stay around the family business and to have to work as hard as they did. They wanted the children to have professions. This was true in several cases.

In the future it is expected that entrepreneurs of all kinds will be better educated than has been the case in the past (Drucker, 1984). Young people now have more access to education however, the education system still has not caught up with the needs of entrepreneurs. These entrepreneurs found little value in their educational backgrounds in terms of preparing them for the experience of initiating a business venture.

## Experience Related to Business Started

From the literature it is recognized that prior experience in a similar business or industry, particularly at the management level is a pre-condition to successful entrepreneurship. This is an unrealistic prerequisite for young founders because they simply have not had time to gain this experience. However, these founders did have an average of 4.5 years of full time experience working in other jobs before launching their own venture; this ranged from 0-8 years.

There appear to be some male/female differences in the degree to which this experience was related to the business started. Four of the 5 men did not have direct work experience relating to their venture. They saw opportunities that interested them and developed businesses around those ideas/opportunities. Only one man had charted a work path which would give him more practical experience in the industry where he wanted to start a business before he took the plunge. The other four started businesses they really did not know very much about at all, but were spurred on by the timing and the opportunity.

The women were more likely to have related work experience - this was true for all five of them. The women were also more likely to be pushed into their own business and thus developed businesses around an area which they already had experience in and knowledge of. Although, one entrepreneur identified an opportunity, did not know anything about the business or industry, so worked in a retail operation for six months to get some retail experience. While she was doing this she negotiated the franchise rights for her store.

The relevance of experience to the business venture started seems to be related in some fashion to the process used to become an entrepreneur. Perhaps 'negative push' entrepreneurs are more likely than 'opportunity pull' entrepreneurs to initiate businesses in their work-related field.

## Self Employment Experience

Five of these young founders (4 of them male) had decided very early in their working lives that they wanted to do something on their own. All five had engaged in some self employment activity prior to starting their own business, 2 while in university (catering and bartending, painting contracts), 2 as moonlighting activities while they were working for somebody else (painting cars, growing mussels), and 1 as a full time freelancer doing makeup artistry the year following graduation from community college. Three of these started full time businesses relating to their self employment activity, mostly indirectly related. Women were less likely to have prior self employment experience, only one in this group.


PREDISPOSITIONS TO ENTREPRENEURSHIP


What motivated these young founders to start their own business?

For six of the founders, a strong desire to own a business had developed early. For one it was a childhood dream. As soon as she started reading fashion magazines she wanted to have her own store in fashion and makeup. She was very independent early (and first born) and recognized that she did not work well for other people. She was the leader and wanted to be in control.

Two discovered after working a short time for someone else that the possibilities for earning money were limited - the potential was greater if you were working on your own.

And others discovered quickly that they simply didn't like working for someone else, that they did not take directions well, they did not like answering to someone else, and they did not like conforming to the standards of the 'corporation'. The predisposition to be independent was stimulated early in their careers, it was a matter then of considering the alternatives and eventually making the self-employment decision.

## Objectives for Starting a Business

The responses to this question category "what were your objectives for starting the business?" fell into 4 groups.

| | |
|---|---|
| Challenge | -1 |
| The potential for making money | -1 |
| To prove it could be done | -3 |
| Independence, self-reliance, didn't want to work for anybody else | -5 |

The overriding objective for these founders derived from their strong need for independence and self reliance. This is evident from comments such as,

> "to not have to rely on anybody for anything ... I didn't want to work for anybody, I didn't want anybody to tell me what to do ... I like to be independent ... I like knowing that my life is in my hands." (T-shirts)

The next most frequently mentioned objective was "to prove it could be done". This was mentioned by three young founders who actually found it motivating and challenging to be surrounded by skeptics, by people who kept saying that it could not be done. Two founders were in industries that were new or undeveloped in Nova Scotia and they were pioneering - they were problem solvers. They really had very little support from the government and industry sectors initially. One founder comments,

> "there was so many skeptics saying that it couldn't be done that I wanted to prove that it could be." (Aquaculture)

Only one person mentioned potential for making money as a prime objective. He saw entrepreneurship as a way of making his life materially better. He says,

> "I was a person looking to better myself, always to better myself, always to look for a better opportunity, to make better money." (Aquaculture)

## The Process

Five of the founders were motivated to change their career directions because they were dissatisfied with their jobs; three of these were pushed into entrepreneurship following disagreements with their employers. These disagreements focused around lack of recognition, reward factors, or company management practices. Two of these founders were pulled into entrepreneurship. Dissatisfied with the way their careers were developing (they wanted something better, more challenging, more monetarily rewarding), they were looking for opportunities. They both were presented with an opportunity and through pursuit of that opportunity developed businesses.

Two of the entrepreneurs were "between things". One back from a 3 year stay in England and one just out of school, they were looking at employment possibilities. Neither entrepreneur had actually aggressively sought employment - the job market was poor, both founders decided to do something on their own and pursued opportunities that they had identified. These eventually turned into businesses but both entrepreneurs present their stories as if things just happened, they are almost not sure how things turned out so well for them in terms of the opportunity.

The remaining three founders were working for someone else but had decided they wanted to have their own businesses. It was as if they were waiting for the right time. They had identified opportunities for ventures of their own already. And then something happened, an event which made them decide to "do it now". In two cases, when conditions changed at work (business changed hands), the time seemed right and they started their businesses. The third entrepreneur had identified an opportunity for manufacturing a product being imported from another part of the country but it was not until he became angry with this supplier, that he decided to go ahead with the business idea.

From the interviews it was apparent that eight of the entrepreneurs probably would have eventually started a venture regardless, but an event - a disagreement with an employer, a poor job market, a change in employment conditions, or the presentation of an attractive opportunity, created the impetus for them to make the decision at that point in time. Something had to happen to veer them off their current pathway, something that would provide the motivation to act in a certain direction.

From this analysis, then, it appears that there are factors which predispose people to look at alternatives to their present situation. These factors could be dissatisfaction with a job, being between things, or a strong desire to be independent through business ownership. These factors lead the founders to look at alternatives, either other employment or self employment. Then an event occurs which triggers the founder to make the decision to go ahead with a venture idea.

There is evidence here that perhaps with younger entrepreneurs, there will be a greater incidence of positive pull factors than negative push factors in the startup decision. This sample is unquestionably too small to draw any definite conclusions but it breaks down to 70% positive pull and 30% negative push. This is the reverse of Shapero's (1975) finding that two-thirds of entrepreneurs were motivated by negative push factors.

In taking advantage of or responding to the presentation of an opportunity or the identification of an opportunity, many of these young founders encountered difficulties. As they admit they lacked the confidence, the credibility, the knowledge, the experience, to go ahead on their own, without overcoming many obstacles. In many cases, there was reliance on parents, clients/friends, partners or a significant other, to provide the emotional support, the financial support, the credibility, the knowledge and experience that these young founders lacked primarily because of their age. This section of the paper examines the problems perceived by this group of young founders.

Only one founder did not have any problems getting his venture started. He only needed $10,000, had $2,000, borrowed $8,000, had security for the loan, paid it back in 6 months, worked in the business with only 1 part-time helper for the first few months, and essentially did not have any problems. The one problem he did have was his age "people begrudge success. A lot of people think I get a lot of help elsewhere, that it's really my father's business or that I have a partner". (Restaurant)

The other founders encountered the following categories of problems:

| | | |
|---|---|---|
| Getting money from the banks | - 5 | 33% of responses |
| Not knowing what I was doing | - 4 | 26% |
| Lack of personal confidence | - 1 | 7% |
|   (wondering if they can make it work) | | |
| Lack of credibility, getting | | |
|   others to believe in me | - 3 | 20% |
| High risk venture | - 1 | 7% |
| Lack of support from | | |
|   community | - 1 | 7% |

Six founders indicated that their problems were exacerbated by the fact that they were either young (4) or female (2).

The two major problems young founders have are inexperience (not knowing what they were doing, how to do things, where to get information, how to be prepared to talk to investors, no experience in dealing with bankers, etc.) and lack of credibility (getting others to support them). There was a feeling among many of these young founders that no one really wanted to do business with them, either on the supplier end (trade credit, money, materials) or customer end (product acceptance). There was perceived risk in dealing with the business started by the young founder, especially in beginning stages. Reactions such as "you're too young to own a store" or "a lot of people thought because I was so young 'holy geez, he's headed for trouble'", created barriers.

## Getting the Business Financed

Except for one young founder, the others all needed to borrow money to get their businesses started and approached the banks. The exception was a business that started really small with overhead kept low, using second hand equipment, etc. The founder used his own personal money to get started, and started on a small scale. The other founders did not have much personal wealth, often a car or some personal affects which they were forced to sell to start the business. Of the nine who approached the banks, 3 were successful in getting money on their first try, 3 were successful after several attempts with up to four different banks, and 3 were totally unsuccessful. Two of this latter group were able to borrow the money from a parent ($1600) and a client/friend ($35,000) who took shares in her business. The third rejected owner was undercapitalized in her high risk aquaculture business for the first year and a half.

Of those with bank financing, 4 of the 6 encountered problems later with the bank either in financing the next project, converting demand loans to lines of credit, or in extending lines of credit. Three of these cases resulted in the founder changing banks to get satisfaction.

These owners were never specifically told that their age was a problem in the negotiations but there was an overriding impression from the anecdotal comments of these founders that the banks perceived some risk in dealing with them and were only willing to go along so far, if at all. As one young founder relates,

> "I thought people were looking for young vigorous people who wanted to go at it but he said (investment partner) 'there's no way'. Other people would have less problem. I think anybody over 30 with experience in their field ... 30 is a magic figure for some people. For a little bit of money, it's worth the risk, or if the idea has little risk, it's different." (Aquaculture)

Two of the young founders had guaranteed loans of $5,000 from the provincial Department of Development under the Youth Entrepreneurial Skills program. Without this money, neither founder would have been able to start their business when they did. Even with this support, one founder was unable to get the additional financing he needed from a bank and had to borrow the money from his mother. In this case the government's support did not mean very much to the banks.

Money is a major problem for young founders because they have not had time to accumulate a lot of personal assets which can be used as collateral security for a bank loan. In most cases the owner had nothing of value. Three parents had to co-sign bank notes and the remainder of the businesses were undercapitalized at the beginning.

Although age was rarely mentioned as a direct problem, it would appear that young women have more difficulties with banks than young men. There were several cases where the banker's reaction was directly related to the fact that the request came from a young woman. Three of the five women cited problems due to sexist reactions. Comments like,

"he treated me like I was a piece of pink fluff in front
of him..." (Clothing)

"he didn't take the shop seriously ... he wouldn't give my
inventory any thought in considering my loan." (Body care
products)

"they treated me like some kind of juvenile idiot. It showed
right off ... And then calling my father! He didn't have
anything to do with it. He didn't even put his name on the
line, ever." (Body care products)

"he literally told me to my face that because I was a woman
they didn't want my account. Women are high risk ... because
'we don't know how long you're going to be in business. You
could get up and get pregnant and decide that you don't want
to have your business any longer and in that respect I can't
take your account...'" (Cosmetics)

The first time this happened to these young people they did not
know how to react. They were more apt to be disappointed and disillusioned, as well as angry. They had to learn that they did not have to
take this kind of treatment from the banks and were usually advised so
by a more seasoned business person.

## HELPS GETTING STARTED

It is obvious from analyzing their problem areas that young
people have not had time to gain the experience, business knowledge, network, political sense, credibility, personal assets, that are required to
mobilize the resources necessary to launch a successful venture. In full
recognition or not, they realized they had to be able to identify people
in the environment who could provide these things for them. In looking
at the descriptions of what helped these young founders most in getting
started it can be seen how this is true.

Parents play a large and key role in helping these young founders. Four of the five female founders and one of the male founders
found support of their parents to be a big help in getting their businesses started. One mother lent her son the additional money he needed
to get started, plus three other parents co-signed bank loans for their
children (all female founders). In addition to the direct or indirect
financial support parents gave to these founders, it was also very important to five of the founders (4 of them female) to have the emotional
support of their parents. To three of these women, it seemed extremely
important to them to gain the approval of their parents on the business
idea before going ahead. Once the parent(s) gave the go ahead, their
approval, the founders pursued the idea full steam ahead. Three others
who did not mention parents, did mention a significant other as having
a strong influence in providing access to money or business knowledge.
One mentioned the franchisor as being extremely influential.

Five founders attribute help to themselves - their own ambition, curiosity, willingness to seek information and advice (not afraid to ask questions), adaptability, and sense of humor as key personal factors which helped them in being able to start their business.

One founder stated it was past experience in a related business which helped most.

From this we can conclude that the role of parents may play a critical role in the startup decision of young founders, maybe even more so if the founder is female. One young founder sums up the important ingredients in a successful startup,

> "Make sure you have enough money to start! That's the biggest thing ... And make sure you have the support of your girl-friend or boyfriend and if you are living at home, the support of your parents ... And if you don't know what you are doing or what you are getting into, ask someone who knows. And if possible hire someone who has been in the business before."
> (T-shirts)

## CONCLUSION

Young entrepreneurs have many problems that older entrepreneurs do not have, or these problems are exacerbated because of the age of the younger group. They do not have the experience and knowledge necessary to easily put a business together. They admit they did not know what they were doing, that often people they are dealing with in business do not tell them that they are on the wrong track, that it is difficult to get money because banks want assets and young people have not had time to accumulate them, therefore they need co-signers, or have to find the money elsewhere. Often times, banks, suppliers, customers do not take them seriously because they are "too young to own a business", the expectation is that these activities are the realm of older people.

For many would-be young founders, it would be impossible to overcome the financial obstacles, the skeptics in an industry, the obstacles in gaining acceptance in a market place, the need for information because of lack of experience and knowledge.

The ingredients stereotypically seen as being important to the successful emergence of "an entrepreneur" are entrepreneurial family background, presence of a role model or mentor, prior business education, business/technical skills, prior business management experience in a related industry, access to capital, access to business networks and support groups, and a good idea. Empirical research indicates that entrepreneurs, in the past, founded their businesses when they were between 30-40 years of age. The reason for this is that it took them 10-15 years to gain the education, skills, management experience, capital accumulation, and support systems (network) deemed pre-requisite for putting together the necessary resources for business formation. Also, the maturity and experience gained during that time contributed to the

level of confidence the entrepreneur had in his/her ability to successfully develop their own business ideas.  These ingredients are less likely to make up part of the young founder's experience.  The experiences
of these young founders challenge much of this and are a cue to the environment that there may be a need for change in how entrepreneurship
is viewed if we want to facilitate the process for more young people.

This discussion is based on a very small sample but some of the
issues identified are worthy of further investigation.  There may be a
need to look at the following issues:

- the important role of parental influence and support in the decision
  making process of young founders.
- the relative importance of choosing a business based on past related
  experience versus pursuing opportunities in new areas for young
  entrepreneurs.
- the question of actual support in the small business environment for
  'young' entrepreneurs.  What are the perceptions and realities?
- the implications of differing use of contacts in getting a business
  established for young founders - personal versus business contacts.
- access to entrepreneurship, education and training for young people
  and the actual benefits of such exposure.
- the issue of sex of the young founders and the process of entrepreneurial entry.  Are there differences?

It seems as if these young people are going to do it anyway -
they have a predisposition to being independently employed and pursuing
opportunities, or to responding favourably to an opportunity when it is
presented.  Their independence should be encouraged and efforts should
be made to facilitate emergence of their businesses.  More than just
parents should believe in the potential of young adults.

As one entrepreneur comments,

> "I reflect on it now and I think there was this person in me
> that wanted to come out ... I believe it's something that
> you have to learn.  I think everybody has the potential to do
> anything that they want to do, it all depends on if you can
> see it.  If someone brings it out in you ... it doesn't
> matter who you are because I'd never have thought that I'd
> be doing this.  Somebody believed that I could do it and
> showed me the way.  I had an opportunity and I didn't let
> it go.  And I think anybody can find those opportunities,
> if they are shown the way."  (Cosmetics - presently a $4
> million business in Atlantic Canada)

## REFERENCES

Drucker, Peter, "Our Entrepreneurial Economy", Harvard Business Review,
     January - February, 1984.

Glaser, Barney G., and Anselm Strauss, The Discovery of Grounded Theory, Ardine Publishing, Chicago, 1967.

Kets de Vries, M.F.R., "The Entrepreneurial Personality, A Person At The Crossroads", The Journal of Management Studies, February 1977.

Ronstadt, Robert C., Entrepreneurship, Text, Cases and Notes, Lord Publishing, Massachusetts, 1984, pp. 95-96.

Shapero, Albert, "The Displaced Uncomfortable Entrepreneur", Psychology Today, November 1975.

Timmons, J.A., Smollen, L.E., and Dingee, A.L. Jr., New Venture Creation, Irwin, Inc., Illinois, 1985, p. 145.

Turner, Barry A., "Some Practical Aspects of Qualitative Data Analysis: One Way of Organizing the Cognitive Processes Associated with the Generation of Grounded Theory", Quality and Quantity, 15, 1981, pp. 225-247.

SUMMARY

RISK CONSIDERATIONS AMONG FRENCH ENTREPRENEURS
AND NON ENTREPRENEURS

Author

V. K. Unni

Address

Department of Management
Illinois State University
Normal, IL 61761
(309) 438-5701

Principal Topics

The risk-taking behavior of entrepreneurs is implied in many of the
earlier writings on entrepreneurship in terms of decision-making
under uncertainty. Studies indicate that potential entrepreneurs
have greater propensity for risk taking. Entrepreneurial literature
also indicate that risk bearing is a major distinguishing characteristic between the function of a manager and those of an entrepreneur. Given the importance of risk considerations the major purpose
of this paper is to determine whether French entrepreneurs and non-
entrepreneurs differ in their risk taking propensities.

Method and Data Base

The study was conducted in France using two groups of participants,
entrepreneurs and non-entrepreneurs. Entrepreneurs were in business
at least for three years and continuing. The entrepreneurs were
selected at random from directories and other comprehensive listings
published by several French national associations. The group of
non-entrepreneurs included banking employees and elementary
teachers. These two groups were identified as non-entrepreneurs
mainly because their career paths are usually professional rather
then entrepreneurial. Wallach and Kogan Choice Dilemmas
Questionnaire (CDQ) was used for the study. The questionnaire was
pretested with a small group of French students attending an
American University. Based on the results, the questionnaire was
translated into French to reduce cultural bias, if any.

## Major Findings

The null hypothesis developed for the study was: entrepreneurs who have been working for the last three years and continuing, will have the same risk-taking propensity as will (a) banking employees, whose career paths are usually professional, and (b) school teachers, who are also more professional oriented than entrepreneurial.

A one-way variance analysis test indicated that the CDQ scores of the three groups were not significantly different from each other. The null hypothesis was accepted; entrepreneurs appear to have the same risk-taking propensity as non-entrepreneurs (both bank employees and school teachers). Data analysis of questionnaire also indicate that entrepreneurs in general were low risk takers and so were the non-entrepreneurs. Research indicates that the pace and character of French entrepreneurship was set by family firms, owned and managed by relatives, whose primary concerns were safety, continuity, and privacy.

The regions under study had also the highest entrepreneurial failures and perhaps one may conclude that there is a relationship between risk propensity and being successful. The study indicates that "successful" entrepreneurs in the region were only low risk takers. Perhaps entrepreneurs who have failed were moderate to high risk takers. Then again, since the data did not include failed entrepreneurs, the results are inconclusive.

## Major Implications

The findings that general risk taking propensity does not distinguish entrepreneurs from non-entrepreneurs is an important characteristic. Lack of information appeared to be an element in risk perception. The amount of possible loss is important in the perception of risk. Risk situations vary and so are the risk taking actions.

STRESS, HEALTH, AND FINANCIAL PERFORMANCE
IN ENTREPRENEURIAL FIRMS

David P. Boyd, Northeastern University
Thomas M. Begley, Northeastern University

ABSTRACT

This paper examines the relationships of work-related stressors,
psychological coping resources, and financial performance on stress and
health problems in a sample of founders and nonfounders of smaller
companies. For company founders, role overload and situational stressors
are the best predictors of stress while sense of mastery is the strongest
mitigator of stress. For company C.E.O.s who are nonfounders, role
overload associates positively with stress while optimistic action
associates negatively. Job stress relates to health complaints while
sense of mastery shows an inverse pattern. Sample respondents were
231 executives in the Smaller Business Association of New England.

INTRODUCTION

This paper will compare the causes and consequences of job stress
in a sample of entrepreneurs and managers of smaller businesses. The
paper will also investigate whether various coping techniques lessen the
adverse effects of work-related stress. For study purposes, an
entrepreneur is defined as the founder of an enterprise. This basic
distinction avoids dependence on subjective criteria such as strategic
preference and orientation toward innovation.[1] The comparison group of
nonentrepreneurs consists of chief executives running smaller business
firms which they did not found.

In previous work reported at this conference, the authors found
that entrepreneurs exhibit high levels of stress.[2] A recent survey by
Enterprise U.S.A. confirms this finding: entrepreneurs list job-related

---

[1]T.M. Begley and D.P. Boyd, "A Comparison of Entrepreneurs and
Managers of Small Business Firms," Journal of Management, in press.

[2]D.P. Boyd and D.E. Gumpert, "The Effects of Stress on Early-Stage
Entrepreneurs," in J.A. Hornaday, J.A. Timmons, and K.H. Vesper (Eds.),
Frontiers of Entrepreneurship Research, Babson Center for Entrepreneurial
Studies, Wellesley, Mass., 1983, pp. 180-191.

stress as the most difficult aspect of their work.[3]  Even when firms have passed the risky start-up stage and external pressures have moderated, stress manifestations persist.[4]

Despite the unremitting nature of the problem, little is known about organizational stressors that precipitate entrepreneurial stress. Most studies of occupational stressors have focused on role conflict and role ambiguity.  These two sources of organizational trauma are closely related to a spectrum of organic disorders and to varying degrees of psychic impairment.[5]

Yet conflicting or ambiguous role expectations do not seem characteristic of owners of smaller businesses since their positional power reduces role frustration.  Parasuraman and Alutto found these role dilemmas more pronounced for individuals at middle and low organizational levels.  For those at high levels, time constraints were the principal stressor.[6]  High level job incumbents might thus become vulnerable to the effects of role overload.  Findings from the Parasuraman and Alutto study also suggest that high-level managers may be more stressed by responsibility for people than responsibility for things.[7]

According to Parasuraman and Alutto, studies of high-level job groups should also investigate factors acting independently of the role set.  Under the rubric of "situational stressors," they include such problems as equipment malfunction, defective materials, employee errors, short lead times, staff shortage, and employee antagonism.[8]

Another salient stressor might be financial performance of the firm.  Numerous studies have established that stress overload impairs individual performance.[9]  However, the reverse hypothesis has not been tested.  Perhaps poor financial performance contributes to owner stress. Even if entrepreneurs increase their exertion and commitment during times of financial distress, eventually the productive aspects of reactivity

---

[3]Enterprise U.S.A., 1 (June 1986), p. 11.

[4]Boyd and Gumpert, op. cit.

[5]C. Orpen, "Type A Personality as a Moderator of the Effects of Role Conflict, Role Ambiguity and Role Overload on Individual Strain," Journal of Human Stress, 42 (1982), pp. 8014.

[6]S. Parasuraman and J.A. Alutto, "An Examination of the Organizational Antecedents of Stressors at Work," Academy of Management Journal, 24 (1981), pp. 48-67.

[7]Ibid.

[8]Ibid.

[9]C.R. Anderson, "Coping Behaviors as Intervening Mechanisms in the Inverted-U Stress-Performance Relationship," Journal of Applied Psychology, 61 (1976), pp. 30-34.

might give way to frustration and exhaustion. The present study will seek to determine whether sustained fiscal constraints exacerbate stress.

In addition to research on antecedent causes of stress, attention should be directed to outcome effects. Mental and physical strain result from prolonged neuro-psychic demands on individual adaptive capacity.[10] This linkage has been documented for a variety of disease states. Most notably, stress has been implicated in the onset and aggravation of coronary artery disease.[11] Mental illness has also been related to occupational stress.[12] However, only one study has targeted the smaller business domain. In that study, Boyd and Gumpert found high prevalence and incidence of physical strain among owners of smaller businesses.[13] The present study seeks to replicate these findings in a new sample. It will also assess the effects of stress on mental strain.

A final purpose of the present paper is to investigate whether coping resources retard the conversion of organizational stressors into felt stress. Recent conceptual models of stress underscore the pivotal role of cognitive appraisal in alleviating felt stress.[14] Yet little is known about the efficacy of available coping techniques. Concern has focused on maladaptive response, especially behavior patterns related to substance abuse. Less attention has been directed to salutary reactions. This study will determine whether selected coping mechanisms have direct main effects on stress.

A number of personality variables appear to affect the stressor-stress sequence. Persons who have a sense of environmental mastery report less psychological distress.[15] Kobasa reports a similar function for self-esteem.[16]

---

[10]G. Blau, "An Empirical Investigation of Job Stress, Social Support, Service Length, and Job Strain," Organizational Behavior and Human Performance, 27 (1981), pp. 279-302.

[11]J.M. Ivancevich and M.T. Matteson, Stress and Work: A Managerial Perspective, Scott, Foresman, Glenview, Ill., 1980.

[12]C.D. Jenkins, "Recent Evidence Supporting Psychological and Social Risk Factors for Coronary Disease," New England Journal of Medicine, 294 (1976), pp. 987-994, 1033-1038.

[13]Boyd and Gumpert, op. cit.

[14]R.R. McCrae, "Situational Determinants of Coping Responses: Loss, Threat and Challenge," Journal of Personality and Social Psychology, 46 (1984), pp. 919-928.

[15]J.H. Johnson and I.G. Sarason, "Life Stress, Depression, and Anxiety: Internal-External Control as Moderator Variable," Journal of Psychosomatic Research, 22 (1978), pp. 205-208.

[16]S.B. Kobasa, "Personality and Resistance to Illness," American Journal of Community Psychology, 7 (1979), pp. 413-423.

Other potential moderators have not been so systematically explored. It has long been acknowledged, for example, that religion plays a role in tempering the impact of felt stress.[17] Yet empirical research in this area is limited. Pearlin and Schooler suggest that beliefs and values can endow the individual with a strategy for manageable suffering, "a strategy that can convert the endurance of unavoidable hardships into a moral virtue."[18] To this end, a religious rationale might be pressed into service. The optimism and resilience of the devotee might keep stress within tolerable bounds. Benson, for example, cites the therapeutic potential of religious meditation for distressed patients.[19]

A sense of financial fulfillment may also palliate the gravity of stress. Psychological satisfaction in this instance would be a function of the disparity between anticipated and actual performance. If achievements do not match aspirations, founders may experience dissatisfaction. This expectation-reality gap may exist even among owners of profitable companies.

The most direct way of coping with work stress is to confront the source of such stress. After studying how the key owner-managers of 90 smaller businesses responded to a natural disaster, Anderson et al. concluded that organizational effectiveness was significantly related to the use of task-oriented coping behaviors.[20] Even if task-oriented action does not eliminate the problem, harmful effects of stress can be buffered by responses that facilitate cognitive restructuring.[21]

The present study will test the efficacy of the psychological coping resources described above.

## SAMPLE

Potential respondents were randomly selected from the Smaller Business Association of New England (SBANE). They were sent a questionnaire soliciting information related to stress level, health, and personal characteristics. They were also asked about their firms'

---

[17]W. Durant and A. Durant, The Lessons of History, Simon and Schuster, New York, 1968.

[18]L.I. Pearlin and C. Schooler, "The Structure of Coping," Journal of Health and Social Behavior, 19 (1978), p. 7.

[19]H. Benson, Beyond the Relaxation Response, Berkeley, New York, 1985.

[20]C.R. Anderson, D. Hellriegel, and J.W. Slocum, Jr., "Managerial Response to Environmentally Induced Stress," Academy of Management Journal, 20 (1977), pp. 260-272.

[21]Pearlin and Schooler, op. cit., p. 6.

financial performance. A letter from the Executive Director of SBANE urged participation in the survey and assured respondents of anonymity. Of the 738 questionnaires mailed in the fall of 1985, 235 were returned in usable form, representing a 32 percent response rate.

Respondents appear to be representative of the SBANE membership. Their demographic characteristics resemble membership profiles compiled by the SBANE staff. In addition, our respondents conform to the typology of SBANE members found in an earlier survey.[22]

## MEASURES

All questions in the instrument used a Likert-type response format. Stress was measured with a five-item scale that addressed perceived job related pressure and tension. It was adapted from Parasuraman and Alutto,[23] who define felt job stress as "a psychological state of disturbed affect" in response to occupational stressors. The scale showed a coefficient alpha of .85.

In addition to stress, three job-related stressors were examined: situational stressors, role overload, and responsibility for people. Situational stressors were assessed with a six-item scale also taken from Parasuraman and Alutto.[24] The scale examined the severity of work situations such as equipment malfunction, defective materials, employee errors, staff shortages, short lead time on jobs, and lack of employee cooperation. The coefficient alpha was .65.

Role overload was measured with three items from Ivancevich and Matteson.[25] The scale had a coefficient alpha of .86. The items inquired how often respondents worked evenings and weekends, how often they were responsible for an unwieldy number of projects or activities, and how often they had more work than could be done in a standard day.

Responsibility for people was also measured with a three-item scale from Ivancevich and Matteson.[26] Scale items assessed how often respondents felt responsible for counseling subordinates, took actions affecting the well-being of others, and had responsibility for the careers of others. The scale's coefficient alpha was .74.

---

[22]T.M. Begley and D.P. Boyd, "Executive and Corporate Correlates of Financial Performance in Smaller Firms," Journal of Small Business Management, 24 (1986), pp. 8-15.

[23]Parasuraman and Alutto, op. cit., p. 46.

[24]Ibid.

[25]Ivancevich and Matteson, op. cit.

[26]Ibid.

Three scales were used to measure various facets of health. Physical health complaints were identified by eight items from the Quinn-Shepard Physical Symptoms Scale.[27] Included were complaints such as headache, neck or back tension, and sleeping difficulty. The items had a coefficient alpha of .74.

Two types of health complaints were assessed: anxiety and depression. Both the anxiety and depression scales were taken from Cobb[28] and were designed to detect tendencies toward these states rather than clinical conditions. The four-item anxiety scale targets symptoms of worry and nervousness. The six-item depression scale focused on the affective component of depressed mood with items such as feeling "blue," and depressed. These symptoms may precede the onset of clinical conditions.[29] Coefficient alphas for the anxiety and depression scales were .76 and .83, respectively.

Several personal characteristics were measured. In addition to the customary ones such as age, education, and sex, five psychological coping resources were assessed: sense of mastery, self esteem, optimistic action, financial fulfillment, and religious beliefs.

Sense of mastery, self esteem, and optimistic action were taken from Pearlin and Schooler.[30] Mastery is a seven-item scale that assesses one's sense of control over life events. Items include "I have little control over the things that happen to me," "There is really no way I can solve some of my problems," and "What happens to me in the future depends mostly on me." The coefficient alpha was .74.

Self esteem measures positive attitude toward self. Five of the six items in Pearlin and Schooler's[31] scale were included. Their scale was derived from Rosenberg's[32] work with the concept. Items include "I feel that I have a number of good qualities," "I feel that I am a person of worth, at least on an equal plane with others," and "I take a positive attitude toward myself." The coefficient alpha was .85.

---

[27]R.P. Quinn and L.J. Shepard, The 1972-73 Quality of Employment Survey, University of Michigan Institute for Social Research, Ann Arbor, 1974.

[28]S. Cobb, Project Analysis Memo #12, University of Michigan Institute for Social Research, Ann Arbor, 1970.

[29]L.R. Derogatis, The Derogatis Stress Profile: A Summary Report, Clinical Psychometric Research, Baltimore, 1984.

[30]Pearlin and Schooler, op. cit.

[31]Ibid.

[32]M. Rosenberg, Society and the Adolescent Self-Image, Princeton University Press, Princeton, NJ, 1976.

Optimistic action is classified by Pearlin and Schooler[33] as a coping response since it refers to a behavioral mode rather than a psychological stance. We took two coping responses from Pearlin and Schooler's optimistic action scale. In our questionnaire, we also included two of their items on selective ignoring. Internal consistency testing showed that the best use of the items resulted in combining three of the four items into a single scale. We labelled this scale "optimistic action." Its coefficient alpha was .51. The three items are "How often do you remind yourself that for everything bad about your work situation there is also something good?" "How often do you talk to others to find a solution to difficulties?" "How often do you notice people who have more difficulties than you do?"

Financial fulfillment is a single-item measure, "How well did your company's performance for the past five years live up to your expectation?" Religious beliefs used a two part measure. Respondents were first asked if religious beliefs play a role in their life. Those who replied "yes" were then asked five questions from the Intrinsic Subscale of the Religious Orientation Scale.[34] Items include "I try hard to carry my religion over into all my other dealings in life," "My religious beliefs are what really lie behind my whole approach to life," and "Religion is especially important to me because it answers many questions about the meaning of life." The scale's coefficient alpha was .82.

The questionnaire sought data on the financial performance of respondents' firms. Three measures were used. One was average yearly return on assets (ROA) from 1981 to 1985. Five response categories were offered: less than 5%, 5-9%, 10-14%, 15-24%, 25% or more. A second measure was growth rate as indicated by revenue trends over the 1981 to 1985 time period. Eight response categories ranging from "decreased" to "increased 31% or more" were used. A third measure was liquidity as indicated by the ratio of current assets to current liabilities. The measure was used in an attempt to capture a profit performance measure other than ROA. Some scholars[35] (e.g., Walsh and White, 1981) suggest that a "Big Business" measure of profitability such as ROA is less applicable to smaller businesses. The following ratios were included: less than 1.0, 1.0-1.24, 1.25-1.49, 1.50-1.99, 2.0-2.49, 2.5-3.0, over 3.0. Response options for the financial measures were recommended by executives of the Small Business Administration and SBANE.

---

[33]Pearlin and Schooler, op. cit.

[34]J. Feagin, "Prejudice and Religious Types: A Focused Study of Southern Fundamentalists, Journal for the Scientific Study of Religion, 4 (1964), pp. 3-13; G. Allport and J.M. Ross, "Personal Religious Orientation and Prejudice," Journal of Personality and Social Psychology, 5 (1967), pp. 432-443.

[35]J.A. Walsh and J.F. White, "Small Business Ratio Analysis: A Cautionary Note to Consultants," Journal of Small Business Management, (October, 1981), pp. 20-23.

Table 1 presents the means and standard deviations for the variables used in the study. The column of means for the whole sample shows that the average respondent was 48 years of age. The average company was 25 years of age and had 1984 revenues of $1-1.9 million. Typical company financial performance shows the 1981-1985 growth rate to be about 15 percent, ROA to be 10-14 percent, and the liquidity ratio to be about 2.0 (assets/liabilities).

Since the study is exploratory, we frame our analysis in terms of open-ended questions rather than specific hypotheses.

Do founders differ from nonfounders in stress, coping resources, and health? Do their firms differ in financial performance and company characteristics? Table 1 presents means and standard deviations for the founder (n=134) and nonfounder (n=97) subsamples. T-tests were performed to determine the statistical significance of the differences in means between the groups. Results indicate that founders and nonfounders do not differ in the area of perceived job stress. Founders, however, report a higher level of role overload than nonfounders. Both groups cite comparable levels of coping resources. Founders register more physical health complaints and a higher level of anxiety. From a financial perspective, founders show higher growth rates and higher ROA than nonfounders. Finally, founders run younger and smaller companies.

What are the strongest predictors of stress among founders? Is the same pattern manifest among nonfounders? To answer these questions, we regressed job stress on three work-related stressors: situational stressors, role overload, and responsibility for people. The results are presented in Table 2. Among both groups, role overload is the strongest predictor of stress. In the nonfounder group, no other variable shows a significant relationship with stress. In the founders, situational stressors also associate with stress. The most notable feature of the comparison is the difference in stress variance explained by work-related stressors: much more variance is explained in founders' stress levels than in nonfounders'.

We sought to learn if variables such as age of the executive, age of the company, or company size might have a differential impact on founders versus nonfounders and therefore account for some of the difference in variance explained. Perhaps, for example, the larger size of the average nonfounder's company might be a stress generator. Results (not shown) of entering these variables into the regressions of stress on the stressors had little impact. In both groups, C.E.O. age made a statistically significant contribution (younger executives reported higher job stress), but the comparative size of the $R^2$s remained unchanged.

TABLE 1

MEANS AND STANDARD DEVIATIONS FOR THE STUDY'S VARIABLES
FOR THE WHOLE SAMPLE AND THE FOUNDER AND NONFOUNDER SUBSAMPLES

| | Whole Sample | | Founders(N=134) | | Nonfounders(N=97) | |
|---|---|---|---|---|---|---|
| | M | S.D. | M | S.D. | M | S.D. |
| Job Stress | 1.92 | 0.69 | 1.95 | 0.76 | 1.89 | 0.57 |
| Situational Stressors | 1.42 | 0.65 | 1.37 | 0.67 | 1.50 | 0.62 |
| Role Overload | 2.23 | 0.97 | 2.40* | 0.99 | 1.98 | 0.88 |
| Responsibility for People | 2.70 | 0.81 | 2.71 | 0.84 | 2.68 | 0.77 |
| Mastery | 3.17 | 0.46 | 3.16 | 0.46 | 3.16 | 0.44 |
| Self Esteem | 3.30 | 0.52 | 3.32 | 0.53 | 3.25 | 0.51 |
| Optimistic Action | 2.67 | 0.65 | 2.70 | 0.66 | 2.64 | 0.64 |
| Financial Fulfillment | 2.04 | 1.01 | 2.07 | 0.99 | 1.98 | 1.04 |
| Religious Beliefs | 4.61 | 4.69 | 4.34 | 4.74 | 5.00 | 4.63 |
| Physical Health Complaints | 1.00 | 0.61 | 1.07* | 0.66 | 0.91 | 0.54 |
| Anxiety | 1.27 | 0.62 | 1.34* | 0.68 | 1.17 | 0.52 |
| Depression | 1.02 | 0.54 | 1.03 | 0.57 | 1.00 | 0.51 |
| Growth Rate (4:11-15%) 5:16-20% | 4.56 | 2.10 | 4.93* | 2.09 | 4.07 | 2.04 |
| Return on Assets (2:10-14%) 3:15-24% | 2.13 | 1.46 | 2.38* | 1.48 | 1.83 | 1.38 |
| Liquidity (3:1.5-1.99) 4:2.0-2.49 | 3.56 | 2.04 | 3.51 | 2.14 | 3.62 | 1.92 |
| Company Age | 24.80 | 26.13 | 12.30* | 12.72 | 42.20 | 29.86 |
| Company Revenues (2=.5M-.99M) 3=1M-1.9M 4=2M-3.9M | 3.32 | 2.20 | 2.40* | 2.05 | 4.53 | 1.74 |
| C.E.O. Age | 47.75 | 11.03 | 48.57 | 11.41 | 46.66 | 10.49 |

*Indicates that a T-test shows a difference in means that is statistically
significant at or beyond the .05 level.

## TABLE 2

### REGRESSIONS OF JOB STRESS ON WORK STRESSORS IN THE FOUNDER AND NONFOUNDER SUBSAMPLES

|  | Founders[a] | Nonfounders |
|---|---|---|
| Role Overload | .406*** | .289** |
| Responsibility for People | .051 | -.021 |
| Situational Stressors | .254** | .035 |
| $R^2$ | .317*** | .091* |

[a] Coefficients are standardized betas.
* < .05; ** <.01; *** <.001.

A second avenue of explanation was to explore the financial performance of the two groups' firms. Since work stressors account for only a small portion of nonfounder stress, perhaps long-term fiscal performance is a more salient stressor. Table 3 presents the results of regressing stress on the financial performance measures in the founder and nonfounder subsamples. Results indicate that these financial performance measures do not predict perceived job stress in either the founder or nonfounder groups. Apparently, firm financial performance does not generate stress.

## TABLE 3

### REGRESSIONS OF JOB STRESS ON FINANCIAL PERFORMANCE INDICATORS IN THE FOUNDER AND NONFOUNDER SUBSAMPLES

|  | Founders[a] | Nonfounders |
|---|---|---|
| Growth Rate | .140[b] | .116 |
| ROA | -.150 | .067 |
| Liquidity | -.153 | -.097 |
| $R^2$ | .049 | .032 |

[a] Coefficients are standardized betas.
[b] None of the coefficients are statistically significant at the .05 level.

Another facet of stress research is to search for factors that prevent stress. Do certain psychological resources mitigate stress generation? Are these factors the same in the founding and nonfounding groups? Table 4 presents the results of regressing stress on five coping resources: sense of mastery, self esteem, optimistic action, financial fulfillment, and religious beliefs. Among founders, a high sense of mastery associates with a low sense of job stress. Sense of mastery apparently imbues founders with the confidence to solve problems in an expeditious and efficacious manner. Very different associations appear among nonfounders. Lower job stress associates more strongly with optimistic action and with religious beliefs. Nonfounders benefit more from indirect problem solving. Two of the three items in the optimistic action scale involve acceptance of the existing situation while religious beliefs entail recourse to internal values. However, the variance explained in both groups is nearly identical.

TABLE 4

REGRESSIONS OF JOB STRESS ON
PSYCHOLOGICAL COPING RESOURCES
IN THE FOUNDER AND NONFOUNDER SUBSAMPLES

|  | Founders[a] | Nonfounders |
|---|---|---|
| Mastery | -.350** | -.142 |
| Self Esteem | .104 | .117 |
| Optimistic Action | -.027 | -.246* |
| Financial Fulfillment | -.074 | .138 |
| Religious Beliefs | -.053 | -.260* |
| $R^2$ | .114* | .138* |

[a] Coefficients are standardized betas.
* $< .05$; ** $< .01$.

Various sets of variables have been separately introduced to examine stress among founders and nonfounders. The question then arises about the relative ability of the variables associated with stress when they compete against one another. Table 5 presents the results of regressing job stress on the range of study variables for founders and nonfounders. With the large number of variables used, multicollinearity could be problematic. The regressions therefore involved stepwise selection of the variable that added the most to the explanatory power of the equation. Beta coefficients in the table are taken from the step in which all statistically significant variables had entered the equation.

Among founders and nonfounders, role overload has the greatest association with stress (Table 5). Beyond that, several variables contribute to founder stress. Situational stressors and size of company

TABLE 5

REGRESSIONS (STEPWISE) OF JOB STRESS ON C.E.O.
AND COMPANY CHARACTERISTICS IN THE FOUNDER AND NONFOUNDER SUBSAMPLES

|  | Founders[a] | | Nonfounders | |
| --- | --- | --- | --- | --- |
| Situational Stressors | (3) | .234** | | -.059 |
| Role Overload | (1) | .347*** | (1) | .353** |
| Responsibility for People | | -.064 | | .076 |
| Mastery | (2) | -.355*** | | -.043 |
| Self Esteem | | .022 | | .028 |
| Optimistic Action | | .030 | (2) | -.307** |
| Financial Fulfillment | | -.139 | | .095 |
| Religious Beliefs | | -.127 | | -.170 |
| Growth Rate | | -.062 | | .149 |
| ROA | | -.053 | | .112 |
| Liquidity | (6) | -.176* | | -.117 |
| Company Age | | -.135 | | -.095 |
| Company Revenues | (5) | .213** | | .043 |
| C.E.O. Age | (4) | -.248** | | -.134 |
| $R^2$ | | .598*** | | .227*** |

[a] Coefficients are standardized betas. Regressions use stepwise inclusion based on incremental contribution to variance explained. Variables in the equations are ones whose contribution to variance explained is statistically significant at the .05 level. Numbers in parentheses indicate order of entry into the equations. $R^2$ indicates the variance explained by the variables that enter the equation.
    * $<$ .05; ** $<$ .01; *** $<$ .001.

revenues relate positively to stress levels. On the other hand, sense of mastery, C.E.O. age, and liquidity ratio relate inversely to founder stress. Among nonfounders, only one additional variable shows: optimistic action relates inversely to stress. We again note a substantial disparity in the variance explained by the variables in Table 5 for founder and nonfounder stress.

A final question in our study concerns entrepreneurial health. Job stress has consistently associated with health problems in large-company populations. Does stress have a similar effect on entrepreneurs? What impact do stressors, coping resources, and financial results have on entrepreneurial health? Are patterns similar for founders and nonfounders? Tables 6 and 7 present the regressions of physical health complaints, anxiety, and depression on stress and the other variables. Stress, which had been the dependent variable in previous tables, is now included with the independent variables as a possible predictor of health complaints.

TABLE 6

REGRESSIONS (STEPWISE) OF PHYSICAL COMPLAINTS, ANXIETY, AND DEPRESSION
ON C.E.O. AND COMPANY CHARACTERISTICS IN THE FOUNDER SUBSAMPLE

| | Physical[a] Complaints | | Anxiety | | Depression |
|---|---|---|---|---|---|
| Job Stress | (1) .439*** | (1) | .456*** | (2) | .260** |
| Situational Stressors | -.024 | | .154 | | .047 |
| Role Overload | .104 | | -.015 | | -.037 |
| Responsibility for People | -.026 | | -.008 | (3) | .231*** |
| Mastery | -.180 | (2) | -.383*** | (1) | -.375*** |
| Self Esteem | -.021 | | -.152 | | .045 |
| Optimistic Action | -.166 | | .008 | | -.044 |
| Financial Fulfillment | .032 | | .036 | (4) | -.219* |
| Religious Beliefs | -.132 | | -.039 | | .045 |
| Growth Rate | .058 | | .018 | | .065 |
| ROA | .142 | | -.090 | | -.066 |
| Liquidity | -.005 | | -.070 | | -.046 |
| Company Age | .066 | | .007 | | .100 |
| Company Revenues | .149 | | .061 | | .096 |
| C.E.O. Age | -.012 | | -.096 | | -.032 |
| $R^2$ | .192*** | | .505*** | | .490*** |

[a] Coefficients are standardized betas. Regressions use stepwise
inclusion based on incremental contribution to variance explained.
Variables in the equations are ones whose contribution to variance
explained is statistically significant at the .05 level. Numbers in
parentheses indicate order of entry into the equations. $R^2$ indicates the
variance explained by the variables that enter the equation.
    * < .05;  ** < .01;  *** < .001.

Results show substantial evidence that stress is a key work-related
associate of health.  In both samples, it consistently enters the
equations predicting physical complaints, anxiety, and depression.  The
magnitude of the coefficients is large.  Mastery makes statistically
significant contributions to four of the six equations.  It reduces
anxiety and depression among founders, and it reduces physical complaints
and depression among nonfounders.  The size of its contribution is larger
in the founders than the nonfounders.  Other variables show little
consistency relating to health.

In the group of founders, job stress is the only effective
associate of physical complaints.  Founders' anxiety is not predicted by
job stress and mastery.  Founders' depression is associated with mastery,
job stress, higher responsibility for people, and lower financial
fulfillment.

In the group of nonfounders, job stress is highly related to physical complaints. It is supplemented by lower sense of mastery and older company age. Anxiety among nonfounders is best predicted by low self esteem, high job stress, and low sense of financial fulfillment. Depression relates to low mastery, high job stress, and low self esteem.

TABLE 7

REGRESSIONS (STEPWISE) OF PHYSICAL COMPLAINTS, ANXIETY, AND DEPRESSION
ON C.E.O. AND COMPANY CHARACTERISTICS IN THE NONFOUNDER SUBSAMPLE

| | Physical[a] Complaints | | Anxiety | | Depression |
|---|---|---|---|---|---|
| Job Stress | (1) | .586*** | (2) | .381*** | (2) | .329*** |
| Situational Stressors | | .060 | | .156 | | -.027 |
| Role Overload | | .065 | | -.062 | | -.193 |
| Responsibility for People | | -.073 | | .091 | | -.119 |
| Mastery | (3) | -.196* | | -.132 | (1) | -.270* |
| Self Esteem | | .140 | (1) | -.357*** | (3) | -.261* |
| Optimistic Action | | -.102 | | -.036 | | -.137 |
| Financial Fulfillment | | -.102 | (3) | -.284** | | -.126 |
| Religious Beliefs | | .004 | | .095 | | -.167 |
| Growth Rate | | -.124 | | .046 | | .001 |
| ROA | | -.146 | | .089 | | -.128 |
| Liquidity | | .104 | | -.147 | | -.074 |
| Company Age | (2) | .226* | | -.077 | | .074 |
| Company Revenues | | -.133 | | -.026 | | -.178 |
| C.E.O. Age | | -.175 | | -.067 | | -.110 |
| $R^2$ | | .413*** | | .420*** | | .371*** |

[a] Coefficients are standardized betas. Regressions use stepwise inclusion based on incremental contribution to variance explained. Variables in the equations are ones whose contribution to variance explained is statistically significant at the .05 level. Numbers in parentheses indicate order of entry into the equations. $R^2$ indicates the variance explained by the variables that enter the equation.
* < .05; ** < .01; *** < .001.

Each of the regression equations explains a sizable portion of the variance in health problems. An exception is the comparatively low amount explained for physical complaints in the founder subsample. In that equation, stress explains its usual high proportion of variance, but its explanatory ability is not supplemented by contributions from other predictors. Stress, and to a lesser extent, mastery are such contributors to health problems among founders and nonfounders that these subsamples show similar patterns. The only notable difference between

these groups is that self esteem contributes prominently to the reduction
of mental health problems among nonfounders but not founders.

## DISCUSSION

This paper first examined differences between founders and
nonfounders in stress, coping resources, health, and corporate financial
performance.  The two groups were similar on stress factors and coping
resources with one exception:  founders reported higher role overload
than nonfounders.  Since role overload later emerges as a key contributor
to job stress, founders seem to be especially susceptible to stress from
this source.  Founders reported more physical problems and more anxiety
than nonfounders even as they reported higher company growth rates and
return on assets.  While it may be tempting to argue that health problems
accompany higher performance, the financial variables did not enter the
equations in Tables 6 and 7 as predictors of health problems.

The paper then examined the relationships between a number of work-
related variables and 1) job stress and 2) health problems in groups of
founders and nonfounders.  Stress levels among founders are more readily
predicted by selected work-related variables than are stress levels among
nonfounders.  Other unmeasured work-related variables may associate more
prominently with nonfounder stress.  Yet it is also possible that
nonfounders simply are not as stressed by their work as founders.
Founders have a keen sense of work involvement since their companies are
their own creations.  In addition, founders may recognize the tenuousness
and vulnerability of a newly created company more than nonfounders, who
have usually taken over established companies.  Founders may therefore be
more sensitive to perturbations in work events.  Nonfounders may be less
stressed by work because the pace may be less frenetic.  Their companies
are generally larger and may have an added hierarchical level, such as a
supervisor or foreman, to buffer problems.  In addition, nonfounders may
be less emotionally committed to their companies and thus suffer less
with the cyclical swings of the business.

Results in both subsamples indicate a lack of relationship between
job stress and financial performance measures for growth, profitability,
and liquidity.  Apparently, financial performance does not relate to
stress levels.  This finding may be influenced by multicollinearity in
the data, that is, the financial performance measures may intercorrelate
highly enough to cancel one another in the regression equations.  While
these measures correlate with one another, examination of Pearson
correlations shows that they do not correlate with stress in the founder
group.  In the nonfounder group, two variables correlate significantly
with stress:  growth ($r=.179$, $p=.04$) and liquidity ($r=-.181$, $p=.05$).
Clearly, founder stress levels are not affected by financial results.
Nonfounder stress levels show some modest associations with financials.

Coping resources prevent stress or modify its effects.  Founders
and nonfounders once again show different patterns in the coping
resources that associate most closely with job stress.  In the founder
group, mastery dominates as the most effective resource.  In the

nonfounder group, optimistic action and religious beliefs are the most effective. As noted earlier, founders appear to have more of a direct problem solving orientation than nonfounders. Since we previously noted the founders' closer associations between work-related stressors and stress, founders may tend to view work problems as a direct challenge necessitating mastery through goal-driven activity. Nonfounders, on the other hand, tend to accept existing conditions with less overt reactivity.

Tables 6 and 7 show clearly that stress is a major covariate with health problems. This result is expected. Not as easily anticipated is the strong contribution made by mastery to mitigating stress levels in both subgroups. Sense of competence and control fosters health maintenance among managers and especially among entrepreneurs.

With the exception of self esteem for nonfounders, other variables do not contribute substantially to predicting health problems. This fact might lead us to dismiss these variables as ineffective. However, we view perceived job stress as a mediating variable between work conditions and health outcomes. In other words, work and personal conditions generate stress, which then relates to health problems. In this view, work conditions need not directly relate to health in order to have predictive value. Rather, they need to predict stress which then relates to health. In this light, role overload, for example, which had little predictive ability in the health equations, is still viewed as a contributor to health problems through its impact on stress. The next logical step in dealing with these variables involves the development of a path analytic diagram or a more complex structural equation model.

In this paper, we have examined a number of aspects of the entrepreneurial work situation. In addition, we have used nonfounders as a comparison group. Entrepreneurs occupy highly stressful jobs which can affect their health. Yet entrepreneurial health is critical to the life of the company. Without a healthy helmsman, the driving force in the company is gone. Continued research on antecedents and outcomes of stress will help ensure the well-being of ventures and venturesome leaders.

# NEW FIRM GROWTH AND PERFORMANCE*

William C. Dunkelberg, Purdue University
Arnold C. Cooper, Purdue University
Carolyn Woo, Purdue University
William Dennis, National Federation of Independent Business

## ABSTRACT

Patterns of growth and performance were analyzed in this longitudinal study of 1178 young firms. Three measures of performance - growth in employment, growth in sales, and personal satisfaction - were considered. Firms which had added employees were compared with those which declined in employment in regard to characteristics of the entrepreneurs, processes of starting, and the nature of the new firms. Factors associated with entrepreneurs' satisfaction or disappointment were also examined.

## INTRODUCTION

This paper reports upon the first two years of a large longitudinal study. It focuses upon two broad questions:

1) What are the patterns of growth or decline for surviving new firms? As entrepreneurs reflect upon their achievements, what are the patterns of satisfaction or disappointment?

2) What factors are associated with growth or decline? How do characteristics of entrepreneurs, processes of starting, and the nature of the new firms relate to subsequent patterns of development? What factors are associated with entrepreneurs' satisfaction or disappointment?

* We would like to acknowledge the work of Jeff Van Hulle, Ann Fraedrich and Laura Gerek for their contributions to the work presented here. The research is sponsored by the National Federation of Independent Business.

This large scale study began in May 1985, when approximately 13,000 questionnaires were mailed to members of the National Federation of Independent Business who reported that they had recently become business owners. The questionnaire focused upon the backgrounds of the entrepreneurs, their processes of starting, and the nature of their new firms. Of the 4814 entrepreneurs who responded, 2994 had first become owners in 1984 or 1985. This longitudinal study examines further developments of these 2994 entrepreneurs, all of whom had been in business for 17 months or less. The median entrepreneur had been in business for 12 months and the interquartile range was 8 for 15 months.

One year later, in May 1986, a follow-up questionnaire was sent. It focused primarily on firm characteristics, including their performance, and changes in employment and sales. It also examined how the firms were managed, including their strategies, financing, allocations of management time, the changes which had been made, and managers' perceptions of the major problems encountered. Responses were obtained from 1178 of those who had originally been in business 17 months or less; this represented a response rate of about 40%. This paper focuses upon these 1178 entrepreneurs and their firms. We believe this to be one of the largest longitudinal studies of entrepreneurship ever undertaken.

The sample involves a broad cross section of new businesses in the United States, representing virtually all industries and all geographic parts of the country. The average firm in the sample at the time of the first questionnaire was quite small, with mean employment, including the entrepreneur, of four.

## PATTERNS OF PERFORMANCE

In examining the performance of these 1178 young firms during their second year of existence, we shall consider three measures of performance:

1) Change in number of employees;
2) Change in sales level;
3) Entrepreneurs' satisfaction, relative to expectations.

Two other possible measures of performance – profitability and survival – were not considered here. We believed that in these young owner-managed firms, reported profits would be largely a residual, after the entrepreneurs had decided what to pay themselves. Reported profits would also often be minimized because of the desire to avoid corporate taxes. In addition, in the early stages of this longitudinal study, we hesitated to probe in regard to personal draws and profits because of concern that this would decrease the overall response rate.

Another possible measure of performance is survival. In that sense, all of these 1178 firms were successful. We are still in the process of gathering data on non-survivors in the original sample and will report at a later time on factors related to survival and nonsurvival.

We shall now consider the patterns of growth and decline for these young firms. At the time of both the first and second questionnaires, firms were asked to report their annual sales and their total employment, both full-time and part-time. (Each part-time employee was counted as 0.5 employees.)

Table 1 shows the growth patterns for the sample. It appears that 17% of the firms contracted employment, 46% were unchanged, and 37% reported employment growth. In sales, only 11% reported a change of less than +5%. For the sample, 68% reported sales growth, with 23% having increases of 100% or more. Only 14% of these surviving firms experienced a decline in sales. Overall, these young firms increased sales more than employment. In assets, 62% of the businesses reported increases; for these firms, their mean increase in assets was 38%. Only 8% of these surviving firms reported a decrease in assets, with a mean decrease of 21%.

Although there were substantial variations, most of these firms did relatively well. Almost two-thirds increased their assets, 37% increased employment, and about two-thirds increased sales.

We now consider the degree of satisfaction of these entrepreneurs, relative to their expectations. As noted in Table 2, sales performance was higher than expected for 27% of the firms, about the same for 43%, and lower for 29%. Profit performance was higher than expected for only 15% of the firms, about the same for 44%, and lower for 40%. The entrepreneurs' overall personal satisfaction was higher than expected for 21%, about the same for 44%, and lower for 33%. On balance, there was some tendency toward disappointment in profits and personal satisfaction.

Growth Versus Decline

We now consider factors associated with performance, specifically examining whether firms which grew were different from firms which declined. We focus upon one of the principal measures of economic impact - employment change - and contrast firms showing declines in employment (17% of the sample) with those showing increases (37% of the sample). Three broad sets of factors which may be associated with growth or decline are considered:

1) The backgrounds of the entrepreneurs;
2) The processes of starting;
3) The characteristics and strategies of the new firms.

Because of the nature of the sample, it is important to use care in interpreting the findings. Recall that all of the firms considered

# TABLE 1

## MEASURES OF SMALL BUSINESS PERFORMANCE

| Change in Employment[a] | % of Firms | Change in Sales[b] | % of Firms |
|---|---|---|---|
| Reduced 50% or more | 2% | 15% or more lower | 14% |
| -50% to -5% | 15% | -15% to -5% | 7% |
| -5% to +5% | 46% | -5% to +5% | 11% |
| 5% to 25% | 7% | 5% to 25% | 17% |
| 25% to 50% | 7% | 25% to 50% | 14% |
| 50% to 100% | 10% | 50% to 100% | 14% |
| 100% to 200% | 9% | 100% to 200% | 10% |
| 200% or more | 4% | 200% or more | 13% |
| | 100% | | 100% |

| Asset Change | | Average Change |
|---|---|---|
| Increased | 62% | +38% |
| Stayed same | 30% | -- |
| Decreased | 8% | -21% |
| | 100% | 100% |

[a] No response was interpreted as no employees in the category in question.

[b] 125 cases for which sales in either or both years were not reported are omitted from the statistics.

TABLE 2

PERFORMANCE AND EXPECTATIONS

|  | Sales | Profits | Personal Satisfaction |
|---|---|---|---|
| Higher than Expected | 27% | 15% | 21% |
| Same as Expected | 43% | 44% | 44% |
| Lower than Expected | 29% | 40% | 33% |
| No Answer | 1% | 1% | 2% |
|  | 100% | 100% | 100% |

here were survivors, so that those which failed are no longer in the sample. Furthermore, these firms may have varied substantially in size at founding or at the time of the first questionnaire. What might be viewed as "poor preparation," such as no management experience, no relevant industry experience, and low capitalization, may have been associated with the starting of very small firms. Firms with no initial employees other than the entrepreneur were unlikely to decline in employment and remain in this sample of survivors. At the same time, some of these tiny firms, characterized by poor preparation, may have shown high percentage rates of growth because of their small bases. This could lead to a portion of the sample being characterized as follows. Poor preparation leads to tiny businesses. Of those which survive, some may show high percentage rates of growth. Therefore, for this portion of the sample, it could appear that poor preparation leads to high performance. We should keep these possible relationships in mind as we examine this total sample of survivors and analyze differences between firms which declined and firms which grew.

## Entrepreneurs' Backgrounds

In analyzing backgrounds of the entrepreneurs, we expected the following factors to be associated with growth: 1) more education; 2) managerial experience; 3) having come from a business organization; 4) having gotten the idea for the new business from a prior job; 5) leaving the prior organization because of plans for the new business (rather than being fired or quitting with no plans); 6) similarity between the new business and the prior organization; and 7) more "managerial" as distinct from "craftsman-like" goals.

In comparing the sample of growth firms and decline firms, no significant differences were observed in regard to most of these background characteristics. (See Table 3.) Findings in regard to the highest level of previous management experience were surprising. Those showing declines were more likely to have managed or owned a business

TABLE 3

ENTREPRENEURS' CHARACTERISTICS

| | Decline Firms (n = 204) | Growth Firms (n = 430) |
|---|---|---|
| **Education** | | |
| High School or Less | 36% | 41% |
| Some College | 38% | 31% |
| Bachelors Degree | 17% | 15% |
| Some Graduate School | 9% | 11% |
| **Management Experience** | | |
| *No Subordinates or Supervised Workers | 54% | 63% |
| Supervised Managers | 8% | 10% |
| *Managed/Owned Business | 33% | 22% |
| **Previous Organization** | | |
| Large Business (> 100) | 17% | 12% |
| Medium Business (100-999) | 7% | 14% |
| Small Business (< 100) | 48% | 51% |
| Had Own Business | 17% | 12% |
| Non-Profit/Not in Labor Force | 11% | 11% |
| **Source of Idea for Business** | | |
| *Prior Job | 42% | 50% |
| Interest/Hobby | 17% | 14% |
| Other | 41% | 36% |

TABLE 3 (continued)

| | Decline Firms | Growth Firms |
|---|---|---|
| **Reason for Leaving Previous Organization** | | |
| Job Discontinued | 12% | 9% |
| Laid Off, Fired | 7% | 7% |
| Quit, No Plans | 7% | 8% |
| Quit, Plans | 53% | 56% |
| Other | 15% | 15% |
| **Similarity to Previous Organization (Very Different)** | | |
| *Products/Services | 40% | 32% |
| Customers | 34% | 33% |
| Suppliers | 35% | 35% |
| **Goals When Starting (Most Important)** | | |
| Do the Kind of Work You Want to Do | 25% | 25% |
| Avoid Working for Others | 21% | 19% |
| Make More Money Than Otherwise | 17% | 19% |
| Build Successful Organization | 31% | 30% |

* $p < .05$

(33% vs. 22%), but less likely to have only managed workers or to have had no subordinates (54% vs. 63%). These puzzling findings may be related to the initial size of the ventures, with those having previously managed or owned a business being more likely to start a new business of substantial size. As hypothesized, those showing growth were more likely to have gotten the idea for the business from a previous job (50% vs. 42%). Also as expected, more of those firms showing decline (40% vs. 32%) were very different from the incubator organizations which the entrepreneurs had left in products or services offered.

## Processes of Starting

In regard to processes of starting, we expected the following factors to be associated with growth: 1) starting the business rather than purchasing it (because of the smaller initial size of the firm); 2) more capitalization; 3) more reliance upon capital from "professional sources" such as outside investors or financial institutions; 4) less ownership by the entrepreneur and family (because of capital from outside investors); and 5) more reliance upon information from professional advisors, such as accountants or attorneys.

In comparing the firms showing growth with those showing decline, there were several significant differences. (See Table 4.) More of those showing growth (70% vs. 55%) had started their firms. For those showing a decline in employment, the entrepreneurs and their spouses were more likely to own 100% of the firm (73% vs. 62%). Of various possible sources of information or help, those showing growth were somewhat more likely to rely upon bankers (56% vs. 49%), but less likely to utilize books (40% vs. 47%).

## Characteristics of Firms

We expected growth and decline to be related to the industries of the new firms and to subsequent management actions taken after the firms were started. Specifically, we expected manufacturing and construction firms to be more likely to grow and retail and non-professional service firms to be more likely to decline. Firms showing growth were expected to rely upon new funds from outside investors and financial institutions. The entrepreneurs were expected to manage their time differently, with those involved with growth firms devoting less time to dealing with customers or producing goods or services. We were uncertain whether changes in strategy, such as changes in relative price levels, new products introduced, or changes in advertising levels would be associated with growth or decline. One possibility is that firms performing poorly would have experienced many changes as their managers searched for success formulas; an alternative possibility is that growing businesses would have been headed by proactive managers who deliberately instituted changes.

In comparing the sample of growth firms with those showing decline, there were a number of differences. (See Table 5.) In regard to industry, the growth firms were less likely to be in retailing (37%

TABLE 4

PROCESSES OF STARTING

|  | Decline Firms | Growth Firms |
|---|---|---|
| How Became Owner | | |
| *Started | 55% | 70% |
| *Purchased | 35% | 24% |
| Initial Capitalization | | |
| $10,000 or less | 30% | 34% |
| $10,000-$49,999 | 43% | 43% |
| $50,000 or more | 27% | 24% |
| Ownership by Entrepreneur and Spouse | | |
| *100% | 73% | 62% |
| 50%-99% | 16% | 20% |
| 49% or less | 7% | 10% |
| Sources of Initial Capital (Some Reliance) | | |
| Personal Savings | 71% | 74% |
| Friends/Relatives | 30% | 30% |
| Individual Investors | 6% | 7% |
| Financial Institutions | 49% | 43% |

TABLE 4 (continued)

| | Decline Firms | Growth Firms |
|---|---|---|
| Sources of Information (Very or Somewhat Important) | | |
| Accountant/Bookkeeper | 70% | 68% |
| Other Business Owners | 60% | 64% |
| *Bankers | 49% | 56% |
| Trade Organizations | 30% | 24% |
| Attorneys | 41% | 44% |
| *Books/Manuals | 47% | 40% |
| Courses/Workshops | 29% | 24% |

* $p < .05$

TABLE 5

FIRM CHARACTERISTICS

|  | Decline Firms | Growth Firms |
|---|---|---|
| Industry | | |
| Construction | 6% | 7% |
| *Manufacturing | 5% | 11% |
| *Retail | 49% | 37% |
| Service | 20% | 21% |
| Sources of New Funds (Some Reliance) | | |
| *Company Earnings | 61% | 74% |
| Existing Investors | 27% | 21% |
| New Investors | 6% | 6% |
| *Financial Institutions | 32% | 41% |
| *Increases in Trade Credit | 36% | 49% |
| Sources of Information and Assistance (Very or Somewhat Important) | | |
| *Accountant | 69% | 78% |
| Other Business Owners | 57% | 59% |
| Bankers | 47% | 48% |
| Trade Organizations | 45% | 42% |
| Attorneys | 29% | 29% |
| Books/Manuals | 60% | 54% |
| Courses/Workshops | 42% | 43% |

TABLE 5 (continued)

|  | Decline Firms | Growth Firms |
|---|---|---|
| Major Changes Made | | |
| *Added Product Lines/Services | 46% | 53% |
| Dropped Product Lines/Services | 25% | 19% |
| Changed Prices Relative to Competitors | | |
| Higher | 17% | 17% |
| *Lower | 20% | 12% |
| Changed Advertising/Promotion | | |
| *More | 26% | 35% |
| *Less | 26% | 13% |
| Allocation of Entrepreneur's Time (Some Time Allocated) | | |
| *Dealing with Employees | 77% | 87% |
| Record Keeping | 82% | 86% |
| Direct Selling | 92% | 93% |
| Production/Provision Services | 65% | 67% |
| Purchasing | 83% | 85% |
| *Planning Firm Growth/Change | 64% | 73% |

* $p < .05$

vs. 49%), but more likely to be in manufacturing (11% vs. 5%). There were some differences in funding sources, with those showing growth being more likely to get new funds from company earnings (74% vs. 61%), financial institutions (41% vs. 32%), or increased trade credit (49% vs. 36%). The growth firms relied more heavily upon information from accountants or bookkeepers (78% vs. 69%). In regard to changes made by management, there were some interesting patterns. Those showing growth were more likely to have added products (53% vs. 46%) and more likely to have increased advertising or promotion (35% vs. 26%). However, those showing declines were more likely to have lowered prices relative to competitors (20% vs. 12%). Thus, the declining firms seemed to be scrambling to hold on through price cuts, while their expanding counterparts build upon their growth through adding products and increasing advertising. In regard to application of the entrepreneur's time, there were two differences. Those whose firms were growing were more likely to devote at least some time to dealing with employees (87% vs. 77%), which was understandable because they were adding employees. They were also more likely to devote at least some time to planning their firm's growth or change (73% vs. 64%). We do not know whether devoting attention to planning was contributing to growth or was a response to the problems associated with growth or change.

### OVERALL SATISFACTION


We now consider the personal satisfactions of the entrepreneurs relative to their expectations. Specifically, we contrast those with higher overall satisfaction than expected (21% of the sample) with those disappointed, relative to their expectations (33% of the sample). These are, of course, subjective measures. Some of the entrepreneurs may have had modest initial goals and others may have hoped that they were founding the next Apple Computer.

We consider here a limited set of variables: 1) sex of the entrepreneur; 2) race; 3) whether the business was started or purchased; 4) industry membership; and 5) amount of capital invested. We had no a priori expectations about how these variables would be related to personal satisfaction, other than industry membership. We did expect those involved in industries which had been growing (such as financial services) to be more satisfied than those positioned in depressed industries (such as agriculture). In regard to initial capital, entrepreneurs starting with more capital invested might have done better, but they might also have had higher expectations, so that it was difficult to judge, on balance, whether they would be more satisfied.

The findings on overall satisfaction, reported in Table 6, showed no significant differences by sex. In regard to race, minority entrepreneurs were disappointed much less than their majority counterparts (23% vs. 34%). Those who purchased their firms included more who were disappointed than those who started their firms (38% vs. 31%). In regard to industry, there were some variations but no industries in which entrepreneurs' satisfaction was significantly

TABLE 6

PERSONAL SATISFACTION AFTER TWO YEARS

| | % of Firms | Personal Satisfaction vs. Initial Expectation | |
| --- | --- | --- | --- |
| | | Higher | Lower |
| ALL FIRMS | | 21% (n = 245) | 33% (n = 390) |
| | | | |
| Sex | | | |
| Female | 19% | 20% | 31% |
| Male | 80% | 21% | 34% |
| | | | |
| *Race | | | |
| Minority | 6% | 20% | 23% |
| Majority | 93% | 21% | 34% |
| | | | |
| *How Became Owner | | | |
| Started | 63% | 22% | 31% |
| Purchased | 30% | 17% | 38% |
| | | | |
| Industry | | | |
| Construction | 8% | 23% | 27% |
| Manufacturing | 10% | 16% | 27% |
| Transportation | 2% | 17% | 28% |
| Wholesale | 5% | 25% | 30% |
| Retail | 42% | 20% | 36% |
| Agriculture | 2% | 26% | 37% |
| Financial Serv. | 6% | 27% | 29% |
| Non-Prof. Serv. | 18% | 21% | 37% |
| Prof. Services | 7% | 23% | 27% |
| | | | |
| Capital Invested | | | |
| Under $5000 | 16% | 27% | 31% |
| $5000-$9999 | 12% | 24% | 34% |
| $10,000-$19,999 | 16% | 22% | 31% |
| $20,000-$49,999 | 26% | 19% | 34% |
| $50,000-$99,999 | 17% | 17% | 37% |
| $100,000-$249,999 | 9% | 20% | 30% |
| *$250,000 or more | 4% | 18% | 44% |

* p < .05

different from the means.  In regard to initial capital invested, those with the most initial capital ($250,000 or more) clearly included the most who were disappointed (44%).  Possibly, these large-scale entrepreneurs had very ambitious goals or were encountering more difficulty in getting their businesses to run smoothly.

## CONCLUSIONS

This longitudinal study provides some insights into how new firms evolve and grow; it also suggests some factors related to these patterns of evolution.  We are now in the process of evaluating the data in a number of ways, including analysis of factors associated with initial size and consideration of how firms of different initial size evolve and grow.  We are assembling data on firms from the initial sample which have discontinued, and are also gathering further data from the third and last year of this longitudinal study.  Thus, if you do not tire of listening to us, we shall be able to report on the continuing survival and evolution of this large sample of young firms.

# EXPECTATIONS VS. REALITY AMONG FOUNDERS OF RECENT START-UPS

Karl A. Egge, Macalester College

## ABSTRACT

This paper probes the extent to which the entrepreneur's expectations were unfulfilled after start-up. It is based on questionnaire results from 150 founders of new firms established in the Minneapolis/ St. Paul area between January 1984 and October 1986. Approximately 50% of the founders agree their revenues were less than expected, their working capital needs were underestimated, and the time it took to become profitable was more than expected. Over 50% agreed their anticipated success and anticipated personal standard of living were less from this business than they had expected. Nearly 67% thought launching their business would go quicker than it did. Statistical analyses of pre start-up variables associated with subsequent shortfalls revealed the importance of venture planning and previous experience. However, a large venture was more likely to have shortfalls.

## INTRODUCTION

It is standard business practice to compare actual performance results with expected or budgeted amounts. This variance analysis is applied here to the difference between what founders had expected and later realized from their new ventures. The attention is on those topics where reality fell short of expectations.

Those of us who teach and work with prospective entrepreneurs must walk a fine line. We want to encourage them, but we want them to have realistic expectations. Our casual empiricism and personal experiences condition our cautionary counsel that starting a new business takes much longer than planned, takes more hours per week than had been expected, and often has more sobering financial results than anticipated.[1] There may be generalized discussions on this topic in books,[1] but even in the journals it is hard to find evidence documenting this conventional

---

[1] See, for example, Jeffrey A. Timmons, New Venture Creation, 2nd ed., Homewood, Ill., Richard D. Irwin, Inc., 1985, p. 600. See also, Robert C. Ronstadt, Entrepreneurship, Dover, MA., Lord Publishing, 1984, Chapter 4.

wisdom. Textbook exhortations like, "the would-be entrepreneur must be realistic,"[2] even if they are surrounded by descriptions of new venture pitfalls, are not likely to jolt the prospective entrepreneur into taking potentially corrective action.

One objective of this paper is to quantify these shortfalls. Another is to understand those pre start-up factors that turn out to be statistically related to them. We who work with prospective entrepreneurs could better justify or reassess our preventive medicines. These might range from delaying a project, encouraging the entrepreneur to first serve as an apprentice, further market research, or forming a team.

Failure in business is feared. Failure in the sense of bankruptcy or business cessations is well documented.[3] However, most research is on the other side of the probability distribution, documenting success or survival.[4] Most new venture outcomes lie between the well-studied extremes of bankruptcy and mega-success. These shortfalls between a founder's expectations and reality during the initial phases of a start-up represent a gap in the literature.

### RESEARCH METHODOLOGY

A four-page questionnaire on new business start-ups was designed for use in this project. It probed these data: 1) Background on the entrepreneur, 2) Information concerning the planning for and start-up of the new business, 3) Comparisons between forecasts and actual results or comparisons between current and a priori beliefs, 4) Statements of advice to prospective entrepreneurs, and 5) Open-ended answers to a question about the most significant mistake made.

---

[2] John G. Burch, Entrepreneurship, New York, John Wiley & Sons, 1986, p. 96.

[3] See, for example, Dun & Bradstreet Corp., The Failure Record Through 1983, and Monthly Failure Report, New York, Dun & Bradstreet Corp. See also Karl Egge, "Entrepreneurial Failures, Results From a Study of Business Bankruptcies in Minnesota," Journal of Private Enterprise, (Fall 1986), pp. 42-50.

[4] D. Kirk Neiswander and John M. Drollinger, "Origins of Successful Start-up Ventures," Frontiers of Entrepreneurship Research, Babson College, 1986, pp. 328-343. See also, Alan, L. Carsrud, Connie Marie Gaglio, and Kenneth W. Olm, "Entrepreneurs-Mentors, Networks, and Successful New Venture Development: An Exploratory Study," Frontiers of Entrepreneurship Research, Babson College, 1986, pp. 229-243. Even well-known texts focus on the correlates of success, e.g., Karl H. Vesper, New Venture Strategies, Englewood Cliffs, NJ, Prentice-Hall, Inc., 1980, p. 55.

## The Sample

The sample population consisted of all new businesses listed in the Monday morning business section of the <u>Minneapolis Star and Tribune</u> for January 1, 1985 through June 30, 1986, and from the monthly publication <u>Minnesota Business Journal</u>, for the same time period. Excluded from the population were expansions of an existing business (e.g., a second store), businesses with an address outside the metropolitan area of the Twin Cities, and franchisees. An important consideration in using these two sources was the identification of the owners.

In November 1986, questionnaires were mailed to 443 owners of new businesses from these two lists. We received 152 completed questionnaires. We attribute this very high (33%) response rate to addressing the entrepreneur. We chose January 1, 1984 as a cut-off date for when the business first opened. Thus, nine questionnaires were not used for this paper. Since the median months opened was 18 at the time of the survey, obviously many had opened prior to the publicly announced opening.

TABLE 1

COMPARISON OF SAMPLES

| Industry Groupings | Macalester Sample, Twin Cities Start-ups (Began in 1984-6) | U of M Sample,[a] Minnesota Start-ups (Began in 1979,82) | Population:[b] (All Business-Begun in MN in 1977) |
|---|---|---|---|
| Ag., Const., & Mfg. | 15% | 39% | 29% |
| Retail | 22 | 15 | 25 |
| Services & Other | 63 | 45 | 46 |
| Total: | 100% | 100% | 100% |
| N: | 152 | 551 | 7,501 |

[a]Paul D. Reynolds, "Organizations: Predicting Contributions and Survival," <u>Frontiers of Entrepreneurship Research</u>, Babson College, 1986, p. 58.

[b]John Tauzell, "Survival of Minnesota New Business in 1977-1980," <u>Review of Labor and Economic Conditions</u>, Minnesota Department of Economic Security, August 1982, pp. 13,14. These are the number of new business formations recorded in the program files of the Minnesota Department of Economic Security.

Table 1 reveals 63% of the sample were in service-related industries. This is higher than Reynolds' sample of new start-ups in Minne-

sota for the years 1979 and 1982.[5]  Corroborating our higher percentage
of service businesses are data from the Economic Report to the Governor,
1987.  Between 1976 and 1984 the top eight industries in employment
growth in the Twin Cities area were service firms, while the declining
industries were manufacturing.[6]

TABLE 2

SELECTED PRE START-UP CHARACTERISTICS OF SAMPLE

| Founders of New Businesses in the Twin Cities, 1984-86 | Percent or Number in Sample |
|---|---|
| Median years since last attended school | 11 years |
| Had 16 or more years of schooling | 57% |
| Woman founder | 44 |
| Previously involved with a business that failed | 21 |
| Previous experience launching or helping to launch a new business | 40 |
| Self-rated good or solid previous business experience in: | |
| Management | 68 |
| Marketing or Sales | 60 |
| Finance and Accounting | 32 |
| Median earnings expected if work for someone else | $35,000 |

Ninety-seven percent of the questionnaires were answered by the
founder.  Among the characteristics of these entrepreneurs are those in
Table 2.  The profile of a typical respondent emerging from Table 2 is:
A male or female (nearly equal chance) about 30 years old and with a
College degree; born in the USA and rates him/herself as a "serious"
academic student when a student; rates his/her previous business experience as "good" or "solid" in management, marketing and sales, and human
resources, but mediocre or no experience in finance-accounting or en-
gineering-production; reports this business experience their first with
a new venture; and, has a "Reservation Wage" of $35,000 per year.  Our

---

[5]Paul D. Reynolds, "Organizations:  Predicting Contributions and
Survival," op. cit., pp. 594-609.

[6]Council of Economic Advisors, Economic Report to the Governor,
1987, State of Minnesota, pp. 88-9.

sample shows 44% women new entrepreneurs, about twice the percentage of women-owned businesses in Minnesota.[7]

## The Venture Planning Phase

Table 3 presents selected start-up planning characteristics of the sample. The picture emerging from Table 3 is one of an entrepreneur who wrote a business plan, but was not likely to have had three or more people playing a major role in the planning of the venture. The entrepreneur was not likely to have had an important or valuable mentor in this phase, and not likely to have consulted an expert in new business start-ups.

TABLE 3

SELECTED START-UP PLANNING CHARACTERISTICS OF SAMPLE

| Founders of New Businesses in the Twin Cities, 1984-86 | Percent in Sample |
|---|---|
| Wrote a Business Plan? | |
| Never | 29% |
| Within three months of start | 38 |
| More than three months from start | 33 |
| Never consulted an expert in new business start-ups nor sought assistance from an agency such as SBA | 49 |
| Selected "income and wealth" or "build an estate" as reasons for starting this business | 39 |
| Had a mentor or a model for this business and rated the mentor 5 or more (1 to 10 highest) | 22 |
| Expected $200,000 or more in first year revenues | 25 |
| Three or more people had a major role in the planning and start-up stage of this venture | 27 |
| Main source of funding was personal savings, and total capital required to open business was $50,000 or more | 12 |

About 70% said only they and/or a spouse owned their business. While one-third claimed they had a mentor who they looked up to and had as a model when they started this venture, about 25% of them rated the importance of the mentor below 5 on a 1 to 10 scale! Nearly 60% of the respondents selected the item "personal savings" as their largest single source of initial financing. Only four founders cited venture capital.

---

[7]Robert D. Hisrich and Candida G. Brush, The Woman Entrepreneur, Lexington, MA., Lexington Books, 1986, pp. 10-11.

A number of questions were asked regarding how long before the business had its first sale or grand opening did the founder perform a certain task. While 30% said they never wrote a business plan, another 10% wrote one a year before their first sale. More than one-third claimed they worked full-time on this venture beginning four or more months before their first sale. More than 50% never went to a bank for funding, and 10% claimed they did not open a business checking account before their first sale. Slightly less than 50% claimed they purchased a Yellow Pages advertisement before their first sale. Nearly 60% said they did not seek assistance from an organization similar to the SBA or SCORE.

In the margins of the questionnaire where these venture-planning questions were asked it was common to find the entrepreneur writing comments. More than a few, who had been checking the category "never" to many of the planning-step questions, wrote they put a business plan together _after_ they opened. Several merely indicated they felt embarrassed checking the column "never" to that line of questions!

SHORTFALLS: EXPECTATIONS VS. REALITY

## Definitions

Our interest is the difference between what an entrepreneur expected or formerly believed, and what turned out or they currently believe. If reality or the current belief is less than or more pessimistic than the _a priori_ belief or expectation, this is termed a shortfall. Neither the extent of the shortfall nor its subsequent importance to the survival or success of the firm is directly addressed. We do not attempt to measure or explain expectations. Neither do we analyze the causes of actual events. A longitudinal study of a sample of entrepreneurs would be the preferred methodology for analyzing the formation of expectations, and the causes of outcomes. Instead, while memories hopefully still are fresh, we ask the founders to recall their former expectations and beliefs before the business began, and contrast those to the current situation. An advantage of this over the longitudinal approach is not picking up the Hawthorne effect.

Several kinds of statements were made to which the entrepreneurs could select: strongly agree, agree, disagree, or strongly disagree. Those selecting either "agree" or "strongly agree" were coded as 1. A shortfall by any measure is represented by a 1.

To protect against someone checking the same response box on the next questions as done on the previous one, the shortfall questions and statements were scattered throughout the questionnaire. One set of statements asked the respondents to look back on the forecasts they had made before they opened, and contrast that to what actually happened. With that in mind, they would agree or disagree with a statement that they had underestimated or miscalculated something. A second set of statements asked the respondents to compare their current beliefs now that their business is opened to the beliefs they recall having before they opened. A third set asked the entrepreneur to choose between whether a fact or perception about their current belief, compared to

327

when they began the business, was either more or less than what they expected. For example, more than one-third of the respondents claimed the excitement over having their own business was less than they had expected. A question about how actual revenues compared to their projected revenues, was used to measure a shortfall.

## Extent of Shortfalls

Table 4 shows four financial-planning shortfalls. Approximately one-half of these founders agreed their revenues were less than anticipated and the amount of working capital was less than needed. Nearly two-thirds agreed it took more time to become profitable than expected. A smaller percentage (29%) agreed they had underestimated the importance of good record keeping. Not surprisingly, there are statistically significant correlations between pairs of financial planning shortfalls. The strongest ones are between revenues being less than expected and profits a longer time coming.

TABLE 4

FINANCIAL PLANNING SHORTFALLS

| Alternative Measures of Financial Planning Shortfalls by Founders of Recent Start-ups[a] | % of Founders Agreeing |
|---|---|
| 1. Revenues projected for first year were less than I expected. | 48% |
| 2. I underestimated "the amount of working capital I needed." | 53 |
| 3. I underestimated "the importance of good record keeping." | 29 |
| 4. "I believe the time it took to become profitable was" more than I expected. | 64 |

[a]Those Pearson Correlation Coefficients, significant at the 5% level, between each pair of financial planning shortfall measures are: 1&4 = .44, 2&3 = .29, 2&4 = .28.

Table 5 shows five measures of personal expectation shortfalls. The first measure reveals about one-fourth of the sample agreeing with the statement they had underestimated how much work there was in launching a new business. Another one-fourth agreed with the statement that all in all they had not "gotten what I wanted out of this business." Forty percent agreed the excitement over having their own business was less than they had expected.

A surprisingly large number indicated their personal success or pecuniary remuneration was less than anticipated. Indeed, three-fourths agreed their personal standard of living had increased less than they had expected.

TABLE 5

PERSONAL EXPECTATION SHORTFALLS

| Alternative Measures of Personal Expectation Shortfalls by Founders of Recent Start-ups[a] | % of Founders Agreeing |
|---|---|
| 1. "I never thought it was going to be so much work." | 26% |
| 2. "All in all, I haven't gotten what I wanted out of this business." | 27 |
| 3. "I am less successful now from this business than I expected I would be by this time." | 55 |
| 4. "I believe the excitement over having my own business was" less than I had expected. | 40 |
| 5. "My personal standard of living (wages, benefits, etc.) increased" less than I had expected. | 74 |

[a]Those Pearson Correlation Coefficients, significant at the 5% level, between each pair of personal expectation shortfall measures are: 1&5 = .24, 2&3 = .42, 2&4 = .22, (2&5, 3&4, 4&5) = .27, and 3&5 = .58.

The Pearson Correlation Coefficients illustrate how interrelated those entrepreneurs' responses were across these measures of personal expectation shortfalls. A highly significant correlation coefficient of nearly .6, between those agreeing they are less successful from this business than expected and those indicating their personal standard of living increased less than they expected, points to a strong linkage between self-rated success and income and wealth. Surprisingly, the correlation between those who underestimated how much work it would be to launch a business and those who felt less successful, or not as excited about their business, was quite low.

Table 6 shows four additional shortfalls. Nearly two-thirds underestimated how long it would take to launch the business. About one-half underestimated the time needed to manage their business' paperwork and personnel issues. About one-third agreed they underestimated the competition. Again, there is a significant positive correlation among these other shortfalls.

OTHER SHORTFALLS

| Other Shortfalls by Founders of Recent Start-ups[a] | % of Founders Agreeing |
|---|---|
| 1. "I thought everything would go quicker than it did." | 63% |
| 2. I underestimated the "time needed to do payroll and tax paperwork," or "time spent recruiting and training employees." | 53 |
| 3. I underestimated the "competition." | 36 |
| 4. "I did not expect the problems I found in finding, hiring, and training personnel." | 28 |

[a]Those Pearson Correlation Coefficients, significant at the 5% level, between each pair of these shortfalls are: 1&3 = .22, 1&4 = .23, 2&3 = .20, 2&4 = .38, and 3&4 = .32.

## Correlates of Shortfalls

The nature of our sample and limitations of the questionnaire limit a full-scale analysis of these shortfalls. The small sample size, perhaps over-representative of service industry ventures, precludes looking at the structure of the industry or the strategy of the venture (e.g., low cost or superior product) as Sandberg and Hoffer would encourage in assessing a new venture's performance.[8]

On the other hand, a reduced-form equation based on the hypothesis that shortfalls depend on the predetermined characteristics of the entrepreneur and on the taking of certain steps or actions in the venture-planning phase can be estimated. We assume other statistical determinants of these shortfalls are random with a mean or zero and with a constant variance. The estimated reduced-form equations yield coefficients whose magnitudes and elasticities are difficult to interpret. They could be determinants of the expectations function, the reality function, or both. For that reason, our interest is merely the sign or direction of the influence on shortfalls.

A preliminary analysis of the responses was made by examining a large correlation matrix as well as performing simple Chi Square analysis. Those results pointed to two classes of variables as being strong determinants of the shortfalls. One class was the experience variables, and the other was planning variables. Several surprising

[8]William R. Sandberg and Charles W. Hoffer, "Improving New Venture Performance: The Role of Strategy, Industry Structure, and the Entrepreneur," Journal of Business Venturing, vol. 2, No. 1, (Winter 1987), pp. 5-28.

relationships were observed. Those who had been involved in a business that recently failed (one-half of whom had been an owner or manager), tended to be among those with more shortfalls. Those planning for and launching larger-scope firms had more shortfalls. About one-half of the sample who said they wrote a business plan wrote it four or more months before their first sale. Our results indicate they were more likely to have shortfalls than those with the "fresher" business plans; i.e., those written within four months of opening.

A dummy dependent variable represented the shortfall measures. The regressors included characteristics about the entrepreneur, such as business experience, education, motivation, and gender. They also included planning type variables including: if a business plan, number of advisors, venture size, source of capital, and anticipated size of the business. Step-wise multiple regressions were estimated.[9]

Table 7 reports regression equation results on eight shortfall measures. The first three concern financial-planning shortfalls. Those who agreed their business' first-year revenues were less than they expected were much more likely to not have written a business plan and to have anticipated a larger-size firm. The variable "revenue expected" was entered numerically and is interpreted here as a venture size measure. An alternative variable showing similar results was a dummy variable equal to 1 for those firms with three or more employees. Larger firms were more likely to have a shortfall. The percent of variance in the dummy dependent variable increases dramatically using the shortfall measure, "I underestimated the amount of working capital I needed." The $R^2$ for cross-sectional data on individuals in this study is low, as is well known and was true in Cooper's study ($R^2 = 9\%$) of optimists and pessimists among new entrepreneurs.[10]

The shortfall in estimating working capital reveals the expected relationships between business experience, education, and planning. Those with 16 or more years of education were much less likely to underestimate their needs. Those with a previous start-up experience were less likely to underestimate their needs. Those with a mentor of value (as defined and discussed earlier) also were less likely to underestimate their needs. Controlling for these education, experience, and planning variables reveals what showed up in our results quite often: the partial or net effect of number of years since last attended school is positive. That is, those out of school longer were more likely to have shortfalls. Here it is in estimating their firm's working capital needs. Again, the venture size variable is positively related to a shortfall.

---

[9] SAS User's Guide:  Basics, Version 5 Edition, Cary, N.C., SAS Institute Inc., 1985.

[10] Arnold C. Cooper, William C. Dunkelberg, Caroloyn Y. Woo, "Optimists and Pessimists:  2994 Entrepreneurs and Their Perceived Chances for Success," Frontiers of Entrepreneurship Research, Babson College, 1986, p. 570.

TABLE 7

STATISTICAL DETERMINANTS OF SELECTED MEASURES OF SHORTFALLS,
EXPECTATIONS AND REALITY BY FOUNDERS IN RECENT START-UPS

Stepwise multiple regressions, dummy dependent = 1 if yes.

| Short Fall Measure (R squared) | Determinants | Coefficient[a] Sign | Signif. |
|---|---|---|---|
| 1) Revenues Expected, 1st Year Were Less Than Expected (.06) | 1. If a Business Plan | − | * |
| | 2. Revenues Expected | + | * |
| 2) Underestimated Amount of Working Capital I Needed (.18) | 1. If Mentor of Value | − | |
| | 2. Years Since School | + | |
| | 3. If 16+ Years Education | − | ** |
| | 4. Previous Start-up | − | * |
| | 5. Revenues Expected | + | |
| 3) Underestimated Importance of Good Record Keeping (.15) | 1. Exper. in Fin-Actg. | − | ** |
| | 2. If a Business Plan | − | * |
| | 3. If a Male | − | ** |
| | 4. Revenues Expected | + | * |
| 4) Didn't Expect the Problems in Finding, Hiring, and Training People (.36) | 1. Exper. in Mgt. | − | ** |
| | 2. Exper. in Mkt-Sales | − | |
| | 3. Larger Venture Size | + | ** |
| | 4. If a Business Plan | − | ** |
| | 5. Revenues Expected | + | ** |
| 5) Underestimated My Competition (.24) | 1. Didn't Use Planning Experts | − | |
| | 2. I was a "Serious" Student | + | ** |
| | 3. Exper. in Mgt. | − | ** |
| | 4. Years Since School | + | ** |
| | 5. If a Business Plan | − | ** |
| | 6. Revenues Expected | − | ** |
| 6) My Standard of Living Increased Less Than I Expected (.10) | 1. If Mentor of Value | − | ** |
| | 2. If Failed Before | + | |
| | 3. Hours Worked Per Week | + | ** |
| 7) Never Thought It Would Be So Much Work (.16) | 1. Didn't Use Planning Experts | − | * |
| | 2. Exper. in Fin-Actg. | − | ** |
| | 3. If a Business Plan | − | ** |
| | 4. Revenues Expected | + | ** |
| 8) I Am Less Successful Than I Expected To Be (.11) | 1. 3 or More Planned Venture | − | ** |
| | 2. If a Male | + | * |

[a]Significance value: * = 10% level, ** = 5% level.

332

The third financial-planning shortfall shown in Table 7 concerns underestimating the importance of good record keeping. Those who earlier in the questionnaire had rated their experience in finance and accounting as quite solid were much less likely to underestimate the importance of good record keeping. Those without a business plan underestimated that problem. We do not have an explanation for why the males were less likely to have this shortfall.

In the middle of Table 7 are the two most robust equations estimated. The first might be thought of as a management type shortfall in that it concerns their agreeing to the statement they did not expect the problems they subsequently had in finding, hiring and training people. Not surprisingly, those experienced in management and those with a business plan were much less likely to have that shortfall. Those with a larger venture, as measured by number of employees or revenues expected, were more likely to represent these management-type shortfalls.

The second robust result concerns the shortfall measure of underestimating the competition. Those experienced in management and with a business plan were less likely to underestimate their competition. The remaining results are more surprising. Those who claimed they had been a serious student when in school and those who had been out of school for a long time were both positively related to this shortfall. Those expecting high revenues did not underestimate the competition.

The remaining set of shortfalls in Table 7 concerns personal planning shortfalls. Those who agreed their personal standard of living had increased less than expected tended to: 1) not have a mentor of value during the planning phase of the business, 2) have worked for a business that previously failed, and 3) claim they worked 60 hours or more per week. We found both those who claimed they worked more than 60 hours per week and those who had agreed with the statement "the work in launching a business was harder than they expected" tended to have many shortfalls. Either they apparently felt they were not rewarded for their sacrifices, or the causation flows the other way from those whose standard of living is less than they expected working harder in order to make up for it.

Typically, those who never anticiated it would be "so much work" had rated themselves less experienced in finance and accoutning, did not write a business plan, and had planned for a larger-size firm. Those claiming they did not use an expert in new business start-ups again show up in this measure of shortfalls as not underestimating the amount of work it takes to launch a business. Because business plan, experience, and venture size are held constant in that equation, this net effect runs counter to our expectations.

The last reported regression result in Table 7 is on the shortfall "I am less successful than I expected to be." Those with three or more people playing a major role in the planning and start-up stage of this venture were much less likely to have had that shortfall. The dichotomous variable was created at 3 or more with the hope it would capture the influence of a non-family member in the planning process. It might measure the impact of a critical, outside, or neutral advisor.

That variable was statistically important, and had the expected sign in many equations not presented herein.

## Mistakes

Respondents were given an open-ended question near the end of the survey to describe the most significant mistake they made since starting their venture. We categorized their answers. We then split the respondents into two groups, one we termed "happy". They were the ones for whom the tone of their answers to the questionnaire was one of satisfaction. The results were intriguing. Those in the less-satisfied group were much more likely to write about mistakes categorized as "unprepared" or "lacked sufficient capital". Two-thirds of them cited one or both of those types of mistakes. On the other hand, the most frequently identified category or mistakes cited by those in the more-satisfied or happy group were "people-related problems" (such as partners, family or employees), and "no mistake written about". Only one-third of them write about a mistake categorized as "unprepared and poor planning" or "lacked sufficient capital".

Another comparison of the type of mistakes by years since school revealed no obvious relationships. A fuller analysis of their responses to the mistake question and their beliefs about advice to future entrepreneurs will be the subject of our next study.

## CONCLUSION

This paper defined, measured, and analyzed a number of shortfalls. These are where expectations for the new venture subsequently did not materialize as anticipated. We found about one-half of the founders of new ventures (open an average of 18 months) agreed with either the statement their revenues were less than expected, or they underestimated the amount of working capital they needed. Nearly two-thirds agreed it took longer to become profitable than they expected. About 30% had underestimated the financial management task concerning the importance of good record keeping. There was a high correlation among these financial planning shortfall measures.

About one-fourth agreed they had underestimated the amount of work it would take to launch their business. More than one-half claimed they were less successful from the business than they expected to be. A huge number (75%) agreed their personal standard of living had increased less than they had expected. About one-fourth did not expect the problems they found in finding, hiring, and training personnel; whereas, one-half underestimated the time needed to do paperwork and recruit and train employees. Those of us with personal knowledge of the development of new ventures probably are not surprised with the finding that two-thirds of these entrepreneurs thought everything would go quicker than it did.

The correlates of these shortfalls often were what we who teach, advise, and work with entrepreneurs had known or suspected. Contrary to

the counter-intuitive finding of Carsrud and others,[11] we found those
with a mentor they looked up to and used as a model when they started [12]
this venture had fewer shortfalls.  Consistent with Cooper's findings,
in which the optimism of new entrepreneurs was a positive function of
experience and preparation, so too our measures of shortfalls were negative functions of experience and venture planning.  Consistent with
Vesper's conclusion[13] that experience and education were positive correlates of success and that teams who found companies do better, so too
our results show higher education, good experience in management and
finance, previous start-up experience, and having three or more people
significantly involved in the planning of a new business were <u>negative</u>
correlates of shortfalls.

We also found some surprising relationships.  Those entrepreneurs in the sample who launched a larger venture in revenues and
personnel than their counterparts were more likely to register shortfalls both in the financial area and at the personal level.  Previous
experience in a failed business unfortunately is positively correlated
with our measures of shortfalls.  Respondents were asked to rank the
three most important reasons they started this business from a list of
six given.  Two reasons in the list concerned making money.  We coded
any response in either item a "1" and in our research labeled that
variable "greed".  It proved statistically insignificant in the regression equation results!

The results and conclusions in this paper should be interpreted
with caution.  It was a small sample, from one metropolitan area,
heavily weighted in the service industries, the ventures were small in
scope, and the research results are not from a longitudinal study.
Nevertheless, while most research is on the causes of the darker shades
of failure, such as bankruptcy and business cessation, little has been
conducted on the lighter shades of failure.  Many more entrepreneurs
experience the lighter than the darker shades, such as reality turning
out below expectations.  Our goal is to learn how to lower the odds of
both shades of failure in new ventures.

---

[11]Carsrud, <u>op. cit.</u>, p. 234.

[12]Cooper, <u>op. cit.</u>, p. 569.

[13]Vesper, <u>op. cit.</u>, pp. 32-40.

335

# REFERENCES

Burch, John G., Entrepreneurship, New York, John Wiley & Sons, 1986, p. 96.

Carsrud, Alan L., Connie Marie Gaglio, and Kenneth W. Olm, "Entrepreneurs-Mentors, Networks, and Successful New Venture Development: An Exploratory Study," Frontiers of Entrepreneurship Research, Babson College, 1986, pp. 229-243.

Cooper, Arnold C., William C. Dunkelberg, Caroloyn Y. Woo, "Optimists and Pessimists: 2994 Entrepreneurs and Their Perceived Chances for Success," Frontiers of Entrepreneurship Research, Babson College, 1986, p. 563-577.

Council of Economic Advisors, Economic Report to the Governor, 1987, State of Minnesota.

Dun & Bradstreet Corp., The Failure Record Through 1983, and Monthly Failure Report, New York, Dun & Bradstreet Corp.

Egge, Karl, "Entrepreneurial Failures: Results From a Study of Business Bankruptcies in Minnesota," Journal of Private Enterprise, (Fall 1986), pp. 42-50.

Hisrich, Robert D., and Candida G. Brush, The Woman Entrepreneur, Lexington, MA., Lexington Books, 1986, pp. 10-11.

Neiswander, D. Kirk, and John M. Drollinger, "Origins of Successful Start-up Ventures," Frontiers of Enterpreneurship Research, Babson College, 1986, pp. 328-343.

Reynolds, Paul D., "Organizations: Predicting Contributions and Survival," Frontiers of Entrepreneurship Research, Babson College, 1986, pp. 594-609.

Ronstadt, Robert C., Entrepreneurship, Dover, MA., Lord Publishing, 1984, Chapter 4.

Sandberg, William R., and Charles W. Hoffer, "Improving New Venture Performance: The Role of Strategy, Industry Structure, and the Entrepreneur," Journal of Business Venturing, vol. 2, No. 1, (Winter 1987), pp. 5-28.

SAS User's Guide: Basics, Version 5 Edition, Cary, N.C., SAS Institute Inc., 1985.

Timmons, Jeffrey A., New Venture Creation, 2nd ed., Homewood, Ill., Richard D. Irwin, Inc., 1985.

Vesper, Karl H., New Venture Strategies, Englewood Cliffs, NJ, Prentice-Hall, Inc., 1980.

CORRELATES OF FIRM AND ENTREPRENEUR SUCCESS
IN TECHNOLOGICALLY INNOVATIVE COMPANIES

Norman R. Smith, University of Oregon
Jeffrey S. Bracker, Arizona State University
John B. Miner, Georgia State University

## ABSTRACT

The Miner Sentence Completion Scale - Form T and an innovative technology survey questionnaire were administered to applicants for development grants under the National Science Foundation Small Business Innovation Research Program. The majority of the applicants were entrepreneurs who had founded their firms, but it was also possible to construct a control group of manager-scientists for comparison purposes. Measures of firm growth, net profit, and individual compensation were developed from the innovative technology survey and used as dependent variables. The survey also provided the information to obtain type of entrepreneur and type of firm scores for the sample members using Smith's typologies. The MSCS-Form T scores yielded strong support for task motivation theory in their relationships to the dependent measures. Evidence was also obtained in support of an Inventor-Entrepreneur type previously suggested by Smith.

## INTRODUCTION

Two prior publications have dealt with certain preliminary results obtained in an extensive study of motivational and other factors relating to the growth and success of entrepreneurial firms and their founders.[1] The present paper extends the previous two by utilizing larger samples, including analyses employing a number of different dependent variables, and presenting results involving a classification system for type of entrepreneur and type of firm.

---

[1]Norman R. Smith and John B. Miner, "Motivational Considerations in the Success of Technologically Innovative Entrepreneurs," Frontiers of Entrepreneurship Research 1984, Babson College, pp. 488-495 and "Motivational Considerations in the Success of Technologically Innovative Entrepreneurs: Extended Sample Findings," Frontiers of Entrepreneurship Research 1985, Babson College, pp. 482-488.

A major feature of the research is an attempt to predict dependent indexes such as firm growth, net profit, and entrepreneur income from a theory of task motivation. This theory is one of four role motivation theories which are stated in parallel form.[2]  The best known of these is the hierarchic or bureaucratic theory which deals with managerial motivation. The others are the professional, group, and of course task theories.

The task theory owes a major debt to McClelland and his achievement motivation theory.[3]  However, there are certain departures from that theory, and accordingly the two should be treated as independent formulations. The task theory applies in a domain where the pushes and pulls of sanctions are built into the task to be performed. Operative pressures and incentives derive from the way the work is structured, not from superiors, or professional norms, or peer group members. The entrepreneurial organization provides the prime model for this type of system. Pulls or positive sanctions are inherent in the prospects for financial reward, community status, and personal satisfaction. Pushes or negative sanctions also operate in the form of the threat of business failure or bankrupcy.

The essential motivational hypothesis of this research has been stated as follows:

> In task systems, task (achievement) motivation should be at a high level among task performers (entrepreneurs, for example), and it should be positively correlated with task success indexes; task motivation should not differentiate in these ways within other types of systems.[4]

Task motivation contains five separate aspects. These motivational components relate to role requirements of positions within the theory's domain. The entrepreneur position is a prime example. The

---

[2]John B. Miner, "Limited Domain Theories of Organizational Energy," Craig C. Pinder and Larry F. Moore, Middle Range Theory and the Study of Organizations, Martinus Nijhoff, Boston, 1980, pp. 273-286.

[3]David C. McClelland, The Achieving Society, D. Von Nostrand Co., Princeton, N.J., 1961; see also David C. McClelland, "Business Drive and National Achievement," Harvard Business Review, Vol. 40, No. 4 (July-August 1962), pp. 99-112.

[4]John B. Miner, "The Uncertain Future of the Leadership Concept: Revisions and Clarifications," Journal of Applied Behavioral Science, Vol. 18, No. 3 (September 1982), pp. 293-307.

five components are:

1. A desire to achieve through one's own efforts and be able to attribute any success to personal causation – <u>self -achievement</u>.

2. A desire to avoid taking risks whenever possible <u>avoiding risks</u>.

3. A desire for some clear index of the level of one's performance – <u>feedback of results</u>.

4. A desire to introduce novel, or innovative, or creative solutions – <u>personal innovation</u>.

5. A desire to think about the future and anticipate future possibilities – <u>planning for the future</u>.

The part of the research relating to task motivation is of a kind that has received considerable attention from those studying entrepreneurship. A rather sizable body of knowledge exists regarding the psychological characteristics of entrepreneurs. Yet, somehow, in spite of many positive findings, a clear picture of the internal dynamics of the successful entrepreneur remains elusive.[5] The intent of this research is to help move toward greater clarity in this area, if at all possible.

A second concern of the study is to investigate further the relationships among Smith's type of entrepreneur and type of firm typologies and both firm success and entrepreneur motivation.[6]

---

[5]Thomas M. Begley and David P. Boyd, "Psychological Characteristics Associated with Performance in Entrepreneurial Firms and Smaller Businesses," <u>Journal of Business Venturing</u>, Vol. 2, No. 1 (Winter 1987), pp. 79-93; Robert H. Brockhaus and Pamela S. Horwitz, "The Psychology of the Entrepreneur," Donald L. Sexton and Raymond W. Smilor, <u>The Art and Science of Entrepreneurship</u>, Ballinger, Cambridge, Mass., 1986, pp. 25-48.

[6]For prior work see Norman R. Smith, <u>The Entrepreneur and His Firm: The Relationship Between Type of Man and Type of Company</u>, Bureau of Business and Economic Research, Michigan State University, East Lansing, Mich., 1967; Norman R. Smith and John B. Miner, "Type of Entrepreneur, Type of Firm, and Managerial Motivation: Implications for Organizational Life Cycle Theory," <u>Strategic Management Journal</u>, Vol. 4, No. 4 (October-December 1983), pp. 332-337.

Type of entrepreneur is viewed as a dimension anchored at one end by an ideal type called the craftsman entrepreneur who is characterized by narrowness in education and training, low social awareness and involvement, a feeling of incompetence in dealing with the social environment and a limited time orientation. At the other end are opportunistic entrepreneurs who exhibit breadth in education and training, high social awareness and involvement, confidence in their ability to deal with the social environment, and an awareness of, and orientation to, the future. A similar typology is posited for the entrepreneur's firm. Rigid firms are unchanging in customer mix, product mix, production methods, production facilities, and markets. Adaptive firms exhibit changes in these areas.

The research hypotheses considered were as follows:

1. Type of entrepreneur and type of firm will be closely related, with opportunistic entrepreneurs heading more
   adaptive firms.

2. Type of entrepreneur and task motivation will be related,
   with opportunistic entrepreneurs having higher task motivation.

3. Measures of firm and personal success will be related to
   type of entrepreneur and type of firm, with the opportunistic entrepreneurs and adaptable firms being successful.

METHOD

## Samples

The source of all samples studied was the National Science Foundation. NSF, and a number of other government agencies as well, provide financial support to small firms for the purpose of helping them develop and bring to market various technological innovations. This program has consistently attracted a considerably larger number of grant applications than are actually funded. Funding, when it does occur, takes the form of a relatively modest seed money grant initially (phase 1), and then subsequently in a relatively small number of cases a more substantial commitment (phase 2).

The samples for this research were derived from lists of phase 1 awardees for the years 1979, 1980, 1981, 1982, and 1983, and the list of rejectees as well for 1982. Initial mailings went to approximately 685 individuals who had submitted grant applications from the same number of firms (there may have been some undetected duplications remaining in this group, since many firms submitted in more than one year). A large number of questionnaires were returned as undeliverable, and in addition it seems likely that some others were not in fact delivered. The effective size of the initial mailing could not have been above 600 and may have been somewhat less.

After three mailings replies which provided either partial or complete information were received from 195 individuals. In 159 of these cases the data included the motivational measure. This latter sample is the primary source of the data reported in this paper. There were 118 individuals of the 159, and 150 of the 195, who were considered to be entrepreneurs in the sense that they answered yes to the question – Were you involved in the original formation of your current company?

A second sample consisted of respondents who had submitted applications to NSF, who were not the entrepreneurs. This group included a few individuals who took over leadership of the firm subsequent to the original entrepreneur's departure. Most, however, were managers and/or scientists at levels below the very top who had nevertheless been responsible for applying to NSF. In many instances these appear to be individuals with somewhat larger firms where the application process had been delegated. These people were called manager-scientists. There were 45 of them in the respondent sample as a whole, and 41 in the base sample utilizing the motivational measure. Being from comparable companies and having played similar roles in the NSF application process, these manager-scientists provide a useful control group for the entrepreneurs.

Measures

Two instruments were completed by the respondents. One was entitled the Innovative Technology Survey. It contained questions dealing with the growth and success of the firm. Also included were a number of questions that provided information permitting the calculation of type of entrepreneur and type of firm scores. The second instrument was the Miner Sentence Completion Scale-Form T, which provides a measure of task motivation and its components.

The success indexes were developed from information provided by the respondents themselves in the Innovative Technology Survey:

1.  Growth in Number of Employees. The number of employees reported for the most recent year, assuming a base starting point of zero.

2.  Growth in Number of Employees/Year. The number of employees reported for the most recent year divided by the number of years the firm had been in business.

341

3. Growth in Sales. The dollar value of sales in thousands of dollars reported for the most recent year, assuming a base starting point of zero.

4. Growth in Sales/Year. The dollar value of sales in thousands of dollars reported for the most recent year divided by the number of years the firm had been in business.

5. Net profit as Percent of Sales. Reported previous year's net profit as a percent of sales on a scale of 1 to 6 as follows:

1 Under 5%            4 15 to 19%
2 5 to 9%             5 20 to 24%
3 10 to 14%           6 25% or more

6. Yearly Income from Position. The present yearly income from position with the company reported on a scale of 1 to 8 as follows:

1 Below $10,000              5 Over $50,000 to $70,000
2 $10,000 to $20,000         6 Over $70,000 to $90,000
3 Over $20,000 to $30,000    7 Over $90,000 to $110,000
4 Over $30,000 to $50,000    8 Over $110,000

The type of entrepreneur score was developed from questions in the Innovative Technology Survey, whereas in past research interview information has been utilized. The measure can yield scores ranging from −14 (extreme craftsman) to +14 (extreme opportunistic). The actual range was much less − from −8 to +6. The type of firm score was developed in a similar manner. The possible range is from −6 (extreme rigid) to +6 (extreme adaptable). This range is reflected in the data of the current study.

Task motivation was measured with the Miner Sentence Completion Scale − Form T.[7] Respondents are to complete 40 items selected to measure the aspects of task motivation. There are eight items intended to tap each of the five components. An overall, total score for task motivation and five subscale scores may be calculated. Each item is scored +, ?, or − depending on whether the response is consistent with the theory's concept of successful entrepreneurship, neutral or unrevealing, or inconsistent with what is expected of successful entrepreneurs. The total score can vary from −40 to +40, although the actual range here was from −16 to +25, subscale scores can vary from −8 to +8.

---

[7]John B. Miner, Scoring Guide for the Miner Sentence Completion Scale − Form T, Organizational Measurement Systems Press, Atlanta, Georgia, 1986.

In order to determine whether the respondents – roughly 27 percent of the total group approached – were representative, a comparison was made across response rounds. The assumption was that any trend from round one to round two to round three would continue on into the non-respondent group. Thus, if differences are not found in the analyses among respondents, they are less likely to be present between respondents and non-respondents.

As Table 1 indicates differences within the respondent group across rounds are almost nonexistent. There is only one. On round one the respondents were more often risk takers than on the other rounds. This makes sense, and may well be a source of bias in other similar surveys as well. Overall, however, the respondent sample would appear on this basis to be representative.

## RESULTS

Table 2 presents the correlations among the MSCS-Form T variables. The results are generally as expected. The Avoiding Risks subscale has the lowest relation to the other measures and Feedback of Results the highest. All of the subscales contribute substantially to the Total Score.

Data on the relationships among the six success indexes are given in Table 3. Both Pearson r and Spearman rho were calculated because most of these measures have a highly skewed distribution with the majority of the cases concentrated at the low end of the distribution and a small number of extreme cases at the high end. This problem of a departure from the assumption of a normal distribution does not exist for the MSCS-Form T data. For both coefficients there are sizable relationships among the two employee growth measures, the two sales growth measures, and the entrepreneur's yearly income. Net profit, however, is if anything negatively related to the other measures. Presumably, this is a function of a trade-off between profit and growth.

Table 4 provides a comparison of the entrepreneurs and the manager-scientist control group. The entrepreneurs exhibit significantly higher task motivation than the controls as hypothesized, but not on all measures and not to the degree one might expect. It is evident that the manager-scientists' firms have grown rapidly. The entrepreneurial firms are really quite small. Also, the manager-scientists' firms have existed roughly five years longer.

In Table 5 the entrepreneurs are split at the median on the Growth in Number of Employees/Year measure. The entrepreneurs with faster growing firms headed firms growing at a rate of 1.5 employees per

# TABLE 1

## Comparison of First (N=94), Second (N=41), and Third (N=24) Round Respondents

| MSCS--Form T Measures | First Round Mean | Second Round Mean | Third Round Mean | F |
|---|---|---|---|---|
| Total Score | 4.65 | 5.56 | 4.79 | .20 |
| Self Achievement | 1.56 | 1.46 | .50 | 1.53 |
| Avoiding Risks | -.02[a] | 1.41 | 1.58 | 6.94** |
| Feedback of Results | -.85 | -.71 | -.92 | .07 |
| Personal Innovation | 2.79 | 2.54 | 2.96 | .29 |
| Planning for the Future | 1.17 | .85 | .67 | .40 |
| **Company Success Measures** | | | | |
| Growth in Number of Employees | 36.12 | 65.62 | 38.14 | .61 |
| Growth in Number of Employees/Year | 5.11 | 6.00 | 3.77 | 1.91 |
| Growth in Sales (in thousands of dollars) | 205.40 | 283.40 | 98.51 | 1.41 |
| Growth in Sales/Year (in thousands of dollars) | 22.01 | 28.20 | 15.44 | .99 |
| Net Profit as Percent of Sales (on a scale with a low of 1 and a high of 6) | 2.24 | 2.04 | 2.41 | .51 |
| Yearly Income from Position (on a scale with a low of 1 and a high of 8) | 4.60 | 4.11 | 4.63 | 1.50 |

**P $<$ .01.
[a]Differs significantly from the other two.

TABLE 2

Correlations Among MSCS--Form T Measures for Entrepreneurs
and Manager Scientists (N=159)

| | | Subscales | | | |
|---|---|---|---|---|---|
| Subscales | Avoiding Risks | Feedback of Results | Personal Innovation | Planning for the Future | Total Score |
| Self Achievement | .09 | .31** | .37** | .09 | .62** |
| Avoiding Risks | | .15 | .13 | .15 | .51** |
| Feedback of Results | | | .26** | .35** | .68** |
| Personal Innovation | | | | .20* | .62** |
| Planning for the Future | | | | | .61** |

*P <.05.   **P <.01.   Median of subscale correlations .18.

year or more. The entrepreneurs with slow growth firms had firms growing at less than the 1.5 figure; in fact, the average was .62 employees
per year. It is apparent that these slow growth firms tend to be very
small indeed. It is also apparent that the entrepreneurs in these firms
do not show the motivational pattern exhibited in Table 4. In fact, the
entrepreneurs with slow growth firms do not differ from the manager-
scientists at all. It is only the entrepreneurs with faster growing
firms that show the entrepreneurial pattern of high task motivation.
Without this motivation entrepreneurs may well survive (the age of their
firms averages almost seven years) but their companies do not grow much.
This would appear to be an important distinction to consider in other
studies of the psychological characteristics of entrepreneurs. If clear
differences are to be obtained it may be well to focus on the entrepreneurs who are in fact doing something with their companies.

The correlational analyses relating motivational measures to
success indexes appear in Table 6. There is no doubt that the hypotheses of the task motivation theory are strongly supported. Only in
the case of Net Profit as Percent of Sales are significant results not
obtained. The Total Score for the MSCS-Form T yields the strongest and
most consistent results, but the Self Achievement subscale performs very
well also. All of the subscales yield some significant findings.

The relationships obtained using the entrepreneur and firm type
measures are given in Table 7. Few are significant. The anticipated
tendency for opportunistic entrepreneurs to have higher task motivation
is not evident, and in fact the opportunistic entrepreneurs do not have

## TABLE 3

Correlations Among Indexes of Company Success for Entrepreneurs

| | Growth in Number of Employees/Year | | Growth in Sales | | Growth in Sales/Year | | Net Profit as Percent of Sales | | Yearly Income from Position | |
|---|---|---|---|---|---|---|---|---|---|---|
| | r | rho | r | rho | r | rho | r | rho | r | rho |
| Growth in Number of Employees | .50** | .79** | .78** | .79** | .62** | .75** | -.28** | -.27** | .30** | .51** |
| Growth in Number of Employees/Year | | | .44** | .63** | .52** | .78** | -.25** | -.23* | .34** | .42** |
| Growth in Sales | | | | | .79** | .89** | -.19 | -.09 | .41** | .56** |
| Growth in Sales/Year | | | | | | | -.14 | -.11 | .38** | .54** |
| Net Profit as Percent of Sales | | | | | | | | | -.02 | .02 |

*P < .05.
**P < .01.

TABLE 4

Comparison of Entrepreneurs (N=118) and Manager—Scientists (N=41)
MSCS—Form T and Indexes of Company Success

| MSCS—Form T Measures | Entrepreneurs | | Manager-Scientists | | |
|---|---|---|---|---|---|
| | Mean | SD | Mean | SD | t |
| Total Score | 5.93 | 8.16 | 1.95 | 5.57 | 3.46** |
| Self Achievement | 1.64 | 2.76 | .61 | 2.34 | 2.14* |
| Avoiding Risks | .80 | 2.58 | .00 | 2.55 | 1.71* |
| Feedback of Results | −.54 | 2.27 | −1.63 | 2.69 | 2.53** |
| Personal Innovation | 2.88 | 2.41 | 2.37 | 1.91 | 1.24 |
| Planning for the Future | 1.15 | 2.89 | .61 | 2.42 | 1.08 |
| **Company Success Measures** | | | | | |
| Growth in Number of Employees | 21.71 | 31.09 | 107.45 | 132.56 | 41.32** |
| Growth in Number of Employees/Year | 3.83 | 6.24 | 9.06 | 10.52 | 14.52** |
| Growth in Sales (in thousands of dollars) | 91.45 | 115.70 | 549.71 | 569.39 | 52.29* |
| Growth in Sales/Year (in thousands of dollars) | 14.42 | 16.85 | 46.21 | 45.56 | 31.68** |
| Net Profit as Percent of Sales (on a scale with low of 1 and a high of 6) | 2.30 | 1.59 | 1.92 | 1.20 | 1.33 |
| Yearly Income from Position (on a scale with a low of 1 and a high of 8) | 4.40 | 1.81 | 4.70 | 1.35 | 1.16 |

*P $<$.05.          **P $<$.01.

greater success on any of the measures. The correlation between entrepreneur type and firm type is significant as hypothesized but it is not
high. There is a tendency for adaptive firms to succeed and grow more
as other studies have shown, however. The relationships again are lower
than in other studies.

## DISCUSSION

The data reported here, which are far more comprehensive, continue to support the task motivation theory in the same manner as the

TABLE 5

Comparison of Entrepreneurs with Faster Growing Firms (N=59),
Entrepreneurs with Slow Growth Firms (N=59),
and Manager-Scientists (N=41)

| | Entrepreneurs | | | |
|---|---|---|---|---|
| | With faster growing firms | With slow growth firms | Manager-Scientists | |
| MSCS--Form T Measures | Mean | Mean | Mean | F |
| Total Score | 10.95[a] | .92 | 1.95 | 44.45** |
| Self Achievement | 3.10[a] | .19 | .61 | 25.69** |
| Avoiding Risks | 1.56[a] | .03 | .00 | 7.05** |
| Feedback of Results | .44[a] | -1.53 | -1.63 | 15.09** |
| Personal Innovation | 3.98[a] | 1.78 | 2.37 | 17.29** |
| Planning for the Future | 1.86[b] | .44[b] | .61 | 4.66** |
| **Company Success Measures** | | | | |
| Growth in Number of Employees | 34.56 | 7.66 | 107.45[a] | 23.04** |
| Growth in Number of Employees/Year | 7.04 | .62[a] | 9.06 | 20.84** |
| Growth in Sales (in thousands of dollars) | 145.45 | 28.23 | 549.31[a] | 28.29** |
| Growth in Sales/Year (in thousands of dollars) | 22.78[c] | 4.64[c] | 46.21[c] | 22.33** |
| Net Profit as Percent of Sales (on a scale with a low of 1 and a high of 6) | 2.09 | 2.53 | 1.92 | 2.17 |
| Yearly Income from Position (on a scale with a low of 1 and a high of 8) | 5.09 | 3.67[a] | 4.70 | 13.52** |

*P < .05.
**P < .01.
[a]This mean differs significantly from the other two.
[b]These two means differ significantly.
[c]All three means differ significantly.

findings reported in the previous papers on this research. When joined
by the substantial support that achievement motivation theory also has
obtained within the entrepreneurial domain the findings becomes very
strong indeed. What is needed now is to move to predictive studies

TABLE 6

Correlations Between MSCS--Form T Measures and Indexes
of Company Success Among Entrepreneurs

Company Success Measures

| MSCS--Form T Measures | Growth in Number of Employees | | Growth in Number of Employees/Year | | Growth in Sales | |
|---|---|---|---|---|---|---|
| | r | rho | r | rho | r | rho |
| Total Score | .18* | .35** | .27** | .49** | .16 | .31** |
| Self Achievement | .09 | .36** | .27** | .49** | .17 | .27** |
| Avoiding Risks | .10 | .11 | .07 | .18* | .05 | .19 |
| Feedback of Results | .25** | .26** | .20* | .28** | .18 | .22* |
| Personal Innovation | .07 | .16 | .12 | .32** | .10 | .08 |
| Planning for the Future | .06 | .18* | .17* | .24* | .02 | .20* |

| MSCS--Form T Measures | Growth in Sales/Year | | Net Profit as Percent of Sales | | Yearly Income from Position | |
|---|---|---|---|---|---|---|
| | r | rho | r | rho | r | rho |
| Total Score | .24* | .39** | .02 | .05 | .35** | .36** |
| Self Achievement | .25* | .35** | .08 | .02 | .31** | .30** |
| Avoiding Risks | .14 | .24* | .02 | .03 | .06 | .06 |
| Feedback of Results | .17 | .21* | .02 | .04 | .24* | .24* |
| Personal Innovation | .08 | .13 | .01 | -.01 | .12 | .09 |
| Planning for the Future | .11 | .25** | .01 | .02 | .31** | .30** |

*P $<$.05.    **P $<$.01.

involving the task theory. Extrapolating from data on the hierarchic
theory, one would expect that task motivation should be found to cause
successful outcomes for entrepreneurs.[8]

---

[8]John B. Miner, "Sentence Completion Measures in Personnel Research: The Development and Validation of the Miner Sentence Completion
Scales," H. John Bernardin and David A. Bownas, Personality Assessment
in Organizations, Praeger, New York, 1985, pp. 145-176.

TABLE 7

Correlations of Entrepreneur Type and Firm Type Variables
with MSCS--Form T Measures and Indexes of Company Success

| MSCS--Form T Measures | Entrepreneur Type (Craftsman----Opportunistic) | | Firm Type (Rigid----Adaptable) | |
|---|---|---|---|---|
| | r | rho | r | rho |
| Total Score | .09 | .10 | .01 | −.03 |
| Self Achievement | .17 | .15 | .09 | .08 |
| Avoiding Risks | −.05 | −.03 | −.15 | −.17 |
| Feedback of Results | .16 | .13 | .02 | −.01 |
| Personal Innovation | .03 | .05 | −.03 | −.04 |
| Planning for the Future | −.01 | −.02 | .07 | .04 |
| **Company Success Measures** | | | | |
| Growth in Number of Employees | .07 | .11 | .13 | .23* |
| Growth in Number of Employees/Year | .16 | .17 | .02 | .10 |
| Growth in Sales (in thousands of dollars) | .02 | .12 | .00 | .22* |
| Growth in Sales/Year (in thousands of dollars) | .15 | .13 | .11 | .22* |
| Net Profit as Percent of Sales (on a scale with a low of 1 and a high of 6) | −.18 | −.17 | .00 | .03 |
| Yearly Income from Position (on a scale with a low of 1 and a high of 8) | .05 | .02 | .20* | .19 |

Correlation between entrepreneur type and firm type
$$r = .30** \quad rho = .30**$$
*P $<$.05.     **P $<$.01.

The results obtained with the type of entrepreneur and type of
firm measures in retrospect are not unexpected. It now seems likely
that this particular sample, with its strong scientific bent, contains a
group of people who are so different from the original sample of manufacturing entrepreneurs from whom the theory was developed, as to make
that theory minimally applicable. Almost 60 percent of the entrepreneurs hold doctoral degrees.

Certain prior findings suggest that the view that opportunistic entrepreneurs foster company growth and craftsman do not fails to apply under certain circumstances.[9] More specifically, the importance of the craftsman orientation for growth appears to depend on the level of economic development of the country and the stage of the life cycle of the firm. Thus, the findings reported here are not entirely without support; there clearly are circumstances under which the original theory does not apply.

The correlation of .30 between entrepreneur type and firm type is well below the values in the .60s obtained previously. Several factors appear to contribute to this result. For one thing there are very few opportunistic entrepreneurs in the sample; less than 20 percent of the group score in the opportunistic direction at all, and none sufficiently to be considered truly opportunistic. This may account for the failure to correlate with the MSCS-Form T measures. The sample entrepreneurs are heavily concentrated in a band with entrepreneur type scores ranging from -4 to 0. The firm type scores for this group vary across the whole range. Over 60 percent of the entrepreneurs fall in this band. This concentration, and the consequent restriction of range on the entrepreneur type measure, contributes to the lower correlation between type of entrepreneur and type of firm measures found in this research.

This particular concentration of scores is also important because it closely matches a group of entrepreneurs that Smith tentatively identified in his early research - a group that is slightly craftsman in orientation. He says -

. . . a new subtype may be appearing. . . . an appropriate name for this type might be Inventor - Entrepreneur. In all of these cases the entrepreneur has taken out a large number of patents. It appears that his orientation is not to attempt to build a business or to turn out the best product. Rather his major concern seems to be to develop an organization, not as an end in itself, but rather as a vehicle to allow him to invent and produce various products.[10]

Something equivalent to these Inventor - Entrepreneurs would appear to be prevalent in the present sample. Perhaps this is an emergent group of Scientist - Entrepreneurs that is responding to the changing technology of our times. Their presence may account for the particular form many of the findings take.

---

[9]Rein Peterson and Norman R. Smith, "Entrepreneurship: A Culturally Appropriate Combination of Craft and Opportunity," Frontiers of Entrepreneurship Research 1986, Babson College, pp. 1-11.

[10]Norman R. Smith, op. cit., pp. 87-89.

REFERENCES

Begley, Thomas M. and Boyd, David P., "Psychological Characteristics Associated with Performance in Entrepreneurial Firms and Smaller Businesses," Journal of Business Venturing, Vol. 2, No. 1 (Winter 1987), pp. 79-93.

Brockhaus, Robert H. and Horwitz, Pamela S., "The Psychology of the Entrepreneur," Donald L. Sexton and Raymond W. Smilor, The Art and Science of Entrepreneurship, Ballinger, Cambridge, Mass., 1986, pp. 25-48.

McClelland, David C., The Achieving Society, D. Von Nostrand Co., Princeton, N.J., 1961.

McClelland, David C., "Business Drive and National Achievement," Harvard Business Review, Vol. 40, No. 4 (July-August 1962), pp. 99-112.

Miner, John B., "Limited Domain Theories of Organizational Energy," Craig C. Pinder and Larry F. Moore, Middle Range Theory and the Study of Organizations, Martinus Nijhoff, Boston, 1980, pp. 273-286.

Miner, John B., "The Uncertain Future of the Leadership Concept: Revisions and Clarifications," Journal of Applied Behavioral Science, Vol. 18, No. 3 (September 1982), pp. 293-307.

Miner, John B., "Sentence Completion Measures in Personnel Research: The Development and Validation of the Miner Sentence Completion Scales," H. John Bernardin and David A. Bownas, Personality Assessment in Organizations, Praeger, New York, 1985, pp. 145-176.

Miner, John B., Scoring Guide for the Miner Sentence Completion Scale - Form T, Organizational Measurement Systems Press, Atlanta, Georgia, 1986.

Peterson, Rein and Smith, Norman R., Entrepreneurship: A Culturally Appropriate Combination of Craft and Opportunity, Frontiers of Entrepreneurship Research 1986, Babson College, pp. 1-11.

Smith, Norman R., The Entrepreneur and His Firm: The Relationship Between Type of Man and Type of Company, Bureau of Business and Economic Research, Michigan State University, East Lansing, Mich., 1967.

Smith, Norman R. and Miner, John B., "Type of Entrepreneur, Type of Firm and Managerial Motivation: Implications for Organizational Life Cycle Theory," Strategic Management Journal, Vol. 4, No. 4 (October-December 1983), pp. 332-337.

Smith, Norman R. and Miner, John B., "Motivational Considerations in the Success of Technologically Innovative Entrepreneurs," _Frontiers of Entrepreneurship Research 1984_, Babson College, pp. 488-495.

Smith, Norman R. and Miner, John B., "Motivational Considerations in the Success of Technologically Innovative Entrepreneurs: Extended Sample Findings," _Frontiers of Entrepreneurship Research 1985_, Babson College, pp. 482-488.

SUMMARY

HIGHLY SUCCESSFUL VENTURES:   EMPIRICALLY DERIVED SUCCESS FACTORS

Author

Gerald E. Hills

Address

Office for Entrepreneurial Studies (M/C 244)
University of Illinois at Chicago
College of Business Administration
2131 University Hall
Box 4348
Chicago, Illinois 60680
(312) 996-2670

Principal Topics and Methodology

This study presents the findings from an empirical search for fundamental success factors in high growth, entrepreneurial firms.  One hundred Chicago area firms over two years were selected as finalists in an Arthur Andersen and Co./University of Illinois at Chicago Small Business of the Year competition.  They survived an extensive screening, with special attention to their record of entrepreneurial decision making, sales growth and profitability.  Average annual sales volume was $16.5 million with an average annual sales increase since 1981 of 54 percent.  The master research proposition was that in highly successful entrepreneurial ventures, there tend to be common underlying factors associated with success.

Most of the information analyzed was provided in an unstructured format.  The nomination form had only three general questions concerning the nature of the business and its products, background information concerning previous operating years and a question about major actions taken and difficulties overcome.  Sales and the number of employees were also provided for each of the previous five years, in addition to whether or not the firm was profitable each year.  The interviewer questionnaire was considerably more specific, with questions that related to the above noted proposition.

In light of the highly qualitative nature of the evidence to be analyzed, content analysis procedures were reviewed to determine their applicability.

Today content analysis has evolved into a scientific method that yields inferences from essentially verbal, symbolic, or communicative data. It is a research technique for making replicable and valid inferences from data to their context. Communication content is transformed through the objective and systematic application of categorization rules. As noted by Rosengren, it is imperative that category formation be determined by the research purpose and hypotheses to avoid bias in the categorization process. Use of good operational definitions for the purposes of categorization is essential. Such definitions should be a valid representation of analyst's concepts and sufficiently precise to guide coders to produce reliable judgments. It was this issue that led the author of this paper to do a modified content analysis. After reviewing many completed nomination forms and questionnaires, it was decided to ensure validity by personally reviewing all of the qualitative questionnaire responses rather than asking less experienced coders to do so. Difficult judgments must be made to place information in categories, judgments that partially rely on experience and business knowledge. Based on this phase, detailed guidelines were developed to assist coders who then reviewed the nomination forms.

Categories were constructed by moving back and forth from theory to data, testing the usefulness of categories in light of the above requirements. This study focuses on Subject matter categories, on the assumption that the appearance of an implicit or explicit definition of, for example, a "market niche" on the nomination form meant that it could be counted for purposes of drawing inferences. The "coding units" are phrases and themes, rather than words or other alternatives.

## Major Findings and Implications

The first factor, distinct competitive advantage, existed in all (100 percent) of the firms that were asked the structured response questions. Also, the author and other coders judged that 86 percent of the other firms possessed one or more such advantages, using content analysis. There was no reference (NR) to this concept by ten firms (or the concept could not be identified) although it may have existed.

It is widely assumed that new ventures and smaller firms tend to have greater success by tailoring their products/services to a "niche" in the marketplace where relatively less competition exists. Seventy-seven percent of the structured answers (SA) confirmed this thesis and 51 percent from the content analysis (CA). Again, the 51 percent may be exceeded in reality, but 51 percent of the seventy nominations (that were content analyzed) alluded to a niche, either in such terminology or in the descriptive information provided. Many methods to encourage employee motivation and productivity were cited, including equity ownership, bonuses, production wage incentives, and by treating employees as "family" with picnics, parties, free coffee and pastries. Peters and Waterman cited as one of their eight basic principles the need to create in all employees an awareness that their best efforts are essential and that they will share in the rewards of the company's success. Ninety-six percent of the CEOs when directly asked indicated that they use a variety of methods, and 31 percent of the nominations submitted alluded to this factor. In the latter case, the nominators did not find this factor to be as central to the success story as it could have been, although it was still referred by by nearly one-third of the nominators.

The remaining four items related to the nature of planning in these successful firms. Existence of a written business plan, use of at least a three of four year planning horizon, seeking "flexibility" over planning, and the existence of stated overall, strategic goal were the factors addressed. In an excellent literature review concerning such variables, several studies concluded that strategic planning in small firms was unstructured, irregular and uncomprehensive. The studies also evidenced little attention to goal setting. In the same review, however, the results were contradictory that attempted to relate the level of firm success to planning, goal setting and the like. Some studies showed that high formality did not enhance performance, that informal planning was more effective, and that higher sales growth firms had shorter planning time horizons than those with low sales growth. This study found that 50 percent of the CEOs responding to a direct question said that <u>maintaining flexibility is more important than planning</u>. Sixty percent of the nominations also evidenced a clear record of adaptive flexibility (although it was not possible to compare this factor to their perception of planning). The remaining items found conflicting results between the direct questions and the content analysis. The <u>existence of a business plan</u> was claimed by 69 per cent of the CEOs in a direct question, but only 17 percent referred to such a plan in the nomination form. Yet it is clear that nearly a third of the CEOs said they had <u>no</u> written plan and that 83 percent made not reference in the nomination form to a plan (where they were presumably citing their success and their most notable practices). These findings infer that many of these highly successful ventures have not found a written business plan to be a key factor for success. Similar findings are associated with the <u>length of the planning horizon</u> used. Thirty-six percent of the CEOs used less than a 3-4 year horizon and only 17 percent alluded to such a planning horizon in the nomination process. Similarly, whereas 81 percent of the CEOs said they have a stated, overall strategic business goal, only 33 percent cited such a goal in their nomination forms. Therefore, even though these results are conflicting, they at least suggest that a sizable minority of highly successful firms succeed without placing great attention on traditional planning practices. These findings underscore the need for further research.

SUMMARY

DEEP VS. SURFACE ENTREPRENEURSHIP IN LARGE COMPANIES

## Author

Vijay Sathe

## Address

Graduate Management Center
The Claremont Graduate School
Claremont, CA 91711
(714) 621-8073

## Principal Topics

This paper describes and analyzes two very different patterns of
entrepreneurship found in large companies. "Surface entrepreneurship" denotes the pattern of entrepreneurial activity found in
companies where entrepreneurship was seen as an important business
objective that management was trying to promote and accomplish. In
contrast, "deep entrepreneurship" denotes the pattern found in companies where entrepreneurship was an important shared value, whether
or not it was seen as a management objective. The distinction has
important implications for the management of large firms.

## Method and Data Base

The data base consists of a in-depth field study in four American
firms over a three year period, and preliminary fieldwork in four
European firms over a one year period. The study is exploratory and
comparative in nature.

## Major Findings

Two of the American firms displayed the pattern of deep entrepreneurship. In these firms, the number of entrepreneurial initiatives
undertaken, the manner in which they were perceived, and the way in
which they were pursued were substantially different than in the two
other American firms that displayed surface entrepreneurship. The
firms with deep entrepreneurship had a higher success rate on ventures launched than did those with surface entrepreneurship. Based
on preliminary data, all four of the European firms displayed surface
entrepreneurship, and are therefore predicted to yield a lower success rate on ventures launched. Planned follow-up fieldwork will
test whether this prediction is borne out.

## Major Implications

Managers seeking to promote entrepreneurship in their organizations need to be aware of the important differences between deep and surface entrepreneurship, and be able to decipher which of the two types they are dealing with. The difficulties of achieving deep entrepreneurship, and some approaches of moving toward it are discussed.

# LEGAL ISSUES IN NEW VENTURE DEVELOPMENT

Catherine A. Brown, University of Calgary
Carmen H. Colborne, University of Calgary
W. Ed McMullan, University of Calgary

## ABSTRACT

This study presents the results of a survey of 100 new venture clients who sought legal assistance from the Small Business Student Clinic at the University of Calgary. The results illustrate that new venture entrepreneurs underestimate the amount of legal support they will require at the early stages of venture development. In a significant number of cases, alterations were made in their business strategy once new legal information was made available. The data also suggests that particular legal issues will dominate at each development stage in the business venture.

## INTRODUCTION

The entrepreneur must do business within a complex set of laws and regulations administered through a variety of enforcement and judicial systems. Municipal, provincial and federal regulatory and enforcement legislation govern almost all aspects of business commerce. The legal issues raised by this legislation may have a significant impact on a particular business venture. The Small Business Student Clinic,[1] a program run by the New Venture Development Group at the University of Calgary was launched in January of 1986 in response to a perceived need for legal assistance in this area. The clinical program itself is aimed at both education and entrepreneurial support. Law students are matched with community entrepreneurs to provide assistance at the early stages of venture development. This legal assistance has included information and reports on a broad range of legal problems. Examples include available tax incentives, business formats, products liability, patents, trademarks, copyright, creditors' rights and

---

[1]See C. Brown and W. Ed McMullan, "Student Legal Assistance for New Ventures", in Frontiers of Entrepreneurship Research 1986, Proceedings of the Sixth Annual Babson Conference, Centre for Entrepreneurial Studies, Babson College, Wellesley, Mass., 1986 (for abstract of paper). Write authors for complete version.

franchising/distribution problems. Using a combination of legal file information and survey data, we attempted to provide some answers to three central questions:

1.  Whether entrepreneurial clients were able to identify legal issues affecting their business, and if so, to what extent;

2.  Whether stage of venture development was related to the type of problems identified by legal personnel; and

3.  Where the clients were not able to identify legal issues,[2] how the identification of these issues by Clinic personnel impacted on the clients' subsequent behaviour and approach to their original business strategy.

### THE STUDY BASE AND THE STAGES OF DEVELOPMENT MODEL

During 1986 approximately 270 clients sought information from the Small Business Student Clinic. The average client received legal information on 3.6 different issues; in total, roughly 975 legal issues were addressed during that period.

Approximately 200 of these clients were asked to respond to a survey on various aspects of the Clinic. The clients were typically surveyed within two to four months of their final visit to the Clinic. At the time of writing, 110 surveys have been completed and returned; a return rate of more than 50%.

Data from the first 100 surveys returned was compiled on a preliminary basis. All but three of this first 100 were early stage ventures of the type targeted by the Clinic. The next three surveys received were used to replace the three outliers. The 100 people surveyed represented 360 legal issues for which information was generated.

---

[2] The phrase "Clinic personnel" refers to all associates of the Clinic who assisted in providing legal support to clients. These included primarily third year law students, but as well, recently graduated students (summer program) and supervisors from the Alberta Bar.

The preliminary review of data revealed that an overwhelming percentage of clients fell into either the preparation phase or into the first year of operations; only three of the initial 100 clients surveyed[3] had established businesses and were improving operating performance or contemplating expansion.

| CONCEPT ONLY | PROTOTYPE DEVELOPMENT | PLANNING | FINANCING & PRE-SELLING | MANUFACTURE | SALES UNDERWAY | OPERATING SYSTEM |
|---|---|---|---|---|---|---|
| PREPARATIONS | | | | OPERATIONS | | EXPANSION |

After adding the three replacement client surveys to round out the sample to 100 respondents, the client files were organized by stages of development in such a manner as to balance the numbers of clients within categories. As a result, prototype development and business planning were grouped together as were the first year of the operation stages described above.

| CONCEPT ONLY | PROTOTYPE DEVELOPMENT AND BUSINESS PLANNING | PRE-SELLING AND FINANCING | EARLY OPERATIONAL |
|---|---|---|---|

The stages may be summarily described in the following way:

1. Concept Only - client is looking into an idea for a new business (27 clients)

---

[3]Notes on each client's file were used to fix the level of development of the venture. Client notes on each file included a description of the venture, steps taken to date in the venture's development and plans for the near-term future.

2. <u>Prototype Development and Business Planning</u> - client is working on development of the product/service, conducting market research or creating a business plan (29 clients)

3. <u>Pre-Selling and Financing</u> - having finalized a business strategy, the client now seeks to pre-sell the products and/or access financing for launch (24 clients)

4. <u>Early Operational</u> - client has been operating a business for less than one year (20 clients)

## ENTREPRENEURS ARE OVERLOOKING LEGAL ISSUES

Twenty-two (22) legal issues common to business start-ups were identified by the authors based on prior experience with start-up clients. These included, for example, business format, licencing, product liability, tax issues, franchising and protection of intellectual property (see Appendix I). Clearly not all issues impacted on every venture. Clinic practice required that clients pre-identify the issues which they wanted to discuss with legal personnel at the Clinic. During the initial interview with the client, legal personnel frequently uncovered additional issues relevant to the client's venture. The additional numbers of issues identified by Clinic personnel were then tallied. Exhibit I illustrates the frequency with which Clinic personnel identified relevant legal problems on which clients had not sought assistance.

## EXHIBIT I

### NUMBER OF LEGAL ISSUES NOT IDENTIFIED BY CLIENT

|  | Total | By Stage of Development | | | |
|---|---|---|---|---|---|
|  |  | 1 | 2 | 3 | 4 |
| No Additional Issues Identified | 9.0% | 7.4% | 6.9% | 8.3% | 15.0% |
| 1 Additional Issue | 30.0% | 33.3% | 24.1% | 25.0% | 40.0% |
| 2 Additional Issues | 17.0% | 29.6% | 13.8% | 12.5% | 10.0% |
| 3 Additional Issues | 26.0% | 11.1% | 34.5% | 37.5% | 20.0% |
| 4 Additional Issues | 18.0% | 18.5% | 20.7% | 16.7% | 15.0% |
|  |  |  |  |  | 100.0% |

Not surprisingly, clients typically were untutored in the law and therefore had limited ability to effectively identify many legal issues that impinged on their ventures. Only in 9% of the cases did clients identify all the issues that the lawyers found relevant to the client's venture. Ninety-one (91%) percent of the time legal personnel were asked to provide information on one or more relevant additional legal considerations. What this suggests is that legal clinics may not only provide early-stage entrepreneurs with information on pre-identified problems, they may also provide entrepreneurs with an understanding of additional relevant legal issues of potential significance to their businesses.

Cross-validation of our finding that the legal personnel identified additional relevant issues came from the follow-up survey of clients. When asked if, as a result of the Clinic, they were made aware of "a potential legal problem of which you were not previously aware", 73% responded in the affirmative. Exhibit II provides responses by stage of venture development.

---

EXHIBIT II

AWARENESS OF NEW LEGAL PROBLEMS

| Made Aware of New Legal Problems | Total | Stage of Development | | | |
|---|---|---|---|---|---|
| | | 1 | 2 | 3 | 4 |
| Yes | 73.0% | 74.1% | 65.5% | 79.5% | 75.0% |
| No | 27.0% | 25.9% | 34.5% | 20.8% | 25.0% |
| | | | | | 100.0% |

---

## Specific Areas of Legal Issues Identified by Clients[4]

Clients were asked to specifically identify those legal issues on which they wanted legal information prior to their interview with Clinic personnel. Each legal problem was then categorized and computed as a percentage of the total number of issues identified by all clients.

---

[4]Based on each client's survey and response and the initial interview sheet prepared by the law student.

EXHIBIT III

CLIENT IDENTIFICATION OF SPECIFIC LEGAL ISSUES

| Categories of Legal Problems | Stage of Development | | | |
|---|---|---|---|---|
| | 1 | 2 | 3 | 4 |
| 1 - Business Format | 36.4% | 21.3% | 25.5% | 48.1% |
| 2 - Intellectual/Industrial Property | 36.4% | 36.2% | 19.1% | 7.4% |
| 3 - Business/Product Liability | 9.1% | 6.4% | 6.4% | 11.1% |
| 4 - Regulatory | 6.1% | 14.9% | 10.6% | 0.0% |
| 5 - Franchising/Financing | 9.1% | 8.5% | 12.8% | 3.7% |
| 6 - Contracts | 3.0% | 10.6% | 14.9% | 14.8% |
| 7 - Taxation | 0.0% | 2.1% | 10.6% | 14.8% |
| 8 - Choosing Professional Advisors | 0.0% | 0.0% | 0.0% | 0.0% |

Overall, the data illustrates that clients most readily identified issues in the business format and intellectual/industrial property areas. One might speculate whether clients' understanding of their legal needs is centered on a desire to protect assets. Further to this point, a review of the files where the business format issues raised by the client in Legal Category 1 and the business/product liability issues in Legal Category 3 were found to be primarily associated with seeking incorporation and limited liability for the venture. Few inquiries were directed towards other business format or other product liability issues, for example, income taxation and packaging/labeling regulatory requirements. Viewed in that context, 45.5% of Stage 1 entrepreneurial issues, 27% of Stage 2 issues, 31.9% of Stage 3 issues and 59.2% of Stage 4 issues all related to the immediate protection of the client's personal assets which might be at risk as a result of the business venture. In total more than 40% of all issues raised by clients appeared to be directed toward this question alone.

The next largest category of issue identification fell into the area of intellectual/industrial property. Again, protection of assets appeared to be the key motivating factor. These clients believed they had an idea, product or service of value. Their questions related to methods of protecting their proprietary position. It is interesting to note that although many of these clients identified the general category into which their legal problem fell, few identified the relevant issue in that category. For example, although all wanted their business idea protected, few realized that a preliminary issue to be addressed was whether their idea infringed on a third party's intellectual property rights.  Another common example of non-identification were clients who sought legal assistance in obtaining patents or other methods of final protection.  Although patent protection may have been an important issue at some point in the venture's development, often a more critical issue was how the client could access development assistance without public disclosure of the trade secrets.  Such public disclosure will, in some cases, preclude patent availability.

Legal issues relating to the protection of assets, either personal property which might be at risk in the venture, or protection of a business concept, represented the vast majority of total issues identified by clients.  In Stage 1, 81.9% of all issues fell into this category, in Stage 2, 63.9%, in Stage 3, 51% and in Stage 4, 66.1% (average 65.7%).  Most clients thus appear able to identify and respond to a perceived need to protect property; fewer were able to identify the myriad of other regulatory controls and legislation which would directly impact on their business venture.

## What Issues are Identified by Legal Personnel?

As a result of interviews averaging approximately 1.5 hours per client, Clinic legal personnel identified what they considered to be the most significant legal problems facing each client at the time.  A further 3 to 5 hours per client was spent researching problems and communicating possible solutions.  Exhibit IV illustrates the total numbers of various legal problems identified for the clientele in each of the four specified stages of development.  As may be obvious to the reader some issues are more dominant in different stages of development than others suggesting some logic for the ordering in the legal priorities of newly developing businesses.

EXHIBIT IV

DOMINANT LEGAL AREAS IN EACH STAGE OF DEVELOPMENT

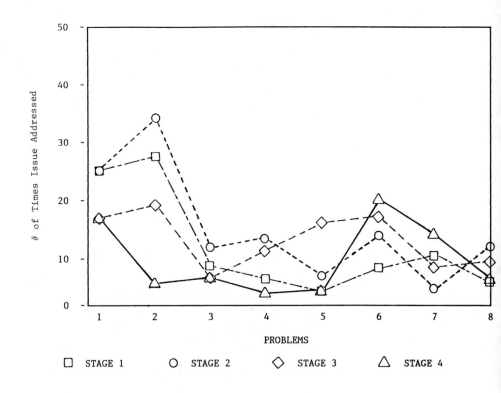

PROBLEMS

☐  STAGE 1          ◯  STAGE 2          ◇  STAGE 3          △  STAGE 4

## Problem Types

1.  Business Format
2.  Intellectual/Industrial Property
3.  Business and Product Liability
4.  Regulatory
5.  Franchising Distributing and Financing
6.  Contracts
7.  Taxation
8.  Choosing Professional Advisors

EXHIBIT V

PERCENTAGE OF LEGAL ISSUES NOT IDENTIFIED BY CLIENT

| Description of Legal Issues | % Not Identified by Client Stage of Development | | | |
|---|---|---|---|---|
| | 1 | 2 | 3 | 4 |
| **1. Business Formats** | | | | |
| Incorporation/Corporate Organization | 38.5 | 50 | 10 | 27 |
| Partnership/Non-Corporate Formats | 33.5 | 60 | 100 | 0 |
| Partnership/Shareholders Agreements | 100 | 100 | 50 | 50 |
| **2. Intellectual/Industrial Property** | | | | |
| Intellectual Property - Infringement | 66.7 | 71.5 | 0 | 0 |
| Intellectual Property - Preliminary Protection | 87.5 | 85.7 | 80 | 100 |
| Intellectual Property - Final Protection | 0 | 17 | 34.4 | 100 |
| Technology Transfer | 80 | 100 | 75 | Ø |
| **3. Business and Product Liability** | 57.2 | 72.8 | 40 | 40 |
| **4. Regulatory** | | | | |
| Municipal Licenses and Tax | 0 | 75 | 80 | 0 |
| Regulatory (non-municipal) | 100 | 0 | 20 | 100 |
| Export/Import | 100 | 100 | Ø | Ø |
| **5. Franchising Distributing and Financing** | | | | |
| Franchise | 0 | 25 | 50 | 0 |
| Financing/Internal Corporate Reorganizations | 0 | 0 | 76.5 | 100 |
| **6. Contracts** | | | | |
| Employer/Employee Legislation | 100 | 50 | 0 | 100 |
| Advertising | Ø | 100 | Ø | 100 |
| Contracts (not otherwise covered in above areas) | 80 | 60 | 60 | 78 |
| Debtor/Creditor Rights | Ø | Ø | Ø | 60 |
| **7. Taxation** | | | | |
| Income Tax Planning | 100 | 66.6 | 50 | 78 |
| Asset Transfers (tax planned) | Ø | Ø | 100 | 10 |
| Income Tax Compiance | Ø | Ø | Ø | 100 |

Ø    No issue in this category was identified either by the clients in the stage of development or the Clinic personnel providing legal assistance to those clients.

0    Each client in the stage of development identified the same legal issues as the Clinic personnel.

## Client Identification Compared to Clinic Identification of Issues

A comparison was made of the legal issues identified by the clients and those identified by the Clinic. Exhibit V illustrates problem areas that clients failed to identify but which were considered important by the Clinic's legal personnel. The lower the percentage the more effective the entrepreneur in identifying relevant legal issues. The higher the percentage, the less effective the entrepreneur.

EXHIBIT V

PERCENTAGE OF LEGAL ISSUES NOT IDENTIFIED BY CLIENT

| Description of Legal Issues | % Not Identified By Client Stage of Development | | | |
|---|---|---|---|---|
| | 1 | 2 | 3 | 4 |
| 1. Business Format | | | | |
| Incorporation/Corporate Organization | 38.5 | 50 | 10 | 27 |
| Partnership/Non-Corporate Formats | 33.5 | 60 | 100 | 0 |
| Partnership/Shareholder Agreements | 100 | 100 | 50 | 50 |
| 2. Intellectual/Industrial Property | | | | |
| Intellectual Property – Infringement | 66.7 | 71.5 | 0 | 0 |
| Intellectual Property – Preliminary Protection | 87.5 | 85.7 | 80 | 100 |
| Intellectual Property – Final Protection | 0 | 17 | 34.4 | 100 |
| Technology Transfer | 80 | 100 | 75 | Ø |
| 3. Business and Product Liability | 57.2 | 72.8 | 40 | 40 |
| 4. Regulatory | | | | |
| Municipal Licences and Tax | 0 | 75 | 80 | 0 |
| Regulatory (non-municipal) | 100 | 0 | 20 | 100 |
| Export/Impert | 100 | 100 | Ø | Ø |
| 5. Franchising Distributing and Financing | | | | |
| Franchise | 0 | 25 | 50 | 0 |
| Financing/Internal Corporate Reorganizations | 0 | 0 | 76.5 | 100 |
| 6. Contracts | | | | |
| Employer/Employee Legislation | 100 | 50 | 0 | 100 |
| Advertising | Ø | 100 | Ø | 100 |
| Contracts (not otherwise covered in above areas) | 80 | 60 | 60 | 78 |
| Debtor/Creditor Rights | Ø | Ø | Ø | 60 |
| 7. Taxation | | | | |
| Income Tax Planning | 100 | 66.6 | 50 | 78 |
| Asset Transfers (tax planned) | Ø | Ø | 100 | 10 |
| Income Tax Compliance | Ø | Ø | Ø | 100 |

Ø   No issue in this category was identified either by the clients in the stage of development or the Clinic personnel providing legal assistance to those clients.

0   Each client in the stage of development identified the same legal issues as the Clinic personnel.

Two observations were made:

1. Although the general areas of business format and intellectual property were identified, clients did not address questions such as shareholder or partnership agreements or critical areas in industrial/intellectual property, particularly in Stage 3. This may result in many clients, for example, losing intellectual property protection since they may be too late to file patent or industrial design registrations.

2. The highest number of issues not identified by clients were in the regulatory area, in the contract area and with respect to taxation issues.

John Slyke, of the Harvard University Graduate Program of Business Administration, in his paper "What Should We Teach Entrepreneurs About the Law?"[5] describes this second grouping of legal issues as "a formidable thicket of constraints, requirements for compliance, and vulnerabilities to actions . . . but (he continues) . . . they also are harsh realities that must normally be faced with little prior experience and extremely scarce resources (i.e. time, money, expertise and access to expert assistance and advice)". He concludes that "The effects of an entrepreneur's decisions and actions, good or bad, with respect to the law are often greatly amplified in future results, consequences, or loss of options".

We attempted to determine whether there was in fact any apparent relationship between the client's failure to identify issues and the impact, if any, on the client's subsequent behaviour and business strategy once the issues were identified by the Clinic. From two to six months after their sessions with the legal Clinic the clients were asked whether they had changed their overall business strategy as a result of new information received from the Clinic. The following exhibit describes client response, and the percentage who altered or abandoned their business strategy as a result of information received. The clients were also asked to indicate if no change occurred despite new information received.

---

[5] In Entrepreneurship: What it is and How to Teach it. A Collection of Working Papers from a Colloquium held at Harvard Business School, 1983.

EXHIBIT VI

CLIENT FOLLOW-THROUGH BEHAVIOUR

| Client Behaviour | Stage of Development | | | | Total |
|---|---|---|---|---|---|
| | 1 | 2 | 3 | 4 | |
| 1 - No Change | | | | | |
|   New Information | 40.7% | 34.5% | 41.7% | 25.0% | 36.0% |
|   No New Information | 22.2% | 31.0% | 12.5% | 10.0% | 20.0% |
| 2 - Alter Business Strategy as a Result of New Information | 22.2% | 34.5% | 41.7% | 65.0% | 39.0% |
| 3 - Abandon Business Strategy as a Result of New Information | 14.8% | 0.0% | 4.2% | 0.0% | 5.0% |
| | | | | | 100.0% |

Fifty-six percent (56%) of all clients indicated they made no change in their business strategy as a result of attending the Clinic. Of this 56%, 36% indicated no change in their original strategy notwithstanding the fact that they acknowledged having received new information on legal issues. It would appear that at least some of this 36% fall into an "adopt risk category"; that is, some clients may have decided to proceed in their venture without fully resolving the legal issues on which they obtained new information.

In total 44% of all clients indicated that they had either altered or abandoned their original strategy as a result of new legal information gained. Of these, 25% were in Stage 3 and 30% in Stage 4.

Five percent (5%) of those clients surveyed abandoned their business strategy altogether. Four of these clients were in Stage 1, one was in Stage 3. Of the five clients abandoning their business strategy, four had failed to identify the critical legal issue which affected their business. One of these clients proposed a product or service which would have infringed on third party intellectual property rights, and another proposed a distribution scheme which would have run afoul of provincial securities legislation.

The data contained in Exhibit IV (dominant legal issues by stage) and Exhibit V (percentage of legal issues not identified by clients) was then compared with client follow-through behaviour in Exhibit VI to illustrate the relationship between changes in behaviour and percentages of issues not identified in dominant legal areas.

Exhibit VII describes the relationship between issues not identified in dominant legal areas by stage and client follow-through behaviour.

EXHIBIT VII

PERCENTAGE OF UNIDENTIFIED LEGAL ISSUES AND CHANGES IN
BUSINESS STRATEGY BY STAGE OF DEVELOPMENT

| Stage of Development | Dominant Legal Areas | % of Legal Issues Not Identified/Total | Client Behaviour | | |
|---|---|---|---|---|---|
| | | | Alter | Abandon | No Change |
| 1 | Format/Liability | 57.3 | 22.2% | 14.8% | 62.9% |
| | Intellectual Ppty. | 58.6 | | | |
| | Taxation | 100 | | | |
| | Contracts | 90.0 | | | |
| | | 76.5 | | | |
| 2 | Format/Liability | 70.7 | | | |
| | Intellectual Ppty. | 68.6 | | | |
| | Contracts | 70.0 | 34.0% | Ø | 65.5% |
| | Regulatory | 58.3 | | | |
| | | 66.9 | | | |
| 3 | Format/Liability | 50.0 | | | |
| | Intellectual Ppty. | 63.1 | | | |
| | Contracts | 30.0 | 41.7% | 4.2% | 54.2% |
| | Franchising/Financing | 63.2 | | | |
| | | 51.6 | | | |
| 4 | Contracts | 84.5 | | | |
| | Format/Liability | 39.0 | | | |
| | Taxation | 62.7 | 65.0% | Ø | 35.0% |
| | Intellectual Ppty. | 66.7 | | | |
| | | 63.2 | | | |

Sixty-five percent (65%) of all those in Stage 4 (early operating) altered their original strategy. This is not surprising. Three of the four major areas which dominate in Stage 4 (see Exhibit VII), i.e. contracts, taxation and final protection of intellectual property, dominate the same legal issues most often not identified by Stage 4 clients.

In Stage 3, 41.7% of clients altered their business strategy. Again, the data reveals a high failure rate in issue identification by the client in almost all the dominate legal areas for Stage 3 ventures.

## Whether Clients Sought Professional Legal Advice

In order to further assess the perceived value, if any, of the new information gained, the clients were asked if they sought legal advice or planned to see a lawyer in connection with their new venture after attending the Clinic. Over 48% of those clients who did not abandon their business plan responded in the affirmative.

---

EXHIBIT VIII

PROFESSIONAL FOLLOW-UP

|  | Saw or Planned to See a Lawyer if Not Abandoning Plan | Did Not See a Lawyer or Do Not Plan To |
|---|---|---|
| Received New Information | 33 (34.7%) | 35 (36.8%) |
| Did Not Receive New Information | 13 (13.7%) | 14 (14.7%) |

---

Of the total number of non-abandoning clients who saw or planned to see a lawyer following attendance at the Clinic (46), 71.7% acknowledged having received new information.

Although no definite conclusions can be drawn it would appear that the new information was perceived of sufficient impact to the venture to require professional legal attention. When broken into stages of development the data also revealed that although 65% of clients in Stage 4 altered their business strategy as a result of new information, only 35% of that group felt the services of a lawyer were required. We have concluded that at least some of the new information provided may have allowed them to find a solution without further legal input. Alternatively, this group may have formed part of the 36% "adopt risk" category previously referred.

# CONCLUSIONS

1.  Legal assistance clinics can help entrepreneurs identify legal issues that might otherwise go undetected.

2.  The most common legal issue identified by entrepreneurs relates to protection of personal assets and business ideas.

3.  Different legal problems tend to dominate at different stages of venture development.

4.  Many clients alter or abandon their original business strategy after receiving legal assistance.

5.  Many entrepreneurs seek professional legal assistance after learning about legal problems from a legal assistance clinic.

6.  It may be worthwhile for researchers to study the costs and benefits associated with abandoning plans and/or changing business strategy since such changes are a frequent consequence of early-stage legal assistance.

## LEGAL ISSUE CLASSIFICATION

1. Business Format

   Incorporation/Corporate Organization
   Partnership/Non-Corporate Formats
   Partnership/Shareholder Agreements

2. Intellectual/Industrial Property

   Intellectual Property - Infringement
   Intellectual Property - Preliminary
       Protection
   Intellectual Property - Final Protection
   Technology Transfer

3. Business and Product Liability

4. Regulatory

   Municipal Licences and Tax
   Regulatory (non-municipal)
   Export/Import

5. Franchising Distributing and Financing

   Franchise
   Financing/Internal Corporate Reorganizations

6. Contracts

   Employer/Employee Legislation
   Advertising
   Contracts (not otherwise covered
       in above areas)
   Debtor/Creditor Rights

7. Taxation

   Income Tax Planning
   Asset Transfers (tax planned)
   Income Tax Compliance

8. Choosing Professional Advisors

# A COMPARATIVE STUDY OF NEW VENTURE FAILURE:  1960 VS. 1980

Albert V. Bruno, Santa Clara University
Joel K. Leidecker, Santa Clara University

## ABSTRACT

The subject of new venture failure is of interest and concern from both a macro and micro level. At the macro level, the relatively high rates of new venture failure consume vital national resources of both a capital and human variety. At the micro level, of course, the individual entrepreneur often experiences significant personal costs when his firm fails.

In this paper, we compare the reasons for failure of two sets of firms. The first set is taken from a sample of technology-based startups founded on the San Francisco peninsula between 1960 and 1963. The second set of firms, is a sample of technology-based firms founded on the San Francisco Peninsula, now called Silicon Valley, between 1980 and 1986.

The comparative analysis focuses on the similarities and differences of causes of failure for failed firms founded in the two time periods. The variables that are compared include:

> Product Timing
> Product Design
> Unclear Business Definition
> Undercapitalization
> Other Financing Considerations
> Management Issues
> The Venture Capital Relationship
> Human Failings

The comparison of the two sets of interviews resulted in considerable consistency. Points of departure are noted in the paper.

## INTRODUCTION

Business failure, a common occurence in market economies, can be devastating to the people and organizations victimized when a company fails. The Dun and Bradstreet corporation compiles exhaustive statistics on business failure in the United States. Their results show that the failure rate has risen steadily since 1978 and by 1983 had reached a level of 110 failures per 10,000 companies.[1] Research findings argue that business failure results from definable causes and that an understanding of these causes can be useful in preventing failure.[2,3,4,5,6,7,8]

The authors have been tracking the performance of 250 firms stated in California's Silicon Valley in the 1960's.[9,10] In a recent article "Patterns of Failure Among Silicon Valley Firms," Bruno, Leidecker and Harder published the findings of their research relative to the failed segment of the 250 firms in the studies cited above.[11] The results, while contributing additional evidence to the growing body of knowledge on why firm fails, also opened new avenues for research. One question that arises is to what extent are failed firms founded in the 1960's different from those founded in other periods such as the 1980's. This

[1] Dun and Bradstreet. "The Business Failure Record." New York: The Dun & Bradstreet Corporation, 1985.

[2] Edward I. Altman, Corporate Financial Distress. New York: John Wiley and Sons, 1983.

[3] Edward I. Altman, R. Haldeman, and P. Narayanan, ZETA Analysis: A New Model to Identify Bankruptcy Risk of Corporations," Journal of Banking and Finance, 1 (June 1977), 29-54.

[4] John Argenti, Corporate Collapse: The Causes and Symptoms. New York: John Wiley and Sons, 1976.

[5] John Argenti, "Corporate Planning and Corporate Collapse," Long Range Planning, 9 (December 1976), 12-17.

[6] Ronald C. Clute, "An Analysis of Accounting-Related Problems in Small Business Failures." The National Public Accountant. Volume 24. (December 1979), pp. 62-71).

[7] Subbash Sharma and Vijay Mahajan, "Early Warning Indicators of Business Failure." Journal of Marketing, Volume 44, No. 4 (Fall 1980), pp. 80-89.

[8] Dawit Kibre, "Myths of Small Business Failure." The CPA Journal, Volume 53, (September 1983), pp. 73-74.

[9] Albert V. Bruno and Arnold C. Cooper, "Patterns of Development and Acquisitions for Silicon Valley Startups," Technovation, Volume 1, (1982), pp. 275-290.

[10] Arnold C. Cooper & Albert V. Bruno. "Success Among High-Technology Firms." Business Horizons, Vol. 20 (April 1977), pp. 16-22.

[11] Albert V. Bruno, Joel K. Leidecker & Joseph W. Harder, "Patterns of Failure Among Silicon Valley Firms." Business Horizons, (forthcoming).

comparative analysis of failure causation serves as the major focus of this paper. A brief review of the failure literature is necessary to position our discussion of the methodology, findings, and implications of this current research.

## LITERATURE REVIEW

Why firms fail, though not as extensively covered in business literature, is perhaps a more important topic than why they succeed. While managers should be aware of factors which could possibly make their firms successful, knowing which factors could possibly lead to the demise of their firm should be more useful from a managerial action point of view. Dun and Bradstreet statistics show that over 400,000 businesses are discontinued each year. According to the Dun and Bradstreet failure causation system, incompetent management is responsible for nearly 90% of these failures.[12]

The first observation that becomes apparent from reviewing the emerging literature, is that no two authors agree on a definition of business failure. Some authors conclude that failure only occurs when a firm files for some form of bankruptcy. Others contend that there are numerous forms of organizational death, including bankruptcy, merger, or acquisition. Still others argue that failure occurs if the firm fails to meet its responsibilities concerning the stakeholders of the organization; this would include employees, suppliers, the community as a whole, customers, as well as the owners.[13]

Other definitions of failure found in the literature include:

1) Firms which liquidate and go out of business without ever filing bankruptcy; 2) Firms which collapse and reduce to a franction of their normal size; 3) Firms which seek a merger partner under conditions of financial distress; 4) Firms which become technically insolvent:  that is cannot pay their bills when due; 5) Firms which are technically insolvent:  meaning that the realizable value of all assets is insufficient to meet total liabilities.

Each of the above under certain circumstances can serve as an adequate definition of failure. The problem is that the definition of failure selected can significantly impact the composition of a data base, the results which are a consequence of examining the data base, as well as compromising conclusions drawn from any comparative analysis. Bankruptcy statistics alone do not reveal the full extent to which business entities experience failure, but in this and previous research by the authors, bankruptcy is utilized as the measure of failure. In our judgment, the declaration of bankruptcy is at least an agreed-upon

---

[12] Dun and Bradstreet. "The Business Failure Record." New York: The Dun and Bradstreet Corporation, 1981.

[13] Sharma and Mahajan, 1980.

"fact." Thus, all firms that have filed for bankruptcy can be classified as failed even though other failures may exist which have not filed for bankruptcy. The data base in this study represents firms identified from bankruptcy records.

There are a number of research methodologies used to interpret and infer causes of failure; each has merit as well as deficiencies. Perhaps the most common is the use of a financial model. This approach seeks to evaluate firm failure in financial terms and attempts to predict failure through the use of ratio analysis. This approach has been widely criticized. The most compelling of the criticisms is based on Argenti's critique of "creative accounting". He argues that the variability of financial statement data generated with creative accounting, intentional or otherwise, limits the predictive validity of these models.[14]

The second most common approach identifies a list of variables that cause failure. Some of these lists are empirically derived through factor or discriminant analysis; others are subjective findings based on interviews with founders, and/or "professionals" associated with failed firms. The major criticism of this applied approach is the nature of the subjective judgment required to produce the list of failure factors. This approach does have value when trying to understand or predict why firms fail; however, it should be supplemented by other methods. Failure can be better understood through the analysis of both the underlying causes and performance indicators which identify symptoms of eventual firm demise. The financial modeling approach is useful for predicting the likelihood of failure, but it does not identify the causes of that failure.

A third approach, which utilizes an interactive model is differentiated from the financially-oriented types in that it attempts to model failure from a total organizational perspective not just from a financial one.[15] This approach is more intuitively appealing because it potentially combines the positive characteristics of the other two methods.

In summary the following general conclusions emerge from the literature on firm failure.

1. Failure is a process that occurs over time; it is not a sudden death.

2. Within failing companies, specific identifiable factors are present which are the causes of failure.

3. Once identified, there factors may be used to predict the propensity for failure.

---

[14] John Argenti, 1976.

[15] Danny Miller, "The Correlates of Entrepreneurship In Three Types of Firms." Management Science, (Vol. 29, No. 7, 1983), 770-789.

4. Knowledge of the presence of these factors can lead to steps intended to avoid or prevent failure.

5. There are both external and internal factors which influence failure.

6. The external factors are those attributable to general economic effects.

7. The internal factors can be linked to the various functional areas of business firms.

8. The single most pervasive causation factor is poor management, which may manifest itself in a variety of ways.

9. General failure factors may influence many businesses across a number of industries; specific failure factors impact firms in specific industries.

## CHARACTERISTICS OF DATA BASES

The data bases which serve as the focus of this research are drawn from two different time periods, 1960's and 1980's.

### 1960's Failures

As noted earlier, the 250 firms that comprise the original data base have served as the focus of several published research studies. These firms can be characterized as being founded by engineers or scientists, as emphasizing R&D, and as having strategies based upon the utilization of new technology. Among the high technology products represented in the data base are semiconductors, instruments, computer peripheral equipment and microwave equipment. As nearly as can be determined, this data base involves almost all of the companies of this type started on the San Francisco Peninsula between January 1, 1960 and July 1, 1969 and might be regarded as a census of that population. Initially data were gathered about these firms through interviews with founders and industry experts and from published sources. The status of these firms has been determined in 1969, 1973, 1976, 1980, and 1984. As of 1984, the number of accumulated failures is 96 firms. We successfully located 11 founders of these 96 failed firms.

The ten firms and their founders which serve as the basis of the 1960's portion of the data base were identified through a process of networking to try to locate one or more of the original founders.

### 1980's Failures

There were four methods used to find persons involved with the 1980's startup firms that failed. A description of each method follows as well as the results of each to date.

The first method was a search through trade journals and the business sections of newspapers in the San Francisco Bay Area for the announcement of any business failures in the high technology area.

This method was very time consuming as it involved looking over several years of newspaper articles on microfilm. Twenty six failed firms were identified using this process. To date no interviews have been completed. There are several reasons why this is the case. First, many of the articles were one or more years old which means that there was no easy method to trace the company or it's key employees and/or founders'. If the failure was a recent one and a founder was located, they have been unwilling to be interviewed due to litigation or because of personal reasons. A number of those located fell into the latter category.

The second source of firms was the Bankruptcy Court. The court in San Jose contains the listing of all filings for bankruptcy in San Mateo, Santa Clara and Alameda counties in Northern California. The first step in this process was to evaluate all bankruptcy filings. Of the total of 63 firms which were verified to be high technology, it was possible to produce telephone numbers of 22 founders. Of the 22, sixteen were successfully contacted, but only two were willing to be interviewed.

A third set of firms was produced through the professional network of the two co-authors. Two problems were encountered with this method. First many of the referrals were provided by third parties. When the person in question was actually contacted, they were unaware as to why they were being contacted and were not interested in giving an interview, even after an explanation as to the nature of the research. The second problem was much the same as that encountered when researching newspaper articles (no followup potential). Despite these obstacles this approach resulted in four completed interviews.

The fourth and most productive source involved founders of failed firms. At the conclusion of an interview with founders of firms started in the eighties or other time periods we asked each subject for the names of other founders or other key employees of failed of 1980's startups. Other unsuccessful entrepreneurs provided leads to six of the twelve individuals in our data base.

The firms in this data base compare favorably with the characteristics of those in the original 1960's group. All are founded by engineers or scientists, emphasize R&D, and have strategies based upon utilizing new technology(ies).


RESULTS


The results of this investigation are summarized in Exhibit 1 (1960's failures) and Exhibit 2 (1980's failures). Where possible, we have sought to maintain consistency in categorization so as to emhance the interpretability of the findings. Each of the factors will now be discussed in turn:

## Product Timing

In both the 1960's and 1980's studies, product timing difficulties were identified by a high percentage of the participants. In the case of four 1960's firms, a minor cause of failure for each was attributed to premature market entry whereas for one 1980's firm, a major cause of failure was attributed to premature market entry. The remainder of the timing causes of failure for the 1980's firms (3 major, 1 minor), were identified as late market entry. This cause of failure is succinctly explained by one of the founders as follows: "The best product in the world will not sell if the market is saturated. A product with a new technology that essentially fills the same consumer needs as other products already on the market has very little chance of success."

A possible explanation for this shift in emphasis from premature entry problems (1960's) to late entry problems (1980's) may be found in the nature of market expectations. In the earlier time frame, perhaps, the "marketplace" had to be sold on technology-based products more so than it had to be in the current era where technology-based products are considerably more commonplace. In addition, as market acceptance was enhanced, the likelihood of more competitors in the marketplace would make late entry, at least from a competitive point of view, a more serious problem, and hence, a more likely cause of failure.

## Product Design

This is also a category which was frequently mentioned in both time periods. Here we are defining product design as problems that are related to product-market timing, but key on an earlier stage in the product development process. For the 1960's two major causes and two minor causes of failure were identified. For the 1980's, three major causes and one minor cause of failure were identified. The underlying explanations for the two periods are similar but several refinements resulted from the 1980's interviews. Two reasons were identified as to why the planned product design time frame and/or budget allocation could not be met. The first was the inability to develop a working prototype from original design criteria. This was noted as a cause in two out of the twelve firms studied. The second version was the inability to produce a marketable product from a working prototype. This was found to be a major cause of failure in one case and a minor cause in another.

## Inappropriate Distribution or Selling Strategy

This category also received a disproportionate share of mentions in the 1960's study but was a major cause of failure in one firm and a minor cause of another in the 1980's study. One explanation for this development is that more channels of distribution are available now than there were in the 1960's. These include OEM's, vertical markets, retailers such as Businessland and Computerland, etc. Given that selling and distribution strategies must be geared toward both the type of product and the type of customer being pursued, the general availability of more choices should make the matching task somewhat easier. However, the reader may speculate that this, a greater set of distribution choices, actually increases the chances of selecting the inappropriate channel.

## Unclear Business Definition

The patterns of failure for this category were the same for both time periods. Although little can be inferred from the results, we conclude that this factor as a cause of failure is actually understated by participants in the study many of whom do not perceive that their business definition is underspecified. This problem seems more likely because high tech startups have founders and CEO's with technical backgrounds who are more technology driven than business oriented.

## Overreliance on One Customer

This category was not identified as a major cause of failure for any of the 1980's firms. It was identified as a minor cause of failure by only one founder. Interestingly, several of the firms in the 1980's sample did have as an initial market focus, the defense industry and yet the overeliance on the government did not create difficulties as it did for four firms in the 1960's. Perhaps, an external factor, such as level of defense spending had an impact. Another explanation may be linked to "learning". One of the well-publicized lessons from early high tech startups (successes or failures) is to avoid overreliance on a single customer. Perhaps that lesson was heeded.

## Initial Undercapitalization

The problems of undercapitalization were cited as major causes of failure for three of the 1960's firms but were identified as a major cause of failure for only one of the 1980's firms. One possible explanation is that capital has been relatively more available, at least partly because of the early successes of some of the 1960's era technology-based companies. Given that this cause is a rather traditional "explanation" for entrepreneurs, the results here are somewhat surprising. The availability of larger amounts and new sources of venture capital in the early 1980's may account for the difference in emphasis.

## Assuming A Debt Instrument Too Early

This was a major cause of failure for only one firm in the 1980's study whereas it was a major cause of failure for three of the 1960's firms. Availability of more venture/equity capital funding is one possible explanation firms did not have to rely on debt financing as early in the growth process. Another explanation could be linked to learning. Founders in the 80's may be more attuned to the nuances and pitfalls of debt financing.

## Problems With The Venture Capital Relationship

This category was identified as a major cause of failure for four of the 1960's firms whereas it was a major cause of failure for one of the 1980's firms and a minor cause of failure for three of these 1980's firms. Several unique observations were made by the 1980's founders. One observed that the "greater the percentage of his personal wealth that a founder contributes to the firm, the greater the belief in the firm by the venture capitalists." Another founder made a "sunk cost" observation when he observed that "the more money invested in a company, the greater the likelihood the investors will continue to support the company... spend $1 to save $10.

## Ineffective Team

This category received a substantial number of mentions for both the 1960's firms (7 major, 2 minor) and the 1980's firms (3 majors, 2 minor). Thus, the concept of building and maintaining a qualified management team with the support of key employees and outside professionals cannot be emphasized enough. Again the apparent reduction in magnitude may be attributed to learning. The prevailing attitude in Silicon Valley in the eighties is one of beware of trying to do it all by yourself.

## Human Failings

This category was cited as an important cause of failure for a number of the 1960's firms (2 major, 2 minor) and was a major cause of failure for a number of the 1980's firms (3 major). Over inflated egos were explicitly identified as explanations for the human failings in the 1980's firms. Another consideration was the inability of founders to recognize their own strengths and weaknesses and act accordingly.

## One-Track Thinking

A unique category was mentioned as a minor cause of failure for one of the 1980's firms. It was explained as being the result of a narrow-minded approach to the applications of a given product by the founder and/or management team. An example of this is a firm which begins production of a particular product, but due to any one of a number of reasons, the assembly line product is not exactly the same as the prototype or it is not accepted in the marketplace as expected. The one-track thinking which is exhibited in this case is to try and force the product into the specific market for which it was originally intended even though it may be better suited to some other type of application. This problem was characterized as being analogous to trying to force a square peg into a round hole rather than trying to find the appropriate round hole.

## Cultural/Social

Another unique cause of failure was identified as a major cause of failure for one of the 1980's firms. This problem arises when a product is designed that results in a serious displacement of a work force (in this case, robots that replace human employees). The founder described a reluctance on the part of his customer base to adopt a product that was otherwise technically and economically feasible.

EXHIBIT 1

Cited Reasons For Failure of Firms Founded in 1960's

| CASE 1: | 1 | 2 | 3 | 4 | 5 | 6 | 7 | 8 | 9 | 10 |
|---|---|---|---|---|---|---|---|---|---|---|
| **PRODUCT/MARKET** | | | | | | | | | | |
| Timing | | m | | | | | | m | | m |
| Design | M | M | m | | | m | | | | |
| Distribution/ Selling | M | | | M | m | | M | m | | |
| Business Definition | | | | | | | M | | m | |
| Over-reliance on | | | | | M | M | | m | m | |
| **FINANCIAL** | | | | | | | | | | |
| Initial Under-capitalization | | | | M | M | | | | | M |
| Assuming Debt Too Early | | M | M | M | | | | | | |
| Venture Capital | | M | M | M | | M | | | | |
| **MANAGERIAL/KEY EMPLOYEE** | | | | | | | | | | |
| Ineffective Team | M | m | M | M | M | | M[1] | m | M[1] | M |
| Personal Problems | | M | | | | | m | M | | m |

[1]Team problems developed primarily after merger.

* M = major reason
* m = miner reason

384

EXHIBIT 2

CITED REASONS FOR FAILURE OF FIRMS FOUNDED IN 1980'S

| CASE #: | 1 | 2 | 3 | 4 | 5 | 6 | 7 | 8 | 9 | 10 | 11 | 12 |
|---|---|---|---|---|---|---|---|---|---|---|---|---|
| **PRODUCT/ MARKET** | | | | | | | | | | | | |
| Timing | | | M | | | | M | | M | m | M | |
| Design | | M | | | m | | | | M | M | | |
| Distribution/ Selling | | | | | M | | | | | | | m |
| Business Definition | | | | | | | | | M | | | m |
| Over-Reliance On One Customer | | m | | | | | | | | | | |
| **FINANCIAL** | | | | | | | | | | | | |
| Initial Under- Capitalization | | m | | | | | | | | | | M |
| Assuming Debt Too Early | | | | | m | M | | | | | | |
| V C Relationship | m | m | | | m | | M | | | | | |
| **MANAGERIAL/ KEY EMPLOYEE** | | | | | | | | | | | | |
| Ineffective Team | | m | M | M | | | | M | m | | | |
| Personal Problems | M | | | | M | | M | | | | | |
| One Track Thinking | | | | | | m | | | | | | |
| **CULTURAL** | | | | | | | | | | | | |
| Product Developed Not "Accepted" by customer | | | | | | | | | M | | | |

\* M = Major reason
\* m - minor reason

EXHIBIT 3

Comparative Table of Failure Research by Source

| Type of Failure Factor | Source Agenti | Altman | D & B | Buckeye, Hudson et al | Bruno Leidecker Harder (1960's) | Bruno Leidecker (1980's) |
|---|---|---|---|---|---|---|
| Problems with Management Team | * | | * | | * | * |
| Shortcomings of the Entrepreneur | * | | * | | * | * |
| Problems with Strategic Planning | * | | | | * | * |
| Weaknesses in the Finance Function | * | * | * | | * | * |
| Operating Problems | | | | | * | * |
| Market Problems | * | | | | | * |
| External Influences On Firms | * | * | | | | * |
| Unclassified Problems | | * | * | * | | * |

# REFERENCES

Altman, Edward I.  Corporate Financial Distress.  New York:  John Wiley and Sons, 1983.

Altman, Edward I., R. Haldeman, and P. Narayanan.  "ZETA" Analysis:  A New Model to Identify Bankruptcy Risk of Corporations,"  Journal of Banking and Finance, 1 (June 1977), 29-54.

Argenti, John.  Corporate Collapse:  The Causes and Symptoms.  New York:  John Wiley and Sons, 1976.

Argenti, John.  "Corporate Planning and Corporate Collapse,"  Long Range Planning, 9 (December 1976), 12-17.

Bank of America.  "Small Business Reporter:  Avoiding Management Pitfalls."  Research Paper, 1981.

Bruno, Albert V. and Arnold C. Cooper.  "Patterns of Development and Acquisitions for Silicon Valley Startups."  Technovation, Vol. 1 (1982), pp. 275-290.

Bruno, Albert V., J.K. Leidecker and J.W. Harder.  "Patterns of Failure Among Silicon Valley Firms."  Business Horizons, (forthcoming).

Buckeye, Jeanne, Roger Hudson, Anonew Van de Fen, and S. Venkaigraman.  New Business Startups, Part II;  A Process Model of Small Business Failure, Strategic Management Research Center, University of Minnesota, 1986.

Clute, Ronald C.  "An Analysis of Accounting-Related Problems in Small Business Failures."  The National Public Accountant.  Vol. 24. (December 1979), pp. 62-71).

Cooper, Arnold C. and Albert V. Bruno.  "Success Among High-Technology Firms."  Business Horizons, Vol. 20 (April 1977), pp. 16-22.

Dun and Bradstreet.  "Business Failure Record."  New York:  The Dun and Bradstreet Corporation, 1981.

Dun and Bradstreet.  "The Business Failure Record."  New York:  The Dun and Bradstreet Corporation, 1985.

Kibre, Dewit.  "Myths of Small Business Failure."  The CPA Journal, Vol. 53, (September 1983), pp. 73-74.

Marris R. and D.C. Mueller.  "The Corporation, Competition, and the invisible Hand."  Journal of Economic Literature, Vol. XVIII (March 1980).

Miller, D. "The Correlates of Entrepreneurship In Three Types of Firms." Management Science, (Vol. 29, No. 7, 1983), 770-789.

Shubash Sharma, Vijay Mahajan. Early Warning Indicators of Business Failure." Journal of Marketing, Volume 44, No. 4 (Fall 1980), pp. 80-89.

SUMMARY

## ON UNDERSTANDING BUSINESS DEVELOPMENT
## IN SMALL TECHNOLOGY-BASED COMPANIES

## Author

Magnus Klofsten

## Address

Linköping University
Department of Management and Economics
S-581 83 Linköping
Sweden
+46-13281000

## Principal Topics

The paper summarizes the results-to-date of an ongoing research of
the development process of technology-based enterprises
(techno-enterprises). The research questions are: what factors are
important for small techno-enterprises to facilitate the development
of a market platform? Which actors are important in different stages in this development process? Is it possible to distinguish
which actors are important in different stages?

## Method on Data Base

The development of concepts and models takes place in part through
longitudinal case studies, and in part through examination of
literature dealing with the subject. Empirical data have been
collected about four techno-enterprises, all of which were founded
in 1980 or thereafter. The initial studies were carried out in
early 1985 and since then roughly thirty personal interviews have
been held with entrepreneurs and other actors, who have had a decisive role in the development of the companies.

## Major Findings

The model used in this research project (see Figure 1) describes the
early development processes in a techno-enterprise. Two distinct
stages are apparent. The initial stage, called the incipient stage,
describes the development to the actual start of the venture: it
leads to the next stage, called the growth stage, which commences
with the launching of the venture, in other words, with the
materialization of the business idea, and continues with the venture's consequent growth.

FIGURE 1

A MODEL OF THE DEVELOPMENT OF A TECHNO-ENTERPRISE

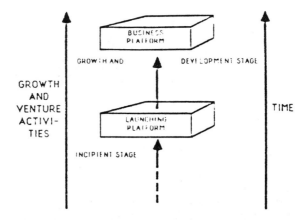

The model also distinguishes between the launching platform and the business platform. The launching platform refers to the special situation existing when the company is launched, in others words, the market situation, the accumulated know-how, the personal network of business associates, the competence of the entrepreneur, and so forth. The business platform, on the other hand, refers to a situation where a critical composite of relationships to other companies, institutions and individuals make of the characteristics of the new market. Relationships are two-dimensional. The first dimension concerns the quantity, how many relationships are necessary? The quantity criterion is directly related to the market structure and the specific nature of the product or innovation. The second dimension concerns the quality, where the content of the relationship is primary, for example, the inherent technology, development potential, contractual terms, and similar properties.

The business platform is arrived at when there is a situation where the company has set up such relationships that its market position can be regarded as secure, on the condition that it is nurtured. The techno-enterprise has attained a market position where it is no longer dependent on external boosting; it can survive of its own power.

The model starts with a situation where an individual notes a possibility to start a business venture. Since the origin of this kind of mental activity is difficult to pinpoint in time, this process is indicated by a dotted line at the bottom of the model in Figure 1. The motivating impetus which leads to action can differ. Some have to do with a recognition of opportunity, such as a desire to operate a business, make money and be one's own boss; or the individual might have discovered an unoccupied market niche, or an unexploited marketing opportunity; or might have been encouraged by friends and associates. A second type of motivating impetus has to do with resolving a negative situation, for example, an impending risk of unemployment, conflicts on the current job or a general job dissatisfaction. As the incipient stage progresses to a launching point, the entrepreneur steadily or zigzaggedly materializes his or her business ambitions. Information about the environment, the needs of the potential market and the technological opportunities will be sought out. The entrepreneur will also strive to establish contacts with actors who can be assumed to be willing to support the future development of the business venture. The initial development process will eventually culminate in the actual founding of an enterprise.

A launching platform for continued progress exists at this point. The company bears the stamp of the persons who were involved in its launching. In a best case situation, the activities intended to establish relationships with supporting actors will have resulted in an acquistion of the necessary complementary resources, such as initial customers, banking services, support from development authorities and similar resources. Business activities will thereafter be concentrated to at least two directions of business.

One direction is outward, it has to do with cultivating and maintaining established relationships and creating new ones. The other type of activity is directed inward to the internal environment; it has to do with creating a credible business plan whose contents are influenced by financial and operational needs expressed by the market and technological potential.

This business plan will be an instrument for internal control and will serve as a basis for communication with customers, vendors, financiers and other associates. This process will continue until the enterprise has sufficient resources to enable its planned expansion. The enterprise now has an inner circle of actors which provides both feedback and the necessary development resources. In other words, a business platform has been established.

# DETERMINING VENTURE CAPITALISTS' DECISION CRITERIA: THE USE OF VERBAL PROTOCOLS[1]

William R. Sandberg, University of South Carolina
David M. Schweiger, University of South Carolina
Charles W. Hofer, University of Georgia

## ABSTRACT

Previous studies have relied on interviews or questionnaires to identify and assess the importance of the criteria used by venture capitalists to evaluate new venture proposals. It is likely that these studies neither fully described the criteria nor captured their application. Two limitations stand out: (1) these studies sought non-conditional criteria and weights, whereas other research indicates that conditional propositions best predict new venture performance; and (2) they sought criteria without examining the venture capitalist's decision process, thus potentially overlooking the logic and wisdom that govern their use.

We propose using verbal protocols, one of the most useful methods for identifying decision processes and criteria. This paper reports on the use of this method in a pilot study of one venture capitalist's venture evaluation process. It identifies his criteria, compares them to those previously identified, explores the relationships among them, and discusses how verbal protocols might be used to extend our knowledge of venture capitalists' decision processes and criteria.

## INTRODUCTION

The paper describes a portion of our ongoing research on the decision processes and criteria used by venture capitalists to evaluate new venture proposals. In particular it presents the results of a pilot study that employed simultaneous verbal protocols to capture a venture capitalist's thoughts as he evaluated three proposals.

---

[1]This study is part of a research project supported by the Center for Entrepreneurial Studies, New York University.

Our immediate purposes are (1) to suggest aspects and dimensions of venture capitalists' decision making that have been neglected in previous research, and why these omissions may be significant; (2) to demonstrate the potential value of the verbal protocol method in research designed to remedy past neglect; and (3) to discuss what our pilot study reveals about one venture capitalist's decision making that could not have been captured in previous research.

## ORIGINS OF THIS STUDY

In his research on new venture performance the first author interviewed venture capitalists concerning their evaluation criteria and decision processes. The results suggested the contingent nature of many of these criteria. Specifically, both the criteria applied and the weight assigned to each criterion appeared to vary from venture to venture. Some criteria seemed virtually absolute, of course, but what a venture capitalist wanted (or would tolerate) in a venture often depended on the characteristics of its industry, the track record of its management, and its proposed business strategy.[2]

Contingent evaluation criteria have their counterpart in the contingent effects of strategy and industry structure on new venture performance. Sandberg[3] found that conditional propositions, such as "Ventures are more successful when they combine differentiation with broad scope in growth industries or with focused strategies in mature industries," are far more powerful predictors of performance than are non-conditional propositions.

Like the venture capitalist's evaluation criteria, a system of strategy propositions must be capable of prescribing actions in a broad range of situations. To do so effectively the propositions must distinguish among these situations; to do so efficiently the distinctions must isolate the determinants of performance.[4] Because venture capitalists need to make accurate evaluations while conserving their own time (typically a critical resource), their evaluation criteria probably also need to isolate the determinants of performance in diverse situations. This line of reasoning led us back to venture capitalists' criteria as a further source of wisdom on new venture performance.

---

[2]William R. Sandberg, New Venture Performance: The Role of Strategy and Industry Structure, Lexington Books, Lexington, Mass., 1986.

[3]Ibid.

[4]Charles W. Hofer, "Toward a Contingency Theory of Business Strategy," Academy of Management Journal, Vol. 18, No. 4 (December, 1975), pp. 784-810.

Unfortunately, prior research and writings have failed fully to capture and convey the richness, subtlety, and discernment embodied in venture capitalists' decision processes and criteria. Nor have they often distinguished among different types of venture capitalists, instead treating this diverse industry as a homogeneous group. Two distinct purposes have motivated prior studies. Some researchers have sought to model the management of venture capital funds or the efficiency of capital markets,[5] while others have sought to understand venture capitalists' decisions in order to aid entrepreneurs in obtaining funds.[6]

These researchers have tried to identify the criteria used by venture capitalists. Some also have tried to assess the weighting attached to each criterion. For the most part, though, these criteria have remained general or vague (e.g., "quality of management") or have revealed the end sought rather than the venture characteristics thought to advance it (e.g., "expected rate of return"). Only sometimes have they been clearly articulated. Rarely have research designs admitted the possibility that different criteria or weightings may be used to evaluate different types of ventures, industries, or entrepreneurs; rarely have the criteria been examined with respect to the different investment or portfolio strategies pursued by venture capitalists.

Early studies used research designs and methods which are incapable of fully capturing decision criteria and processes. Their interviews and questionnaires did serve to identify many criteria used by venture capitalists, but provided little basis for comparison across studies. Recent studies have converged on a common set of criteria and sharpened somewhat the understanding of how venture capitalists weigh those criteria. Nevertheless, methodological limitations weaken their usefulness. We shall examine two of the most comprehensive and sophisticated of these studies.

Few researchers have attempted to measure the criteria used in evaluating specific ventures. Tyebjee and Bruno[7] are an exception:

---

[5]For a review of such studies, see David J. Brophy, "Venture Capital Research," in Donald L. Sexton and Raymond W. Smilor, Eds., The Art and Science of Entrepreneurship, Ballinger Publishing Co., Cambridge, Mass., 1986, pp. 119-143

[6]For example, Jeffry Timmons and David Gumpert, "Discard Many Old Rules About Getting Venture Capital," Harvard Business Review, Vol. 60, No. 1 (January-February, 1982), pp. 273-280.

[7]Tyzoon T. Tyebjee and Albert V. Bruno, "A Model of Venture Capitalist Investment Activity," Management Science, Vol. 30, No. 9 (September, 1984), pp. 1051-1066.

they had 41 venture capitalists each select and report on one or more proposals which they had given "serious consideration." Each subject rated his or her proposal(s) on 23 evaluation criteria using a four-point scale. (Tyebjee and Bruno developed the criteria from the literature and their own, separate survey of 46 venture capitalists.) Subjects also evaluated the riskiness and expected returns and reported their actual decision on each proposal. A total of 90 proposals were evaluated, each solely by the venture capitalist who reported it.

Tyebjee and Bruno used factor analysis to identify five venture characteristics (comprising 21 of the 23 listed criteria) that explained 60.4% of the variation in the rating items. The characteristics are listed here in order of their importance, measured by percentage of variance explained:[8] (1) market attractiveness, which "depends upon the size, growth and accessibility of the market and on the existence of a market need"; (2) product differentiation, a combination of the entrepreneur's technical skills and the product's uniqueness, patentability, and high profit margin; (3) managerial capabilities, comprising the entrepreneur's references and his or her skills in management, marketing, and finance; (4) environmental threat resistance, or the venture's protection against obsolescence, down-side risk, economic cycles, and subsequent entrants; and (5) cash-out potential, reflecting the venture capitalist's ability to liquidate the investment.

Each proposal's average scores on these five characteristics were regressed on expected return and perceived risk. Expected return was related primarily to market attractiveness and secondarily to product differentiation (both positive); perceived risk was related primarily to managerial capabilities and secondarily to resistance to environmental threats (both negative). Cash-out potential was not significantly related to either assessment.

Tyebjee and Bruno's findings were a major research contribution because they established key characteristics in replicable form. We were interested, too, in the prominence of strategy-related criteria, which were the essence of market attractiveness and resistance to environmental threats and were the major part of product differentiation. Yet we could not prudently accept the criteria ratings or rankings because of several methodological limitations.

First, their 41 respondents evaluated 90 proposals, an average of 2.2 apiece. As a result, the criteria weights of some venture capitalists were counted more heavily than others simply because they submitted more proposal evaluations. Assuming a respondent uses a consistent set of criteria and applies them consistently to all proposals he or she evaluates, unequal sample representation can bias results. The contrary assumptions (inconsistent criteria, inconsistently applied) also pose a problem: they suggest a contingent evaluation process, a possibility not accomodated in Tyebjee and Bruno's research design.

---

[8]Ibid., p. 1059.

Second, each proposal was evaluated by only one participant. If criteria or their application vary from one proposal to another, a participant's responses become a function of the proposal as well as of the participant. Without common proposals in the set, one cannot assess the extent to which this may have occurred.

Third, all evaluations were reported retrospectively. Tyebjee and Bruno acknowledged the possibility of "post-hoc rationalization of the decision" to invest or not to invest.[9] Other possible errors or biases in retrospective reporting of decisions and decision processes are summarized by Huber and Power.[10] They include the perceptual and cognitive limitations of people, such as limited recall and a tendency to reconstruct the past in terms of their "espoused theories" of how they make decisions.

A study by MacMillan, Siegel, and Subba Narasimha represents a more recent, comprehensive examination of venture capitalists' criteria.[11] Using a two-stage research design, they first developed a list of 24 criteria classified under five headings: (1) entrepreneur's personality, (2) entrepreneur's experience, (3) product characteristics, (4) market characteristics, and (5) financial considerations.[12] Then their questionnaire elicited responses from 100 venture capitalists who rated the importance of each criterion on a four-point scale.

It is noteworthy that the highest level of importance on this scale was "essential," meaning a venture would not be funded if it did not satisfy that criterion. (Our review has not uncovered prior research that permitted the identification of noncompensatory (essential) criteria. Yet any such criteria are central to a venture capitalist's decisions.) MacMillan et al. identified the ten criteria most frequently described as "essential" and found that six involved the entrepreneurs themselves. Further analysis revealed the ten most deadly combinations of flaws -- that is, criteria pairs that would combine to disqualify a proposal from consideraton. In each instance at least one of the two criteria related to the entrepreneur's personality or experience.

---

[9]Ibid., p. 1055.

[10]George P. Huber and Daniel J. Power, "Retrospective Reports of Strategic-level Managers:  Guidelines for Increasing their Accuracy," Strategic Management Journal, Vol. 6, No. 2 (April, 1985), pp. 171-180.

[11]Ian C. MacMillan, Robin Siegel, and P.N. Subba Narasimha, "Criteria Used by Venture Capitalists to Evaluate New Venture Proposals," Journal of Business Venturing, Vol. 1, No. 1 (Winter, 1985), pp. 119-128.

[12]A sixth set of statements called for respondents to select the one essential characteristic of a venture team from a list of three, plus "none of the above."

A factor analysis yielded six factors that explained 60.2% of the variance in criteria ratings. Although competitive risk was most important, it was the only factor readily interpretable as essentially product-or market-related. Bail out risk related mainly to financial prospects; investment risk combined the entrepreneur's attention to detail and track record with the market's growth rate and the prospect of a 10 year return of 10 times the investment; management risk include the entrepreneur's handling of risk, capacity for intense effort, and familiarity with the market. Implementation risk comprised a functioning prototype, demonstrated market acceptance of the product, and the entrepreneur's articulateness in discussing the venture. Finally, leadership risk consisted solely of the entrepreneur's demonstrated leadership ability.

Contrary to Tyebjee and Bruno, then, MacMillan et al. reported a strong corroboration of the conventional wisdom regarding the dominant role of the entrepreneur's characteristics in influencing venture capitalists' decisions. They concluded that a business plan's content concerning product, market, and competition was "necessary, but not sufficient."[13] It is less apparent to us, however, that the entrepreneur emerges so clearly from several of their factors. In particular, investment risk and implementation risk contained significant elements of product and market considerations as well as entrepreneurial characteristics.

MacMillan et al. investigated the differences among venture capitalists' criteria. A cluster analysis enabled them to address areas of doubt created by earlier research design and methodological limitations. They found three broad types of venture capitalists: purposeful risk managers, 40% of the sample, who seek "entrepreneurs with demonstrated leadership skills" and risk-reducing product/market characteristics; determined eclectics, one-third of the sample, who seem deliberately to impose a minimum of restrictions on what ventures they will consider; and parachutists, one-quarter of the sample, who seem willing to invest as along as their exit will be easy.[14]

While the researchers' interpretations of the clusters are interesting and quite plausible, their greatest contribution to the field is their verification of significant differences among the criteria weights espoused by different venture capitalists. Whether these differences are enacted in investment decisions remains an open question that MacMillan et al. say will be tested in a later study. Another open question is whether the respondents vary their criteria or weightings according to the circumstances of a specific venture.

Other researchers have addressed some of the issues raised in this discussion of the two principal studies. Robinson sought to enhance the "understanding of venture capital activity as an 'industry'"

---

[13]MacMillan et al., op. cit., p. 119

[14]Ibid., pp. 127-128

by analyzing its structural context, the operant strategic assumptions of its participants, and the strategies of individual firms.[15] He also examined evaluation criteria through respondents' weightings of 15 items describing the company, product, environment, and entrepreneur or team. Factor analysis produced five factors: the management team, the fit between management's technical skills and the industry's requirements, the venture's resource needs versus the personal skills and motivation of its management, the venture's financial history, and professional references. Despite identifying several dimensions along which venture capital firms are becoming more diverse, Robinson concluded that "an increasingly differentiated...industry will remain virtually uniform in their fundamental deal evaluation criteria."[16] This conclusion must be regarded as informed speculation on his part, however, as he did not establish uniformity in current criteria. And to the extent that the industry becomes more heterogeneous, as Robinson expects, the strategies of its participants (and hence their venture evaluation criteria) should become more heterogeneous as well.

Indeed subsequent analysis of Robinson's data has indicated that different criteria weights are used by different groups of venture capitalists.[17] Among the differences were these: less experienced venture capitalists emphasized high growth potential while more experienced ones emphasized a capable venture management; corporate or institutional funding disposed venture capitalists to seek earlier exit opportunities than were sought by venture capitalists who relied on private funding; venture capitalists who spend little time assisting their investees seek stronger organizational/managerial skills than do those who devote substantial time to management assistance. These and other differences noted by the researchers[18] suggest the existence of strategic groups within the venture capital industry. While further analysis is required to delineate such groups with confidence, the evidence seems sufficient to establish that venture capitalists are not a homogeneous group and that their criteria weights are one aspect of difference among them.

Consensus Findings and Common Limitations of Recent Research

Despite certain important differences among their findings, the three principal studies (Tyebjee and Bruno, MacMillan et al., Robinson)

[15]Richard B. Robinson, Jr., "Emerging Strategies in the Venture Capital Industry," Journal of Business Venturing, Vol. 2, No.1 (Winter, 1987), p. 55.

[16]Ibid., p. 73.

[17]Frank L. Winfrey, Richard B. Robinson, Jr., and John A. Pearce II, "Criteria for New Venture Investment Across Different Strategic Groups Within the Venture Capital Industry," unpublished paper, 1987.

[18]Ibid.

share fundamental agreement and limitations. The most important area of consensus is the identity of venture capitalists' criteria. MacMillan et al. noted the close parallels between their six factors and the five identified by Tyebjee and Bruno, and Robinson likewise found that criteria differed "very little" from Tyebjee and Bruno's.[19] Both Robinson and MacMillan et al. differed from the earlier study, however, by reporting that the entrepreneur (or team) outweighed product/market characteristics in venture capitalists' decisions. Robinson and MacMillan et al. both found evidence of diversity among respondent firms, reflected in their own strategies and in how they applied their evaluation criteria.

In describing these three studies we have detailed some limitations in research design and method that prevent them from conclusively identifying the criteria and weightings used by venture capitalists. These included unequal influence of respondents and problems of retrospective reporting (Tyebjee and Bruno), and the use of questionnaire responses rather than actual evaluations (MacMillan et al., Robinson).

Each study also is vulnerable to the conscious and unconscious errors and biases that may accompany self-reporting. As MacMillan et al. noted, respondents may be influenced to make what they believe to be desirable responses.[20] An additional problem is present in self-reports on decision criteria, however. Other researchers have found that self-reporting tends to overstate the number of criteria actually used and to understate the weighting of the most important criteria.[21] Venture capitalists frequently state that "the entrepreneur" or "management" accounts for most of their decision, yet self-reported criteria weights show many criteria involved and none truly dominant. The abundance of significant criteria in self-report surveys is consistent with the aforementioned tendency to overstate the number of criteria used. One wonders, are venture capitalists more accurate chroniclers of their decision criteria, or might they too rely on only a few criteria in practice?

Finally, none of the cited research directly examined the decision process, a broader concept that involves both the criteria and how and when they are applied. To the extent that those studies attempted to address issues of process, they inferred process from outputs.[22] Decision researchers note the shortcomings of this approach:

> It is gradually becoming clear that human decision making cannot be understood by simply studying final decisions. The perceptual, emotional and cognitive processes which ultimately lead to the choice

---

[19]Robinson, op. cit., p. 73.

[20]MacMillan et al., op. cit., p. 122.

[21]Michael J. Stahl and Thomas W. Zimmerer, "Modeling Strategic Acquisition Policies: A Simulation of Executives' Acquisition Decisions," Academy of Management Journal, Vol. 27, No. 2 (June, 1984), pp. 369-383.

of a decision alternative must also be studied if
we want to gain an adequate understanding of human
decision making.[23]

By studying the processes that lead to venture capitalists'
decisions, one might uncover evidence of several interesting phenomena.  For example, the sequences in which information is sought
and criteria are applied could reveal venture capitalists' priorities and possible tradeoffs among criteria.  Prevalent patterns in
information seeking could guide the organization and presentation
of material in business plans, too.  Tradeoffs might point to areas
an entrepreneur could bolster to offset a less readily corrected
weakness.  Greater understanding of the decision processes also could
enable identification of noncompensatory (i.e., essential) criteria
and of the conditions governing contingent criteria or weightings.

In the remainder of this paper, we will explain how simultaneous verbal protocols might overcome these shortcomings and report
on our pilot study using this approach.

SIMULTANEOUS VERBAL PROTOCOLS

Researchers have used simultaneous verbal protocols to trace
the processes involved in investment trust decisions, strategic decisions, the design of management information systems, and other problem-
solving and decision-making activities.[24]  Simultaneous verbal protocols are transcripts of individuals' conscious thought processes.[25]
This methodology commonly involves asking subjects simply to "think
aloud" while solving a problem or making a decision.  Typically their

---

[22]Researchers sometimes use an "input-output" approach to infer
decision processes.  Although this approach has serious limitations, it
is more effective than the use of outputs alone.  None of the studies
discussed herein measured or controlled for inputs (i.e., proposed ventures), so none could be termed an input-output study.  Instead, each
studied only self-reported criteria or decisions on unspecified, non-
standard ventures.

[23]O.Svenson, "Process Descriptions of Decision Making,"
Organizational Behavior and Human Performance, Vol. 23 (1979), p. 86

[24]For further examples and citations, see David M. Schweiger,
"Is the Simultaneous Verbal Protocol a Viable Method for Studying
Managerial Problem Solving and Decision Making?" Academy of Management
Journal, Vol. 26, No. 1 (March, 1983), pp. 185-192.

[25]The following explanation is based on David M. Schweiger, Carl
R. Anderson, and Edwin A. Locke, "Complex Decision Making:  A Longi-
tudinal Study of Process and Performance, "Organizational Behavior and
Human Decision Processes, Vol. 36 (1985), pp. 245-272.

verbalizations are tape-recorded, transcribed, and then content analyzed via some coding scheme devised for the specific research questions. Coded protocols have been used in both exploratory and hypothesis testing research and appear to be "an accurate and unobtrusive methodology" for studying managerial decision making at the individual level.[26]

The usefulness of verbal protocols depends on the validity of the reports given by the subjects. As with any self-report research methodology, subjects may not provide valid responses. Ericsson and Simon[27] have specified the conditions under which verbal reports are most likely to be accurate: (a) the information to be reported is the focus of attention; (b) the task or cognitive processes are not highly routinized through habit or repetition; (c) only a short time elapses between performance and verbalization; (d) verbalization does not require excessive encoding (i.e., processing, reconceptualizing, interpretation, inference, etc.); (e) reports are oral; (f) subjects are free from cognitive overload and distractions; (g) the questions and instructions are clear and specific; (h) completeness in reporting is encouraged.

The deliberations of a venture capitalist, tape-recorded as he evaluates a proposal for the first time, closely approximate these ideal conditions. Certainly the venture capitalist focuses on evaluating the proposal and the cognitive processes are not highly routinized; simultaneous recording enables oral reporting and eliminates any time lag. Verbalization requires no encoding beyond what the venture capitalist normally and freely does, provided no attributions, categorization, or other mental processes are specifically required. Venture capitalists normally isolate themselves long enough to read a proposal and limit interruptions during that time. Finally, clear and specific instructions and complete reporting are relatively easy to ensure in this instance. Therefore the verbal protocol is an appropriate method for studying the venture capitalist's decision process.

A PILOT STUDY

As part of a broader investigation of venture capitalists' decision processes, we have performed a pilot study using simultaneous verbal protocols for one venture capitalist as he evaluated three venture proposals. Our purpose in this pilot study, of course, was not to reach final conclusions as to the decision processes and criteria used by venture capitalists. Rather, we sought to determine the practicability and potential value of this methodology to entrepreneurship and venture capital research. Thus our "findings" really are indications

---

[26]Schweiger, op. cit., p. 190.

[27]K.A. Ericsson and H.A. Simon, "Verbal Reports as Data," Psychological Review, Vol. 87 (1980), pp. 215-251.

of what verbal protocols can reveal that would not have been captured in previous research.

## Subject and Methodology

The subject was a general partner in an SBIC that had made more than a dozen investments in the 5+ years since its founding. Most of these investments had been first-stage or seed capital financings. The SBIC's total portfolio value and typical investment size placed it somewhat (but not substantially) below the average for venture capital firms.[28]

Two of the authors visited the subject in his office and spent 15 minutes briefing him on the purpose of this study and instructing him on "thinking aloud" and complete reporting. They did not mention any hypotheses or opinions on the research topic, nor did they discuss entrepreneurs or new ventures in any form. By prearrangement the venture capitalist had saved three proposals that had reached him during the previous few days. The researchers gave him a tape recorder and left his office, returning only after he had completed his evaluation of all three proposals. At that time, they interviewed him for about 25 minutes, asking specific questions about his firm's investment policies, internal workings, and similar matters that will be of interest in their broader research.

Transcripts of the tape-recorded verbalizations were coded according to a scheme jointly developed by the authors, using previous research to guide their choice of categories. Each "thought unit" (a single idea expressed by the venture capitalist) was assigned to a category that described its subject matter. It was also identified as being either an examination of the plan or a reflection on its contents, and placed sequentially in the overall process. The assignments and placements were arrived at through discussion by two of the authors.

## Results

The venture capitalist's decision process with respect to one venture is represented in Figure 1. The thought units are arranged in sequence, as indicated by the arrows connecting them. Each thought unit is placed beneath a column heading that describes the information it sought or the evaluation it made. Most of the headings are self-explanatory, but a few require comment. ACTION refers to units that are not related to any one category, but involve the venture capitalist's initiation of the process or his overall conclusions and plans for further action. GENERAL USE OF FUNDS refers to how the proceeds of the financing deal would be used, while THE DEAL refers to the pricing and structuring of the financing. ADEQUACY OF THE PLAN refers to the document's content, organization, style, format, etc. (The headings of empty columns on each page are omitted.)

---

[28]Because we have promised confidentiality and are presenting only one venture capitalist's protocols, we cannot describe him any more precisely or completely.

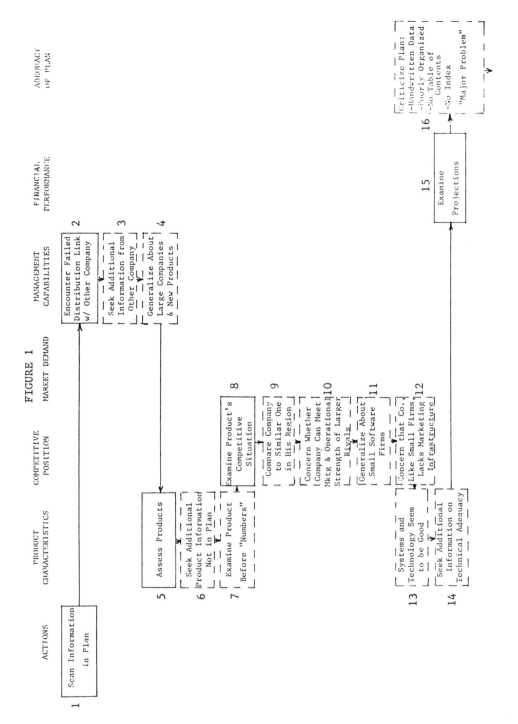

FIGURE 1

| ACTIONS | PRODUCT CHARACTERISTICS | COMPETITIVE POSITION | MARKET DEMAND | MANAGEMENT CAPABILITIES | FINANCIAL PERFORMANCE | ADEQUACY OF PLAN |

1 Scan Information in Plan

2 Encounter Failed Distribution Link w/ Other Company

3 Seek Additional Information from Other Company

4 Generalize About Large Companies & New Products

5 Assess Products

6 Seek Additional Product Information Not in Plan

7 Examine Product Before "Numbers"

8 Examine Product's Competitive Situation

9 Compare Company to Similar One in His Region

10 Concern Whether Company Can Meet Mktg & Operational Strength of Larger Rivals

11 Generalize About Small Software Firms

12 Concern that Co. Like Small Firms Lacks Marketing Infrastructure

13 Systems and Technology Seem to be Good

14 Seek Additional Information on Technical Adequacy

15 Examine Projections

16 Criticize Plan:
-Handwritten Data
-Poorly Organized
-No Table of Contents
-No Index
"Major Problem"

403

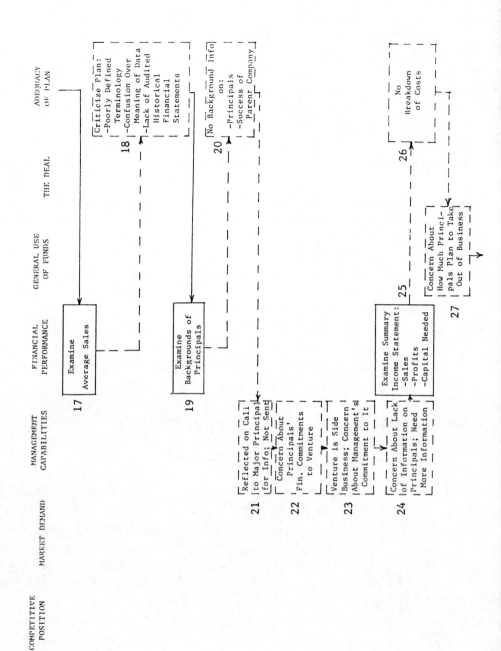

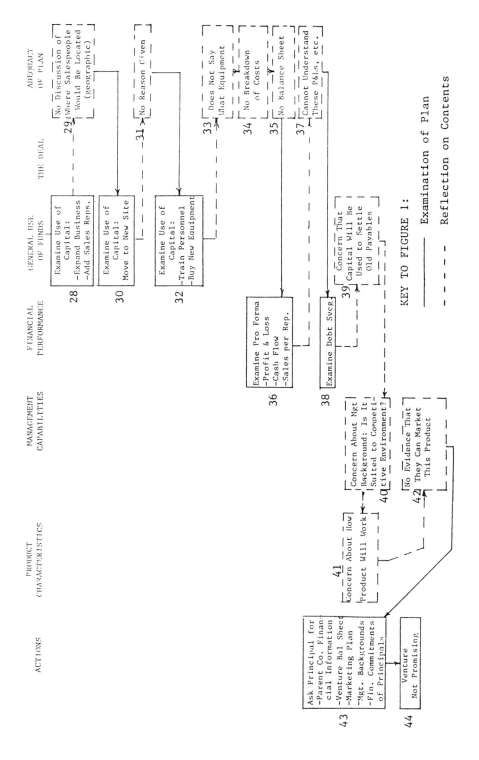

405

The sequence of thoughts reveals several interesting aspects of his decision making. Early on we see conscious choices to examine the product (#5) and to continue doing so before "the numbers" (#7). This decision led him to consider the venture's competitive position (#8), with thought given to a similar company in the area (#9) and to his own, experience-based theories about the marketing and operational disadvantages of smaller companies (#10-12). He returned to specific consideration of the product (#13-14) before examining the financial projections (#15).

This sequence, deliberately undertaken, suggests a desire to establish a context for assessing the financial projections. We believe it also provided a basis for assessing management capabilities. Although the venture capitalist did not articulate this purpose, he made the mental link some time later (#40 and #42). Even if a venture capitalist does not consciously assign top priority in his overall evaluation to the product and competitive position, we believe his early impressions of the venture's feasibility may influence his subsequent evaluations of management capabilities.

In this instance we sense the venture capitalist's mounting skepticism of those capabilities. He rather severely criticized the business plan's organization and presentation (#16 and #18) just before examining the backgrounds of the principals (#19), and immediately noted the absence of these data (#20) despite his specific request that they be included (#21). There followed three more reflections on management capabilities, including repeated concern over the lack of data (#24). Nearing the end of his evaluation, the venture capitalist returned to the issue of management capability in the specific venture context (#40 and #42).

Without denying the impact of management capabilities on this venture capitalist's decision, we note the prominence of strategic and financial evaluations and reflections in this protocol. Of 44 thought units, 11 related to strategy (product, competition, and market) and 10 to financial performance or use of funds. At the very least, these units established the venture context, as recounted above. It is possible that they played a far greater role in this venture capitalist's evaluation. (Space does not permit discussion of his other protocols, but our preliminary analyses indicate similarly important roles for strategic and financial considerations.)

## Conclusions

Examining decision processes, rather than merely criteria, is vital to capturing venture capitalists' wisdom. This pilot study has demonstrated the potential richness of data available through simultaneous verbal protocols. In our next stage of research, we are collecting various data on the participants and are using a standard set of venture proposals to permit identification of decision process differences attributable to (1) differences among ventures and (2) different strategies or practices among venture capitalists.

Brophy, David J., "Venture Capital Research," in Donald L. Sexton and Raymond W. Smilor, eds., The Art and Science of Entrepreneurship, Ballinger Publishing Co., Cambridge, Mass., 1986, pp. 119-143.

Ericsson, K.A. and H.A. Simon, "Verbal Reports as Data," Psychological Review, Vol. 87 (1980), pp. 215-251.

Hofer, Charles W., "Toward a Contingency Theory of Business Strategy," Academy of Management Journal, Vol. 18, No. 4 (December, 1975), pp. 784-810.

Huber, George P. and Daniel J. Power, "Retrospective Reports of Strategic-level Managers: Guidelines for Increasing their Accuracy," Strategic Management Journal, Vol. 6, No. 2 (April, 1985), pp. 171-180.

MacMillan, Ian C., Robin Siegel, and P.N. Subba Narasimha, "Criteria Used by Venture Capitalists to Evaluate New Venture Proposals," Journal of Business Venturing, Vol. 1, No. 1 (Winter, 1985), pp. 119-128.

Robinson, Richard B., Jr., "Emerging Strategies in the Venture Capital Industry," Journal of Business Venturing, Vol. 2, No. 1 (Winter, 1987), pp. 53-77.

Sandberg, William R., New Venture Performance: The Role of Strategy and Industry Structure, Lexington Books, Lexington, Mass., 1986.

Schweiger, David M., "Is the Simultaneous Verbal Protocol a Viable Method for Studying Managerial Problem Solving and Decision Making?" Academy of Management Journal, Vol. 26, No. 1 (March, 1983), pp. 185-192.

Schweiger, David M., Carl R. Anderson, and Edwin A. Locke, "Complex Decision Making: A Longitudinal Study of Process and Performance," Organizational Behavior and Human Decision Processes, Vol. 36 (1985), pp. 245-272.

Stahl, Michael J. and Thomas W. Zimmerer, "Modeling Strategic Acquisition Policies: A Simulation of Executives' Acquisition Decisions," Academy of Management Journal, Vol. 27, No. 2 (June, 1984), pp. 369-383.

Svenson, O., "Process Descriptions of Decision Making," Organizational Behavior and Human Performance, Vol. 23 (1979), pp. 86-112.

Timmons, Jeffry and David Gumpert, "Discard Many Old Rules About Getting Venture Capital," Harvard Business Review, Vol. 60, No. 1 (January-February, 1982), pp. 273-280.

Tyebjee, Tyzoon T. and Albert V. Bruno, "A Model of Venture Capitalist Investment Activity," Management Science, Vol. 30, No. 9 (September, 1984), pp. 1051-1066.

Winfrey, Frank L., Richard B. Robinson, Jr., and John A. Pearce II, "Criteria for New Venture Investment Across Different Strategic Groups Within the Venture Capital Industry," Academy of Management, New Orleans, 1987.

SUMMARY

VENTURE CAPITAL IN WESTERN EUROPE

Author

Tyzoon T. Tyebjee
Lister Vickery

Addresses

Leavey School of Business
Santa Clara University
Santa Clara, CA 95053
(408) 554-4716

European Institute of Business Administration
INSEAD
77305 Fontainebleau
Cedex, FRANCE

Principal Topics

A comparative analysis of venture capital flows in ten Western
European countries. The level of activity is related to four
characteristics of the country environments, namely culture, size of
technology sector, financial markets and government incentives to
risk capital.

Method and Data Base

The study is descriptive and relies on secondary sources of data.

Major Findings

Venture capital though a growing institution in Europe is still
relatively small by American standards. Where it has thrived,
namely in France, Netherlands and the United Kingdom it has been
accompanied by strong fiscal incentives or loss guarantees, a viable
stock market for new companies and a cultural legitimacy for the
business entrepreneur.

Major Implications

Many countries are captivated by the spectacular success of venture
capital in the United States. If a country wishes to develop venture
capital, it must develop an environment conducive to attracting this

type of investors. This means measures to provide fiscal advantages and loss guarantees to prime the pump, a secondary stock market which accommodates the needs of small companies, and public information programs which reinforce the role of the business entrepreneur as a valuable economic force.

SUMMARY

HOW VENTURE CAPITALISTS VALUE
ENTREPRENEURIAL COMPANIES

Author

    James L. Plummer

Address

    QED Research, Inc.
    125 California Avenue, Suite 200
    Palo Alto, CA 94306
    (415) 321-9827

Principal Topics

Venture capitalists must value companies every day, but almost none has tried to write down how they do it. Venture capital has been an "apprenticeship industry." The only way to learn it has been by working for or with an old hand in the industry. However, many of the old hands are a little shy on financial analysis skills. With the venture capital field growing so fast, there is a need for a compilation of the rules of thumb in common use in the industry. There is also a need to try to reconcile those rules of thumb with modern financial analysis techniques. Academic literature contains some excellent work on evaluation criteria used by venture capitalists, but nothing on valuation itself.

Method and Data Base

This paper describes a small portion of the results of two surveys of venture capitalists that were carried out in 1986. These results form a part of a forthcoming book entitled QED Report on Venture Capital Financial Analysis: Valuation, Pricing, Performance, and Risk Management (QED Research, Inc., 1987).

Major Findings and Implications

The methods used to value normal growth closely-held companies focus either on the tangible assets of the company, or on the stream of future earnings of the company over many years. These methods do not work for valuing entrepreneurial companies with high growth potential because entrepreneurial companies are idea-based and growth-based rather than asset-based companies. This paper begins by describing the differences between valuation of high growth entrepreneurial companies and valuation of normal growth companies.

Summary descriptions are given of the three most popular valuation methods used by venture capitalists: 1) the conventional VC valuation method, 2) the First Chicago method, which is a simplified decision analysis approach, and 3) the revenue multiplier method, including a potential refinement in this method.

THE INFORMAL VENTURE CAPITAL MARKET:
ASPECTS OF SCALE AND MARKET EFFICIENCY

William E. Wetzel, Jr., University of New Hampshire

## ABSTRACT

The informal venture capital market, the market in which entrepreneurs raise equity-type financing from private investors (business
angels) is virtually invisible. Data drawn from existing research support the inference that private investors manage a venture investment
portfolio aggregating in the neighborhood of $50 billion. The "typical"
angel-backed venture appears to raise about $250,000 from three or more
private investors. The data also support the conclusion that the informal venture capital market is handicapped by the high cost of information by many investors' unfamiliarity with the techniques of venture
financing. The paper concludes with a discussion of Venture Capital
Network, Inc., an experimental effort to enhance the efficiency of the
informal venture capital market.

## INTRODUCTION

Entrepreneurial ventures require access to capital, venture capital in particular. Consequently, the performance of the venture capital markets is a matter of concern to entrepreneurs and to venture investors. These concerns extend to issues of public policy in a society
that increasingly depends upon entrepreneurs and venture investors for
its economic vitality.

The market for venture capital consists of three major segments:

* the public equity market,

* the professional venture capital market, and

* the market for informal venture capital.

The public equity market and the professional venture capital
market are visible, efficient, and well understood. The informal venture
capital market on the other hand, is often misunderstood. It is composed
of a virtually invisible population of individual investors who provide
equity-type financing for entrepreneurial ventures of all types, including those that ultimately raise funds from professional venture
investors or the public equity market.

Despite their low profile, wealthy individuals (business angels) appear to represent the largest venture capital resource in the United States. There are, however, compelling reasons to believe that the high cost of information about investors and investment opportunities, and limited familiarity with the techniques of successful venture investing, constrain the flow of informal venture capital.

Unanswered questions about the market for informal venture capital include the number and characteristics of individual venture investors, the size of the capital pool they control, the intensity of their interest in venture investing, the investment decision models they employ, the number and characteristics of the ventures they finance, the size and structure of their investment transactions, the performance of their portfolios, the relative efficiency of the informal venture capital market, and the extent of regional differences in the market for informal venture capital. Scattered pieces of data suggest the answers to some of these questions.

The following discussion deals with two issues: the scale of the informal venture capital market and market efficiency. The discussion draws on existing research to extract and synthesize data that provide a reasonable basis for inferences about scale and efficiency. The paper concludes with a discussion of Venture Capital Network, Inc. (VCN), an experimental effort to enhance the efficiency of the informal venture capital market.

## SCALE ESTIMATES: SUPPLY-SIDE INDICATORS

A sense of the scale of the informal venture capital market provides the background for addressing other questions. Readers who are uncomfortable with inferences drawn from limited data, data that are at best suggestive, will be uncomfortable with the following discussion. Better data do not exist.

The supply side of the informal venture capital market is composed of a diverse and diffuse population of individuals of means, many of whom have created their own successful ventures. For discussion purposes, individual venture investors (business angels) are defined as follows:

1) Net worth over $1 million and annual income over $100 thousand.

2) Substantial business and financial experience.

3) Capable of evaluating the merits and risks of prospective investments.

4) Unaffiliated with portfolio ventures, i.e., excludes founders, friends, and relatives.

5) Willing to take substantial financial risks to earn substantial returns.

6) Willing to commit funds for extended periods to earn substantial returns.

There are no directories of individual venture investors and no public records of their investment transactions. Despite the lack of hard data, clues to the scale of informal venture investing can be found.

## Millionaires & Mega-Millionaires

U.S. News and World Report reported that the U.S. population included 833,000 millionaires at the end of 1985, and that the number would exceed one million by the end of 1986. (1) Based on these figures, millionaires comprise less than 1/2 of 1 percent of the United States population. The net worth of ninety-five percent of U.S. millionaires is between $1 million and $10 million. The following excerpts from the article are pertinent to a discussion of informal venture capital:

"The typical millionaire is a self-made entrepreneur in his early 60s - fewer than 10 percent are under 40. He works 10 or 12 hour days and, more frequently than not, his business caters to the ordinary needs of ordinary Americans."
******
"The average annual income of millionaires is $121,000, of which three fourths comes from earned income"
******

"Eighty percent of American millionaires come from middle or working-class families."
******

"In fact, 85 percent of America's millionaires own their own business or a share in a private company."
******

---

(1) U.S. News & World Report, January 13, 1986

Case in point:  Samuel Moore Walton, Bentonville, Arkansas, claimed by Forbes (2) to be the wealthiest individual in the United States, opened a discount store with his brother James in Rogers, Arkansas in 1962.  He now operates 950 Wal-Mart stores.  Walton Enterprises, the family investment company, is valued at $4.5 billion.

The Forbes Four Hundred (3) richest people in America represent a combined net worth of about $156 billion.  Their average net worth is $390 million and the net worth of the 400th mega-millionaire is $180 million.  Compared to 80 percent of all millionaires who apparently are self-made, only 44 percent (174) of the Forbes Four Hundred built their fortunes without benefit of a significant inheritance.  The six wealthiest individuals on the Forbes list are all self-made and represent a combined net worth in excess of $14 billion.

In a study of consumer finances, Avery and Elliehausen (4) found that the net worth of 1.3 million U.S. families (almost 2%) is at least $1 million.  According to their data, most wealth is saved out of accumulated earnings, not inherited.  The wealth, income, and asset distribution of the top one percent of U.S. households (840,000 families) are displayed in Table I and provide an approximation of the potential supply of informal venture capital.

(2)  Forbes, October 27, 1986
(3)  Ibid
(4)  Robert B. Avery & Gregory E. Elliehausen, "Financial Characteristics of High Income Families," Federal Reserve Bulletin, March, 1986

TABLE I

WEALTH, INCOME, AND ASSET DISTRIBUTION OF U.S. HOUSEHOLDS

| | Top 1/2% | Next 1/2% |
|---|---|---|
| Number of Households | 420,000 | 420,000 |
| Net Worth (millions) | >$2.5 | $1.4 - $2.5 |
| Family Income (thousands) | >$280 | $150 - $280 |
| Percent owning non public business - no management interest (3% of all families) | 46% (193,200) | 28% (117,600) |
| Mean holding of owners | $621,279 | $263,437 |
| Mean percent of assets for owners | 14% | 10% |

Based on the data in Table I, 311,000 families (37% of the top 1% of U.S. households) have invested $151 billion in nonpublic businesses in which they have no management interest. The nature of these investments was not discussed by the authors. If one third could be described as venture financing, existing informal venture investments are in the neighborhood of $50 billion. Credence is provided to this inference by Avery and Elliehausen's data describing attitudes toward financial risk and liquidity of the "super rich" (top 1/2%) and the "very rich" (next 1/2%). These data are displayed in Table II.

## TABLE II

### ATTITUDES TOWARD FINANCIAL RISK AND LIQUIDITY

|  | Top 1/2% | Next 1/2% |
|---|---|---|
| **Financial Risk** | | |
| Take substantial financial risk to earn substantial return (6% of all families) | 10% | 5% |
| Take above-average financial risk to earn above-average return (11% of all families) | 34% | 36% |
| **Liquidity** | | |
| Tie up money for long term to earn substantial return (12% of all families) | 26% | 22% |
| Tie up money for intermediate term to earn above-average return (26% of all families) | 47% | 56% |

Based on stated attitudes toward risk and liquidity and the fact that the top one percent of U.S. households have invested over $150 billion in nonpublic businesses in which they have no management interest it is not unreasonable to believe that venture-type financing in the portfolios of the top one percent may be at least $50 billion.

## Informal Risk Capital in the Sunbelt

Research conducted by Applied Economics Group, Inc. (AEG) (5) provides further clues to the supply of informal venture capital. AEG examined how and where small firms in SBA Regions III, IV, and VI obtain equity capital for start-up and growth. Regions III, IV, and VI include Delaware, District of Columbia, Maryland, Pennsylvania, Virginia, and West Virginia; Alabama, Florida, Georgia, Kentucky, Mississippi, North Carolina, South Carolina, and Tennessee; and Arkansas, Louisiana, New Mexico, Oklahoma, and Texas respectively.

(5) Robert J. Gaston & Sharon Bell, Informal Risk Capital in the Sunbelt, Applied Economics Group, Inc., Knoxville, TN, 1986.

417

AEG estimated that Regions III, IV, and VI contain 99,000 informal venture investors. In a typical year 68,700 of these individuals provide equity capital to entrepreneurial ventures, an average of one $38,000 investment every eighteen months for each investor. The annual dollar value of these investments totals $2.6 billion, ten times the capital invested in these regions by venture capital firms. AEG's data indicate that informal investors extend another $2.5 billion to portfolio firms in the form of loans and loan guarantees. The typical firm in AEG's sample raised $220,500 of equity and near-equity financing, typically from three informal investors.

Since Regions III, IV, and VI represent 28.6 percent of the U.S. population, extrapolation suggests that there are about 345,000 informal venture investors in the United States, an inference not inconsistent with Avery and Elliehausen's data. AEG estimates the median net worth of informal investors at $750,000 and their median family income at $70,000. According to AEG's data, informal investors commit some 10-24 percent of their net worth to venture investments. If there are 345,000 informal venture investors in the U.S. with an average net worth of $750,000, and with 10-24 percent of their net worth available for venture investments, the aggregate informal venture capital pool is between $25 billion and $62 billion.

SCALE ESTIMATES: DEMAND-SIDE INDICATORS

The demand side of the informal venture capital market is almost as elusive as the supply side. The ventures funded by individual investors appear to fall into two broad categories. The first includes technology-based inventors and start-up firms of all types requiring less than $1 million of seed capital. A few of these ventures survive and grow fast enough to become substantial companies in a short period of time, five years or less. These "high potential" ventures typically attract second and third round financing from professional venture capital firms before being acquired by a larger company or undertaking a public stock offering.

The second category is made up of established, privately-held firms that are growing faster than internal cash flows and retained earnings can support. Seldom can even the most profitable firms rely exclusively on retained earnings when growth rates exceed twenty percent per year. The most dynamic small firms are growing at annual rates exceeding 100 percent. Between 1980 and 1984, sales growth for the Inc. 500 Fastest-Growing Private Companies (6) averaged 94 percent per year.

_____

(6) Inc., December, 1985

## Small Technology-Based Firms

Indications that self-made individuals play an important role in the financing of both categories of ventures can be traced at least back to the 1960s. Baty (7) found that wealthy individuals were the largest source of capital for new, technology-based companies. Baty found that individual investors were not only more likely to supply initial risk funds than venture capital organizations, but were likely to supply them on more liberal terms. He also discovered that initial investors in new, research-based enterprises were predominantly affluent individuals, and that those who were "self-made" tended to be more venturesome than those with inherited wealth. Self-made investors tended to invest in the industries in which they had made their wealth.

Brophy (8) examined sources of financial support for new, technology-based firms incorporated and operating from 1965-1970. In a sample of Boston-area firms, Brophy found that "private individuals" (excluding founders, friends, and relatives) provided 14.3% of total financing and "SBICs and private venture capital firms" provided 15.1%. Regional differences were evident in Brophy's data. Figures for a sample of Ann Arbor/Detroit firms were 15.7% and 2.3% respectively.

Charles River Associates (CRA) (9) examined the composition of external funds received by small, technology-based firms making initial public offerings from 1970 to 1974. CRA found that "unaffiliated individuals" accounted for 15% of external funds while "venture capitalists" accounted for 12%. When the data were segmented by stage (age of venture), CRA found that unaffiliated individuals provided 17% of external funds during the start-up year, while venture capitalists provided 11%. CRA excluded "individuals" who act informally as providers of venture funds from their examination capital market imperfections. Yet CRA speculated that "they may represent the largest source of venture capital in the country."

(7)    Gordon Baty, Initial Financing of the New Research-Based Enterprise in New England, Federal Reserve Bank of Boston, Boston, MA, 1964
(8)    David T. Brophy, "Venture Capital Research," Encyclopedia of Entrepreneurship, Prentice-Hall, Englewood Cliffs, N.J., 1982
(9)    Charles River Associates, Inc., An Analysis of Capital Market Imperfections, prepared for the Experimental Technology Incentives Program, National Bureau of Standards, Washington, DC, 1976

## Start-up Ventures

Shapero's study (10) of the initial financing of new ventures in Columbus, Ohio and Louisville, Kentucky sheds more light on the characteristics of angels. Shapero collected data from thirty-three private individuals who had made investments in start-up or very young companies. Shapero found that individuals most likely to invest in new ventures were those who had "made it themselves," first generation money. He also found that the decision to consider an investment is highly related to personal knowledge of the business field or the entrepreneur, or a high regard for the third party who brought the investment opportunity to the investor for review.

## SEC Data

Two reports prepared by the Securities & Exchange Commission (11) (12) support the conclusion that individual investors are a significant source of risk capital. Corporate private placements reported to the SEC in 1981 under Rule 146 exceeded $1 billion. A sample of Form 146 filings revealed that corporate issuers were engaged primarily in high technology or in other manufacturing or nonfinancial services. They were generally young companies employing few workers. Eighty-seven percent of the investors in corporate issues were individuals or personal trusts. Note that Rule 146 data exclude offerings exempt from filing because of their intrastate nature (Rule 147) or financing by closely held firms under small offering exemptions (Rules 240 and 242.)

On April 15, 1982, Regulation D replaced the exemptive provisions of Rules 146, 240, and 242. Issuers claiming exemption under Regulation D during its first year offered $15.5 billion of securities in over 7,200 filings. Corporations accounted for 43 percent of the value ($6.7 billion) and 32 percent of the offerings (2,304). Under Rule 504 of Regulation D (limited offerings under $500,000), 1,103 corporations reported offering securities totalling $220 million. The typical corporate issuer under Rule 504 had five or fewer employees (60.7%) and an operating history of two years or less (68.8%).

---

(10) Albert Shapero, The Role of the Financial Institutions of a Community in the Formation, Effectiveness and Expansion of Innovating Companies, Shapero-Huffman Associates, Columbus, OH, 1983.
(11) U.S. Securities and Exchange Commission, Report of the Rule 146 Exemption in Capital Formation, Washington, D.C., 1983.
(12) U.S. Securities and Exchange Commission, An Analysis of Regulation D, Washington, D.C., 1984.

Drawing on the data cited above, some simple mental exercises suggest the scale of the informal venture capital pool. If the average net worth of millionaires is between $1 million and $2 million, then, excluding borrowed funds, the total wealth controlled by the one million or more U.S. millionaires is between $1 trillion and $2 trillion. If the average millionaire commits 10 percent of his or her net worth to venture investing, the total informal venture capital pool is between $100 and $200 billion. If only one fourth of U.S. millionaires have any interest in venture investing, the pool of informal venture capital controlled by these 250,000 individuals lies in the $25 to $50 billion range, about twice the capital managed by professional venture investors.

It appears that each year over 100,000 individual investors finance between 20,000 and 50,000 firms for a dollar investment totalling $5 billion and $10 billion. The typical firm financed by angels raises about $250,000 from three or more investors. The typical investor provides between $25,000 and $50,000 per firm, about half in the form of equity and half in near-equity (loans and loan guarantees). During 1985 professional venture investors financed about 2,500 firms for a total of about $2.5 billion, an average of about $1 million per firm.

## CAPITAL MARKET EFFICIENCY

Perceptions that gaps exist in the equity markets serving entrepreneurs led to passage of the Small Business Investment Act of 1958. The Act created the Small Business Investment Company (SBIC) program. Though capital gaps have never been documented convincingly, perceptions of gaps endure, at least in the minds of entrepreneurs. Perceived capital include product development financing for technology-based inventors, start-up financing for ventures that fail to meet the size and growth criteria of professional venture investors, and equity financing for closely held firms that are growing faster than internal cash flows can support.

Research documenting entrepreneurs' perceptions of capital gaps include work by Obermayer (13) and Wilson (14). Recent efforts to deal with the gap include the Small Business Investment Incentive Act of 1980, the Small Business Innovation Development Act of 1982, and the SEC's Regulation D.

---

(13) Judith H. Obermeyer, The Capital Crunch: Small High-Technology Companies and National Objectives During a Period of Severe Debt and Equity Shortages, Research & Planning, Inc., Cambridge, MA, 1983.
(14) Ian G. Wilson, Financing High Growth Companies in New Hampshire, Department of Resources and Economic Development, State of New Hampshire, Concord, N.H., 1984.

The capital gap folklore is based upon the observable behavior of financial institutions, including SBICs and professional venture capital firms. However, the folklore overlooks the investment record of informal venture investors - business angels. Angels not only exist, they tend to invest in precisely the areas perceived as gaps in the capital markets for entrepreneurs. For an expanded discussion of angel financing see Wetzel (15) (16).

Despite the apparent size of the informal venture capital pool, the effect of capital gaps can be created when markets fail to function efficiently. Modern financial theory rests on assumptions of efficient markets - markets in which information about sources of funds and about investment opportunities is fully and freely available to buyers and sellers of capital. The evidence suggests that this necessary condition is far from fulfilled in the angel segment of the venture capital markets. In the absence of efficient markets, capital cannot flow from less productive to more productive investment opportunities.

"At the heart of free market systems is the issue of whether or not prices accurately reflect all the information necessary for scarce resources to be efficiently allocated among an infinite variety of alternative and competing uses." (17)

Bean, Schiffel and Mogee (18) found little support for assertions that technological innovation by new/small firms is impeded by an inadequate supply of capital. However, they noted that the majority of venture capital firms do not fund start-up companies, a pattern that still prevails. Venture Capital Journal (19) reported that thirteen percent of the funds disbursed by all venture capital firms in 1985 were "seed" or "start-up" investments. Seed and start-up investments represented 12.6 percent of Venture Magazine's (20) November, 1986 Index of Venture Capital Activity. One of Bean, Schiffel and Mogee's observations is worth quoting.

(15) William E. Wetzel, Jr., "Angels and Informal Risk Capital," Sloan Management Review, Summer, 1983.
(16) William E. Wetzel, Jr., "Informal Risk Capital: Knowns and Unknowns," The Art and Science of Entrepreneurship, Ballinger Publishing Co., Cambridge, MA, 1986.
(17) J. Fred Weston & Thomas E. Copeland, Managerial Finance, 8th ed., Dryden Press, Hinsdale, IL, 1986.
(18) A. S. Bean, D. Schiffel, & M. E. Mogee, "The Venture Capital Market and Technological Innovation," Research Policy, Vol. 4, 1975.
(19) Venture Capital Journal, February, 1986.
(20) Venture, November, 1986.

"The issue of little knowledge of the venture capital/new technological enterprise is multifaceted. Entrepreneurs and potential entrepreneurs seem to need better information on financial sources while capital suppliers seem to need better information on new-venture/technological investment opportunities." (21)

The CRA study also found "no evidence of substantial market imperfections that restrict the flow of funds to small, technology-based firms." Recall, however, that CRA excluded from their study of capital market imperfections "individuals who act informally as providers of venture funds." Despite their conclusions, CRA made the following point:

"It is not clear whether the existing system for generating and disseminating information about investment opportunities is efficient. In other words, it is not clear whether it could be improved in a cost-effective manner." (22)

Networks and Market Efficiency

Data describing the channels through which information about opportunities for investment in new/small companies is transmitted to individual investors can be found in several studies. Without exception, cite the dominant role of informal networks of trusted friends and business associates in the referral process.

Early in the development of the venture capital industry in the United States, Rubenstein (23) found that private investors were more dependent on informal networks than were large venture capital institutions.

"The fraternity of individual backers of small businesses appears to be rather close knit, at least on a local level. A good deal of information is passed about by word of mouth. If one investor who enjoys considerable prestige among his associates, believes a situation to be promising and recommends it to others, his friends may participate merely on the basis of his recommendations ...."

---

(21) Bean, Schiffel, & Mogee, op. cit.
(22) Charles River Associates, Inc., op. cit.
(23) A. H. Rubenstein, Problems of Financing and Managing New Research-Based Enterprises in New England, Federal Reserve Bank of Boston, Boston, MA, 1958.

The significance of a respected lead investor in attracting the participation of associates was evident in a case study of the Taplin & Montle Development Fund, an informal association of individual investors in the Boston area (24). The work of Baty (25) and Shapero (26) also document the catalytic role played by respected lead investors.

The importance of informal venture investment networks was cited by the Panel on Venture Capital of the U. S. Department of Commerce Technical Advisory Board (27). The Panel reported that they:

> ".... became increasingly aware of an informal network of people, institutions, and relationships that are significant in the process of financing new enterprises."

> ".... it is apparent that the network does not operate with the same degree of effectiveness in every geographic region of the country."

Subsequent research has documented both the significance of informal networks and regional differences in the effectiveness of these For example, Hoffman (28) explored the process by which individual investors identify, evaluate, and structure investments in new, small companies. Data were collected from thirty-nine investors in Waco and Austin, Texas. Hoffman found that friends and business associates referred more new and small companies to these investors than any other source. He also found that differences in the venture capital investment process between more developed and less developed areas relate more to the dynamics of the local venture capital networks than to the absolute availability of venture capital, the number of venture capitalists, the opportunities to invest, or the absolute propensity to invest. Shapero 29 also found that the nonexistence of investor networks was an important difference between communities in the propensity to invest.

---

(24) William E. Wetzel, Jr., "The Taplin & Montle Development Fund: A Case Study in Finance," Frontiers of Entrepreneurship Research, Babson College, Wellesley, MA, 1983
(25) Baty, op. cit.
(26) Shapero, op. cit.
(27) Financing New Technological Enterprise, Report of the Panel on Venture Capital, Commerce Technical Advisory Board, U. S. Department of Commerce, Washington, D.C., 1970
(28) Cary A. Hoffman, The Venture Capital Investment Process: A Particular Aspect of Regional Economic Development, unpublished Ph.D. dissertation, The University of Texas, Austin, TX, 1972.
(29) Shapero, op. cit.

In a study of informal risk capital in New England, Seymour and Wetzel (30) collected data from one hundred thirty-three individual investors who fit the description of business angels. These investors reported risk capital investments totalling over $16 million in 320 ventures between 1976 and 1980, an average of one deal every two years for each investor. The average size of their investments was approximately $50,0C0, while the median size was about $20,000. Sixty percent of their investments represented participations with other individuals in larger transactions.

Fifty-two percent of the New England sample cited "business associates as a frequent source of investment opportunities, fifty percent cited "friends," and forty-one percent cited "active personal search." The next most common source, "investment bankers," was cited as a frequent source by fifteen percent of the sample. All other sources, including business brokers, commercial bankers, attorneys, and accountants were insignificant. Since individual investors tend to found in clusters, these data may understate the significance of professional intermediaries in the referral process. While most investors learn of investment opportunities from friends and business associates, the typical opportunity may be introduced to one member of the cluster by a banker, broker, attorney, or accountant.

New England investors "totally dissatisfied" with existing channels of communication between entrepreneurs and individual investors outnumbered "definitely satisfied" investors by over four to one. Fifty-eight percent expressed a "strong interest" in a service that would direct investment opportunities to their attention. Thirty-eight percent expressed a "moderate interest" in such a service.

In their Sunbelt study, AEG (31) found that informal investors' most common and reliable sources of investment information were friends and business associates. One third of the Sunbelt investors were dissatisfied with information channels currently available. The average investor wanted to invest 83 percent more than he did but could not find sufficiently attractive opportunities. Given sufficient opportunities, funds available from investors in the three regions would total about $9 billion per year. Extrapolated to the United States, the total would exceed $30 billion annually.

---

(30) Craig R. Seymour & William E. Wetzel, Jr., Informal Risk Capital in New England, prepared for the Office of Advocacy, U. S. Small Business Administration, University of New Hampshire, Durham, N.H., 1981.
(31) Gaston & Bell, op. cit.

Krasner and Tymes (32) replicated the Seymour and Wetzel study (33) in the San Francisco Bay area. Data were collected from forty-one tors, thirty of whom were private individuals and eleven were professional venture capitalists. California investors relied upon the same informal network of friends and business associates for most of their investment opportunities. However, sixty-one percent of the California investors were either "definitely satisfied" or "basically not totally satisfied" with the effectiveness of existing channels of communication between entrepreneurs and investors. Only twenty-eight percent of New England investors shared those opinions.

## VENTURE CAPITAL NETWORK - AN EXPERIMENT IN CAPITAL FORMATION

Perceptions of the scale and inefficiency of the informal venture capital market, combined with the significance of entrepreneurial ventures to the vitality of the U. S. economy in general and the New England in particular, prompted the formation of Venture Capital Network, Inc. (VCN). VCN is a not-for-profit corporation managed by the Office of Small Business Programs of the University of New Hampshire. VCN's essential purpose is to introduce entrepreneurs to individual venture investors and to venture capital firms interested in early-stage financing. VCN places no geographic restrictions on its services.

VCN is neither an investment advisor nor a broker-dealer of securities, and has received the appropriate "no-action" letters from the SEC. VCN provides only an information service for entrepreneurs and investors. VCN neither evaluates nor endorses the merits of investment opportunities presented through its services. VCN conducts no investigations to verify the accuracy or completeness of information provided by entrepreneurs and investors. VCN reports to entrepreneurs the reasons cited by investors for rejecting their investment proposals.

From the inception of operations in July, 1984 through June, 1986, VCN arranged in excess of one thousand introductions for over two hundred entrepreneurs from thirty states and over three hundred investors from thirty-three states. VCN maintains no systematic contact with clients once introductions have been concluded. However, at least seven entrepreneurs are known to have raised funds from VCN investors.

(32) O. J. Krasner & Eleanor R. Tymes, "Informal Risk Capital in California," Frontiers of Entrepreneurship Research, Babson College, Wellesley, MA, 1983.
(33) Seymour & Wetzel, op. cit.

Financial support for VCN has been provided by the Business and Industry Association of New Hampshire, the University Center for Technical Assistance, the U. S. Economic Development Administration, the Ellis L. Phillips Foundation, and a group of sponsoring organizations. Sponsors include Deloitte Haskins & Sells; Peat, Marwick, Mitchell & Co.; Price Waterhouse; and the Shawmut Bank of Boston, N.A.

## VCN Entrepreneurs and Investors

Entrepreneurs most likely to benefit from participation in VCN require between $50,000 and $750,000 of equity-type financing. They are often referred by VCN by accountants, attorneys, bankers, and venture capitalists. Entrepreneurs are required to submit an Executive Summary of their business plan when they register with VCN. Over 90 percent of the ventures seeking financing through VCN are under five years old.

VCN investors are primarily affluent individuals. Seed capital venture funds represent about one fifth of VCN's investor clients. VCN clients are required to certify that they are accredited investors as defined in Rule 501 of the SEC's Regulation D (Rules Governing the Limited Offer and Sale of Securities Under the Securities Act of 1933) or that they have such knowledge and experience in financial and business matters that they are capable of evaluating the merits and risks of prospective investments, as specified in Rule 506 of Regulation D.

## VCN Counterparts

VCN provides assistance to not-for-profit organizations replicating VCN outside New England. Through September, 1986 working relationships had been established with the Indiana Institute for New Business Ventures, Inc. the State University of New York at Plattsburgh, St. Louis University, the Atlanta Economic Development Corp., Northern Michigan University, the Ontario, Canada, Chamber of Commerce, the Kenan Institute for Private Enterprise at the University of North Carolina, and the Technology Commercialization Center at Northwestern University.

Additional groups exploring the creation of VCN counterparts are located in Arkansas, Minnesota, Mississippi, New Jersey, Oregon, South Carolina, Texas, Washington, Wisconsin, and Wyoming. Ultimately VCN expects to establish VCN-International, a service that will link regional networks, thereby contributing to the efficiency of the international market for informal venture capital.

## Lessons from VCN's First Two Years

VCN is still an experimental project. While early results are encouraging, it can scarcely be claimed that VCN has had a major impact on the flow of informal venture financing in New England. Several lessons are emerging. First, VCN's experience confirms the diverse and diffuse nature of the informal investor population. Informal venture investors are tough to reach. Second, new concepts do not sell themselves. They need to be explained, often on a face-to-face basis. Where this had occurred participation tends to follow. Third, building a track takes time. But performance builds the credibility and awareness that in turn lead to spreading interest. VCN's second two years are expected to be significantly more productive than its first. Fourth, the intensity of an individual's interest in venture investing appears to be dependent in part upon the investor's familiarity with the techniques of successful venture investing, as well as upon the availability of opportunities. Venture investing is not a full-time occupation for informal investors. Learning the tricks of the trade takes time and time is scarce. Faced with more familiar alternatives, otherwise qualified venture investors may pass up opportunities to back entrepreneurs. This dimension of market efficiency was not anticipated when VCN was launched. During its second two years VCN will experiment with a variety of methods to overcome this perceived obstacle. Much has been learned during VCN's first two years. Overriding the lessons is the conclusion that VCN's original premises are still sound.

## CONCLUSION

The informal venture capital market poses many unanswered questions. Issues of scale and market efficiency have been addressed in this paper. The available data suggest that the informal venture capital market is twice the size of the professional venture capital market. The number of ventures financed by informal investors appears to be at least ten times the number of ventures financed by professional venture capital firms.

Market efficiency is a more difficult issue to address. Limited information about investors and investment opportunities appears to be a significant obstacle to the financing of particular types of entrepreneurial ventures. The flow of informal venture capital appears to be further constrained by unfamiliarity with the techniques of successful venture investing on the part of entrepreneurs and potential informal investors. If VCN and its counterparts endure as sulf-sufficient enterprises it will demonstrate that market efficiency can be improved in a cost-effective manner. That fact alone would confirm the inefficiency of the random process that currently brings entrepreneurs and investors together. Gaps between private and social rates of return from innovation justify public as well as private efforts to enhance capital market efficiency, especially efforts directed at entrepreneurial ventures where the gaps are greater than for large firms.

Of equal significance, the survival of VCN and its counterparts will provide an international roster of informal venture investors. With this unique data base in hand, other unanswered questions can be addressed: questions about the characteristics of business angels, the investment decision models they employ, the characteristics of the ventures they finance, the structural characteristics of their venture investments, the performance of their portfolios, and questions concerning regional differences in the informal venture capital markets.

SUMMARY

THE STRUCTURE OF THE INVESTMENT NETWORKS
OF VENTURE CAPITAL FIRMS

Authors

William D. Bygrave

Address

Tomasso 224
Babson College
Babson Park
(Wellesley), MA 02157
(617) 239-4567

Principal Topics

Venture capital firms are linked together in a network by their
joint investments in portfolio companies.  Through connections in
that network, they exchange resources with one another.  The most
important of those resources are the opportunity to invest in a
portfolio company (good investment prospects are always scarce), the
spreading of financial risk, and the sharing of knowledge.  This
paper examines the structure of the networks formed by the joint
investments of venture capital firms in portfolio companies.
Theoretical models are developed for those networks.  Actual networks are compared with those models.

Method and Data Base

The joint investments of 464 venture capital firms in 1501 portfolio
companies were examined.  The venture capital firms were classified
according to the degree of technological innovativeness of their
portfolio companies, the number of companies in their portfolios,
and the state in which their head office was located.  Sociograms
were developed for the top 21 venture capital firms investing mainly
in high innovative technology companies and for the top 21 firms
investing mainly in low innovative technology companies.  The
intrastate networks and the interstate networks are presented and
compared.

It is a privilege to thank Venture Economics for its collaboration
on this project.

## Major Findings

It was found that the top 21 venture capital firms investing mainly in high innovative technology companies (HIVCs) comprise a tightly coupled network. And of that group, none is more tightly bound than the 9 HIVCs located in California. In contrast, the group of top 21 firms that invest mainly in low innovative technology companies (LIVCs) is more loosely bound. It is reasoned that HIVCs are more tightly bound together because they shoulder more uncertainty and therefore have a greater need to share information with one another. Furthermore, it is reasoned that the HIVCs in California are more tightly bound together than the HIVCs in the Northeast because there is a higher concentration of HIVCs in California (a finding that is predicted by the resource exchange model).

The pattern of the network of HIVCs is quite different from that of LIVCs. Whereas the HIVCs are clustered along coastal corridors in California and the northeast, with lots of coast to coast links, the LIVCs are more evenly distributed across the U.S.A. in general, the empirical findings are consistent with the predictions of the models for intragroup and intergroup networks.

## Major Implications

Venture Capitalists. It is vital to be well-connected to other venture capital firms. They are important sources of information and investment opportunities. For HIVCs, the California group is central in the network, so links to them are valuable. Communications in a tightly-coupled system are swift, so it is likely that information is disseminated very quickly among members of the group. It probably facilitates the setting of a "market rate" for venture capital. A disadvantage of a tightly bound system is that information flowing among the members has a redundancy and sameness about it, so to ensure a supply of fresh information members should have as many links as possible to other organizations and individuals other than venture capitalists.

Entrepreneurs. When entrepreneurs submit a proposal for funding to venture capital firms, they can assume that news will spread fast to other firms. Thus, they should not use a "bird-shot" approach, rather they should select their targets with the "rifle" precision. The proposal should be submitted to a few firms that are known to specialize in the type of product or service that the entrepreneur is planning to make. Entrepreneurs should be concerned about more than the price of the deal. When top 61 firms invest in portfolio companies, they bring information, contacts, and "deep pockets" to those companies. Those factors are significant in nurturing a growing company.

Policy Makers. The networks of HIVCs and LIVCs are quite different. The HIVCs cluster around oases of high-technology entrepreneurship in the northeast and California, where as the LIVCs are more evenly spread throughout the U.S.A. There is a relationship between the so called "bi-coastal regions of prosperity" and the location of HIVCs. Innovative entrepreneurship, of the sort that HIVCs invest in, is crucial to economic growth. That is not to say that HIVCs cause economic growth, but they are an essential ingredient.

This study found cliques among the venture capital firms. But it found no evidence that the top 61 venture capital firms exclude other venture capital firms from their coinvestments of first-rounds of capital. More research is needed before conclusions can be drawn about the power and influence of the top firms.

SUMMARY

## THE ROLE OF BANKERS IN START-UP
## AND EARLY STAGE VENTURES

Authors

    Roger W. Hutt
    Barry L. Van Hook

Address

    Department of General Business
    College of Business
    Arizona State University
    Tempe, AZ 85287
    (602) 965-3229

Principal Topics

The paper examines the business relationship that exists between
entrepreneurs and the bankers who lend them money.

Method and Data Base

Personal interviews were conducted with a representative of each of
nine banks headquartered in the Phoenix, Arizona metropolitan area.
Two of the banks has a single location, while in addition to their
home offices, seven banks operated a combined total of 363 branches
throughout the state.

Major Findings

Finding of the study are presented as answers to the following
questions:

1.    How does the relationship between the entrepreneur and the
    banker begin?  The entrepreneur-banker relationship is most
    frequently initiated through referral from such professionals
    as certified public accountants and attorneys and from mutual
    acquaintances.

2.    In addition to loans, what assistance (both formal and infor-
    mal) does the banker provide to the entrepreneur?  The types of
    assistance mentioned most frequently were introduced to poten-
    tial customers and suppliers, help obtaining additional
    financing, and help with planning, forecasting, or budgeting.

3. How do bankers rate various aspects of the business opportunity? Bankers in the study assigned their highest ratings to experience of the management team, market description, and the demand for the product or service. Other highly rated factors were the founding team's recognition of its own weaknesses, the proposed use of the proceeds, and the composition of the venture's investor group.

4. How do bankers view the entrepreneurial environment in Phoenix? Respondents ranked the following environmental helps one through five in terms of importance: market contacts, supplier assistance, capable local advisors, capable local manpower, and technical education. These same environmental helps were also ranked in the top five positions in Phoenix, however, the exact rank order differed from that of the ranking according to importance. Market contacts, for example, was ranked first in terms of importance, but second in the degree it is present in Phoenix.

## Major Implications for Practitioners

An implication of the study is that entrepreneurs should be aware that bankers prefer to have new borrowers referred to them. Also, when selecting a lending institution, entrepreneurs should determine if various informal services, such as introducing borrowers to potential customers, are provided.

## Major Implications for Future Reseach

Future studies of the entrepreneur-banker relationship should examine bankers' understanding and perceptions of start-ups and early stage expansions in specific industries.

SUMMARY

# FINANCING NEW VENTURES:  A LIFE CYCLE MODEL

## Authors

Rein Peterson
Joel Shulman

## Addresses

York University
North York, Ontario M3J1P3
(416) 736-5091

Babson College
Wellesley, MA 02157
(617) 239-4436

## Principal Topics

Our paper examines financial capital structures of new and/or
smaller ventures using a large international data base.  We propose
a corporate capital structure life cycle model which takes into
account the size of a growing firm, the preferences of its owners,
agency costs, and the prevailing economic climate.

## Method and Data Base

Our data base consists of 4,400 small firms from 12 countries with
firms ranging in size from 0-100 employees.  Six of the countries
can be considered developed (Canada, Japan, Netherlands, United
Kingdom, United States and West Germany), and six countries can be
considered less developed (Brazil, Cameroon, Colombia, Indonesia,
Keyna, and Spain).

## Major Findings

Most new ventures in our study appear to be initially dependent on
relatives/friends and personal equity for expansion and working
capital needs.  As these firms become more established they are able
to rely more heavily on venture capital and traditional sources of
bank debt for financial support.  Informational asymmetries, as part
of Agency Cost theory, help explain why financial institutions may
be reluctant to lend funds to new ventures without detailed formal
information (such as financial statements).  Furthermore, total
costs of available funds for new ventures (including direct and
indirect costs) are presumed to be quite high.

Liquidity levels for young firms are hypothesized to be lowest in between stages II and III of our model. This finding is true for all countries included in our sample. However, we note that our sample of U.S. small ventures were able to acquire bank debt at an earlier stage than firms in less developed countries. Finally, we conclude that, in general, new small business ventures do not, and should not, have equal access to bank financing because of the agency and transaction costs which we have outlined.

DURATION OF THE COMPARATIVE ADVANTAGE ACCRUING
FROM SOME START-UP FACTORS IN HIGH-TECH ENTREPRENEURIAL FIRMS[1]

Jérôme Doutriaux, University of Ottawa
Farhad Simyar, University of Ottawa

## ABSTRACT

Past studies of technology-based entrepreneurial firms have shown the effect of a number of start-up factors on the growth and success of the firm: past managerial experience, similarity of products or markets with those of the previous employer of one of the founders, start-up financing, to name just a few. This paper reports on the duration of the effect of some of these factors on the development of the entrepreneurial firm: do they have a permanent effect, or does the comparative advantage that they confer to the firm fade away after two, four or more years? This study is based on the start-up and growth characteristics of 73 high-tech firms, located in various parts of Canada, founded between 1965 and 1980 by one or several entrepreneurs in the microelectronics, communication and related fields.

## INTRODUCTION

Technology-based entrepreneurial firms have been singled out as a special class of small businesses because they have shown a higher potential for growth and job creation and a lower disappearance rate than other small firms[2]. They also tend to be more innovative than larger companies in the same fields[3]. And, being "knowledge

---

[1]This research project is funded by grant from the Social Science and Humanities Research Council of Canada. The views and opinions expressed in this paper are those of the authors and not necessarily endorsed by the granting agency.
This study owes much to the hard work and dedication of Colleen Bigelow, B.A., MBA.

[2]Doutriaux, J., "Evolution of the Characteristics of (High Tech) Entrepreneurial Firms", Frontiers of Entrepreneurship Research Conference, Babson College, 1984, page 368.

[3]Cooper, A., "Rand D is more efficient in small companies", Harvard Business Review, June 1984.

industries", they are considered very important from an economic point of view in Canada because of their potential for shifting the country's orientation from a natural resource base to a technology base.

High tech entrepreneurial firms have, however, not behaved according to commonly known and previously established characteristics of other small firms. The short product life cycle, limited financial entry barrier, strong and increasing competition in the international arena, and the vast sums of funds spent on innovativeness and research and development by the multinationals and their parent countries, have produced a highly volatile, competitive and turbulent environment for these firms.

The start-up process and early growth of high tech entrepreneurial firms has been extensively researched both in Canada and abroad. Of particular interest has been the identification of the special factors, characteristics, conditions which seem to contribute to success: past experience of the founders, number of founders, start-up financing, special links with the previous employer of one of the founders, type of technology and type of market, to name just a few. Potential entrepreneurs, established enterprises venture capitalists, government agencies, have shown a lot of interest in these studies which provide an empirical base of knowledge for the development of new ventures and the establishment of policies supportive of the new venture creation process.

This research project builds upon the existing knowledge base to assess empirically the duration of the effect of some of the start-up factors on the development of the entrepreneurial firm: do they have a permanent effect, or does the comparative advantage that they confer to the firm fade away after two, four or more years? The study is based on the start-up and growth characteristics of 73 high tech firms founded between 1965 and 1985 by one or several entrepreneurs in the microelectronics, communications or related fields, and located in various regions of Canada.

After a short review of the literature on "success factors", the data-base on which this project is based will be described. The analysis of the time-phased effect of some start-up factors will then be given.

### START-UP FACTORS AND SUCCESS - SOME BACKGROUND WORK

A number of studies have examined the underlying factors which may contribute to the success of technologically-oriented entrepreneurial firms. These factors are related to the choice of business, start-up characteristics, and operational characteristics during the initial growth period of the firm. Vesper[4] has shown that the choice of busi-

---

[4]Vesper, K.H., New Venture Strategies, Englewood Cliffs, N.J.: Prentice Hall, 1980.

ness is likely the most important determinant of success. And a number of researchers have shown the effect of the R&D and technology strategy, marketing effort, growth of assets and financial strategy on the operations of the firm[5]. Of interest here, however, are the actual conditions at start-up which may provide an a-priori comparative advantage to the new firm.

One of the first studies of start-up factors was done ten years ago by Cooper and Bruno[6]. They found that successful entrepreneurial high tech firms had multiple founders whose skills were complementary and who provided each other with psychological support. They also found that the founders of successful firms entered markets and utilized technologies similar to those of their previous employers. In addition, the greater the size of the founders previous organization, the greater the success of their new firm. These results were confirmed by a number of researchers. In particular, Lamont[7] showed that previous entrepreneurial experience was a definite asset, Tyebjee and Bruno[8] and Roberts[9] found that lower levels of start-up capital were related to subsequent lower sales, and Litvack and Maule[10] noted that initial public sector contracts were instrumental in steering firms in a successful path. The importance of marketing and financial management skills has also been noted[11].

---

[5]See for example, Litvak, I.A., and C.J. Maule, "Successful Canadian Entrepreneurship and Innovation, Six Case Studies", and T.T. Tyebjee and A.V. Bruno, "A Comparative Analysis of California Start-ups from 1978 to 1980", both at Frontiers of Entrepreneurship Research Conference, Babson, 1982, and W.E.Wetzel and I.G. Wilson, "Seed Capital Gaps: Evidence from High Growth Ventures", Frontiers of Entrepreneurship Research Conference, Babson, 1985.

[6]Cooper, A.C., and A.V. Bruno, "Success Among High Technology Firms, Business Horizon, April 1977, pp. 16-22.

[7]Lamont, L.M., "What Entrepreneurs Learn from Experience", in Entrepreneurship and Venture Management, C.M. Baumback and J.R. Mancuso Eds, Prentice Hall, 1975, pp. 254-260.

[8]Tyebjee and Bruno, op.cit.

[9]Roberts E.B. and H.A. Wainer, "Some characteristics of Technical Entrepreneurs", IEEE Transactions on Engineering Management, vol. EM-18, No 3, 1971.

[10]Litvak and Maule, op.cit.

[11]Oakey, R., High Technology Small Firms, St. Martin's Press, New York, 1984.

Recent studies of the effect of start-up factors[12] have tried to measure in a systematic manner the embodied characteristics of an innovation, a market, a young firm and its founders. These studies tend to confirm previous results and propose more precise measurements of some of the start-up characteristics which have just been listed. Our study, however, will make direct use of these former characteristics.

Thus far, we have explored various causes of success investigated by researchers without defining what success means. The literature on definition of success of entrepreneurial small firms in high-technology innovations sector is very rich. Success has been measured by various variables, indicating different dimensions of quantitative and qualitative yardsticks of performance. Litvack and Maule[13] view the success of an entrepreneurial high tech firm merely as its survival after the initial five years of operations. E.B. Roberts[14] states that "survival is not the same as success"; he describes success as growth, sales, profitability and the like. Cooper and Bruno[15] distinguish successful firms from the unsuccessful ones on the basis of sales growth rate. Tyebjee and Bruno[16] and Doutriaux[17] used the level of sales achieved as a measure of success. Weiss[18] considered four ratios to measure success. These were year-by-year comparisons of sales growth ratios, profit to sales ratios, return on investment ratios and investment intensity ratios. On the other hand, Dunkelberg and Cooper[19] used the growth rate in employment as a measure of success. It is apparent from the above survey that these yardsticks of success are simple dimensional or at best non-exhaustive of potential success measures. Stuart and Abetti[20],

---

[12]Stuart, R. and P.A. Abetti, "Field Study of Start-up Ventures, Part II: predicting initial success", Frontiers of Entrepreneurship Research Conference, Babson College, 1986, p. 21.

[13]Litvack, I.A. and C.J. Maule, "Entrepreneurial Success or Failure, Ten Years Later", Business Quarterly, Winter 1980.

[14]Roberts, E.B., "How to Succeed in a New Technology Enterprise", Technology Review, December 1970, p. 22.

[15]Cooper A.C. and A.V. BRuno, op.cit.

[16]Tyebjee and Bruno, op.cit.

[17]Doutriaux, op.cit., and Doutriaux, J., Growth Pattern of Academic Entrepreneurial Firms, Working Paper 86-56, Faculty of Administration, University of Ottawa, 1986.

[18]Weiss, L.A., "Start-up Business: A Comparison of Performance", Sloan Management Review, Fall 1981.

[19]Dunkelberg, W.C. and A.C. Cooper, "Pattern of Small Business Growth", Academy of Management Proceedings, 1982, pp. 409-413.

[20]Stuart and Abetti, op.cit.

in their study of 24 new technical US ventures, have tackled the question of success in a more comprehensive manner. They use the following four different dimensions to view success:

1 - Subjective versus objective, i.e. judgement versus cash flow.

2 - Bimodal, multimodal versus continuous, i.e. a yes or no category versus relative category such as return on investment.

3 - Financial versus non-financial, i.e. profitability ratios versus contribution to society.

4 - Meeting or not meeting expectations, i.e. expectation and goals set by management whether conservative or challenging.

None of these researchers have used the usual financial and accounting ratios to evaluate the effectiveness and efficiency of young firms. Even if these ratios are extremely useful when evaluating established businesses, they are difficult to use and to interpret in the case of very young firms because of the lack or poor definition of financial and accounting data, and because these ratios are impractical to evaluate the dynamics of a rapidly changing firm.

We are currently conducting a research project on some measures of success of technology-based firms. This project is not completed yet; in the meantime, we will use the annual level of sales as a measure of success, in spite of its shortcomings, in evaluating the efficiency and technical soundness of a new firm.

DATA COLLECTION PROCESS

The purpose of this study is to examine the duration of the effect of some of the start-up factors of high tech entrepreneurial firms. Do some of the characteristics of the founders, technology, market, provide a permanent advantage to the firm, or does that initial advantage fade away after two, four or more years? The primary focus is on companies operating in the micro-electronics and communication fields in Canada, created between 1965 and 1980. The study focuses on their first eight years of operation (less if they are not yet eight years old). This research stems from a pilot study conducted by Doutriaux[21] in order to identify the evolution of the organization structure and growth patterns of high tech firms in Ottawa, Canada. This study involved personal interviews with a sample of 14 companies. It was limited in scope and sample size. However, the intention was to employ its findings in the design and implementation of a more extensive research project with broader scope and a larger sample size. The approach used in the present study is based on the findings of this pilot study and

_____

[21]Doutriaux, 1984, op.cit.

utilizes the experience gained from that experiment.

A total of 508 Canadian high-tech firms were invited to participate in the initial phase of the current study by completing the short questionnaire with selected information concerning the company's origins and its current operations. Approximately 11% of the questionnaires were returned by Canada Post. Of the remaining 449 companies, 163 returned the completed questionnaire, allowing for a response rate of 32.1%. A large percentage (67.5%) of the responding companies originated as entrepreneurial ventures. An additional 9 firms were founded as independent new ventures, but with the assistance and the financial sponsorship of another company or companies.

**Seventy-three** of these **110** entrepreneurial firms, or 66.4%, were founded between 1965 and 1980 and are currently involved in some degree of manufacturing activity. These firms therefore met the sample criteria established for the major study and were asked to participate in Stage 2, the data collection process. The second stage attempted to gain more comprehensive and detailed information regarding the early years of the firms in this sample. Together with the data obtained in the preliminary survey, this information was used to help identify some of the variables which, alone or together, affect the dynamics of growth and prospects for success and survival of Canadian entrepreneurial high-technology firms.

The research instrument was an 18 page questionnaire composed of 42 detailed questions and tables to be answered by the participating companies, aided by an interviewer (researchers or research assistants). The questionnaire covered the following areas, with several questions in each section for year one through year eight of operation[22]:

- origins and status of founders at start-up
- products and markets
- line of activity
- export activity
- personnel
- strategy
- evolution
- financial information
- critical events (mergers, major discovery, etc.)

## CHARACTERISTICS OF THE FIRMS IN THE SAMPLE

Of the 73 firms that meet the criteria for the major study, the majority (73.96%) are located in Central Canada (44 in Ontario, 10 in Quebec). Whereas 18 companies represent the Western provinces, only one

---

[22]If a company was in operation for less than eight years, the questions were to be answered for year one through to the current year.

is located in the Maritime region.

The average age of the entrepreneurial firms established between 1965 and 1980 is 10.84 years. As shown in Table 1 below, one half of the companies have been in operation for at least ten years. The 6 youngest high-tech firms were established in 1980, with the 2 oldest companies starting operations in 1966.

Table 1

Age of Entrepreneurial Firms

| Age | Number of Companies | % of Companies |
|---|---|---|
| 5-6 years | 10 | 14% |
| 7-8 years | 12 | 16% |
| 9-10 years | 14 | 19% |
| 11-15 years | 27 | 37% |
| 16-20 years | 10 | 14% |
| Total | 73 | 100% |

As required by the selection criteria, all of the firms in the sample are currently involved in some degree of manufacturing activity. It is of interest to note, however, that slightly more than half of these companies manufactured during their first year of operation and that only 4 originated as strictly manufacturing firms. Designing was the most common activity of the sample firms during their first year of operation (Table 2), followed by manufacturing, research and development, assembly and provision of services.

In many cases, the entrepreneurs felt that the initial product or service offered by their new venture was relatively innovative in comparison with others available on the market at the time. Forty-five percent of the sample rated their product or service as a unique innovation, while 16% classified theirs as identical or very similar to existing products or services.

Table 2

Original and Current Activities of Entrepreneurial Sample

| Type of Activity | 1st Year of Operation* | Current Year of Operation* |
|---|---|---|
| . Design | 67% | 89% |
| . Manufacturing | 53% | 100% |
| . Assembly | 33% | 76% |
| . Research & development | 42% | 84% |
| . Distribution or sales | 23% | 63% |
| . Servicing products sold | 18% | 63% |
| . Provision of services | 29% | 44% |
| . Other | 5% | 4% |

* (percentage of total firms)

Over half of the firms originally entered markets that were occupied by three or fewer competitors and 20% of the total sample faced virtually no competition for their major product or service line in the company's first year of operation.

Because of the age range of the sample high tech companies, as well as their different activities and experiences, the sales levels reported in the study vary considerably. The median level of annual sales revenues for the firms' initial year of operation was $78,000 and slightly over $2 million for their most recent fiscal year. Whereas over 82% of the firms currently export, approximately 29% did sell their goods or services to other countries in their first year of operation.

The large majority of the sample companies currently undertake research and development activities, which represent an average of 19% of annual sales. While this average does not differ greatly from that of the firms' first year of business, considerably fewer of the companies performed R&D when they were first established.

In terms of employees, the largest high tech venture in the sample has grown from a three-man operation to an employer of over 1,200 people in the past fifteen years. Most of the firms, however, have remained relatively small, with half of the firms employing less than 40 people.

The study included questions concerning the entrepreneurs' previous experience in the start-up of new ventures, as well as their functional experience prior to the establishement of their entrepreneurial high tech firms. Seventy-three percent of the companies reported that none of their founding members had had past involvement in starting a new enterprise and that this had been their first entrepreneurial experience. In the remaining companies, at least one of the original founding members had previously taken part in a new venture start-up.

As shown in Table 3 below, a large number of the entrepreneurial firms were founded by individuals whose expertise was in technical areas, particularly in engineering and design. In almost half of the cases, the combined experience of the original founders included prior marketing familiarity. Past experience in other managerial functions, however, such as financial management, planning and corporate strategy, and government contracting, was cited by considerably fewer of the respondents in the survey.

The mean amount of capital used to establish the firms was approximately $52,000. The initial capital investment varies considerably within the sample, ranging from $500,000 to no capital investment being made in the case of a small software consulting firm. The median of $16,000 is probably a more appropriate indicator of the amount of capital used to establish the high-tech entrepreneurial firms in the sample.

Sixty-three of the respondents provided information concerning the sources of capital used to establish their new ventures. Personal savings of the founders was the sole source of capital of 24 of these firms, and represented 62% of the total initial capital of the sample companies. Bank loans, the second largest source of start-up capital, accounted for approximately 20%. Relatively few of the firms secured financing from investment groups, government programs or other sources.

Table 3

Previous Functional Experience of Founders

| Functional Area | Number of Companies (N=71) | % of Companies |
|---|---|---|
| • Financial management | 21 | 30% |
| • Marketing | 34 | 48% |
| • Production | 33 | 46% |
| • Engineering & design | 55 | 77% |
| • Research & development | 41 | 58% |
| • Planning/corporate strategy | 14 | 20% |
| • Government contracting | 14 | 20% |
| | 212 | |

The apparent hesitancy and/or inability of high-tech entrepreneurial firms to take advantage of venture capital is also reflected in this study. While the number of companies in the sample securing venture capital has increased from 4 at the start-up phase to 13 in the last year of operation, the great majority (80.6%) have not used this source of financing. On the average, approximately 94% of the equity of the firms was held by the original founding members in the first year of business. This has declined to 76% in the current year of operation, with 6% of the total equity being held by venture capitalists and the balance by other individuals.

Most of the founding members have tended to maintain a centralized approach to decision making responsibility within their firms. Slightly over 90% of the sample companies indicated that this responsibility was held by a centralized management team when the firm was first established. This frequency, however, has fallen to 66% in the last year of operation, indicating that as some of the sample firms have evolved, they have adopted a less authoritative and more decentralized internal structure.

RESULTS OF THE STUDY

A total of eight start-up characteristics are being investigated in this study:

- the amount of start-up capital used by the firm;
- the level of marketing experience present in the founding team at time of start-up;
- the level of financial experience present in the founding team at time of start-up;
- the similarity of the market served by the new firm, compared

to the market of one of the founders' previous employer;
- the similarity of the technology used by the new firm, compared with the technology used by one of the founders' previous employer;
- the number of persons in the original founding team;
- whether any of the founders had any previous entrepreneurial experience;
- the level of public sector sales (contracts) during the first year of operation.

As shown in Table 4, close to 60% of the firms in the sample started with less than $25,000 in capital, and over 40% had no marketing and/or no financial expertise at time of start-up. Most firms were using a technology similar or complementary (72% of the cases) to the technology used by one of the founders' previous employer, and the markets served by the new firms were often (55% of the cases) similar or complementary to the markets served by previous employers.

Table 4

Statistics on Start-up Factors

| Start-up Factor | | Number of firms | % |
|---|---|---|---|
| Start-up Capital: | -less than $25,000. | 36 | 59 |
| | -$25,000. to $100,000. | 13 | 21 |
| | -over $100,000. | 12 | 20 |
| Marketing Experience at time of start-up | -No expertise | 27 | 40 |
| | -some expertise | 41 | 60 |
| Financial Experience at time of start-up | -No expertise | 29 | 44 |
| | -some expertise | 37 | 56 |
| Market similar to previous employer's | -Different | 31 | 45 |
| | -Similar or complementary | 38 | 55 |
| Technology similar to previous employer's | -Different | 20 | 28 |
| | -Similar or complementary | 50 | 72 |
| Team Founding? | -One founder | 19 | 27 |
| | -More than one founder | 51 | 73 |
| Prior start-up experience by one or several founders | -yes | 21 | 29 |
| | -no | 53 | 71 |

A majority of the firms (73%) were started by a team rather than by a single individual, and only a minority of the new companies (29%) were profiting from the experience of someone who had already started another firm.

Many of these start-up characteristics are related to each other. As shown by the Chi-squares reported in Table 5, there is a strong relationship between the amount of start-up capital and the prior start-up experience, the marketing experience and the financial experience of the founding team, the similarity of the market served by the new company with the market of one of the founders, and the size of the founding team. As expected, there is also a strong relationship between prior start-up experience, and experience in marketing and in finance. It is interesting to note that starting firms operating in a

Table 5

Relationship Between Start-up Factors[1]

| Start-up Factors | Start-up Factors | | | | | | |
|---|---|---|---|---|---|---|---|
| | $X_1$ | $X_2$ | $X_3$ | $X_4$ | $X_5$ | $X_6$ | $X_7$ |
| $X_1$, Start-up Capital (3 groups) | – | 57 | 56 | 58 | 59 | 61 | 65 |
| $X_2$, Marketing experience (2 gr.) | 7.9* | – | 66 | 64 | 65 | 67 | 66 |
| $X_3$, Financial experience (2 gr.) | 5.6** | 4.4* | – | 62 | 63 | 65 | 64 |
| $X_4$, Similar Market (2 gr.) | 8.8* | 8.3* | 2.9** | – | 69 | 69 | 67 |
| $X_5$, Similar Technology (2 gr.) | .1 | .7 | 2.9** | 2.6*** | – | 70 | 68 |
| $X_6$, Founded by Team (2 gr.) | 4.7** | .6 | 0 | 2.5*** | .0 | – | 70 |
| $X_7$, Prior Start-up exp. (2 gr.) | 5.0* | 4.5* | 7.2* | .3 | .4 | 2.1*** | – |

Notes:   [1]: above diagonal, number of observations
              below diagonal, value of chi-square statistics
      *: significant at 5% level
     **: significant at 10% level
    ***: significant at 15% level

market similar to the market served by one of the previous employers of one of the founders also have a good level of expertise in marketing, finance, and entrepreneurship. It is suprising, however, to note that there is little relationship between the size of the founding team and the levelof marketing and financial experience found in that team. One could have hypothesized that one of the reasons for teamwork when creating a new firm would be to get complementary technical and managerial skills. This is obviously not the case here.

As noted in a previous section, the success of our entrepreneurial firms will be measured by the level of sales attained each year during their first eight years of operations. In order to be able to compare companies with various start-up dates, all the sales data were converted to constant dollars (Table 6). In constant 1971 dollars, our firms went from average sales of 121 thousand dollars in their first

## Table 6

### Statistics on Annual Level of Sales ($1000., constant 1971 dollars)

|  | Number of observation | Mean | Standard deviation | Minimum | Maximum |
|---|---|---|---|---|---|
| year 1 | 62 | 121 | 181 | 0 | 1025 |
| year 2 | 58 | 204 | 259 | 0 | 1090 |
| year 3 | 57 | 347 | 398 | 10 | 1741 |
| year 4 | 49 | 457 | 491 | 10 | 2014 |
| year 5 | 51 | 591 | 639 | 10 | 2811 |
| year 6 | 50 | 862 | 984 | 21 | 4960 |
| year 7 | 47 | 1088 | 1182 | 15 | 4585 |
| year 8 | 32 | 1034 | 1194 | 22 | 5060 |

year of operation, to over a million dollars in their eighth year of operation.

The study of the relationship between each start-up factor and the success of the firm was done through regression analysis (for the amount of start-up capital used by the firm) or through an analysis of variance (for all the other factors considered). The results (F statistics and degrees of freedom of each test) are reported in Table 7.

The amount of start-up capital has a significant effect on the level of sales of the firms during their first three years of operation. After that time, there seems to be little difference between the firms which started with little or with a lot of initial capital. Our data also show that the amount of start-up capital has a significant effect on the number of employees of the firm during its first six years of operations.

The level of start-up capital therefore confers a comparative advantage to the young firm, but that comparative advantage is of limited duration.

The use of outside capital at time of start-up does not seem to have an effect on the sales of our firms. It is known that outside capital is one of the major determinants of the success of a firm, but that capital is usually called in to finance the growth of the firm rather than its start-up.

Whereas prior financial experience seems to have little effect on the level of sales, prior marketing experience seems to lead to higher sales during the first three years of existence of the firms. Our data shows that types of experience, however, are related to the size of the firms in terms of number of employees during the first three years of the firms. It is not clear at this point why "financial experience" should have an effect on the number of employees. The comparative advantage given to a firm by initial financial and marketing expertise fades away in a few years because, presumably, by that time, the other

447

Table 7

Relationship Between Start-up Factors and Annual Sales Level[1]

| Start-up factor | | Year of operations | | | | | | | | |
|---|---|---|---|---|---|---|---|---|---|---|
| | | 1 | 2 | 3 | 4 | 5 | 6 | 7 | 8 | Most recent year |
| Amount of start-up capital ($) | F | 18.9* | 13.8* | 17.6* | .0 | .0 | .7 | .0 | .2 | .0 |
| | d.f. | 48 | 44 | 44 | 36 | 39 | 37 | 34 | 34 | 53 |
| Outside capital at start-up (yes/no) | F | 1.1 | 1.4 | 1.3 | .1 | .4 | .1 | .0 | .1 | 1.5 |
| | d.f. | 50 | 46 | 46 | 37 | 39 | 37 | 35 | 34 | 53 |
| Marketing experience at start-up (yes/no) | F | 4.7* | 3.5* | 3.5* | 1.3 | .5 | 1.5 | .2 | .5 | 1.8 |
| | d.f. | 53 | 49 | 49 | 42 | 45 | 43 | 39 | 38 | 58 |
| Finance experience at start-up (yes/no) | F | .9 | .6 | .5 | .5 | .3 | .2 | .0 | .3 | .7 |
| | d.f. | 52 | 48 | 48 | 41 | 44 | 42 | 38 | 37 | 57 |
| Market similar to previous employer's (yes/no) | F | 2.4*** | .3 | .0 | 1.1 | .7 | .3 | .4 | 1.5 | .5 |
| | d.f. | 57 | 53 | 53 | 46 | 48 | 46 | 43 | 41 | 61 |
| Technology similar to previous employer's (yes/no) | F | 1.5 | .4 | .2 | .0 | .1 | .2 | 1.6 | .5 | .5 |
| | d.f. | 58 | 54 | 54 | 46 | 48 | 46 | 43 | 41 | 62 |
| Founded by a team (yes/no) | F | 1.0 | 1.7 | 1.5 | 1.1 | 1.7 | 2.6 | 2.1 | 2.5 | 3.4** |
| | d.f. | 59 | 55 | 55 | 47 | 49 | 47 | 44 | 42 | 63 |
| Prior start-up experience (yes/no) | F | .8 | 1.8 | 1.8 | .6 | .1 | .7 | .8 | .4 | 4.4* |
| | d.f. | 55 | 51 | 51 | 43 | 45 | 43 | 41 | 40 | 61 |
| Public sector sales in first year[2] (yes/no) | F | 4.54* | 6.1* | 9.1* | 6.2* | 2.2*** | 6.0* | 12.5* | 13.2* | 2.2*** |
| | d.f. | 58 | 54 | 53 | 45 | 47 | 46 | 42 | 41 | 60 |

Notes:   [1]:  in constant 1971 Canadian Dollars
         [2]:  sales in current dollars except for most recent year
         *:  significant at 5% level
        **:  significant at 10% level
       ***:  significant at 15% level

firms have hired comparable expertise.

It is surprising to note that the similarity of the new firm's market or technology with those of the previous employer of one of the founders does not seem to lead to a real comparative advantage in terms of level of sales. Our data shows that similarity of technology does lead to higher growth in sales and in employees during the first four year of operations and therefore contributes to the development of the firm. The results of the lack of effect on the level of effect on the level of sales are at odds with the literature and will be further investigated.

Our data does not indicate any early comparative advantage from team founding or from prior start-up experience. We must, however, note a significant effect on the level of sales during the most recent year of operations. This last result corresponds to findings reported in the literature. According to our data, there is a strong relationship between team founding and the number of employees of the firms during their first eight years of operations, and between prior start-up experience and the growth in the number of employees during the first four years. The difference in the effect of these two start-up factors on sales and on level of employees is surprising and will necessitate more research.

Public sector sales in the first year of operations is strongly related to the annual level of sales attained by our firms during at least their eight first years. The reasons for this result will be investigated in more depth, but it tends to show that, in Canada at least, governments contracts and government purchasing can have a very supportive effect on high technology firms.

## CONCLUSIONS

This study has shown that if the success of a technology-based entrepreneurial firm is measured in terms of its annual sales level or in terms of its total employment, some start-up factors provide a comparative advantage to the young firm: the amount of start-up capital, marketing and financial experience, similarity of the technology with the technology of one of the previous employers, and public sector sales in the first year. This comparative advantage, however, tends to fade away after three or four years, because presumably by that time, the other firms have hired the required managerial expertise.

Even if some start-up factors seem to put the new firm on a stronger footing, it is not always clear which factor contributes most to the growth of the firm because they are not independant of each other. Subsequent research will be necessary to assess their individual contribution.

Cooper, A., "Rand D is more efficient in small companies," Harvard Business Review, June 1984.

Cooper, A.C., and A.V. Bruno, "Success Among High Technology Firms," Business Horizon, April 1977.

Doutriaux, J., "Evolution of the Characteristics of (High Tech) Entrepreneurial Firms," Frontiers of Entrepreneurship Research Conference, Babson College, 1984.

Doutriaux, J., Growth Pattern of Academic Entrepreneurial Firms, Working Paper 86-56, Faculty of Administration, University of Ottawa, 1986.

Dunkelberg, W.C., and A.C. Cooper, "Pattern of Small Business Growth," Academy of Management Proceedings, 1982.

Lamont, L.M., "What Entrepreneurs Learn from Experience," in Entrepreneurship and Venture Management, C.M. Baumback and J.R. Mancuso Eds, Prentice Hall, 1975.

Litvack, I.A., and C.J. Maule, "Entrepreneurial Success or Failure, Ten Years Later," Business Quarterly, Winter 1980.

Litvack, I.A., and C.J. Maule, "Successful Canadian Entrepreneurship and Innovation, Six Case Studies," Frontiers of Entrepreneurship Research Conference, Babson College, 1982.

Oakey, R., High Technology Small Firms, St. Martin's Press, New York, 1984.

Roberts, E.B., "How to Succeed in a New Technology Enterprise," Technology Review, December 1970.

Roberts, E.B., and H.A. Wainer, "Some characteristics of Technical Entrepreneurs," IEEE Transactions on Engineering Management, Vol. EM-18, No. 3, 1971.

Stuart, R., and P.A. Abetti, "Field Study of Start-up Ventures, Part II: predicting initial success," Frontiers of Entrepreneurship Research Conference, Babson College, 1986.

Tyebjee, T.T., and A.V. Bruno, "A Comparative Analysis of California Start-ups from 1978 to 1980," Frontiers of Entrepreneurship Research Conference, Babson, 1982.

Vesper, K.H., New Venture Strategies, Englewood Cliffs, N.J.: Prentice Hall, 1980.

Weiss, L.A., "Start-up Business: A Comparison of Performance," Sloan Management Review, Fall 1981.

Wetzel, W.E., and I.G. Wilson, Seed Capital Gaps: Evidence from High
Growth Ventures, Frontiers of Entrepreneurship Research Conference,
Babson, 1985.

# CHARACTERISTICS OF SUCCESSFUL HIGH-TECH START-UP FIRMS

L.N. Goslin, Portland State University

## ABSTRACT

A research study of high-tech start-up firms explored the characteristics of successful firms. The specific objectives of the research were to understand: (1) background characteristics of the firm and its founders; (2) criterion for success, characteristic entrepreneurial/management styles and organizational structures; (3) marketing strategies used and (4) the means of financing and the characteristics of venture funding.

The research analyzed the personal decision-making styles of the respondent entrepreneur-founder, the decision-making style of the firm as a whole, and strategies and method used to maintain a technological advantage (for those firms which tend to be technology driven).

In 30 percent of the cases studied, the respondent had been involved in previous start-up ventures. The primary source of motivation for the respondent founder was the desire for independence or to create, personal satisfaction or personal challenge. These criteria may be construed as unattainable when employed by another firm.

## OVERVIEW[1]

This paper provides an interim report on an ongoing research study on the characteristics of high-tech start-up firms. The study gathered information on:

o specific background characteristics of the firm and its founders;
o criterion for success;

---

[1]The author wishes to express appreciation for the contributions of: Dr. Q. Clarkson, research design; S. Kiehl, field survey; and Dr. G. O'Leary, observations on high-tech management.

o characteristic management styles and organizational
  structures used;
o marketing strategies used by the start-up;
o primary means of financing; and
o specific characteristics of venture funding were applicable.

The survey results are classified according to the respondent
firms' own declared success criteria. These mutually exclusive success criterion classification groups are:

o profitability;                  o product focus;
o financial stability;            o market share/growth;
o sales;                          o personal criteria.

The report reviews the methodology employed and presents information on:

o general results;
o personal decision-making style;
o decision-making style of firm;
o strategies; and
o mechanism to maintain competitive advantage.


## METHODOLOGY


A sample of high-technology firms was drawn from a directory,
_Advanced Technology in the Pacific Northwest_, published by Quanix.[2] A
sample of over 200 high-tech start-up firms was selected. A mail survey of this sample was made with a response rate from the sample of 37
percent. The criteria for the firm's selection for the sample were:

o less than five years old;
o in the high-tech sector of the economy; and
o located in the state of Idaho, Oregon or Washington.

A twelve-page questionnaire was used including both closed-
and open-ended questions under the four broad headings of:

1. Background Information;
2. Management,
3. Product/Marketing; and
4. Financing.

The preliminary analysis consisted of descriptive statistics
such as frequency counts of each response and measures of central
tendency of the various responses. Further analysis with cross
tabulations of different variables revealed relationships of interest.

---

[2]_Advanced Technology in the Pacific Northwest_, Quanix Data
Services, Portland, Oregon, 1985.

Finally, the Pearson Product Moment Correlation was utilized to determine the strength and significance of the various relationships.

GENERAL RESULTS

### The Entrepreneur

The respondent high-technology firms were more than three years old and an established functioning organization (75 percent). The entrepreneur respondents were either one of the original founders or the sole founder of the firm (97 percent). In 45 percent of the cases, the entrepreneur alone was the key person or founder of the firm.

In 30 percent of the firms, the entrepreneur had been involved in previous start-up ventures. Of these, the number of previous ventures ranged from one to six, while the number of previous successes ranged from zero to three. In 48 percent of the cases, the founder was successful in all previous ventures; the founder was never successful regardless of the number of attempts in 13 percent of the cases, and 35 percent were succesful in at least half of his/her previous attempts.

The primary source of motivation for the entrepreneur founder (57 percent) was the desire for independence. An additional 12 percent indicated the desire to create something, personal satisfaction or the personal challenge as primary sources of motivation. These are also indicative of a desire for independence, as they may be construed as unattainable when employed by another firm. Financial gain was primary for some (13 percent), with the remaining indicating a variety of sources ranging from dissatisfaction with the previous employer to the window of opportunity.

The educational background of the respondents breaks down as follows:

o Bachelors degrees (60 percent);
o Masters degrees (19 percent);
o MBA's (10 percent);
o Ph.D.'s (10 percent); and
o No degree (16 percent).

Due to the fact that many respondents indicated only their highest degree attained, it is impossible to determine a characteristic mix of educational attainment for the individual entrepreneur.

It should be noted that 38 percent of the degrees held are in engineering with an additional 17 percent in the hard sciences (mathematics, physics, etc.). The accounting/finance area accounted for 11 percent of the degrees, management accounted for 12 percent, while marketing accounted for a mere 3 percent.

Eighty-one percent of the respondents indicated that the start-up was not a spinoff of the firm by which they were most recently employed. It is interesting to note that the product/market choice of the start-up was closely tied to the founder's most recent experience in 53 percent of the total cases and in 45 percent of those cases where the start-up was not a spinoff. Of those cases where the product/market choice was not related to the most recent experience, 42 percent of the respondents indicated a perceived market need, with the remainder indicating a variety of non-market oriented motives.

## Product Marketing

In 96 percent of the situations, the firms are still producing the original product/service. The remaining 4 percent of the firms changed their product/service due to misjudgments of demand or misreading the market situation.

Ninety-three percent of the firms are still serving their original markets. The remaining 7 percent indicated that their original target market was incorrect. The reasons given covered a wide variety of issues.

The primary target market indicated by 44 percent of the respondents was the industrial market, followed by the consumer market in 14 percent and military in 9 percent of the cases. Other markets mentioned each had 5 percent or less of the responses.

Less than one half (45 percent) of the start-up firms initially conducted market research of any type. Of these firms, 33 percent relied on secondary research, 32 percent relied on personal interviewing and 21 percent utilized telephone or mail surveys.

On the whole, the average firm wants to double its current market share from 28 to 50 percent; it intends to accomplish this end primarily by market penetration (34 percent) or product expansion (32 percent). The operational details of explicit actions to accomplish these ends were not mentioned.

## Financing

As could be expected, 71 percent of the entrepreneurs indicated the primary original source of start-up capital was personal. Equity capital of various types accounted for 18 percent of the original capital source. Of those receiving equity capital, 85 percent received the first round of venture capital at start-up. To date, 17 percent of the firms have had at least two rounds of venture funding. Surprisingly, most respondents (62 percent) are not planning on going public. The following reasons were offered for the lack of interest:

o The primary reason, "not necessary";
o "Maintaining control";

o Acquisition or merger were probable; and
o Inappropriate size or structure.

## Management

The group of entrepreneur managers surveyed indicated that their criteria for success in starting their firms were:

o profitability (25 percent);
o product focus (13 percent);
o market share/growth (9 percent);
o sales (31 percent);
o personal criteria (31 percent); and
o financial stability/breakeven (9 percent).

Sixty-five percent of the respondents indicated that they were able to achieve this criterion in a time frame 12 months or less.

Stability of focus was indicated by sixty percent who felt that the criterion would not change over time. Of those (40 percent) that indicated that it would in fact change, the future criteria were:

o market share/growth (41 percent);
o product focus (21 percent);
o personal criteria (14 percent); and
o profitability (10 percent);
o financial stability/breakeven (7 percent).
o sales (7 percent);

Various management and firm characteristics were analyzed through the use of Lickert scales. The respondents were asked to respond to each characteristic on two different time scales--one describing the said characteristic at start-up and the second describing the characteristic at the present time.

The four factors of major consideration displayed as graphs for discussion are:

1. personal decision-making style (of the founder);
2. the decision-making style of the firm (as a whole);
3. strategies; and
4. method used to maintain a technological advantage (for those firms which tend to be technology driven).

The following measure of central tendency was used to illustrate different styles in reference to the time scales of the four factors.

```
Intuitive          1 . . 2 . . 3 . . 4 . . 5   Data Based
Participatory                                   Nonparticipatory
Market Driven                                   Technology Driven
Engineering                                     High R & D
  Follow-on
```

Each of the success criteria--profit, financial stability, sales, product focus, market share, personal--is displayed as the abscissa on a series of graphs. Each graph reflects the mean evaluation of the respondent group.

PERSONAL DECISON-MAKING STYLE

The personal decision-making style of all the founders, regardless of the criteria of success, has shifted from intuition-based decision making to more data based. The least shift with experience are persons who view the personal subjective reasons as the criterion of success.

FIGURE 1

PERSONAL DECISION-MAKING STYLE

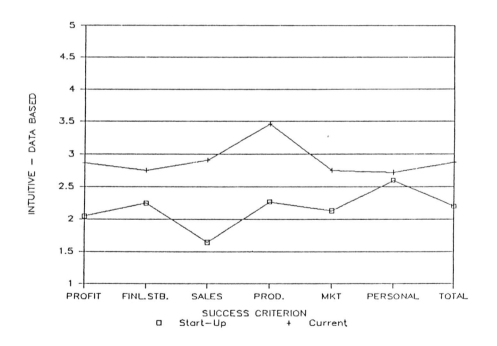

DECISION-MAKING STYLE OF THE FIRM

The decision marketing style of the firms illustrates an interesting and provocative pattern of value shifts with experience. The available analytical insight does not permit anything other than conjecture. Additional analysis and follow up will be done to determine the underlying factors where possible.

FIGURE 2

DECISION-MAKING STYLE OF THE FIRM

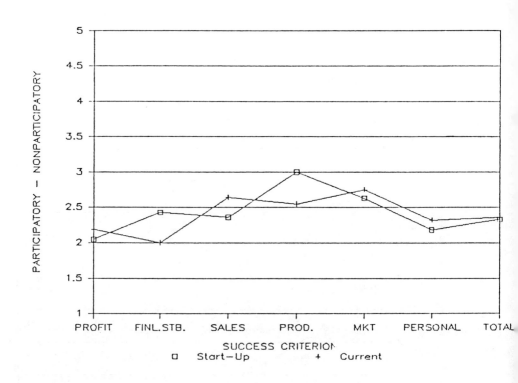

STRATEGIES

The review of the information of strategies to achieve market success reveal an overwhelming indication of the shift from technology focus to market focus with experience; however, a mediating tendancy intervenes as the entrepreneur-manager is forced to reassess and consider the future.

FIGURE 3

STRATEGIES

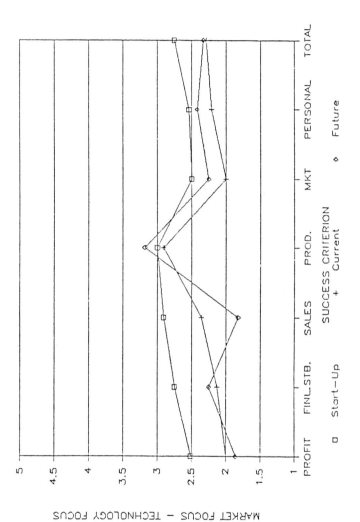

The perception of current thinking in all categories of entrepreneur is that there is a strong requirement to invest in R & D to maintain momentum toward success.

FIGURE 4

MECHANISM TO MAINTAIN TECHNICAL EDGE

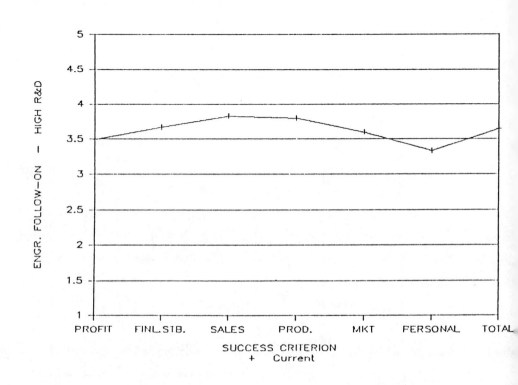

SUCCESS CRITERION
+    Current

Reviewing some of the "popular" literature for insights does provide a bit of corroborating insight. Not a lot, but some.

The current thinking and literature is divided the mix of characteristics of entrepreneurs. Blotnick talks of entrepreneurs as being impatient, yet persistent and thick-skinned to repeated setbacks. He states "people who prefer to minimize risk are better off in an organization."[3] In other words, they should remain in large organizations rather than strike out on their own. The research results of this sample of high-tech start-up firms doesn't seem clearly to support that particular view.

In "The Making of a Maverick," Carbone describes an entrepreneur: "usually show an inclination toward hard work and achievement early in life, an inclination that does not diminish over time."[4] Entrepreneurs are take-charge people.

The entrepreneur's training is obtained while working for someone else. This is accomplished by listening and learning and by establishing personal relationships. The information gained in this sample would seem to agree with that observation

The president of Compaq, Ron Canion, feels "entrepreneurial success is far less dependent these days on the brilliant insights and force of personality of hard-charging chief executive officers."[5] and he is not alone. When 90 West Coast companies were asked for their No. 1 priority in running their business, fully two-thirds cited the development of a strong management team. Our results suggest that the entrepreneur "did it on their own"; team building was important, but not highlighted.

When Canion, Bill Murto, and Jim Harris, all senior managers at Texas Instruments, Inc., were looking to form Compaq, they wanted seasoned professionals for their management team. Canion and his two co-founders invited their new managers to join them and key company decisions are hammered out using consensus management. The smart-team concept at Compaq works throughout the company.

The entrepreneurs of AST Research, Quantum and Linear Technology share a similar philosophy to the founders of Compaq. Linear was founded by a group of executives and engineers. Their

---

[3]Srully Blotnick, "Restlessness and Risk," Forbes, Vol. 137 (June 16 1986), p. 187.

[4]T.C. Carbone, "The Making of a Maverick," Management World Magazine, Vol. 15 (June 1986), p. 32.

[5]Joel Kotkin, The "Smart Team" at Compaq Computer, Inc. (February 1986), p. 45.

first move was to assemble a "strong managment team much larger and more experienced than a relatively small new company would initially require."[6]  AST Research and Quantum have similar stories.

This information does not seem to be supported by Figures 1 and 2; the value of further data analysis and refinement appears appropriate.

Overall, however, the research study does throw additional light on the thinking, perceptions, and values of start-up entrepreneurs in the high-tech arena.

_____

[6]Kotkin, p. 54.

## REFERENCES

Advanced Technology in the Pacific Northwest, Quanix Data Services, Portland, Oregon, 1985.

Blotnick, Srully, "Restlessness and Risk," Forbes, Vol. 137 (June 16, 1986), pp. 186-7.

Carbone, Dr. T.C., "The Making of a Maverick," Management World Magazine, Vol. 15 (June 1986), pp. 32-2.

Kotkin, Joel, The "Smart Team" at Compaq Computer, Inc. (February 1986), pp. 48-55.

Montagno, Ray, Donald Kuratko, and Joseph Scarcella, "Perception of Entrepreneurial Success Characteristics," American Journal of Small Business, Vol. 10 (Winter 1986), pp. 25-32.

Pollock, Marilyn and John Pollock, "Are You a Risk Taker?" Venture Magazine, Vol. 8 (July 1986), p. 24.

# MATURATION IN THE MICROCOMPUTERS SOFTWARE INDUSTRY: VENTURE TEAMS AND THEIR FIRMS

Richard D. Teach, Georgia Tech
Fred A. Tarpley, Jr., Georgia Tech
Robert G. Schwartz, Mercer University
Dorothy E. Brawley, Mercer University

## ABSTRACT

This paper examines the maturation of the microcomputer software industry by looking at both changes in the venture teams and changes in the firms. It contrasts and compares new principals with founding principals on a number of dimensions. The existence of formal business and marketing planning and its affect on performance is examined. The rate of sales growth for individual firms is determined and found to be declining.

## INTRODUCTION

Over the last several years the authors have reported the results of annual surveys on microcomputer software firms. In the initial 1984 study, the authors characterized the demographics of software entrepreneurs and their firms.[1] In a more recent study, the question of the composition of software venture teams was addressed.[2] The earlier studies reported that the educational level of entrepreneurs was extremely high, with almost half having an advanced degree. In addition the degree fields were found to be quite varied. It was discovered that women accounted for less than fifteen percent of the principals in the surveyed firm. In addition, it was noted that software entrepreneurs came in almost equal numbers from large non-entrepreneurial firms and from small entrepreneurial firms.

In the original study the authors found that over two-thirds of the firms were headed by venture teams as opposed to individual entrepreneurs. Team formation was a way to aggregate both financial and human capital with the former appearing to be a much stronger reason for venture team creation than the latter. Previous managerial experience at a mid-management level significantly enhanced the sales performance of the firm. Neither prior top management nor other experience in a firm enhanced sales. Finally, it was found that previous experience in the software industry by a venture team member was the most significant contributor to the sales success of the firm.

In a more recent study, the authors examined "Entrepreneurial Myopia: The Software Case".[3] This study documented the disquitude that entrepreneurs were encountering as their firms matured. This was primarily shown in terms of the great gap between perceived length of the product life cycle on the part of the entrepreneurs and the realized product life cycle in the market place. It was concluded that only those firms that engaged in market and/or business planning and allocated a portion of their receipts to product development stood a good chance of escaping the twin dangers of short product life cycles and becoming a single product firm.

Further observations indicated that differentiable products, combined with unique market niches, along with management dealing from the strength of experience appeared to lead to superior performance in the market place. This observation was the beginning of what appeared to be a mitigating of the entrepreneurial experience and a quickening to the more mature management phase of the firms' venture teams.

Indicators of: change in the make-up of the venture teams, enhanced firm performance and the formal planning process were observed and tested. This paper reports on these observations and their significance to the continued and differential changes in the maturing firm and industry.

## VENTURE TEAM COMPOSITION

The professionalization of the management cadre in the micro-computer software industry was further demonstrated by comparing the educational level and background of the new additions to the venture teams as opposed to the founding members. As one would expect, there was a dropping off at both ends of the educational spectrum. The virtual disappearance of the "computer jock" without a college degree was mirrored by the significant reduction in the number of new team members with a doctorate.

TABLE 1

Educational Levels of Principals

| | Educational Level | | | | |
| | Less than College degree | Bachelor | Masters | Ph.D. | Prof. |
|---|---|---|---|---|---|
| Founders | 24 | 93 | 69 | 25 | 9 |
| | 10.9% | 43.3% | 31.4% | 11.4% | 4.1% |
| New Principals | 1 | 28 | 26 | 2 | 0 |
| | 1.8% | 49.1% | 45.6% | 3.5% | 0% |

Chi Sq = 11.87            Sig. = .0198

The educational backgrounds of the new team members as compared to the founders showed a movement toward an education in business and away from an educational background in the sciences, including computer science. Those reporting bachelors degrees in the sciences fell from over 22% of the founders to only 7% for the new additions. The same figures for those reporting bachelors in computer science were over 18% and less than 5% respectively. At the masters level, the flight from science was even more pronounced. From 19.2% of the founders to 4.3% for the new additions. Surprisingly, the percentage with masters degrees in computer science remained almost constant with 13.7% and 13% respectively. The net winner at both the bachelors and masters level were those reporting degrees in business. At the bachelors level, the percentage increased from 15.5% to 20.9%. At the master's level from 42.5% to 69.6%.

The message was clear. One's chances of joining a microcomputer software firm as a principal were greatly enhanced if one had an educational background in business. The founders were trying to complement the technical skills of the firm with managerial skills by adding persons with professional management credentials.

TABLE 2

Educational Fields of Principals

| | Degree Fields | | | | | | |
| | Bus | Eng | Comp | Lib Arts | Sci | Other | Total |
|---|---|---|---|---|---|---|---|
| BS Orig Found. | 23 15.5% | 38 25.7% | 15 10.1% | 29 19.6% | 33 22.3% | 10 6.9% | 148 |
| MS | 31 42.5% | 12 16.4% | 10 13.7% | 2 2.7% | 14 19.2% | 4 5.4% | 73 |
| BS New Prin. | 31 20.9% | 14 32.6% | 2 4.7% | 11 25.6% | 3 7.0% | 4 9.3% | 43 |
| MS | 16 69.6% | 2 8.7% | 3 13.0% | 3 13.0% | 1 4.3% | 1 4.3% | 23 |

This observation was further confirmed by an examination of the previous positions held by the new members of the venture team. As was mentioned above in the earlier surveys, principals tended to come more from middle management, operations and staff rather than top management. The latest survey revealed again that a large portion of venture team members come from middle management (a third) but when the original founders were compared with the new team members it was found that the percentage coming from previous positions in top management had increased from 21% to 36%. Indeed for the new team members, previous positions in top management had replaced previous positions in middle management as the major source of principals. This was accomplished not by a large drop in the percentage coming from middle management (approximately 32% in both sub-samples) but by a significant reduction in those whose previous experience had been in staff and operations. This is detailed in Table 3 below.

TABLE 3

Principals' Previous Positions

|  | Previous Positions | | | | | |
|  | Top Mgt | Mid Mgt | Lower Mgt | Oper. Staff | Clerical | Total |
|---|---|---|---|---|---|---|
| Orig. Found. | 44 20.9% | 69 32.7% | 36 17.1% | 59 28.0% | 3 1.4% | 211 |
| New | 19 | 17 | 9 | 8 | 0 | 53 |

Chi Sq = 7.4                      Sign. = .0564

This research showed that not only was the venture team becoming more professional with additions with previous top management experience but also there had been a change in the percentage concentration of the new team members versus founders in terms of certain functional areas. The winners have been marketing and finance, with marketing being predominate. While only 12.5% of the original founders came from the marketing area, almost double that, 23.5% of the new principals came from a marketing position. A similar shift occurred in terms of finance. Although the numbers were smaller, the actual percentage was greater. In finance, only 6.8% of the founders came from this functional area while 17.6% of the new principals had finance backgrounds. This shift was compensated in a large part by the almost

TABLE 4

Functional Areas of Principals

|  | Functional Area | | | | | | | |
|  | Mrkt | Sales | Fin | Eng | Mfg | R&D | Other | Total |
|---|---|---|---|---|---|---|---|---|
| Orig Found | 24 12.5% | 23 12.0% | 23 6.8% | 41 21.4% | 5 2.6% | 36 18.8% | 50 26.1% | 192 |
| New Prin | 12 23.5% | 7 13.7% | 9 17.6% | 9 17.6% | 1 2.0% | 2 3.9% | 11 21.6% | 51 |

Chi Sq. = 15.6                      Sig. = .0289

disappearance of "R&D" as a source of new principals. Founders with R&D backgrounds made up 18.8% of the principals while a meager 3.9% of the new principals had an R&D background.

This further documents the contention that management was not only being professionalized but much of this professionalization was coming in marketing and finance; areas which tend to increase in importance as firms mature. The slippage in R&D as a source of principals was to be expected as an industry moves out of its product development stage and towards maturity.

As much as some things change, others remain the same. This survey confirmed the results of the earlier surveys indicating that large non-entrepreneurial and small entrepreneurial firms tend to be equal contributors of both new principals and founders. No statistical significance was found in either the size of the previous firm or its classification as entrepreneurial or non-entrepreneurial.

As an interesting sidebar, it was found that the microcomputer software industry was becoming less male dominated.

TABLE 5

Sex of the Principals

|  | Men | Women | Total |
|---|---|---|---|
| Founders | 200 (87.3% | 29 (12.07%) | 229 |
| New Principals | 47 (77.0%) | 14 (23.0%) | 61 |
| Total | 247 | 43 | 290 |

Chi Sq. 4.04 Sig. = .0445

Whereas only 12.7% of the founders were women, that percentage has almost doubled among the new additions to the venture team (23%).

PLANNING

The professionalization of the management team was not only indicated by the educational credentials of the team but by the actions of the firm. A reasonable surrogate for the degree of professionalization was the level of business and/or marketing planning.

In order to determine if business and/or marketing planning was an important co-variant with the size of the firm as measured by sales, the firms were divided into subsets: those who wrote formal business plans; marketing plans; both business and marketing plans and those who engaged in no formal planning processes. In order that the results not be dominated by the extremes of very large and very small firms, all firms with sales less than $100,000 as well as those with sales in excess of $5,000,000 were removed for this analysis. The latter group consisted of only two firms, one of which reported sales in excess of $15,000,000. The inclusion of these extreme values tremendously increased the variance while adding little to the base of our knowledge.

Slightly over one half (65 out of 128) of the responding firms, having sales within the selected range, provided answers to both the current years sales as well as indicating the existence or lack of a formal business plan. Twenty-one firms or 32.3% did no formal business planning. These firms had average sales of $729,000 (SD 712,000). The balance or 44 firms, 67.7% produced formal business plans. Their average sales were $1,236,000 (SD 1,076,000). An ANOVA analysis showed these two groups to be different at the .0545 level.

The number of firms fitting these constraints and responding to the question regarding marketing plans were slightly larger, as 73 firms met this criterion. These firms were more evenly split with 35 firms, 47.9% producing no formal marketing plans. The sales differences were even more pronounced in the case of the existence of marketing plans. Planners had average sales of $1,310,000 (SD 1094 thousand) and non-planners reported sales of only $664,000 (SD 679 thousand). An ANOVA analysis showed these two groups to be different at the .0038 level of significance.

It appeared that planning paid off in that the firms which did neither formal business nor marketing planning only had average sales of $55,600 (SD 534,000).

Of the two types of planning, those firms having only a marketing plan had greater sales than firms having only a business plan. Surprisingly, having only a formal marketing plan was only slightly less rewarding than having both. The expected sales reported by firms with both formal business plans and formal marketing plan was only $80,000 higher than the sales reported by firms producing only formal marketing plans.

The same message held when sales growth was taken into account. The authors took the difference in reported sales by firm between last year and the current year as a measure of growth. When the individual firm growth was split between firms which did formal business planning and those which did not, the business planner showed considerably more growth. Planners experienced an average growth of $457,000 in the past year while non-business planners experienced only $149,000 in sales growth. This difference was significant at the .0128 level. When the split was made between non-market planners and market planners the difference in sales growth was even more pronounced. Firms which did no formal market planning reported sales growth of only $190,000 while those who prepared formal marketing plans reported sales growth averaging $483,000. A significance level of .0051 was achieved for this difference.

On reflection, the results were less surprising than originally thought. The microcomputer software industry has turned into a marketing industry. Marketing is the name of the game and market planning, whether standing alone or integrated into the business planning process, is the significant co-variant with firm sales.

## SALES GROWTH

By whatever measure used, the microcomputer software industry has experienced a cycle of extraordinary growth. For the responding firms, ratios of sales growth were calculated for the period 1979 to 1986. In addition, the sales growth ratio was calculated for the 1987 forecasted sales. A sales ratio is a link relative or the current year's sales divided by the previous year's sales. First noticed by the authors was the size of the ratios of the sales growth over this entire period of time. From a meager growth ratio of approximately 1.6 in 1979, these firms, on average, achieved a growth ratio of 4.3 or a growth rate of 330% in 1983. Since that time there has been a halving of the growth ratio but before excessive sympathy is extended to the industry this still translates to a growth rate of well over 100% per year. The firms were asked to forecast their sales for 1987. This rate was just slightly below the actual sales growth rate for 1986.

It would appear that we have witnessed the initial explosive growth cycle in the microcomputer software business. One would expect these extraordinary growth rates reported by the responding firms to be unsustainable. A retardation in growth rates would be expected to occur as maturity set in (see Figure 1). However, it is still amazing that sales more than doubled last year and are expected to double again next year.

It is heartening to see that the 1987 forecast indicates a realism concerning future sales growth that has not always been the hallmark of software firms. This may be another indication of the professionalization of management and the movement away from the entrepreneurial environment which dominated the industry in its earlier years.

## THE CHALLENGE OF TECHNOLOGICAL CHANGE

As the microcomputer software industry approaches its 10th anniversary, the industry may be facing its most transforming technological change. The authors took the opportunity of this survey to try to develop some prospective data on how firms were planning to respond to 32 bit architecture based on the Intel 80386 and the Motorola 68020 microprocessors. There are two tasic advantages of this new technology. One is its increased processing speed due to a wider bus and the increase in cycle speed. The second advantage is the tremendous

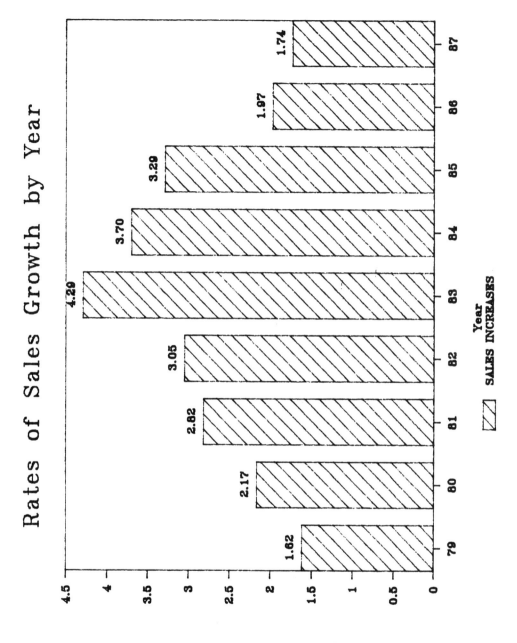

Rates of Sales Growth by Year

increase in addressable memory. Taken together this should allow desktop microcomputers, based on this 32 bit architecture, to reach the speeds and power of many of the current mini-computers. For this to occur, however, microcomputer software that takes full advantage of the improvement in hardware technology must be developed. This a much more difficult problem than porting existing software to run on these new machines. This is both a threat and an opportunity for existing microcomputer software firms.

The survey asked specific questions on whether firms were currently spending development funds on software for this new architecture. Twenty-six firms out of the sample of 128 were found to have spent development funds on software related to the new technology. An additional 40 firms indicated that they expected to begin work in 1987 and 17 more expected to start on or before 1991. The remaining 45 either did not report or indicated no interest in spending development dollars on this new technology. The authors anticipate tracking firms as this new technology is introduced later this year and in the future.

It was interesting to examine the firms that, last year, invested in 80386 and 68020 product development and compare these firms with those which reported that they planned to begin investing next year and within the next five years. Firms currently spending money on 80386 and 68020 software tended to be larger than firms in general and larger than the firms planning to start spending on this development next year or within the next five years. The firms that reported that they currently have no plans to spend development money on neither the 80386 nor the 68020 software were by far the smallest. A similar breakout was made as to the firm's commitment to formal planning. Firms who reported spending on 80386 and 68020 software development were much more likely to do formal planning. Of course the common co-variant was firm size.


CONCLUSION


In this paper the maturing and moving towards professional management in the microcomputer software industry was examined. The new principals added to the firm were compared to the founding principals. They were more likely to have a bachelors or a masters degree and less likely to have less than a college degree or a doctorate. They were much less likely to have a degree in science but much more likely to have been awarded their bachelors or masters degree in business. New principals were much more likely to have come from top management positions than were the founders. New principals were more likely to have had responsibilities in marketing and finance and much less likely to come from R&D. New principals were more likely to be female than founding principals.

Firms which formally plan, either business, marketing or both did better in terms of reported sales than those firms which did not. Marketing planning seemed to be extremely critical. Firms which engaged in marketing planning alone did better than firms which did business planning alone.

Sales growth in the microcomputer software industry has been and remains extremely high.  Sales growth rates peaked in 1983, at approximately 330% for the firms in the survey.  In 1986, sales were essentially doubling.

As the microcomputer industry enters the tenth year of existence we find a strong and still fascinating preteen.  But the growth rates are declining, as they must, and the responsibilities and problems that come with maturity are starting to surface.

The most dramatic event in the industry in the early teen years will be the coming of the Intel 80386 as well as the Motorola 68020 chip machines.  The authors will be watching with great fascination to see how this young industry reacts.

## REFERENCES

Teach, Tarpley and Schwartz, "Who are the Software Entrepreneurs"? Frontiers of Entrepreneurship Research, 1985.  Hornady, Skils, Timmons and Vesper; Editors.  Published by Center for Entrepreneurial Studies at Babson College, Wellesley, MA., 1985, pages 435-451.

Teach, Tarpley and Schwartz, "Software Venture Teams" A paper submitted to Business Development Review.  A publication of Commercial Development Association, Washington, D. C.

Teach and Tarpley, "Entrepreneurial Myopia:  The Microcomputer Software Case."  A paper presented at the American Marketing Association Conference entitled; "The Marketing and Entrepreneurial Interface," chaired by Professor Gerald Hills, University of Illinois at Chicago Circle, July, 1986.

SUMMARY

## THE CHARACTERISTICS OF ENTREPRENEURIAL
## SOFTWARE DEVELOPMENT VENTURES

Authors

Philip S. Barton*
Donald H. Peters

Addresses

| University of Auckland | *Box 25-003 |
| Private Bag | St. Heliers |
| Auckland | Auckland |
| New Zealand | New Zealand |
| (9) 737-999 | (9) 587-153 |

Principal Topics

This paper describes a "recipe" for software ventures that identifies some of the major factors by which ventures and their founders can be distinguished. A detailed description of the grounded
method employed that resulted in this framework is also offered.

Method and Data Base

When the project was begun there were no known studies on entrepreneurial software development ventures; it was therefore necessary to
adopt an exploratory methodolgy. Merton-type focused interviews
were made of 40 ventures which were chosen non-randomly so as to
represent the rich variety of the industry in New Zealand. An additional 15 interviews - with entrepreneurs, venture capitalists, and
industry commentators - were made prior to the case-building meetings in order to familiarize the researchers with the nature of
software venturing. Content analysis of the voluminous unstructured interview notes was used in order to define the constructs
most valuable in characterizing ventures. The cases were finally
coded according to their representation of the various characteristics in the recipe and submitted to a variety of clustering
techniques.

Major Findings

The research uncovered 10 'personal' constructs and 23 'venture'
constructs that served to distinguish ventures.

## The Personal Constructs

- Age of the entrepreneurs
- Their tertiary qualifications
- "Business" versus Software orientation of the venturers
- Previous software development experience
- Number of previous ventures
- Degree of "push" from last job as a motivation to venture
- The importance of monetary gain
- The importance of the need to prove an idea
- Parental role model
- Existence of previous <u>employment</u> in an "entrepreneurial" firm

## The Venture Constructs

Strategy related Constructs

- Degree of risk-taking inherent in strategy
- Financial return aimed for
- Importance of export versus local market to firm
- Importance of PC software in mix of work
- Importance of minicomputer software in mix of work
- Importance of mainframe software in mix of work
- Degree of concentration on generic applications
- Degree of concentration on vertical markets
- Degree of concentration on customized software
- Computer centered as opposed to User centered
- Was there a single catalyst project for the venture?
- To what degree is the total venture concerned with the development of software?
- Degree to which the venture sells its own work
- Staff size
- Number of entrepreneurs
- Existence of a pair of founders (1 "business partner", 1 boffin)
- Relative reliance on Venture Capital as opposed to cashflow and initial capital for financing

Maturity and "Style" Constructs

- Flavor of operation (e.g.: casual, formal, disorganized, etc.)
- Status:
  * Aborted
  * Failed
  * Being Planned
  * Operating
  * Meeting the majority of the aims of it founders (i.e.: being successful)
- Number of distinct projects undertaken by the venture
- Proportion of staff who are/were founders
- Number of years of operation
- Degree to which growth is the venture's aim

Computer analysis of the coded cases showed that the most significant variables in distinguishing cases from one another were those that defined the firm's strategy with respect to the size of computer that was being primarily written for, and the type of software being produced. Clusters obtained were immediately logical and the relationship between the ventures in each group was meaningful.

## Major Implications

Software ventures and their entrepreneurs vary quite considerably over a large number of distinguishing characteristics. These identifying variables, taken together, form a "recipe" that is amenable to further testing with quantitative methods.

SUMMARY

## VENTURE CAPITAL-BACKED VERSUS NON-VENTURE CAPITAL-BACKED COMPANIES IN THE COMPUTER INDUSTRY

Authors

    Antony C. Cherin
    Michael Hergert

Address

    College of Business Administration
    San Diego State University
    San Diego, CA 92182-0094
    (619) 265-5657

Principal Topics

    It has been stated that venture capitalists bring value added to
    the entrepreneurial management of those firms which they husband.
    This paper reports a test of this thesis by examining the risk-
    adjusted stock market performance of venture-backed firms relative
    to non-venture-backed firms. The evidence suggests that,
    regardless of firm size, venture capitalists do not provide value
    added to their client firms.

Method and Date Base

    The venture capital community is the set of capital market institu-
    tions which supplies entrepreneurial capital needs. The close rela-
    tionship between the venture capitalist and an entrepreneurial
    management team is one of the major distinctions separating the
    former from a passive investor. Pratt views three characteristics
    which define the association between venture capitalist and
    entrepreneur. In the present context, the most important is:
    "...an active, ongoing involvement by the venture capitalist who
    brings personal value-added to the capital investment." (Pratt,
    1981, p. 7) This idea is further highlighted in an article from
    Forbes about a Connecticut venture capital firm, Oak Investment
    Partners: "Like any good venture capital outfit...Oak offers more
    than money. Founder Edward Glassmeyer and Stewart Greenfield pro-
    vide contacts, managerial experience and plain old hand-holding that
    often outweigh their financial commitment. 'You can't survive in
    this business if it's just the money,' says Glassmeyer." (Bryne,
    1983, p. 194)

This study explores one primary question: Do venture-backed companies in the computer industry perform significantly better than non-venture-backed companies in this industry? The hypothesis that there is no difference is tested from 1981 to 1983. Further, a test is made to analyze the extent to which firm size plays a part in explaining variation in performance.

Two frequently discussed portfolio theory concepts, monthly holding period returns (HPRs) and the ensuing Sharpe composite measure of portfolio performance, were employed.

A stock HPR is the percentage return earned during a specified period of time and was calculated as follows:

$$HPR = \frac{P_t - P_{t-1} + D_t}{P_{t-1}} \times 100\%$$

where:

$P_t$ = The stock price at the end of the month;
$P_{t-1}$ = The stock price at the beginning of the month; and
$D_t$ = Any dividend paid during the month.

The Sharpe concept represents a risk-adjusted performance measure. A modified form of this measure was calculated in the following manner:

$$Modified\ Performance\ Measure = \frac{\bar{r}}{SD}$$

where:

$\bar{r}$ = The mean return (the average monthly HPR for a firm's stock)
$SD$ = The standard deviation around this return.

In demonstrating differences in portfolio performance it is important to implement some measure of relative dispersion as a means of quantifying risk. Forming a ratio with the average HPR in the numerator and the standard deviation around this mean return in the denominator yields a risk-adjusted performance measure.

Venture Capital Journal maintains an index of 100 public companies that have received venture capital backing. Because venture capitalists have been very active in the computer equipment industry, the 40 computer firms in the index were singled out. Then firms with the same SIC codes were selected from Dun and Bradstreet's Million Dollar Directory. This yielded a list of 78 additional firms, 34 of which had also received venture capital backing, a further indication of venture capital activity in this industry. The final sample varied between 69 and 77 publicly traded companies depending on the year of the study. In each year the sample was divided into two groups: the venture-backed companies and the non-venture-backed companies. Stock prices and dividends were gathered from the Standard and Poor's Daily Stock Price Record. T-tests and analysis of covariance were the statistical techniques utilized to test for differences in the mean performance measures of the venture-backed firms and the non-venture-backed firms and to control for company size.

## Major Findings

The table below presents the results of the t-tests.  There were significant differences between the venture-backed and the non-venture-backed groups in 1982 and 1983.  Here, the non-venture-backed group performed better than the venture-backed group.  In absolute terms, the venture-backed group was higher (less negative) than the non-venture-backed in 1981.

Modified Performance Measures (MPMs) for
Venture-Backed (VBFs) and Non-Venture-Backed Firms (NVBFs)

| Year | Group | Number of Cases | Mean MPM | Standard Deviation of the Mean MPM | t Value | p-Value |
|------|-------|-----------------|----------|-------------------------------------|---------|---------|
| 1983 | VBFs  | 48 | .236 | .356 | − 2.44 | .017* |
|      | NVBFs | 19 | .468 | .338 | | |
| 1982 | VBFs  | 50 | .127 | .232 | − 3.04 | .003* |
|      | NVBFs | 20 | .304 | .188 | | |
| 1981 | VBFs  | 48 | − 0.015 | .260 | 0.18 | .860 |
|      | NVBFs | 21 | − 0.029 | .361 | | |

* Significant at a 5 percent confidence level.

To ensure that company size and the status of venture capital backing were not acting together to determine performance, a covariate, total assets, was introduced.  Analysis of covariance revealed that size had no significant impact on performance over the three year period.  In short, performance measure differences between venture-backed and non-venture-backed firms cannot be attributed to differences in company size.

## Major Implications

The primary conclusion of this research is that publicly-held, venture-backed companies in the computer industry do not seem to perform significantly better than their non-venture-backed counterparts on a risk-adjusted basis.  Furthermore, this result cannot be attributed to differences in firm size.

Contrary to intuitive expectations, the non-venture-backed firms
actually outperformed those with venture capital affiliations in two
of the three years examined. This would seem to indicate that the
value added by venture capitalists does not filter down into better
stock market performance for publicly held firms. This raises many
questions about the magnitude of he benefits provided by venture
capitalists. Although it is impossible to conclude that they do not
provide significant value added to their clients, it makes this area
an important topic for future research.

THE BLUE BROTHERS--AN ACT TO WATCH:  THE MAGIC OF TRANSFORMING A
PATTERN OF VENTURING BY DEFECTING SCIENTISTS INTO
FRUITFUL CORPORATE-SPONSORED VENTURES

Daryl G. Mitton, San Diego State University

ABSTRACT


In August, 1986, Neal and Linden Blue acquired GA Technologies,
Inc., from Chevron Corporation for roughly $50 million.  Through its
thirty-one year existence, GA (originally General Atomic) has been a
prolific generator of technological innovations and opportunities.  Over
twenty-five of these opportunities have been transformed into successful
ventures by GA's defecting scientists.  During this three-decade pattern
the firm has lost nearly $1 billion.  Only since 1982 has it shown a
profit.  Its latest reported annual sales and earnings are $155 million
and $2.6 million, respectively.  Meanwhile, GA's incubation-generated
counterparts have annual sales and earnings of roughly $1 billion and $20
million, respectively.

The Blue brothers propose to stop this brain drain and, instead,
turn the inventory of technologies which GA now holds and is continuing
to generate, into lucrative, corporate-sponsored ventures.

This is a three part study:  (1) an examination of the GA
environment that causes the proliferation of technologies and
opportunities that rivals that of its publicly sponsored neighbor, the
University of California, San Diego, in producing commercializable
technologies and enterprising alumni; (2) an examination of the specific
ventures spawned by defecting GA scientists and the circumstances
attributing to this phenomenon; and (3) an examination of the strategies
the Blues are employing to transform the corporation-generated
technologies into corporate-sponsored ventures.

INTRODUCTION


Neal and Linden Blue bought GA Technologies from Chevron
Corporation in August, 1986.  It was a high leveraged buyout and
represents a significant change in the historical ownership pattern of GA
Technologies.  Previously, since its inception in 1952 as General Atomic,
a corporate subsidiary of General Dynamics Corporation, it has had a
succession of very large corporate owners.  Owners after General Dynamics
were, first, Gulf Oil Corporation, then a 50/50 partnership of

Gulf and Royal Dutch/Shell, then Gulf again as single owner, and more recently, Chevron Corporation.

The giant oil companies defined a very narrow and limiting objective on what had been a broad exploratory research program. Both the pursued objective and the neglected side activities ended in a very significant financial drain on the oil companies, even though their pockets were deep enough to absorb the losses.

The Blue brothers, the new owners, do not have a huge corporate back-up. Although the Blues own or control a number of corporations, including their privately held Cordilla Corporation, a Denver based real estate, oil, gas and utilities firm, these holdings do not at all compare in order of magnitude to such firms as Gulf, Shell, or Chevron. The Blue Brothers, however, have an entrepreneurial zeal, and Neal Blue intends to be the hands on owner-manager.

This new ownership represents the most promising entrepreneurial thrust for the firm since the early days of John Jay Hopkins, the founding president of General Dynamics. It was under Hopkins' direction that a brilliant group of scientists were brought together in 1955, in his newly-formed General Atomic subsidiary, to explore the possibilities of peacetime use of atomic energy.

This firm became notorious for both its unique technological discoveries and the defection of its scientists, who took their know-how and set up sound commercial ventures independent of GA. Coincident with this phenomenon, which has continued for thirty years, was an accumulated loss in General Atomic of close to $1 billion. At the same time, very significant aggregate gains have been produced by the technology-oriented ventures spawned by GA. These now number over twenty-five firms, and well over fifty firms if second, third, and forth generation enterprise are included.

It is the Blues' intent to stop the brain drain and attain financial and commercial viability with the storehouse of technology and developing technology within the firm. It's a tall order considering the patterns of the past. This challenging mission makes the Blue brothers an act to watch.


THE STAGE


The stage for this unfolding drama was set in 1952. At that time entrepreneur John Jay Hopkins incorporated General Atomic. He wanted to capture the name and the concept for broad application of atomic energy for peacetime pursuits. Concurrently, he changed the name of his Electric Boat Company of Groton, Connecticut, to General Dynamics, again to be more representative of what his firm was becoming. It was an aggregate of enterprises not only in boat and submariine building, but airframe manufacturing, electronics, and the soon to be activated atomic energy and space endeavors.

Hopkins had been the guiding executive of Electric Boat since the onset of United States involvement in World War II with the bombing of Pearl Harbor. This firm, which had built over 150 liberty ships in World War I, distinguished itself by building 82 submarines in World War II, more than all other private shipyards combined.

After the war, Hopkins eagerly accepted the challenge of building the first atomic powered submarine. The cause of the atomic submarine had been pushed by then Captain Hyman G. Rickover. His fanaticism was catching to Hopkins, who increased his design force to 712 people from the only 190 it had been at the peak of WWII. Hopkins not only produced the Nautilus, but a succession of atomic powered submarines--the Skate, Triton, Skipjack, and Scorpion.

Concurrent with Hopkins' submarine triumph, he added diversity to his organization through the acquisition of other firms: First, Canadair (F-86 Sabre), then Consolidated Vultee Aircraft (the sixth largest airframe manufacturer), and Stromberg-Carlson (electronics). With positions in sea and air power firmly entrenched, he sought to extend his lead in atomic power.

In 1955, he activated the General Atomic division. He directed his senior vice president, Gordon Dean, the one time head of the Atomic Energy Commision, to find a man to run it. Dean hired Vienna born, Harvard educated physicist Frederic de Hoffmann. Dr. de Hoffmann was right for the role Hopkins intended. He was a charismatic, visionary philosopher-scientist. He attracted a dozen other prominent scientists, including Edward Teller (father of the hydrogen bomb) to his board of advisors. He hired Ed Creutz as director of research. Creutz was a physicist turned metallurgist with a brilliant professional track extending back through the Atomic Energy Commission, Carnegie Tech, Los Alamos, and Oak Ridge. By 1958, General Atomic had 250 scientists with over 50 Ph. D's. (At their peak employment in the mid 1970's, GA reached over 3,000.) Besides laying the groundwork for acquiring scientific talent, Hopkins busied himself securing a location for the scientists' workplace which would be second to none. He obtained 300 acres of prime Torrey Pines pueblo land overlooking the Pacific Ocean, a gift from the City of San Diego. This was immediately adjacent to the land set aside for the soon to be established research-oriented University of California, San Diego, in 1961. This was the setting of Hopkins' laboratory of pure and applied research, General Atomic.

THE CRITIC'S CORNER

This is, in a sense, a historical review. The actors and actions cover over thirty years. To bring this drama back to life and into perspective, over twenty key characters were interviewed--scientists and executives from the very earliest people employed up to the present. Also contacted were people in second, third, and fourth generation firms. Various firms' documents and cross-reference of information have been used, when possible, to verify the information presented.

This ongoing study is considered complete enough to supply answers, at least in part, to the following questions: (1) What was the company environment that (a) caused such a proliferation of technologies and opportunites--a proliferation that rivals the producing of commercializable technologies of our most prestigious universities, and (b) caused the defection of scientists to set up their commercial ventures external to GA?  (2) What enterprises have been spawned by the defecting scientists of GA, what technologies do they represent, and how succesful have they been?  and (3) What strategies will the Blues employ to transform the corporation-generated technologies into corporate-sponsored ventures which will return an economic gain to GA?

PAST PERFORMANCES

On July 19, 1955, just a little over a year after the successful launching of the first atomic powered submarine, Nautilus, John Jay Hopkins announced the activation of the General Atomic Division of General Dynamics.  Division president Frederic de Hoffmann, research director Ed Creutz, and H. Burke Fry, director of administration, huddled in a La Jolla hotel to plot their strategy.  They attracted a group of the nation's leading scientists to a symposium on atomic energy in the summer of 1956.  The scientists explored the basic types of power reactors theoretically possible--and their commercial application.  They also reviewed the theories and work in fusion.  From this group General Atomic recruited prestigious consultants as well as a cadre of working scientists.  Many were Nobel laureates.  Among those put into service in one capacity or another were:  Dr. Edward Teller, theoretical and experimental physics and electronics and father of the hydrogen bomb; Dr. Hans Bethe, theoretical physics and Nobel Laureate; Dr. Peter Fortescue, engineering and physics from England; Dr. Manson Benedict, nuclear physics from MIT; Dr. Freeman Dyson, physics from Princeton; Dr. Theodore Taylor, theoretcial physics from Los Alamos; Dr. Robert F. Mehl, physics and metallurgy from Carnegie Institute of Technology; Dr. Frederick Seitz, physics, from University of Illinois; Dr. Richard Courant, aerodynamics, from New York University; Dr. Fred L. Whipple, astrophysics, from Harvard; Dr. Robert Duffield, chemist, from University of Illinois; and Dr. Marshall Rosenbluth, expert on fusion.  This concentrated pool of talent would serve as a basis for giving direction and guidance for basic nuclear research.

The Warmup--General Dynamics

It was Hopkins' hope to discover new forms of power.  His corporate purpose, specifically, was "The comprehensive exploration of the basic forces of the universe and their translation into useful work under the seas, on the sea, on land, in the air, and in space..." General Dynamics' early lead in nuclear research would lay a groundwork for the destiny Hopkins saw for his firm--a corporation bigger even than General Motors.

This was an era of optimism regarding nuclear energy in general. The Nautilus success was followed by talk of atomic powered aircraft and space vehicles. There were few negative attitudes--in fact, a preponderance of enthusiasm prevailed regarding peacetime use of atomic energy. Many of the nation's brightest science graduates actively sought careers in this field.

The atmosphere at GA was particularly inviting as the firm let its scientists delve into uncharted fields of basic research in a stimulating environment, free of the pressure of producing immediate profits. It was a time, too, when all the other divisions of General Dynamics appeared to be doing very well, reporting substantial profits and growth.

Hopkins earmarked $25 million for the San Diego laboratory. More would follow as the other divisions' prosperity financed this newest developing division. One could anticipate the far reaching impact this division was to have from de Hoffman's remarks at the ground breaking ceremony at the Torrey Pines site in 1956. Pointing out over the Pacific, he predicted how their work would free hydrogen from the ocean water to provide energy at low cost for even the most impoverished nations.

Their start was impressive. de Hoffmann grew a talented staff dominated by Ph.D.'s. He took pride in the fact that many of his researchers were comfortable in a number of scientific disciplines--philosophers as much as scientists.

They approached the design of atomic reactors from a purely theoretical standpoint. For example, early on they were able to produce a small training, research, and isotope-producing reactor at General Atomic which they named TRIGA. It was a clever design, inherently safe, powered by a special self-regulating fuel, uranium zirconium hydride, which would shut it down if anything went wrong. This reactor, over 60 of which have been produced to date, is extremely successful, sought after by universities, hospitals, research institutions and developing nations. GA also produced the fuel for the TRIGA.

In those early days they also laid the groundwork for the ideal structure of a fail safe, land-based reactor. It would be helium gas-cooled to avoid any possibility of melt down, even though at that time melt down was not a public concern.

It looked like the mission, strategy, and structure for the new division had created a winner. The in-place leadership would make it work. Hopkins coupled his big picture vision with creativity, intuition, confident decision making, pragmatism, and substantial material support. de Hoffmann attracted and embraced competence and provided a free atmosphere for pure research and its hoped-for eventual application. All systems were go--a supportive, attractive, freedom-oriented work environment, goals that were seen as world benefiting and achievable; all located in a community where the life-style and the climate are nonpareil.

Then in May 1957, John Jay Hopkins died. He was replaced by Frank Pace who was the complete opposite of Hopkins--conservative, deliberate, indecisive, anxious to be liked, insecure, and unable to direct. The change in leadership made a significant difference in corporate consequence. Pace gave no real guidance to any of his managers. He presided over General Dynamics as their Convair division, in building its first civilian jet transports, accumulated the biggest loss in U. S. corporate history at that time--over $425 million. Corporate dividends were discontinued in June, 1961. In February, 1962, the board replaced Pace with Roger Lewis. Lewis took measures to rewin lost contracts and beef up the other divisions. He gave what encouragement and guidance he could to the General Atomic division, but the firm was now burdened with a $350 million debt. The cash cows of General Dynamics which were to feed General Atomic were too sick to nourish anything.

When de Hoffmann subsequently outlined his program for the future, estimating costs to be about $50 million a year for years to come, Lewis decided it was time to sell the division. He successfully sold the General Atomic division to Gulf Oil in 1968 for around $40 million.

The Main Act--Oil Company Dominance

It was logical for an oil company such as Gulf to buy General Atomic. The oil industry faces a foreseeable destiny: the eventual depletion of oil reserves. Finding alternate energy sources is, therefore, a constant concern. In the 1960's, nuclear energy was the clear alternate energy source. Therefore, when Gulf took over General Atomic, it is not surprising that the basic focus of the division would narrow, becoming very specific and commercially oriented: design and build efficient nuclear reactors and supply fuel for these reactors as well as reactors already in operation. The technology and scientific know-how for this undertaking were certainly in place at GA. What was so surprising, at least in retrospect, was that they gave so little priority to the continuance of research not directly related to reactors.

This new orientation, however, meant the end of the "think tank" environment that had prevailed. de Hoffmann and Creutz's operating philosophy had been: smart people, little structure--get out of the scientist's way and ideas will flow from concept to hardware. They had not pressed for immediate commercialization. General Dynamics' Roger Lewis had taken a slightly harder line when money got tight, but essentially the free atmosphere which facilitated recruiting the world's best scientists had prevailed. General Dynamics was able to keep the world class laboratory and its scientists together. By the time it was sold it was a first class "discovery machine" as well as a saleable property.

The Gulf Oil Corporation culture was different: prepare budgets and hold the line in those budgets; set benchmarks on programs and adhere to those deadlines. The main thrust was the continuing development of the high temperature gas-cooled reactor. Any programs too far off this goal were considered a distraction. de Hoffmann met with the Gulf board to try to obtain more money for fundamental research. No luck.

The two cultures never really merged.  de Hoffmann left and reappeared as president of GA's neighbor, Salk Institute of Biological Research, one of the nation's outstanding biomedical research laboratories, where he has repeated his feat of attracting outstanding scientists to the staff.

Gulf's philosophy was both good news and bad news.  The bad news was that it started a defection of scientists who sought greater freedom and a chance to continue on work in which they were interested.  The good news was that it did give focus to the gas-cooled reactor, which gave every indication of being a commercially feasible product.  Although developing it required big money, the private funding de Hoffmann had put together and the deep pockets of the oil company promised a commercial payoff.

For a very large corporation, their decision made some sense.  The high temperature gas-cooled reactor was a theoretically sound design which avoided many of the hazards of water-cooled reactors.  General Atomic appeared headed for successes that would have a positive influence on bottom line.  One reactor had been built and another one started in the 60's.  The first was a 40 megawatt unit built for Philadelphia Electric.  It had been built quickly and was on line a very high percentage of the time by any power plant standards.  However, it proved too small to  maintain economically.  The second plant, the Fort St. Vrain, built for Public Service of Colorado, was designed at 330 megawatts.  Although completed close to schedule, it was built with a major design flaw:  the circulation water seal was faulty.  Water would seep into the reactor, necessitating shut down to get the water out. With the thick insulation on the reactor, it took forever to dry it out. Further, the Nuclear Regulatory Commission applied tougher and redundant safety features on the reactor.  Making engineering changes after basic completion became a nightmare.  Costs ratcheted upward from these factors alone.  In addition, the confident de Hoffmann had an "up and running " date built into the contract.  Non-operating penalty payments mounted, since the reactor did not go on line until 1979.

The early optimism regarding the program had triggered continued expansion of the GA workforce to over 3,000 by the mid 1970's.  In 1974, Gulf invited Royal Dutch/Shell into a 50-50 partnership to share the anticipated costs and rewards of the expanding business.  Shell paid approximately $80 million for their 50 per cent interest.  Gulf had figured that they would need eight reactor contracts on their books to break even.  By 1975, they had 10 contracts (over $10 billion in sales).

The mid 1970's signaled many new problems besides the excessive down time of Fort St. Vrain.  The glamour of "atoms for peace" was replaced by concern and protest over the environmental hazards of nuclear energy.  Conservation measures had lowered the demand for energy, and the energy produced was being used more efficiently.  Natural gas got cheap and utilities were switching to gas turbines as a source for electric power.  Escalating inflation resulted in high financing and construction costs for reactors.  These higher costs way exceeded GA's contracted estimates.  Royal Dutch/Shell senior executives, after a reasoned and careful study, canceled all the reactors on order even though this

resulted in their paying over $200 million in total cancellation
compensation to utility firms.  If this action had not been taken, there
is little doubt it would have brought GA as well as a number of utilities
involved to their knees.  Interestingly, since 1975, no new nuclear
energy facilities have been ordered, and at present there is no shortage
of electric energy production.

For Shell, the nuclear reactor business had become mainly an
exercise in sharing costs.  The partnership formed in 1974 was dissolved
in 1982 with Shell taking 56 acres of prime Torrey Pines real estate
worth roughly $1 million per acre as their share.  Gulf continued to
operate the division under the new name GA Technologies.

Faced with the fact that no further reactors would be built,
there was retrenchment and redirection.  Dr. Harold Agnew, a very
prestigious scientist and former director of Los Alamos Labs, was brought
in as president.  He was clearly his own man, intimidated by neither the
scientists nor the oil executives.  He continued the consolidation of the
workforce to about 2,000 and sought out commercially viable
opportunities.  Agnew can clearly be credited with keeping GA from dying.
He resurrected nuclear research, obtained support contracts, and started
a service business which has shown promise since the Three Mile Island
and Chernobyl incidents.

After Shell pulled out, he was able to expand contracts with the
Department of Defense, which had been prohibited when Shell, a foreign
company, was part owner.  Agnew's own talents and interests were broad
and varied.  He understood the inventory of scientific talents at GA and
was able to secure contracts that used these talents effectively.  For
example,  GA took on the task of determining how to dispose of the nerve
gas stock-pile left over from WWII.  By 1983, GA was showing a profit for
the first time.

In 1984, Gulf was acquired by Chevron in a "white knight" rescue
to prevent Gulf's takeover by T. Boone Pickens.  Chevron did not want to
be in the nuclear business and was anxious to pay down the $10 billion
debt incurred in the acquisition.  Chevron's management decided to sell
GA.  GA's management studied the possibilities of a high leveraged buy-
out.  Circumstances seemed right for it--the firm was still rich in
technical know-how; it was capable of supporting the debt that would be
incurred; and GA's assets, including choice real estate, were carried on
the books at significantly less than market value.  Nonetheless, GA
executives decided against a management buy-out.  Harold Agnew joined
those retiring and Dr. Kerry Dance assumed the presidency.  At this point
the Blue brothers bought GA on a high leveraged buy-out for about $50
million.


THE REACTIONS TO PAST PERFORMANCES


The original thrust of General Atomic was to attract, hold, and
effectively tap the best scientific talent for nuclear research and its
application.  From the beginning through 1975,  an impressive staff was

built, numbering about 3500 at its peak. Through the years, however, there were a sufficient number who did not stay. This section is a history of those who defected and an attempt to understand why the defections occurred. The corporate culture actually changed dramatically several times through the more than thirty year history. This analysis will cover three cultural phases: 1) The General Dynamics Division build-up; 2) The oil companies' nuclear reactor pursuit; and 3) The oil companies' retreat.

## The General Dynamics Buildup

The first defection occurred in 1958. Dr. Heinz F. Poppendick, an authority on heat transfer, reports that he became disillusioned with too much freedom, too many research directions, and not enough applications orientation. He could see no practical commercial horizon. He left to establish Geoscience, Ltd., an operational test laboratory using applied physics in heat transfer and fluid mechanics. It has contracts with the Air Force, General Dynamics, General Electric, and NASA, among others. In the mid 1960's, Poppendick proposed still a second firm, Thermonetics, which manufactures thermal instruments.

In 1959, Myron Eichon, the only non-degree staff member, was moonlighting, doing work for a UCSD professor who needed to measure Silicon 32 in ocean sediment. He was successful in developing very sensitive intrumentation for detecting traces of radioactivity. He reported this to Dr. Rod Sharp, head of Chemical and Metalurgical Instrumentation, who thought it was a great idea for a business base, but de Hoffmann turned it down as being outside the company charter. Sharp and Eichon quit in early 1960 to form Sharp Laboratories. This firm was subsequently sold to Beckman Instruments and spawned nine additional firms through three generations. Ivac (medical instruments, acquired by Eli Lilly for $60 million) was incubated out of Sharp. Imed (medical instruments), Vitalmetrics (electronic monitors and surgical instruments), Camino Lab (medical instruments), and Pacific Device (medical device assembly) came out of Ivac. Imed was sold to Warner Lambert for $465 million and spawned Ultramed (cataract surgical tools), IZONE (ozone generators), and Winchester Partners and Henry & Company, both venture capital firms. Myron Eichon went on to found many more firms, including Hydroproducts (underwater instruments sold to Honeywell), Cronover Engineering (ceramic systems sold to Hewlett-Packard), Continental Controls (sold to Bendix), and Brooktree (digital to analog to digital integrated circuits).

In the latter days of General Dynamics' ownership and tighter money, four scientists from the Orion project (plasma high energy fluid dynamics) and computer science left to establish S Cubed Corporation (System, Science, and Software). They were joined later by others from GA. They were essentially a high technology military group who felt that they could do better on their own, free of GA's high overhead. In 1984 they were purchased by Maxwell Laboratories, Inc.

This first phase could be characterized by a rapid development of viable technology--some of which was certainly transferable to commercial profitability. When there was not an outlet for this expression from within the firm, the entrepreneurial scientists left and did their own things free of the large corporate drag.


## The Oil Companies' Nuclear Reactor Pursuit

Commercialization became primary with Gulf's acquisition of GA, but the focus was limited toward the high temperature, gas-cooled reactor. One of the obvious "misfits" was the accelerator physics department. Its original intent was to study the scatter pattern of neutrons in the graphite reactor. Once that was resolved, de Hoffmann wanted to continue basic accelerator research, but Gulf saw this as a distraction from their purpose. The chairman and the assistant chairman of this department were the first defectors after the Gulf acquisition. The assistant chairman set up a firm called Enviromed, Inc., in late 1968, which was relatively short-lived.

Dr. J. Robert Beyster, the department chairman, had obtained several contracts in Washington from the forerunner of the Department of Energy. Beyster felt he could duplicate a think tank on his own, but make it a profitable enterprise as well. He was right! He formed Science Applications, Inc., in 1969. He did essentially what de Hoffmann had done--attracted brilliant scientists. Their mission, however, was to attract commercially profitable contracts. It was a simple formula, but it was extremely successful. Current sales are in excess of $500 million and profits are over $15 million. Jim Young, also from GA, had joined Beyster in SAI at the start. In 1974, he left to form a similar firm, Jaycor, which now has revenue of over $50 million. The rich scientific base of SAI has resulted in the spawning of other successful firms: Spectron Development Laboratories (laser technology), Photon Research (electro optics), Horizon Technology, Inc. (weapons effect work), Sparta (strategic defense initiative work), Stonehouse (defense study work), and Titan Corporation (advanced technology in command-control-communications and intelligence)--which, since its founding in 1981 has reached over $100 million in sales and over 2000 employees.

General Atomic, as part of its fusion research, had developed a strong electro-magnetic pulse capability. The resulting discharge could wrap or form metal. The process was called magneform. Gulf was not interested and Magneform was sold as a division to Maxwell Laboratories. The GA people involved went to Maxwell.

In 1971, Jack Bass, who worked on water level instrumentation, took the technology to form Bass Engineering, Inc., which was later sold to Interocean Systems.

In late 1972, GA's Radiation Technology Division was sold to form IRT Corporation (nuclear radiation and industrial radiology). Victor Van Lint and Robert Mertz, who were working in this division on electro-magnetic flux pulse effect (weapon effect), joined the new venture. IRT has current sales of $40 million. In 1986, Mertz founded Four Pi Systems (automatic circuit board X-ray).

In 1974, GA sold its Reverse Osmosis Division to Universal Oil Products as UOP Inc. Fluid Systems Division (water purification). All key employees transferred over.

This second phase is best characterized by emerging and maturing technologies within the corporation that clearly were ready for bold commercialization. Since they were not a part of the firm's defined narrow focus on nuclear reactor or nuclear reactor fuel, they were discarded or sold at a discount price. The argument offered in defense of their strategy was that big corporations hunt elephants and they could not be concerned with operations having "small" markets. Even so, some of their technologies appear to have been elephants in mice's clothing.

The Oil Companies' Retreat from Reactors

By 1975, the signals were clear--no reactors would be built. Retrenchment took place by cutting programs and personnel. For example, Ron Stinson, who was one of the brightest of the project engineers, and a group of employees volunteered for severance and set up Management Analysis Company (strategic consulting service to utilities and energy companies). They now have over $30 million revenue.

In 1976, Richard McCormack left to form RAMCO, Inc. (reactor power program management). He left this line of work and founded Thermal Energy Storage (storage using salt hydrates). In 1982, Infrasonics (high frequency infant ventilators) was formed by Jim Hitchin, an original employee of Thermal Energy Storage.

Hugh Stewart, who was vice-president of engineering for gas cooled reactors left in 1978 to set up NUTEVCO (energy consulting).

In the process of working with graphite reactors, GA became very knowledgeable about pyrolytic carbon. It was determined that it was a very versatile material and capable of being used for surgical implants, since the body rejected it less than either plastic or metal. However, even though the resulting Carbo Medical Division showed great promise and substantial profits, it was sold in 1979 for royalty payments instead of being developed. It became the Carbo Medics Division of Intermedics. They have been particularly successful in making a trouble-free mechanical heart valve, which accounts for a significant part of Intermedics' $214 million sales. Jack Bokros, who led the project, left to join Intermedics, as did most of the staff. Even though this was a tempting non-reactor product for Gulf, they did not feel that they could risk the liability, should the product precipitate litigation.

In 1980, Ernesto Corte founded Gamma-metrics. It uses GA technology--neutron monitoring equipment for the instantaneous analysis of bulk materials such as coal and limestone, and GA receives royalties for its use.

Also in 1980, John Neill formed Advanced Energy Concepts to perform engineering research primarily for Gas Cooled Reactor Associates. The firm was short-lived, however. Further, Ray Dandl and later, Gareth

Guest, formed <u>Applied Microwave Plasma Concepts</u> to develop electron cyclotron heating for fusion. This firm, too, is no longer active.

A group from GA's Computer Service Division formed <u>Base-Eight, Inc.</u>, in 1982. They are computer consultants.

Also in 1982, GA sold or released its interest in two joint ventures with foreign firms: <u>GEA Power Cooling Systems, Inc.</u> (gas turbine recuperators and power plant cooling towers-North American market) to a group in Bochum, Germany; and <u>Pyropower Corporation</u> (fluidized bed combustion boilers-North American market) to A.Ahlstrom in Finland. The involved GA employees transferred with the deal. Pyropower has a backlog of about $100 million.

In 1983, GA sold its Electronic Marketing Systems Division, <u>Emark, Inc.</u> (gasoline station and bulk oil terminal control systems) to Marsh Industries. GA employees transferred with the sale. In 1984, Rod Morrison, who had developed a radiation detector for measuring rain and moisture-pack, took the technology and set up <u>Sunburst Energy Systems.</u> Also, the service personnel unit performing radiation monitoring to nuclear reactors in the field set up <u>Spectrum RMS, Inc.</u>, to continue the work.

<u>Nuclear Medicine,Inc.</u>, (radioactive pharmaceuticals for inoperative cancer) was founded by John Russell and Richard Moore, nuclear scientists from GA. Russell had left in 1978 to teach and do nuclear medical research at Georgia Tech, where his university work led him into nuclear medicine.

In early 1986, Paul Sager took his robotics know-how, learned from his analytic engineering and fusion work at GA, and founded <u>Pacific Robotics</u> (industrial robots). Sager took advantage of GA's early retirement offer as Chevron wound down the operation prior to sale. Conceivably many other retirees will emerge with new ventures.

Through this third phase, with the reactor business shot down, GA had no central credible purpose. It was a period when scientists were taking their golden handshakes and their technologies to form commercial enterprise. Nonetheless, during this phase, Harold Agnew was able to achieve and sustain profitability by searching out project contracts for the very significant technologies and scientists remaining.


THE NEW ACT


The Blue brothers bought GA Technologies from Chevron in August, 1986, for about $50 million. This purchase signaled a significant change in structuring of GA. For the first time since the early days of its inception, ownership and operating control are once again closely linked, as they had been in the first years of GA's life. For nearly thirty years, however, from the days of General Dynamics' President Frank Pace and his distant, non-directing style, throughout the ownership by the oil companies, a non-trusting "we-they" relationship between the scientists and management had prevailed.

With Neal Blue as resident-owner-president of GA Technologies, this newly integrated, autonomous enterprise should sponsor a new culture. The Blues are proven entrepreneurs. Through their Cordilla Corporation, they own four utility companies in four states. They also own controlling interest in Harvard International Resources, Ltd., a large privately held oil and gas company in Canada, as well as extensive real estate holdings. Linden Blue has also been past CEO of Beech Aircraft and Gates Learjet.

In their new ownership role, the Blues have been able to hit the ground running. The general direction in which both Harold Agnew and Kerry Dance had been pointing GA is similar to the Blues' intent--a significant increase in defense work. In the six months preceding the announcement of purchase, but while negotiations were underway, a Defense Programs Group was formed. Dr. Thomas Dillon, former deputy assistant secretary for nuclear energy in the Department of Energy, headed up the group. This is now the Advance Defense System Division.

The advisory board put in place by Kerry Dance has been augmented by the Blues with the addition of Alexander Haig, former NATO Commander and Assistant to President Nixon. Others on the Board are General John Vessey, former chairman of the Joint Chiefs of Staff; Simon Ramo, founder and director emeritus of TRW; William R. Gould, former chairman and CEO of Southern California Edison Company; and former presidents of GA, Harold Agnew and Kerry Dance. This is a savvy and prestigious group to provide practical guidance and help in securing contracts in both the defense and energy industries. The Blues also have an internal "institute" to evaluate the commercial potential of their technologies.

GA is already involved in particle beam and free electron lazer projects and proposals with McDonald Douglas, TRW, Boeing, and Teledyne Brown. It has also delivered experimental electro-magnetic launchers in contracts with the Air Force and Army, and is managing operator of the San Diego Supercomputer Center at UCSD.

Its work with nerve gas destruction, radiation monitors, weapons effects, corrosion-resistant ceramic materials, superconducting magnetics, thermionics, the small research reactor TRIGA and its fuel, and other mainstay projects continues.

All of the inventory of technologies lend themselves to the "star wars" nature of the Strategic Defense Initiative. GA has great expectations in further expansion of contracts in this area.

GA, of course, continues to improve its technology in high temperature gas-cooled reactors and fusion research. The disasters of Three Mile Island and Chernobyl spell the continuing need for a second generation of nuclear reactors--particularly with the realization that fossil fuel is finite. GA's modular High Temperature Graphite Reactor, with its helium coolant, encapsulated fuel, and graphite core, offers inherent safety from nuclear contamination of the atmosphere--a probable design choice for future reactors. Their fusion program, directed by internationally renowned Dr. Tihiro Ohkawa, has a $200 million backlog of work supported primarily by the Department of Energy.

In the meantime, the spin-off of by-products of GA's research continues. During the Blue's negotionations in March, 1986, they let a significant technology go in the golden handshake of Norbert Elsner, metallurgist, and the formation of Electro Technology, Inc. The new firm will transfer industrial waste heat into energy as well as develop "remote" devices, using thermalelectrics for underwater and in-space power supplies. These plutonium-fueled devices are power sources for much space program work and certainly appear critical in SDI technology.

In December, 1986, GA sold its proprietary circulating bed combustion technology (used for hazardous waste incineration) as well as its prototype plant and laboratory equipment to Ogden Corporation. Brian Baxter and his staff will become Ogden Environmental Services.

This commercialization by other companies will no doubt stop soon. It is Neal Blue's intent to commercialize the technologies within the company--setting up subsidiaries, perhaps, but allowing the technology to contribute to profit. Blue is emphasizing a policy that individual remuneration will be directly tied to individual performance which contributes to the firm's bottom line. To accomplish this, technologies will have to be transformed into profit centers and equity may have to be shared. One thing is certain: with the deep pockets of the oil companies gone, Blue will have to make quick decisions as to whether to promote or abandon technologies. Those activities which cannot be sustained by profitable funding will be gone. Right now GA is working hard for $400 million in congressional funding for continuing research into gas-cooled reactors in the hopes of beating out either liquid metal reactors or light-water reactors as the government's favored second generation reactor technology.

The Blue brothers are setting the stage to take advantage of existing and developing technologies. At last at GA Technologies an entrepreneurial spirit may be teamed with a proven scientific and innovative spirit.


BACK STAGE DISCUSSION


Several general conclusions can be drawn from this study:

1) Leadership can make a significant difference in corporate consequence. Entrepreneurial leadership has a positive effect on profit and corporate growth. Non-entrepreneurial leadership has a negative effect. John Jay Hopkins grew General Dynamics by accepting technological challenge combined with financial leverage, commitment, and focus. He sponsored and sparked a remarkable research-oriented organization, which, in spite of major adversities, is still contributing significant technological discoveries thirty years later. Frank Pace, on the other hand, withered it by offering little direction or control. The

firm suffered huge losses and incurred a large debt.  The oil executives' indifference to what they regarded as fringe technology cost the firm many commercial opportunities as the defecting scientists ventured on their own.  Similarly, the entrepreneurial Blues are markedly increasing sales and profit compared to their bureaucratic corporate predecessors.

2) It behooves corporate owners and city fathers alike to encourage research and research-oriented organizations.  Research both sponsors growth and the spawning of new ventures.  In either event, the result is beneficial in attracting investment money to the community and increasing payroll and tax base.  In this study roughly 50 firms can trace their origin to GA Technologies.  These firms represent over $1 billion in annual revenues and $20 million in profit; and GA has revenues and profits of roughly $150 million and $3 million, respectively--and rising.  In spite of the lost technology and scientist, GA remains a technology-rich enterprise.

3) Proven "know-how" is a sound base for high technology ventures.  Of the fifty spawned firms in this study, only three have discontinued operations.  The rest survive, indeed thrive, in one form or another.

4) Projecting the fruits of asset management is often more important than projecting the outcome of operations management in making acquisition decisions.  The uncertainties of future operations appeared to cause GA executives to back away from a buy-out.  The certainties of asset value drove the Blue brothers to want the deal.

5) "Know-how, know who, no money" is often a proven combination for success.  The Blue brothers' lives are exemplar of continuous entrepreneurial activity.  They observe the above stated tenets of the seasoned entrepreneur.  They know how to nurture and guide an organization to growth.  They know how to structure a deal to advantage.  They know value when they see it--and take action to obtain it.  They know talent when they see it, too.  They know people of prestige, know-how, and power can help guide technology, business, and aid in obtaining new business.  These dimensions have all been borne out in their past business careers as well as the indicated favorable start they have at GA.  They possess a talented scientific team and an advisory board second to none in science, space, defense, industry, and energy.  Their financial contacts provided leverage to buy a very viable technology-laden organization with little money down and a property whose land value (at roughly $1 million per acre) exceeds the price they paid for the going concern.

All in all, the Blue Brothers is an act to watch!

# ENTRY STRATEGIES OF CORPORATE VENTURES
## IN EMERGING AND MATURE INDUSTRIES

Alex Miller, University of Tennessee
Robert Wilson, University of Tennessee
William B. Gartner, Georgetown University

## ABSTRACT

An analysis of 110 corporate ventures in the PIMS, STR4 database explored the question of first-mover advantages, that is: Do corporate ventures that enter early in emerging industries achieve competitive advantages over corporate ventures that enter afterwards? Three types of corporate ventures were studied: firms entering early into emerging industries (Pioneers), firms entering late into emerging industries (Ranchers), and firms entering late into mature industries (Settlers). Results showed Pioneers achieved important competitive advantages in market share, product and service quality, and product differentiation, but Pioneers' short run (first four years) financial performance was no better than the performances of later entrants.

## INTRODUCTION

From the old saying "the early bird gets the worm" to Peter Drucker's recent reissue of Nathan Bedford Forrest's call to be "fustest with the mostest," being first, being competitive is part of America's zeitgeist.[1] The idea that the first entrant in an industry achieves important competitive advantages is fundamental to most strategists' thoughts on business behavior.[2][3][4] For example, in

---

[1] P. Drucker, *Innovation and Entrepreneurship*. Harper & Row, New York, 1985.

[2] I. Ansoff, & Stewart, J., "Strategies for Technology-Based Business," *Harvard Business Review*, Vol. 45, No. 6 (Nov.-Dec., 1967), pp. 77-83.

[3] M. Porter, *Competitive Strategy*. The Free Press, New York, 1980.

[4] M. Porter, *Competitive Advantage*. The Free Press, New York, 1985.

Michael Porter's book <u>Competitive Advantage</u>, eight important first-mover advantages were identified, with the implication that early entrants with these advantages should have higher and achieve earlier profits than later entrants.[5]

The purpose of this paper is to explore the value of first-mover advantages to corporate new ventures. Previous research on eight-year-old businesses in the PIMS SPI database showed that early entrants had returns on investments (ROIs) that were 30% higher than later entrants and that early-entrant ROIs were near the 22% returns of mature businesses.[6] Our research uses a PIMS sample of younger corporate ventures (four years old) to analyze whether better financial performance is apparent early on. Do early entrants in an industry become profitable earlier and achieve higher profits than later entrants? Do early entrants gain important competitive advantages?

The concept of first-mover advantages recognizes issues of market timing and product life cycle (PLC). Market timing is the order in which businesses enter an industry (being first, second, third, etc.). PLC is the stage of the industry's growth (emerging, growth, maturity, and decline).[7] A business can enter an industry early or late. In choosing to enter late, a business has the option of waiting until the industry matures, that is, waiting until the industry reaches another stage of the PLC. We suggest three types of entry strategies based on market timing and PLC.

<u>Pioneers</u>       Businesses that are early entrants into emerging and growing industries

<u>Ranchers</u>       Businesses that are later entrants into emerging and growing industries

<u>Settlers</u>       Businesses that are entrants into mature and declining industries

In this framework, the Pioneers should be the firms which achieve first-mover advantages and have better financial performance than the later entrants.

---

[5]M. Porter, <u>op. cit.</u>, note 4, pp. 186-189.

[6]A. Miller, & Camp, B., "Exploring Determinants of Success in Corporate Ventures," <u>Journal of Business Venturing</u>, Vol. 1, No. 1 (Winter 1985), pp. 87-106.

[7]C.W. Hofer, "Toward a Contingency Theory of Business Strategy," <u>Academy of Management Journal</u>, Vol. 18, No. 4 (December, 1975), pp. 784-810.

## Sample

The corporate ventures analyzed for this study came from the PIMS, STR4 database. The corporate ventures analyzed were non-service businesses of Fortune 500 companies with the first four years of financial data. A complete description of the types of businesses in the PIMS, STR4 database can be found in three earlier studies.[8][9][10] A discussion of the validity and usefulness of PIMS based research can be found in two reviews.[11][12] A corporate venture in the STR4 database is defined as "a business marketing a service or product that the parent company has not previously marketed and that required the parent company to obtain new equipment or new people or new knowledge. A business is defined as a division, product line, or other profit center within its parent company selling a distinct set of products or services to an identifiable group of customers in competition with a well-defined set of competitors."[13]

We studied 110 firms, of which 40, 46, and 24 were Pioneers, Ranchers, and Settlers, respectively. The characteristics of market entry and PLC used to differentiate the three types of firms in the sample were defined in the following manner.

> (1) Early Market Entry. The <u>first business</u> to develop such products or services or one of the <u>pioneers</u> in developing such products or services. (PIMS question 106)

> (2) Late Market Entry. An <u>early follower</u> of the pioneer(s) in a still growing, dynamic market, or a <u>later entrant</u> into a more established market situation. (PIMS question 106)

---

[8]R. Biggadike, "The Risky Business of Diversification," <u>Harvard Business Review</u>, Vol. 57, No. 3 (May-June 1979), pp. 103-111.

[9]E.L. Hobson, & Morrison, R.M., "How do Corporate Ventures Fare?" In J.A. Hornaday, J.A. Timmons & K.H. Vesper (Eds.), <u>Frontiers of Entrepreneurship Research</u>, Babson College, Wellesley, MA., 1983, pp. 390-410.

[10]I.C. MacMillan, & Day, D.L., "Corporate Ventures into Industrial Markets: Dynamics of Aggressive Entry," <u>Journal of Business Venturing</u>, Vol. 2, No. 1 (Winter 1987), pp. 29-40.

[11]C.R. Anderson, & Paine, F.T., "PIMS: A Re-examination." <u>Academy of Management Review</u>, Vol 3., 1978, pp. 602-611.

[12]R. Ramanujam, & Venkatraman, N., "An Inventory and Critique of Strategy Research Using the PIMS Database," <u>Academy of Management Review</u>, Vol 9., 1984, pp. 138-151.

[13]E.L. Hobson, & Morrison, R.M., <u>op. cit.</u>, Note 9, p. 390.

(3) Early PLC.  Introductory (Primary demands for product just starting to grow; products or service still unfamiliar to many potential users) and Growth states (demands growing at 10% or more annually in real terms; technology or competitive structure still changing).  (PIMS question 105)

(4) Late PLC.  Maturity (Products or services familiar to vast majority of prospective users; technology and competitive structure reasonably stable) and Decline states (products viewed as commodities; weaker competitors beginning to exit).  (PIMS question 105)

Pioneers were defined as firms with characteristics 1 and 3. Ranchers were defined as firms with characteristics 2 and 3.  Settlers were defined as firms with characteristics 2 and 4.

## Measures and Analysis

Values for each of the measures used in this analysis are averages of the first four years of data.  The use of a four-year average is typical of most PIMS-based research because it reduces the problem of significant changes in single-year data.[14][15]

Competitive advantage was measured by using typical PIMS measures for market share, product quality, service quality, product differentiation, advertising, sales force, relative costs, and relative prices.[16][17]

Financial performance was measured in four ways: (1) a four-year average of ROI, (2) a four-year average of return on sales, (3) a four-year average of cash flow on investment, and (4) V, a measure of progress toward ROI over time, Beta x $R^2$.  We believe V to be an important measure of performance for new corporate ventures because it measures improvement in performance over time rather than achieved performance.  Since the achieved performance measures for all three types of firms were negative during their first four years, (and since profitabilty for corporate ventures takes an average eight years to achieve[18]), a measure of change in performance over time, V, would better reflect which new corporate ventures will more rapidly achieve profitability in the future.  A description of all of the measures used in the study are found in Appendix 1.

---

[14]C.R. Anderson, & Paine, F.T., op. cit., Note 11.

[15]R. Ramanujam, & Venkatraman, N., op. cit. Note 12.

[16]C.R. Anderson, & Paine, F.T., op. cit., Note 11.

[17]R. Ramanujam, & Venkatraman, N., op. cit. Note 12.

[18]R. Biggadike, op. cit., Note 8.

An analysis of variance was used to analyze differences among the three types of firms. Pairwise comparisons of the firms (1 versus 2, 2 versus 3, 1 versus 3) were made using Scheffe's test. A summary of the statistics on the three types of firms appears in Table 1.

RESULTS

The statistics listed in Table 1 indicate that Pioneers gain significant competitive advantages over later entrants, but Pioneers do not achieve better short-run financial performance.

FIGURE 1

PIONEERS ACHIEVE HIGH MARKET SHARES

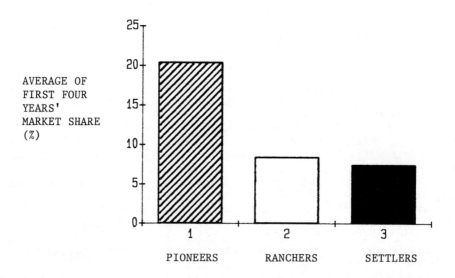

Pioneers achieved market shares nearly twice those of Ranchers and nearly three times those of Settlers. In mature businesses, this difference in market shares among the three types of firms would also translate into different ROIs as well, that is, a market share of 20% should produce an ROI of 14%, while a market share of 7% would produce an ROI of 10%.[19] Efforts to increase market share in the beginning of the business's life may be the reason why Pioneers do not have better financial performance than later entrants. Studies of mature

---

[19]R. Buzzell, Gale, B., & Sutton, R., "Market Share - A Key to Profitability," Harvard Business Review, Vol. 52, No. 1 (Jan.-Feb., 1975), pp. 97-106.

TABLE 1

SUMMARY STATISTICS ON THREE TYPES OF FIRMS

| Measure | Pioneers (Mean) | (SD) | Ranchers (Mean) | (SD) | Settlers (Mean) | (SD) | F Value | Sig. (p.) | Significant comparisons (Alpha of .10) |
|---|---|---|---|---|---|---|---|---|---|
| Market Share | 20.47 | 25.30 | 8.48 | 9.38 | 7.50 | 8.76 | 6.44 | .002 | 1-2, 1-3 |
| Product Quality | 42.76 | 38.97 | 17.93 | 43.53 | 16.83 | 42.04 | 4.68 | .011 | 1-2, 1-3 |
| Product Diff. | 55.92 | 34.46 | 44.93 | 29.21 | 35.35 | 32.01 | 3.28 | .040 | 1-3 |
| Service Quality | 3.63 | 1.09 | 3.25 | .96 | 3.12 | .59 | 3.38 | .038 | 1-2 |
| Advertising | 3.03 | 7.07 | .85 | 1.60 | .64 | 1.36 | 2.98 | .050 | 1-2 |
| Sales Force | 5.23 | 9.45 | 1.09 | 1.73 | .68 | .87 | 6.91 | .002 | 1-2, 1-3 |
| Relative Cost | 129.95 | 77.36 | 117.77 | 50.65 | 111.20 | 22.64 | .84 | .433 | |
| Relative Price | 118.24 | 66.23 | 101.55 | 14.14 | 103.35 | 30.97 | 1.72 | .184 | |
| ROI | -110.68 | 42.51 | -17.27 | 52.62 | -24.67 | 137.28 | .25 | .776 | |
| Return on Sales | -110.07 | 404.71 | -16.75 | 34.92 | -17.18 | 45.94 | 1.82 | .167 | |
| Cash Flow on Investment | -.25 | .24 | -.23 | .23 | -.06 | .48 | .96 | .392 | |
| V - Progress Toward ROI | .64 | .28 | .49 | .33 | .59 | .33 | 2.49 | .088 | 1-2 |

businesses have found that gaining market share adversely affects profitability.[20][21]

FIGURE 2

PIONEERS ACHIEVE HIGH PRODUCT QUALITY AND DIFFERENTIATION

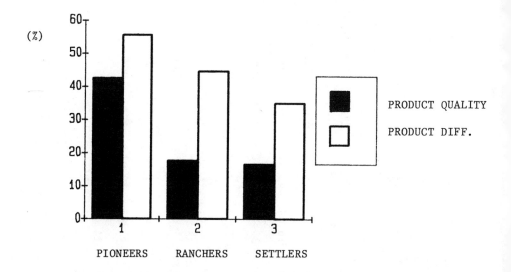

PIONEERS    RANCHERS    SETTLERS

Porter suggests that first movers will be able to establish the competitive rules of an emerging industry by defining technology and product standards.[22]  The first mover has the opportunity of producing and selling products with special characteristics that later entrants must adopt to compete in that industry.  While later entrants are struggling to match the standards of the first mover, the first mover can continue to go down the learning curve.  The first mover should have an advantage, then, in producing better quality goods. The results concerning product quality and differentiation seem to bear this out.  Pioneers produce significantly better products and a wider range of products than later entrants.  In mature businesses, high quality can be translated into high ROI as well.[23]  As the

[20]B. Hedley, "Strategy and the Business Portfolio," Long Range Planning, Vol. 10 (1977), pp. 9-15.

[21]B.D. Henderson, Henderson on Corporate Strategy, Mintor Books, New York, 1979.

[22]M. Porter, op. cit., Note 4, p. 188.

[23]R. Buzzell, Gale, B., & Sutton, R., op. cit., Note 19.

industry matures, the Pioneers may be able to transform the quality and differentiation advantage into better performance as well.

FIGURE 3

PIONEERS ACHIEVE HIGH SERVICE QUALITY

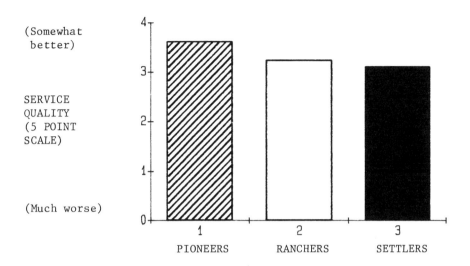

FIGURE 4

PIONEERS SPEND MORE ON MARKETING

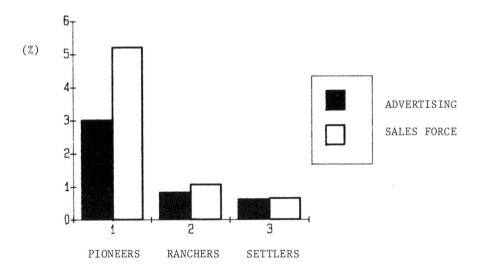

Pioneers achieved better service quality than later entrants. Service quality is a measure of the business's ability to stay close to customers, that is, provide support services which accompany the business's products. Pioneers may be able to achieve this position because of the emerging nature of the industry and the newness of the products. Customers may need training and support early in the PLC to use these new products effectively because the products are unfamiliar to them. The position of being close to customers may enable Pioneers to continue to innovate and develop more and better products to meet the needs to their customers.[24]

Pioneers spend more on advertising and sales forces than do later entrants. This result appears to support earlier studies which demonstrate that successful entrants enter industries aggressively.[25] [26] [27]

FIGURE 5

PIONEERS DO NOT ACHIEVE PRICE OR COST ADVANTAGES

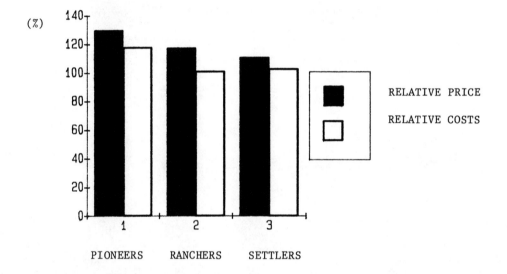

[24]M. Porter, op. cit., Note 4.

[25]R. Biggadike, op. cit., Note 8.

[26]E.L. Hobson, & Morrison, R.M., op. cit., Note 9.

[27]I.C. MacMillan, & Day, D.L., op. cit., Note 10.

Differences in relative costs and prices among the three types of firms were found to be insignficant. Pioneers do not achieve cost or price advantages over later entrants. Porter suggested that first movers may bear substantial costs that later entrants may not have to bear, such as: gaining regulatory approvals, developing needed raw materials and new types of machinery, achieving code compliance, developing an infrastructure, etc.; therefore, Pioneers would not be able to achieve cost advantages in the early stages of the industry's growth.[28]

We had assumed that Pioneers would be able to charge higher prices for new products. It was surprising to find this was not the case. New products do not appear to receive higher prices. Established substitutes may exist which provide a price ceiling which new products are not likely to rise above.

FIGURE 6

PIONEERS DO NOT HAVE HIGHER ROI'S THAN LATER ENTRANTS

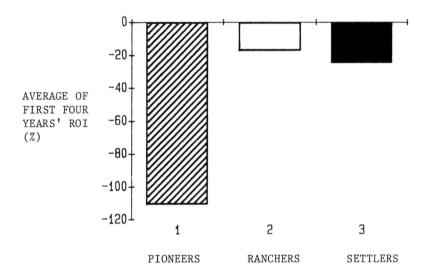

AVERAGE OF FIRST FOUR YEARS' ROI (%)

PIONEERS          RANCHERS          SETTLERS

Pioneers appear to have significantly worse performance than later entrants as shown in Figure 6. Because the variation in performance for the three types is so large (standard deviations of 42.51, 52.56, and 137.28 for Pioneers, Ranchers, and Settlers, respectively), there was no significant statistical difference in financial performance among the three types of firms. Pioneers had financial performance similar to that of later entrants on two other

---

[28] M. Porter, op. cit., Note 4.

measures (return on sales and cash flow on investment) as well. Our measure of progress toward improving ROI, V, indicated that Pioneers are making significant gains in ROI versus later entrants. We believe that this ROI improvement measure suggests that Pioneers steadily improve their financial performance and eventually surpass the financial returns of Ranchers and Settlers as the Miller and Camp study indicates.[29] But, Porter's assumption that early entrants become profitable earlier and achieve higher profits than do later entrants (in the short run) does not appear to be true for this set of corporate ventures.

We believe that the reason Pioneers do not show early and high profits is that substantial investments in gaining competitive advantages as first movers (in market share, product and service quality, etc.) are made in the beginning years of the business. This assumption has been supported in other studies that demonstrate that firms that enter industries aggressively achieve stronger competitive positions.[30][31][32]

## IMPLICATIONS

Pioneers do achieve important competitive advantages over later entrants. Pioneers have higher market shares, higher quality and more differentiated products, and better service. Pioneers appear to be positioned to achieve higher profits in the future. Our suggestion to corporate managers is to: BE FIRST. Corporate ventures that pioneer in emerging industries are much stronger competitively.

Managers of corporate ventures who expect immediate profits from pioneering in emerging industries will be dissapointed. As earlier studies have indicated, growing a corporate venture to where it is profitable requires over eight years.[33] Immediate profits were not forthcoming from any of the three types of businesses (Ranchers had the highest ROI of −17.27%). Pioneers will not generate early and higher profits.

Only market timing appeared to affect the results, that is, choosing to pioneer had significant consequences for the business's competitive position. Once an industry has been pioneered, the choice of entering the industry in its emerging, growth, mature, or declining

---

[29] A. Miller, & Camp, B., op. cit., Note 6.

[30] R. Biggadike, op. cit., Note 8.

[31] E.L. Hobson, & Morrison, R.M., op. cit., Note 9.

[32] I.C. MacMillan, & Day, D.L., op. cit., Note 10.

[33] R. Biggadike, op. cit., Note 8.

stages does not seem to influence the competitive position of later entrants. Ranchers did not achieve a stronger competitive position over Settlers, and vice versa.

We were very surprised that PLC had no affect on financial performance or competitive advantage. We would have assumed that firms entering emerging and growing markets would have higher profits than those of firms entering mature and declining markets because the emerging and growing markets provide more "room to grow" for the entering firms. Entering firms in growing markets should face less stringent competition and therefore achieve higher profits. Further studies need to be done to explore why PLC has no effect.

Additional studies need to be done to ascertain whether the competitive position attained by Pioneers translates into higher profits for these firms as they get older.

We recognize that competitive strategy for corporate ventures cannot be boiled down to such a simple rule as: be first. Anecdotal evidence suggests that Pioneers do not always achieve significant competitive advantages over later entrants (e.g., Bowmar in electronic calculators). Being first into an industry is not an guarantee that a business will be successful. Being first must also entail achieving competitive advantages as well. The mechanisms for how Pioneers go about achieving competitive advantages needs to be explored.

We believe that new businesses entering emerging industries are more likely to try out different types of competitive strategies because they are new themselves and exploring new and unfamiliar territory. The nature of Pioneering may be more than being first, it may also entail establishing new ways of competing as well.

## REFERENCES

Anderson, C.R., & Paine, F.T., "PIMS: A Re-examination." Academy of Management Review, Vol 3., 1978, pp. 602-611.

Ansoff, I, & Stewart, J., "Strategies for Technology-Based Business," Harvard Business Review, Vol. 45, No. 6 (Nov.-Dec., 1967), pp. 77-83.

Biggadike, R., "The Risky Business of Diversification," Harvard Business Review, Vol. 57, No. 3 (May-June 1979) pp. 103-111.

Buzzell, R., Gale, B., & Sutton, R., "Market Share - A Key to Profitability," Harvard Business Review, Vol. 52, No. 1 (Jan.-Feb., 1975), pp. 97-106.

Drucker, P. Innovation and Entrepreneurship. Harper & Row, New York, 1985.

Hedley, B., "Strategy and the Business Portfolio," Long Range Planning, Vol. 10 (1977), pp. 9-15.

Henderson, B.D., Henderson on Corporate Strategy, Mintor Books, New York, 1979.

Hobson, E.L., & Morrison, R.M., "How do Corporate Ventures Fare?" In J.A. Hornaday, J.A. Timmons & K.H. Vesper (Eds.) Frontiers of Entrepreneurship Research, Babson College, Wellesley, MA., 1983, pp. 390-410.

Hofer, C.W. "Toward a Contingency Theory of Business Strategy," Academy of Management Journal, Vol. 18, No. 4 (December, 1975), pp. 784-810.

MacMillan, I.C., & Day, D.L., "Corporate Ventures into Industrial Markets: Dynamics of Aggressive Entry," Journal of Business Venturing, Vol. 2, No. 1 (Winter 1987), pp. 29-40.

Miller, A. & Camp, B., "Exploring Determinants of Success in Corporate Ventures," Journal of Business Venturing, Vol, 1, No. 1 (Winter 1985), pp. 87-106.

Porter, M. Competitive Strategy. The Free Press, New York, 1980.

Porter, M. Competitive Advantage. The Free Press, New York, 1985.

Ramanujam, R., & Venkatraman, N., "An Inventory and Critique of Strategy Research Using the PIMS Database," Academy of Management Review, Vol 9., 1984, pp. 138-151.

# APPENDIX 1

## A DESCRIPTION OF MEASURES USED IN THIS STUDY

Market Share - The respondent's market share as a percent of the total sales in the market actively served by the business averaged for years 1 through 4.

Product Quality - The percent of sales from superior products sold less the percent of sales from inferior products sold averaged for years 1 through 4.

Product Differentiation - The sum of the percent of sales from superior products sold and the percent of sales from inferior products sold averaged for years 1 through 4.

Service Quality - The respondent's ranking of the quality of the customer services provided to end users (five-point scale, 1 = much worse, 2 = somewhat worse, 3 = about the same, 4 = somewhat better, 5 = much better) in relation to that provided by the three largest competitors averaged for years 1 through 4.

Advertising - The respondent's advertising and sales-promotion expenses as a percent of the total sales in the market actively served by the business averaged for years 1 through 4.

Sales Force - The respondent's sales-force expenses as a percent of the total sales in the market actively served by the business averaged for years 1 through 4.

Relative Cost - The respondent's cost as a percent of the weighted average of the leading three competitors' costs averaged for years 1 through 4.

Relative Price - The respondent's price as a percent of the weighted average of the leading three competitors' prices averaged for years 1 through 4.

ROI - (Net income + taxes)/total assets averaged for years 1 through 4.

Return on Sales - (Net income + taxes)/total sales averaged for years 1 through 4.

Cash Flow on Investment - (Net income + taxes + depreciation)/total assets averaged for years 1 through 4.

V (Progress Toward ROI) - Beta x $R^2$. The slope of the regression line (Beta) constructed from the first four years' of ROI, adjusted by the variability in the data ($R^2$).

# REDIRECTION DECISIONS IN SUCCESSFUL CORPORATE VENTURES

Tait Elder, University of Minnesota
Janette M. Shimanski, University of Minnesota

## ABSTRACT

A change of direction made after a substantial investment of time and money is examined for eight different innovations in the same corporation. All had become financially successful, returning many times their original investment while growing in size and breadth. In each example the decision to change was precipitated by a major failure. This failure appeared in retrospect to have been regarded as a lack of fit between an original product concept and real needs in growth markets which were unappreciated until revealed by actual use of a product. Capabilities and market insights derived in the course of the product development process were essential to the selection of an ultimately successful direction. A key redirection decision is analyzed in a standardized format for each venture. Provisional conclusions in the form of propositions to be tested by further research deal with false starts, discovery of growth markets, and the ambients for the redirection process.

## INTRODUCTION

In the past few decades, the number of new ventures has increased dramatically, although there is some disagreement on the quantification of this statement. In 1985 over 250,000 new businesses were reported in the U.S. representing a 20% increase over 1980 levels.[1] This rapid surge in new venture activities has been marked by a substantial number of businesses or new ventures which fail each year. Kibre (1983) reports that about 55% of new businesses fail within the first five years, with an additional 31% failing within ten years' time.[2] In other words, only one seventh of all new businesses

---

[1]William E. Bundell, "Failure: Spotlight on a Neglected Side of Business," Wall Street Journal, Section 2 (December 15, 1986), pp. 25-26.

[2]Dawit Kibre, "Myths of Small Business Failure," The CPA Journal, Vol. 53 (September 1983), pp. 73-74.

are in operation ten years after initial commercialization.  Among
those still operating, many are falling short of original expectations
for ROI, profit margins, or sales growth.

The corresponding record of failure for internally generated
corporate ventures is not so publicly detailed, although Sykes (1986)
has analyzed discontinued internal ventures of Exxon Enterprises.[3]
Many failures are not even counted, and successes are often buried in
some corporate operating unit without external fanfare.  The literature of corporate ventures is highly fragmented, and much has been
written for different readerships about the reasons for failure and
success.  This is illustrated by the 48 journal references given in
the review paper by Burrows (1982)[4] which are evenly divided into
three groups:  a cluster of general management journals, several
technical management publications, and a mixture of news, marketing,
planning, psychology and advertising magazines.  In addition there
were 13 varied books and monographs.

A high incidence of failure has provided a great deal of
research material.  The focus of the present work is different:  a
study of eight corporate ventures which have been financially successful by any measure.  The data base is open literature of historical
events, augmented by trade publications, reports to stockholders and
inputs from participants or close observers.  The purpose of this
retrospective look is to determine patterns of historically successful
entrepreneurial efforts in a common corporate situation, in order to
discover how to manage more effectively the interim successes and
failures with which current ventures must deal.

The paper is organized into four major sections.  First, some
measures used in the literature for determining venture success and
failure are reviewed, along with factors traditionally associated with
either outcome.

In the second section, nomenclature is developed to describe
corporate venture creation, establishing a convenient framework for
presenting the eight historical case summaries in a standardized
format.  This model is also represented graphically.

In the third the redirection decisions selected are presented
in abstract form, and common factors are identified.

The final section is devoted to discussion and conclusions,
with a particular interest in possible areas for future research.

---

[3]Hollister B. Sykes, "The Anatomy of a Corporate Venturing
Program:  Factors Influencing Success", _Journal of Business Venturing_,
Vol. 1, No. 3 (Fall 1986) pp. 275-293.


[4]B.C. Burrows, "Venture Management--Success or Failure?" _Long
Range Planning_, Vol. 5, No. 6 (1982) pp. 84-99.

CORPORATE SUCCESS AND FAILURE

## Criteria

Bruno, Leidecker and Harder list four factors which partially explain the problems which they identified in studying venture failure: establishing an appropriate sampling frame, reticence of founders to discuss failure, inability of founders to understand and articulate causation, and multidimensionality of failure.[5] These have their counterparts in any retrospective studies of success as well. In addition, both poor documentation detail and lack of comparability between financial summaries expressed at different times are typical of new corporate venture units. Bias may arise from many causes, including the fact that some of the contributing elements may be unknown even to the principals.

Several investigators have addressed the problem of defining success and failure in a way which is meaningful for ventures. Table 1, which is not presented as comprehensive, illustrates selected measures from the literature. In this table, independently published success and failure criteria are displayed in a common ranking which approximates their relative degree of difficulty or financial achievement.

In Table 1, the breakeven condition is highlighted. A hypothetical venture which achieves at least breakeven qualifies as a success by some possible measures.[6,7] Alternatively, breakeven could be designated a failure when compared with criteria cited by others.[8,9] One may well question the validity of a success criterion

---

[5]Albert V. Bruno, Joel K. Leidecker and Joseph W. Harder, "Patterns of Failure Among Silicon Valley High Technology Firms," _Frontiers of Entrepreneurship Research_, Babson College, Wellesley, MA, 1986, pp. 677-694.

[6]William R. Sandberg and Charles W. Hoffer, "The Effects of Strategy and Industry Structure on New Venture Performance," _Frontiers of Entrepreneurship Research_, Babson College, Wellesley, MA 1986, pp. 224.

[7]Robert W. Stuart and Pier A. Abetti, "Field Study of Start-Up Ventures--Part II: Predicting Initial Success," _Frontiers in Entrepreneurship Research_, Babson College, Wellesley, MA 1986, pp. 21-39.

[8]Edward B. Roberts, "New Ventures for Corporate Growth," _Harvard Business Review_, (July-August) 1980, pp. 134-142.

[9]Eric von Hippel, "Successful and Failing Internal Corporate Ventures: An Empirical Analysis," _Industrial Marketing Management_, Vol. 6, 1977, pp. 163-174.

TABLE 1
RANKING OF SUCCESS AND FAILURE CRITERIA

Measures of Success

ROI over 30%[6]

ROI exceeding that of
  lower risk investments[7]

Satisfy corporate ROI,
  profit and growth
  expectations[8]

ROE above breakeven
  but less than 30% [6]

Make 10% profit
  before tax[9]

ROE above breakeven[6]

Measures of Failure

Fail to satisfy ROI, profit
  and growth expectations[8]

Fail to make 10% profit 3
  or more years after
  start-up[9]

0 _____ Breakeven ROE[6] _____

Financial success
  weighted by employment
  and assets[7]

Nonfinancial success
  factors[7]

Survival[10,11,12]

Significant losses[6]

Discontinued[5,6,9,12]

[10]Dun and Bradstreet, The Business Failure Record, Dun and Bradstreet Corporation, New York, NY, 1985.

[11]Paul D. Reynolds, "Organizations: Predicting Contributions and Survival," Frontiers in Entrepreneurship Research, Babson College, Wellesley, MA, 1986, pp. 594-609.

[12]James D. Hlavecek, "Toward More Successful Venture Management," Journal of Marketing, VOl. 38 (October 1974), pp.56-60.

defined as mere survival accompanied by continuing annual losses; however, a number of large and well known corporations now find their entire operations to be in exactly that situation, and their stocks still trade on national exchanges.

The above comments do not imply that the criteria of Table 1 are invalid representations of the basis of real life judgments of ventures. Fast found, in a study of 18 corporate venture organizations, that the primary and consistent basis for measuring the perceived success of a corporate venture was matching the <u>current management expectation of performance</u>, whether that expectation was for protracted investment or for rapid growth in profits.[13]

Both von Hippel and Stuart and Abetti have stated that a long time frame--seven to twelve years--is needed to judge a venture on the basis of purely financial success criteria. The present study has followed this guidance; it has also avoided the difficulty of establishing comparable standards of success in different ventures by the selection of historical cases for which unequivocal financial success was demonstrated by major contributions to corporate sales and profits over a period of years.

## Factors Influencing Success and Failure

Prior studies have identified many structural or procedural elements which can be related to success or failure: market, product, innovation, personnel, leadership, control, strategy and management support systems. Block[14] (1982) lists 29 reasons which have been reported for venture failure in corporations. At the end of the list he notes, "There have also been outstanding successes where many of these elements have been present." The development process, including problems or experience with idea generation, product concept development, or dealing with the rest of the organization tends to be of more interest in the behavioral sciences, in memoirs or in more philosophical treatments.[15,16] Block and MacMillan[17] have proposed that an important goal of new venture business plans should be to produce and build on new knowledge, including redirection or replanning based on a

---

[13]Norman D. Fast, <u>The Rise and Fall of Corporate New Venture Divisions</u>, UMI Research Press, Ann Arbor, MI, 1977.

[14]Zenas Block, "Can Corporate Venturing Succeed?" <u>Journal of Business Strategy</u>, Vol. 3, No. 2 (1982) pp. 21-33.

[15]Ian C. MacMillan, "Corporate Ideology and Strategic Delegation" <u>Journal of Business Strategy</u>, Vol. 3, No. 3 (Winter 1983) pp. 71-76.

[16]Thomas J. Peters, "Putting Excellence into Management" <u>Business Week</u> (July 21, 1980) pp. 196-205.

[17]Zenas Block and Ian MacMillan, "Milestones for Successful Venture Planning", <u>Harvard Business Review</u> (September-October 1985) pp. 184-196.

growing body of understanding. The present study exemplifies this operational approach in historical examples, with particular emphasis on key decisions which later are seen to have had great moment.

## THE CORPORATE VENTURE DECISION SEQUENCE

In order to compare decisions and their impact for a variety of situations, some logical framework is needed to describe the background and consequences. In the original examination of venture successes, certain regularities or recurring patterns in the decision process were observed. Figure 1, which diagrams a typical decision sequence, introduces terminology useful in analyzing the case summaries. The three labeled arrows show essential stages: Definition, Development, and Redirection. These are connected by appropriate decision points.

### Definition

The core contained in the top arrow of Figure 1 is an idea for a new product or business. The caption "Definition" signifies that before a decision to proceed can be made some information must usually be assembled, e.g., patentability, general market knowledge, financial requirements. At this stage the general corporate resources such as facilities, procedures, and administration are helpful. In addition, specific corporate strengths pertinent to the idea--such as supplier relationships, scientific or manufacturing capability or customer contacts--help in the process of definition.

It is at this point that individual entrepreneurial skill is most important, for the utilization of many corporate resources and inherent strengths is not always easy. Most corporate resources were established for specialized needs, and diverting them for assessing an untried idea necessitates a certain amount of subversion.

The first decision may occur early or late, depending on the idea and organization. Because of the focus here on ventures, we ignore the two most probable outcomes: either that the idea may be picked up immediately by an existing operating business (transferred), or that it be shelved. Instead we assume that the venture proceeds to the Development stage.

### Development

A first decision to "proceed" leads to the second arrow captioned "Development". This entails not only further feasibility studies, but tangible progress in making prototypes. For our purposes, we assume that in this stage actual products are made. This process thus is able to generate both new capabilities and insights about what the product can do, how it performs in field or simulated usage, what its probable manufacturing cost may be, and how well it is accepted by the originally postulated users. Incidental to this is

# FIGURE 1.
## CORPORATE VENTURE DECISION SEQUENCE

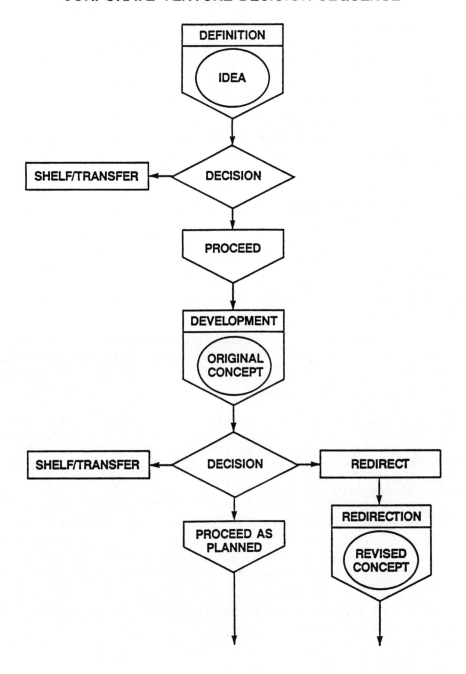

the development of new expertise in the venture people involved in the product, customer and management areas.

The timing of the second Decision is not necessarily at some end point of the Development process. In fact, it is not predictable, although certain events tend to trigger such a decision. When this decision occurs, the totality of what has been learned in the develop- ment step as of that time may be indispensible to making the decision wisely. Again we deliberately ignore the option to shelve or transfer the originally developed product/market concept and consider the two other alternatives shown:

1) Proceeding as planned, because the original idea appears valid, or

2) Redirection, to a revised concept for further develop- ment.

Our interest focuses now on those instances in which this last option has been selected.

Issues in Redirection

There are three issues in a decision to change direction: the occasion for decision or the trigger, the participants in the decision, and the definition of a new direction. The trigger may be internal to the venture (associated with either some problem or some new opportunity) or it may be external, such as general financial pressures on the corporation.

The actual participants in a management decision may be literally the responsible level of management. In venture redirec- tion, however, inputs to this decision come sometimes directly from top management, sometimes directly from users, and almost always from two or more functional groups in the venture itself.

The new definition of the business direction calls for preparation and planning similar to that for the original definition-- but it contains essential new inputs from the experiences of the development process. As a consequence redirection tends to be far more experientially based.

THE ROLE OF REDIRECTION IN EIGHT CORPORATE VENTURES

The findings discussed in this paper are based on analysis of the following eight independent corporate ventures which had succeeded as businesses within one large midwest organization.[18,19] Although

---

[18]Virginia Huck, Brand of the Tartan: The 3M Story, Appleton- Century-Crofts, Inc., New York, NY (1955).

they built on corporate strengths, all were truly new businesses
rather than extensions of existing product lines.

1) Waterproof sandpaper
2) Ceramic pigment signs
3) Highway centerline tapes
4) Resilient industrial adhesives
5) Moisture proof tape
6) Library copiers
7) Plastic matting
8) Inert electrically insulating liquids

## Sample Selection

The selection criteria for the above examples were: published
measures of performance, elapsed time since initial commercialization,
and variety in markets and technologies involved.

The first criterion, measures of performance, was intended to
verify the "success" of each venture included for analysis. An
understandable reticence on the part of corporations to encourage
public access to detailed financial records led to the happy choice of
historical samples whose success was beyond question in regard to ROI,
profit margin, and ultimate sales growth expectations. Figure 2,
from the 1965 Annual Report of Minnesota Mining and Manufacturing
Company, identifies 29 product areas which were important in that
year. Almost a third of these were derived over time from products
described in the above cases.

The second criterion, time since initial commercialization,
was used to ensure that long term measures of success had actually
been met. All of the ventures examined are at least twenty years
beyond initial commercialization.

The final criterion of variety was used to avoid simply
examining different aspects of the same business or team. Although
all of the markets served were essentially industrial, in several the
products were eventually sold to end users including consumers. The
technologies and products had some overlap in manufacturing techniques, but each involved a radically different performance specification.

## Case Summary Format

All the case summaries were analyzed in the pattern of Figure
1, in which three stages were identified in detail: original Definition, Development of actual product, and Redirection and the elements
of that decision.

---

[19]Minnesota Mining and Manufacturing Company, Our Story so Far,
St. Paul, MN (August 1977).

# FIGURE 2

## MAJOR 3M BUSINESSES IN 1965

### 3M diversified products for industry, business and home

"Scotch" brand pressure sensitive tapes and tape dispensers

Gift wrap products

Magnetic tapes, including video, computer, audible range and instrumentation tapes

"Scotchgard" stain repellers

Specialty chemicals and resins

Coated abrasives

"Scotch-brite" abrasive materials

Adhesives, coatings and sealers

Electrical insulating tapes, resins and corrosion protection materials

Electro-mechanical products

Thermoelectric and radiant heating products

Technical ceramics

Advanced magnetic tape systems

Wollensak magnetic tape recorders and home and commercial music systems

Photographic film, equipment and supplies

Carbonless "Action" paper

Roofing granules

Outdoor signing materials and services

"Scotchpak" and "Scotchpar" polyester films

"Tartan" surfacing materials

Medical products—surgical tapes, drapes, masks, dental materials

Copying machines and supplies

Visual communications products

Microfilm equipment and supplies

Lithographic plates, chemicals and printing preparation materials

"Scotchlite" reflective sheeting

"Scotchcal" marking film

Decorative laminating materials

Highway striping resins and tapes

Source: 3M 1965 Annual Report

519

Each summary centered on a redirection decision for a particular venture. For this purpose a venture is defined as a new product development effort involving uncertainty and significantly large risked cost. Patterns observed in the development process for some businesses led to selective re-examination of all for similar behavior--or its absence. One pattern discovered in the sample selection process is that once a business was successful financially it expanded into a succession of related areas.

## Eight Cases of Venture Success through Redirection

**Waterproof sandpaper**. 3M developed a water resistant, abrasive-coated sheet which failed to meet the needs of existing abrasives customers such as furniture finishers who preferred dry abrasion or oil-compatability. The business was redirected to appeal to automobile refinishers who valued the product's performance in abrading metal while generating minimal dust.

**Ceramic pigment signs**. An original weatherproof sign concept was developed, but failed to meet a real need given its limited color availability. A local roofing shingle manufacturer's request for more stable construction granules led to feasibility tests and a huge opportunity in colored roofing granules for 3M.

**Highway centerline tapes**. Based on a local highway engineer's request for brighter highway centerlines, 3M developed a glass pigmented tape which provided retroflective brightness. The reflective highway centerline tapes failed the durability tests of harsh weather and traffic conditions. The business was then redirected by utilizing the glass pigment tape technology to develop reflective sheeting for highway signs.

**Resilient industrial adhesives**. Adhesives consisting of rubber dissolved in gasoline were developed to bond cloth automobile roofs to the framing. Although the bonding was successful, the flammable solvent was unacceptable in large-scale manufacturing. This led to the development of non-flammable solvents which opened the door to many other automotive and other industrial uses.

**Moistureproof tape**. A need to bond sheets of cellophane to form a waterproof sheath for refrigerator car insulation led to a cellophane-based pressure sensitive tape. The market for this application was insignificant, but the availability of a moisture proof tape led to innumerable applications in the home and office.

**Library copiers**. A thermographic copy machine developed and sold for copying material from bound books was bulky, costly, and had only a small number of users. The product was changed to a portable model and a direct distribution system to offices was developed. These changes resulted in pioneering success in the office copier market.

**Plastic matting**. A non-woven matting for floor covering was sold into many small applications. Several product performance problems included curling, limited widths, and floor damage. A new application was identified as entranceway matting which was later developed and sold through an internal operating division in the building maintenance market.

Inert electrically insulating liquids. The use of fluorochemical fluids for transformers and relays was limited since alternative products were cheaper and of acceptable quality. However, a chance discovery that coatings of such materials could be used as stain repellents for fabrics and leathers led to a stain protector against both oil and water soluble stains.


## Common Factors

There were several features which the eight cases had in common. First, the initial product was made and offered for sale, but failed to meet the originally stated need, to deliver the promised performance, or to have a customer group of economic size. Second, a new direction came from trying the original product in a new and unanticipated application. It did not usually appear immediately.

The new direction also led to growth in sales, which then led to substantial alteration of the product form to match the new customer need. Since the development capability included both facilities and knowledgeable, motivated people, a great deal of effort could quickly be applied to exploring new directions which might justify further effort.

Although the nominal decision makers varied from one case to the next, preparation for the redirection decision involved two or more of the venture functional groups. In at least half of the cases top management was personally involved in the redirection; and in almost half one user's view was involved explicitly in defining the new course.

The direction change, essentially a new insight to make use of developed capability, came relatively quickly after it was recognized. On the other hand, implementation in the form of different product performance or manufacturing took place more slowly. In the course of meeting revised specifications in technology, product and manufacturing there were analogous redirections continually occurring on a smaller scale: substituting a raw material, tailoring product quality to customer need, or shifting to less expensive processes. The effective handling of these changes, as each new need became apparent from a constantly expanding base of insight and capability, demonstrated in practical terms the utility of entrepreneurial management to every venture function.

A basis for growth external to the venture was present in every case, whether the new direction was simply a new solution to an old problem (roofing shingles, adhesion, carpets) or filling a previously unimportant or unidentified need (auto body finishing, highway signs, office copies, stain repellents, mending). The growth was driven by the fact that at the time the product was introduced the number of customers or their level of need was increasing. These external growth factors would probably have been completely absent even ten years earlier.

Curiously enough, in all but one case (flammable adhesives), the originally conceived product eventually became a part of the product line, even though in most cases it only contributed moderate additional success.

## DISCUSSION

To put the foregoing into perspective, we review next the results of an earlier and broader historical survey of sources of industrial innovation in the first half of this century. Table 2 presents a summary of 71 inventions from the John Jewkes study of innovations.[20] In over half of the instances, the driving force for commercialization of these inventions was autonomous individuals. The laboratories of manufacturing companies accounted for only one third of the total selected, although successful inventions in the form of new materials from the companies outnumbered those from autonomous individuals two to one.

The Jewkes study used the word Invention in essentially the meaning used on our Figure 1 for the word Idea. Their definition of Development included both expansion on an original concept and determination of commercial feasibility in market terms. Notably, their word Development also included "another invention" which was required when "blockage" occurred--which probably corresponds to our terms of redirection and failure, respectively, as a part of the overall development process.

In both our study and that of Jewkes, the role of time is necessarily understated greatly. Time and timing of events are both absolutely vital, but in retrospective summaries they are unknowable in faithful detail. Both our "revised concept" and Jewkes' "another invention" may take a disastrously long time to appear. The persistent inventors in the Jewkes study often encountered new players who brought both insights and capabilities which had been needed. When these new contributors entered, financial success was simply distributed differently. In any event, the fact that Jewkes' stories ended in success shows that the expenditure rate between any blockage and the appearance of a new invention was not insupportable.

In corporate ventures, the situation is quite different. A brilliant new concept delayed by one or more years in a failing corporate venture may find that there is no longer an existing venture upon which to rebuild. It was in recognition of this situation that

---

[20]John Jewkes, David Sawers and Richard Stillerman, The Sources of Invention, Second Edition, W.W. Norton and Company, Inc., New York, NY 1969.

Table 2

INVENTIONS CLASSIFIED BY ORIGINAL COMMERCIALIZATION IMPETUS AND BY TOPIC

| Manufacturing Companies | Autonomous Individuals | Other Combinations |
|---|---|---|

MATERIALS, including plastics and biologicals

| Manufacturing Companies | Autonomous Individuals | Other Combinations |
|---|---|---|
| Acrylic Fibers, Orlon | | Bakelite |
| | Krilium | |
| Chlordane | Cellophane | Stainless Steels |
| DUCO Lacquers | Insulin | Tungsten Carbide |
| Freon Refrigerants | Penicillin | |
| Perspex, Plexiglass | Streptomycin | |
| Neoprene | Titanium | |
| Nylon | | |
| Polyethylene | | |
| Semi-synthetic Penicillins | | |
| Silicones | | |
| Synthetic Detergents | | |
| Polyester Fiber, Dacron | | |
| Tetraethyl Lead | | |

PROCESS IMPROVEMENTS

| Manufacturing Companies | Autonomous Individuals | Other Combinations |
|---|---|---|
| Continuous Hot-strip Rolling | Catalytic Cracking | Continuous Casting |
| Float Glass | Chromium Plating | of Steel |
| Oxygen Steel Making | Cotton Picker | Shell Moulding |
| | Electric Precipitation | |
| | Hardening of Liquid Fats | |
| | Photo-typesetting | |
| | Quick Freezing | |
| | Sulzer Loom | |

OTHER INVENTIONS

| Manufacturing Companies | Autonomous Individuals | Other Combinations |
|---|---|---|
| Cellophane Tape | Air Conditioning | Electronic Digital |
| Crease-resistant Fabrics | Air Cushion Vehicles | Computers |
| Diesel-Electric Locomotion | Automatic Transmissions | Long Playing Record |
| Fluorescent Lighting | Ball Point Pen | Radar |
| Modern Artificial Lighting | Cinerama | Rockets |
| Television | Cyclotron | |
| Transistor | Domestic Gas Refrigeration | |
| | Electron Microscope | |
| | Gyro-Compass | |
| | Helicopter | |
| | Jet Engine | |
| | Kodachrome | |
| | Magnetic Recording | |
| | Moulton Bicycle | |
| | Polaroid Land Camera | |
| | Power Steering | |
| | Radio | |
| | Rh. Disease Treatment | |
| | Safety Razor | |
| | Self-winding Wrist-watch | |
| | Synthetic Light Polarizer | |
| | Wankel Engine | |
| | Xerography | |
| | Zip Fastener | |

[Adapted from Jewkes et al (1969) pp. 66, 73, 75]

Figure 1 described two of the decision alternatives with the words shelf (rather than quit) and transfer (rather than divest). In other words, it is sometimes possible in a corporation to retain the ability economically to build later on the insights and capability resulting from a failed venture development process, where a needed creative addition eventually gives guidance. Furthermore, the alternatives of joint ventures, vendor agreements, or even licensing may retain financial benefit to the original corporation from business expansion outside of the corporate mission.

## Corporate Characteristics

In order to deal simply with the historical data in this study, we have assumed a corporate venture to be one originating in any company with sufficient resources to afford funding for growth. Even in the earliest case, 3M was a small company but profitable. All of the cases discussed above originated in areas of emerging if not wholly new technology. An existing company was a valuable if not indispensible source of early support. In fact, the practical consequence of the genius of Thomas Edison was greatly leveraged by his repeated ability to fund the development process.

The management of a successful operating business is accustomed to being resourceful in solving customer problems. It understands financial criteria and measures an expenditure by its expected reward. When an idea is shown by profits--or even by growing sales-- to be beyond the unproven investment stage, such a company has a high comfort level of expenditure.

In an established company, there are also existing relationships of trust and credibility. These are important to venture personnel initiating a new idea, for it is through such informal relationships that many corporate resources are made available.

Existing company employees also tend to think in terms of continuity and personal ambition, so that simply quitting when a new idea falters is less desirable than re-using it. Finally, the political climate of a corporation usually develops both supporters and detractors, and this may have kept a contested decision alive longer.

## Selective Features of 3M

The outcomes of our eight cases were undoubtedly influenced by a rare if not unique ambient for entrepreneurial activity which was present within 3M for the entire time in which these cases transpired. Personal philosophies of the senior management, notably William L. McKnight, set the tone for the corporation during this period:

1) Personal involvement of top management with individual employee business activities
2) Basic premise that the company needed to develop people with initiative

3) Belief that success could follow repeated failures through persistance

4) Tolerance of wide excursions if conducted with minimal expenditure and aimed at profitable growth

5) Focus on customer need, coupled with suspicion of theory--either in technology or marketing

6) Increasing realization of the profit potential of holding basic patents on products which satisfy growing customer requirements.

The epoch of 1920-1970 was a propitious one for small new endeavors within 3M. Even during the Depression, the company sustained some business areas because they were cost-effective to customers--and the businesses were small enough not to be driven completely by the national economy. Further, there were relatively few companies then competing in the New Product Development "industry".

## Conclusions

Since the study base is composed of simplified historical summaries of a qualitative and incomplete nature, formal conclusions are not warranted. However, hypotheses which may be tested by later research are stated as propositions.

Proposition 1. <u>False Starts</u>: In the development of a corporate venture, product-market concepts which fail in performance or acceptance are commonplace, being more probable and more numerous in proportion to the degree of innovation entailed.

Proposition 2. <u>Discovery of Growth Markets</u>: The major utility of the development effort of such failures is the foundation of capability and insight which is essential to the discovery of other commercial directions which are more promising both in entry timing and in identification of unanticipated growth market opportunities.

Proposition 3. <u>Breadth of Participation and Vision</u>: Utilization of new perspectives requires participation by several people having visceral experience with the product in use--functional group members of the venture team and a variety of potential users. The breadth of eventual exploitation depends on the resourcefulness of senior management in broadening the corporate mission or in finding other ways to profit from innovative beginnings (e.g., joint ventures).

Proposition 4. <u>Staying Power and Cost</u>: Since an old direction is usually seen to be failing long before some better utilization of new capability or insight is found to be viable, venture spending rates should be radically controlled to allow "staying in the game". Quitting tends to assure permanent failure.

Proposition 5.  <u>Independent Follow Through</u>:  After a venture is viable, operating units should be free to exploit aspects of the new direction in the form of related products timed to be profitable early rather than new long term investments.  No single organizational unit can carry an innovative venture to its full breadth of exploitation.

Proposition 6.  <u>Corporate Need</u>:  Corporations are capable of both initiating innovations and exploiting successful businesses.  They fail to approach the full profit potential of their own new enterprises unless redirection in some form is used to join these two strengths.

# SPECIFYING INTRAPRENEURSHIP

R. Jeffery Ellis, Babson College
Natalie T. Taylor, Babson College

## ABSTRACT

Intrapreneurial venturing is an important response to lack of innovativeness and uncompetitiveness of large corporations. Reports now have been made of the use of this phenomenon in 38 companies involving 117 corporate ventures. Content analysis was used to review this published practice to date. Cases were found to represent four distinct types of ventures and intrapreneurial activities could be synthesized as ten composite variable "driving forces." An array of venture types with the six most reported forces explained the overwhelming majority of variance in the data and provide an experience derived framework for advancing the management and study of intrapreneurship. Propositions are offered for further investigation.

## SAMPLE AND METHOD

A literature review demonstrated that the study of intrapreneurship is embryonic with few conceptual parameters identified. Limited opportunity has been provided for deductive, hypothesis testing. To embrace the fullest experiences of the phenomenon with reasonable overall depth, the ABS Inform database was employed covering principle articles from more than 660 management and business periodicals worldwide from 1971 to date. The key words "intrapreneur," "corporate venture," "corporate start-up," "corporate entrepreneur," and the limiter "case study" selected a total of 37 articles. Library searches have confirmed that no material accounts have been excluded from this sample. Of these articles, seven were rejected as anomalous, thus arriving at an effective database of 30 articles for this study.

Exhibit 1 presents the resulting sample, identifying 38 companies and 117 ventures. Many additional companies and some ventures were also mentioned in passing. A total of 58 projects were addressed in depth in the articles. For 32 more, the data were fragmentary and for 27, only cursory information was available. Inspection confirmed

The authors gratefully acknowledge the research assistance of James Ascanio and Carl Hedberg, Babson College MBA 1987.

a bias toward success exemplars.  The sample can be regarded as a compendium of reported "best practice" concerning intrapreneurism.

Initially, these accounts were reviewed judgementally to assess the nature of intrapreneurship as a reported phenomenon. Formal content analysis was then conducted first to distinguish overall patterns or categories underlying the variation in the sample. Second, general themes were identified on the grounds of frequency of mention.  Finally, the categories and themes so described were cross tabulated and inferences drawn.

Three investigators worked independently within designated steps in the content analysis.  Consistency checks demonstrated reliability of the analysis.  Co-researchers cross checked one with the other findings and inferences.

## SPECIFYING INTRAPRENEURSHIP

Categories were sought to partition total variance in projects so that variance within chosen categories was minimized and variance between categories maximized.  This process led inevitably to identification of four distinct types of ventures:  corporate ventures (frequency = 51), business ventures (frequency = 21), product/market extension ventures (frequency = 36), and efficiency ventures (frequency = 9).  Implications of these venture types for strategy, structure, process and risk were then postulated and evaluated against the data.

Six composite variables descriptive of the intrapreneurial activity common to all reported cases were then distinguished and later termed "driving forces."  These were Organizational Conditions, Sponsorship, Venture Process, Management Profile, Rewards and Awards.

The four venture types and six most frequently mentioned driving forces explain nearly all the significant variance in reported experience.  Venture types and driving forces form the basic parameters for specifying intrapreneurial venture activity embraced in this sample.

### Venture Types

Working from first principles, the venture types were examined conceptually along four dimensions:  strategy, structure, process, and risk.  A corporate venture was postulated to pursue a strategy of unrelatedness to present activities, to adopt the structure of an independent unit and to involve a process of assembling and configuring novel resources.  A business venture was reasoned to take place mostly at a level beneath corporate ventures and result in semi-autonomous units reflecting a process of configuring resources moderately related to those held in diverse locations in the corporation. Product/market extensions were postulated to involve a strategy of closely related ventures, adding units to an existing structure and needing a marshalling or sharing of facilities held within the business. At the lowest level, a venture whose objectives were to increase efficiency modified existing operations, leaving structure unaltered and strategy unaffected. Risk was postulated to parallel the type of venture, ranging from high for corporate ventures to low or non-existent for efficiency ventures. These postulates are adumbrated in Table 1.

TABLE 1:  VENTURE TYPES - POSTULATED DISTINCTIONS

| VENTURE TYPE | STRATEGY | STRUCTURE | PROCESS | RISK |
|---|---|---|---|---|
| Corporate | Unrelated venture | Independent unit | Assembling and configuring of novel resources | Unique - very high |
| Business | Mostly related business | Semi-autonomous unit | Resources held in diverse corporate locations | High |
| Product/Market Extension | Closely related new product, new market | Added to existing structure | Remarshalling or sharing facilities within the business | Moderate |
| Efficiency | Integral | Unaltered structure (Inside business) | Modifying existing operations | Low |

For the 18 ventures described in the greatest detail in the database, a pilot test was undertaken. Using integer value dummy variables, a close correspondence (about 80 percent of instances) was found between venture type, structure and process. Strategy was determined by a composite score reflecting the extent to which the venture was related to the host's production, marketing and technological activities. A correlation of 0.82 for 17 degrees of freedom ($p < .01$ significance) indicated a link between venture type and strategic relatedness of venture. Risk could not be operationalized but support for the construct was suggestive in that many corporate ventures were reported as failures (Sykes, 1986), while only one business venture failed (Pinchot, 1985a, Convergent Technologies) and no product/market or efficiency failures were reported, although sample bias is a factor to be weighed in this determination. It was tentatively accepted that there was a real distinction between the four venture types and that strategy relatedness, structure, process and risk all vary by venture type.

## Driving Forces

Composite variables common to all intrapreneurial ventures were derived by listing all significant mentions of actions under a 'lexicon' of descriptor headings. When collated, several themes were displayed strongly throughout the sample. These thematic descriptors were derived directly and systematically from the data and are sur- mised to represent, therefore, respondent statements of the "driving forces" for intrapreneurship as a whole. Each of ten forces is described below, together with its incidence in the data and the role that it played.

- **Goals** for intrapreneurship in any formal sense were only reported for the 3M company, but a determined, although unquantified commitment to selling new ventures or creative efficiencies was noted commonly (often after one or more ven- tures had arisen and shown the meaning of the concept).

- **Motives** were concerned with the reasons for selling and managing ventures. Evidence was fragmented but, in general, it was clear that managements were otherwise unable to inno- vate at the pace required to continue to be competitive. Motives were sometimes stated clearly for corporate ventures that involved major, irretrievable funding (Hardymon et al., 1983; Silver, 1979) but were more often implicit for ventures at lower levels.

- **Organizational conditions** stressed the exchange of information between different parts of the organization. This was to help stimulate ideas and facilitate cohesion around ventures when they materialized. The spawning of a climate for intrapreneurship was also addressed and concerned the readiness of organizations for intrapreneurship and idea stimulation. For lower level ventures this was reported fre- quently in the guise of creativity sensitizing and brain- storming sessions, for example. Attitude change also formed part of readiness for intrapreneurism where shibboleths were questioned, such as the inevitability of maturity of product life cycles and where a dislodging of staid norms was attempted by 'fun-days' (Baum, 1986), for example. These latter mechanisms were reported, particularly, for formerly conservative organizations and lower level ventures.

- Sourcing was concerned with where and how the particular venture concept originated. Examples in the data include usage of waste by-products (Marketing News, 1986), seeking customers for services previously provided only for internal corporate use (Data Communications, 1985), accidents demonstrating otherwise overlooked technical properties of substances (Polhill, 1985), customer initiated requests

(Donath, 1986; Polhill, 1985), company initiated customer
investigations (Donath, 1986; Pinchot, 1985a) and systematic
attempts by some companies to monitor technical and market
advances at large (Hardymon et al., 1983; Urrows and Urrows,
1983).

-    **Sponsorship** involved support of the venture from higher
levels. Senior levels sponsored projects in the deliberate
sense of agreed budgets and other resource allocations.
Perhaps more vital, however, was a more informal sponsorship
by managers just above the level of the venture who were pro-
tectors, mentors and facilitators through the organization.
In some cases, some of these activities were formalized
through a designated "office for venturing."

-    **Management profile** embraced the characteristics of
manager(s) directly involved with development of the venture.
These are the people who translated concept into profitable
activity. They "made it happen" with all that implies organi-
zationally.

-    **Venture process** was concerned with coordination of the
venture and its interactions with the organization at large.
Team building and maintaining activities were reported frequently together with the degree of autonomy of the
"intrapreneurial unit."

-    **Control** was carefully addressed only in the case of the
3M Company, but appeared a necessary theme throughout to
sustain ventures. Reportedly, control at 3M is positive and
facilitating, "Numbers are used to set goals and measure performance rather than to deny expenditures or punish for unmet
expectation." (Williams, 1986) Emphasis is placed upon
achieving balance between strategic and operational considerations. The role of controllers is seen as facilitation of
the intrapreneurial process by costing out new ventures and
helping managers prioritize opportunities.

-    **Awards** were also a conspicuous feature of the 3M
intrapreneurship system, but other companies reported
adopting awards activities as well. In 3M a variety of
awards are offered for recognition of individual as well as
team results, for specific functional areas (Donath, 1986;
Johnson, 1986; Kuzela, 1984; Williams, 1986) as well as for
general innovation. More specific award schemes include one,
for example, for the origination and transfer of ventures
within and between foreign subsidiaries (Polhill, 1985).

-    **Rewards** was a dominant theme and provided pecuniary and
career gains as well as other returns. Rewards both induced
further intrapreneurial activity and recognized its successful occurrence.

While further themes did appear sporadically (such as people orientation and active management style), their mentions were few, judged
incidental, and often could be incorporated adequately by refining the
scope of the themes identified above.

## Driving Forces by Venture Type

It was postulated that driving forces take different forms
according to venture type. To evaluate, reports for the six most
extensively mentioned driving forces were taken directly from the
database and arranged on the matrix of venture types by driving forces. Table 2 summarizes statements of preponderant reports for these
most extensively described driving forces. Inspection of the table
indicates general support for a different characterization of
intrapreneurship for each venture type.

The following tendencies existed through the four levels of
ventures:

- **Organizational conditions** reported separateness for corporate ventures and autonomy for business ventures. Decentralization and the pushing of responsibility and authority
to the lowest levels were reported for product/market and
efficiency ventures, respectively. Independence was
described for corporate ventures (such as freedom to buy in
anything from any source) while discipline mixing was
reported for business ventures, cross fertilization of functions for product/market ventures and idea generation and
attitude change for efficiency ventures.

- **Sponsorship** varies from chief executive and board insti-
gation of top level ventures to line manager encouragement
and driving of ventures at operating levels. For business
ventures it is reported that nurturing and real commitment
(psychological as well as resources) by senior management is
characteristic. For product/market ventures general manager
tolerance of initiatives and support with money and resources
is typical. Chief executive officers promulgate the concept
of intrapreneurship from the top to the bottom of the organization although the exact form of sponsorship is shown here
to vary by venture type.

- **Management profile** varied clearly by venture type.
Corporate ventures tended to comprise proven technologists
and accomplished professional managers. It was difficult to
discriminate evidence concerning management profile for business and product/market ventures. Broadly, business ventures
emphasized hands-on management and team building and this was
reported to a lesser degree for product/market ventures. The
intrapreneur as radical risk taker and rule breaker seemed to
occur more forcefully at lower managerial levels and for
product/market ventures. Resourceful individuals of any rank
close to operations drove efficiency ventures.

TABLE 2 – VENTURE TYPE – MAJOR LITERATURE REPORTS

| Primary Literature Focus | Organizational Conditions | Sponsorship | Management Profile | Venture Process | Rewards and Awards |
|---|---|---|---|---|---|
| Corporate | Separate company Independent (helps creativity) Visionary | The board, typically Funding and general intention defined but details undefined | Managers and technologists drawn from any source (independently of main sponsor) | Teams small and focused (mirrors independent start-ups) | Some reports of equity participation in revenues or internal royalty system (mostly unspecified) |
| Business | High autonomy Disciplines mixed through corporation | Ventures nurtured through commitment and discourse with senior levels | Takes hands-on responsibility to turn dream into profitable reality Personal drive to implement through to market Team builder | Boundary crossing teams Initially informal teams, then more formality Teams help set directions | Career rewards Greater access to discretionary resources |
| Product/Market Extension | Decentralization Cross fertilization of functional areas | General managers tolerant of independent initiative Money and resources made available | Team leader Creative, risk taker, master gamesman, tenacious, bucks rules, learns rapidly from failure, hard headed, thick skinned Crosses functional lines | Multifunctional teams Leader driven | Access to greater latitude within available resources |
| Efficiency | Responsibility and authority pushed to "lowest levels" Idea generation Attitude changing | Senior management zealously promote innovation. Line managers encourage and drive innovation | Opportunities independent of rank Individual, rather than team | Individual driven Top down education for innovation | Employee awards Bonuses |

    —   **Venture process** showed a progression from corporate ventures to efficiency ventures in decreasing scale, diminishing complexity, lesser novelty and shorter elapsed time. Teams went from "whole start-up companies" through self-directing teams of managers, leader driven multifunctional teams to particular individuals for many efficiency ventures.

    —   **Rewards and awards** varied from possible equity participation for corporate ventures, through longer term career rewards and access to fresh funds for business ventures, to greater latitude within normal allocations for product/market ventures, to shorter term bonuses and employee awards for efficiency ventures.

The above description embraces the overwhelming majority of variance in the database's cases and their content, and is offered as an efficient typography for the management and study of intrapreneurship.


## PROPOSITIONS


In this research a coarse grained sieve was used to examine the phenomenon of intrapreneurship. Overall, it was concluded that the phenomenon provides a set of sound and useful ideas for managing organizational innovation. Additional definition to the field was provided through the concepts of venture type and driving forces as identified and developed. Intrapreneurship serves different purposes at different levels in the organization because of the different circumstances that hold at each level. These findings pose propositions to address in subsequent work, some amenable to finer grain methodologies.

1.    Intrapreneurial ventures can be well specified by the interplay of venture types and driving forces.

2.    Intrapreneurial ventures exist in four distinct forms: corporate ventures, business ventures, product/market ventures and efficiency ventures.

3.    Each venture type embraces different configurations of strategy, structure, process and risk, as defined in this paper.

4.    Ten driving forces are significant and available in managing an intrapreneurial venture.

5.    The driving forces each take on different forms according to each venture type and configure differently for each venture type.

The findings and propositions developed by this research project promise, despite the inevitable exploratory methodology, a sound foundation for progressing study of the fascinating and vital field of intrapreneurship.

## REFERENCES

Available from the authors on request.

EXHIBIT 1

| Company | Venture(s) | Data Depth | Reference | Reject | Venture Type |
|---------|-----------|-----------|-----------|--------|--------------|
| Campbell Soup | a) Le Menu | Significant | Baum (1986) | | pdt/mkt ext. |
| | b) Prego | | | | pdt/mkt ext. |
| | c) Misc. other new products & product lines | | | | pdt/mkt ext. |
| | d) salmon aqua-culture process | | | | efficiency |
| | e) waste water heating system | | | | efficiency |
| | f) chicken boning equipment | | | | efficiency |
| Clark Equipment | | | Behre (1974) | discusses evolution of inter-national marketing programs | |
| Quantum | Hardcard disc reader | Fragmentary | Brandt (1986) | | business |
| Grace | a) Rotolite | Cursory | Burstein | | corporate |
| Olin | a) Continental | Cursory | et al. | | corporate |
| Tenneco | a) J.B. Systems | Cursory | (1985) | | corporate |
| Kodak | a) syncoa (batch trans-mission soft-ware) | Fragmentary | Data Communi-cations (1985) | | business |
| | b) local network digitized images | Cursory | | | business |
| 3M | a) light control film | Fragmentary | Donath (1986) | | business |
| | b) market informa-tion system–auto repair business | Fragmentary | | | pdt/mkt ext. |
| | c) Career Develop-ment Plan | Fragmentary | | | pdt/mkt ext. |
| Anaconda | --- | --- | Evans (1976) | conglom-erate trading of busi-ness | |

| Company | Venture(s) | Data Depth | Reference | Reject | Venture Type |
|---|---|---|---|---|---|
| Prospect Associates | a) minority health care contract | Cursory | Fenn (1986) | | pdt/mkt ext. |
| | b) worksite health care program | Cursory | | | pdt/mkt ext. |
| | c) Dental Research Institute | Cursory | | | pdt/mkt ext. |
| Unspecific | General | Significant | Finch (1985) | | |
| Exxon | a) Exxon Enterprises | Fragmentary | Hardymon et al. | | corporate |
| Genstar | a) Sutter Hill | Fragmentary | (1983) | | corporate |
| General Electric | a) GEVENCO | Fragmentary | | | corporate |
| AT&T | a) Epicenter software concept | Significant | Hoffer (1986) | | business |
| | b) Conversant systems venture | Significant | | | business |
| | c) NDT (resistivity testing) | Significant | | | business |
| | d) Medical Diagnostic X-ray image transmission | Significant | | | business |
| | e) Medical information Systems Venture | Significant | | | business |
| Digital Equipt. | f) Fire resistant paper stock | Significant | | | business |
| Polaroid | g) package of vacation diversions | Fragmentary | | | business |
| AFG | a) Hi-T R - photovoltaic glass | Fragmentary | Hubbard (1985) | | pdt/mkt ext. |
| | b) Comfort-E R - photovoltaic glass | Fragmentary | | | pdt/mkt ext. |
| | c) Mini Float R Glass System | Fragmentary | | | business |
| 3M | R&D Laboratories | Fragmentary | Johnson (1986) | | all |
| Lotus | a) partnerships | Fragmentary | Jubak (1986) | | corporate |
| | b) agreements | | | | corporate |
| | c) acquisitions (Dataspeed; Software Arts) | | | | corporate |
| | d) equity investment (Arity) | | | | corporate |
| | e) joint research agreement (Teknowledge) | | | | corporate |

| Company | Venture(s) | Data Depth | Reference | Reject | Venture Type |
|---|---|---|---|---|---|
| Savings and Loans Banks | "unregulated" banking subsidiaries | Significant | Kulczycky (1982) | banking specific and con-fined to product concept informa-tion | |
| 3M | a) asphalt shingle business | Fragmentary | Kuzela (1984) | | business |
| | b) glass bead bus. | Cursory | | | business |
| | c) Post-It | Cursory | | | pdt/mkt ext. |
| Dupont | a) Photo Products Department | Fragmentary | | | pdt/mkt ext. |
| | b) synthetic films | Fragmentary | | | pdt/mkt ext. |
| | c) printed circuits manufacturing | Fragmentary | | | efficiency |
| Allied Air Products | a) metal cooling process | Cursory | | | |
| | a) root constituent extraction | Cursory | | | |
| 3M | General | Significant | Lehr (1986) | | |
| | | | LeRoux (1986) | discusses risk man-agement (self insurance) | |
| Castle and Cooke | a) Fruit'n Juice bars | Fragmentary | Marketing News (1986) | | pdt/mkt ext. |
| | b) Fruit & Cream | Fragmentary | | | pdt/mkt ext. |
| | c) Fruit Sorbet | Fragmentary | | | pdt/mkt ext. |
| | d) Pineapple sauce | Fragmentary | | | pdt/mkt ext. |
| South-western Bell | a) Silver Pages directory | Fragmentary | Management Review (1986) | | pdt/mkt ext. |
| | b) Floating Clips | Fragmentary | | | efficiency |
| | c) "Bone's Pair Frogger" | Fragmentary | | | efficiency |
| Stew Leonard's dairy and supermarket | General | Fragmentary | McKendrick (1986) | | efficiency and pdt/mkt ext. |

| Company | Venture(s) | Data Depth | Reference | Reject | Venture Type |
|---|---|---|---|---|---|
| Control Data | a) Global Tech | Cursory | Nelton | | business |
| | b) Control Data Business Advisors | Cursory | (1984) | | business |
| Levi-Strauss | a) Winter Jeans | Cursory | | | pdt/mkt ext. |
| | b) Maternity wear | Cursory | | | pdt/mkt ext. |
| | c) Two Horse brand jeans | Cursory | | | pdt/mkt ext. |
| Hewlett-Packard | Low resolution oscilloscope | Significant | Pinchot (1985a) | | pdt/mkt ext. |
| Convergent Technologies | Workslate computer | Significant | | | pdt/mkt ext. |
| Radio Shack | TRS 80 computer | Cursory | | | business |
| DuPont | Automatic clini- cal analyzer | clini- Cursory | | | business |
| AT&T | remote telephone switch | Cursory | | | efficiency or pdt/mkt ext. |
| Hewlett-Packard | Low resolution oscilloscope | Significant | Pinchot (1985b) | | pdt/mkt ext. |
| 3M | Post-it Notes | Significant | | | pdt/mkt ext. |
| 3M | a) retro reflec-tive materials | Significant | Polhill (1985) | | pdt/mkt ext. |
| | b) capsule slow release plant foods | Significant | | | business |
| General – over 20 company citations | General | Significant | Rind (1980) | | |
| AT&T | a) multiline electronic telephone syst. | Cursory | Robson (1985) | | pdt/mkt ext. |
| | b) 400 computer modem | Cursory | | | pdt/mkt ext. |
| Silicon General | Hybrid semi-conductors medium | Fragmentary | | | business |
| General Mills | Product variants | Cursory | | | pdt/mkt ext. |
| | | | Rydge's (1985) | unavail-able (1 page) | |

| Company | Venture(s) | Data Depth | Reference | Reject | Venture Type |
|---|---|---|---|---|---|
| Charter Co. | | | Tell (1984) | reference to annuity insurers using up-front cash to finance unrelated corporate ventures | |
| Some 30 or 40 large companies mentioned | | Cursory | Urrows & Urrows (1983) | | |
| Data Corp. | a) Lexis legal search | Fragmentary | | | pdt/mkt ext. |
| | b) Direct Imaging | Cursory | | | pdt/mkt ext. |
| | c) Admark printing | Cursory | | | pdt/mkt ext. |
| 3M | a) insurance program savings | Fragmentary | Williams (1986) | | efficiency |
| | b) eliminated cost of extended credit terms and reduced duties | Fragmentary | | | efficiency |
| | c) eliminated 10% of departmental computer runs | Fragmentary | | | efficiency |
| General Electric | a) Biological energy corp. | Fragmentary | Wilson (1983) | | corporate |
| | b) reprogrammable semiconductors | Fragmentary | | | corporate |
| Acme Cleveland | a) robotics | Fragmentary | | | corporate |
| | b) laser systems | Fragmentary | | | corporate |
| | c) computer graphics | Fragmentary | | | corporate |

| Company | Venture(s) | Data Depth | Reference | Reject | Venture Type |
|---------|-----------|------------|-----------|--------|--------------|
| Signode | a) transponder | Significant | Schaffhauser | | pdt/mkt ext. |
| | b) microwave tray | Significant | (1986) | | pdt/mkt ext. |
| | c) plastic snow fence | Significant | | | business |
| GM | EDS-Jt. Ven. | Cursory | Shanklin | | corporate |
| GE | Hitech-Jt. Ven. | Cursory | (1986) | | corporate |
| GM | Fanuc-Jt. Ven. | Cursory | | | corporate |
| General: Value Eng. 3M, Control Data, Gulf and Western, Allied, Bohlen Technik | Corporate venture capital fund (external) | Significant | Silver (1979) | | corporate |
| Dylex, Inc. | | | Stern (1986) | Canadian specialty apparel retailing turnaround expert | |
| Exxon | a) Air Polution Control (1 venture) | Significant | Sykes (1986) | | corporate |
| | b) Health Care (1 venture) | Significant | | | corporate |
| | c) Advanced Mat. (2 ventures) | Significant | | | corporate |
| | d) Energy Conv. & Storage (3 ventures) | Significant | | | corporate |
| | e) Information Systems (11 ventures) | Significant | | | corporate |
| | f) Energy Conv. & Stor. Syst. (5 ventures) | Significant | | | corporate |
| | g) Advanced Mat. Components & Systems (7 ventures) | Significant | | | corporate |
| | h) Information Systems & Syst. Components (7 ventures) | Significant | | | corporate |

ENTREPRENEURSHIP IN LARGE CORPORATIONS
A CASE HISTORY

Roy Serpa, Borg-Warner Chemicals, Inc.

ABSTRACT


In 1979 Dr. James Brian Quinn of Dartmouth College stated that
"to solve the world's problems, we need innovation on a large scale.  Our
only hope is to make room for the innovative approaches of entrepreneurs
in our large corporations."  The same year the subsidiary of a major oil
company launched a new plastic fabricating business.  The planning for
and implementation of this start-up and its early operation were executed
in an entrepreneurial fashion.  The unique organization, management and
administration of this business was an example of the innovative
approaches that can be taken by large corporations.  This and similar
innovations are critical to the revitalization of our major corporations
if many of them are to survive the major rationalization and restructuring that will continue throughout the remainder of the 1980's.

This paper will present the history of this entrepreneurial
activity from the idea stage through start-up, growth and expansion.  A
perspective will be provided into the formation of this new organizational culture as well as the special efforts that were required to
maintain the arm's length operation of this autonomous corporate
sponsored small business.

INTRODUCTION


During this decade a major subject of discussion in industry and
academia has been the need for an entrepreneurial management style within
large corporations.  Peter Drucker has made the dire prediction that
"today's businesses, especially the large ones, simply will not survive
in this period of rapid change and innovation unless they acquire entrepreneurial competence."  In his book, Innovation and Entrepreneurship, he
contends that entrepreneurship is a practice that has a knowledge base
and can be pursued systematically.  However, during the past ten years
there have been few examples of the application of entrepreneurial
management styles to successfully launching new ventures by large
corporations.  The aversion to risk taking that exists in many large
corporations has discouraged new venture formation at a time when it is
needed most to revitalize our economy and create new jobs.

Although there are no statistics available, the common perception exists that except for the "excellent companies" very few large companies are capable of successful new venture creation and operation. The purpose of this paper is to encourage new venture formation by demonstrating that "entrepreneurial competence" can be developed within large corporations and can contribute to the development of new profit opportunities.

The following case history supports Drucker's contention that entrepreneurship can be pursued in a systematic manner.

BACKGROUND

During the 1960's several oil companies entered the plastic fabrication business in an effort to increase plastic resin consumption and add value to their raw materials. They learned very quickly that plastics fabrication was a very different business than the energy or plastic resin business. Usually these businesses were managed by entrepreneurs who had many years of experience in the marketing and manufacturing of fabricated plastics. Their organizations can be characterized as aggressive, decisive, and flexible with few management levels and low overhead. The oil companies had attempted to manage their fabrication businesses in the same manner as they managed their energy and resin businesses with a slow decision process, rigid policies and procedures and high overhead burdens. Not surprisingly, few oil companies were successful and during the late 1960's and early 1970's several abandoned these ventures after significant losses.

Among the companies that disposed of their plastics fabrication ventures was one of the top ten U.S. oil companies that will be referred to as Company X throughout this paper. The knowledge and experience acquired from this unsuccessful venture subsequently served as a resource to the planning and preparation for re-entering the plastics fabrication business in the late 1970's. In this instance forward integration was not motivated exclusively to acquire a captive outlet for its plastic resin. The objective was to learn how to operate successfully in the plastics fabrication business and to build a significant opportunity to add value and profit to the resin business over a ten year period. This venture would be part of a strategy to diversify into plastics fabrication that would ultimately encompass multiple product lines, penetrate several markets and establish production facilities in several geographic areas. It would be a start-up into a new market for plastic resins using proprietary production technology.

During the early 1970's Company X was a major supplier to a plastics fabrication market segment, one of the fastest growing areas for its resin. This segment appeared to offer an attractive forward integration route. However, due to its previous unsuccessful venture and the fact that Company X could not contribute anything unique to the market, it chose to monitor this market segment and concentrated on increasing its resin sales as a merchant supplier.

In 1975 at an international plastics exhibit, one of Company X's business development managers observed samples of a unique plastics fabricated part that was being used in the above mentioned market segment in Europe. The part was produced using proprietary technology developed by a European manufacturer. Although it had been produced and marketed there for more than ten years and in Japan for over five years, the part had never been commercialized in the U.S. Upon his return from the exhibit the business development manager reported what he had observed and recommended consideration of this product and technology as a new business opportunity. Discussion with the European manufacturer followed and in 1976 Company X purchased a one year option to license the technology for the U.S. During the option period Company X retained the services of a nationally recognized engineering consulting firm to conduct an extensive market research and feasibility study. It also hired a consultant with extensive experience in plastics fabrication and marketing. As a result of positive findings and recommendations from the consultants, Company X decided to pursue the opportunity. It negotiated and signed a long term exclusive license providing rights to manufacture and market the fabricated part in the U.S.

## THE WHITE PAPER

Early in 1977 the manager of the business development function prepared and submitted a New Business White Paper to Company X's senior management. This indvidual, a long term career employee, was one of the participants in Company X's earlier ill-fated venture into plastics fabrication. The "white paper" presented a basic concept of how to structure and manage what the author termed "a small emerging business venture." Senior management approved the concept and the required authorization for expenditures that were to guide and fund the venture for its first five years of operation.

The "white paper" stressed that a new business venture required unique management skills, decision making processes, controls and procedures, and marketing systems unlike those that existed in Company X. The new venture must avoid the tendency to manage and operate as an extension of the base business and avoid overhead allocations for services unrelated to and unneeded by a new business. In order to minimize risk the new business should access the advantages of services available from Company X without being burdened with its limitations.

The "white paper" referred to the prime competitive weapons of most small businesses as their speed of response and flexibility facilitated by short chains of command and rapid decision making processes. In order to reach its full potential, the new business was to be managed as autonomously as possible. Otherwise, it would become a second priority in a continual competition with the base business for the latter management's time.

The new venture must have the flexibility, speed of response, and other competitive attributes characteristic of the industry in which it would operate. The structure through which the venture's independence was to be maintained and at the same time Company X's services were to be made available, as needed, was considered a key success factor. The formation of a wholly owned subsidiary was proposed as the most appropriate organizational structure for managing and operating the new fabrication business. The subsidiary company was to be headed by a president who would be the operating head, the business manager and principal decision maker of the new venture. The president would report to a Board of Directors that would be composed of executives and business development managers of Company X who had been sponsors of the new venture. The head of business development at Company X would be the acting chairman of the board and serve as the supervisor of the President. The primary duties of the chairman were to guide and advise the President, manage the interface between the subsidiary and the parent company, and act as liaison between the members of the board and the President between board meetings. A key function of the chairman was to insure that the President (venture manager) and the subsidiary operated without any undue influence or direction from Company X's executives, managers or functional personnel.

The "white paper" went on to identify the guidelines for the selection of the venture manager. This decision was considered the most crucial to influencing the success of the venture. The assumption that the base business's sound management skills would be transferable to the new business was considered largely erroneous. The management tools were the same but the setting would be quite different. Although a manager was skilled, successful and productive in the base business in technology, marketing, finance or general management, equal effectiveness would not be assured in a small emerging business situation. On the contrary it was felt that the management style and functional specialization normally developed from long associations within a large corporation could well be obstacles to successfully managing this type of venture. Based on the foregoing it was decided that the venture manager would not be recruited from within Company X.

The guidelines for selecting the venture manager included the following:

1.  The manager must have some previous experience in the venture's industry.

2.  The manager must devote full time to building the venture's business.

3.  The manager must have a strong personal bond to the business, both a financial stake and an emotional commitment.

4.  The manager must believe that the reward is worth the effort.

The "strong personal bond" of the venture manager must be fostered by the confidence and support demonstrated and accountability expected by the board of directors in his decisions and actions in operating the venture. The manager's emotional commitment to the businesss must equate business and self such that it is "his" business.

The manager's additional strong personal stake was financial. The reward system must be commensurate with the success of the business and would include one or a combination of the following:

1.  Low salary/high bonus.

2.  Phantom stock options.

3.  Stock purchase/repurchase plan.

It must be sufficiently related to venture success to be highly motivational and should reflect the same high risk/reward components typically facing the owner-operator. System 1 was eventually selected for this venture.

Aside from the selection of the venture manager, no single action was more critical to the successful launching of the new venture than the preparation, executive commitment and implementation of the concepts and strategies of the "white paper." It established a context for the creation of a new organizational culture, a culture that would be significantly different from the base business and in keeping with the entrepreneurial nature of the new venture.

## ORGANIZATION AND PREPARATION

During the summer of 1977 the search for the venture manager was conducted using the guidelines outlined in the "white paper." The search was not an easy one since the most qualified individuals were well established in their companies and were reluctant to take on a new high risk venture. The most qualified candidate and ultimately the one hired was contacted through an industry aquaintance and not through an executive search firm. This individual had more than twenty years of experience in the market segment where the new product would be specified and sold. He had a strong marketing background and was considered a decisive, hard-working manager with excellent leadership qualities. The challenge of the opportunity to run his own business combined with the financial offer appealed to him. With his agreement the decision was made to hire the consultant who had worked on the market research study as assistant general manager responsible for manufacturing. These well qualified professional managers initiated a teamwork relationship that would characterize the new venture well into the future.

Both managers immediately outlined a plan to search for a site for the production and office facility, familiarize themselves with the process and equipment required for manufacture, procure it and install it. At first the approach was to lease a building in the Southeast (the location recommended by the feasibility study conducted earlier). Unfortunately due to the special requirements of the process, a suitable building could not be located. This situation necessitated that a site be purchased and a building be constructed. It also required that the scope of the project be expanded and additional funds be appropriated for the new venture. Fortunately, there was no consequent delay since the production equipment which was to be manufactured in Europe under the supervision of the licensor would not be available before the building was completed.

In the Winter of 1977 the subsidiary was formed, the board of directors elected and the strategic and financial plan for 1978 approved. The venture manager and the acting chairman initiated a close working relationship that was to work effectively from this point through the preparation for and start-up of the venture to the period of commercialization of the new product. During this delicate period the mode of operation was in conformity with the spirit and concept of the "white paper."

An interesting challenge to this method of operation occurred at the outset of the venture when the purchase of the manufacturing equipment was handled by the base business purchasing function as a service to the new subsidiary. The purchasing agent was reluctant to place orders for such expensive, sophisticated equipment with one supplier (located overseas) without requesting competitive bids. It was necessary for the acting chairman to meet with him and his superiors to explain that this matter must be handled as a special situation since the purchase had been authorized by the subsidiary board and was not under the jurisdiction of base business policy. Of course, the fact that the equipment was proprietary was another convincing factor.

As soon as a suitable site was located, the land purchase and the construction of the building were authorized by the board. Here again, the venture manager called upon the resources of the base business in the area of real estate and engineering. In each case services were procured on a fee basis.

The venture manager and his assistant rented a small office near the building site to monitor progress. They prepared a critical path diagram for construction, technical development and marketing events. While the building and equipment were under construction they began to develop a more detailed marketing plan. One major complication that confronted them was that the technical literature for the product was in a foreign language therefore requiring translation and conversion to U.S. units and design concepts. The decision was made to hire a consultant with extensive knowledge of the U.S. market to assist in preparing the technical literature that would be required.

Although the venture manager and chairman were in frequent telephone contact, it was thought advisable to have the board of directors meet once each month to be informed of progress and to have them available to support the organizational effort as needed. The meetings were brief (about 2 hours) and usually consisted of a status report presented by the venture manager and a discussion of future actions. The meetings that took place during 1978 allowed the board to get to know the venture manager very well and to gain confidence in his ability. It also allowed him to get to know them and to build relationships with individuals within the base business who would be able to provide support on an as requested basis. The working relationship between the venture manager and the acting chairman evolved into a close

partnership wherein both had confidence and respect for each other. The
venture manager made all tactical decisions on his own but relied on the
chairman for guidance and advice on strategic decisions. The chairman
acted as the major internal sponsor for the venture within the base
business and kept the board members informed on an informal basis between
meetings. There was a clear cut understanding established at the outset
that no one within the base business was to make requests of or to
provide guidance or advice to the venture unless the chairman agreed to
the action. This arrangement contributed greatly to avoiding unnecessary
involvment by the base business executives, managers, and functional
personnel.


## START-UP


During the Fall of 1978 the building was completed, the start-up
team was recruited and the production line assembled in Europe, inspected
and shipped. The Human Resources personnel from the base business were
helpful in determining suitable pay scales based on geographical and
industry factors as well as in recruiting the new employees. These
services were requested by the venture manager and billed on a fee
basis. It is worthy to note that the venture manager had developed such
strong personal relationships with functional personnel at the parent
company that often he received much more service support than was billed
to the venture. The monthly visits to the parent company to meet with
the board during the past year had provided him with the opportunity to
cement these favorable relationships.

The start-up team was carefully selected. It consisted of a
general foreman and six hourly personnel. The foreman had previous
plastics fabrication experience. He was sent to Europe to become
informed about the manufacturing process and equipment. After two weeks
of training by the licensor he returned to begin orienting the hourly
personnel before the equipment arrived. In addition, training was
conducted in plant and personnel safety. These early steps were to forge
what turned out to be an outstanding operations team and an enthusiastic,
industrious corporate culture.

In addition to the operations team, the first marketing representative and an accountant were hired. The former was a previous
associate of the venture manager who had experience in the targeted
market segment. He began to contact potential distributors and to
develop a tactical product promotion plan. The latter individual was a
female with accounting experience who began to establish an accounting
system with the assistance of accounting personnel at the parent
company. This versatile individual eventually managed administration and
purchasing as well as accounting.

In November the production line arrived and was assembled. On
December 1st it began operation. To mark the occasion the December board
meeting was held at the venture facility with the President and senior
executives of the parent company present. The high point of the occasion
was the meeting in the production area with all personnel present. The

chairman presented a wine (not champagne) toast to the venture team and to the success of the business.

That same month a second marketer joined the venture. This individual had over twenty years of sales experience in the targeted market segment and again was a former associate of the venture manager. He arranged meetings with potential distributors and began calling on major specifiers. Technical literature was completed and the product promotion program was launched.

As is a common occurrence in technology based businesses, initial operation of equipment does not result in acceptable quality product. In this case it took approximately two months before production problems could be overcome and a specification product could be produced. This achievement was facilitated by assistance from the individual who had developed the process in Europe. The initial production was used for selective field test demonstrations.

About this time the venture manager initiated a one page monthly newsletter that presented a brief overview of all venture activities. Copies of this newsletter were sent to all employees as well as board members. This newsletter served as an excellent communication vehicle both internally and externally. It also indicated the high level of confidence the venture manager had in his team.

As the start-up progressed, a major issue emerged. The equipment in place would provide the business with one production line and therefore if serious production problems developed with this sophisticated process or sales increased more quickly than anticipated, the venture would be unable to meet the demand that was being created. This issue was presented to the board with the proposal that a second production line be purchased. There were divergent opinions expressed by members of the board. The venture manager supported by the chairman and part of the board believed that the potential risk of lost business dictated that a new production line be ordered immediately since there was a nine month lead time. The remainder of the board felt that buying a second line at this point was premature and it would substantially increase the financial risk of the venture. The advantages and disadvantages of both courses were debated. Subsequently, the chairman requested a motion for affirmative action that was proposed, seconded and passed unanimously. This event was a strong positive indication of the problem solving style of the board that would characterize its function for the next two critical years. It also served as a vote of confidence for the venture manager.

As the venture became operational, the board decided to change the schedule for meetings to every other month in order to allow the venture manager to spend more time with his business.

THE FIRST ORDER

As the first quarter of 1979 ended, agreements were being negotiated with several distributors, inquiries were being processed and the first mailing to 10,000 prospective specifiers of the product was completed. The most significant event was the press conference that took place in New York City announcing the introduction of the new product to the U.S. market. The planning and preparation for this event turned out to be more complicated than anticipated. No one in the venture or in the parent company had any experience with a press conference to announce a new product. Fortunately, the chairman had used the services of a New York City public relations firm in a previous assignment. This firm had experience with press conferences and provided a plan that could be implemented by the parent company's public relations function on the venture's behalf. The press conference was successful with the attendance of twenty-two editors from major business and plastics industry publications. The venture manager and his assistant were the featured speakers. The product and their enthusiasm for the new business generated considerable interest and good coverage in the press.

The production team became more comfortable with the process and a significant product inventory was established. A potential application for the product was identified at one of the parent company's sites and prospects for other orders looked good. Post production complications in assembling the product surfaced and considerable effort was expended to develop new systems to overcome them.

Although production and marketing capabilities were in place and functioning, three months had passed without the generation of any sales revenue. Then in April it happened; the first order was received and billed for $1,786.

CRISIS AND GROWTH

During the second quarter of 1979 distributors were appointed, promotions programs continued and the second production line was ordered for delivery in early 1980. Fortunately, the order for product from the parent company was received providing an excellent case history for the product in the U.S. and contributing $115,036 of revenue.

From mid-1979 to mid-1980 the new venture confronted its first crisis. Sales grew very slowly; much more slowly than had been predicted. Acceptance was slow in coming because of the nature of the product, the need for evaluation and specification before sales and the fact that it was new to the U.S. market. There was considerable pressure for direct involvement by people from the base business. Due to an organizational change in early 1980 a new business development manager took over as acting chairman of the board and pressure for direct involvement intensified. The thrust of this effort was partially neutralized by transferring a marketing manager from the base business to the subsidiary reporting to the venture manager in mid-1980.

It was at this time that concerns about using distributors rather than company representatives and other questions about the marketing strategy surfaced. In retrospect two aspects of the marketing plan may

have been misdirected. One was to market the product through
distributors supported by a small number of company representatives.
Although the distributors had excellent market relationships, the fact
that the product was unknown in the U.S. market required a considerable
amount of attention and promotion to gain the confidence of the potential
customers. This level of effort was more than most distributors were
willing to provide. A larger number of company representatives may have
been a better strategy. However, as in any small start-up company,
control of costs was a preoccupation of management who were concerned
that the early years would result in significant losses and thus head
count and expenses should be kept to a minimum.

The other aspect of the plan that could have been reoriented was
the decision not to seed the market with a product imported from Europe
but to wait until domestic production became available. The thinking was
that U.S. specifiers and buyers would be reluctant to consider the
imported product and would prefer to evaluate the new product that would
be produced domestically. Here again, there was a mitigating circumstance in that the level of activity in other areas would have made it
difficult to support the introduction of the imported product during this
period.

The efforts with product promotion yielded continued interest
that would take time to result in orders. Selective case histories
demonstrating performance, exhibits at industry fairs, advertising and
direct mail campaigns along with emphasis on educating and working with
distributors were the tactics that occupied the marketing team. At the
same time the manufacturing team concentrated on upgrading and refining
the production process.

These activities were bound to pay off, and they did. In the
third quarter of 1980 awareness of the product's value to the customer
was growing rapidly and the number of potential orders increased dramatically. Not unexpectedly sales began to grow significantly during the
fourth quarter of 1980 and the first quarter of 1981. In January of 1981
the venture showed its first monthly operating profit and for the first
time had an order backlog stretching to the middle of March. Plans were
made to expand the existing facility and its production capacity.

The hourly labor force was increased from the start-up team to
fifteen hourly employees. The second process line was put into
operation. During the second quarter preliminary plans began for a
second production facility to be located in the Southwest. It was
expected to be operational in 1982.

Sales continued at a strong pace until the Fall. From then until
late 1982, business dropped off significantly due to the recession. In
spite of this situation, construction of the new facility continued and
although delayed, was completed in 1983.

The business recovered after the recession and has grown to the
point that another new facility will be completed in 1987 to serve the
West Coast market. Ten years after the commitment to start a new

venture the business will have grown to having three facilities serving the U.S. market for a product that did not exist previously.

## CONCLUSIONS

The success of this business illustrates that large corporations do possess the capability of planning, launching and operating new ventures. However, it also demonstrates that new organizational models, management styles and operating approaches will be required. Several major factors had a positive influence on the creation and operation of this new venture in its formative years. They were:

1. The approval and commitment that Company X's senior management provided to the concepts and strategy presented in the "white paper,"

2. The selection of the venture management and their ability to build a team that was dedicated to making the venture successful,

3. The implementation of the concept and strategy of the "white paper" by the venture manager and the board chairman especially in the maintenance of the autonomous relationship between the venture and the base business in the early years,

4. The persistence and continuous commitment of Company X's senior management to support the growth of the new venture during the periods of crisis.

These factors offer broad implications to the management of large corporations. They place priority upon new and different concepts and strategies that are usually not employed in existing businesses, the selection of management with unique management styles and the need for continuous commitments to new ventures during periods of crisis. To succeed in new ventures and to create new profit opportunities, large companies must become more entrepreneurial while the current financial environment places priority upon improved productivity and profit from established businesses. Drucker perceives no dilemma here since he believes that contemporary management must be entrepreneurial. However, few managers share this view of convergence. It appears that those managers who can effectively deal with this issue will prepare their companies for growth and profit in the 1990's while those who cannot will not survive that period.

SUMMARY

DEVELOPING CORPORATE ENTREPRENEURS -
THREE AUSTRALIAN CASE STUDIES

Author

John E. Bailey

Address

Centre for the Development of Entrepreneurs
David Syme Business School
Chisholm Institute of Technology
P.O. Box 167
East Caulfield 3145
Victoria
Australia
(03) 211 3710

Principal Topics

This paper documents three case studies of Australian corporations
in which a variety of programs of intrapreneur development have been
launched. The cases firstly outline the backgrounds to the companies and their need for corporate entrepreneurs; secondly they provide details of the various entrepreneur development processes used
and thirdly, they explore the results of corporate entrepreneurial
activity. The paper concludes with a discussion of the lessons
learned from the various cases and the methodologies employed.

Major Findings

The three organizations which are the subject of the case studies
are a large multinational manufacturing company, a large international chartered accounting firm and one of Australia's largest
companies involved in transport and associated services.

A variety of entrepreneur development activities were employed
within these organizations during 1986. A comparison of the
author's experiences in each company provides three major findings
or lessons. These are:

1. A proportion of participants in development programs for corporate entrepreneurs should be expected to withdraw from the

programs unless very careful pre-briefing and selection processes are applied. Participants withdraw for a variety of reasons but the predominant reason appears to be excessive workloads caused when normal activities are coupled with planning for entrepreneurial ventures.

2. Programs which employ training workshops coupled with personal counseling of intrapreneurs or teams, are more likely to produce well developed business plans and successful ventures than are programs which operate with training workshops only.

3. Changes to the cultures of organizations may be as valuable an outcome of development programs for corporate entrepreneurs as are the ventures launched by the participants. A firm which encourages its entrepreneurs through a development program, provides evidence to other staff that the culture of the organization is receptive to innovative ideas and activities.

SUMMARY

## INTRAPRENEURSHIP: EXAMPLES OF USING EXTERNAL TECHNOLOGIES FOR INNOVATION

Authors

  Elizabeth Gatewood
  Frank Hoy
  William Boulton

Address

  Small Business Development Center
  University of Georgia
  Chicopee Complex
  Athens, Georgia 30602
  (404) 542-6801

Principal Topics

  Although the literature contains numerous studies on organizational
  innovation, most research addresses the issue of internal development of innovation.  While authors have mentioned the option of
  external acquisition of technologies for innovation, this has not
  been a strong area of research interest.  Yet external sources are
  employed by firms engaging in new business start-ups.  This paper
  will contrast the practices of two firms in their use of external
  sources for start-ups.  A third firm will be used to illustrate how
  the use of external sources can change in response to a change in
  strategy.

Method and Date Base

  Using a clinical research methodology, data were collected on eight
  firms from published documents and seventeen interviews with personnel
  from the firms to produce in-depth case studies.  The firms in the
  sample differed on a number of different dimensions:  Size, industry
  characteristics, preference for innovation or efficiency, etc.
  However, all the firms used external sources of technology to some
  degree.

Major Findings

  All of the firms used external sources of technology to innovate;
  however, the importance of external sources to the innovative effort
  of the firms varied.  Some firms predominantly used internal development; external sources were only used to fill gaps or as "a

missing piece of a puzzle." One firm, however, based its innovation effort almost totally on external sources. Some firms used a more equally balanced approach of internal development and acquisition of external sources for innovation. Some firms used external sources for reasons other than start-up needs.

The importance of the role external sources played was affected by the history of the firm. If a firm relied on internal development or the use of external sources or some combination, and it had been successful in that approach, it continued to use that approach. However, major changes in the environment and/or organization could produce a change in the importance of external sources.

## Major Implications

External sources of technology can play an important role in new business start-ups. The benefits of using external sources should be evaluated against the benefits of using internal development.

Since firms use external sources of technology to innovate, a better understanding of the phenomenon could lead to a better understanding of the innovation process and intrapreneurism. One suggestion for future research would be to develop a large, randomly drawn sample from the business population that would allow for generalizations to be made to the population.

# FACTORS INFLUENCING ENTREPRENEURIAL EVENTS
## IN JAPANESE HIGH TECHNOLOGY VENTURE BUSINESS

Dennis M. Ray, California State University at Los Angeles
Dominique V. Turpin, IMEDE, Lausanne, Switzerland

## ABSTRACT

In this study of the founders of a new generation of Japanese high technology firms, we seek to understand the process of starting a high technology company in Japan. The focus of the research is on the entrepreneurial event following the spirit if not quite the model of Albert Shapero. The sample was drawn from the Nikkei Press Group which publishes an annual directory in Japanese of over 1,700 "high technology" venture business firms. A close examination of this directory reveals that there are somewhere between 100 and 200 firms that are both high technology and less than ten years old. From this list, we selected 100 firms for a single mailing of a Japanese language questionnaire and received completed questionnaires from 46.

The survey consisted of eight questions, six of which were multi-part questions covering the time frame for the formation of the company; circumstances which led to the formation of the company; sources of advice, the goals and motivations of the founder; social factors which played a role in the decision to form the company; how others perceived the decision; and the background and work experience of the entrepreneur. Interesting similarities and differences were found between U.S. and Japanese high technology entrepreneurs.

## INTRODUCTION

Few kinds of businesses hold the promise of high technology business. This is particularly true in Japan where a generation of entrepreneurs in the electronics industry not only created world leading computer and consumer electronics firms, but spearheaded Japan's movement to a leading position in the international economic system.

In this study of the founders of a new generation of Japanese high technology firms, we week to understand the process of starting a high technology company in a country better known for its technological and industrial achievements than for its spirit of entrepreneurship.

While the entrepreneur is the object of our study, our approach is not psychological. Rather our focus is on the entrepreneurial event following the spirit if not quite the model of Albert Shapero who was the first to direct research attention to the event. In other words, instead of looking at the personality of the entrepreneur, we are trying to identify what are the events that influence the decision for Japanese high-tech entrepreneurs to form their own company.

## RESEARCH DESIGN

### The Sample

While the Nikkei Press Group publishes an annual directory in Japanese of over 1,700 "high technology" venture business firms,[1] a close examination of this directory reveals that there are somewhere between 100 and 200 firms that are both high technology and less than ten years old.[2] Out of this list, we selected 100 firms for a single mailing of a Japanese language questionnaire and received completed questionnaires from 46 which is especially high rate of response for Japan or any country outside of the United States.

Aside from the enticing nature of the questionnaire, the high response rate can probably be attributed to the fact that one of the authors had lived in Japan for five years and had already interviewed a

---

[1] Bencha Bijinesu Joho (Data on Venture Businesses), Tokyo: Nihon Keizai Shimbunsha Ed, 1986.

[2] The expression, bencha bijinesu (venture busines) is used freely in Japan and does not always correspond to what would be called entrepreneurship in the United States and in Europe. It appears that linguistic and cultural barriers apply, and that these are mainly responsible for the ambiguity of the expression. The Venture Enterprise Center (VEC) in Tokyo has tried to rub out part of the ambiguity by making a distinction between "venture like" and "new venture" businesses. The main differences would be the age of the company, "new ventures" being less than twenty years old. Other criteria include company rate of growth, technical and financial independence, market potential, ratio of R&D expenditures to turnover, ratio of personnel engaged in R&D to total number of employees, and entrepreneurial spirit of the company founder(s). The criteria defined by VEC were used for selecting the sample of our survey. However, for comparative purposes with Western ventures, it was decided to restrict our studies to companies being less than ten years old. For more details on VEC criteria, see Bencha Bijinesu Doko Chosa Hokoku (Report on the Present Conditions of Venture Business), Tokyo: VEC, 1983.

Similarly, "high-technology" is also an ambigious term in Japan. For clarification purposes, high technology refers in this study to the following industries: microelectronics, mecatronics, optoelectronics, lasers, new materials, and information processing.

significant number of the respondents as part of his doctoral dissertation research on Japanese entrepreneurship. The response rate from entrepreneurs previously interviewed was 22 of 37 (60%) while the response rate from entrepreneurs not previously interviewed was only 24 of 63 (38%). This suggests that personal contact is not only a critical variable in doing business in Japan but also in the research of business phenomena.

## The Questionnaire

The survey consisted of eight questions, six of which were multi-part questions. The questions explored these dimensions of entrepreneurial events:

- The time frame for formation of the company.
- Circumstances which led to the formation of the company at the time it was formed.
- Sources of advice.
- Goals and motivations which led to the formation of the company.
- Social or environmental factors which played a role influencing the decision to form a company.
- How entrepreneurs perceived their entrepreneurial activities.
- How others perceived their activity.
- Family background and work experience of the entrepreneur.

In four of the eight questions the following scale was offered to the entrepreneur to apply to each factor in multi-faceted questions:

| Factor Importance | Numerical Value | Transformed Value |
|---|---|---|
| Critically Important | 1 | 4 |
| Very Important | 2 | 3 |
| Moderately Important | 3 | 2 |
| Slightly important | 4 | 1 |
| No Importance | 5 | 0 |

On the questionnaire, the numerical value of "1" was equated with "critically important" in order to reflect first or primary importance in the mind of the respondent. However, in the analysis and presentation of the results, it seemed more appropriate to assign "0" to a factor with no importance and "4" to critically important factors. This corresponded with the tendency of the respondents to simply not answer those portions of the questions which had no importance to them. All results are reported using transformed numbers unless otherwise specified in the text.

## Displacing Events

Out of 46 respondents in our sample, only 7 (or 15 percent) acknowledged the impact of some displacing event in their decision to become entrepreneurs. Of these, just 2 respondents considered the displacement to be very important and only 3 considered it moderately important.

559

Displacing events, like much social phenomena in Japan, may be ambiguous and have a subtle quality about them which our questionnaire could not capture. For example, after the 1973 Oil Crisis, recession and financial difficulties caused some large Japanese corporations to make drastic cuts in their global expenses, including R&D budgets. As some development projects were abandoned, individuals who were particularly involved decided to form their own company. This happened for example at Nippon Telegraph and Telephone (NTT) when Dr. K. Iwata, director of a research project on computer graphics, decided to leave NTT after top management decided to cut funds for his research project. As a result, Dr. Iwata established Graphica, which is today a leading company in computer graphics. Other high technology entrepreneurs in Japan may have had their research project displaced while their own position remained secure. This reflects, for example, the experience of Dr. Y. Yamano, an engineer formerly in charge of a research project on plasma display technology at Sony Corporation. When management decided to put an end to the project, Dr. Yamano took this opportunity to continue the project by establishing his own company, Dixy Corporation.

Interestingly enough, in the seven displacements, an opportunity was acknowledged to have arisen and probably played a role in the decision to launch a business, although in two of these cases the opportunity was classified as "slight." This suggests that necessity is not only the mother of invention but awakens one to opportunities in the marketplace.

In one case, a "critically important" opportunity was created by a friend and in all five of the displacements which were very important or moderately important, friends became the source of business opportunity. It appears that when someone is displaced in the Japanese economy of high technology, friends can be of a precious aid. This hardly comes as a surprise when one realizes that very often different complementary technical skills are needed to start up a venture in the field of high technology. This phenomenon of "team entrepreneurship" is of course not a unique Japanese phenomenon, as it can also be observed in the U.S.A. and in Europe. However, due to the strong propensity of the Japanese to work together, the phenomenon may be more common in Japan.

An examination of the 29 respondents who claimed that they had "no alternative but to form a company," found that in four cases there was no acknowledgment of the role of an opportunity in the decision to form a company. In three of these four cases, however, the respondents considered friendship as playing a "critical" role in the decision to form a company. Did these individuals come to aid of distressed friends? Only a follow-up study can answer this question with certainty, but it appears that in as many as nine cases in a sample of 46 (or just under 20 percent) the web of friendship obligation is involved in company formations. The relationship between friendship and entrepreneurship is a question which requires further research, particularly in the case of Japan where groupism and mutual obligation is part of a long tradition.

The respondents who felt they had "no alternative" to launching their company were tentatively classified as experiencing a subjective displacing event. The validity of this classification was checked in several ways. First, we cross-checked between objective and subjective events. All seven respondents who experienced a displacing event also indicated that they had "no alternative." Second, we cross-checked between those who might have had a high level of social marginality, as measured both by a social marginality scale and discrete variables refleting discontent with their previous position. We found a statistical relationship between social marginality and perceptions of "no alternative" at the .01 level of significance. This is summarized in Table 1.

TABLE 1

CROSS TABULATION BETWEEN SOCIAL MARGINALITY AND NO ALTERNATIVES

|  | Socially Marginal | Not Socially Marginal | Total |
|---|---|---|---|
| No Alternative | 20 | 4 | 24 |
| No Response | 7 | 10 | 17 |
| Total | 27 | 14 | 41 |

A form of social marginality that we did not explore in our questionnaire was the impact of education on high technology entrepreneurs since there are a number of surveys on the educational background of Japanese entrepreneurs. What these surveys clearly show is that new entrepreneurs are highly educated; half of them are university graduates. But the most successful entrepreneurs in Japan are not graduates from the country's elite universities but usually come from little-known local universities or local colleges. The Japanese university elite, graduates from Todai (Tokyo University), Keio, Waseda or other prestigious universities, prefer to join major Japanese companies or serve in a ministry where they are sure to receive the utmost job security and social prestige. A position in the Japanese Ministry of Finance, MITI or in a large business group is indeed the summit of social success in Japan. Therefore, few of these individuals will undertake the risks of entrepreneurship. However, entrepreneurship may be a useful vehicle for ambitious non-scholars to overcome low social status. Third, we cross-checked whether age was related to having "no alternative" on the grounds that the respondents might be experiencing some type of Japanese mid-life crisis and found no statistical relationship between age and perceptions of "no alternative." Finally, we cross-checked whether they strongly perceived an opportunity in the marketplace.

## Opportunity Pull

Opportunities come in all shapes and sizes from marginal to fully developed and irresistable. The later might include a clearly identified niche, a product waiting to be produced, customers asking to be supplied, talented friends who become available at the critical moment of decision, and an inheritance of more than enough money to launch the venture.

In this study, both the intensity and scope of an opportunity was examined. The variables included in our assessment of the pull of an opportunity were:

- Var. A: "Someone offered me an attractive deal or contract."

- Var. B: "I saw a commercial opportunity."

- Var. C: "My former company neglected to develop a commercial opportunity."

- Var. D: "The money to form this company became available.

- Var. E: "Close friends wanted me to form a company with them."

First, we attempted to ascertain the scope and intensity of opportunities in general. The results are presented in Table 2. The term "objective opportunity" refers to the first four variables listed above.

Second, we examined the distribution of opportunities by types and the results are presented in Table 3.

TABLE 2

NATURE OF CONTENT OF OPPORTUNITY
IN OPPORTUNITY DRIVEN ENTREPRENEURS IN JAPAN

| Intensity | Perception of Objective Opportunities | Opportunity Tied to Friends | Both Conditions | Total of Cases |
|---|---|---|---|---|
| Critically Important | 6 | 5 | 4 | 15 |
| Very Important | 5 | 0 | 1 | 6 |
| Moderately Important | 7 | 1 | 2 | 10 |
| Slightly Important | 1 | 1 | 1 | 3 |
| Sub-Totals of Cases | 19 | 7 | 8 | 34 |

Note:  No double counting despite the fact that some respondents responded to several of the variables.  Only the strongest measure of intensity is recorded here.

TABLE 3

OPPORTUNITY PULL AMONG JAPANESE ENTREPRENEURS

| Variables: | A | B | C | D | E |
|---|---|---|---|---|---|
| Critically Important | 7 | 0 | 5 | 2 | 9 |
| Very Important | 3 | 4 | 5 | 3 | 1 |
| Moderately Important | 6 | 2 | 7 | 8 | 5 |
| Slightly Important | 7 | 1 | 7 | 8 | 4 |
| Sub-Totals (Cases) | 23 | 7 | 24 | 21 | 19 |

The results are interesting because they point out the very concrete nature of opportunity recognition among opportunity driven entrepreneurs in Japan. Very few saw a general commercial opportunity (variable B); the pattern was far more common that they responded to a market ignored by their former company (variable C).

In this context, it is important to note several economic conditions. First, never before has the world experienced three simultaneous major technological revolutions - electronics, biotechnology and new materials - as being experienced in the advanced developed countries like Japan. The rapid development of multiple technologies creates a very large number of opportunities for technological start-ups. Second, these new technologies can be combined at different levels to open other major technological horizons. For example, electronics can be coupled with optics, mechanics or even biology to open vast technological fields like opto-electronics, mechatronics, or bio-electronics. The Japanese are particularly creative in this area. Third, large-scale Japanese companies have been accumulating technologies and patents at an incredible rate for the last thirty years. Not only does Japan remain a net importer of technology through license agreements and other purchases of technology, but Japan registers more patents per year than the United States. A single company cannot cover every possible technological "cross-over" that it has developed or purchased and choices have to be made on which technologies to commmercialize. This creates opportunities for Japanese entrepreneurs.

Whereas R&D teams in large Japanese companies tend to focus on technologies with the largest potential, individuals may recognize opportunities adequate for starting a company and many of Japan's new generation of entrepreneurs have decided to exploit technologies and market niches untapped by their former employers.

Role Models

If displacing events are not a major factor in explaining Japanese entrepreneurial events, then we need to explore other variables. The literature suggests that an unusually high percentage of entrepreneurs had fathers who were themselves entrepreneurs or farmers. Here again, our findings are not consistent with the pattern of entrepreneurial phenomena in other countries. Only five respondents had fathers who were entrepreneurs and another seven had fathers who were farmers, representing just over one quarter of the sample. However, if other categories of self-employment are considered, 43 percent of the sample had fathers who offered an entrepreneurial-like role model. these results are summarized in Table 4.

TABLE 4

FATHER'S OCCUPATION OF JAPANESE HIGH TECHNOLOGY ENTREPRENEURS

| Occupation | Frequency | Percentage |
|---|---|---|
| Entrepreneur | 5 | 10.9 |
| Farmer | 7 | 15.2 |
| Other self-employed | 8 | 17.4 |
| Deceased | 5 | 10.9 |
| Sub-total Non-employee | 25 | 54.3% |
| Employee | 14 | 30.4 |
| Public servant | 3 | 6.5 |
| Other employee (architect) | 1 | 2.2 |
| Sub-Total Employee | 18 | 39.1% |
| Unemployed | 1 | 2.2 |
| Unable to classify | 2 | 4.4 |
| Total | 46 cases | 100% |

An intriguing finding which deserves more attention in comparative research on entrepreneurship is that five (11 percent) of the respondents had fathers who died when they were young. While there is considerable criticism of psychodynamic models of entrepreneurial behavior, perhaps a minority of entrepreneurs can be explained in terms of such models and that a subset of the psychodynamic model is the role of the missing father.

Other role models, such as observing colleagues or others form companies, were examined and found to have only a limited role. These are reported in Table 5.

TABLE 5

NON-FAMILIAL ROLE MODELS FOR JAPANESE HIGH TECHNOLOGY ENTREPRENEURS

|  | Observed Colleague | Observed Non-Colleague |
|---|---|---|
| Critically Important | 1 | 1 |
| Very Important | 2 | 4 |
| Moderately Important | 5 | 5 |
| Slightly Important | 7 | 3 |
| Not Important | 31 | 33 |
| Total | 46 | 46 |

## The Spin-Off Phenomena

Over 90 percent of the new high technology companies studied by Cooper (1972) had at least one founder who had previously worked in the same industry. Approximately 85 percent of the new firms in the U.S. had initial products or services that drew on the founder's previous technical experience. U.S. experience clearly demonstrates that established organizations serve as incubators for new companies which do business in the same market. In Japan, 83 percent of the founders acknowledged that their firm was a "spin-off" from their previous experience. If all members of the founding team had been surveyed, the percentage undoubtedly would have been higher. The results are summarized in Table 6.

TABLE 6

SPIN-OFF PHENOMENA AMONG JAPANESE HIGH TECHNOLOGY ENTREPRENEURS

| Category | Frequency | Percentage |
|----------|-----------|------------|
| Spin-off | 38 cases | 82.5 |
| Not a spin-off | 7 cases | 15.2 |
| Unable to classify | 1 case | 2.1 |

Not only is experience in the target industry strongly associated with entrepreneurial events, it is also associated with the building of successful companies. Nearly 83 percent of the high technology entrepreneurs in Japan who acknowledged that their firm was a spin-off had either strong contact with the market or research and development.

TABLE 7

JOB EXPERIENCE OF JAPANESE SPIN-OFF ENTREPRENEURS

| Job/Career Orientation | Frequency | Percentage |
|------------------------|-----------|------------|
| Administration | 5 | 11.4 |
| Sales & Marketing | 13 | 29.6 |
| Finance & Accounting | 0 | 0 |
| Research & Development | 20 | 45.4 |
| Production | 4 | 9.1 |
| Export | 1 | 2.2 |
| Other | 1 | 2.2 |
| Total | 44 | 100.0 |

Note: From among the 38 spin-offs, one respondent held up to three positions and four held two positions, for a total of 44 positions.

Furthermore, those in positions of authority were twice as likely to launch a spin-off enterprise as those without substantial authority.

TABLE 8

CROSS-TABULATION BETWEEN SPIN-OFF ENTERPRISE AND LEVEL OF AUTHORITY
IN PREVIOUS EMPLOYMENT FOR 45 JAPANESE HIGH TECHNOLOGY ENTREPRENEURS

|              | Authority | No Authority | Total |
|--------------|-----------|--------------|-------|
| Spin-off     | 26        | 12           | 38    |
| Non-spin-off | 0         | 7            | 7     |
| Totals       | 26        | 19           | 45    |

Particularly intriguing is the fact that in all cases on non-spin-offs, the entrepreneurs lacked authority. In four of the seven cases of non-spin-offs, the entrepreneur had a father who was self-employed or had died when the entrepreneur was young; in all but one case the entrepreneurs acknowledged some perception of an opportunity (not a universal phenomenon in our sample); and in every case, the entrepreneur seems to be driven by a need to create, a high internal locus of control or a need for power.

The literature on entrepreneurship in the United States also suggests that entrepreneurship begets entrepreneurship and that most spin-offs are more likely to be generated by smaller as opposed to larger companies. This was definitely not the pattern among Japanese high technology entrepreneurs. One third of the spin-offs had incubator organizations that employed over 1,000 people and 59 percent came from incubator firms with over 250 employees. A reason for that may be that big business in Japan has been instrumental in developing the major technological breakthroughs that have inspired potential entrepreneurs.

TABLE 9

SIZE OF INCUBATOR ORGANIZATIONS

| Number of Employees | Frequency |
|---------------------|-----------|
| Under 10 | 1 |
| 11-100 | 7 |
| 101-250 | 8 |
| 251-500 | 5 |
| 501-1000 | 5 |
| Over 1000 | 13 |
| No Response | 7 |

While smaller firms do act as incubators for entrepreneurs, as more and more high technology venture businesses thrive, smaller-sized firms may begin to play an incubator role in high technology.

Feasibility:  Other Aspects

There is a very wide range of phenomena which shape the feasibility of entrepreneurship in a particular country.  While we will not try to describe these factors in Japan, we did explore how the respondents themselves perceived their immediate social environment with regard to entrepreneurship.  Somewhat surprisingly, we found that the majority of our sample perceived positive support for entrepreneurship in their immediate environment.  This is summarized in Table 10.

TABLE 10

PERCEPTIONS OF THE ENVIRONMENT FOR ENTREPRENEURSHIP

| Orientation | Frequency | Percentage |
|---|---|---|
| **Favorable** | | |
| Very Favorable | 6 | 13.0 |
| Moderately Favorable | 10 | 21.7 |
| Slightly Favorable | 17 | 36.9 |
| Neutral with Favorable Bias | 3 | 7.5 |
| Sub-Total: | 36 | 78.2 |
| Neutral | 2 | 4.3 |
| Unable to Classify | 3 | 7.5 |
| **Unfavorable** | | |
| Slightly Unfavorable | 5 | 10.8 |
| Total | 46 | 100.0 |

The significant aspect of this finding is that the high technology entrepreneurs did not find their environment unfavorable or negative. However, interviews conducted earlier with a similar sample showed that some constraints imposed on the entrepreneurs by former employers could be interpreted very negatively in the Western context. Perhaps this contradiction may be explained by the fact that many entrepreneurs tend to be optimistic by nature. Only additional research could tell to what extent the environment was really supportive of entrepreneurial initiative and to what extent do entrepreneurs reconstruct their reality, through selective perception and other devices, to fit their present needs.

The five respondents who perceived their environment as unfavorable scored at least moderately strong on two or more of these scales: social marginality, the need to create, or the need for self-actualization.

It is highly probable that a percentage of those with high levels of "social marginality," "needs to create," or a "need for self-actualization" are going to find resistance to these needs within their immediate social environment. However, in Japan, most high technology entrepreneurs do not.

If displacing events are not a strong factor in explaining high technology entrepreneurship in Japan, how are we to explain the phenomenon? First, our research found that the single most important of 49 variables to Japanese entrepreneurs was the desire to "create an opportunity for myself." In fact, the five of the most important variables were related to self-actualization and creativity. In order of descending importance they include:

- Create an opportunity for myself.
- Create an organization that reflects my values.
- Reached a critical point in my life.
- Create an opportunity to grow and develop my talent.
- Unable to exercise full creativity in previous position.

The tremendous success and achievement of the Japanese economy and the centuries of Japanese social and ethnic continuity point in the direction that Japan ranks at or near the top of countries in meeting the hierarchy of needs of its people. Not only does the social structure work against entrepreneurship, but success itself defuses that latent entrepreneurial drive most all of us possess. The one level of human need which the Japanese system does not adequately meet is the need for creativity and self-actualization. The need for creativity and self-actualization is probably not widely distributed in any country and its distribution is further restricted by social pressures towards conformity which vary from country to country but are universal. Thus, the apparent driving force behind Japanese entrepreneurship is a phenomenon unlikely to be widely distributed anywhere in the world and certainly not in Japan.

Second, it may well be that the Japanese are able to achieve within the framework of large organizations what other countries must accomplish through entrepreneurial development. Large Japanese companies, for example, have tended to play a stronger role in fostering employment through long-term employment security than their U.S. counterparts. Japanese firms are able to sustain a high level of innovation and invention within large organizations. Further, Japan has maintained a high level of economic growth for an advanced industrial economy through the dynamic qualities of their major corporations. As a "public good," entrepreneurship is usually discovered when other approaches have been tried and failed to stimulate jobs, technical innovation and economic growth. As other advanced developed countries seek to renew themselves, they ought to look at both the entrepreneurial option and how Japan creates these economic benefits within the context of large organizations.

Third, the impetus of Japanese economic development going back to the Meiji Restoration has been to "catch up with the West." Today, Japan has achieved most of its task and has defined a new challenge to become the world's leading country in sciences and technology by the year 2000. To the extent that entrepreneurship will facilitate this goal, we may expect to see more support for high technology entrepreneurship in Japan.  However, should high technology spin-offs prove to be disruptive of this goal, as some large U.S. electronic firms maintain, then technical entrepreneurship in Japan might be a rather limited phenomenon.

# ENTREPRENEURSHIP AND VENTURE CREATION -
## AN INTERNATIONAL COMPARISON OF FIVE COMMONWEALTH NATIONS

Leo Paul Dana, McGill University[1]

## ABSTRACT

Entrepreneurship may be initiated as a response to particular situational circumstance, environmental factors external to the entrepreneur. Governments, being in a position to introduce policies, and therefore influence the environment, may directly and indirectly enhance or repress venture creation. This paper examines the setting in five international contexts of various government intervention. The research involves five countries which were all once part of the British Empire, but which have evolved in various directions: Australia, British Virgin Islands, Cayman Islands, Malaysia, and Singapore. Today, each has developed differing policies promoting entrepreneurship in various ways, and to varying degrees. Indeed opportunities and constraints vary according to the environment, and governments do affect environments differently.

## INTRODUCTION

Traditional research postulated that entrepreneurship is a function of personal entrepreneurial qualities.[2] Yet psychology studies indicate that a genetic endowment may be redirected or tamped down or perhaps encouraged by the environment. [3] Recent research suggests that the

---

[1]The researcher expresses appreciation to the Australian Department of Industry, Technology and Commerce, the Economic Development Board of Singapore and the Malaysian Industrial Development Authority.

[2]For a thorough discussion see G.T. Solomon, "The Characteristics of Entrepreneurs and Small Business Owner-Managers", Proceedings, Creativity, Innovation and Entrepreneurship Symposium, George Washington University, March 21-22, 1985.

[3]John Leo, "Behavior", Time (January 12, 1987), p. 53.

environment may inherit or encourage venture creation.[4]  Wilken[5] and Shapero[6] are among those whose research emphasizes the cultural-societal environment as a major factor influencing entrepreneurship.  Dana[7] suggested an open society with social mobility which might therefore serve as a motivating force for the entrepreneur.

Peterson and Peterson[8] concentrated instead on entrepreneurship as a function of the political-regulatory environment, concluding that government paperwork requirements in Canada have become a burden on managerial time of owner-managers.  Levi and Dexter[9] have also found that government intervention hinders opportunity.  Dana[10] noted how the relaxation of regulation helps reduce barriers to entry, thereby increasing opportunity.

This paper looks at entrepreneurship policies developed by each of five governments, and how each affects the environment for small venture creation.  All five nations studied once depended on Great Britain for policies, but in recent years various levels of autonomy have been achieved.

METHODOLOGY

This paper is a descriptive study which necessitated field research in each of the five countries for talks with government officials, chambers of commerce representatives, and entrepreneurs.  Data gathering would otherwise have been incomplete.  Especially in developing nations, in order to be thorough,  one must often investigate and clarify in person on

---

[4]Peter E. Drucker, "The Discipline of Innovation", Harvard Business Review (May-June 1985), pp. 67-72.

[5]Paul H. Wilken, Entrepreneurship - A Comparative and Historical Study, Norwood, New Jersey, Ablex, 1979.

[6]Albert Shapero, "The Entrepreneurial Event in Calvin A. Kent (ed.), The Environment for Entrepreneurship, Lexington, 1984.

[7]Leo Paul Dana, "A Cross-Cultural Comparison of Attitudes Towards Owner-Operated Small Business", presented to the Canadian Society for the Comparative Study of Civilization, at the Learned Societies Conference, McMaster University, Hamilton, May 1987.

[8]R. Peterson and M. Peterson, "The Impact of Economic Regulation and Paperwork", Regulation Reference Working Paper Series, Ottawa, Economic Council of Canada, 1981.

[9]M. Levi and Albert Dexter, "Regulated Prices and their Consequence", Canadian Public Policy IX, 1983, pp. 24-31.

[10]Leo Paul Dana, "Flight Plans", Policy Options VII, June 1986, pp. 34-37.

location.  Gross[11] and Mitchell[12] are among many authors recognizing the need to be on location to verify conflict, misleading or inaccurate information.

## ENVIRONMENT FOR ENTREPRENEURSHIP IN AUSTRALIA[13]


In Australia, 500,000 small businesses account for 40% of private employment in urban areas.  These often generate more direct jobs per unit of invested capital than larger firms.  Yet small business may face disadvantages vis-a-vis the large multinationals in Australia, such as a lack of easy access to credit; lack of economies of scale.  For such reasons, the Australian government seeks to provide small businesses with an access to expertise and facilities relevant to their efficient operations and viable development.

Thus, the Australian state government assumes responsibility for the provision of direct services to small businesses in aspects such as counselling, training and information, while the federal government serves as coordinator and provides support functions such as research, publication and training materials.  The federal Department of Industry and Commerce also chairs and services the unit called the Small Business Working Party. The unit meets regularly in order to monitor development in programs assisting small business; provide a communication channel between governmental agencies, develop and implement a joint program of assistance to small business; develop policies and proposals for submission to the Standing Committee of Officials to the Industry Ministers' Conference.

Consequently the result has been a fully identifiable inter-government program to facilitate small business start-ups and operation in Australia.  A nationwide management training program has been established, based upon the distribution of training packages.  Central and state governments together have published a wide range of small business textbooks, management aids and small business profiles.  Total sales are in the vicinity of one million copies.

---

[11]Andrew C. Gross, "Analyzing Third World Markets" in McDougall and Drolet (eds.) Marketing 77:  The Canadian Perspective, Fredericton, New Brunswick:  Canadian Association of Administrative Sciences (June 1977), pp. 159-171.

[12]Lionel Mitchell, "Third World Government Marketing and the Survival of Small Economies", Proceedings, Administrative Sciences Association of Canada, International Business Division, June 1-3, 1986, pp. 28-41.

[13]For a detailed study, see:  Leo Paul Dana, "The Spirit of Entrepreneurshhip and the Commonwealth of Australia", presented at the 1987 International Council for Small Business World Conference, Simon Fraser University, Burnaby, B.C., forthcoming in the Journal of Small Business Management.

The Department of Industry, Trade and Commerce in Australia also organizes Small Business Awards to encourage venture creation and to recognize success.

The Department of Trade also tries to promote small business through a New Small Exporter Scheme whereby small business can apply for free expert assistance to develop export plans, survey export markets, make foreign contacts and participate in trade events overseas.

## ENVIRONMENT IN THE BRITISH VIRGIN ISLANDS

Unlike the U.S. Virgin Islands, the British ones are poorer and less developed. Airline service to the islands has been reduced with the cessation of flights by the now defunct British Caribbean, the only airline with jet service to the islands, and the only direct link with the United States mainland. Banking and commercial facilities are very limited. The currency is the U.S. dollar, and interest rates are normally based on points above current New York Prime Rates.

The government appears eager to stimulate its economy by improving the environment for entrepreneurship: Personal income tax is 5% on the first $7,500 of income, 10% on the next $7,500, 15% on the subsequent $10,000 and 20% on all income exceeding $25,000. To facilitate accounting, paperwork and auditing, tax is charged on gross income, with no credit for any personal allowances.

The company tax rate is 15% on chargeable income, but rates of 10% and 1% may apply. Dividends paid to shareholders and interest paid to non-residents are exempt from local tax.

The British Virgin Islands impose no wealth/capital tax, as exists for example in the Province of Quebec, Canada.

To protect its citizens, the government discriminates openly against non-residents: All businesses require a Trade Licence. Its cost is $10 or less for residents, but $300 for business persons residing in the British Virgin Islands for less than five years.

To encourage development by local entrepreneurs, citizens pay land tax of $3 per year on the first acre and $1/acre on all remaining property. Foreigners pay $20 for the first acre and $10 each for remaining acreage.

In order to encourage venture creation, a tax concession is available to all: Under the Pioneer Services and Enterprises Ordinance, entrepreneurs may obtain a tax holding of up to ten years while capital equipment for such enterprises may be imported free of customs duty.

Further concessions may be granted under the Hotels Aid Ordinance for building hotel rooms, with a tax-free period of up to 20 years.

The Cayman Islands are, by choice, a British Colony. They are self-governing, with a stable government committed to supporting its increasing reputation as an international finance centre.

To encourage entrepreneurship in the Cayman Islands, the Cayman Islands Companies Law, 1961, as amended, allows for the creation of investment companies, trading companies, ship registration, off-shore insurance, and royalties, patent and trademark operations, as well as local activities. Directors and officers may be of any nationality and need not reside in the Cayman Islands.

Whereas Peterson and Peterson[14] concluded that small businesses are a victim of paperwork burden in North America, the opposite is true in the Cayman Islands. Entrepreneurs in the Caymans have minimal paperwork and accounting reporting to do.

In the Cayman Islands, there is no direct taxation either on income or capital. There is no inheritance tax or death duty, no mutation tax nor capital transfer tax. The entrepreneur in the Caymans thus benefits from capital and income appreciating at an accelerating rate which would not be possible in jurisdictions of heavy taxation. Furthermore, a small business in the Caymans may obtain a guarantee from the government for exemption from taxation which may be introduced by future legislation for a period of up to 20 years.

## ENVIRONMENT FOR ENTREPRENEURSHIP IN MALAYSIA AND SINGAPORE

Despite close geographical proximity and periodic common history, Malaysia and Singapore contrast greatly in their attitudes towards entrepreneurship, perhaps due to cultural differences.[15] The ancestors of the Malays converted to Islam in the fifteenth century, shortly before the arrival of the Portugese in 1511. The latter were interested in ruling the area, for the purpose of using it as a base for spice trade. European rule was perpetuated with the arrival of the Dutch in 1641 and finally the British, who also confined their interest to mercantilism. These lived in urbanized areas, along with immigrant Chinese entrepreneurs.

The native Malays, calling themselves the Sons of the Soil, remained by choice, mostly in rural areas, and only relatively recently

---

[14]Peterson and Peterson, op. cit.

[15]Leo Paul Dana, "Evaluating Policies Promoting Entrepreneurship - A Cross-Cultural Comparison of Entrepreneurship Case Study: Singapore and Malaysia", Journal of Small Business and Entrepreneurship IV, Winter 1986-1987, pp. 36-41.

began the process of industrialization.[16]  In 1948, the Malayan peninsula, excluding Singapore, was formed into a very decentralized federation, becoming independent in 1957.  The reason for Singapore's exclusion was Malay concern of possible dominance by Singapore.  Nevertheless, in 1963, Singapore united with Malaya, Sarawak and Sabah (British North Borneo) to become Malaysia.  Singapore ironically found itself dominated by the Malays, and tensions arose due to cultural differences.  Malaysia adopted one official language, Bahasa Malaysian, and one official state religion, Islam, with stringent traditional requirements and cultural peculiarities such as four wives sharing one husband.  Consequently, Singapore opted for independence in 1965.  It hence recognized multiple languages and secularism in its constitution, and its industrializing elites pursued free enterprise industrial policies with tax incentives.  Agriculture has become an insignificant sector in the economy, with three-fifths of the workforce employed in service industries, and two-fifths in manufacturing.

Entrepreneurship in Singapore can be traced back to the flourishing Singa pura (lion city), a prosperous trading state in the fourteenth century.  This prosperity, however, ended with the conquest by Malacca.  In 1819, Sir Stamford Raffles, governor of Sumatra for the East India Company, purchased the island and turned it into a haven for entrepreneurs, a free emporium, a port open to merchants regardless of ethnic origin.  Singapore was thus reborn in the spirit of entrepreneurship, to promote the same; it grew to be the home of venture capitalists from different social, linguistic, racial and religious backgrounds.  Each culture brought along its respective ideology, attitudes and work habits.

In 1826, Singapore was incorporated as part of the British Straits Settlements, until it fell to invasion by the Japanese in 1942.  At the termination of World War II, it returned to the British, and enjoyed steady progress towards autonomy, aided by the British government.  It attained self-rule in 1959, and became completely independent from the U.K. in 1963, when it became part of the Federation of Malaysia for a period of two years.  The union was short-lived due to the abovementioned tensions between the Malayan leaders of the federation and Singapore's Chinese-dominated government.

Since the division, the two young countries have had contrasting environments for business.  Sharma and Jain[17] noted that during the decade 1973 to 1982 (most recent comparative data available) Singapore had 26 strikes while Malaysia had 467 strikes.

Malaysia has a population of 15,680,000 in 329,293 square kilometers; Singapore has a higher density, notably more urbanized, a population of 2,500,000 in 581 square kilometers.

---

[16]Leo Paul Dana, "Industrial Development Efforts in Malaysia and Singapore", Journal of Small Business Management, July 1987 (forthcoming).

[17]Sharma, Basu and Hem C. Jain, "Industrial Relations Practices and Multinational Corporations", Proceedings, Administrative Sciences Association of Canada, International Business Division, 1986, pp. 164-175.

## Singapore

In 1985, the Acting Minister of Trade and Industry introduced the Small Enterprise Bureau of Singapore, with programs to help small business, for which the Government of Singapore had allocated S$100,000,000 (Singapore dollars), with more funds forthcoming if necessary.[18] A division of the Singapore Economic Development Board, this Small Enterprise Bureau helps promising enterprises upgrade themselves and head for success, under the guidance of consulting advisors if necessary. Its primary mission is to assist entrepreneurs to upgrade their business, evolving their operations into efficient, well organized, technically competent and effectively managed enterprises, thereby contributing to the local economy.

The Small Enterprise Bureau has a General Assistance Department to help small enterprises become aware of and make full use of various assistance schemes available and also to assist entrepreneurs to develop business plans or proposals. It guides entrepreneurs to sources of information, potential financing, government incentives, grants, and even to consultations to develop business plans and marketing plans. Not only beginners are guided, but also those wishing to diversify or expand existing businesses. The General Assistance Department will also assist in forming a Cooperative where there are several in a given trade who need a united and concerted effort to organize the planning, administration, production and marketing functions.

Singapore's Small Enterprise Bureau promotes and facilitates business development and joint ventures, by providing a joint venture matching service backed by grants for business development and acquisition of new technology. Entrepreneurs in Singapore may thus benefit from strategic alliances with small businesses elsewhere. The bureau also provides specialized assistance to entrepreneurs. Financially, for example, under the Small Industries Finance Scheme, it provides working capital loans, machinery loans and even factory loans through sixteen credit institutions. Working capital loans are repaid over eight years, the amount of a loan not to exceed 70% of the machinery cost. Factory loans, which can be up to 85% of the value of the factory, are paid back over a period of up to ten years.

The Small Enterprise Bureau also provides services in credit control, insurance, bookkeeping and debt collection as well as finance. When an entrepreneur encounters a cash flow difficulty, the bureau makes available export as well as domestic factoring. The bureau pays the entrepreneur cash for approved invoices, and then assumes the credit risk and the cost of collection. In 1986, interest rates for financing through the Small Enterprise Bureau were 6% for export financing and 7 3/4% for the loans. The entrepreneur in Singapore can also apply to the bureau for a grant.

---

[18]B.G. Lee Hsien Loong, "Address by the Chairman of Committee on Small Enterprise Policy", at the seminar on "Management Productivity in the Small and Medium-Sized Enterprises", Singapore, November 12, 1985.

Malaysia

The federal government's goal is to emphasize and orient policy measures and programs to sustain socio-economic development and to ensure long-term economic stability as well as to undertake measures aimed at the eradication of poverty and restructuring of the social environment through government intervention. Its aim is to concentrate on industry as the main engine of growth. The government's agency for the promotion and coordination of the above is the Malaysian Industrial Development Authority. It handles all enquiries, plays the role of advisor to entrepreneurs, and evaluates applications for manufacturing licences, incentives, and import duty exemption. It also evaluates applications for tariff protection and quantitative restrictions.

Approved projects obtain tax reliefs. Accelerated depreciation allowance was also introduced, whereby from basis year 1986 the incentive is in the form of an initial allowance of 20%, and an annual allowance, to encourage investment in capital expenditures. Provided approval is obtained from the Minister of Finance double deduction is allowed on Export Credit Insurance premiums, and double deduction is possible for promotion of export. This includes expenses incurred in overseas advertising, supply of free samples abroad, fares in respect of travel and accommodation and sustenance expenses incurred by Malaysian businessmen going overseas, but within government guidelines. All details pertaining to such guidelines are available from the Malaysian Industrial Development Authority. The authority appears to have a centralized concentration of power. Its chairman as of January 1, 1986 has been Dato' Ahmad Sarji bin Abdul Hamid, also the Secretary General of the Ministry of Trade and Industry and a member of the board of Petronas, Permodalan Nasional Berhad and the National Sports Council as well as a member of the Foreign Investment Committee, Capital Issues Committee, the Committee on Invisible Trade and the Panel on Takeovers and Mergers.

For specific financing, the New Investment Fund of Malaysia was set up by the Ministry of Finance. In theory, it is similar to Singapore's Small Industries Finance Schemes, facilitating loans to entrepreneurs, but in fact in Malaysia, priority is given to export-oriented projects and those that generated new productive capacity only.[19] Its lending rate is 1.25% per annum over the Base Lending Rate of commercial banks. The entrepreneur in Malaysia is required to approach a commercial bank for queries on eligibility. Effective New Investment Fund Lending Rate in 1986 was approximately 11% (based on Base Lending Rate of 9.75% plus 1.25% New Investment Fund Surcharge). Meanwhile in Singapore the entrepreneur could obtain financing through the Small Business Bureau at rates as low as 6% during 1986 while the researcher was there researching this paper.

---

[19]Industrial Financing, Kuala Lampur, Malaysia, Government of Malaysia, Malaysian Industrial Development Authority, 1985.

Li Choy[20], professor of business at the National University of Singapore, remarked that Singapore has a very open economy with a social structure allowing success in business. Social mobility is thus relatively highand entrepreneurial success is highly regarded, as noticed also by the researcher of this paper, and the system is self-reinforcing as the Small Business Bureau helps more entrepreneurs succeed, setting a model for future interest in entrepreneurship.

In Malaysia, however, brochures and other literature published by the Malaysian Industrial Development Authority appear to be more preoccupied with internal concerns rather than an awareness of the entrepreneur's needs and concerns. Thus, whereas Singapore has helped its entrepreneurs and now the entrepreneurs are helping the economy, Malaysia remains a relatively poor country where the entrepreneur appears to have less of a role in economic policy. The Small Business Bureau of Singapore is a facilitator, while the Malaysian "Authority" emphasizes rules. Both offer loans, but interest rates are significantly higher in Malaysia.

It appears, therefore, that Singapore has better succeeded in promoting an environment conducive to entrepreneurship. Its slogan is "Who Says Small Business Can't Have Big Dreams?" Assistance is available to entrepreneurs and social mobility serves as a motivating force. Indeed, the entrepreneur in Singapore is facilitated by the government's Small Business Bureau, as well as the social and cultural environments which sustain it, and social mobility through entrepreneurship reinforces it.

The cultural and social environment in Malaysia differs greatly. The official religion is Islam, requiring women to cover their hair and skin in public. Malaysian women are less visible in positions of authority than their Singapore counterparts. Malaysia is still poor, with little social mobility, and an increasing gap between the income levels of rich and poor. The official religion of Malaysia being Islam, non-Moslem minorities continue to endulge in entrepreneurial endeavours perhaps because of the lack of social mobility possibilities other than entrepreneurship, such that there exists relative social blockage.[21] However, government intervention in Malaysia may suppress entrepreneurship more than encourage it. For example, whereas the Singapore Economic Development Board tells the entrepreneur how to set up a business in nine pages of text, in Malaysia 79 pages are devoted to policies.


CONCLUSION


The objectives of this study encompass an examination of the role of government in affecting the environment for entrepreneurship in five countries all with policies originating under the Union Jack. Today, each country has a different approach.

---

[20]Chong Li Choy, "The Entrepreneur as a Social Person", Journal of Small Business and Entrepreneurship IV, Fall 1986, pp. 34-40.

[21]E. Hagen, The Economics of Development, Homewood, Illinois, Dorsey, 1968.

Australia provides educational material on how to set up and maintain small business; it has a special program for small exporters. The British Virgin Islands gives tax incentives in the form of little accounting necessaryand little taxation, but giving preferential treatment to its citizens. The Cayman Islands have minimal corporate reporting and no direct taxation, for residents and aliens alike. Malaysia and Singapore, briefly united as one country, broke up due to cultural tensions. Both attempt to promote venture creation, but Singapore does so through a body called a "Bureau" which facilitates business start-ups and helps the entrepreneur; whereas Malaysia does so through a governmental unit referred to as an "Authority", which emphasizes rules and regulations, with apparently minimal assistance to the entrepreneur.

By researching and comparing policies of different nations, it may become possible to adopt certain elements and perhaps adapt them to other countries as well,[22] hence modifying existing environments and perhaps encouraging entrepreneurship.

## REFERENCES

Dana, Leo Paul, "A Cross-Cultural Comparison of Attitudes Towards Owner-Operated Small Business", presented to the Canadian Society for the Comparative Society of Civilization, at the Learned Societies Conference, McMaster University, Hamilton, May 1987.

Dana, Leo Paul, "Evaluating Policies and Promoting Entrepreneurship - A Cross-Cultural Comparison of Entrepreneurship. Case Study: Singapore and Malaysia", Journal of Small Business and Entrepreneurship IV, Winter 1986-1987, pp. 36-41.

Dana, Leo Paul, "Flight Plans", Policy Options VII, June 1986, pp. 34-37.

Dana, Leo Paul, "Industrial Development Efforts in Malaysia and Singapore", Journal of Small Business Management, July 1987 (forthcoming).

Dana, Leo Paul, "Marketing History", Policy Options VIII, April 1987, p. 37.

Dana, Leo Paul, "The Spirit of Entrepreneurship and the Commonwealth Government of Australia", presented at the 1987 International Council for Small Business World Conference, Simon Fraser University, Burnaby, B.C., reprinted in abridged form in the Journal of Small Business Management (forthcoming).

Drucker, Peter E., "The Discipline of Innovation", Harvard Business Review (May-June, 1985), pp. 67-72.

---

[22]Leo Paul Dana, "Marketing History", Policy Options VIII, April 1987 p. 37.

Gross, Andrew C., "Analyzing Third World Markets", in McDougall and Drolet (eds.), Marketing 77: The Canadian Perspective, Fredericton, New Brunswick: Canadian Association of Administrative Sciences, (June 1977), pp. 159-171.

Hagen, E.E., The Economics of Development, Homewood, Illinois, Dorsey, 1968.

Industrial Financing, Juala Lampur, Malaysia, Government of Malaysia, Malaysian Industrial Development Authority.

Leo, John, "Behavior", Time (January 12, 1987), p. 53.

Levi, M. and Al Dexter, "Regulated Prices and their Consequences", Canadian Public Policy IX, 1983, pp. 24-31.

Li Choy, Chong, "The Entrepreneur as a Social Man: Implications for Entrepreneurial Promotion and Development in Singapore", Journal of Small Business and Entrepreneurship IV, Fall 1986, pp. 34-41.

Loong, B.G. Lee Hsien, "Address by the Chairman of Committee on Small Enterprise Policy" at the seminar on "Management Productivity in the Small and Medium-Sized Enterprises", Singapore, November 12, 1985.

Mitchell, Lionel, "Third World Government Marketing and the Survival of Small Economies", Proceedings, Administrative Sciences Association of Canada, International Business Division, June 1-3, 1986, pp. 28-41.

Peterson, R. and M. Peterson, "The Impact of Economic Regulation and Paperwork", Regulation Reference Working Paper Series, Ottawa, Economic Council of Canada, 1981.

Shapero, Albert, "The Entrepreneurial Event in Calvin A. Kent (ed.), The Environment for Entrepreneurship, Lexington, Mass.: D.C. Heath, 1984.

Sharma, Basu and Hem C. Jain, "Industrial Relations Practices and Multinational Corporations", Proceedings, Administrative Sciences Association of Canada, International Business Division, June 1-3, 1986, pp. 164-175.

Wilken, Paul H., Entrepreneurship - A Comparative and Historical Study, Norwood, New Jersey, Ablex, 1979.

SUMMARY

CREATING AND REVITALIZING SMALL FIRMS:
A SURVEY ON ENTREPRENEURIAL BEHAVIOR IN ITALY

Author

    Daniele Boldizzoni

Address

    Instituto Studi Direzionali
    Via Mazzini, 127
    28040 Belgirate (Novara)
    Milano 796476
    ITALY
    (0322) 76375

Principal Topics

The paper examines: 1) the problems encountered and the skills, knowledge, behavior and management practices used by small entrepreneurs at times of critical change in the evolution of their businesses, notably at start-up and re-birth or revitalization; 2) the links between the process whereby a firm is created and that in which it is reborn and revitalized.

Method and Data Base

The paper gives the results of a survey carried out in two stages using:

1) a structured questionnaire given to a sample of owners of manufacturing firms with a minimum of 20 and a maximum of 150 employees, representative in terms of size and industry of the small business universe covered by the survey;

2) a highly detailed check-list that was completed at indepth interviews with a pre-selected group of 30 entrepreneurs who had all experienced at least two life cycles in the development of their businesses, and hence at least one revitalization stage.

Data were analyzed using cross-tabulations and factor analysis.

The most interesting findings emerging from the survey are that:

1) In the small businesses covered in the survey, the role and activities of the entrepreneur do not closely match the firm's problems, and tend to be particularly out of line at innovation and revitalization stages. Activities are somewhat more closely matched to problems in firms undergoing development and expansion.

2) The small entrepreneur's development and training process seems to be more geared to "skill enrichment" than to "skill enlargement." In other words, it is based more on building on the few "core" skills the owner had at the outset, rather than on acquiring an increasingly broad range of management skills in line with the growth of the business.

3) Owners engaged in innovation and revitalization seemed to be particularly jealous of preserving their original skills and instead of changing "genetically" from owner to manager, sought to adapt themselves while still maintaining their distinctive competence.

4) In plotting the firm's evolution, a number of different paths to growth emerged, starting from the individual traits and management culture of the entrepreneur and then diverging in terms of his acquisition and use of management skills and the development of distinctive competence.

5) Revitalization, in particular, is not based so much on the search for and development of a new competence as on the adaptation of the original distinctive competence that was successfully used to start up the firm and which were strengthened as it expanded.

SUMMARY

THE ROLE OF ENTERPRISE AGENCIES IN SUPPORTING ENTREPRENEURSHIP:
THE SCOTTISH EXPERIENCE

Author

    Frank Martin

Address

    University of Stirling
    Stirling FK9 4LA
    Scotland
    (0786) 73171

Principal Topics

This paper seeks to argue that the rapid development of Local
Enterprise Agencies with Scotland is an important link in the small
business network, and that their cumulative actions add to the climate of enterprise in Scotland. In so doing they help support the
development of entrepreneurship in that country.

Method and Data Base

A data base of agency activities developed by the Scottish
Development Agency was drawn on to provide extensive background
information on; the activities, funding and strategies of the agencies. A questionnaire was sent to all 32 agencies to provide information on their strategies towards the development of
entrepreneurship.

Major Findings

The Local Enterprise Agencies (LEA's) have effectively become the
first link in the business support network within Scotland. As yet
their principal client group are first time business start ups. To
this group the LEA's provide, as their principal activities, business counselling and training. However to effectively promote the
development of entrepreneurship the nature of the client group needs
to develop and mature into one where they are moving into new markets
with new or improved products. The need to move to a more proactive
strategy to assist this process is recognized by the LEA's, and definite signs are emerging of this process taking place, as witnessed
by the responses to the questionnaire showing 15 LEA's as dealing
with businesses which fit the definition of entrepreneurship given
at the start of the questionnaire.

## Major Implications

If the LEA's are to take on this more proactive role the level of training and funding available to the LEA's will have to be both maintained and enhanced. By so doing the agencies can ensure that level of competence and continuity so vital to developing a long term relationship with the area and the businesses they serve.

One possible outcome of this might be a significant reduction in the amount of small business start ups who fail to both survive and succeed.

SUMMARY

EMPIRICAL OBSERVATIONS ON THE NEW SOCIAL
ENTREPRENEURSHIP IN BRAZIL

Authors

    Fernando Quezada
    Alvaro Mello

Addresses

    Massachusetts Centers of Excellence Corporation
    One Ashburton Place, Rm. 2110
    Boston, Massachusetts 02108 USA
    (617) 727-7438

    Fundacao Getulio Vargas
    EAESP
    Av. 9 de Julho 2029
    CEP 01313
    Sao Paulo, SP, BRAZIL
    (011) 284-2311

Principle Topics

This paper examines the types and levels of opportunities which have become increasingly available for entrepreneurial initiatives in Brazil. Particular attention is given to the deliberate structuring of legal and economic policy measures to enable the small-scale, informal sector entrepreneurs to have access to these opportunities. Principal topics covered include a discussion of the Microenterprise Statute of 1984; Entrepreneurship in the face of the Brazilian economic reality; risk capital in Brazil; and Brazilian experiences in social entrepreneurship.

Method and Data Base

Interviews were conducted with selected entrepreneur support and promotion programs specifically established to reach out to otherwise disenfranchised elements. These programs were profiled with regard to key characteristics. Observations on these programs were linked with measures of compatibility with the emerging national policies which are intended to remove barriers to entrepreneurial initiatives.

Entrepreneurial efforts among the poor are natural outcomes of their needs for survival. Because support programs can be designed to tap the spontaneous energies of this sector, social entrepreneurship outreach has great potential at this time in Brazil's socio-political transition. The programs analyzed in this paper, however, demonstrate that as beneficial as partnerships are between government, industry and universities, the trust level between these sectors is not yet sufficient. Even as monetary incentives for social entrepreneurship efforts become more available, there is a wide range of strategic and structural alternatives as program models from which to choose. Any efforts to scale up assistance programs to reach more significant numbers of existing and potential entrepreneurs must be balanced by control and uniformity on one hand and on decentralization and flexibility on the other. Finally, while it may be clear that both government and industry have much to gain from creating a stable and more prosperous climate for entrepreneurship to thrive among the poor, sustained involvement on the part of universities increased extramural funding.

# ENTREPRENEURIAL ACTIVITY AND EDUCATIONAL BACKGROUND

Jeffrey C. Shuman, Bentley College
John A. Seeger, Bentley College
Nicholas C. Teebagy, Bentley College

## ABSTRACT

Academic institutions and their programs have substantial and significant impact on the entrepreneurial experiences and careers of their students. Over 4100 undergraduate and graduate alumni with backgrounds in business, accountancy, liberal arts, or engineering, from four colleges, were identified as practicing entrepreneurs, ex-entrepreneurs, or serious non-starters, and compared along five entrepreneurial dimensions --- demographic factors, entrepreneurial type, entrepreneurial role, career path, and time commitment.

## INTRODUCTION

The question of the best educational preparation for an entrepreneurial career is widely debated in both the academic and popular press. Reflecting his concern for education, Vesper expressed his belief that, "The most likely entrepreneurs to fail would be those with experience but no education. The second most likely entrepreneurs to fail would be those with education but no experience. Conversely, those entrepreneurs who had both experience and education would be associated with the most profitable business enterprises."[1] This makes the education issue an important one.

Between 1975 and 1985, the number of colleges or universities in the United States offering entrepreneurship courses increased from 104 to 253.[2] But what about the student's broader education --- does educational background affect entrepreneurial activities? Do academic institutions and their programs influence those activities differently?

---

[1]K. Vesper, "Introduction and Summary of Entrepreneurship Research," in Kent, C. A., Sexton, D. L., and Vesper, K. H., Encyclopedia of Entrepreneurship, Prentice Hall, Englewood, NJ, p. xxi.

[2]K. H. Vesper, "New Developments in Entrepreneurship Education," in Donald L. Sexton and Raymond W. Smilor, The Art and Science of Entrepreneurship, Ballinger Publishing Company, Cambridge, MA, 1985, p. 379.

While the flow of academic research on entrepreneurs and the entrepreneurial process has increased steadily over the past several years, no systematic investigation has been undertaken with a focus on the role played by formal education on entrepreneurial activities. The research reported in this paper builds upon a previous study by considering whether certain kinds of educational environments retard or help entrepreneurial development and success?[3]

## PROJECT DESIGN AND DATA BASE

The data for this study were abstracted from a larger database of 4135 respondents. All of the respondents were alumni of four colleges (Bentley College, Babson College, Rensselaer Polytechnic Institute and Georgetown University) who were participants in Phase I of the National Entrepreneurship Study directed by Robert Ronstadt at Babson College. As noted by Ronstadt, "... the resulting database represents the largest database that has been created primarily for research purposes."[4] Relatively high response rates were experienced from all four schools. These response rates were for one mailing only (i.e., no follow-up):

| College | Number Surveyed | Respondents | Rate |
|---------|-----------------|-------------|------|
| Bentley | 3,000 | 505 | 17% |
| Babson | 5,250 | 1,311 | 25% |
| Georgetown | 3,500 | 664 | 18% |
| Rensselaer | 8,500 | 1,655 | 19% |
| TOTAL | 20,250 | 4,135 | 20% |

We assume these respondents represent most (or even all) of the entrepreneurially inclined alumni from the original mailing. Respondents are not assumed to typify all of the colleges' alumni.

Respondents were included in our sample if:

a) they were age 27 or older (leveling was needed to account for differences in graduation cut-off dates used by the four colleges),
b) had graduated since 1946, and

c) they identified themselves as either --
practicing entrepreneurs (PE's) - people who are primary forces

---

[3]See Jeffrey C. Shuman, John A. Seeger, Judith B. Kamm, and Nicholas C. Teebagy, "An Empirical Test of Ten Entrepreneurial Propositions," Frontiers of Entrepreneurship Research - 1986, Babson College, Wellesley, Ma, 1986, pp. 187 - 198.

[4]Robert Ronstadt, "Phase One of the National Entrepreneurship Study," a report submitted to the Board of Research, Babson College, August, 1986, p. 2.

in starting, acquiring, or franchising a new and independent
organization for profit or non-profit,

ex-entrepreneurs (ExE's) - individuals who had been practicing
entrepreneurs in the past but were working for someone else at
the time of the survey (July of 1985), or

serious non-starters (SNS's) - individuals who investigated
starting an entrepreneurial venture but decided against it.

Not included in the analysis are respondents indicating that
they had never seriously considered or had any entrepreneurial desires
and/or experiences.

To test for any differences between students with associates or
bachelors degrees and those with advanced degrees, respondents were separated by degree level and entrepreneurial category:

|  | BABSON | | BENTLEY | | G'TOWN | | R.P.I. | | TOTAL | | GRAND |
|  | U | G | U | G | U | G | U | G | U | G | TOTAL |
|---|---|---|---|---|---|---|---|---|---|---|---|
| PE's | 396 | 369 | 166 | 62 | 101 | 113 | 411 | 500 | 1,074 | 1,044 | 2,118 |
| ExE's | 71 | 80 | 45 | 16 | 24 | 31 | 65 | 104 | 205 | 231 | 436 |
| SNS's | 57 | 110 | 63 | 25 | 38 | 59 | 42 | 121 | 200 | 315 | 515 |
| TOTAL | 524 | 559 | 274 | 103 | 163 | 203 | 518 | 725 | 1,479 | 1,590 | 3,069 |
| GRAND TOTAL | 1,083 | | 377 | | 366 | | 1,243 | | 3,069 | | |

NOTE: If a respondent does not have a graduate degree, we
know he/she graduated from the college shown. However,
if a respondent has a graduate degree, we know that
at least one of his/her degrees were from the designated college.

## ENTREPRENEURIAL DIMENSIONS

The survey questionnaire was designed to provide data on the
five entrepreneurial dimensions considered important in the literature.
Data was analyzed along each dimensional element both within and across
schools, as well as within and across the three major categories of
entrepreneurial experience.

### Demographic Factors

The demographic factor dimension looks at the respondent's age,
gender, marital status, and citizenship. Also studied are their ages
when they first seriously considered becoming an entrepreneur and their

ages when they started their ventures.  From the data provided it was possible to calculate each respondents' entrepreneurial career length.[5]

## Entrepreneurial Type

Respondents were asked to identify the type of entrepreneur they were in each of their entrepreneurial endeavors.  The focus of this dimension is to identify whether respondents pursued independent venture situations, were successors to family/non family business(es), franchisor/franchisee activities, corporate entrepreneuring, or self-employed.

## Entrepreneurial Role

The entrepreneurial role dimension considers whether the respondents chose to venture forth on their own, with a partner(s), as the lead entrepreneur, or as a member of an entrepreneurial team.

## Career Path

The career path dimension looks at the respondents work background in relation to their entrepreneurial activities.  If a respondent had a career prior to entrepreneuring, consideration is given as to whether that career was explicitly chosen as preparation for their own venture, was directly relevant experience, or unrelated to their entrepreneurial activities.

## Time Commitment

One measure of the commitment an entrepreneur makes to his/her venture is the time they allocate to the business during the prestartup, startup, and poststartup periods.  Data was collected as to whether the respondents considered involvement, are or were involved with their initial venture mainly on a part- or full-time basis.

## SCHOOL PROFILES

Presentation of the data by schools is complicated by the fact that the schools' alumni are not homogeneous populations.  Undergraduate and graduate degree holders sometimes show different characteristics, and the three entrepreneurial categories of respondents often differ from one another.  In the descriptions that follow, the word "alumni" is used to indicate relationships which hold for all of a school's entrepreneurial respondents;  "U" and "G" discriminate between undergraduate and graduate degree holders.  All comparative statements are based on Chi-square tests or analysis of variance showing significant differences between schools at the level of $p < .05$ or less;  where significance meets the tighter standard, $p < .01$, the statement is marked with an asterisk.  (See Tables 1 and 2 for comparative percentage responses.)

---

[5]See Robert Ronstadt, "The Corridor Principle and Entrepreneurial Time," unpublished research paper, Babson College, Wellesley, MA, 1986.

## Georgetown University

Of the four schools participating, only Georgetown has a noticeable proportion of women in its entrepreneurial alumni. Of its undergraduate alumni PE's, 6.9 percent are women (*); 12.5 percent of its ex-entrepreneurs and 26.3 percent of its serious non-starters are women (*). Georgetown's graduate degree holding alumni show similar percentages of women in the ExE (*) and SNS categories. Fewer of Georgetown's practicing entrepreneurs are married (U *); the same is true of its serious non-starters (G *).

### TABLE 1: SIGNIFICANT DIFFERENCES BETWEEN SCHOOLS
### Percentages of Undergraduate Respondents, by School

All relationships shown here are significant at the level p < .05 (unmarked in the left-most column) or p < .01 (marked with an asterisk in the left-most column).

| | | Babson | Bentley | G'town | R.P.I. |
|---|---|---|---|---|---|
| **Demographics** | | | | | |
| * | Married (Practicing Entr's) | 82.0% | 84.3% | 71.3% | 88.1% |
| * | Married (Serious Non-Starts) | 87.5 | 88.9 | 65.8 | 90.5 |
| | Widowed (Practicing Entr's) | 1.3 | 4.8 | 0 | 2.3 |
| * | Male (Practicing Entr's) | 97.0 | 94.6 | 93.1 | 98.8 |
| * | Male (Serious Non-Starters) | 86.0 | 93.7 | 73.7 | 100.0 |
| | Male (Ex-Entrepreneurs) | 100.0 | 95.6 | 87.5 | 98.5 |
| * | Divorced (Ex-Entrepreneurs) | 28.2 | 6.7 | 8.3 | 17.5 |
| * | Career Length in years (PE) | 14.5 | 14.2 | 10.0 | 15.0 |
| | Career Length in years (ExE) | 9.9 | 10.7 | 3.5 | 9.6 |
| | | | | | |
| **Entrepreneurial Type** | | | | | |
| * | Independent (Practicing) | 72.2 | 55.4 | 62.0 | 72.5 |
| * | Independent (Ex-Entr's) | 68.7 | 31.7 | 60.9 | 57.1 |
| * | Family Business Successor (PE) | 19.1 | 4.2 | 22.0 | 13.9 |
| | Corporate Entrepreneur (PE) | 18.8 | 21.1 | 19.2 | 27.4 |
| | | | | | |
| **Entrepreneurial Role** | | | | | |
| * | Founder (Practicing Entr's) | 64.9 | 48.8 | 46.5 | 60.1 |
| | Director (Serious Non-Starts) | 8.8 | 3.2 | 21.1 | 9.5 |
| | | | | | |
| **Career Path** | | | | | |
| * | Had Prior Full-Time Career (PE) | 79.6 | 88.2 | 68.8 | 86.0 |
| * | Chose Prior Career to Prepare | 28.4 | 25.2 | 34.9 | 16.1 |
| | | | | | |
| **Time Commitment** | | | | | |
| | Part-Time before Start-up (ExE) | 47.0 | 45.2 | 71.4 | 65.5 |
| | Part-Time at Start-up (ExE) | 24.2 | 42.9 | 52.4 | 48.1 |
| | Full-Time at Start-up (PE) | 66.5 | 53.4 | 65.9 | 66.8 |

## TABLE 2:  SIGNIFICANT DIFFERENCES BETWEEN SCHOOLS
### Percentages of Graduate Degree Holders Responding, by School

All relationships shown here are significant at the level p < .05
(unmarked in the left-most column) or p < .01 (marked with an asterisk in the left-most column).

|  | | Babson | Bentley | G'town | R.P.I. |
|---|---|---|---|---|---|
| **Demographics** | | | | | |
| * | Male (Ex-Entrepreneurs) | 90.0% | 100.0% | 87.1% | 100.0% |
|  | Male (Serious Non-Starters) | 86.4 | 96.0 | 79.7 | 93.3 |
| * | Married (Serious Non-Starts) | 78.2 | 88.0 | 64.4 | 87.5 |
|  | Career Length in Years (ExEs) | 6.0 | 6.2 | 4.9 | 8.5 |
| **Entrepreneurial Type** | | | | | |
| * | Independent (Practicing Entr's) | 72.8 | 55.0 | 58.4 | 66.3 |
|  | Family Business Successor (PE) | 12.5 | 5.0 | 14.2 | 7.7 |
|  | Franchisee (Practicing Entr's) | 8.4 | 1.7 | 4.4 | 4.2 |
| * | Self-Employed (PE) | 36.5 | 50.0 | 32.7 | 27.5 |
| **Entrepreneurial Role** | | | | | |
| * | Founder (Practicing Entr's) | 60.7 | 56.5 | 42.5 | 55.2 |
|  | Co-Founder (Practicing Entr's) | 43.9 | 25.8 | 36.3 | 43.2 |
| **Career Path** | | | | | |
|  | Had Prior Full-Time Career (PE) | 86.7 | 87.7 | 80.4 | 89.9 |
| * | Had Prior Full-Time Career (ExE) | 79.2 | 87.5 | 67.7 | 93.0 |
|  | Chose Prior Career to Prepare (PE) | 20.4 | 28.0 | 27.8 | 16.1 |
|  | Chose Career to Prepare (SNSs) | 11.1 | 35.7 | 25.0 | 8.4 |
|  | Prior Career Relevant to New (PE) | 72.9 | 78.0 | 77.8 | 81.8 |
| **Time Commitment** | | | | | |
|  | Part-Time at Start-up (PE) | 38.3 | 51.8 | 35.3 | 31.3 |
|  | Part-Time after Start-up (PE) | 26.4 | 37.5 | 33.3 | 23.4 |
|  | Full-Time at Start-up (PE) | 56.2 | 46.4 | 56.9 | 68.1 |
|  | Full-Time after Start-up (PE) | 64.9 | 62.5 | 63.7 | 74.9 |

Georgetown alumni in the practicing entrepreneur category are
more involved in family businesses than people from other schools (*),
and correspondingly less likely to call themselves founders of a firm
(*).  Among the schools' ex-entrepreneurs, the length of the entrepreneurial career is substantially shorter for Georgetown alumni:  undergraduates left their careers after a mean of 3.5 years (*), compared
with a mean career length of 10.1 years for the other schools' alumni.

Fewer Georgetown alumni PE's reported having full-time careers
prior to beginning their entrepreneurial work (U *);  the same is true for
its former entrepreneurs who have graduate degrees (*), but not for undergraduates.  Undergraduate ExE's reported a high proportion of part-time
workers, both before and at the beginning of their entrepreneurial careers.

The pattern of responses from Georgetown alumni appears to describe a population heavily oriented toward family business, with graduates more likely to join family firms immediately after schooling. The less successful of its entrepreneurs begin their work on a part-time basis; the more successful ones (assuming that practicing entreprepreneurs are more successful than those who have left the trade) begin on a full-time basis.

## Babson College

Like their Georgetown counterparts, Babson College's practicing entrepreneurs report a heavy involvement with family business (U *). Unlike the other schools' people, however, Babson respondents report themselves as independent entrepreneurs (*) and as founders of their businesses (*). Babson's graduate degree holders also contain a heavier proportion of franchisees and a lower proportion of PE's whose prior full-time career was relevant to their entrepreneurial work.

Demographically, Babson's undergraduates are distinguished from the other schools' only by a very high divorce rate among its _former_ entrepreneurs; 28 percent of its ExE's are divorced, while the other three schools' average is 11 percent.

## Bentley College

Divorce is apparently not a factor in the decision of Bentley College's undergraduates to terminate an entrepreneurial career: fewer than seven percent of these ExE's are divorced. Bentley's undergraduates show a lower proportion of practicing entrepreneurs in family business (*) or in independent firms (*) or in franchised operations. Bentley's alumni holding graduate degrees follow this same pattern, but balance it with a heavy proportion of self-employed entrepreneurs (*).

A high proportion of Bentley's undergraduate PE's worked at full-time careers before venturing into entrepreneurial work (*). The school's practicing entrepreneurial alumni with graduate degrees are notable for their high proportion of part-timers, both at and after the start of their ventures, and for their correspondingly low proportion of full-time workers (*).

## Rensselear Polytechnic Institute

At the opposite end of the scale from Bentley's part-timers are the graduate degree holders among RPI's practicing entrepreneur alumni. Over 68 percent of these respondents started their ventures on a full-time basis (*); 75 percent were full-time after the start (*). Ninety percent of these PE's (and 93 percent of the ExE's (*)) had full-time careers before starting their entrepreneurial ventures. Significantly more of the RPI people reported that their previous career was relevant to their new work. But substantially fewer (U *) chose their first careers explicitly as preparation for their own later venturing.

RPI graduate degree holders reported the smallest proportion of self-employed entrepreneurs (*); undergraduate alumni reported the largest proportion of independent entrepreneurs (*) and of corporate entrepreneurs (at 27 percent of respondents).

## CONCLUSIONS

Along all five of the dimensions measuring entrepreneurial activity of responding alumni, significant differences mark the graduates of these four schools. Some of the differences are consistent with and may be associated with the different educational emphases of the subject colleges.

It is beyond the range of this paper to document the varied characteristics of the four schools in the time period pertinent to this study -- from the end of World War II up to 1975. We take as given the public images of the four: Georgetown as a major urban university strong in the liberal arts and sciences; Babson as a specialist in business education; Bentley (which was only beginning in the early '70s to establish itself beyond its original discipline) as a specialist in accounting; and RPI as a major center of engineering education.

**Demographic differences** lead us to suspect that Georgetown was the only one of these schools with a fair representation of women in its student body in the pertinent time period. Significant differences in gender and marital status of the schools' entrepreneurs may be associated with the "male bastion" aura of the other three institutions at the time.

Distinct differences appear also in **entrepreneurial type**. The high proportions of Babson and RPI alumni reporting themselves as independent entrepreneurs are consistent with the business and engineering emphasis of those schools. The low number of independent operators and successors to family business management from Bentley is consistent with the accounting image, as is the high proportion of Bentley's self-employed alumni. RPI's high number of corporate entrepreneurs matches the engineering tendency to spin off new ideas for further development within the employing company.

Differences in **entrepreneurial role** are less pronounced, but Babson's higher proportion of founders and co-founders appears consistent with the image of the aggressive businessperson. Georgetown boasts a large number of serious non-starters who have thought about becoming directors of new ventures.

**Career path** differences are pronounced. Georgetown has many more alumni moving directly into entrepreneurial work from school; of its people who choose other careers, more make the choice explicitly to prepare themselves for later venturing. Very few RPI graduates choose a career for that purpose, but more RPI entrepreneurs report their prior work was relevant to their later careers; the engineering model is apparent. Many of Bentley's serious non-starters picked their jobs to prepare themselves for entrepreneuring, but have never made the move: the stereotype of the professional accountant is clear.

In terms of **time commitment**, wide differences appear between undergraduate and graduate degreed alumni and between entnrnepreneurial types. Georgetown's ExE undergraduates are distinctly part-timers, while its practicing entrepreneurs and graduate degreed people are mainstream full-time. Bentley's graduate degree alumni, true to the accountant's role, are predominately part-time, both at and after the start of their ventures. RPI's advanced-degree alumni, in the image of the high-tech start-up, are full-time workers at the start and after.

## FUTURE RESEARCH

Further analysis of the database used in this study will continue to add to our knowledge of entrepreneurs and the entrepreneurial process. As noted by Ronstadt:

> The principal objective of the National Entrepreneurship Study is to test basic hypotheses about the process of entrepreneurship. These hypotheses will include the discovery and validation of facts as well as emerging concepts and theories that explain and predict activities associated with the creation of new enterprises.[6]

Research now underway builds upon the analysis presented here by focusing on the career differences/similarities that exist by field of study. The analysis examines respondents' entrepreneurial careers by degree held (field of study) across all institutions. For example, it is expected that this will enable investigation of whether and how, people with a bachelor of engineering degree differ from those with a bachelor of arts degree. Or, do alumni with a master of business administration degree have different/similar entrepreneurial experiences of those with a master of engineering or a doctorate of jurisprudence?

With the addition of additional respondents from other institutions, having distinct fields of program emphasis, it is hoped that regression and factor analyses will yield a model capable of predicting entrepreneurial activity.

---

[6]Ronstadt, "National Entrepreneurship Study," P. 7.

## REFERENCES

Ronstadt, Robert C., "Phase One of the National Entrepreneurship Study," a report submitted to the Board of Research, Babson College, Wellesley MA, 1986.

Ronstadt, Robert C., "The Corridor Principle and Entrepreneurial Time," working paper, Babson College, Wellesley, MA, 1986.

Shuman, J. C., Seeger, J. A., Kamm, J. B., and Teebagy, N. C., "An Empirical Test of Ten Entrepreneurial Propositions," <u>Frontiers of Entrepreneurship - 1986</u>, Babson College, Wellesley MA, 1986, pp. 187 - 198.

Vesper, Karl H., "Introduction and Summary of Entrepreneurship Research," in Kent, C. A., Sexton, D. L., and Vesper, K. H., <u>Encyclopedia of Entrepreneurship</u>, Prentice Hall, Englewood Cliffs, NJ, 1982, p. xxi.

Vesper, Karl H., "New Developments in Entrepreneurship Education," in Sexton, D. L., and Smilor, R. W. <u>The Art and Science of Entrepreneurship</u>, Ballinger Publishing Company, Cambridge, MA, 1985, p. 379.

SUMMARY

## PERCEPTIONS OF SUCCESS IN BUSINESS START-UP AND THE IMPACT OF ENTREPRENEURIAL EDUCATION

Authors

    Ivan E. Brown, Jr.
    Ron L. Christy
    Arleen F. Banowetz

Address

    The Center for Entrepreneurship and Department of Management
    The Wichita State University
    Post Office Box 88
    Wichita, KS 67208
    (316) 689-3214 or
    (316) 689-3000

Principal Topics

This paper examines the relationship between entrepreneurship education and entrepreneurial success - both perceived and actual success - in business start-up.

Method and Data Base

The data base for the study was a sample of business owners who have taken the course, "Entrepreneurship: Your Future in Business (YFIB)," at The Wichita State University between 1978-85. The population is broken down in the table below.

| | # | % | Response Rate |
|---|---|---|---|
| Business Owners | 602 | 16% | 53% |
| Non-Business Owners | 2729 | 71% | 35% |
| Unknown (address changes) | 489 | 13% | |
| Total Population | 3820 | 100% | |

Fifty-three percent of the business owners responded to a survey about their businesses. Over half of the business owners' surveys were not utilized in this analysis because their data had not yet been coded and entered into the computer or some of the data relevant to this analysis was missing.

Because of the large population, our plan for a longitudinal study, and our desire to gather a large volume of data, we chose a survey method to collect data. The survey has three basic parts. The first part obtains demographic and psychological data about all students. An affirmative response to a question in this section about business ownership means the respondent will receive the second and third parts of the questionnaire. The second part obtains information about the start-up and current status of their business, and the third part asks questions about the helpfulness of "Your Future in Business."

## Major Findings

According to most previous research, there is a positive association between entrepreneurship training and entrepreneurial success. Our analysis indicated that entrepreneurs who started businesses after taking YFIB tended to attribute their success more to organizational factors (cost control, marketing), whereas those who started before taking YFIB tended to attribute their success to individual factors (persistence, motivation). This was especially true for entrepreneurs who were thirty years of age or younger, unmarried, or first and only born in the family. Regardless of when they took the course, females tended to attribute their success to organizational factors.

These findings suggest a "socialization effect." It would seem that the course provides a substitute for something missing in the student's previous socializations. For example, for middle born children who are socialized to share with others in the family (organization). The class opens their awareness to their own individualitic needs. In the study, middle born entrepreneurs who started after taking YFIB tended to attribute their success to individual factors. This finding reversed the general finding in the analysis.

In addition, those who started after YFIB were less likely to experience positive growth in sales, especially if one of the following conditions existed: the firm was less than four years old; the entrepreneur was thirty years of age or younger; the entreprenuer was not married; or the entreprenuer had taken only two or fewer college business courses. As the age of the firm or age of the entrepreneur increased, or the entrepreneur's marital status changed, or the entrepreneur took more college business courses, the likelihood of positive sales growth increased.

Analysis of the mean sales growth performance of entrepreneurs who started before and after revealed an "accelerator effect." Those who started after taking YFIB tended to change their mean sales growth by twofold, both positively and negatively. One possible explanation may be that the class helped to accelerate the performance of the successful entrepreneur, while it helped to decelerate the performance of the less successful entrepreneur. A concern raised by many educators is that some prospective entrepreneurs are encouraged to enter business when they probably should not. Although our findings confirm the legitimacy of this concern, our analysis also revealed some implications for entrepreneurship educators who assist people in the entrepreneurial process.

## Implications for Entrepreneurship Education

In an article published in the American Journal of Small Business, Robert Ronstadt encouraged the development of entrepreneurship programs, as opposed to single classes, to train high performance entrepreneurs. Our findings demonstrate the importance of this point. At the very minimum, educators should encourage students to take additional business courses, and if possible, entire programs in entrepreneurship. Indeed, if higher education is serious about entrepreneurial training, it must be programmatic in orientation. The implementation of complete curriculums is necessary to fulfill the university's obligation to train high performance entrepreneurs.

## Implications for Research

As the sample size of this research increases, we should be able to delineate more finely the relationship between entrepreneurial training and success. For now, it is clear that we need to develop more measures of success and begin to determine the other variables that eventually influence an entrepreneur's success.

## Implications for Practitioners

For the entrepreneur, one implication is clear: take more college business and entrepreneurship courses before venturing. Additional classes will give the practitioner time to nurture a business idea, and provide greater opportunities for interaction with professors, other entrepreneurs, and students.

SUMMARY

CAN BUSINESS SCHOOLS PRODUCE ENTREPRENEURS?:
AN EMPIRICAL STUDY

Author

    Russell M. Knight

Address

    School of Business Administration
    The University of Western Ontario
    London, Ontario, Canada
    N6A 3K7
    (519) 661-3299

Principal Topics

The purpose of this study was to examine the reasons why a sample of 231 graduates from the Western Business School chose to become entrepreneurs. Research issues examined include whether parents or other mentors served as entrepreneurial role models and reasons they left former corporate employers to establish their own firm. The influence of entrepreneurial ventures prior to graduation from university and other reasons contributing to their decision to become entrepreneurs were also investigated. Also, information on their type and size of venture, sources of financing used and other background details were gathered to provide an overall picture of entrepreneurial graduates from one particular business school.

Method and Data Base

Questionnnaires were administered to 231 graduates from Honours Business Administration (Undergraduate) and Masters of Business Administration classes from Western. Locating entrepreneurial graduates was a difficult problem since alumni records were often incomplete for these individuals. Data were analyzed using SPSS cross-tabulations and factor analysis.

Major Findings

In general, Western's entrepreneurial alumni left positions in the corporate world to enter their own business. Their primary reasons were a desire to be their own boss, to build something of their own and frustration with the corporate environment. They tended to use their own savings as the primary source of funds to start the venture. Almost half had entrepreneurial fathers while a third had entrepreneurial role models other than parents.

In suggesting changes in the business school curriculum in the direction of entrepreneurship, graduates highly recommended case studies of entrepreneurs, especially alumni who, by being present in class during discussion of the cases, could act as role models for current students. Graduates felt their business school program had partially prepared them for an entrepreneurial career, but more could be added, in all courses, not just those on entrepreneurship. They suggested the entrepreneurship option should be stressed much more, at Western and all business schools and many offered to help in doing this.

TECHNOLOGY-BASED NEW VENTURES
FROM SWEDISH UNIVERSITIES: A SURVEY

Christer Olofsson, Linköping University
Göran Reitberger, Temaplan Företagsutveckling AB
Peter Tovman, Royal Institute of Technology, Stockholm
Clas Wahlbin, Linköping University

## ABSTRACT

This paper reports on a survey of technology-based companies started since 1980 by Swedish university researchers.

The over-all rate of company formation has doubled between the 1980-82 and the 1983-85 periods. There is also a stronger growth of companies started in the second period, reflecting a smaller share of "on-the-side" companies. The change is the effect of (1) changes in attitudes in society at large, in the universities, and at sponsors of technological research, (2) the much increased availability of risk capital in Sweden since 1982, and (3) the creation of science parks and other elements of infrastucture at many universities. The companies have a distinct high technology character, and were often started by senior researchers. Development work for customers, and consulting, are main lines of operatioh at present.

In total, some of the prerequisites for a further growth by second and higher order spin-offs in the decades to come are there.

## INTRODUCTION

In the past decade, there has been an increasing interest in technology-based companies started by university researchers. There are several reasons for this. Society at large has an interest that research results and other knowledge of researchers are commercialized with a short time lag. Apart from the direct economic effects of such firms, they may be suitable vehicles to diffuse innovations and knowledge into industry in general, thereby having an indirect importance that outweighs the direct effects. In addition to the direct and indirect economic effects, the added contacts between academia and industry are beleived to have positive effects on academia, e.g. by stimulating more "reality-oriented" research. At the same time, there are possible negative effects: More short-sighted research, researchers leaving universities because of the higher earnings outside, to name a few.

In this paper, we describe and analyze the creation and growth of technology-based companies started by university researchers. Particularly, we are interested in differences between universities in rates of company starts, and in the growth (or non-growth) of the companies. In the paper, we concentrate on reporting empirical data and analyses of these data. The method is also reported in some detail, since it is essential for judging the validity and reliability of the results.

While there are earlier studies of company starts from Swedish universities[1], there has been no study made on a cross-sectional basis covering several universities. Therefore, a first aim of the study is simply to describe the phenomenon with comparable data for different universities. Our interest is in firms that are started in order to commercialize research knowledge, and that are started by researchers employed by the university. We have no requirement that the founders must leave the university completely when starting the company. Due to the problems of determining whether a company is based on research results from research of the founder(s) or on general knowledge, e.g. from the research of other people, we have included also companies that we know have weak links to original research. Two categories of companies are not included: Companies started by students or graduates not employed by the university, and departments of "outside" companies located in e.g. research parks. The study is further limited to a target group of companies started 1980-86.

## METHOD OF THE STUDY

The survey covers all academic institutions in Sweden that award a M.Sc. degree, i.e. all institutions that have an institute of technology. In some cases, the institute of technology is a part of a university, in some cases it is a free-standing institution. Since in Sweden departments are often "mixed" in the sense that they serve both the institute of technology and other parts of a university, we have surveyed the university, i.e. the broader entity. One university has been included because of a recent activity in encouraging bio-tech start-ups. All institutions surveyed have Ph.D. programmes and are active in research in science and technology. Some characteristics of the institutions surveyed are detailed in Table 1. It should be noted that the Swedish M.Sc. is an integrated 4.5-year education, generally started the year that the student reaches 19 or 20 years of age.

---

[1]See e.g. Douglas H. McQueen & J. Torkel Wallmark, "Spin-off Companies from Chalmers University of Technology", Technovation, Vol. 1 (1982), pp. 305-415 and Christer Olofsson & Clas Wahlbin, "Technology-Based New Ventures from Technical Universities: A Swedish case", in Hornaday et. al., eds., Frontiers of Entrepreneurship Research 1984, pp. 192-211.

TABLE 1

SOME CHARACTERISTICS OF INSTITUTIONS SURVEYED

| Institution | Whole institution | | | Science & technology part | | | |
|---|---|---|---|---|---|---|---|
| | Year of start | No of stud's (1000) | Out-lays MSEK | No of stud's (1000) | Out-lays MSEK | Pc of total outl | No of M Sc lines |
| Chalmers UT | 1829 | 4.0 | 462 | 3.8 | 460 | 99 | 8 |
| Linköping U | 1967 | 5.5 | 378 | 2.3 | 167 | 44 | 5 |
| Luleå U | 1971 | 2.4 | 215 | 1.2 | 158 | 73 | 5 |
| Lund U | 1668 | 13.8 | 1187 | 3.1 | 495 | 42 | 7 |
| Royal IT | 1827 | 4.6 | 568 | 4.6 | 568 | 100 | 10 |
| Umeå U | 1964 | 5.4 | 558 | 0.6 | 105 | 19 | - |
| Uppsala U | 1477 | 9.1 | 854 | 1.2 | 314 | 37 | 2 |

Data refer to the 1983/84 situation; source: annual report of
The National Swedish Board of Universities and Colleges.
Number of students is equivalent full-time student load.
Outlays in science and technology include a proportional
share of cost for library, computer centre, cleaning etc.

Chalmers UT = Chalmers University of Technology, Gothenburg
Linköping U = Linköping University, Linköping
Luleå U     = Luleå University, Luleå
Lund U      = Lund University, Lund
Royal IT    = Royal Institute of Technology, Stockholm
Umeå U      = Umeå University, Umeå
Uppsala U   = Uppsala University, Uppsala

The survey covers the research universities in Sweden, except
those in Stockholm and Gothenburg. In these two cities, Chalmers UT and
Royal IT are free-standing institutions, concentrating on science and
technology and on the traditional Swedish M.Sc. education since the
early 20th century. At all other universities, the M.Sc. education was
started in the 1960's or early 1970's. Luleå is a regional university in
the north of Sweden, and science and technology account for three
quarters of the budget. At the northern university of Umeå, science and
technology account for only 20 per cent of total outlays. The two old
universities of Lund and Uppsala, and the young in Linköping, all have
roughly 40 per cent of their activity in science and technology.

When measuring the number of company start-ups, there are some problems involved. We therefore discuss in some detail how the companies included in the data base were arrived at.

In most cases, there were lists available of companies started by researchers and by others, compiled by the universities, and these lists were used. In some cases, names of companies were compiled also by mail questionnaires to the institutions. The final lists are reasonably inclusive as concerns economically significant company starts by researchers in the period 1980-85, but not for 1986 up to the fall when the survey was undertaken. The lists vary in the degree that they contain also companies started by students upon graduation, departments of large firms moving into research parks, spin-offs from other companies etc. This is reflected both in variations in the response rate and in differences in the share of those responding that belong to the target group in Table 2.

## TABLE 2

### DETAILS OF RESPONSE IN MAIL QUESTIONNAIRE SURVEY

| Institution | Mail-ing | Cases in data-base | Resp rate, pc | Cases in target group | Of which: Start 80-85 | Start 80-85 meeting size cr |
|---|---|---|---|---|---|---|
| Chalmers UT | 50 | 37 | 74 | 33 | 33 | 16 |
| Linköping U | 29 | 25 | 86 | 23 | 21 | 15 |
| Luleå U | 27 | 14 | 52 | 7 | 7 | 4 |
| Lund U | 62 | 45 | 73 | 36 | 32 | 21 |
| Royal IT | 105 | 40 | 38 | 30 | 25 | 16 |
| Umeå U | 54 | 30 | 56 | 25 | 20 | 10 |
| Uppsala | 41 | 23 | 56 | 18 | 16 | 8 |
| All | 368 | 214 | 58 | 172 | 154 | 90 |

Target group = Technology-based firms started 1980-86 by researchers employed at the university.
Size criterion = Turnover in second year of operation 100 thousand SEK or more in 1986 prices according to consumer price index.
Of the 64 firms not meeting the size criterion, 23 did not state their turnover in the second year.

Further, the lists vary as to the degree that they contain very small companies, started e.g. to take care of small amounts of extramural consulting and teaching, etc. This variation is reflected in Table 2 in the drop between the number of target group companies started 1980-85 and those that also meet the criteria of a turnover of 100 thousand SEK or more in their second year of operation. In some cases, half of the answers from target group companies were from such very small companies. Another problem in some few cases is that they have roots at several universities. We have judgementally assigned a company to one university only. Lastly, the lists vary in their inclusion also of companies not based on technology, e.g. management consulting firms. We have refrained from excluding such companies.

All companies in the lists received a mail questionnaire asking for basic data on turnover, employment, etc. 1980-86, and plans for 1987. Of a total of 368 questionnaires mailed, 214 were sent back and included in the data base, giving a response rate of 58 per cent. Considering the number of non-target companies in the lists, we consider the over-all response rate fair. Special efforts were undertaken to get answers from target group companies meeting the size criterion, and we believe that the coverage of such firms started 1980-85, i.e. those firms in the right-hand column in Table 2, is reasonably inclusive. (As mentioned above the lists vary in their coverage of 1986 starts.)

A sample of companies answering were interviewed by telephone. 36 such interviews were completed in the target group for the present analysis.

RATE OF COMPANY FORMATION

A Comparison between the Universities Surveyed

Inspection of the data suggests that there is a marked difference in the over-all rate of formation between the 1980-82 and the 1983-85 periods, as well as in the growth of companies started these years (see Table 4 below). Therefore, we study the rate of formation for these two periods separately.

In gross terms, there were 59 target group companies formed 1980-82, and 95 1983-85, i.e. the rate of formation has nearly doubled. In order to compare between universities surveyed, we use data only on target group companies formed 1980-85 that also meet the size criterion (see the discussion above). This means that we underestimate the rates by 54 and 34 per cent in the two periods, since the number meeting the size critera are 27 and 63, respectively. The distribution over universities is shown in Table 3, together with an index number showing the number of starts per year and 100 MSEK 1983/84 outlay in science and technology (see Table 1).

TABLE 3

NUMBER OF COMPANIES STARTED 1980-85 MEETING SIZE CRITERION

| Institution | No. of starts | | No. of starts per year and 100 MSEK sc & techn outlay | |
|---|---|---|---|---|
| | 1980-82 | 1983-85 | 1980-82 | 1983-85 |
| Chalmers UT | 6 | 10 | 0.43 | 0.72 |
| Linköping U | 6 | 9 | 1.20 | 1.80 |
| Luleå U | 0 | 4 | 0 | 0.84 |
| Lund U | 3 | 18 | 0.20 | 1.21 |
| Royal IT | 8 | 8 | 0.47 | 0.47 |
| Umeå U | 2 | 8 | 0.63 | 2.54 |
| Uppsala U | 2 | 6 | 0.21 | 0.64 |
| All | 27 | 63 | 0.39 | 0.93 |

The rate of formation of "significant" companies has more than doubled between the two periods. The marked increase is there for most of the institutions. Chalmers has the longest tradition of reserachers starting companies on the Swedish scene, a result of the fact that professor Wallmark started encouraging his students in electrical engineering to go on their own. In Linköping, the phenomenon took off in the late 1970's. Chalmers and Linköping have about the same numbers started, and both have increased the rate. In relative terms, Linköping is highest in both periods among those institutions that have an institute of technology. The Royal institute of Technology in Stockholm has had an even rate of companies formed. Chalmers and Linköping, and to a lesser degree The Royal institute, have actively encouraged the formation of technology-based companies, and have set up various facilitating organisations and elements of infrastructure.

Lund has made the most ambitious effort in the creation of infrastructure by the building of the science park, Ideon. It is a project with a total cost of 500 MSEK, and it was conceived in late 1982. The first companies moved in in late 1983. Ideon has a focus on both university spin-offs and research departments of large firms. We believe that the very strong increase in company formation from Lund University is to a large degree a result of the Ideon effort.

Umeå and Uppsala both have a bio-tech focus in their efforts to encourage research-based companies, and judging from our data, the efforts seem to have paid off. The Umeå rate is exceptionally high in relative terms during the 1983-85 period. (It should then be noted that the medical part of the universities are not included in our base for calculating relative rates.)

## A Comparison with Cambridge University

In a study of technology-based firms started in Cambridge[2], 17 per cent of 128 identified firms started in 5.5 years (1979 - mid-1984) were by individuals coming straight from the university or still remaining in it. Adding an estimated 15 per cent not reached, these figures give an estimated rate of formation of 4.5 companies per year by university researchers. Calculating per thousand students in science and technology, the number is 0.76 per year. (Cambridge had ca 12,160 full-time equivalent students 1980-83, and a 49 per cent share in science and technology in recent years.)

In our data, we have no good estimate of the share of target group companies not reached, since our lists covered very small companies to a varying degree. Not trying to adjust for non-response, there are 154 target group firms started 1980-85 in the universities surveyed, or 1.53 per year and thousand students in science and technology. The Swedish universities most comparable to Cambridge in size, age and share in science and technology are Lund and Uppsala (see Table 1). The number of target group companies per year and thousand sicence and technology students is 0.91 and 0.89 at these universities.

We conclude that the rate of company starts by university researchers in Sweden is at least on par with the Cambridge example during the 1980's, and that special efforts at some universities seem to have paid off in terms of the number of new firms started. In the concluding section of the paper, we turn to the general factors behind the high over-all rate and the increase during the period studied.

## SOME CHARACTERISTICS OF COMPANIES STARTED

Below, we report on some characteristics of target group companies as described by interview data. Since the interviewed companies do not represent a random sample of the total population - we attempted an even number from each university - the data reported below should be viewed as indications.

---

[2]Segal Quince & Partners, The Cambridge Phenomenon, Cambridge, Segal Quince & Partners, 1985

Five out of ten companies state their main operation as development work for customers. Three out of ten do mainly consulting, while one to two of ten have own products as their main line of operation. Six out of ten, however, do have a product of their own on the market. The high-tech character is obvious: Over 20 per cent are in computer software, close to 20 per cent in electronics including computer hardware, and close to 20 per cent in biotechnology.

Large companies is the main customer group for four out of ten companies, and in total two thirds have other companies as their main customers. Close to 20 per cent have public agencies as their main customers, while 10 per cent have research laboratories.

40 per cent are one-man/woman starts, while 25 per cent were started by a group of two people. In two cases out 10, there is somebody not from the university in the founding group. A third of the companies state that they have no connections to the university today, while a little less than a third have "medium strong" conncetion, and the rest claim strong connections. Strong connections are particularly common in biotech and electronic instruments.

About half of the central founders have their education from an institute of technology, roughly evenly divided between M.Sc., Ph.D. and licentiate (a Swedish "in-between" exam). The rest come from various backgrounds, and roughly two thirds of them have a Ph.D. The median age of the central founder at the start of the company is 38 years. 20 per cent were 30 years or younger, slightly over 30 per cent 40 years or older. Comparing to non-university starts, both the education and the age is high[3].

In a third of the companies, there has been some change of the ownership structure, mostly in the respect that one founder has left the company, and someone else has come in. Venture capital and other sources of external capital have entered in a few cases. In those, however, the amounts of capital are large.

GROWTH OF THE COMPANIES

Below, we describe the growth of the companies studied. We describe all target group companies, i.e. also those that do not meet the size criterion. It should then be noted that we most probably have an underrepresentation of very small companies, since the lists used in the survey cover such firms to a varying degree, and since special effort was taken to secure answers from large target group companies.

---

[3]James M. Utterback & Göran Reitberger, Technology and Industrial Innovation in Sweden - A Study of New Technology-Based Firms, MIT-CPA, Cambridge, Mass., 1982

## The Average Growth

In Table 4, the average turnover and number of persons employed in companies started each year 1980-86 is shown. The different growth in the two periods 1980-82 and 1983-85 is easily noted. The average growth rates are quite impressive, but it should be noted that the turnover per employee most often is still small.

TABLE 4

AVERAGE GROWTH OF COMPANIES STARTED 1980-86

| Year of oper | Aver value of | Year of start 1980 | 1981 | 1982 | 1983 | 1984 | 1985 | 1986 |
|---|---|---|---|---|---|---|---|---|
| 1 | Turnover | 0.36 | 0.18 | 0.50 | 0.58 | 0.50 | 1.10 | 0.34 |
|   | Employees | 2.06 | 2.00 | 2.87 | 3.05 | 2.62 | 5.37 | 2.44 |
| 2 | Turnover | 0.62 | 0.43 | 0.52 | 1.39 | 1.79 | 1.71 | |
|   | Employees | 2.52 | 2.25 | 3.18 | 4.81 | 4.82 | 5.73 | |
| 3 | Turnover | 0.68 | 0.78 | 0.74 | 2.59 | 3.29 | | |
|   | Employees | 2.71 | 2.38 | 3.76 | 7.52 | 7.00 | | |
| 4 | Turnover | 1.08 | 0.74 | 0.84 | 4.39 | | | |
|   | Employees | 3.05 | 2.64 | 4.28 | 9.09 | | | |
| 5 | Turnover | 1.64 | 0.97 | 1.16 | | | | |
|   | Employees | 4.29 | 3.00 | 4.41 | | | | |
| 6 | Turnover | 2.84 | 1.18 | | | | | |
|   | Employees | 4.85 | 3.38 | | | | | |
| 7 | Turnover | 2.80 | | | | | | |
|   | Employees | 5.33 | | | | | | |
| Growth pc pa | Turnover | 35 | 29 | 31 | 77 | 84 | | |
|   | Employees | 16 | 11 | 12 | 37 | 45 | | |

Turnover is average turnover in MSEK in 1986 prices.
Employees is number of people employed.
Growth is compound annual growth in per cent from second year of operation up to last year entered.

The average number of people employeed in 1986 was 6.0, meaning that total employment in target group companies surveyed was around 1000.

## The Distribution of Growth

In Table 5, the shares of companies that have a smaller turnover than 100 thousand SEK, between 100 thousand and 1 MSEK, and 1 MSEK or more (in 1986 prices) in different years after the start are shown for companies started in the two periods 1980-82 and 1983-86, respectively. As can be seen in the table, the companies started in the two periods start with approximately the same shares of very small companies. For the early starts, the share of very small firms decreases with a fairly slow trend, and even six to seven years after the start, a quarter of the firms are still very small. In the late start group, the share of very small firms decreases rapidly with the age of the firm, and in the fourth year only six per cent remain very small. Thus, it seems that the "seriousness" of the company starts have increased over the years. The same conclusion can be drawn from the share of firms having a turnover of 1 MSEK or more. While there is a gap already in the first year of operation between early and late starters, this gap widens with the age of the company. For the early starters, data suggest that there is a spurt in the growth after five years, and this is borne out by the median turnover.

TABLE 5

DISTRIBUTION OF GROWTH OF COMPANIES STARTED 1980-86

| Year of opera-tion | Firms started 1980-82 | | | | Firms started 1983-86 | | | |
| --- | --- | --- | --- | --- | --- | --- | --- | --- |
| | Share, pc, w turnover | | | Median turnov | Share, pc, w turnover | | | Median turnov |
| | < 100 th SEK | 100-999 th SEK | ≥ 1 MSEK | MSEK | < 100 th SEK | 100-999 th SEK | ≥ 1 MSEK | MSEK |
| 1 | 50 | 42 | 8 | 0.09 | 44 | 31 | 15 | 0.12 |
| 2 | 47 | 39 | 14 | 0.14 | 21 | 50 | 29 | 0.31 |
| 3 | 44 | 33 | 23 | 0.25 | 13 | 43 | 42 | 0.62 |
| 4 | 32 | 44 | 23 | 0.31 | 6 | 38 | 56 | 1.00 |
| 5 | 34 | 34 | 32 | 0.35 | | | | |
| 6 | 23 | 20 | 57 | 1.40 | | | | |
| 7 | 26 | 11 | 63 | 1.80 | | | | |

Turnover in 1986 prices according to concumer price index

The rate of technology-based company starts in the 1980's by researchers at Swedish universities is at least on par with that of the noted European example of Cambridge. It remains to be seen whether the large impact of second- and higher order starts, i.e. spin-offs from the spin-offs, etc., will be there also in Sweden. Such spin-offs is a main factor behind what has been labelled "The Cambridge Phenomenon".

The most noteworthy change during the 1980's is the apparent change in the character of university spin-offs that has taken place since 1982: the rate of spin-off has approximately doubled, and there has been a shift towards more "serious" companies (as opposed to companies "on the side") which is reflected in the growth of the companies. This change is the result of several developments in the 1980's that have had an impact on the ease of starting a company and on the incentive to do so for university researchers:

An over-all favourable attitude to entrepreneurship and business in general has developed, in contrast to the thinking over a long period in the 1970's. On the university side, it has been accepted that researchers have some business going on while they still work full-time at the university. It has even been declared desirable by some leading representatives of the universities. STU, The National Swedish Board for Technical Development, who is a main sponsor of technological research, has taken a favourable attitude towards more immediate benefits from technological research in the form of e.g. spin-off companies.

During the period from 1982 and onwards, most of the Swedish venture capital funds have been started[4]. It has never been so easy to get access to venture capital, whether from such funds or from other sources, as during these years. Venture capital funds as well as corporate venture capital and new venture divisions have shown a genuine interest in university research and actual and potential spin-offs. The availability of capital has made it possible to start firms also around business ideas that need a large amount of capital for R&D work before there is a product on the market.

The infra-structure has been developed by adding industrial parks close to several universities and by providing different types of services important to the entrepreneurs in their early years. As mentioned above when discussing the start-up rates at the different universities surveyed, such programs seem to have contributed very much to the increase.

---

[4]See Christer Olofsson & Clas Wahlbin, "The Swedish Venture Capital Market - An Early Appraisal" in Hornaday et. al., eds., Frontiers of Entrepreneurship Research 1985, pp. 191-210

Most of the factors have been discussed since around 1980, but the concrete manifestations of them have not come until some years later. The earlier start-ups have had an important role in the sense that they have served as role models. In particular, early starts that have grown have demonstrated that it is possible to plan from the outset for growth.

To conclude, it seems that many of the factors for a "take-off" in the form of second- and higher order spin-offs in the decades to come are there on the Swedish scene.

## ACKNOWLEDGEMENTS

The study reported in this paper has been sponsored by STU, The National Swedish Board for Technical Development. The participation of Olofsson and Wahlbin is supported by a grant from STU to the research programme Technology, Innovation and Entrepreneurship at Linköping University. The authors want to thank Margareta Wahlbin for editing and coding the data.

## REFERENCES

McQueen, Douglas H. & J. Torkel Wallmark, "Spin-off Companies from Chalmers University of Technology", Technovation, Vol. 1 (1982), pp. 305-315

Olofsson, Christer & Clas Wahlbin, "Technology-based New Ventures from Technical Universities: A Swedish case", in John A. Hornaday, Fred Tarpley, Jr., Jeffry A. Timmons & Karl H. Vesper, eds., 1984, Frontiers of Entrepreneurship Research 1984, Wellesley, Mass., Babson College, pp. 192-211

Olofsson, Christer & Clas Wahlbin, "The Swedish Venture Capital Market: An Early Appraisal", in John A. Hornaday, Edward B. Shils, Jeffry A. Timmons & Karl H. Vesper, eds., 1985, Frontiers of Entrepreneurship Research 1985, Wellesley, Mass., Babson College, pp. 191-210

Segal Quince & Partners, The Cambridge Phenomenon, Cambridge, Segal Quince & Partners, 1985

Stankiewics, Rikard, Academics and Entrepreneurs - Developing University-Industry Relations, London, Francis Pinter, 1986

Utterback, James M. & Göran Reitberger, Technology and Industrial Innovation in Sweden - A Study of New Technology-Based Firms, MIT-CPA, Cambridge, Mass., 1982

FACULTY ENTREPRENEURSHIP IN
RESEARCH UNIVERSITY ENVIRONMENTS

David N. Allen, The Pennsylvania State University
Barbara J. Bird, Case Western Reserve University

## ABSTRACT

Much has been said about how major universities can play an important role in promoting the creation of local new firms. A key actor in the university related new firm creation process is the faculty member. This paper presents analysis based on surveys of research productive faculty at two major state supported universities. Entrepreneurial activity is a low interest among faculty, although evidence suggests that interest is steadily increasing. Important value conflicts characterize the wide gap between entrepreneurial and academic research worlds.

## INTRODUCTION

Universities are some of the most enduring institutions in history. They are immense repositories of knowledge and expertise, primarily embedded in the resources of faculty. As the U.S. economy continually moves in the direction of entrepreneurial and technological development, the role of the university has diversified beyond traditional instructional and research missions. Commercial and political pressures coming primarily from outside the university seek to gradually adapt universities into more flexible, responsive institutions. Current attention on "competitiveness" will only heighten these pressures.

The purpose of the paper is to explore one aspect of the current movement to redirect and expand faculty resources. The university entrepreneurial environment, as seen from the perspective of active faculty researchers, is examined with data collected at two major universities, The University of North Carolina and North Carolina State University. A short discussion of the role of universities, in general, and faculty, in specific, serves as the point of departure. Much has been written about university participation in technology-based startups. And, as so often occurs in a new area of research, little consensus exists on the influence of universities. Using survey data, faculty entrepreneurial behavior and institutional level concerns are examined. The discussion of the findings primarily focuses on value differences between academic and industry roles.

## Universities and Economic Development

Considerable myth and misunderstanding seems to surround general notions about universities and economic development. The situation seems even more confused concerning faculty roles in entrepreneurial development. Couple the high status ascribed to the academic profession with popular media emphasis on a few highly successful ventures, and it is easy to see how great expectations emerge.

Little disagreement exists about the need to enlarge the role of higher education in society. Many also believe that the potential of universities in technological development has been ignored.[1] When the discussion turns to faculty entrepreneurship, however, disagreement about the potential becomes common, albeit muddled by anecdotal success stories and a lack of data.

Faculty entrepreneurship is but one of many approaches for commercializing the research conducted at universities. A five part schema for describing these arrangements[2] has been adapted for purposes of this discussion. First, industry sponsors "basic" research that does not have a direct commercial process or product development outcome. The second approach is more focused on a specific proprietary interest which has direct commercial expectations. A third approach is some type of boundary spanning or liaison program much like the service-oriented extension activities of state universities. A fourth model is that of a free standing, separately governed center or institute that exhibits many characteristics of a corporate laboratory or contract research operation. The last approach is direct university involvement (or tacit approval) with individuals or industrial partners to commercialize university faculty research through a new business. Recently many state governments have begun to act as catalysts to provide financial and expertise support networks to promote faculty research commercialization.[3]

## Universities and Faculty Entrepreneurship

It is within the domain of the last category of university research commercialization where our interests lie. The variations of university support, and activities that are approved, are virtually

---

[1]Robert Premus, Location of High Technology Firms and Regional Economic Development, U.S. Congress, Joint Economic Committee, Washington, D.C., 1982.

[2]Government-University-Industry Roundtable, New Alliances and Partnerships in American Science and Engineering, National Academy of Sciences, Washington, D.C., 1986.

[3]Charles B. Watkins, "Programs for Innovative Technology Research" in State Strategies for Economic Development, National Governor's Association, Washington, D.C., 1985, pp. 2-35.

limitless. Today universities are increasing venturing with their faculty to provide investment capital, physical plant, human resources, management expertise and other assistance to provide a supportive environment for entrepreneurship. For example, of the over 220 business incubators in the U.S., about one quarter are university sponsored, with many more in the planning stage.

The university plays other formal and informal roles in encouraging entrepreneurship. Many universities provide formal curriculum to encourage and support entrepreneurship, with an increasing number of courses and majors in new venture development.[4] Furthermore, as part of entrepreneurship courses or more standard marketing or policy courses, some faculty encourage students to do fieldwork projects with new ventures or entrepreneurial organizations. Similarly, entrepreneurship is moving out of business schools into engineering and science colleges. For example, a course at Case Western Reserve University pairs MBA students with senior engineering students to determine the market feasibility of their senior engineering projects. Interested students are forming entrepreneurship clubs to provide support for student entrepreneurs and often providing assistance to new ventures in the community. These clubs are linked to a national organization (the Association of Collegiate Entrepreneurs) which holds a yearly conference for hundreds of students and faculty. Another formal role that universities play is supporting entrepreneurially oriented faculty.

As part of their role in the university and as an extension of their research interests, individual faculty contribute to new venture development in a number of ways. First, they act as consultants to organizations. A 1969 survey of college and university faculty in all disciplines found that 60 percent serve as paid and unpaid consultants to large and small, profit and non-profit organizations, with 19 percent consulting more than four hours a week.[5] Consulting is more likely at universities than colleges, at high prestige institutions, and among senior faculty members.[6] However, the extent of faculty consultations with new ventures and small business remains uncertain. In general, smaller organizations tend to be less connected to university resources[7] and therefore less likely to employ faculty as consultants.

---

[4]Karl H. Vesper, "New Developments in Entrepreneurship Education" Donald Sexton and Raymond Smilor (eds.), The Art and Science of Entrepreneurship, Ballinger Publishing, Cambridge, MA, 1986, pp. 379-387.

[5]John D. Maver and Charles V. Patton, "The Correlates of Consultation: American Academics in 'the Real World'," Higher Education, Vol. 5, 1976, pp. 319-335.

[6]National Science Board, University-Industry Research Relationships: Myths, Realities and Potentials, National Science Foundation, Washington, D.C., 1982.

[7]David N. Allen and Victor Levine, Nurturing Advanced Technology Enterprises, Praeger Publishers, New York, 1986.

A survey of the members of the Academy of Management (faculty in management and business schools) interested in entrepreneurship found that 41
percent served as paid consultants, 41 percent served as unpaid consultants to new ventures, while 62 percent (paid) and 50 percent (unpaid)
consulted with small businesses.[8]

Faculty consulting is important to entrepreneurship for several
reasons. First, it provides a direct avenue for personal contact that
avoids organizational rigidity. Faculty are highly isolated from
industry counterparts,[9] and consulting breaks down those barriers.
Second, consulting often leads to a more formal research arrangement
between industrial partners and faculty.[10] Third, and perhaps most
pertinent to entrepreneurship, consulting may gradually ease the faculty
person into a business venture. The process of being pulled into product development and a new firm is described by Bullock:[11]

> From doing initial consultancy work, the academic
> starts to realize that he can "routinize" what he is
> doing...as a result a consultancy package begins to
> emerge...What he is doing in this process is reduc-
> ing the high-level, analytical content...and bring-
> ing it down to something more simple and robust,
> which is suitable for the commercial market...a com-
> mon way (to devise a product) is to abbreviate still
> further the report into testing reports, and from
> there into design reports, until the academic is
> actually designing products for customers...If that
> succeeds, then slowly the academic will direct
> efforts more toward this product...From there we
> tend to see companies getting into assembly, and
> possibly into manufacturing, relying on specific
> supply contracts placed by clients who have already
> bought their consulting work.

---

[8]William B. Gartner and Barbara J. Bird, "Academic Interest in
Entrepreneurship: A Survey of the Academy of Management" Paper presented
at the Babson Entrepreneurship Research Conference, Philadelphia, PA,
1985.

[9]J. D. Eveland, Communication Networks in University-Industry
Cooperative Research Centers, National Science Foundation, Washington,
D.C,, 1985.

[10]Herbert I. Fusfeld, "Overview of University-Industry Research
Interactions" in Thomas Hangfitt and Sheldon Hackney (eds) Partners in
the Research Enterprise, University of Pennsylvania Press, Philadelphia,
PA, 1983, pp. 10-22.

[11]Matthew Bullock, "Cohabitation: Small Research-Based Companies
and the University" Technovation. Vol. 3, 1985, pp. 35.

Other faculty roles include being a director or investor in new ventures. The Academy survey[12] found that 23 percent of management faculty interested in entrepreneurship were directors and 30 percent had invested in new ventures (in the small business sector 17 percent were directors and 19 percent were investors). While restricted to management faculty, these results are indicative of a multidimensional faculty involvement in new ventures. Before examining the data on faculty entrepreneurship, it is important to assess the university as an incubator organization.

## Universities as Incubator Organizations

At the face of it, universities appear to have many of the characteristics that would provide a supportive environment for entrepreneurship, especially for technology-based firms. The university is particularly well equipped with the resources to parent new ventures: faculty dedicated to advancing knowledge in key scientific, engineering, management, and social areas; highly skilled and motivated student labor, which can be obtained at a relatively low cost; fully equipped, often state-of-the-art laboratories; and a host of other facilities that can be shared (e.g., computers, libraries, media access, etc.). Furthermore, since federal funding has been systematically cut back, an increasing amount of the research currently conducted by faculty and students is funded by industry, with the stated or unstated objectives of technology transfer.

From a new venture's point of view, the university is an important resource for technical information (faculty research activities, faculty consultants, joint research efforts, access to libraries, computers, and laboratories) and a magnet for attracting and training employees (college graduates, degree programs for employees, part-time teaching opportunities, and cultural advantages). While small firms tend to be less connected to university resources, younger firms do not differ from more established firms in the value they place on these resources.[13] Furthermore, firms with growth plans tend to place higher value on these resources than firms that are stable.[14]

Historical evidence seems to support the efficiency of some university business incubation environments. One study shows that 156 of 216 high technology companies in the Boston area were created at M.I.T.

---

[12]op cit., Gartner and Bird.

[13]op cit., Allen and Levine

[14]ibid.

research facilities.[15] Cooper[16] states that in Boston, Austin and Ann Arbor "substantial percentages of new firms...were direct spin-offs from a university or one of its laboratories." However, he also found[17] that only six of 243 firms founded in Silicon Valley during the 1960s had executive level ties to university faculty. Miller and Cote[18] contend that universities are poor incubators because research and faculty members have little contact with the marketplace. Universities are seen as inhabited by individuals lacking a sense of creative opportunism, the primary distinction being "passive suppliers" versus "active developers."[19]

Little doubt exists that higher education institutions can play a significant value added role to technology-based startups. The extent of that activity and explanations for the variation in activity remain elusive. To shed some light on these issues faculty at two major institutions in North Carolina were surveyed.

## THE RESEARCH CONTEXT

The two schools chosen for analysis are interesting for two reasons. First, Rogers,[20] has argued that North Carolina universities have favorable policies to assist (and presumably start up) local firms. Second, these two universities form two of three corners of the Research Triangle Park (RTP). After 25 years of planned growth at RTP, it can be confidently stated that it is one of the most successful technology parks in the world. About 50 firms employ over 20,000 people in this 6,500 acre area. Together the two universities employ nearly 4,000 faculty and provide instruction to 45,000 students.

---

[15]Marshall I. Goldman, "Building a Mecca for High Technology," _Technology Review_, (May/June 1984).

[16]Arnold C. Cooper, "The Role of Incubators in the Founding of Growth Oriented Firms," _Journal of Business Venturing_ Vol. 1, No. 1, 1985, pp. 75-86.

[17]Arnold C. Cooper, _The Founding of Technologically-Based Firms_. The Center for Venture Management, Milwaukee, WI, 1970.

[18]Roger Miller and Marcel Cote, "Growing the Next Silicon Valley," _Harvard Business Review_, (July/August 1985), pp. 114-123.

[19]ibid., p. 116.

[20]Everitt M. Rogers, "The Role of the Research University in the Spin-Off of High-Technology Companies," _Technovation_, Vol. 4, 1986, pp. 169-181.

## Methodology and Sample

Faculty members at the University of North Carolina, Chapel Hill and North Carolina State University, Raleigh, were surveyed about their actual and potential entrepreneurial activities. The research offices of both institutions provided a list of faculty who had received an external grant or contract during the last two years. Sponsored research could have been funded through industry, foundations or government bodies. A total of 767 faculty (373 at NCSU and 394 at UNC) were sent surveys through the campus mail. Returned surveys were sent to the out-of-state office of a consulting firm. A 25 percent response rate was achieved (93 from NCSU and 97 from UNC). The 190 responses were reduced by 19 in order to limit the analysis to four disciplinary areas. The sample used for analysis purposes is divided between physical sciences (17.5%), biological sciences (38.6%), engineering (22.2%), and professional schools (21.6%).[21]

The faculty in this study are generally characteristic of research oriented faculty at major state higher educational institutions. The majority are male (94.6%), held more than a masters degree (98.3%), and are full professors (55.6%). Approximately one of three (29.0%) are associate professors and 15.4 percent are assistant professors. On average they are 44 years old, have been employed by their institution 10.25 years, and spend 60 percent of their time conducting research. Nearly thirty percent (29.7%) currently hold a patent.

## Research, Consulting and Entrepreneurial Activity

These research productive faculty were asked a series of questions pertaining to contacts with clients or parties arising from research and consulting activities. Slightly more than 70 percent (71.3%) had a personal paying consultancy within the last two years. This figure is similar to findings reported by Maver and Patton[22] and the National Science Board.[23] A much smaller percentage (7.6%) were involved in business commercialization activity "to develop, test or produce a product, service, process or technique for market."

Respondents were also asked about their future research, consulting, and commercialization plans: (1) within the next year; and (2) at some time in the future beyond the next year. The data indicate future changes for both activities; consulting activity is expected to decrease

---

[21]Biological Sciences include agricultural sciences, engineering includes match and computer science, and professional schools are composed of law and medicine.

[22]op cit., Maver and Patton.

[23]op cit., National Science Board.

and entrepreneurial activity is expected to increase. In the next year about half (49.7%) expect to be doing personal outside consulting while beyond one year expectations for consulting are even less (43.3%). Entrepreneurial activity will involve 5.7 percent of the sample in the next year, while in the longer run, 15.7 percent desire to start up a firm based on their research activity. The analysis above is based on time constraints, the two previous years and one future year, and a general desirability question. Questions broader than the suggested time frames were also asked.

About 13 percent (13.5%) of these productive faculty said that their research or consulting activity has already led them to commercialize a product or service. About one-third (32.1%) said their research or consulting activity could lead them to commercialize a product or service. Almost twenty percent (19.3%) said their work could not lead to commercialization and 35.1 percent were uncertain.

Faculty members' perceptions about potential commercialization have, to some degree, been validated by individuals in a position to commercialize their research. Respondents were asked whether they had "been approached by a friend, client, industry representative or corporation acquaintance to pursue some aspect or potential of their research or consulting activity." Nearly one quarter of the respondents (24.4%) said they had been offered financial support to commercially pursue their ideas. Other indicators of interest are: 15.5 percent offered a position in a firm, 13.1 percent approached to buy rights to a commercializable product or service; 12.5 percent invited into a partnership agreement for commercialization, and 11.9 percent to act as an agent to license their product.

## Institutional Level Concerns

To this point the descriptive findings have been presented in aggregate matter. The purpose of the aggregate reporting was to show the current and potential scope of commercialization activity. In this section we concentrate on institutional level impacts on and results of commercialization. To better understand the makeup of the respondents, an activity focus variable was created. The three hierarchical values of activity focus are: (1) those faculty who at some time in the last two years were involved in an existing business or business startup related to their research (11.7%); (2) those who engage in a personal paying consultancy, but not as an existing or startup business (69.8%); and (3) those not engaged in a research related business or personal consultancy (27.5%), i.e., the last two years were occupied by sponsored research.

Some variation in activity focus is due to the respondents disciplinary focus. Compared to the entire sample, engineering faculty are more likely to be involved in commercialization and less in sponsored research (Table 1). Professional school faculty are not apt to be involved in commercial ventures. Consulting activity varies little by disciplinary focus.

TABLE 1

Disciplinary Focus by Activity Focus

| Frequency Row Percent Column Percent | Entrepre- neurial | Consulting | Sponsored Research | Total |
|---|---|---|---|---|
| Physical Sciences | 4 13.3 20.0 | 20 66.7 19.2 | 6 20.0 12.8 | 3 17.5 |
| Biological Sciences | 7 10.6 35.0 | 38 57.6 36.5 | 21 31.8 44.7 | 66 38.6 |
| Engineering | 8 21.0 40.0 | 25 65.8 24.0 | 5 13.1 10.6 | 38 22.2 |
| Professional Schools | 1 2.7 5.0 | 21 56.8 20.2 | 15 40.5 31.9 | 37 21.6 |
| Total | 20 11.7 | 104 60.8 | 47 27.5 | N=171 100.0 |

Chi Square = 12.7 sig. at .05.
Cramer's V = .19

The impact of activity focus on institutional concerns occurs at two levels, university and departmental. Respondents were asked to assess policies, practices and procedures at the two levels relative to their (your) "ability to commercialize a product or service or engage in entrepreneurial activity." Respondents were evenly split concerning their feelings about university level policies. An equal one third said either that the university level policies were supportive, of no effect, or restrictive. No statistically significant differences were found by activity focus or disciplinary focus. Departmental level policies were seen as less restrictive, but not more supportive; the difference being a greater number felt that departmental policies had no effect. Again, no statistically significant differences were seen by activity focus or disciplinary focus.

An important concern, especially from the perspective of a university executive, is addressed by the question: "Could the commercialization potential of your research or consulting activity lead you to alter your relationship with the university?" As seen in Table 2, the tentative evidence[24] suggests a weak to moderate, statistically significant relationship between activity focus and altering university relationship. Perhaps most notable is that few university faculty are

_____

[24]Due to the low frequencies in some cells the relationship must be considered tentative.

certain about their expectation of changing or not changing their relationship with the university. A considerable number of faculty express uncertainty as to the future relationship, although less than half (45.0%) of the commercialization faculty do not expect to alter their university relationship.

TABLE 2

Expectation of Altering University Relationship by Activity Focus

| Frequency<br>Row Percent<br>Column Percent | Entrepre-<br>neurial | Consulting | Sponsored<br>Research | Total |
|---|---|---|---|---|
| No Change | 9 | 72 | 37 | 118 |
| Expected soon | 7.6 | 61.0 | 31.4 | 70.7 |
| | 45.0 | 72.0 | 78.7 | |
| Uncertain, but | 8 | 22 | 10 | 40 |
| Possible | 20.0 | 55.0 | 25.0 | 23.9 |
| | 40.0 | 22.0 | 21.3 | |
| Change Expected | 3 | 6 | 0 | 9 |
| Soon | 33.3 | 67.7 | 0.0 | 5.4 |
| | 15.0 | 6.0 | 0.0 | |
| | 20 | 100 | 47 | N=167 |
| Total | 12.0 | 59.9 | 28.1 | 100.0 |

Chi Square = 10.8 sig. at .05
Cramer's V = .18

A final question asked of respondents concerns intention "to go into business to commercialize your (their) product or service if you (they) had the opportunity." The relationship between opportunistic intention and activity focus shows the tentative nature of many faculty. Overall nearly 40 percent (38.1%) of all faculty would not consider going into business, and 46.4 percent were uncertain. Faculty engaged in consulting are quite similar to their solely research oriented colleagues. Nearly half of both the research and consulting oriented faculty (48.9 and 46.5% respectively) were uncertain as to whether they would go into business given the opportunity.

Summary of Findings

The findings presented based on a mailed survey to productive research faculty show the scope of faculty entrepreneurship. First, few faculty are actually involved in entrepreneurial activities related to their research. Although future intent is evident, whether entrepreneurial activity actually is undertaken is unresolved. Evidently, faculty are intrigued with entrepreneurship, but uncertainty, even under favorable conditions, remains high. Even though many faculty members have at least tentative interest in entrepreneurship, about 70 percent do not expect to alter their relationship with the university. The reluctancy to alter the university relationship is low even among those who in the last two years have engaged in commercial ventures.

## CONCLUSION

Dissimilarities in the worlds of sponsored research and entrepreneurship suggest a set of value differences that help explain the low level of faculty entrepreneurial activity. Academic values of knowledge creation and dissemination are reinforced in the tenure and promotion process and yearly raises. The intrinsic rewards of publishing works with students and acceptance in scholarly circles is vastly different than the world of commerce. In entrepreneurial realms knowledge is embodied in a finished, marketable product or service. Distribution of process or product formuli or configurations is tantamount to lack of control over important proprietary resources. Although intrinsic rewards for performance and completion obviously exist, objective criteria such as economic return are not easily determined in scholarly arenas. In essence, the principal investigator mentality (characterized by collegial behavior and control over the research agenda) vastly differs from the entrepreneurial mentality. Entrepreneurs seek to maintain control and have to respond to market needs. Researchers turned entrepreneurs often find the transition difficult and many settle for consulting and R&D shops rather than full commercialization.

Although value differences are clearly apparent, a small percent of faculty are willing to venture into the commercial world. Others seem interested in eventually following the faculty entrepreneurial colleagues. Many more are perplexed by the choices commercialization poses. The high degree of faculty uncertainty about whether or not they would commercialize their research, given the opportunity, suggests a lack of information or competency in assessing product and service market potential. This is not unexpected given the fact that most faculty are appreciably removed from commercial contexts. Even a high level of consulting activity does not mean that commercial concerns are being examined; we suspect that technical concerns are the mainstay of consulting agendas. Consulting can be a bridge to the commercial world, but few maybe willing to walk where the guiderails of the market are poorly delineated.

The findings do suggest, however, that a small percentage of faculty are ready to commercialize their research by starting a firm. Universities that believe these people to be renegades probably have little to fear. The university attitude a decade ago could be characterized as "reign them in so they do not stray from the research path." Today the threat of a "brain drain" has been turned on its head. If universities do not provide the flexibility needed to venture into business, faculty will be tempted to go to those institutions that are responsive to their commercialized desires. Put another way, by being flexible and responsive, universities can actually achieve a "brain

gain." The evidence from this study shows that few actual or aspiring
entrepreneurial faculty desire to alter their existing relationships
with the university. These faculty will, over the long run, likely
remain research productive, if for no other reasons than to retain a
competitive edge for their own firm and promote themselves as leaders in
their profession.

Universities have other good reasons to support faculty entrepreneurship. Innovative universities are looking at these ventures as new
markets for research that may gradually substitute for declining enroll-
ments. Universities also seek curry favor with donors; successful
entrepreneurs are likely to give back to their institution. The alarm
voiced by many academics a few decades ago, concerning the changing
mission of the university brought on by industrial collaboration, seems
to have lost its ring. We suspect that debate about faculty
entrepreneurship will also become moot as the university's role as a
creator of new value becomes more prevalent in our post-industrial
economy.

# REFERENCES

Allen, David N. and Levine, Victor, <u>Nurturing Advanced Technology Enterprises</u>, Praeger Publishers, New York, 1986.

Bullock, Matthew, "Cohabition: Small Research-Based Companies and the University," <u>Technovation</u>, Vol. 3, (1985), pp. 27-38.

Cooper, Arnold C., <u>The Founding of Technologically-Based Firms</u>, The Center for Venture Management, Milwaukee, WI, 1970.

Cooper, Arnold C., "The Role of Incubators in the Founding of Growth Oriented Firms," <u>Journal of Business Venturing</u>, Vol. 1, No. 1, (1985), pp. 75-86.

Eveland, J. D. <u>Communication Networks in University-Industry Cooperative Research Centers</u>, National Science Foundation, Washington, D.C., 1985.

Fusfeld, Herbert I., "Overview of University-Industry Research Interactions," in Thomas Hangfitt and Sheldon Hackney (eds.), <u>Partners in the Research Enterprise</u>, University of Pennsylvania Press, Philadelphia, PA, 1983, pp. 10-22.

Gartner, William B. and Bird, Barbara J., "Academic Interest in Entrepreneurship: A Survey of the Academy of Management," Paper presented at the Babson Entrepreneurship Research Conference, Philadelphia, PA, 1985.

Goldman, Marshall I., "Building a Mecca for High Technology," <u>Technology Review</u>, (May/June, 1984).

Government-University-Industry Roundtable, <u>New Alliances and Partnerships in American Science and Engineering</u>, National Academy of Sciences, Washington, D.C., 1986.

Miller, Roger and Cote, Marcel, "Growing the Next Silicon Valley," <u>Harvard Business Review</u>, (July/August, 1985), pp. 114-123.

Maver, John D. and Patton, Charles V., "The Correlates of Consultation: American Academics in 'the Real World'," <u>Higher Education</u>, Vol. 5, (1976), pp. 319-355.

National Science Board, <u>University-Industry Research Relationships: Myths, Realities and Potentials</u>, National Science Foundation, Washington, D.C., 1982.

Premus, Robert, <u>Location of High Technology Firms and Regional Economic Development</u>, U.S. Congress, Joint Economic Committee, Washington, D.C., 1982.

Rogers, Everitt M., "The Role of the Research University in the Spin-Off of High-Technology Companies," Technovation, Vol. 4, (1986), pp. 169-181.

Vesper, Karl H., "New Developments in Entrepreneurship Education," in Donald Sexton and Raymond Smilor (eds.), The Art and Science of Entrepreneurship, Ballinger Publishing, Cambridge, MA, 1986, pp. 379-387.

Watkins, Charles B., "Programs for Innovative Technology Research," in State Strategies for Economic Development, National Governor's Association, Washington, D.C., 1985, pp. 2-25.

SUMMARY

## THE VENTURE GENERATING POTENTIAL OF A UNIVERSITY

Authors

    Cristina Castro
    W. Ed McMullan
    Karl H. Vesper
    Michael Raymont

Address

    New Venture Development Group
    Faculty of Management
    University of Calgary
    443 Scurfield Hall
    2500 University Drive NW
    Calgary, Alberta  T2N 1N4
    (403) 220-6117

Principal Topics

The objective of this study was to assess the number and type of spin-offs at the University of Calgary where it is hoped more will occur in the future as a result of entrepreneurial research, education, encouragement and assistance efforts.

Method and Data Base

Although one may define a university spin-off in a number of different ways, for the purposes of this study a university spin-off has been defined as any new business which meets the four following conditions:

    a)  has an off-campus office outside a private resident with a separately listed telephone number;

    b)  was based upon knowledge or technology associated with the university

    c)  involved a faculty member, research associate or graduate student as a principle office of the venture;

and  d)  was started concurrent with or immediately after membership in the university community.

An attempt was made to identify spin-offs in three different stages of existence a) projects that had identifiable spin-off potential; b) early-stage venture in the process of becoming spin-offs and c) ventures that had already achieved spin-off status.

Sources of information were:

° questionnaires were sent to 21 different departments
° published lists of companies
° two campus organizations, the New Venture Development Group and Technology Transfer office which identified some of the spin-offs.

## Major Findings

A total of 48 existing ventures were identified. The top ten companies together employed 260 out of a total of 324 in all the 48 spin-offs found. The faculty of Science produced the largest number of spin-offs with 18 (37.5%) followed by the Engineering School with 13 (27.1%), with the remainder from other departments of the campus. The greatest amount of job creation came from the Petroleum and Chemical Engineering Spin-off (138 jobs) followed by Mechanical Engineering (37) and Biology (36).

There are 13 ventures in the process of spinning out. The vast majority are very recent formations. All are engaged in activity related to the formation of a new venture such as prototype development, business planning and the search for capital, and 21 who indicated that they had a research project with potential to be commercialized.

## Major Implications

° The process of finding spin-offs is an exercise in detective work.
° The impact of university spin-offs on the city of Calgary is still light.
° The New Venture Development Group is attempting to increase the spin-off rate.

# FRONTIERS
# OF
# ENTREPRENEURSHIP
# RESEARCH

# TOPICAL INDEX 1981-1987

Prepared by
**NEIL C. CHURCHILL**
1986-87 Paul T. Babson Professor of Entrepreneurial Studies
Babson College
and
**JOHN A. HORNADAY**
Director, Center for Entrepreneurial Studies
Babson College

# CONTENTS OF TOPICAL INDEX

CONTENTS OF TOPICAL INDEX (continued)

TOPICAL INDEX:   1981 - 1987

START-UPS--DATA ON CHARACTERISTICS, RATE
OF FORMATION, ETC. (Continued)

Hills, Gerald E.
    Market Analysis and Marketing in New
    Ventures:  Venture Capitalists' Perceptions          1984          43


Hutt, Roger W. and William E. Miller
    New Ventures in the Food Industry                    1981          463


Katz, Jerome A.
    Entry Strategies of the Self-Employed:
    Individual Level Characteristics and
    Organizational Outcomes                              1984          396


Mitton, Daryl G.
    The Anatomy of a High Tech Service Venture:
    Roadmap to Entrepreneurship for the Aspiring
    Manager                                              1983          96


Roberts, Edward B.
    Business Planning in the Startup
    High-Technology Enterprise                           1983          107


Shapero, Albert and Joseph Giglierano
    Exits and Entries:  A Study in Yellow Pages
    Journalism                                           1982          113


Shuman, Jeffrey C., Gerald Sussman, and
    John J. Shaw
    Business Plans and The Start-Up of Rapid
    Growth Companies                                     1985          294


Stevenson, Lois
    Towards Understanding Young Founders                 1987          275


Stuart, Robert W. and Pier A. Abetti
    Field Study of Start-Up Ventures:
    Strategy, Innovation and Organization
    Versus Market                                        1985          18


Stuart, Robert W. and Pier A. Abetti
    Field Study of Start-Up Ventures--Part II:
    Predicting Initial Success                           1986          21

START-UPS--DATA ON CHARACTERISTICS, RATE
OF FORMATION, ETC. (Continued)

VENTURE CAPITAL--CHARACTERISTICS OF VENTURE CAPITAL
INDUSTRY, ROLE IN BUSINESS FORMATION, ETC.

McMullan, Wallace Edward, Richard Long, and
    Jay Tapp
    Entrepreneurial Share Transaction
    Strategies           1984    32

Neiswander, D. Kirk
    Informal Seed Stage Investors    1985    142

Olofsson, Christer and Clas Wahlbin
    The Swedish Venture Capital Market –
    An Early Appraisal    1985    191

Sahlman, William A. and Howard H. Stevenson
    Capital Market Myopia    1985    80

Sandberg, William R., David M. Schweiger and
    Charles W. Hofer
    Determining Venture Capitalists' Decision
    Criteria: The Use of Verbal Protocols    1987    392

Schell, Douglas W.
    The Development of the Venture Capital
    Industry in North Carolina:  A New Approach    1984    55

Stevenson, Howard H., Daniel F. Muzyka and
    Jeffry A. Timmons
    Venture Capital in a New Era:  A Simulation
    of the Impact of Changes in Investment
    Patterns    1986    380

Timmons, Jeffry A.
    Survey of the Most Active Venture Capital
    Firms    1981    199

Timmons, Jeffry A.
    Venture Capital in Sweden    1982    294

Timmons, Jeffry A., Norman D. Fast, and
    William D. Bygrave
    The Flow of Venture Capital to Highly
    Innovative Technological Ventures    1983    316

## FINANCING START-UPS OTHER THAN THROUGH VENTURE CAPITALISTS (Continued)

## MANAGING THE BUSINESS--TURNAROUND, HARVEST CONTRACTIONS, ACQUISITION, ETC.

# CORPORATE VENTURING (Continued)

## INCUBATORS AND OTHER UNIVERSITY SUPPORT TO ENTREPRENEURSHIP

Allen, David N., Eugene J. Bazan,
    and Janet Hendrickson-Smith
    Gritty and Flashy Entrepreneurship in
    the Atlanta Metropolitan Area             1986    303

Brown, Richard L.
    NASA's Interest in Entrepreneurs        1981    353

Colton, R. M. and G. G. Udell
    Implications of the Stevenson-Wydler
    Technology Innovation Act of 1980
    Public Law 96-480        1983    422

Dana, Leo Paul
    Entrepreneurship and Venture Creation -
    An International Comparison of Five
    Commonwealth Nations        1987    573

Gatewood, Elizabeth, Frank Hoy,
    and Charles Spindler
    Functionalist vs. Conflict Theories:
    Entrepreneurship Disrupts the Power
    Structure in a Small Community    1984    265

Jansson, David G. and Robert D. Hisrich
    Entrepreneurship in Puerto Rico    1981    179

Kirchhoff, Bruce A. and William E. Knight
    Government's Role in Research and
    Development        1981    321

Knight, Russell M. and W. Ker Ferguson
    The Success of Ontario's SBDC Program    1984    73

Krasner, O. Jay and Charles L. Wood
    Free Trade Zones and Entrepreneurship    1981    372

Mueller, Charles E.
    Poverty and Entrepreneurship    1981    384

## FACTORS INFLUENCING ENTREPRENEURSHIP & START-UPS
## (GOVERNMENT) (Continued)

Obermayer, Judith H.
    Government R&D Funding and Startups             1981     337

Schell, Douglas W.
    Entrepreneurial Implications of the Small
    Business Investment Incentives Act           1982     270

Schwartz, Robert G. and Richard D. Teach
    Primary Issues Effecting the Development
    and Growth of a Professional
    Infrastructure for Emerging Technology
    Start-ups: The State of Georgia Experience     1984     126

Wahlbin, Clas
    Supporting New Venture Development:
    The Experience of Swedish Regional
    Development Funds                   1983     529


## WOMEN & MINORITIES IN ENTREPRENEURSHIP

Bearse, Peter J.
    An Econometric Analysis of Black
    Entrepreneurship                   1984     212

Birley, Sue, Caroline Moss, and Peter Saunders
    The Differences Between Small Firms Started
    by Male and Female Entrepreneurs Who
    Attended Small Business Courses         1986     211

Hisrich, Robert D. and Marie O'Brien
    The Woman Entrepreneur              1981     21

Hisrich, Robert D. and Marie O'Brien
    The Woman Entrepreneur as a Reflection of
    the Type of Business             1982     54

Hisrich, Robert D. and Candida Brush
    The Woman Entrepreneur:  Implications
    of Family Educational, and Occupational
    Experience      1983      255

Hisrich, Robert D. and Candida G. Brush
    Women and Minority Entrepreneurs:  A
    Comparative Analysis      1985      566

Hisrich, Robert D. and Candida G. Brush
    Women Entrepreneurs: A Longitudinal Study      1987      187

Kirchhoff, Bruce A., Richard L. Stevens
    and Norman I. Hurwitz
    Factors Underlying Increases in Minority
    Entrepreneurship      1982      39

Mescon, Timothy S., George E. Stevens
    and George S. Vozikis
    Blacks as Entrepreneurs: The Liberty
    City Experience      1984      249

Sexton, Donald L. and Calvin A. Kent
    Female Executives Versus Female
    Entrepreneurs      1981      40

Sexton, Donald L. and Nancy B. Bowman
    Validation of a Personality Index:
    Comparative Psychological Characteristics
    Analysis of Female Entrepreneurs, Managers,
    Entrepreneurship Students and
    Business Students      1986      40

Smith, Norman R., Gary McCain, and Audrey Warren
    Women Entrepreneurs Really are Different      1982      68

Watkins, Jean M. and David S. Watkins
    The Female Entrepreneur:  Her Background and
    Determinants of Business Choice
    - Some British Data      1983      271

# FAILURES AND EX-ENTREPRENEURS

# ENTREPRENEURIAL EDUCATION

## CROSSCULTURAL STUDIES